WITHDRAWN

AMERICAN EDUCATION

Its Men,

Ideas,

and

Institutions

Advisory Editor

Lawrence A. Cremin
Frederick A. P. Barnard Professor of Education
Teachers College, Columbia University

AMERICAN EDUCATION: *Its Men, Ideas, and Institutions* presents selected works of thought and scholarship that have long been out of print or otherwise unavailable. Inevitably, such works will include particular ideas and doctrines that have been outmoded or superseded by more recent research. Nevertheless, all retain their place in the literature, having influenced educational thought and practice in their own time and having provided the basis for subsequent scholarship.

FREE SCHOOLS

A Documentary History of the Free School
Movement in New York State

BY
THOMAS E. FINEGAN

ARNO PRESS & THE NEW YORK TIMES
New York * 1971

L182
G5
F55

Reprint Edition 1971 by Arno Press Inc.

Reprinted from a copy in
  The University of Illinois Library

American Education:
  Its Men, Ideas, and Institutions - Series II
ISBN for complete set: 0-405-03600-0
See last pages of this volume for titles.

Manufactured in the United States of America

Library of Congress Cataloging in Publication Data

Finegan, Thomas Edward, 1866-1932.
    Free schools.
    (Fifteenth annual report of the Education
Department, v. 1) (American education: its men,
ideas, and institutions. Series II)
    Reprint of the 1921 ed.
    1. Public schools--New York (State).
I. Title. II. Series: New York (State).
University. Annual report of the Education
Department, no. 15, v. 1. III. Series:
American education: its men, ideas, and
institutions. Series II.
L182.G5F55   372.9'747   73-165737
ISBN 0-405-03606-X

FREE SCHOOLS

A Documentary History of the Free School
Movement in New York State

BY
THOMAS E. FINEGAN
*Deputy Commissioner of Education and Assistant
Commissioner for Elementary Education*

ALBANY
THE UNIVERSITY OF THE STATE OF NEW YORK
1921

THE UNIVERSITY OF THE STATE OF NEW YORK

Regents of the University
With years when terms expire

1926 PLINY T. SEXTON LL.B. LL.D. *Chancellor* – – Palmyra
1927 ALBERT VANDER VEER M.D. M.A. Ph.D. LL.D.
    Vice Chancellor – – – – – – – Albany
1922 CHESTER S. LORD M.A. LL.D. – – – – – Brooklyn
1930 WILLIAM NOTTINGHAM M.A. Ph.D. LL.D. – – Syracuse
1921 FRANCIS M. CARPENTER – – – – – – Mount Kisco
1923 ABRAM I. ELKUS LL.B. D.C.L. LL.D. – – – New York
1924 ADELBERT MOOT LL.D. – – – – – – Buffalo
1925 CHARLES B. ALEXANDER M.A. LL.B. LL.D.
    Litt.D. – – – – – – – – – – Tuxedo
1919 JOHN MOORE LL.D. – – – – – – – Elmira
1928 WALTER GUEST KELLOGG B.A. LL.D. – – – Ogdensburg
1920 JAMES BYRNE B.A. LL.B. LL.D. – – – – New York
1929 HERBERT L. BRIDGMAN M.A. – – – – – Brooklyn

President of the University and Commissioner of Education
JOHN H. FINLEY M.A. LL.D. L.H.D.

Deputy Commissioner and Assistant Commissioner for Elementary Education
THOMAS E. FINEGAN M.A. Pd.D. LL.D.

Assistant Commissioner and Director of Professional Education
AUGUSTUS S. DOWNING M.A. L.H.D. LL.D.

Assistant Commissioner for Secondary Education
CHARLES F. WHEELOCK B.S. LL.D.

Director of State Library
JAMES I. WYER, JR, M.L.S.

Director of Science and State Museum
JOHN M. CLARKE D.Sc. LL.D.

Chiefs and Directors of Divisions

Administration, HIRAM C. CASE
Agricultural and Industrial Education, LEWIS A. WILSON
Archives and History, JAMES SULLIVAN M.A. Ph.D.
Attendance, JAMES D. SULLIVAN
Educational Extension, WILLIAM R. WATSON B.S.
Examinations and Inspections, GEORGE M. WILEY M.A.
Law, FRANK B. GILBERT B.A., *Counsel*
Library School, FRANK K. WALTER M.A. M.L.S.
School Buildings and Grounds, FRANK H. WOOD M.A.
School Libraries, SHERMAN WILLIAMS Pd.D.
Visual Instruction, ALFRED W. ABRAMS Ph.B.

FIFTEENTH ANNUAL REPORT

OF THE

EDUCATION DEPARTMENT

VOLUME I

THE UNIVERSITY OF THE
STATE OF NEW YORK

ALBANY, April 19, 1919

Honorable Thaddeus C. Sweet

 Speaker of the Assembly, Assembly Chamber, Albany, N. Y.

Sir: Pursuant to law, the annual report of the Education Department is herewith submitted to the Legislature.

    Very respectfully yours
      PLINY T. SEXTON
       Chancellor of the University
      JOHN H. FINLEY
       President of the University and
       Commissioner of Education

TABLE OF CONTENTS

	PAGE
Preface	3

Chapter I. The Early Schools 7
    Completion of fifty years of free schools; schools during the period of English rule; private schools; Clinton's interest; establishment of academies; The University of the State of New York; the school act of 1795; development of the country; enlargement of democratic views; Colonial schools and colleges in New York; schools under the Dutch; the first Dutch school; schools under the English; Latin schools; establishment of King's College; Columbia University; schools of Long Island; old and modern schools in New Rochelle.

Chapter II. Education after the Revolution 25
    The University of the State of New York; board of regents; interest of Clinton, Hamilton, Livingston and Jay; the school law of 1795 and 1796.

Chapter III. The Law of 1812 34
    Governor Thompson appoints committee; enactment of law; its principal provisions; the rate bill system; full text of committee report; full text of law.

Chapter IV. The Period of 1826-46 52
    Social and educational progress; recommendations of various governors; speech of Thaddeus Stevens; his career; Massachusetts system; George H. Martin; public education in Rhode Island; Dr Charles Carroll; Egerton Ryerson; enactment of a general school law in New York City; early legislative references to free schools.

Chapter V. Constitutional Convention 1846 83
    General Marion's views on education; Doctor Potter's address; convention for revising the constitution; free schools for free government; common school state convention; address by Horace Mann; addresses by Superintendent Henry, Professor Thompson and others; biography of members of committee on education; journal of constitution relating to schools; vote on free schools; editorial comment; views of superintendents, teachers and others.

Chapter VI. Free School Bill of 1849 162
    Views of state superintendent, county superintendents; discussion in Legislature; record of vote in the Assembly; in the Senate; copy of law; record of vote of people by counties; general comment; memorial of Onondaga county teachers; newspaper comment.

Chapter VII. The Fight for Resubmission 231
    Superintendent Morgan's report; press comment.

Chapter VIII. The Act of Resubmission, 1850 265
    Message of Governor Fitch; petitions to the Legislature; legislative record; report of Senate committee on literature; opinion of Attorney General; the Pompey petition; report of Assembly committee; minority report of the Assembly committee; resubmission law.

PAGE

Chapter IX. The Campaign before the November Election in 1850 314
    Action by Monroe county teachers; address of W. L. Crandall; public meeting in Syracuse; convention of town superintendents; the Free School Clarion; free school peppercorns; Peter Plowshare; address to the State; free school state convention; public meeting of women in Syracuse; press comment; annual convention of Mechanics Mutual Protection; further press comment; Henry H. Martin; address by an old schoolmaster; record of vote on repeal of law by counties.

Chapter X. The Free School Law of 1851 419
    Superintendent Morgan's official report; views of Superintendent Randall; press comment; memorial from Westchester county board of supervisors; Monroe county mass meeting opposes free schools; state convention of town superintendents; resolutions; Senate and Assembly records; official record of vote.

Chapter XI. Educational Developments after the Law of 1851.. 486
    Proposal to establish department of public instruction; official reports; views of educators; school statistics; opposition to use of public funds for private schools; report of committee on colleges, academies and common schools on petition of certain Roman Catholics of New York, Utica, Syracuse and other cities; judicial decision on free school law; interesting legislation 1853–68; views of Governors.

Chapter XII. Abolishing the Rate Bill 537
    Official reports; press comment; the act of 1867; comments on the passage of the law; compulsory education.

Chapter XIII. The Important Educational Laws of 1917 565
    President Finley reports to the Board of Regents; copies and abstracts of the seventeen laws enacted.

Chapter XIV. The Evening Schools of Colonial New York City 630
    Discussion by Doctor Seybolt; list of schools.

Chapter XV. The New York Colonial Schoolmasters 653
    Names of masters; other records.

PREFACE

It is a long step in the development of an educational system from the first school organized in 1638 by Adam Roelantsen to the present system meeting the demands of more than 2,000,000 children. The liberal facilities provided for the children of today through the present school system have not been attained without a bitter struggle. The friends of free schools and of generous educational opportunity were compelled to fight every inch of the road in developing the school system of the State.

In collecting the material of this volume it was not the intention of the author to write a history of the struggle which resulted in the adoption of free schools but it was his intention to bring together, from various sources, valuable material which is now inaccessible and make it available for teachers, students of education, and even the general reader. While much labor was involved in the preparation of this volume, the author found great pleasure in the performance of such work. A careful study of this volume will give courage to those who carry responsibility in the organization of educational reforms.

The accepted doctrine in America today is that all the property of the state must educate all the children of the state and that each child in the state has not only the inherent right to attend school but that, in the interests of the state itself, must attend. The history revealed through the sources given in this volume will show that New York has made a rich contribution to the establishment of this accepted American principle.

The author wishes to express his appreciation to Mr C. W. Bardeen, editor of the School Bulletin, Syracuse, N. Y., and to Major Fred Engelhardt and Dr Sherman Williams of the Education Department for valuable assistance in the preparation of this volume.

T. E. F.

FREE SCHOOLS

Chapter 1

THE EARLY SCHOOLS

As this year marks the completion of fifty years of free schools in New York State, it is proposed to devote this report to a study of the issues which led to the establishment of free schools throughout the State. There is an abundance of material relating to the organization and development of free schools which should be made available to the students of public education. The results of a study of this subject and the documents relating thereto will not only increase the general appreciation of New York's educational system, but will be of great service in an interpretation of new educational problems and in their proper solution. As soon as the Revolution was ended, and peace with the mother country agreed upon, the subject of education received attention.

For a period of one hundred twenty-five years, or from the beginning of English rule in 1664, there had been no action by the government providing for the maintenance of schools. Private schools, church schools and charity schools had been established, but these were of uncertain tenure and were not attended by the great majority of children. Governor Clinton appreciated that the greatest need of a democracy was an educated citizenship. In his first message to the Legislature, he recommended that provision be made for the education of the children of the State. The Legislature, acting favorably upon that recommendation, created The University of the State of New York and conferred upon that body the power to charter academies. These academies were authorized for the express purpose of providing educational facilities for children of the prosperous and aristocratic classes. It was well known that the great majority of the children of the country would be excluded from attendance upon such institutions. Public opinion did not then demand the establishment of schools for the education of all children.

Public schools were authorized throughout the State and maintained very generally as early as 1795. State aid was given for the support of these schools at this time, for a period of five years. Upon the discontinuance of state aid the schools gradually declined in number and almost wholly disappeared.

Democracy, however, was working a new era in our national history which followed the termination of the War of 1812. There was not that sharp division in relation to republican institutions which had previously existed. The opinion that the people did possess the capacity for self-government was commonly accepted. The men who were guiding the affairs of state possessed a vision of the possibilities of the future of the Nation and, under their leadership, the great natural resources of the country were developed, commercial and manufacturing industries were established and great national subjects such as internal improvements, the tariff, the army and the navy, the establishment of banks, the currency, the reorganization of the territory of the national domain and other questions bearing upon the expansion and development of the material interests of the country were considered by the Congress, became political issues of vital importance to the country and aroused the intellectual interest of the people generally. Thus there was a quickening influence of the national spirit and a development of national consciousness and obligations.

It was in this period that the leaders of public opinion began to give careful consideration to the questions which would elevate and improve the social conditions of the masses and there was accordingly a demand for popular educational facilities. In response to this demand, the Legislature of our State enacted a law establishing the foundation of our state system of common schools. The establishment of this system of schools was a great advance movement in the development of our republican institutions but it did not meet the vital needs of a great nation of free men. After a struggle of nearly seventy-five years, but not until the Civil War had been fought, free schools were established and the principle that the property of the State shall educate the children of the State became the fundamental law in American education.

To understand fully the establishment and development of this principle, and the organization and growth of our great public school system, it is necessary to make a study not only of the first schools organized in the State but of the schools maintained in the colonial period.

The writer prepared a paper on the schools of the colonial period for the meeting of the New York State Historical Association held at Cooperstown in 1916 and the material in that paper has such bearing upon this subject that it is given here. It is as follows:

COLONIAL SCHOOLS AND COLLEGES IN NEW YORK

New York was settled by the Dutch during the first half of the seventeenth century. A great struggle for liberty had shaken Europe during the preceding century and the burden of that struggle had fallen upon the people of the Netherlands. The Calvinists ruled the country and the founders of New Netherland were adherents of the Calvinistic party. A fundamental principle of the democracy of Calvinism from the beginning of the teaching of that doctrine was that each individual should be able to read. Under that doctrine each person was held to be equally concerned in religious matters and to be personally accountable for his own conduct. The Bible contained the rules of conduct which should regulate the lives of all people, and each person should therefore be able to read that Book and not be dependent upon others for a knowledge of its teachings. In the countries, therefore, under the control of Calvinism there were established the basic principles of compulsory education laws so general in all progressive countries at the present time.

Before Holland began her settlement of New York the Dutch had maintained public schools in some of their cities for more than one hundred fifty years and a school system had been perfected which provided schools not only in all the cities but throughout all the rural regions. These schools afforded instruction for every girl as well as for every boy in that land. Such schools were public schools and were maintained in accordance with regulations prescribed by the public authorities. They were under dualistic control, the church and the state, with the ecclesiastical influence predominating. Although tuition was generally charged for attendance upon these schools, they were nevertheless properly regarded as public schools. They were public schools in the sense that they were open to all children of the country, were supported in part by public taxation, and were in their management and control subject to the public authorities. The curriculum was simple, including reading, writing and religious instruction. Sometimes the elements of arithmetic were also taught. The civil authorities determined the books to be used, the qualifications of the teachers, the general policy of the schools, and they also employed the teacher and paid his salary. Poor children were received without the payment of tuition. In addition to these schools, universities had been established affording a system of higher education and exerting a mighty influence upon the life of the nation.

The people of Holland, at the close of the sixteenth and the beginning of the seventeenth centuries, were leaders in agriculture, horticulture, dairying, manufacturing, commerce and industrial pursuits generally. Her men of trade and finance, of letters and science, her artists and inventors, her lawyers and statesmen were among the leaders of the world. The achievements of her army and navy gave her a national standing second to no other nation. Her people were generous and tolerant, yet they appreciated the value of their liberties and freedom and possessed the courage to protect and maintain them. No people of that period occupied a more commanding position throughout the world in industrial, commercial and financial affairs and no country enjoyed the exercise of greater civil, political and religious liberties.

This brief review of the civilization of the country from which the founders of New York came and of the social and institutional life of that country furnishes us a knowledge of the type of citizens who laid the foundations of our great commonwealth. We see Holland, the fatherland, as a country possessing all the institutions required to administer to the social necessities of the people of that day. She is known to have been, at that time, a land of homes, hospitals, orphanages, churches and schools. The people of that land were happy and contented, prosperous and thrifty, cultured and religious. There was no political issue which divided the people. They regarded their country, its customs and institutions, with devoted and patriotic affection. These people were therefore unlike the representatives of most nations that sought homes in the new world in the seventeenth century. They came to American shores, not because they were oppressed at home, not to avoid persecution, not to find a refuge where they might peacefully live in accordance with the dictates of their consciences, not as adventurers and plunderers; but they came on their own initiative to reap the advantages which their country's expanding commerce and the commercial opportunities of the times and conditions afforded.

Where the Dutch made settlements in America, they established schools of the type of those which existed in Holland. In the creation of an institution, in their adopted country, which would have such a vital influence upon their happiness and liberties as the public school, it was natural that they should introduce the type of school which had been the bulwark of their freedom and civilization in the mother country. There was no organized government in the new land and the governmental authority exercised in the

Collegiate School for Boys as it appeared in 1918 (organized as early as 1638); 243 W. 77th street, **New York**

The boys of the Collegiate School attending chapel (1918)

Collegiate School for Boys (1918); game in gymnasium

Dutch settlements was that which Holland exercised through the West India Company. The government was vested in a supervisory body known as the lord directors and a director general and council who exercised such power as the lord directors conferred upon them.

The first school established by the Dutch was at New Amsterdam. It is settled beyond question that this school was organized not later than 1638 and probably several years earlier. Many writers have claimed that the school was organized in 1633. It is known that Adam Roelantsen, who taught the school in 1638, was in New York in 1633 and there is much evidence upon which to base the claim that this school was organized in that year. This pioneer American school was maintained through the entire period of Dutch rule but, upon the advent of the second period of English rule in 1674, passed into the control of the Reformed Dutch Church of New York City and that institution has continued the maintenance of the school to the present time. It is now known as the Collegiate School for Boys and is located at 243 West 77th street, New York City. This school has therefore had a continuous existence for a period of nearly three centuries extending down through the perilous days of our Colonial and National life, and stands as an institution of first historical importance in this country in the development of elementary education.

When Dutch settlements were first established the children were undoubtedly instructed at home. This practice was continued by many parents even after schools were organized. But schools were soon established and the early municipal records show that schools were organized in each of the villages of Beverwyck (Albany), Brooklyn, Flatbush, Flatlands, New Haarlem, Wiltwyck (Kingston), and New Utrecht, which were chartered during the Dutch period. Schools were also organized in the unchartered villages of Dutch antecedents such as Schenectady, Boswyck, Kinderhook and others.

The expense of the maintenance of the school at New Amsterdam was shared by the company and by the city. The company paid the salary of the master and the city provided the building for the school and for the master. In the Dutch villages, it appears that subscriptions, which were regarded as compulsory, were received and that revenue was provided from excise sources. There is evidence to show that in some of these villages the company contributed to the salary of the teacher. In accordance with the practice in Holland, poor children were received without the payment of tuition.

In view of the religious instruction required the church exercised a strong influence over the school. The church authorities therefore examined and licensed the teachers, prescribed the catechism, approved the textbooks used, and supervised the instruction to see that its requirements were satisfied.

These schools were called official schools but in addition to these there were several schools in New Amsterdam under private management. There were probably more children under instruction in these schools than there were in attendance upon the city school. The parents who patronized these private schools were required to pay tuition as there was no public support given to the maintenance of such schools. The master provided his own school building, but the schools were of the same general type as the official schools. Private schools were not generally conducted in the smaller settlements. No master could legally open even a private school at New Amsterdam unless authorized to do so by the director general and council. When one Van Corlaer opened a school without the required permission, Director General Stuyvesant closed it. The patrons of Van Corlaer's school then petitioned the burgomasters and schepens to have the school opened as the children had forgotten what had been taught them. These inferior officers presented the petition to Director General Stuyvesant who declined to authorize the reopening of the school. Van Corlaer then petitioned Director General Stuyvesant direct but his petition was again denied and his teaching career thus ended. This incident illustrates the official or public status of a school which we could call private.

Official records supply reliable information on the qualifications, personality and work of the teacher. The masters very generally possessed intellectual attainments which properly equipped them for the service which they were required to perform. Adam Roelantsen was the first teacher. He left a bad record for he was constantly in trouble and frequently arrested. The court records show that he was guilty of slander, of violating the custom laws and of immoral conduct. The teachers of New Amsterdam were better known than those of the other settlements and, with the exception of Roelantsen, they were all of good reputation. While there were occasional lapses from the deportment exacted from those charged with the responsibility of directing the youth of the land, the number of such lapses and the seriousness of the offenses were no greater than those of other citizens whose positions in the community required them to be of exemplary habits.

When a master taught but six hours in a day, he had much spare time which he might use for other purposes. When he taught evenings as well as in the day time he was employed but nine hours. The means of recreation and diversion were so limited that any time not required for the performance of his school duties might be used for other purposes. It was the custom, therefore, for teachers to be employed in various other occupations outside of school hours. Through this outside service the master was able to supplement his income and meet the living expenses of his family. The master was therefore commonly employed as reader and precentor in the church, and as sexton. He frequently served as court messenger or town clerk, and he served legal processes and drew legal papers.

The compensation of a master was not uniform throughout the settlements. Neither was it exorbitant nor was it generally paid in currency. The salary of a master was commonly paid in beaver skins, wampum or seawan, wheat, peas or rye. As the value of these articles fluctuated more or less, the actual amount received by the master was often less than he had expected to receive. Sometimes it was more. The value of beaver skins and of grain fluctuated less than the value of wampum. The salary to be paid was expressed either in Holland coin or in equivalent values of the commodities substituted for the accepted currency. The *florin* or *guilder* was the unit and was equivalent to 40 cents of our money. It consisted of 20 *stivers* and a stiver therefore was equivalent to 2 cents. It was customary in all the settlements to provide the master with living quarters which were usually in the schoolhouse. He was given a fixed salary and required to give instruction to the poor children without tuition. He was allowed to receive tuition from other children but the amount was fixed by the authorities.

The amount received by masters for their services is shown in a general way by the records of certain contracts. In 1660 at Brooklyn the salary of a master was fixed at 150 guilders, or $60, a year, and in 1662 at Boswyck 400 guilders, or $160, a year. In an official estimate of the expenses of a proposed settlement in 1664 the item for the schoolmaster, who was also to serve as precentor and sexton, was fixed at 360 guilders, or $144, a year. In 1650 the salary of Verteusz in New Amsterdam was made 420 guilders or $168, a year. Verteusz was also paid 100 guilders, or $40, for board, though it was not usual to pay the board of a master. In 1655 at New

Amsterdam the amount was fixed at 520 guilders, or $208, a year. The letter to Evert Pietersen setting forth his duties as master may be regarded as providing the average salary of that date (1664). Under Pietersen's contract he was to receive 432 guilders, or $172.80, a year. The fees which he might charge pay students were as follows: for pupils taught a b c, spelling and reading, 120 stivers, or $2.40, a year; for pupils taught reading and writing, 200 stivers, or $4, a year; for pupils taught reading and writing and ciphering, 240 stivers, or $4.80, a year. If the master had twenty pay students he therefore received in addition to his regular salary $75.25. On this basis of computation Pietersen's income from teaching was $248 a year in addition to his living apartments. The salaries of the masters and the fees due them from parents were not always promptly paid as many instances are records of petitions to the court for the salary due from the city and of suits entered because of the failure of parents to pay tuition. Cases in which real hardships have been inflicted upon the families of masters are to be found because of these lapses. Unfortunately a state department of education possessing powers to adjudicate such questions and to direct payment thereof had not yet been created.

What kind of an institution was a typical Dutch colonial school? No picture of one of these schools is known to be in existence and no written description of one of these early institutions prepared during the time of their existence has been discovered. An examination of official records of various kinds, however, reveals certain facts in connection with the character of the schools maintained during the Dutch period. These facts, combined with our knowledge of the Dutch people and of the conditions of the Dutch period, enable us to present an accurate description of a school which is typical of those which were maintained in the Dutch settlements.

Were we permitted to look upon one of these schools today we should see a small building erected near the Dutch church. It would not be recognized as a school building of the twentieth century type and regarded by all citizens as the object of greatest pride in the community. The lots purchased by the council on which to erect a building generally ranged from 20 by 22 feet to 30 by 15 feet. I feel a sense of personal pride in stating that the largest building of which we have record was the one constructed at Beverwyck (Albany) on a lot 34 by 19 feet. In New Amsterdam the director general and council, in a spirit of liberality, voted that it would be more convenient if the schoolhouse were erected

A teacher's desk in a Dutch school, as pictured by David Van Der Kellen jr, in De Oude Tijd

A Dutch school as pictured by David Van Der Kellen jr, in De Oude Tijd

As Roelantsen appears to a modern artist of Dutch antecedents

on part of the graveyard. As small as these buildings may appear to have been for school purposes even, they also contained the living apartments of the schoolmaster's family. In the early part of the Dutch period special buildings for school purposes were not always erected and in such cases the school was conducted in the church steeple, in the church, in some public room when not in use for its regular purpose, or in rented quarters. At one time, when a more suitable place was not available, the school in New Amsterdam was conducted in the kitchen of the prosecuting officer of the city. No attention was given to the heating, lighting or sanitation of such buildings. At times, therefore, they were too warm and at others too cold. The furniture and equipment consisted of a chair and desk for the master, benches without backs upon which the children sat, and tables upon which they wrote. These, of course, were of the simplest and rudest type. If we could look into the interior of one of these desolate rooms we should see the master seated at his desk with his hat upon his head and dressed in the well-known Knickerbocker costume, the boys seated on one side of the room with their caps upon their heads, and the girls seated on the opposite side of the room. As the population of the settlements increased, assistant teachers were employed so that in many schools there was more than one teacher. It further appears that women, as well as men, were employed as assistant teachers.

The children usually began to attend school when they were from seven to eight years of age. It was intended that they should receive the prescribed instruction in a period of three years and they were generally required to leave school at the end of that period to make room for others. If a child had not completed the work prescribed when he reached the age of twelve years, he was generally compelled to attend evening school. It was the custom in all the Dutch settlements to open school in the morning at eight o'clock and continue the session until eleven. An intermission of two hours was then taken and the school reconvened at one o'clock and continued until four o'clock. The evening session opened at six o'clock and closed at nine o'clock. Three sessions of three hours each were therefore held each day. The same hours were not always prescribed for the summer which were prescribed for the winter. The school was conducted for six days in the week and was continued the entire year without vacation. School was not in session on Wednesday and Saturday afternoons, nor was it in session on St Nicholas Day (December 6), Christmas, New Year.

Easter and probably other days requiring special observance under Dutch custom. It will thus be observed that the maintenance of school was regarded as a matter of serious importance and it could not be charged that a child was wasting valuable time during vacation period. It may be parenthetically stated that there is so much merit in the prescribed school hours of the colonial Dutch school and its continuous session throughout the year that we might, with great profit to the interests involved in American education, incorporate such features in a modified form into our present state systems of education in this country.

The curriculum prescribed for these schools will, of course, indicate in a general way the object which the authorities had in mind in the establishment of schools. In a letter issued June 7, 1636, by the classis of Amsterdam, containing instruction for ministers, comforters of the sick, and schoolmasters going to the Indies, is the following statement bearing upon the curriculum of the schools maintained in the Dutch possessions:

He is to instruct the youth both on shipboard and on land, in reading, writing, ciphering, and arithmetic, with all zeal and diligence; he is also to implant the fundamental principles of true Christian religion and salvation, by means of catechizing; he is to teach them the customary forms of prayers, and also to accustom them to pray; he is to give heed to their manners, and bring these as far as possible to modesty and propriety, and to this end he is to maintain good discipline and order, and further to do all that is required of a good, diligent and faithful schoolmaster.

The records indicate that the colonial authorities usually issued a letter of instruction to teachers when they were first employed. When Evert Pietersen was employed as teacher at New Amsterdam in 1661, on the advice of the director general and council, the burgomaster issued him the following instruction:

1 He shall take good care, that the children, coming to his school, do so at the usual hour, namely at eight in the morning and one in the afternoon.

2 He must keep good discipline among his pupils.

3 He shall teach the children and pupils the Christian prayers, commandments, baptism, Lord's supper, and the questions with answers of the catechism, which are taught here on every Sunday afternoon in the church.

4 Before school closes he shall let the pupils sing some verses and a psalm.

5 Besides his yearly salary he shall be allowed to demand and receive from every pupil quarterly as follows: For each child, whom he teaches the a b c, spelling, and reading, 30 st.; for teaching to read and write, 50 st.; for teaching to read, write and cipher, 60 st.; from those who come in the evening and between times pro rata a fair sum. The poor and needy, who ask to be taught for God's sake, he shall teach for nothing.

6 He shall be allowed to demand and receive from everybody, who makes arrangements to come to his school and comes before the first half of the quarter preceding the first of December next, the school dues for the quarter, but nothing from those, who come after the first half of the quarter.

7 He shall not take from anybody, more than is herein stated. Thus done and decided by the Burgomasters of the City of Amsterdam, in N. N., November 4, 1661.

The program of instruction in the Dutch colonial schools was, therefore, a simple one. The backbone of the course of study was religious instruction. The main purpose for which schools had been established and maintained in the mother country was to inculcate in each soul the essential principles upon which Calvinism was founded. They believed that the preservation of their religious and civil liberties depended upon the rigid enforcement of such policy. The Dutch settlers in America were actuated by similar motives in the organization of schools here. The teaching of reading was only a means to this end. Children were therefore taught to read primarily to enable them to read the Scriptures. Formal prayers were provided for the opening and the closing of each session of the school. The children were required to learn these prayers and to recite them at the appropriate time each day. They were required to learn the Lord's prayer and to be able to recite that prayer when called upon. The children were also required to learn the "twelve articles of the Christian faith" and "the confession of sins" as established under the Calvinistic creed and also the ten commandments. They were required to commit to memory the two catechisms prescribed by the church and known as the small and the large catechisms. Certain selections from the Scriptures had been compiled for Sunday reading and they were required to learn these as well as certain psalms. The text used in teaching children to read was that which included the prayers and other religious matter which they were required to learn. The importance which the Dutch attached to religious instruction will be appreciated as this program of work in the schools is considered. In addition to this thorough religious instruction which was mandatory and given without fail, instruction was also mandatory in reading and in writing. Instruction in the subjects which have been enumerated was required of all children, both boys and girls. In addition to these subjects, the course of study included arithmetic. The teaching of arithmetic, however, was not mandatory and was taught in those schools only where there was an apparent need for the children to possess a knowledge of that subject. A knowledge of arithmetic was regarded as essential for those children only who expected to engage in commercial affairs. New Amsterdam and Albany gave instruction in arithmetic, but it was not generally provided in the schools of other settlements and all children in the schools in these two settlements did not receive such instruction. The master was required to examine or catechise his pupils once a week in the presence of the minister and the elders.

It will be readily understood, since the major part of the course of study related to religious instruction, why the schoolmaster was so closely associated with the work of the church. The schoolmaster generally performed the duties of reader (voorleger), precentor (voorsanger) and clerk. Dr William H. Kilpatrick of Columbia University, in his admirable treatise on the Dutch schools of New York, which has been of great service to me in the preparation of this paper, uses his imagination so skilfully in describing the service of the schoolmaster of a Dutch colonial school on Sunday that I have taken the liberty of quoting it here. It is as follows:

The master would on Sunday morning open the church, " place the stools and benches in the church or meeting house in order," put on the " psalm board " the psalms to be sung before the sermon, and ring the first bell. Then he would return to the schoolhouse (his home) where the children had in the meanwhile assembled, march with them to the church, and have the older ones sit about him to assist in the singing. The second bell would then be rung, after which he would " read a chapter out of the Holy Scriptures." "After the third ringing of the bell he shall read the ten commandments and the twelve articles of our faith, and then take the lead in the singing." It was the master's duty to secure proper behavior and attention during the church services. After the morning service there was an intermission for dinner. Then the pupils assembled in the schoolroom, where the older ones were questioned on the morning's sermon, and all on the catechism. This being done they marched to the church for afternoon service.

We are to understand, of course, that these early schools were not supplied with textbooks so generously and in such attractive and satisfactory pedagogical form as our modern schools. Textbooks were imported from Holland and invoices of these books, as well as inventories of the stock of book dealers, have been preserved in official records. Some of these books may now be found in book collections. These books were generally Bibles, psalm books, cathechisms, song books and arithmetics. One of the celebrated books was known as " The Arts of Letters." This was the a b c book used by the children who first entered school. Slates formed a part of the school equipment from the beginning. In 1665 a slate containing a frame was inventoried in an estate at Albany at a value of 10 guilders, or $4. The value of one without a frame was 4 guilders, or $1.60. No question was raised by the board of health or by the mothers' club on the use of the slate from a sanitary standpoint.

Discipline was severe and punishment was inflicted for slight offenses. The chief instruments of torture were those used in Holland and, unfortunately for the Dutch boys in America, brought to this country with the other essential equipment of a public school. These were a heavy wooden stick shaped like a paddle called a *plak* and the renowned switch as celebrated and necessary in public schools throughout the civilized world as the master himself and which was called the *roede*.

This review of the colonial schools covers the period included within the forty years of Dutch rule. It relates to elementary schools only. In 1674 the school at New Amsterdam, as we have already stated, passed into the control of the Reformed Dutch Church of that city and was continued under the management of that church. The schools in the other settlements were continued as city schools until the Revolution. The development of the Dutch system of elementary schools was discontinued when English rule became dominant. The influence of the schools which had been established, however, and the democratic principles upon which they had been constructed exerted an influence not only upon the life of the colony but even later upon the life of the State.

The population of New York increased more rapidly under the English than it had under the Dutch. New Amsterdam in 1674, which had then become New York, contained among its citizens representatives of eighteen nationalities. Elementary school facilities were not provided in accordance with the growth of the colony and the needs of its people. The general assembly, during the period of its existence, did not enact a single provision to promote elementary education. In 1713 John Sharpe, chaplain of the king's forces, expressed the educational needs of New York as follows:

There is hardly anything which is more wanted in this country than learning, there being no place I know of in America where it is less encouraged or regarded.

In 1741, in addition to the Dutch school, which was still in operation, there were six private English schools conducted in New York City. These were not, however, of a very stable class. Twenty-one years later, in 1762, there were two Dutch schools, ten English schools, one French school, and one Hebrew school. None of these were public schools and the only civil jurisdiction claimed over these schools was the right to license the teachers.

In the beginning of the eighteenth century the Society for the Propagation of the Gospel in Foreign Parts, an agency of the Church of England, was chartered by the king and began its propaganda for the establishment of society charity schools in America. In 1689 William Huddleston established a private school and after the founding of Trinity Church he brought his pupils to the church where the rector gave them instruction. Huddleston was an active worker and an official of Trinity Church. The private school which Huddleston had organized undoubtedly was the origin of Trinity School and was merged with that school in 1709 — the date which is usually given as the date of the founding of that school. Huddleston was chosen the teacher of Trinity School in that year. He conducted the school in his home and in the steeple of Trinity Church. The mayor and the common council permitted him to use the city hall for his school from 1714 to 1717. The following year the pupils of the school were assigned seats in Trinity Church. The interest of the church in the school constantly increased and in 1732 the church appointed a committee to inspect such school. Until 1740 this school had been regarded as the charity school of the S. P. G. but after that date it gradually became known as Trintty Church School, and in 1763 received the name " Trinity School — New York." The support of the Society for the Propagation of the Gospel to this school and its work in New York City was discontinued in 1784, and the school was continued under the general control and management of the authorities of the Protestant Episcopal Church. It has developed into a leading college preparatory school and has been for more than a century under the control of a corporation organized by an act of the Legislature in 1806 known as " The New York Protestant Episcopal Public School." The name of this corporation signifies the sources of support of this school.

Other schools were established by the society largely in territory adjacent to New York, and between 1710 and 1776, the society maintained continuously from five to ten elementary schools each having an average attendance of 40 pupils. It is known that schools were organized at Rye, White Plains, North Castle, West Chester, Yonkers, New Rochelle, Staten Island, Hempstead, Oyster Bay, Jamaica, Southampton, Brookhaven and Johnstown. The main purpose of these schools was to give religious instruction and to increase the prestige and influence of the Church of England. The

Trinity School as it appeared in 1918 (organized 1689); 139-47 W. 91st street, New York

The boys of Trinity School attending chapel (1918)

Gymnasium of Trinity School (1918)

curriculum in these schools did not differ materially from that of the Dutch schools. The text used was, of course, in English instead of Dutch. One material distinction between these schools and the schools of the Dutch period was that the teachers of the schools established by this society were licensed by the Bishop of Canterbury (later the Bishop of London) instead of the classis of Amsterdam.

Latin schools were maintained in nearly all the cities of Holland for the purpose of giving students desiring to pursue advanced study a thorough knowledge of the Latin and Greek languages. To accomplish this end pupils were prohibited from reciting in Dutch. The records show that a Latin school was established in New Amsterdam in 1652 and continued for two years. Jan M. de la Montague was the master. But little is known of the history of this school. On May 20, 1658, the directors of the West India Company presented a statement to the director general expressing the desirability of establishing a Latin school, and on September 19, 1658, the burgomasters and schepens of New Amsterdam also presented a petition to the council for a master of a Latin school. It was set forth in this petition that the nearest school where the children of the colony could receive instruction in Latin was at Boston and that the burghers could not afford to send their children to that place for such schooling. It was urged that if a Latin school were established in New Amsterdam the city would furnish a building and that pupils from neighboring settlements, as well as from that city, would attend the school. On April 10, 1659 the board of directors at Amsterdam selected Alexander Carolus Curtius as the teacher of a Latin school in New Amsterdam and on the 25th of that month he sailed from Holland. The exact date on which the Latin school was opened does not appear, but the school was in session on July 4, 1659. At that date Curtius appeared before the burgomasters, was paid 50 guilders and immediately requested that his salary be raised as he had but few pupils. Curtius was a physician and practised medicine in addition to conducting the school. He served as teacher of this school two years, as he was dismissed in July 1661. Time will not permit a review of his career as teacher of this school. It was a period of trouble for him and for the officials who were responsible for the management of the school. He was constantly requesting increased pay, he declined to pay proper claims against him, was charged by the court with cheating in a hog trade, and it further appears that he overcharged pupils for tuition. This offense was repeated after warning and he was dismissed. The school appears to have been successful but there was much trouble about his discipline. One parent complained that the boys fought among themselves and tore the clothes from each others bodies, and therefore requested that the master punish the boys and prevent such conduct. Another parent informed the master that he did not want his children punished. The master thereupon appealed to the burgomasters for the enactment of an ordinance defining his powers in such cases. These conflicting parental views on school discipline suggest that human nature was quite similar in some respects in the seventeenth century to what it is in the twentieth century. From some of my experiences during the past twenty-five years I am able to sympathize somewhat with the burgomasters who were called upon to settle that question.

The Latin school was not in operation for nearly a year but in 1662 the Rev. Aegidius Lewyck was appointed rector of the school and reopened it. He probably continued the school until 1664 when the colony passed under English rule. The support and management of these Latin schools was quite similar to that of the elementary schools. It appears that the salary of the Latin teachers was about twice that paid the elementary teachers.

In 1702 an act was passed " for the encouragement of a grammar free school in the city of New York." There is no record, however, that this school was established until 1704, but in April of that year George Muirson was licensed and authorized to teach such school. In the following October, his salary of 25 pounds was paid. In the early part of 1705, Mr Muirson went to London and Andrew Clarke was chosen his successor by the common council. There is no record of any kind indicating service by Mr Clarke and no further record of the work of the school. It was undoubtedly discontinued upon the retirement of Mr Muirson and its charter, which expired in 1707, was not renewed.

No further action to promote education was taken by the legislative authority of the colony until 1732, when the general assembly passed "An act to encourage a public school in the city of New York for teaching Latin, Greek and mathematics." Alexander Malcolm was the master of this school and conducted it for six years. Under the terms of this act, the city and county of New York was entitled to ten pupils, the city and county of Albany to two, the county of Kings to two, and each of the other counties to one pupil. This may be looked upon as the germ of the law of

The old Drumm house built in Johnstown in 1763 for the home of Edward Wall, the teacher of the first school in that part of the Mohawk valley

1912, which established 3000 state scholarships in the colleges of the University of this State and it may also be regarded as an indication of the development of public sentiment looking toward the establishment of a state system of education. The law authorized the establishment of the school for a period of five years and upon the expiration of that term, a bill to extend the school for one year was bitterly opposed but passed the General Assembly by only one majority.

The first grammar school founded west of Albany was probably at Cherry Valley in 1743.

It is stated by some authors that the efforts to establish Latin schools in New York in 1702 and 1732 may be traced as the origin of the establishment of Kings College. We find no evidence to sustain this theory. But one college was established during the colonial period — Kings College in 1754. A sharp controversy arose over the establishment of this institution. One party favored a charter granted by the king of England and the other party favored a charter granted by the colonial legislature. The former party succeeded and the charter was granted by King George II. Time will not permit a discussion of the issue which arose on the proposition to found the college. William Livingston, who was an adherent of the philosophy advocated by the followers of John Locke, was the leader of this opposition. He opposed with great zeal and effectiveness an appropriation of state funds for an educational institution which was to be controlled by a religious denomination. We see here the germ of the doctrine that public education is a matter of state concern and one of the basic principles upon which public school systems in the several states of this country have been constructed. The first class matriculated in this institution contained eight students. The course of study covered four years — the time of standard courses in all colleges and universities of the present day.

The college was organized by Dr Samuel Johnson, its first president. He was succeeded by Dr Myles Cooper, a graduate of Oxford, who conducted the institution until the outbreak of the Revolution when the doors of the college were closed for eight years. It is not possible to estimate the value of the services rendered by this institution, not only to New York but to the Nation as well. Many of the leaders of the State and of the Nation, in the constructive period of our national government following the Revolution, were educated and trained in this institution for the service which they rendered mankind. After the conclusion of peace, the college was reorganized, by an act of the Legislature, under the name of Columbia College, in honor of the discoverer of America. From an institution of eight students in 1754, Columbia has grown to be not only one of the largest universities but one of the most powerful and influential forces in the preservation and development of the advancing civilization of the world.

Under the Dutch rule there was a gradual separation between the influence of the church and of the civil authorities, and this movement extended to the secular control of the schools. During the century following the rule of the Dutch, this movement gained in strength with the people and developed into an open opposition to the ecclesiastical control not only of the schools but of civil affairs generally. Thus we find that after the adoption of the Duke's Laws on Long Island the people voted revenues for the support of the school at town meetings and also selected teachers by popular vote. The development of the spirit of democracy in the new republic founded after the close of the Revolution was such that the fundamental democratic spirit upon which the Dutch schools of the colony had been organized and maintained was made the basis of the establishment of a school system on such broad and comprehensive interest in human affairs that it administers to the intellectual necessities of ten million people.

As an illustration of the growth and development of the school system the accompanying pictures of school buildings in the city of New Rochelle are included. One of these pictures represents a building as it stands today, which was used for a public school in that city over one hundred years ago. This building is a fair illustration of the type of building and type of school which met the educational needs of the times in which this building was constructed.

The two pictures which follow — a modern elementary school building in New Rochelle (there being ten elementary school buildings in the city), and a modern high school building — are fair illustrations of the type of schools which are needed at the present time to meet the intellectual necessities of the people.

Building used as a schoolhouse in the city of New Rochelle more than a century ago. It is still standing as shown in the picture. This building served the intellectual necessities of that community in the early days

The building of the Johnstown Academy, incorporated by the Regents January 27, 1794

This picture indicates one of the ten elementary schools required in the city of New Rochelle for its present educational necessities

NEW ROCHELLE HIGH SCHOOL

This is a picture of the high school maintained in the city of New Rochelle to meet present day demands

Chapter 2
EDUCATION AFTER THE REVOLUTION

Immediately after the close of the Revolution, the subject of public education began to receive the attention of the foremost men of the country. In our own State, Clinton, Hamilton, Livingston, Jay and others advocated the adoption of means for the education of the masses. The British evacuated New York City in November 1783 and within two months thereafter the State Legislature was in session and Governor Clinton was stating to that body in his official message that the most important subject for their consideration was the necessity of providing for the education of the youth of the State. In 1784 and within six months after the defeated British forces had marched from New York City, the lawmaking body of the State enacted two laws which have exerted a mighty influence in the development of New York's public school system. These were the acts creating the University of the State of New York and the one to provide funds for the support of the schools. The first official statement setting forth the needs of a system of public schools came from the Board of Regents in 1787. A committee of that body of which Alexander Hamilton and Ezra L'Hommedieu were members submitted a report which contained the following statement: " Your committee feels bound to add that the erecting of public schools for teaching reading, writing and arithmetic is an object of very great importance, which ought not to be left to the discretion of private men, but be promoted by public authority."

Governor Clinton, in his annual messages, continued to impress upon the Legislature the importance of providing elementary schools. The Board of Regents in its annual reports to the Legislature joined with Governor Clinton in setting forth the supreme need of establishing schools throughout the State. In the reports for 1793, 1794 and 1795, the Regents again took strong ground upon this question and, in the latter year, the Legislature responded favorably. It may seem strange now that the Legislature acted with much deliberation upon a question of such pressing and momentous importance to the people. There was reason enough for such delay. The long struggle of the Revolution had impoverished the people; the population of the State was only 340,000; the expense of inaugurating a school system was a consideration at that day which properly made wise men cautious;

there were those who believed that parents should meet the entire expense of the education of their children; there were those who were indifferent to the proposition; and there were others who were positively opposed not only to the State's assuming direction of public education but even to the idea of educating the masses. Public sentiment, however, was fast ripening upon this question.

The Assembly of 1795 appointed a committee to consider that part of Governor Clinton's message which related to his recommendation on the establishment of a system of common schools. This committee reported a bill which became a law and was the beginning of the foundation on which the State school system was constructed. This law authorized **an annual appropriation of fifty thousand dollars for a period of five years**, to be apportioned to the localities which maintained schools. Each town was required to raise by taxation a sum equal to one-half the amount apportioned to it from the State fund. Localities were authorized to form associations for the purpose of maintaining schools and to elect two trustees to have charge of the general business affairs of the schools. The towns were required to elect from three to seven commissioners who were given supervision and direction of the schools and the power to determine the qualifications of teachers and to apportion the school funds. This scheme had no general directory or supervisory force and no cohesive power within itself and therefore completely broke down. It appears that about fifteen hundred schools had been organized within the five years for which appropriations had been authorized and that as many as sixty thousand children had attended them. They failed, however, to command sufficient respect and influence to induce the Legislature in 1800 to renew the appropriation for their support and were therefore discontinued in that year.

The full text of the law and the amendment to it made by the Legislature of 1796 are as follows:

Chapter 75
An Act for the encouragement of schools.

Passed the 9th of April, 1795

Be it enacted by the People of the State of New York, represented in Senate and Assembly That out of the annual revenue arising to this State from its stock and other funds, excepting so much thereof as shall be necessary for the support of government, the sum of twenty thousand pounds, shall be annually appropriated for the term of five years for the purpose of encouraging and maintaining schools in the several cities and towns in this

State, in which the children of the inhabitants residing in this State shall be instructed in the English language or be taught English grammar, arithmetic, mathematics and such other branches of knowledge as are most useful and necessary to complete a good English education; which sum shall be distributed among the several counties in the manner following until a new apportionment of the representation of the legislature of this State shall be made that is to say,

The city and county of New York shall be entitled to receive the sum of one thousand eight hundred and eighty eight pounds.

The county of Kings the sum of one hundred and seventy four pounds.

The county of Queens the sum of seven hundred and forty four pounds.

The county of Suffolk the sum of eight hundred and forty pounds.

The county of Richmond the sum of one hundred and seventy four pounds.

The county of West-Chester the sum of one thousand one hundred and ninety two pounds.

The county of Dutchess the sum of two thousand two hundred pounds.

The county of Ulster the sum of one thousand four hundred and forty pounds.

The county of Orange the sum of nine hundred and forty four pounds.

The county of Columbia the sum of one thousand three hundred and ninety pounds.

The county of Rensselaer the sum of one thousand one hundred and ninety two pounds.

The county of Washington the sum of one thousand one hundrd and fifty two pounds.

The county of Clinton the sum of two hundred pounds.

The county of Albany the sum of one thousand five hundred and ninety pounds.

The county of Saratoga the sum of one thousand and ninety two pounds.

The county of Herkimer the sum of nine hundred and thirty pounds.

The county of Montgomery the sum of eleven hundred and ninety two pounds.

The county of Otsego the sum of eight hundred and forty four pounds.

The county of Onondaga the sum of one hundred and seventy four pounds.

The county of Tioga the sum of three hundred and forty eight pounds and

The county of Ontario the sum of three hundred pounds and the treasurer of the State is hereby required to pay the said several sums of money to the treasurers of the respective counties or their respective orders on the third Tuesday of March in every year or as soon thereafter as the said monies shall come into his hands provided nevertheless that the first of the said annual payments shall be made on the third Tuesday of March in the year one thousand seven hundred and ninety six. And if the annual revenue of the State after deducting what may be necessary for the support of government shall not be sufficient for the payment of the whole of the said sum of money in any one year, then the treasurer of the State shall pay the same out of any monies not otherwise appropriated which may be or may come into the treasury, and if the whole of the said monies not otherwise appropriated shall not be sufficient for that purpose then every such payment shall be made to each county respectively in the same proportion as the whole of said money is hereby directed to be paid before the next apportionment of the representation on the legislature and after such next appropriation shall be made, every payment of the several counties shall be in proportion to the number of electors for members of assembly in each county. And the treasurers of the respective counties are hereby authorized to retain in their hands the sum of three pence in the pound for every pound of the monies which may come into their hands by virtue of this act as a compensation for their services in receiving and paying the same.

And whereas It will be expensive and inconvenient to enumerate the inhabitants of the several towns in every year. Therefore

Be it further enacted That it shall be the duty of the supervisors in each and every of the counties of this State, at their meeting on the last Tuesday of May or within ten days thereafter in every year to apportion the said respective sums among the several towns in their respective counties after having deducted the fees of the treasurers of their respective counties for receiving and paying the same, according to the number of taxable inhabitants which shall appear to be in several towns in each county, by the tax lists, directed to be annually returned to them by the act entitled "An act for defraying the public and necessary charge in the respective counties of this State and if at their said time of meeting no such tax list shall be returned to them, by the assessors of any one or more of the towns in any county then it shall be lawful for the supervisors to estimate the number of taxable inhabitants in any such town or towns according to the best information that they shall be able to obtain; and when such apportionment shall be completed the supervisors shall certify to each town the sum of money allotted to that town by virtue of this act; and a copy of such certificate, subscribed and sealed by them, shall be delivered to each supervisor present, who shall file the same in the office of the clerk of the town, for which he shall be supervisor, and when any one or more of the supervisors are absent, it shall be the duty of the clerk of the supervisors to transmit such certificates to the clerks of the several towns whose supervisors were not present at such annual meeting, and such clerks shall file the same in their respective offices.

And be it further enacted That the mayor, aldermen and commonalty of the city of New York in common council convened shall yearly and every year during the continuance of this act cause to be raised by a tax in the said city and county a sum equal to one half of the sum appropriated for encouraging and maintaining schools in the city and county for New York by virtue of this act in the same year to be added to and applied in the same manner with the money so appropriated as aforesaid, which said sums of money so to be raised shall be assessed levied and collected and paid according to the directions of the act entitled "An act for the more effectual collection of taxes in the city and county of New York."

And be it further enacted That the supervisors of each of the several other counties of this state shall yearly and every year during the continuance of the act cause to be raised by a tax in each town in the same county a sum equal to one half of the sum to be allotted to the same town in the same year out of the money so appropriated to the county by the State in the same year by virtue of this act to be added to and applied in the same manner with the money so to be allowed to the same town in the same year by virtue of this act which said sums of money shall be raised levied collected and paid to the treasurer of the same county together with and in the same manner as the necessary and contingent charges of the said county are to be raised collected and paid by virtue of the act entitled An act for defraying the public and necessary charge in the respective counties of this State.

And be it further enacted that it shall and may be lawful for the mayor aldermen and commonalty of the city of New York in common council convened from time to time during the continuance of this act to cause as well the money so appropriated for encouraging and maintaining schools in the city and county of New York as the money to be raised in the said city and county for the same purpose by virtue of this act to be applied as well as for the encouragement and maintaining of the several charity schools as of other schools in which children shall be instructed in the English language or taught English grammar arithmetic mathematics and such other branches of knowledge as are most useful and necessary to complete a good English education whether the children taught in such charity school shall be the children of white parents or descended from Africans or Indians in such manner as the common council shall think proper and in conformity with the intent of the act and shall on or before the first day of November in the year of our Lord one thousand seven hundred and ninety six and on or before the first day of November in every year thereafter during the continuance of this act cause an account of the application and distribution of the said monies to be filed in the office of the secretary of the State who shall deliver the same to the legislature at their next session.

And be it further enacted That on the distribution of the monies assigned to or to be raised within the city and company of New York amongst the different schools in the said city that if one or more of the said schools should refuse to receive their respective proportions of the money so assigned or raised as aforesaid then in that case the same shall be appropriated to the charity schools in the said city at the discretion of the said common council.

And be it further enacted That the supervisors of the county of Albany shall yearly and every year during the continuance of this act cause to be raised by a tax in the city of Albany a sum equal to the half sum to be appropriated for encouraging and maintaining schools in the said city by virtue of this act in the same year to be added to and applied the same manner with the monies so appropriated as aforesaid which said sum of money so to be raised shall be assessed levied and collected and paid to the treasurer of the same county together with and in the same manner as the necessary and contingent charges of the same county are to be raised collected and paid by virtue of the act entitled An act for defraying the public and necessary charge in the respective counties of this State.

And be it further enacted That it shall be lawful for the mayor aldermen and commonalty of the city of Albany in common council convened from time to time during the continuance of this act to cause as well the money so appropriated for encouraging and maintaining schools in the city of Albany as the money to be raised in the said city for the same purpose by virtue of this act to be applied for the encouragement and maintenance of the schools in which children shall be instructed in the English language or taught English grammar arithmetic mathematics and such other branches of knowledge as are most useful and necessary to complete a good English education in such manner as the common council shall think proper and most agreeable to the intent of this act on or before the first day of November in the year of our Lord one thousand seven hundred and ninety six and on or before the first day of November in every year thereafter during the continuance of this act cause an account of the application of the said monies to be filed in the office of the secretary of this State who shall deliver the same to the legislature at their then next session and the treasurer of the said county of Albany is hereby directed to pay as well the money so to be allotted to as to be raised in the said city of Albany for encouraging and maintaining schools in the said city of Albany to the order of the mayor aldermen and commonalty of the city of Albany to be by them appropriated as aforesaid.

And be it further enacted That it shall be lawful for the freeholders and inhabitants in the several towns in the State who may be qualified by law to vote at town meeings to elect at their respective annual town meetings not less than three nor more than seven persons who shall have the superintendence thereof and shall determine concerning the distribution of the monies allotted or raised in the same town for the purpose of encouraging and maintaining schools by virtue of this act in the manner hereafter directed provided that for the present year the supervisor and town clerk and assessors shall be commissioners.

And be it further enacted That the city of Hudson in the county of Columbia shall be considered as a town for all the purposes contemplated in this act: And the freemen of the said city being inhabitants thereof shall annually elect commissioners of schools in like manner as last above prescribed, and at such time in every year as they are by law directed to elect aldermen assistants, and other officers in and for the said city and the said commissioners when so elected and qualified as above prescribed shall continue in office for the like time perform the like duties, exercise the like powers and proceed in doing business in like manner as the commissioners of schools in the several towns in the State; and every certificate or other matter in writing which is hereby directed to be filed in the office of the clerk of any town, shall in and for the said city be filed in the office of the clerk of the city and that the city of Albany in the county of Albany shall be considered as a town in the distribution to be made by the supervisors of the same county of the money appropriated to the same county by this act.

And be it further enacted That for the purpose of deriving a benefit from the monies hereby appropriated it shall be lawful for the inhabitants residing in the different parts of any town to associate together for the purpose of procuring good and sufficient schoolmasters, and for erecting or maintaining schools, in such and so many parts of the town where they may reside as shall be found most convenient and in which shall be taught such branches of learning as are intended to receive encouragement from the monies hereby appropriated. And all such persons as may associate together for the purposes above mentioned, shall appoint two other persons to act in their behalf as trustees of every school. *Provided nevertheless* that no person shall be appointed a trustee of any such school who may be, in any other manner authorized or empowered to carry this act into effect and the said trustees shall whenever they judge it necessary confer with the commissioners of schools for the town or ward where they may reside concerning the qualifications of the master or masters that they may have employed or may intend to employ, in their school, and concerning every other matter which may relate to the welfare of their school or to the propriety of erecting or maintaining the same, to the intent that they may obtain the determination of the said commissioners whether the said school will be entitled to a part of the moneys allotted to or raised in that town by virtue of this act and whether the abilities and moral character of the master or masters employed or intended to be employed therein are such as will meet with their approbation. And the said trustees of the said several schools shall on the third Tuesday in March in every year or within four days thereafter make a return certified under their respective hands to the commissioners of schools for the town where their respective schools may have been kept containing the name or names of the master or masters who in the year next preceding may have instructed in the school for which they were appointed trustees and the time or times when they severally began and left off instructing in the said school and the number of days they may have severally instructed therein, and the terms upon which they have severally agreed to instruct, in the same and the names of the scholars who in that year have been instructed therein and the number of days which they have severally attended the school and the time or times with which the school has been kept in that year *provided nevertheless* That the name of any child who shall be under the age of four years shall not be inserted in any such returns and if after the receipt of the said returns it shall appear to the said commissioners that there is no material error, fraud or deception in them they shall collect into one sum the whole number of days for which each and every scholar that may attended any one of the said schools shall have been instructed therein, and shall apportion the monies allotted to and raised in that town for that purpose aforesaid according to the whole number of days for which instruction shall appear to have been given in each of the said schools in such manner that the school in which the greater number of days of instruction shall appear to have been given shall have a proportionally larger sum and if it shall at any time appear to the said commissioners that the abilities or moral character of the master or masters of any school are not such that they ought to be entrusted with the education of youth or that any of the branches of learning taught in any school are not such as are intended to receive encouragement from the monies appropriated by this act the said commissioners shall notify in writing the said trustees of such notification and no longer shall any allowance be made to such school unless the same thereafter be conducted to the approbation of the said commissioners and where more masters than one shall have been employed in any school the said commissioners shall apportion the monies allotted to that school among the said several masters according to such agreement as shall have been made with them by the trustees of said school or by any other person or persons who may have procured them.

And be it further enacted That nothing herein contained shall be construed to prevent the inhabitants residing near the limits or borders of any town from associating with inhabitants residing in any adjoining town for the purposes above mentioned and in every such case the trustees of the school shall be residents of the town shall make the like distribution to such school as is hereinbefore prescribed with respect to the other schools in such town.

An be it further enacted That the said commissioners in every town shall provide a book in which they shall make an entry of every school under their superintendence the names of the trustees and the names of masters the time of application made to them by the trustees and the time of approbation of the said commissioners as well of schools already established during the continuance of this act and shall on the last Tuesday in May in every year from the return of the trustees with such vouchers as may be necessary determine the sums due to the trustees of the respective schools and shall give to the trustees of each school an order on the treasurer of the county for the sum of which they shall so determine to be due and the treasurer of the county is hereby required to pay the same.

And be it further enacted That the commissioners in the several towns within this State shall on or before the first day of July in the year one thousand seven hundred and ninety-six and in every year thereafter during the continuance of this act delivered to the treasurer of their respective counties a schedule containing the number of schools the masters names the number of scholars taught and the number of days of instruction in the school of which they were the commissioners and the treasurers of the several counties shall on or before the first day of November in every year transmit the same to the secretaries office and the secretary shall lay the same before the legislature at their next meeting.

And whereas special provisions hath already been made for the encouragement of learning in the several colleges and academies in the State. Therefore

Be it further enacted That nothing in this act contained shall be so construed as to extend to any college or academy which is or hereafter shall be incorporated under the authority of the regents of the university or by virtue of any law of the State.

And be it further enacted That this act shall be in force and take effect, from and after the first Tuesday of April one thousand seven hundred and ninety-five.

Chapter 49

An act to amend the act entitled An act for the encouragement of schools.

Passed the 6th of April, 1796

Whereas it is provided by the twelfth section of the act entitled An act for the encouragement of schools that the inhabitants of two adjoining towns may associate for the purpose of erecting schools in conformity to the said act and that commissioners of the town in which the school is kept shall make the like distribution to such school as to schools wholly composed of children belonging to the town in which the school is kept which in many instances is likely to operate unequally between the inhabitants of said towns. For remedy whereof

Be it enacted by the People of the State of New York represented in Senate and Assembly That the commissioners of the adjoining towns in which such association shall take place shall respectively furnish monies to such school in the same manner as is directed with regard to other schools in proportion to the number of scholars from each town respectively and the trustees of the school in the town where such school is so kept shall direct a separate account of the days of instruction that shall be so given to scholars that belong to such adjoining town and deliver the same to the commissioners of schools of such adjoining town and the said commissioners shall pay the proportion of said money to said trustees accordingly.

And be it further enacted That the children of the inhabitants of any town where there is an academy incorporated or to be incorporated, and shall be taught in such academy only reading writing and common arithmetic shall be considered as scholars of common schools are considered by the act entitled "An act for the encouragement of schools" and shall have the like benefit as other scholars belonging to the common schools in the same town as the gratuity of this state and the tax to be raised in the same town.

Chapter 3
THE LAW OF 1812

Each year thereafter the Governor in his messages and the friends of the schools who were in the Legislature pressed the issue to the front until the year 1811 when Governor Tompkins was authorized to appoint another committee to report to the Legislature the following year " a system for the organization and establishment of common schools." This committee gave the question most careful consideration. They evidently made an exhaustive study of the plans pursued in other countries and submitted to the Legislature of 1812 a report which forms one of the most important educational documents in the history of the State. The committee also submitted with its report the draft of a bill to carry into effect the recommendations made in its report. This bill was enacted in to law by the Legislature of 1812. Its principal provisions were as follows:

1 The present plan of school districts was provided. The territory in each town was divided into such districts by three commissioners chosen for this special purpose at the town meeting.

2 A complete and effective school organization was created in each district, consisting of three trustees, a collector and a clerk.

3 The principle that all teachers should possess moral character and certain scholastic qualifications was established and local officers known as town commissioners and inspectors were created to determine such qualifications and also to inspect the schools.

4 The office of state superintendent of common schools was created, being the first office of the kind to be established by any state in the Union. This officer was given sufficient directory and supervisory authority to initiate proceedings to set the machinery of each district into operation and the power to bind the schools together into one strong, aggressive force to accomplish the purposes for which the State created it.

5 Each district was required to provide a schoolhouse and site, to keep the building in repair and to furnish necessary appendages and fuel. A tax could be laid upon the property of the district for this purpose.

6 Trustees were authorized to employ a teacher and fix the compensation.

7 The money apportioned to a district from the school funds could be used only in the payment of teachers' salaries.

These were the broad lines upon which the schools were to be conducted and each of these general provisions has been continued in the management of our school system through the century which followed. This fact is evidence of the wisdom and the keen vision which was possessed by our forefathers who constructed the machinery for the operation of an organization so vast in its importance, touching as it does the most cherished interests of every fireside in the Commonwealth.

In addition to these provisions of the law there are certain important fundamental principles of State policy involved which should be briefly considered.

1 That public education was a State function and that public schools should be fostered and maintained under State supervision, was determined.

2 That in the accomplishment of this purpose a State system of tax-supported schools should be established and officers chosen in the several localities to execute the State's policy in relation to public education.

3 That where the funds of the State go, the authority and supervision of the State must follow.

A comparison of the essential features of the school system adopted in 1812 with the school system developed in Holland in the sixteenth and seventeenth centuries and also with schools maintained in the Dutch villages of New York during the period of Dutch rule will reveal types of schools which are strikingly similar. There was, however, one predominant influence in the Holland and in the Dutch colonial schools which was absolutely eliminated in the system of 1812. This was the ecclesiastical power. It will be observed that the secular influence which had gained such great ground throughout the civilized world where the people were responsive to the influences of democracy was in complete control of the schools.

The Rate-bill System

There were three sources from which the necessary revenues for meeting the expenses of maintaining schools were derived: (1) the district imposed a tax for the expense of providing a schoolhouse, fuel etc., and the tuition of indigent children; (2) the fund apportioned by the State, which was about twenty dollars for each district, was to be applied exclusively toward the payment of the salary of the teacher; (3) the balance necessary to meet the deficiency in the salary of the teacher was assessed upon the parents of the children who attended school. The children of the indigent were exempt from the payment of tuition. This assessment upon parents authorized in 1814 was the inauguration of what was known as the rate-bill system.

This plan often placed a burden upon the poor which they were not able to meet. To avoid it, they must acknowledge that they were indigent. The tuition was then assumed by the district and entry of the payment thereof made in the public records. The children affected were therefore publicly branded as indigent children and the recipients of charity. The whole plan was repugnant to the proper spirit of democratic institutions in the dawn of the nineteenth century. It was doubtless an inheritance from Holland. In that country, during the seventeenth century, as we have already observed, the poor children were admitted to school upon request without the payment of tuition. A similar plan prevailed in the Dutch schools in America. While the establishment of a system of common schools was an expression of the democracy which prevailed after the close of the Revolution, our democratic tendencies had not yet reached that development where human rights were always to be regarded as superior to property rights. We were not yet ready to adopt the principle that it is the obligation of the State to provide for the education of all its children.

This very question which seems so simple now was one of the most troublesome in the development of the public school system. It is probably within the truth to say that no other question agitated the public mind to a greater extent and was a source of greater feeling among the people for so long a period of time. It was a subject of bitter controversy in the legislative halls of the State for over a half century before a solution was reached.

The report of the committee appointed by Governor Tompkins, and the law which was enacted upon the basis of such report, are such important documents in the development of our educational history that the full text of each is included herein. These documents are as follows:

Monday, February 17th, 1812
The house met pursuant to adjournment.

A message from his excellency the Governor, delivered by his private secretary, was read, and is in the words following, to wit:

GENTLEMEN: Pursuant to the power, vested in me, by the act passed April 9, 1811, Jedediah Peck, John Murray, junior, Samuel Russel, Roger

Skinner and Robert Macomb, were appointed Commissioners, to report a system for the organization and establishment of Common Schools. The system they have devised, is now submitted to the consideration of the Legislature.

DANIEL D. TOMPKINS

Albany, Feb. 17, 1812

To D. D. Tompkins, Governor, &c.

The Commissioners appointed, "to Report a system for the organization and establishment of Common Schools, and the distribution of the interest of the School Fund, among the Common School of this state," beg leave to present the accompanying report and draught of a bill.

JOHN MURRAY, Jun., *Chairman*

ROBERT MACOMB, *Sec'ry.*

Albany, February 14, 1812

The Commissioners appointed by the Governor, pursuant to the Act passed April 9th, 1811, to report a system for the organization and establishment of Common Schools and the distribution of the interest of the School Fund among the Common Schools of this State, beg leave respectfully to submit the following

Report—

PERHAPS there never will be presented to the legislature a subject of more importance than the establishment of common-schools. Education, as the means of improving the moral and intellectual faculties, is, under all circumstances, a subject of the most imposing consideration. To rescue man from that state of degradation to which he is doomed, unless redeemed by education; to unfold his physical, intellectual, and moral powers; and to fit him for those high destinies which his Creator has prepared for him, cannot fail to excite the most ardent sensibility of the philosopher and the philanthropist.—A comparison of the savage that roams through the forest, with the enlightened inhabitant of a civilized country, would be a brief, but impressive representation, of the momentous importance of education.

It were an easy task for the commissioners to show, that in proportion as every country has been enlightened by education, so has been its prosperity. Where the heads and the hearts of men are generally cultivated, and improved, virtue and wisdom must reign, and vice and ignorance must cease to prevail. Virtue and wisdom are the parents of private and public felicity, vice and ignorance of private and public misery.

If education be the cause of the advancement of other nations, it must be apparent to the most superficial observer of our peculiar political constitutions, that it is essential, not to our prosperity only, but to the very existence of our government. Whatever may be the effect of education on a despotic, or monarchial government, it is not absolutely indispensable to the existence of either. In a despotic government the people have no agency whatever, either in the formation or in the execution of the laws. They are the mere slaves of arbitrary authority, holding their lives and property at the pleasure of uncontrolled caprice. As the will of the ruler is the supreme law, fear, slavish fear, on the part of the governed, is the principle of despotism. It will be perceived readily, that ignorance on the part of the people can present no barrier to the administration of such a government; and much less can it endanger its existence. In a monarchial government the operation of fixed laws is intended to supersede the necessity of intelligence in the people. But in a government like ours where the people is the sovereign power; where the will of the people is the law of the land, which will is openly and directly expressed; and where every act of the government, may justly be called the act of the people, it is absolutely essential that that people be enlightened. They must possess both intelligence and virtue; intelligence to perceive what is right, and virtue to do what is right. Our republic, therefore, may justly be said to be founded on the intelligence and virtue of the people. For this reason it is with much propriety, that the enlightened Montesquieu has said, " in a republic the whole force of education is required."

The commissioners think it unnecessary to represent in a stronger point of view, the importance, and absolute necessity of education, as connected either with the cause of religion and morality, or with the prosperity and existence of our political institutions. As the people must receive the advantages of education, the enquiry naturally arises, how this end is to be attained. The expedient devised by the legislature, is the establishment of common-schools which being spread throughout the state, and aided by its bounty, will bring improvement within the reach and power of the humblest citizen. This appears to be the best plan that can be devised, to disseminate religion, morality and learning throughout a whole country. All other methods, heretofore adopted, are partial in their operation, and circumscribed in their effects. Academies and universities, understood in contradistinction to common-schools, cannot be considered as operating impartially and indiscriminately, as regards the country at large. The advantages of the first are confined to the particular districts in which they are established; and the second, from causes apparent to every one, are devoted almost exclusively to the rich. In a free government, where political equality is established, and where the roads to preferment is open to all, there is a natural stimulus to education; and accordingly we find it generally resorted to, unless some great local impediments interfere. In populous cities, and the parts of the country thickly settled, schools are generally established by individual exertion. In these cases, the means of education are facilitated, as the expenses of schools are divided among a great many. It is in the remote and thinly populated parts of the state, where the inhabitants are scattered over a large extent, that education stands greatly in need of encouragement. The people here living far from each other, makes it difficult so to establish schools, as to render them convenient or accessible to all. Every family, therefore, must either educate its own children, or the children must forego the advantages of education.

These inconveniences can be remedied best by the establishment of common-schools, under the direction and patronage of the state. In these schools should be taught, at least, those branches of education which are indispensably necessary to every person in his intercourse with the world, and to the performance of his duty as a useful citizen. Reading, writing, arithmetic, and the principles of morality, are essential to every person, however humble his situation in life. Without the first, it is impossible to receive those lessons of morality, which are inculcated in the writings of the learned and pious; nor is it possible to become acquainted with our political constitutions and laws; nor to decide those great political questions, which ultimately are referred to the intelligence of the people. Writing and arithmetic are indispensable in the management of one's private affairs, and to facilitate one's commerce with the world. Morality and religion are the foundation of all that is truly great and good, and are consequently of primary importance. A person provided with these acquisitions, is enabled to pass through the world respectably and successfully. If, however, it be his intention to become acquainted with the higher branches of science, the academies and universities established in different parts of the state, are open to him. In this manner, education, in all its stages, is offered to the citizens generally.

In devising a plan for the organization and establishment of common-schools, the commissioners have proceeded with great care and deliberation. To frame a system which must directly affect every citizen in the state, and so to regulate it, as that it shall obviate individual and local discontent, and yet be generally beneficial, is a task, at once, perplexing and arduous. To avoid the imputation of local partiality, and to devise a plan, operating with equal mildness and advantage, has been the object of the commissioners. To effect this end they have consulted the experience of others, and resorted to every probable source of intelligence. From neighboring states, where common-school systems are established by law, they have derived much important information. This information is doubly valuable, as it is the result of long and actual experience. The commissioners by closely examining the rise and progress of those systems, have been able to obviate many imperfections, otherwise inseparable from the novelty of the establishment, and to discover the means by which they have gradually risen to their present condition.

The outlines of the plan, suggested by the commissioners, are briefly these. That the several towns in the state, be divided into school districts, by three commissioners, elected by the citizens qualified to vote for town officers: That trustees be elected in each district, to whom shall be confided the care and superintendence of the school to be established therein: That the interest of the school-fund be divided among the different counties and towns, according to their respective population, as ascertained by the successive census of the United States: That the proportion received by the respective towns, be subdivided among the districts, into which such towns shall be divided, according to the number of children in each, between the ages of five and fifteen years inclusive: That each town raise, by tax, annually, as much money as it shall have received from the school-fund: That the gross amount of monies received from the state and raised by the towns, be appropriated, exclusively, to the payment of the wages of the teachers: That the whole system be placed under the superintendence of an officer, appointed by the Council of Appointment. These are the great outlines of the plan; the details will appear more fully by the annexed sketch of a law, submitted to the consideration of the legislature.

This being the plan devised by the commissioners, let us next enquire what means the legislature have assigned to carry it into effect. This will be explained by a reference to the report of the comptroller of the state, made to the legislature, the 11th of February instant, By this it appears that the SCHOOL-FUND is composed of the following items:

Bonds and mortgages for part of the consideration money of lands sold by the Surveyor-General..........................	$240,370.67
3000 shares of the capital stock of the Merchants' Bank........	150,000.00
300 shares of the capital stock of the Hudson Bank............	15,000.00
Mortgages for loans..	101,924.52
Bond of Horatio G. Spafford and sureties for a loan..........	3,000.00
Bond of the Mechanics' Bank in the city of New-York.........	10,000.00
Arrears of interest due on the bonds and mortgages of the fund.	35,831.13
Balance in the Treasury on the 31st December, 1811, belonging to this fund...	2,338.37
Dolls.	558,464.69

REVENUE

The revenue of the School-Fund for this year is estimated at $45,216.95 arising from the following sources.

Annual interest on bonds and mortgages......................	$21,766.95
Dividends on bank stock.....................................	14,850.00
Probable collections from persons refusing to do military duty.	1,600.00
Proceeds of the Clerk's Office of the Supreme Court..........	7,000.00
	45,216.95

It further appears, by the same report, that of the 500,000 acres of land which are directed, by law, to be sold for the benefit of the school-fund, the Surveyor-General has already sold 198,507$\frac{656}{1000}$ acres, leaving 301,492$\frac{344}{1000}$ acres yet to be appropriated to that purpose. As soon as this fund shall have produced a revenue of $50,000, that revenue, by the act of April 2d, 1805, is to be divided among the different counties of the state.

It will readily be perceived by the legislature that if the common-school establishment, were intended to be maintained by this fund exclusively, the fund would fall far short of being adequate to the object. A brief statement will make this fact very apparent.

Let us suppose that the school-fund were arrived at that point, when by law it is to be divided — There will then be 50,000 dollars of public money to be distributed among the schools; and as, by the contemplated plan, a sum is to be raised, annually, by tax equal to the interest of the school-fund, the gross amount of monies which the school will receive, will be $100,000. There are in this State, 45 counties, comprising, exclusively of the cities, 449 towns. It will be very evident, therefore, that the proportion of each town must necessarily be small. As, however, the school-districts are authorized to raise, by tax, a sum sufficient to purchase a lot, on which the school-house is to be built; to build the school-house; and to keep the same in repair; and as the school-monies are devoted, exclusively, to the payment of the teacher's wages, the sum, however small, which each district will be entitled to, will be, from these considerations, so much the more efficacious. It will however, be evident to the legislature, that the funds appropriated, by the state, for the support of the common-school system, will, alone, be very inadequate:

And the commissioners are of opinion, that the fund in any stage of it, even when the residue of the unsold lands shall be converted into money bearing an interest, never will be alone adequate to the maintenance of common-schools; as the increase of the population, will probably be, in as great, if not a greater ratio, than that of the fund. But it is hardly to be imagined, the legislature intended that the state should support the whole expence of so great an establishment. The object of the legislature, as understood by the commissioners, was to arouse the public attention to the important subject of education, and by adopting a system of common-schools, in the expence of which the state would largely participate, to bring instruction within the reach and means of the humblest citizen—And the commissioners have kept in view the furtherance of this object of the legislature: for by requiring each district to raise, by tax, a sum sufficient to build and repair a school-house; and by allotting the school-monies solely to the payment of the teacher's wages, they have, in a measure, supplied two of the most important sources of expence. Thus every inducement will be held out to the instruction of youth.

As to the particular mode of instruction best calculated to communicate to the young mind the greatest quantity of useful knowledge, in a given time, and with the least expence, the commissioners beg leave to observe, that there are a variety of new methods lately adopted, in various parts of Europe, of imparting instruction to youth, some of which methods have been partially introduced into the United States. The Lancastrian plan, as it is called, which has lately been introduced into some of the large towns of the United States, merits the serious consideration of the legislature. As an expeditious and cheap mode of instructing a large number of scholars, it stands unrivaled. And the subjoined certificates of the trustees of the New-York Free-School, together with those of divers tutors, carry with them the evidence of its vast utility and success. The commissioners, therefore, recommended that a number of Lancaster's books, containing an account of his mode of teaching, &c. be printed, by order of the legislature, and distributed among the several towns in this state with the annexed certificates of recommendation.

The legislature will perceive, in the system contained in the bill submitted to their consideration, that the commissioners are deeply impressed with the importance of admitting, under the contemplated plan, such teachers only, as are duly qualified. The respectability of every school must necessarily depend on the character of the master. To entitle a teacher to assume the control of a school, he should be endowed with the requisite literary qualifications not only, but with unimpeachable character. He should also be a man of patient and mild temperament. "A preceptor," says Rousseau, "is invested with the rights and takes upon himself "the obligations of both father and mother." And Quintilian tells us "that to the requisite literary and moral endowments, he must "add the benevolent disposition of a parent."

To enable a teacher to perform the trust reposed in him, the above qualifications are indispensable. When we consider the tender age at which children are sent to school; the length of time they pass under the direction of the teachers; when we consider that their little minds are to be diverted from their natural propensities, to the artificial acquisition of knowledge; that they are to be prepared for the reception of great moral and religious truths;

to be inspired with a love of virtue and detestation of vice; we will forcibly perceive the absolute necessity of the above qualifications in the master. As an impediment to bad men getting into the schools, as teachers, it is made the duty of the town-inspectors strictly to enquire into the moral and literary qualifications of those who may be candidates for the place of teacher. And it is hoped that this precaution aided by that desire which generally prevails of employing good men only will render it unnecessary to resort to any other measure.

The commissioners at the same time that they feel impressed with the importance of employing teachers of the character described, cannot refrain from expressing their solicitude as to the introduction of proper books into the contemplated schools. This is a subject so intimately connected with a good education, that it merits the serious consideration of all who are concerned in the establishment and management of schools. Much good is to be derived from a judicious selection of books, calculated to enlighten the understanding not only, but to improve the heart. And as it is of incalculable consequence to guard the young and tender mind from receiving falacious impressions, the commissioners cannot omit mentioning this subject as a part of the weighty trust reposed in them. Connected with the introduction of suitable books, the commissioners take the liberty of suggesting that some observations and device touching the reading of the Bible in the schools might be salutary. In order to render the sacred volume productive of the greatest advantage, it should be held in a very different light from that of a common school-book. It should be regarded as a book intended for literary improvement not merely, but as inculcating great and indispensable moral truths also. With these impressions, the commissioners are induced to recommend the practice introduced into the New-York Free-School, of having select chapters read at the opening of the school in the morning, and the like at the close in the afternoon. This is deemed the best mode of preserving the religious regard which is due to the sacred writings.

It will naturally occur to the legislature, as the interest of the school-fund is to be divided every year among the counties and towns as soon as it shall amount to 50,000 dollars annually, that this sum must be forth-coming on a fixed day, annually, to meet the contingencies for which it is appropriated. Without a certainty in the payment of the annual appropriation, the whole system will be impeded in its operation. By a recurrence to the report of the Comptroller, it will appear that the greatest part of the revenue of the school-fund arises from sources which preclude the probability of certainty in the receipt. The interest arising from monies loaned on mortgage, the net proceeds of the officers of the clerks of the supreme court, &c. cannot be counted on with any certainty as to time. This inconvenience must be, in some way, remedied. And the most advisable method that occurs to the commissioners will be, by the annual appropriation, by the state, of a sum equal to the interest of the school-fund, the state having recourse to the debtors of the fund for arrears of interest for its reimbursement.

The commissioners have deemed it proper to recommend to the legislature the appointment of an officer, whose duty it shall be to superintend, generally, the interest, and watch the operations of the common-school system. They are induced to this measure by the consideration that the system is sufficiently important to justify the measure.

The commissioners cannot conclude this report without expressing, once more, their deep sense of the momentous subject committed to them. If we regard it as connected with the cause of religion and morality merely, its aspect is awfully solemn. But the other view of it, already alluded to, is sufficient to excite the keenest solicitude in the legislative body. It is a subject, let it be repeated, intimately connected with the permanent prosperity of our political institutions. The American empire is founded on the virtue and intelligence of the people. But it were irrational to conceive that any form of government can long exist without virtue in the people. Where the largest portion of a nation is vicious, the government must cease to exist, as it loses its functions. The laws cannot be executed where every man has a personal interest in screening and protecting the profligate and abandoned. When these are unrestrained by the wholesome coercion of authority, they give way to every species of excess and crime: One enormity brings on another, until the whole community becoming corrupt, bursts forth into some mighty change, or sinks at once into annihilation. " Can it be," said Washington, " that providence has not connected the permanent felicity of a nation with its virtue? The experiment, at least, is recommended by every sentiment which ennobles human nature."

And the commissioners cannot but hope, that that Being, who rules the universe in justice and in mercy, who rewards virtue and punishes vice, will most graciously deign to smile benignly on the humble efforts of a people in a cause purely his own; and that he will manifest his pleasure in the lasting prosperity of our country.

JEDIDIAH PECK
JOHN MURRAY, JUN.
SAM'L. RUSSEL } *Commissioners*
ROGER SKINNER
ROBERT MACOMB

Dated Albany, February 14, 1812

Chapter CCXLII

An act for the establishment of common schools.

Passed June 19, 1812

I *Be it enacted by the People of the State of New York, represented in Senate and Assembly,* That there shall be constituted an officer within this state, known and distinguished as the superintendent of common schools, which superintendent shall be appointed by the council of appointment, and shall keep his office at the seat of government, and shall be allowed an annual salary of three hundred dollars, but not to be under pay until he shall give notice of the first distribution of the school money, payable in the same way as is provided for other officers, by the act, entitled "An act for the support of government."

II *And be it further enacted,* That it shall be the duty of the superintendent aforesaid, to digest and prepare plans for the improvement and management of the common school fund, and for the better organization of common schools; to prepare and report estimates and expenditures of the school monies, to superintend the collection thereof, to execute such services relative to the sale of the lands, which now are or hereafter may be appropriated, as a permanent fund for the support of common schools, as may be by law required of him; to give information to the legislature respecting all matters referred to him by either branch thereof, or which shall appertain to his office: and generally to perform all such services relative to the welfare of schools, as he shall be directed to perform, and shall, prior to his entering upon the duties of his office, take an oath or affirmation for the diligent and faithful execution of his trust.

III *And be it further enacted,* That no distribution of the interest of the school fund shall take place amongst the common schools in this State, until it shall arise to fifty thousand dollars a year; and it shall not be lawful for the superintendent aforesaid to distribute any more than fifty thousand dollars a year until he shall find he will be able to distribute sixty thousand, and the sum of sixty thousand until the interest shall arise to seventy thousand, and so on as often as the interest shall increase ten thousand dollars, it shall be lawful for the superintendent to add to the sum last distributed ten thousand dollars more; and in all cases when he shall find he will be enabled to add ten thousand dollars to the sum last distributed, the next year, it shall be his duty to send a notice to the county clerk, and for said county clerk to notify the several town clerks in his county previous to such increase of monies to be distributed in the same form and manner as is provided in the fifth section of this act, to be made previously to the first distribution.

IV *And be it further enacted,* That the interest of the school funds which shall accumulate annually between the time of the first distribution of fifty thousand dollars, and sixty thousand dollars, and seventy thousand dollars, and so on from time to time, shall by the comptroller, be loaned and re-loaned in the same form and manner, and on the same security as he is now by law directed to loan the monies belonging to the common school fund of this State, and shall become principal in said funds.

V *And be it further enacted,* That the superintendent of common schools shall, in the month of January, which will be thirteen months before the first distribution of the interest of the school fund, send a notice in writing to each of the county clerks in this state, informing them that there will be a distribution of the interest of the school fund in the month of February, which will be thirteen months after the date of said notice, stating the amount that will be assigned to each county. And it shall be the duty of the said county clerks, to send a like notice to the clerk of the board of supervisors, and to each town clerk in his county, stating the amount of money to be distributed, and the time when, which notice the town clerk shall read at the opening of the next town meeting, to the intent that the town meeting may direct by their vote the supervisor, to levy on said town, at the next meeting of the board aforesaid, the sum for the support of common schools, required by this act to entitle said town to its proportion of the interest of said fund to be distributed; and the supervisor of each town so complying, shall, on or before the first Tuesday of June after, in each year, deliver a notice in writing, of such compliance, to the clerk of the board of supervisors of the county, and said clerk shall, at the opening of the next meeting of said board, report the several notices so received to the board of supervisors aforesaid, whose duty it shall be to apportion the county's proportion of said monies amongst the several towns that shall have directed the raising of such school monies, according to the population of each town as ascertained by the census of the United States having so complied, and file a list of the names of such towns, with the several sums allotted to each of them, in the office of the county treasurer, and the said county treasurer shall pay to the school commissioners of each such town its proportion of said school money according to said list. And the board of supervisors shall cause to be added to the sum raised in each of said towns, to pay the contingent expense of the respective towns, a sum equal to the sum which such town is to receive of the school monies aforesaid, with the addition of five cents on a dollar, of said sum for collection fees, and direct the collector in his warrant to pay the same, when collected, into the hands of the school commissioners of the several towns, reserving his fees, and take their receipts therefor; which receipt shall be his voucher of having paid such sum, and the treasurer shall file the same in his office, without fee or reward: *Provided always,* That the respective towns may, at their town meetings direct as much more money to be raised than is equal to their respective proportion of the school money as they may deem proper for the purposes aforesaid, not exceeding double said sum.

VI *And be it further enacted,* That the inhabitants living within the limits of the several towns within this state, and within the cities of Hudson and Schenectady, who by law have, or may have a right to vote in town meetings, shall, on the days of their annual town meetings, choose, by ballot, three of the inhabitants of their respective towns, commissioners, to superintendent and manage the concerns of the schools within said towns respectively, and to perform all such services relative to schools as they shall be directed to perform; that said commissioners, before they enter upon the execution of their office, shall respectively take an oath or affirmation, for the diligent and faithful execution of their trust, which commissioners shall be allowed for their services so much as the inhabitants of said towns respectively shall direct, and the same shall be paid out of the monies raised for town expenses. And the inhabitants of said towns respectively, shall choose a suitable number of persons within their respective towns, not exceeding six, who, together with the commissioners aforesaid, shall be inspectors of the schools of said towns respectively; which inspectors shall examine the teachers, and the respective schools, and no person shall be employed as a teacher in any one of the schools, in any of the districts of this State, who shall not have been previously examined by the inspectors aforesaid, and have received a certificate, signed by at least two of said inspectors, importing that he is duly qualified to teach a common school, and is of good moral character. And it shall be the further duty of the inspectors to examine into the state of the schools in their respective towns, both as it respects the proficiency of the scholars, and the good order and regularity of the schools; and from time to time to give their advice and directions to the trustees, as to the government of the same.

VII *And be it further enacted,* That the commissioners aforesaid are hereby authorized and empowered to divide their respective towns into a suitable and convenient number of districts, for keeping their schools, and to alter and regulate the same from time to time, as there may be occasion; and whenever it may be necessary and convenient to form a district out of two or more adjoining towns, such district may be formed by the commissioners from all such towns parts of which may be included in such district, and may be in like manner altered or changed at their pleasure; and every such district shall be under the superintendence of the inspectors of the town in which such school-house shall be situated, and numbered accordingly. And where it shall be convenient for any neighborhood adjoining to any other state, where such neighborhood has been in the habit of sending their children to a school in such adjoining state, it shall be lawful for said commissioners to set off such neighborhood by themselves, and such neighborhood shall be entitled to their share of the monies amongst the several districts in the town where said neighborhood shall be situate, in proportion to the number of children in such neighborhood between the ages of five to fifteen years; and it shall be lawful for such neighborhood to meet together and appoint one trustee, who shall make a report to said commissioners on or before the first day of May in each year, containing the number of children in such neighborhood from five years to fifteen inclusive, and the number educated in said school in the preceding year; and it is hereby made the duty of the commissioners aforesaid to describe and number each district within their respective towns, and deliver the same in writing to the clerk of such town, who is hereby required to record the same in the town records. And whenever a district shall be altered, pursuant to this act, it shall be the duty of the said commissioners to make a new description corresponding with such alteration, and the same shall be recorded in manner aforesaid.

VIII *And be it further enacted,* That whenever any town in this state shall be divided into school districts, according to the directions of this act, it shall be the duty of one of the school-commissioners of said town, within twenty days after, to make a notice in writing, describing said district, and appointing a time and place for the first district meeting, and deliver said writing to some one of the freeholders or inhabitants, liable to pay taxes, residing in said district, whose duty it shall be to notify each freeholder or inhabitant residing in said district, qualified as aforesaid, by reading such notice in the hearing of each such freeholder or inhabitant, or leaving a copy thereof at the place of his abode, at least six days before the time of such meeting; and if any such freeholder or inhabitant shall neglect or refuse to give such notice, he shall pay a fine of fi,ve dollars, to be recovered in the same manner, and for the same purpose, as is provided in the ninth section of this act. Such district meeting shall have power, when so convened, by the major vote of the persons so met, to adjourn from time to time as occasion may require, and to fix on a time and place to hold their future annual meetings, which annual meeting they are hereby authorized and required to hold, and to alter and change the time and place of holding such annual meeting as they or a majority of them, at any legal meeting, may think proper. And at such first meeting, or any future meeting, the said freeholders and inhabitants, or a majority of them so met, are hereby authorized and empowered to appoint a moderator for the time being, to designate a site for their school-house, to vote a tax on the resident inhabitants of such district as a majority present shall deem sufficient to purchase a suitable site for their school-house, and build, keep in repair, and furnish it with necessary fuel and appendages; also to choose three trustees to manage the concerns of such district, whose duty it shall be to build and keep in repair their school-house, and from time to time, as occasion may require, to agree with and employ instructors, and to pay them; also to choose one district clerk to keep the records and doings of said meeting, whose doings shall be good in law, who shall be qualified by oath or affirmation, as the several town clerks are; likewise one collector, who shall have the same power and authority, and have the same fees for collecting, and be subject to the same rules, regulations and duties, as respects the business of the district, which by law appertaineth to the collectors of towns in this state; and the said trustees, clerks, and collectors shall not be compelled to serve more than one year at any one time; and it shall be the further duty of the trustees of each district as soon as may be after the district meeting have voted a tax, to make a rate bill or tax list, which shall raise the sum voted, with five cents on a dollar for collector's fees, on all the taxable inhabitants of said district, agreeable to the levy on which the town tax was levied the preceding year, and annex to said tax list or rate bill a warrant, which warrant shall be substantially as followeth:

County of .... ss. To .... collector of the .... district, in the town of .... in the county aforesaid, greeting: In the name of the people of the state of New-York, you are hereby required and commanded to collect from each of the inhabitants of said district, the several sums of money written opposite to the name of each of said inhabitants, in the annexed tax list, and within ...... days after receiving this warrant, to pay the amount of the monies by you collected into the hands of the trustees of said district, or some one of them, and take their or his receipt therefor. And if any one or more of said inhabitants shall neglect or refuse to pay the sum, you are hereby further commanded to levy on the goods and chattels of each delinquent, and make sale thereof according to law. Given under our hands and seals this .... day of 181

[L. S.]
[L. S.] Trustees
[L. S.]

IX *And be it further enacted,* That the trustees of each district, or a majority of them, whenever they shall deem it expedient, may call a special meeting of the inhabitants of said district, to transact any business which may come regularly before them: *Provided always,* That such trustees shall give five days notice, in writing, to the inhabitants of said district respectively.

X *And be it further enacted,* That every person and persons, being duly chosen and appointed as aforesaid, to serve in any of the offices aforesaid, who shall refuse to serve therein, and to take the oath, (if any by law be required) to said office respectively belonging, if he be able to execute the said duties, shall pay the sum of five dollars, with costs, to be recovered by an action of debt brought by the school commissioners of the town or any individual, on this statute, before a justice of the peace in the county where the defendant shall dwell, in the ordinary mode of proceeding before magistrates; which money, when collected, after deducting the costs, shall be subject to the order of the commissioners of the town where the defendant was so chosen and appointed to office as aforesaid, for the use of the common schools in said town; and every such officer, duly chosen and appointed as aforesaid, having accepted (or not declared his refusal to accept) the office he is appointed to, and who shall neglect the performance of the trust committed to him, shall pay the sum of ten dollars, and the same shall be recovered in manner aforesaid, with costs of prosecution, and when collected, shall be disposed of in manner aforesaid.

XI *And be it further enacted,* That if any person who is not duly qualified, according to this act, to vote in any town-meeting, shall vote for the choice of officers, granting of taxes, or any other matters contemplated in this act, such persons so offending, and being thereof convicted before any court having competent jurisdiction, shall be fined in a sum not exceeding five dollars, and not less than three dollars, at the discretion of the court, and shall pay all costs and charges of prosecution; and the fine, when collected, shall be disposed of in the manner directed in the preceding section.

XII *And be it further enacted,* That the several persons appointed within any town to any office instituted by this act, may hold their offices until the annual meeting next following such appointment, and until others shall be appointed in their places; and whenever it shall happen that the said offices, or any of them, shall be vacated, either from neglect of appointment, refusal to serve, death, or removal from the district or town, or incapacity of such as may be thus appointed, such vacancy or vacancies may be supplied in the way and manner prescribed in the sixth section of the act, entitled " an act relative to the duties and privileges of towns," in similar cases, which officers, thus appointed, shall be regarded the same in all respects as if appointed by the inhabitants of such district or town.

XIII *And be it further enacted,* That from and after the passing of this act, the interest of the common school fund, arising under the several acts of this state, as from time to time shall become due, shall be paid to the treasurer of this state, which, together with all such monies as are by law pledged and appropriated for the encouragement and support of common schools, shall be distributed and applied pursuant to this act, and not otherwise: and to the end that the said monies may be inviolably applied in conformity to this act, and may never be diverted to any other purpose, an account shall be kept by the treasurer of the receipts and dispositions thereof, separate and distinct from other accounts.

XIV *And be it further enacted,* That the several towns in this state which shall conform to the provisions of this act, shall be entitled to such monies, to be distributed to them severally, according to the number of inhabitants in each town, to be ascertained by the respective census under the constitution of the United States, subject nevertheless to a distribution thereof, by said town, to the several school districts therein, pursuant to this act.

XV *And be it further enacted,* That the several school districts within the several towns in this state which shall conform to the provisions of this act, shall be entitled to the monies deposited with the commissioners as aforesaid, to be distributed to said districts severally, according to the number of children within each district, between the ages of five and fifteen inclusive, as shall appear from the returns of the trustees aforesaid, made pursuant to this act; and it is hereby made the duty of said commissioners, annually, on or before the first day of May, to apportion the monies aforesaid to the several school districts, in manner aforesaid; but in each district, composed of more than one town, each of the several parts shall draw its proportion, according to its number of children as aforesaid, from the town in which such part shall be situate; for which purpose, it shall be the duty of the trustees of such district, not only to make a general report as is hereinafter directed, but a report of the number of children in each part, to their several town commissioners respectively, and to pay over to each of said districts its share thereof, on the order of one or more of the trustees of such district, taking a receipt therefor; which monies shall be applied and expended by said trustees in paying the wages of the teachers to be employed, and for no other purpose; and further, that the accounts of the said commissioners shall annually be audited and settled by the board appointed by law to settle accounts of overseers of the poor in the respective towns: *Provided,* That after the first year, no order shall be accepted, nor shall the commissioners aforesaid deliver the monies, directed to be delivered as aforesaid, until two of the trustees of such district shall have certified in writing, under their hands in the words following, viz: We, the trustees of the   school district within the town of   do certify, that the school in said district hath been kept for three months at least, during the year ending on the first day of May last, by an instructor duly appointed and approved in all respects, according to law, and that all the monies by us drawn from the commissioners for said year, appropriated for schools, have been faithfully applied and expended in paying the wages of said instructor.— Dated

Trustees.

Provided always, That nothing shall be so construed as to prevent any persons attending said schools, whom the trustees aforesaid may deem proper to admit: *Provided further,* That whenever the aggregate expense of paying the instructors in schools, in any of the towns in this State, shall in any year equal or exceed the fund deposited with the commissioners as aforesaid, although any one or more of the districts in such town shall not have kept a school within the year, or not long enough to expend its proportion of such monies which otherwise would have belonged to such district, the monies thus unexpended and remaining with the commissioners aforesaid, shall be paid to and applied in the districts which have complied with the law, and which shall have expended, in paying instructors, a sum exceeding their proportion, regard being had, as far as may be, to their respective rights; but if such aggregate expense shall not equal the funds for any given year, then the monies shall remain with the commissioners aforesaid, to be added to and distributed with the monies next to be appropriated under this act.

XVI *And be it further enacted,* That if the trustees appointed under this act shall make a false certificate, by means whereof the school monies aforesaid shall be fraudulently obtained from the commissioners, each person signing such false certificate shall forfeit the sum of twenty dollars to the commissioners of such town to which such trustees shall belong, to be recovered by action of debt on this statute, in the name of the said commissioners, who are hereby required to prosecute therefor accordingly; and the sum when recovered, shall be applied for the benefit of the common schools in said town.

XVII *And be it further enacted,* That the trustees of the several school districts shall, annually, on the first day of May, make and transmit to the commissioners of the town wherein their respective districts are situated, a report, specifying the length of time a school hath been kept in said district; the amount of monies received; the manner the same hath been expended; and, as nearly as may be, the number of scholars taught therein, and the number of children, from five years old to fifteen inclusive, except Indian children otherwise provided for by law; whereupon the commissioners of the several towns aforesaid shall, on or before the first day of July, annually, make a town report to the clerk of the county wherein such town shall be situate, which report shall embrace the same objects as are contained in the report of the trustees as aforesaid; and the clerks of the several counties in this state shall, on or before the first day of November, annually, make a county report, in manner aforesaid, comprising the several reports received by them as aforesaid, and transmit the same to the superintendent of common schools; whereupon the said superintendent shall annually, on or before the first Tuesday in February, make a report to the legislature, embracing all the objects contemplated in this act: *Provided always,* That the several duties enjoined on the several county treasurers and county clerks, shall be done without fee or reward; and if any of the said treasurers or clerks shall refuse to do any of said duties, he or they shall forfeit and pay the same fine which is imposed, as aforesaid, on the town commissioners and trustees of districts; which fine shall be recovered in the same way, and applied to the same purpose, as the fines imposed on said commissioners and trustees.

XVIII *And be it further enacted,* That out of the school money apportioned by the superintendent, from time to time, to the county of Albany, the city of Albany shall have its proportion, with the towns in the county, according to the population thereof, and shall be paid by the county treasurer into the hands of the trustees of the Lancaster school, in said city, who shall give their receipt therefor, to be applied to the education of such poor children, belonging to said city, which may be, in the opinion of the said trustees, entitled to gratuitous education: *Provided,* That the said trustees shall receive into said school, all the children of every poor person residing in said city, and in no wise turn away any child that shall be, for that purpose, presented to them, from time to time; and that said trustees shall account to the county treasurer of said county for the faithful application of said money, according to the true intent and meaning of this act; and shall make a true report of the state of the school, with the number of scholars educated in said school, in the year last passed, to the county clerk, on the first day of July in each year, to be incorporated into the county report to be made to the superintendent of common schools.

XIX *And be it further enacted,* That the clerk of each town and of the cities of Hudson and Schenectady, shall, at any time after the passing of this act, on application of any six freeholders of such city or town, warn a town-meeting, giving at least eight days notice of such meeting in the manner now provided by law, for the purpose of electing commissioners of schools.

XX *And be it further enacted,* That in all cases in which any new town or towns may have been erected, or shall hereafter be erected, from a part of any other town or towns since the census aforesaid, it shall be the duty of the supervisors of such towns, to meet on the day of the month, and at the place directed by law for erecting such town, or at such other time and place as they may agree upon, and shall then and there apportion the money to be divided between the said towns, in the same proportion as the poor of the town, and the money belonging to them, shall be divided

Chapter 4
THE PERIOD 1826-46

All social and educational progress passes through three stages. First, the need becomes a conscious conviction in the minds of a few leaders who endeavor, through constant agitation, to enlighten the general public. Second, the demand for legal sanction arises from a few communities that begin to see the advantages their people might gain by adopting such principles. Then third, the injustice and inequalities developed by this method of legal sanction becomes apparent to all and the demand for legal compulsion results. This was true in the evolution of free schools. The leaders of the State from an early date began to appreciate that " education in all its branches but particularly in that which includes the common schools is the highest object of public concern." Although in this earlier period a statewide free school system was not advocated, one can not help but appreciate that in these messages of the governors we begin to hear the " voice in the wilderness." The following are extracts from the messages of the several Governors from 1826 to 1842 on the " State and education."

De Witt Clinton, 1826

The first duty of government, and the surest evidence of good government, is the encouragement of education. A general diffusion of knowledge is the precursor and protector of republican institutions; and in it we must confide as the conservative power that will watch over our liberties, and guard them against fraud, intrigue, corruption, and violence. In early infancy, education may be usefully administered. . . .

An important change has taken place in the free schools of New York. By an arrangement between the corporation of that city and the trustees of the free school society those establishments are to be converted into public schools, to admit the children of the rich as well as of the poor, and by this annihilation of factitious distinctions, there will be strong incentive for the display of talents, and a felicitous accommodation to the genius of republican government. . . .

To break down the barriers which poverty has erected against the acquisition and dispensation of knowledge, is to restore the just equilibrium of society, and to perform a duty of indispensable and paramount obligation. And under this impression, I also recommend that provision be made for the gratuitous education in our superior semenaries of indigent, talented and meritorious youth.

I consider the system of our common schools as the palladium of our freedom; for no reasonable apprehension can be entertained of its subversion, as long as the great body of the people are enlightened by education. To increase the funds, to extend the benefits, and to remedy the defects of this excellent system, is worthy of your most deliberate attention.

WILLIAM L. MARCY
Governor of New York, 1832–38

DeWITT CLINTON
Governor of New York, 1818–22, 1824–28

De Witt Clinton, 1828

Permit me to solicit your attention to the two extremes of education, the highest and lowest, and this I do in order to promote the cultivation of those whom nature has gifted with genius, but to whom fortune has denied the means of education. Let it be our ambition, (and no ambition can be more laudable) to dispense to the obscure, the poor, the humble, the friendless, and the depressed, the power of rising to usefulness and acquiring distinction.

With this view, provision might be made for the gratuitous education in our colleges, of youth eminent for the talents they have displayed, and the virtues they have cultivated in the subordinate seminaries. This would call into activity all the faculties of genius — all the efforts of industry — all the incentives to ambition, and all the motives to enterprise, and place the merits of transcendent intellect on a level at least with the factitious claims of fortune and ancestry.

William L. Marcy, 1834

Republics should be ever mindful of this important truth, that to be free, man must be educated. Without a knowledge of his rights, he will never properly estimate nor long maintain them. Our enjoyments as individuals — our usefulness as members of society — our privileges as citizens of a free government, are all founded on education. These obvious propositions show at once the vast importance of our system of public instruction, and the necessity of so improving it as to give to its operations the utmost extension and the greatest efficacy. While we are reposing our hopes for the continuance of civil liberty upon the general intelligence of the people, it becomes our duty to see that this foundation is laid broad and deep. . . .

I fear there is too much reason to regret that more zeal is not felt, and greater efforts made, to improve the condition of our primary schools throughout the State; yet there are places where their importance is duly appreciated, and vigorous exertions have been made for their advancement. Justice requires that the example of the city of New York should not be passed without notice and commendation. This city imposes annually a general tax, which now produces about ninety thousand dollars, for the support of its public free schools. They are under the management of a board instituted by the common council, called the Public School Society. This board are careful to select competent teachers, and to cause the schools under their charge to be often visited, and the course of instruction in them to be properly directed and vigilantly supervised by intelligent committees.

William L. Marcy, 1835

Upon the whole I think we have reason to be satisfied with the present condition of our higher schools and seminaries. In regard to the common schools, considering their great importance in a political and moral point of view, the efforts of the Legislature should not be intermitted until the system shall be so improved as to secure to the children of all classes and conditions of our population such an education as will qualify them to fulfil, in a proper manner, the duties appertaining to whatever may be their respective pursuits and conditions of life.

William L. Marcy, 1836

In a government like ours, which emanates from the people, where the entire administration in all its various branches is conducted for their benefit and subject to their constant supervision and control, and where the safety and the perpetuity of all its political institutions depend upon their virtue and intelligence, no other subject can be equal in importance to that of public instruction, and none should so earnestly engage the attention of the Legislature. Ignorance, with all the moral evils of which it is the prolific source, brings with it also numerous political evils, dangerous to the welfare of the State. It should be the anxious care of the Legislature to eradicate these evils by removing the causes of them. This can be done effectually only by diffusing instruction generally among the people. Although much remains here to be done in this respect, the past efforts of legislation upon the subject merit high commendation. Much has been already accomplished for the cause of popular education. A large fund has been dedicated to this object, and our common school system is established on right principles. But this is one of those subjects for which all cannot be done that is required, without a powerful cooperation on the part of the people in their individual capacity. The providing of funds for education, is an indispensable means for attaining the end; but it is not education. The wisest system that can be devised cannot be executed without human agency. The difficulty in the case arises, I fear, from the fact that the benefits of general education can only be fully appreciated by those who are educated themselves. Those parents who are so unfortunate as not to be properly educated, and those whose condition requires them to employ their time and their efforts to gain the means of subsistence, do not, in many instances, sufficiently value the importance of education. Yet it is for their children, in common with all others, that the common school system is designed; and until its blessings are made to reach them, it will not be what it ought to be. If parents generally were sensible of the inestimable advantages they were procuring for their children by educating them, I am sure the efforts and contributions which are required to give full efficiency to our present system, would not be withheld. If I have rightly apprehended the indications of public opinion on this subject, a more auspicious season is approaching.

At this time, a much larger number of individuals than heretofore, are exerting their energies and contributing their means to impress the public mind with the importance of making our system of popular instruction effective in diffusing its benefits to all the children in the State. I anticipate much good from the prevalence of the sentiment that the efforts of individuals must cooperate with the public authorities to ensure success to any system of general education.

William L. Marcy, 1837

Education in all its branches, but particularly in that which includes the common schools, is the highest object of public concern; and the duty of promoting and extending it, is in all respects, the most important that can engage your attention. The subject assumes at this time a new interest, because more ample means than the State has hitherto possessed are placed within your control, and may be devoted to extend the blessings of popular education. . . .

I should not do justice to the patriotism and public spirit of the times, if I should pass unnoticed and uncommended, the individual efforts now exerted, in a higher degree and in a more efficient manner than heretofore, for the promotion of popular instruction. Convinced that the security of property and the preservation of civil rights — that domestic happiness and public prosperity are sustained and promoted by diffusing education through all ranks of the people, men of literature are devoting their talents, and men of wealth are freely contributing their means to give success to the cause of public instruction; and assisted, as I doubt not they will be, by the powerful cooperation of the Legislature, its rapid advancement may be confidently anticipated.

William L. Marcy, 1838

All classes of our constituents will look with much anxiety and high hopes to your proceedings on the subject of education. As the friends of civil liberty, and the possessors of the legislative power of a free people, we are commanded by the dictates of reason, and the voice of duty, to provide liberally and efficiently for popular instruction. An ignorant people would not long retain, if by chance they should acquire, civil liberty, and would never rightly appreciate its benefits. To the intelligence of those who have preceded us, are we mainly indebted for our free institutions, and all the blessings that attend them; and it is only upon the intelligence of those who must be the future guardians of these institutions, that we can confidently rest our hopes of having them perpetuated and improved. Popular education is, therefore, identified with civil liberty. We owe to both the devotion of our best faculties, and the wisest application of the means placed at our disposal for sustaining and promoting them. . . .

Elementary instruction is only the first stage in the progress of education, and but little is accomplished if there be no advance beyond it. To make ample provision for conducting all the children in the State through this stage, should undoubtedly continue to be, as it hitherto has been, the first and main object of the Legislature; yet all that public sentiment demands and the public good requires, will not be achieved until needful facilities are furnished to a career of self-instruction.

William H. Seward, 1840

Although our system of public education is well endowed, and has been eminently successful, there is yet occasion for the benevolent and enlightened action of the legislature. The advantages of education ought to be secured to many, especially in our large cities, whom orphanage, the depravity of parents, or some form of accident or misfortune seems to have doomed to hopeless poverty and ignorance. Their intellects are as susceptible of expansion, of improvement, of refinement, of elevation, and of direction, as those minds which through the favor of Providence are permitted to develop themselves under the influence of better fortunes; they inherit the common lot to struggle against temptations, necessities, and vices; they are to assume the same domestic, social and political relations; and they are born to the same ultimate destiny.

The children of foreigners, found in great numbers in our populous cities and towns, and in the vicinity of our public works are too often deprived of the advantages of our system of public education, in consequence of prejudices arising from difference of language or religion. It ought never to be forgotten that the public welfare is as deeply concerned in their education as in that of our own children. I do not hesitate, therefore, to recommend the establishment of schools in which they may be instructed by teachers speaking the same language with themselves and professing the same faith. There would be no inequality in such a measure, since it happens from the force of circumstances, if not from choice, that the responsibilities of education are in most instances confided by us to native citizens, and occasions seldom offer for a trial of our magnanimity by committing that trust to persons differing from ourselves in the language or religion. Since we have opened our country and all its fullness to the oppressed of every nation, we should evince wisdom equal to such generosity by qualifying their children for the high responsibilities of citizenship.

William H. Seward, 1842

It was among my earliest duties to bring to the notice of the Legislature the neglected condition of many thousand children, including a very large proportion of those of immigrant parentage in our great commercial city; a misfortune then supposed to result from groundless prejudices and omissions of parental duty. Especially desirous at the same time not to disturb in any manner the public schools which seemed to be efficiently conducted, although so many for whom they were established were unwilling to receive their instructions, I suggested, as I thought, in a spirit not inharmonious with our civil and religious institutions, that if necessary, it might be expedient to bring those so excluded from such privileges into schools rendered especially attractive by the sympathies of those to whom the task of instruction should be confided. It has since been discovered that the magnitude of the evil was not fully known, and that its causes were very imperfectly understood. It will be shown you in the proper report, that twenty thousand children in the city of New York, of suitable age, are not at all instructed in any of the public schools, while the whole number in all the residue of the State, not taught in common schools, does not exceed nine thousand. What had been regarded as individual, occasional and accidental prejudices, have proved to be opinions pervading a large mass, including at least one religious communion equally with all others entitled to civil tolerance — opinions cherished through a period of sixteen years, and ripened into a permanent conscientious distrust of the impartiality of the education given in the public schools. This distrust has been rendered still deeper, and more alienating, by a subversion of precious civil rights of those whose consciences are thus offended.

Happily in this, as in other instances, the evil is discovered to have had its origin no deeper than in a departure from the equality of general laws. In our general system of common schools, trustees chosen by taxpaying citizens, levy taxes, build school houses, employ and pay teachers, and govern schools which are subject to visitation by similarly elected inspectors, who certify the qualifications of teachers; and all schools thus constituted participate in just proportion in the public moneys, which are

WILLIAM H. SEWARD
Governor of New York, 1839-43

conveyed to them by commissioners also elected by the people. Such schools are found distributed in average spaces of two and a half square miles throughout the inhabited portions of the State, and yet neither popular discontent, nor political strife, nor sectarian discord, has ever disturbed their peaceful instructions or impaired their eminent usefulness. In the public school system of the city, one hundred persons are trustees and inspectors, and by continued consent of the common council, are the dispensers of an annual average sum of $35,000, received from the Common School Fund of the State, and a sum equal to $95,000 derived from an undiscriminating tax upon the real and personal estates of the city. They build school houses chiefly with public funds, they appoint and remove teachers, fix their compensation, and prescribe the moral, intellectual and religious instruction which one-eighth of the rising generation of the State shall be required to receive. Their powers, more effective and far reaching than are exercised by the municipality of the city, are not derived from the community whose children are educated and whose property is taxed, nor even from the State, which is so great an almoner, and whose welfare is so deeply concerned, but from an incorporated and perpetual association which grants upon pecuniary subscription the privileges even of life membership and yet holds in fee simple the public school edifices, valued at eight hundred thousand dollars. Lest there might be too much responsibility, even to the association, that body can elect only one half of the trustees, and those thus selected appoint their fifty associates.

The philanthropy and patriotism of the present managers of the public schools, and their efficiency in imparting instruction, are cheerfully and gratefully admitted. Nor is it necessary to maintain that agents thus selected will become unfaithful, or that a system that so jealously excludes popular interference, must necessarily be unequal in its operation. It is only insisted that the institution, after a fair and sufficient trial, has failed to gain that broad confidence reposed in the general system of the State, and indispensable to every scheme of universal education. No plan for that purpose can be defended, except on the ground that public instruction is one of the responsibilities of the government. It is, therefore, a manifest legislative duty to correct errors and defects in whatever system is established. In the present case, the failure amounts virtually to an exclusion of all the children thus withheld, I cannot overcome my regret, that every suggestion of amendment encounters so much opposition from those who defend the Public School System of the metropolis, as to show that in their judgment it can admit of no modification, either from tenderness to the consciences or regard to the civil rights of those aggrieved, or even for the reclamation of those for whose culture the State has so munificently provided; as if society must conform itself to the public schools, instead of the public schools adapting themselves to the exigencies of society. The late eminent Superintendent, after exposing the greatness of this public misfortune, and tracing it to the discrepancy between the local and general systems, suggested a remedy, which, although it is not urged to the exclusion of any other, seems to deserve dispassionate consideration. I submit, therefore, with entire willingness to approve whatever adequate remedy you may propose, the expediency of restoring to the people of the city of New York — what I am sure the people of no other part of the State would, upon any consideration, relinquish — the education of their children. For this purpose it is only necessary to vest the control of the common schools in a board to be composed of commissioners elected by the people; which board shall apportion the school moneys among all the schools, including those now existing, which shall be organized and conducted in conformity to its general regulations and the laws of the State, in the proportion of the number of pupils instructed. It is not left doubtful that the restoration to the common schools of the city, of this simple and equal feature of the common schools of the State, would remove every complaint, and bring into the seminaries the offspring of want and misfortune, presented by a grand jury, on a recent occasion, as neglected children of both sexes, who are found in hordes upon the wharves and in corners of the streets, surrounded by evil associations, disturbing the public peace, committing petty depredations and going from bad to worse, until their course terminates in high crimes and infamy.

This proposition, to gather the young from the streets and wharves into the nurseries which the State, solicitous for her security against ignorance, has prepared for them, has sometimes been treated as a device to appropriate the school fund to the endowment of seminaries for teaching languages and faiths, thus to perpetuate the prejudices it seeks to remove; sometimes as a scheme for dividing that precious fund among an hundred jarring sects, and thus increasing the religious animosities it strives to heal; sometimes as a plan to subvert the prevailing religion and introduce one repugnant to the consciences of our fellow citizens; while in truth, it simply proposes, by enlightening equally the minds of all, to enable them to detect error wherever it may exist, and to reduce uncongenial masses into one intelligent, virtuous, harmonious and happy people. Being now relieved from all such misconceptions, it presents the questions whether it is wiser and more humane to educate the offspring of the poor, than to leave them grow up in ignorance and vice; whether juvenile vice is more easily eradicated by the court of sessions than by common schools; whether parents have a right to be heard concerning the instruction and instructors of their children, and taxpayers in relation to the expenditure of public funds; whether in a republican government, it is necessary to interpose an independent corporation between the people and the schoolmaster, and whether it is wise and just to disfranchise and entire community of all control over public education, rather than suffer a part to be represented in proportion to its members and contributions. Since such considerations are now involved, what has hitherto been discussed as a question of benevolence and of universal education, has become one of equal civil rights, religious tolerance, and liberty of conscience. We could bear with us, in our retirement from public service no recollection more worthy of being cherished through life, than that of having met such a question in the generous and confiding spirit of our institutions, and decided it upon the immutable principles on which they are based.

The establishment of free schools was not only contested in New York State but was opposed in practically all the older states. An interesting sidelight in behalf of free schools is the able address by Thaddeus Stevens, delivered before the Pennsylvania Legislature in April 1835, and extracts from the history of the educational movements in Rhode Island and in Massachusetts indicating the difficulties that these states encountered in the free school movement.

A Plea for Public Schools by Thaddeus Stevens

Mr Speaker: I will briefly give you the reasons why I shall oppose the repeal of the school law.

This law was passed at the last session of the legislature with unexampled unanimity, but one member of this house voting against it. It has not yet come into operation, and none of its effects have been tested by experience in Pennsylvania. The passage of such a law is enjoined by the constitution; and has been recommended by every governor since its adoption. Much to his credit, it has been warmly urged by the present executive in his annual messages delivered at the opening of the legislature. To repeal it now, before its practical effects have been discovered, would argue that it contained some glaring and pernicious defect, and that the last legislature acted under some strong and fatal delusion, which blinded every man of them to the interests of the Commonwealth. I will attempt to show that the law is salutary, useful and important, and that consequently the last legislature acted wisely in passing and the present would act unwisely in repealing it; that, instead of being oppressive to the people, it will lighten their burdens, while it elevates them in the scale of human intellect.

It would seem to be humiliating to be under the necessity, in the nineteenth century, of entering into a formal argument, to prove the utility, and, to free governments, the absolute necessity of education. More than two thousand years ago the Deity, who presided over intellectual endowments, ranked highest for dignity, chastity, and virtue among the goddesses worshipped by cultivated pagans. And I will not insult this house or our constitutents by supposing any course of reasoning necessary to convince them of its high importance. Such necessity would be degrading to a Christian age, a free republic.

If then, education be of admitted importance to the people, under all forms of government, and of unquestioned necessity, when they govern themselves, it follows, of course, that its cultivation and diffusion is a matter of public concern, and a duty which every government owes to its people. In accordance with this principle, the ancient Republics, who were most renowned for their wisdom and success, considered every child born subject to their control, as the property of the State, so far as its education was concerned; and during the proper period of instruction they were withdrawn from the control of their parents and placed under the guardianship of the Commonwealth. There, all were instructed at the same school; all were placed on perfect equality, the rich and the poor man's sons; for all were deemed children of the same common parent of the Commonwealth. Indeed, where all have the means of knowledge placed within their reach, and meet at common schools on equal terms, the forms of government seem of less importance to the happiness of the people than is generally supposed; or rather, such a people are seldom in danger of having their rights invaded by their rulers. They would not long be invaded with impunity. Prussia, whose form of government is absolute monarchy, extends the blessing of free school into every corner of the kingdom — to the lowest and poorest of the people. With a population equal to our whole Union, she has not more than 20,000 children who do not enjoy its advantages. And the consequence is, that Prussia, although governed by an absolute monarch, enjoys more happiness, and the rights of the people are better respected than in any other government in Europe.

If an elective Republic is to endure for any great length of time, every elector must have sufficient information, not only to accumulate wealth and take care of his pecuniary concerns, but to direct wisely the legislature, the ambassadors, and the Executive of the nation — for some part of all these things, some agency in approving or disapproving of them, falls to every freeman. If, then, the permanency of our Government depends upon such knowledge, it is the duty of government to see that the means of information be diffused to every citizen. This is a sufficient answer to those who deem education a private and not a public duty — who argue that they are willing to educate their own children, but not their neighbor's children.

But while but few are found ignorant and shameless enough to deny the advantages of general education, many are alarmed at its supposed burdensome operation. A little judicious reflection, or a single year's experience, would show that education, under the free-school system, will cost more than one-half less, and afford better and more permanent instruction than the present disgraceful plan pursued by Pennsylvania. Take a township 6 miles square and make the estimate; such townships, on an average, will contain about 200 children to be schooled. The present rate of tuition generally (in the country) is $2 per quarter. If the children attend school two quarters each year, such township would pay $800 per annum. Take the free-school system — lay the township off into districts 3 miles square; the farthest scholars would then have 1½ miles to go, which would not be too far. It would require four schools. These will be taught, I presume, as in other States, three months in the winter by male and three months in the summer by female teachers; good male teachers can be had at from $16 to $18 per month and board themselves; females at $9 per month. Take the highest price, $18, for three months would be $54, and then for females at $9 for three months, $27, each school would cost $81; or four to a township, $324. The price now paid for the same is $800; saving for each township of 6 miles square, $476 per annum.

If the instruction of 200 scholars will save by the free-school law $476, the 500,000 children in Pennsylvania will save $1,190,000! Very few men are aware of the immense amount of money which the present expensive and partial mode of education costs the people. Pennsylvania has half a million of children, who either do, or ought to go to school six months in the year. If they do go, at $2 per quarter, their schooling costs $2,000,000 per annum! If they do not go when they are able, their parents deserve to be held in disgrace. Where they are unable, if the State does not furnish the means, she is criminally negligent. But by the free-school law, that same amount of education which would now cost $2,000,000, could be supplied at less than one-third of this amount. The amendment which is now proposed as a substitute for the school law of last session, is, in my opinion, of a most hateful and degrading character. It is a reenactment of the pauper law of 1809. It proposes that the assessors shall take a census, and make a record of the poor. This shall be revised, and a new record made by the county commissioners, so that the names of those who have the misfortune to be poor men's children shall be forever preserved, as a distinct class, in the archives of the country! The teacher, too, is to keep in his school a pauper book, and register the names and attendance of poor scholars; thus pointing out and recording their poverty in the midst of their companions. Sir, hereditary distinctions of rank are sufficiently odious; but that which is founded on poverty is infinitely more so. Such a law should be entitled "An act for branding and marking the poor, so that they may be known from the rich and proud." Many complain of this tax, not so much on account of its amount, as because it is for the benefit of others and not themselves. This is a mistake; it is for their own benefit, inasmuch as it perpetuates the Government and insures the due administration of the laws under which they live, and by which their lives and property are protected. Why do they not urge the same objection against all other taxes? The industrious, thrifty, rich farmer pays a heavy county tax to support criminal courts, build jails, and pay sheriffs and jail keepers, and yet probably he never has, and never will have, any personal use of either. He never gets the worth of his money by being tried for a crime before the court, by being allowed the privilege of the jail on conviction, or receiving an equivalent from the sheriff or his hangman officers! He cheerfully pays the tax which is necessary to support and punish convicts, but loudly complains of that which goes to prevent his fellow-being from becoming a criminal, and to obviate the necessity of those humiliating institutions.

This law is often objected to, because its benefits are shared by the children of the profligate spendthrift equally with those of the most industrious and economical habits. It ought to be remembered that the benefit is bestowed, not upon the erring parents, but the innocent children. Carry out this objection and you punish children for the crimes or misfortunes of their parents. You virtually establish castes and grades founded on no merit of the particular generation, but on the demerits of their ancestors; an aristocracy of the most odious and insolent kind — the aristocracy of wealth and pride.

It is said that its advantages will be unjustly and unequally enjoyed, because the industrious, money-making man keeps his whole family constantly employed, and has but little time for them to spend at school; while the idle man has but little employment for his family, and they will constantly attend school. I know, sir, that there are some men, whose whole souls are so completely absorbed in the accumulation of wealth, and whose avarice so increases with success, that they look upon their very children in no other light than as instruments of gain — that they, as well as the ox and the ass within their gates, are valuable only in proportion to their annual earnings. And, according to the present system, the children of such men are reduced almost to an intellectual level with their colaborers of the brute creation. This law will be of vast advantage to the offspring of such misers. If they are compelled to pay their taxes to support schools, their very meanness will induce them to send their children to them to get the worth of their money. Thus it will extract good out of the very penuriousness of the miser. Surely a system which will work such wonders, ought to be as greedily sought for, and more highly prized, than that coveted alchemy which was to produce gold and silver out of the blood and entrails of vipers, lizards, and other filthy vermin.

Why, sir, are the colleges and literary institutions of Pennsylvania now, and ever have been, in a lanquishing and sickly condition? Why, with a fertile soil and genial climate, has she, in proportion to her population, scarcely one-third as many collegiate students as cold, barren New England? The answer is obvious; she has no free schools. Until she shall have you may in vain endow college after college; they will never be filled, or filled only by students from other States. In New England free schools plant the seeds and the desire of knowledge in every mind, without regard to the wealth of the parent or the texture of the pupil's garments. When the seed, thus universally sown, happens to fall on fertile soil, it springs up and is fostered by a generous public until it produces its glorious fruit. Those who have but scanty means and are pursuing a collegiate education, find it necessary to spend a portion of the year in teaching common schools; thus imparting the knowledge which they acquire, they raise the dignity of the employment to a rank which it should always hold, honorable in proportion to the high qualifications necessary for its discharge. Thus devoting a portion of their time to acquiring the means of subsistence, industrious habits are forced upon them and their minds and bodies become disciplined to a regularity and energy which is seldom the lot of the rich. It is no uncommon occurrence to see the poor man's son, thus encouraged by wise legislation far outstrip and bear off the laurels from the less industrious heirs of wealth. Some of the ablest men of the present and past days never could have been educated, except for that benevolent system. Not to mention any of the living, it is well known that that architect of an immortal name, who plucked "the lightning from heaven and the sceptre from tyrants," was the child of free schools. Why shall Pennsylvania now repudiate a system which is calculated to elevate her to that rank in the intellectual, which, by the blessing of Providence, she holds in the natural world? To be the keystone of the arch, the " very first among her equals?" I am aware, sir, how difficult it is for the great mass of people, who have never seen this system in operation, to understand its advantages. But is it not wise to let it go into full operation and learn its results from experience? Then, if it prove useless or burdensome, how easy to repeal it. I know how large a portion of the community can scarcely feel any sympathy with, or understand the necessity of the poor; or appreciate the exquisite feelings which they enjoy when they see their children receiving the boon of education, and rising in intellectual superiority above the clogs which hereditary poverty had cast upon them. It is not wonderful that he whose fat acres have descended to him, from father to son in unbroken succession, should never have sought for the surest means of alleviating it. Sir, when I reflect how apt hereditary wealth, hereditary influence, and perhaps as a consequence, hereditary pride are to close the avenues and steel the heart against the wants and the rights of the poor, I am induced to thank my Creator for having from early life bestowed upon me the blessings of poverty. Sir, it is a blessing, for if there be any human sensation more ethereal and divine than all others, it is that which feelingly sympathizes with misfortune.

But we are told that this law is unpopular; that the people desire its repeal. Has it not always been so with every new reform in the condition of man? Old habits and old prejudices are hard to be removed from the mind. Every new improvement which has been gradually leading man from the savage, through the civilized, up to a highly cultivated state, has required the most strenuous, and often perilous exertions of the wise and good. But, sir, much of its unpopularity is chargeable upon the vile arts of unprincipled demagogues. Instead of attempting to restore the honest misapprehensions of the people, they cater to their prejudices, and take advantage of them to gain low, dirty, temporary, local triumphs. I do not charge this on any particular party. Unfortunately almost the only spot on which all parties meet in union is this ground of common infamy. I have seen the present chief magistrate of this Commonwealth violently assailed as the projector and father of this law. I am not the eulogist of that gentleman; he has been guilty of many deep political sins; but he deserves the undying gratitude of the people for the steady, untiring zeal which he has manifested in favor of common schools. I will not say that his exertions in that cause have covered all, but they have atoned for many of his errors. I trust that the people of this State will never be called on to choose between a supporter and an opposer of free schools. But if it should come to that; if that should be made the turning point on which we are to cast our suffrages; if the opponent of education were my most intimate personal and political friend, and the free-school candidate my most obnoxious enemy, I should deem it my duty as a patriot, at this moment of our intellectual crisis, to forget all other considerations, and I should place myself unhesitatingly and cordially in the ranks of Him whose banner streams in light. I would not foster nor flatter ignorance to gain political victories which, however, they might profit individuals, must prove disastrous to our country. Let it not be supposed from these remarks that because I deem this a paramount object that I think less highly than heretofore of those great important cardinal principles which for years past have controlled my political action. They are, and ever shall be, deeply cherished in my inmost heart. But I must be allowed to exercise my own judgment as to the best means of effecting that and every other object which I think beneficial to the community. And, according to that judgment, the light of general information will as surely counteract the pernicious influence of secret, oath-bound, murderous institutions as the sun in heaven dispels the darkness and damp vapors of the night.

It is said that some gentlemen here owe their election to their hostility to general education — that it was placed distinctly on that ground, and that others lost their election by being in favor of it; and that they consented to supersede the regularly nominated candidates of their own party, who had voted for this law. May be so. I believe that two highly respectable members of the last legislature, from Union county, who voted for the school law, did fail of reelection on that ground only. They were summoned before a county meeting, and requested to pledge themselves to vote for its repeal as the price of their reelection. But they were too high minded and honorable men to consent to such degradation. The people, incapable for the moment of appreciating their worth, dismissed them from their service. But I venture to predict that they have passed them by only for the moment. Those gentlemen have earned the approbation of all good and intelligent men more effectually by their retirement than they could ever have done by retaining popular favor at the expense of self-humiliation. They fell, it is true, in this great struggle between the powers of light and darkness; but they fell, as every Roman mother wished her sons to fall, facing the enemy with all their wounds in front.

True, it is, that two other gentlemen, and I believe two only, lost their election on account of their vote on that question. I refer to the late members from Berks, who were candidates for reelection; and I regret that gentlemen whom I so highly respect and whom I take pleasure in ranking among personal friends, had not possessed a little more nerve to enable them to withstand the assaults which were made upon them; or if they must be overpowered, to wrap their mantles gracefully around them and yield with dignity. But this, I am aware, requires a high degree of fortitude, and those respected gentlemen, distracted and faltering between the dictates of conscience and the clamor of the populace, at length turned and fled. But duty had detained them so long that they fled too late, and the shaft which had already been winged by ignorance overtook and pierced them from behind. I am happy to say, sir, that a more fortunate fate awaited our friends from York. Possessing a keener insight into futurity and a sharper instinct of danger, they saw the peril at a greater distance and retreated in time to escape the fury of the storm, and can now safely boast that " discretion is the better part of valor," and that " they fought and ran away, and live to fight — on t'other side."

Sir, it is to be regretted that any gentleman should have consented to place his election on hostility to general education. If honest ambition were his object, he will ere long lament that he attempted to raise his monument of glory on so muddy a foundation. But, if it be so, that they were placed to obstruct the diffusion of knowledge, it is but justice to say, that they fitly and faithfully represent the spirit which sent them here, when they attempt to sacrifice this law on the altars which, at home, among their constituents, they have raised and consecrated to intellectual darkness; and on which they are pouring out oblations to send forth their fetid and noxious odors over the 10 miles square of their ambitions! But will this legislature, will the wise guardians of the dearest interests of a great Commonwealth, consent to surrender the high advantages and brilliant prospects which this law promises, because it is desired by worthy gentlemen, who, in a moment of causeless panic and popular delusion, sailed into power on a Tartarean flood? A flood of ignorance darker, and, to the intelligent mind, more dreadful than that accursed pool at which mortals and immortals tremble! Sir, it seems to me that the liberal and enlightened proceedings of the last legislature have aroused the demon of ignorance from his slumber; and, maddened at the threatened loss of his murky empire, his discordant howlings are heard in every part of our land!

Gentlemen will hardly contend for the doctrine of cherishing and obeying the prejudices and errors of their constituents. Instead of prophesying smooth things and flattering the people with the belief of their present perfection, and thus retarding the mind in its onward progress, it is the duty of faithful legislators to create and sustain such laws and institutions as shall teach us our wants, foster our cravings after knowledge, and urge us forward in the march of intellect. The barbarous and disgraceful cry which we hear abroad in some parts of our land, " that learning makes us worse — that education makes men rogues," should find no echo within these walls. Those who hold such doctrines anywhere would be the objects of bitter detestation if they were not rather the pitiable objects of commiseration, for even voluntary fools require our compassion as well as natural idiots.

Those who would repeal this law because it is obnoxious to a portion of the people would seem to found their justification on a desire of popularity. That is not an unworthy object when they seek that enduring fame which is constructed of imperishable materials. But have these gentlemen looked back and consulted the history of their race to learn on what foundation and on what materials that popularity is built which outlives its possessor, which is not buried in the same grave which covers his mortal remains? Sir, I believe that kind of fame may be acquired by deep learning, or even the love of it, by mild philanthropy or unconquerable courage. And it seems to me that, in the present state of feeling in Pennsylvania, those who will heartily and successfully support the cause of general education can acquire at least some portion of the honor of all these qualities combined, while those who oppose it will be remembered without pleasure and soon pass away with the things that perish.

In giving this law to posterity you act the part of the philanthropist, by bestowing upon the poor as well as the rich the greatest earthly boon which they are capable of receiving; you act the part of the philosopher by pointing if you do not lead them up the hill of science; you act the part of the hero if it be true as you say that popular vengeance follows close upon your footsteps. Here, then, if you wish true popularity, is a theater in which you may acquire it. What renders the name of Socrates immortal but his love of the human family exhibited under all circumstances and in contempt of every danger? But courage, even with but little benevolence may confer lasting renown. It is this which makes us bow with involuntary respect at the name of Napoleon, of Caesar, and of Richard of the Lion Heart. But what earthly glory is there equal in luster and duration to that conferred by education? What else could have bestowed such renown upon the philosophers, the poets, the statesmen, and orators of antiquity? What else could have conferred such undisputed applause upon Aristotle, Demosthenes, and Homer; on Virgil, Horace and Cicero? And is learning less interesting and important now than it was in centuries past, when those statesmen and orators charmed and ruled empires with their eloquence?

Sir, let it not be thought that these great men acquired a higher fame than is within the reach of the present age. Pennsylvania's sons possess as high native talents as any other nation of ancient or modern time. Many of the poorest of her children possess as bright intellectual gems if they were as highly polished as did the scholars of Greece or Rome. But too long, too disgracefully long, has coward, trembling, procrastinating legislation permitted them to lie buried in " dark, unfathomable caves."

If you wish to acquire popularity, how often have you been admonished to build not your monuments of brass or marble but make them of ever-living mind. Although the periods of yours or your children's renown can not be as long as that of the ancients, because you start from a later period, yet it may be no less brilliant. Equal attention to the same learning, equal ardor in pursuing the same arts and liberal studies, which has rescued their names from the rust of corroding time and handed them down to us untarnished from remote antiquity, would transmit the names of your children and your children's children in a green, undying fame down through the long vista of succeeding ages until time shall mingle with eternity.

Let all, therefore, who would sustain the character of the philosopher or philanthropist sustain this law. Those who would add thereto the glory of the hero, can acquire it here, for in the present state of feeling in Pennsylvania, I am willing to admit that but little less dangerous to the public man is the war club and battle-ax of savage ignorance, than to the Lion-hearted Richard was the keen scimiter of the Saracen. He who would oppose it, either through inability to comprehend the advantages of general education, or from unwillingness to bestow them on all his fellow-citizens, even to the lowest and the poorest, or from dread of popular vengeance, seems to me to want either the head of the philosopher, the heart of the philanthropist or the nerve of the hero.

All these things would be easily admitted by almost every man, were it not for the supposed cost. I have endeavored to show that it is not expensive; but, admit that it were somewhat so, why do you cling so closely to your gold? The trophies which it can purchase, the idols which it sets up, will scarcely survive their purchaser. No name, no honor can long be perpetuated by mere matter. Of this Egypt furnishes melancholy proof. Look at her stupendous pyramids, which were raised at such immense expense of toil and treasure! As mere masses of matter they seem as durable as the everlasting hills, yet the deeds and the names they were intended to perpetuate are no longer known on earth. That ingenious people attempted to give immortality to matter, by embalming their great men and monarchs. Instead of doing deeds worthy to be recorded in history, their very names are unknown, and nothing is left to posterity but their disgusting mortal frames for idle curiosity to stare at. What rational being can view such soulless, material perpetuation, with pleasure? If you can enjoy it, go, sir, to the foot of Vesuvius; to Herculaneum and Pompeii, those eternal monuments of human weakness. There, if you set such value on material monuments of riches, may you see all the glory of art, the magnificence of wealth, the gold of Ophir, and the rubies of the East, preserved in indestructible lava, along with their haughty wearers — the cold, smooth, petrified, lifeless beauties of the " Cities of the Dead."

Who would not shudder at the idea of such prolonged material identity? Who would not rather do one living deed than to have his ashes forever enshrined in ever-burnished gold? Sir, I trust that when we come to act on this question we shall all take lofty ground — look beyond the narrow space which now circumscribes our visions — beyond the passing, fleeting point of time on which we stand; and so cast our votes that the blessing of education shall be conferred on every son of Pennsylvania — shall be carried home to the poorest child of the poorest inhabitant of the meanest hut of your mountains, so that even he may be prepared to act well his part in this land of freemen, and lay on earth a broad and a solid foundation for that enduring knowledge which goes on increasing through increasing eternity.

THADDEUS STEVENS
(From The American Portrait Gallery)

Thaddeus Stevens

Thaddeus Stevens, "The Great Commoner," was born in Peacham, Caledonia county, Vermont, April 4, 1793. He was lame and delicate in childhood. His parents were extremely poor, but his mother labored untiringly to secure an education for him. Through her exertions, he was enabled to attend the country district school during the few months of each year that it was open. The boy was ambitious, and desirous to learn, and by close application he succeeded in preparing for college. He entered Dartmouth College, from which he was graduated with honor in 1814. During that year he removed to York, Pa., where he studied law and taught in an academy at the same time. In 1816 he was admitted to the bar, and soon rose to a high rank as a practitioner.

Mr Stevens did not take an active part in politics until 1828. In the exciting presidential campaign of that year he espoused the cause of John Quincy Adams, and subsequently became an active member of the Whig party. In 1833, he was elected to the Pennsylvania legislature, and was reelected to the same office in 1834, 1835, 1837 and 1841. During his membership in this body he delivered his notable speeches on the common school system and the act for establishing a school of art. He early became distinguished by his opposition to slavery. In 1836 he was a member of the convention to revise the state constitution. He took an active part in all the debates, but refused to sign the constitution, because it restricted suffrage on account of color. In 1838 he was appointed a canal commissioner, then one of the most important offices in the government, on account of the vast expenditures being made for internal improvements. In 1842 he removed to Lancaster and devoted the next six years to the practice of his profession. He also became largely engaged in the manufacture of iron. In 1848 he was elected a Representative from Pennsylvania to the thirty-first Congress. He was also elected to the thirty-second Congress in 1850. He strongly opposed the repeal of the Missouri Compromise, the Fugitive Slave Law, and the Kansas-Nebraska Bill.

Mr Stevens was again elected to Congress in 1858, and held his seat until his death. In the latter years of his life he was a recognized leader of the Republican party. He was among the earliest to declare the abolition of slavery the only alternative of the government, and took a leading part in all measures for emancipating the negroes and for giving them citizenship, and advocated the arming and disciplining of 150,000 of them as soldiers. He presented the indemnity act, and the fourteenth amendment to the constitution. The Emancipation Proclamation was urged upon the President by him, and during the war he advocated and carried acts of confiscation, and proposed the most rigid and severe measures against the confederates.

During three sessions of Congress, Mr Stevens served on the important committee on ways and means, and also served on various other committees of importance. He was chairman of the committee on the reconstruction of the thirty-ninth and fortieth Congresses; of the special committee on the Pacific Railroad; of the committee on appropriations; of the committee on a postal railroad to New York; the special committee on reconstruction; and of the committee on free schools in the District of Columbia. He served on the committee on the Niagara ship canal, and was a member of the committee on the death of President Lincoln. He assisted in drafting the articles of impeachment against President Johnson, and was chairman of the committee of seven who managed the case on the part of the House. He was a delegate to the Baltimore convention of 1864, and to the Philadelphia "Loyalists' Convention" of 1866. In 1867 he received from Middlebury College the degree of LL.D.

Mr Stevens died at Washington, D. C., August 11, 1868.

The following extracts of "Evolution of the Massachusetts Public School System" (George H. Martin) briefly outlines the history of the free school movement in that state.

When the lawmakers of 1647 spoke of grammar schools, they meant such schools as they had already started, and these were such as they had been educated in at home. Winthrop came from Groton, in Suffolk. At Bury St Edmunds, close by, was a free grammar school founded by Edward in 1553. At Eye, in the same colony, was one founded before 1556; while at Sunbury there was another, founded by one William Wood a year before Columbus discovered America.

John Cotton came from old Boston. There was a free grammar school, and Cotton, a few years before, had been one of a committee to select an usher for it. Eddicott, of Salem, came from Dorchester. There was a school founded in 1579, "a free school with a learned master for children of all degrees." Dudley, of Roxbury, came from Northampton. There was a school, founded in 1541, to teach boys who desired to learn, freely.

To James G. Carter, of Lancaster, belongs the honor of first attracting attention to the decadence of the public schools, the extent of it, the cause of it, and the remedy for it. Within a year after he graduated from college he began an aggressive campaign in favor of free schools, which he continued for seventeen years, until his triumph was complete in the establishment of normal schools, and Horace Mann came to follow up his victory.

His first efforts were through the press. He described the condition of the public schools; he showed how they had sunk in the character of their instruction and instructors; with convincing logic he showed how the academies and private schools were largely responsible for this decline; in eloquent terms he painted the wisdom and self-denial of the founders of the State, and contrasted them with the degeneracy of their children; and with the ardor of his age, and a sagacity and insight beyond his years, he argued for inductive teaching in all the schools, and proved conclusively that there could be no such teaching until competent teachers could be provided. Then, rising to the height of his subject, he outlined a plan for a seminary for teachers, of which Prof. Bryce said, in 1828, it was "the first regular publication on the subject of the professional education of teachers which he had heard of." These papers were widely circulated and favorably received. They were reviewed by Theophilus Parsons in the Literary Gazette, and by Prof. Ticknor in the North American Review, and bore almost immediate fruit in the legislation of 1824 and 1826.

Meanwhile the support of the schools was falling more and more into the hands of the districts, and the executive functions came to be performed, by the district committees, with the results which we have learned to deplore. The law of 1826, therefore, introduced no new idea into the school history of the State; it made universal and compulsory what had already become familiar to many communities. But it did more than this; it elevated the school interests by differentiating them, specializing these functions, as the care of the roads, of the poor, of taxing, had long before been specialized.

The law of 1789 was a long step forward, by making it somebody's business to know what the schools were doing. This law was a longer step forward, by making the somebody a special body, and giving to it new and more extended powers. It is not strange that the law met with vigorous opposition. Petitions came to the next legislature urging its repeal, but it was not repealed.

So arrogant had the little district become, so jealous of their imagined rights, though they had had a corporate existence but thirty-seven years, that they complained of the new law as being arbitrary and oppressive, because it gave back to the town a part of the powers which had always belonged to it, but which the districts had usurped.

The law was not repealed, but a sop was thrown to the districts, which in practice went far to neutralize all the good effects of the law. This was the authority given to the prudential committee to select the teacher. The power had been long exercised; now it was legally conferred. The town committees neglected their restrictive duties, so that in many towns the new legislation was practically inoperative.

One other feature of the legislation of 1827 should be noticed in passing. For the first time in the history of the State is the entire support of the schools by taxation made compulsory. From 1647 such support had been voluntary. For many years it had been universal.

From the beginning legislation had recognized the principle so aptly stated by Mr Carter, that all the property of the town was liable for the education of all the children of the town. Now, after one hundred and eighty years, the principle is enacted into a law. So slowly are institutions evolved and perfected in a government by the people.

Mr Carter's plans for school improvement included two means as of primary importance; a school fund, and a seminary for the training of teachers. The efforts of the friends of reform to secure these two ends were unremitting. The measures were forced upon the attention and consideration of the Legislature every year from 1827, until opposition and reluctance yielded to importunity, and both were secured.

In 1834 a bill was reported and enacted establishing a school fund. The fund was to consist of all money in the treasury derived from the sale of lands in the State of Maine, and from the claims of the State on the United States for military services, and half of all money thereafter to be received from the sale of Maine lands, the fund not to exceed a million dollars. Profiting by the example of Connecticut and New York, the distribution of the money among the towns was upon two conditions: the towns must raise by taxation at least one dollar for each person of school age — four to sixteen years — and must make to the State the statistical returns required by law. The fund was thus made a means not only of aiding the towns, but also of securing that information concerning the state of education which was necessary to intelligent legislation.

Dr Charles Carroll, in his " Public Education in Rhode Island," makes the following comments on the history of free schools in Rhode Island.

Reviewing earlier events briefly: A free school law enacted in 1800 was repealed in 1803. A committee of the General Assembly in 1818 reported as inexpedient Governor Knight's proposition to establish free schools for youth employed in factories. A committee of the General Assembly, appointed in 1821 to collect school statistics, failed to report. A constitution that provided for a permanent school fund was rejected by the freemen in 1824.

The General Assembly, in 1825, referred a proposed " act for the establishment of lotteries for the purpose of raising a fund for the support of free schools " to the next session.

The American and Gazette in 1828, took up the fight for free schools in earnest. January 4, it said:

" There is one subject of much more importance to Rhode Island than the election of a President, and that is the establishment of free schools. To be sure, those who would favor a military despotism would not be anxious to disseminate education, but this is a question involving the dearest interest of present and future generations, and all others ought to be made to yield to it."

Anticipating the opening of the January session of the General Assembly, the same newspaper, on January 11, said:

" Among all the subjects which will come before them (the General Assembly) the bill for establishing free schools stands pre-eminent. This deserves an early and deliberate consideration. Happily no real difference of opinion exists as to the expediency of establishing free schools, and we do not believe that if the question were taken by ayes and noes, a single member of the House would answer in the negative. There are three or four members in the Senate we should anticipate a negative vote from, in accordance with their uniform objections to every measure of public opinion and improvement. The only question that will produce difference of opinion is the mode of establishing schools, the ways and means by which they are to be supported — whether it shall depend upon a somewhat precarious revenue derived from lotteries, etc., or whether to this sum shall be added an equal or proportional amount raised by the several towns in such manner as they may think proper. As to the plan proposed by Mr Waterman, the benefits of which are to be experienced by the children of the great-grandchildren of the present generation, no man who is a father can listen to it a moment. We do not believe in the maxim 'Let posterity take care of itself,' but it surely is a correct principle that we should first provide for the present rising generation. Let free schools be established to the extent our present means will allow, and future generations will provide for preserving and enlarging the system. There is no instance in which a system of free schools, once fairly established, has been abandoned. It can, moreover, be plainly shown that the voluntary tax to be raised by each of the towns to entitle them to an equal or larger sum from the treasury, will not exceed the amount they already pay for the schools kept within their limits. Under the contemplated bill they will, therefore, receive double the benefits they now experience, at no greater expense than they already voluntarily incur for the education of their children."

The Rhode Island School law of 1845 and the labors of Henry Barnard marked the beginning of a new epoch in Rhode Island school history — "new," because, historians to the contrary notwithstanding, there were schools in Rhode Island and a history of schools before Rhode Island called Henry Barnard; "an epoch" because the change from old to new was fraught with so much import, and "the beginning," because so much of what Henry Barnard projected was destined to be realized only years after his retirement.

Scholars in the early free schools of Providence were assessed for fuel and required to furnish ink. In 1833 the fuel assessment was abolished. Newport assessed against scholars a small tuition charge, but provided free textbooks and stationery. By statute in 1839 school committees were empowered, "whenever an amount of money sufficient to pay for fuel, rent and other incidental expenses of public schools shall not be provided by any town by taxation or otherwise," "to assess a sum sufficient to pay such expenses upon those who send scholars to the schools, in such manner as they may deem just, exempting from assessment such as they consider unable or too poor to pay."

The evil of rate bills. Commissioner Potter, in 1850, recommended abolition of rate bills. "There can be no doubt," he said, "That the present rate bill system is one great obstacle in the way of a more general attendance. In several of the larger towns the schools are now made entirely free by town taxation, but in many of the towns the state and town appropriation are insufficient and the remainder is assessed on scholars."

In 1868 rate bills, after the current year, were abolished.

The fight for free schools in Rhode Island covered a period of half a century. "Abolition of tuition and free textbooks were necessary to make the public schools absolutely and completely free for all. Free schools must precede effective compulsory attendance laws, and compulsory attendance is necessary to insure universal education. Unless the state assumes the entire burden of school support, maintenance by sub-divisions of the state must be mandatory to insure schools in every section. The abolition of districts was an administrative reform, supplementing the mandatory town school support law."

Egerton Ryerson D.D. LL.D.

The Reverend Egerton Ryerson was the son of Colonel Joseph Ryerson, who, having fought on the side of the British in the American Revolution, was exiled to Canada in 1783. Colonel Ryerson was one of the pioneers in penetrating into that part of Canada that was then an unbroken wilderness and at Charlotteville on March 24, 1803, his fourth son, Egerton, was born. The boy received the very elementary education then afforded in his native county but this was supplemented by the extensive reading and study which he continued throughout his life. On his twenty-second birthday he was ordained a deacon in the Methodist Episcopal Church and during his experience as a circuit rider, he continued his study, often finding his only opportunity to read while on horseback. He became prominent in the affairs of the Methodist conference and on three occasions was sent to England to represent the Canadian Methodist Church in its negotiations with the English Methodists.

In 1827 he wrote a series of letters to the press which established his reputation as a skilful and able controversial writer, a reputation which was fully sustained later.

From 1840 to 1844, he was president of the then newly established "University of Victoria College" at Cobourg.

The first Canadian school bill was passed in 1841 and in 1844 Doctor Ryerson was appointed chief superintendent of education for Upper Canada, a position which he held for over twenty years. He was an ardent advocate of public schools and in 1846 obtained the enactment of a law, one feature of which was the support of the schools by a uniform rate upon property. During his service as superintendent of education, Doctor Ryerson was instrumental in obtaining additional legislation which provided for free common schools and which encouraged and gave aid in the establishment of academies and universities. He made four trips to Europe and one to the United States for the purpose of studying educational systems and of obtaining models and works of art for the educational museum which had been established under his jurisdiction. It has

EGERTON RYERSON DD. LL.D.
Chief Superintendent of Education for Upper Canada,
appointed 1841; served for over twenty years
(From Barnard's Journal of Education)

been said of him that " What national education in England owes to Sir J. K. Shuttleworth, what education in New England owes to Horace Mann, that debt education in Canada owes to Egerton Ryerson. . . . Through evil report and good report he has resolved, and he has found others to support him in the resolution, that free education shall be placed within the reach of every Canadian parent for every Canadian child."

On April 11, 1842, the Legislature extended the provision of the general school law to apply to the city of New York. It is of interest to note that sections 9 and 12 indicate that schools in New York City were supported by tax on property.

Laws of New York, 65th Session, 1842, Chapter 150

An act to extend to the city and county of New York, the provisions of the general act in relation to common schools.

Passed April 11, 1842

The People of the State of New-York, represented in Senate and Assembly, do enact as follows:

1 There shall be elected in each of the wards of the city and county of New-York two commissioners, two inspectors and five trustees of common schools, who shall be elected by ballot, at a special election to be held on the first Monday of June in each year, by the persons qualified to vote for charter officers in the said wards, and to be conducted in the same manner, by the same inspectors, at the same ward districts, and subject to the same laws, rules and regulations, as now govern the charter elections in said city. The commissioners of common schools so elected shall constitute a board of education for the city of New-York; a majority of whom shall constitute a quorum. They shall elect one of their number president of said board who shall preside at the meetings thereof, which shall be held at least as often as once in three months, and they may appoint a clerk whose compensation shall be fixed and paid by the supervisors of said city and county. The commissioners so elected in each ward shall be the commissioners of schools thereof, with the like powers and duties of commissioners of common schools in the several towns in this state, except as hereinafter provided. The said inspectors of common schools so elected in the several wards shall have the like powers, and be subject to the same duties with the inspectors of common schools of the several towns of this state, except as hereinafter provided. The trustees of common schools so elected in their respective wards shall be the trustees of the school districts, which may be formed and organized therein, with the like powers and duties as the trustees of school districts in the several towns in this state, except as hereinafter provided.

2 All such provisions of the third, fourth, fifth, and sixth articles of Title two, Chapter fifteen, Part first of the Revised Statutes, and of the several acts amending, and in addition to and relating to the same, not inconsistent with the provisions in this act contained, shall be, and the same are, hereby declared applicable to the city and county of New-York.

3 For all the purposes of this act, each of the several wards into which the said city and county of New-York now is or may be hereafter divided, shall be considered as a separate town, and liable to all the duties imposed, and entitled to all the powers, privileges, immunities, and advantages granted by the said third, fourth, fifth, and sixth Articles of Title two, Chapter fifteen, Part first of the Revised Statutes, to the several towns in this state, so far as the same are consistent with this act.

4 The forty-fourth section of an act entitled "An act to amend the second Title of the fifteenth Chapter of the first Part of the Revised Statutes, relating to common schools," passed May 26, 1841, is hereby repealed; and all the other sections of the said act, not inconsistent with the provisions of this act, are hereby declared applicable to the city and county of New York.

5 No compensation shall be allowed to the commissioners, inspectors, or trustees of common schools for any services performed by them, but the commissioners and inspectors shall receive their actual and reasonable expenses while attending to the duties of their office, to be audited and allowed by the supervisors of said city and county.

6 The said commissioners of common schools of each ward are hereby authorized to appoint a clerk, whose compensation shall be settled and paid by the board of supervisors.

7 Whenever the trustees elected in any ward shall certify in writing to the commissioners and inspectors of common schools thereof, that it is necessary to organize one or more schools in said ward, in addition to the schools mentioned in the thirteenth section of this act, it shall be the duty of said commissioners and inspectors to meet together and examine into the facts and circumstances of the case; and if they shall be satisfied of such necessity, they shall certify the same under their hands to the said board of education, and shall then proceed to organize one or more school districts therein, and shall procure a school house and all things necessary to organize a school in such district, the expense of which shall be levied and raised pursuant to the provisions of section nine of this act; and the title of all lands purchased by virtue of this act, with the buildings thereon, shall be vested in the city and county of New York.

8 Whenever the clerk of the city and county of New York shall receive notice from the superintendent of common schools, of the amount of moneys apportioned to the city and county of New York, for the support and encouragement of common schools therein, he shall immediately lay the same before the supervisors of the city and county aforesaid.

9 The said supervisors shall annually raise and collect, by tax upon the inhabitants of said city and county, a sum of money equal to the sum specified in such notice, at the same time and in the same manner as the contingent charges of the said city and county are levied and collected; also a sum of money equal to one-twentieth of one per cent of the value of real and personal property in the said city liable to be assessed therein, to be applied exclusively to the purposes of common schools in said city; and such further sum as may be necessary for the support and benefit of common schools in said city and county, to be raised, levied, and collected in like manner, and which shall be in lieu of all taxes and assessments to the support of common **schools for said city and county.**

10 The said supervisors shall, on or before the first day of May in every year, direct that a sum of money equal to the amount last received by the chamberlain of said city and county from the common school fund, be deposited by him, together with the sum so received from the school fund, in one of the incorporated banks in the said city and county (such bank to be designated by the said supervisors), to the credit of the commissioners of common schools in each of the said several wards, in the proportions to which they shall respectively be entitled, and subject only to the drafts of the said commissioners respectively, who shall pay the amount apportioned to the several schools enumerated in the thirteenth section of this act, to the treasurer of the societies or schools entitled thereto, or to some person duly authorized by the trustees of such societies of schools to receive the same.

11 So much of the seventh Article of Title second, Chapter fifteen, Part first of the Revised Statutes, and the several acts amending and in addition to, and relating to the said article as is especially applicable to the city and county of New York, and all other acts, and all provisions therein, providing for or directing, or concerning the disbursing or appropriation of the funds created for or applicable to common school education in the city and county of New York, and all and every provision for raising any fund, or for the imposition of any tax therefore, so far as the same are inconsistent with this act, are hereby repealed.

12 All children between the ages of four and sixteen, residing in said city and county, shall be entitled to attend any of the common schools therein; and the parents, guardians, or other persons having the custody or care of such children, shall not be liable to any tax, assessment, or imposition for the tuition of any such children, other than is herein before provided.

13 The schools of the Public School Society, the New York Orphan Asylum school, the Roman Catholic Orphan Asylum school, the schools of the two Half Orphan Asylums, the school of the Mechanics' School Society, the Harlem school, the Yorkville Public school, the Manhattanville Free school, the Hamilton Free school, the Institution for the Blind, The School connected with the alms house of said city, and the school of the Association for the Benefit of Colored Orphans, shall be subject to the general jurisdiction of the said commissioners of the respective wards in which any of the said schools now are or hereafter may be located, subject to the direction of the board of education, but under the immediate government and management of their respective trustees, managers, and directors, in the same manner and to the same extent as herein provided in respect to the district schools, herein first before mentioned, in said city and county; and so far as relates to the distribution of the common school moneys, each of the said schools shall be district schools of the said city.

14 No school above mentioned, or which shall be organized under this act, in which any religious sectarian doctrine or tenet shall be taught, inculcated, or practised, shall receive any portion of the school moneys to be distributed by this act, as hereinafter provided; and it shall be the duty of the trustees, inspectors and commissioners of schools in each ward, and of the deputy superintendent of schools, from time to time, and as frequently as need be, to examine and ascertain, and report to the said board of education, whether any religious sectarian doctrine or tenet shall have

been taught, inculcated, or practised in any of the schools in their respective wards; and it shall be the duty of the commissioners of schools in the several wards to transmit to the board of education, all reports made to them by the trustees and inspectors of their respective wards. The board of education, and any member thereof, may at any time visit and examine any school subject to the provisions of this act, and individual commissioners shall report to the board the result of their examinations.

15 It shall be the duty of the said board of education to apply, for the use of the several districts such moneys as shall be raised to erect, purchase, or lease school houses, or to procure the sites therefor; and also, to apportion among the several schools and districts provided for by this act, the school moneys to be paid over to the commissioners of schools in each ward, by virtue of the tenth section of this act, and shall file with the chamberlain of said city and county, on or before the fifteenth day of April, in each year, a copy of such apportionment, and stating the amount thereof to be paid to the commissioners of each ward; which apportionment shall be made among the said several schools and districts, according to the average number of children over four and under sixteen years of age, who shall have actually attended such school the preceding year. But no such school shall be entitled to a portion of such moneys, that has not been kept open at least nine months in the year, or in which any religious sectarian doctrine or tenet shall have been taught, inculcated, or practised, or which shall refuse to permit the visits and examinations provided for by this act.

16 The commissioners of schools of the respective wards, when they have received from the chamberlain of said city and county, the money apportioned to the several schools and districts in their several wards, shall apply the same to the use of the schools and districts in their several wards, according to the apportionment thereof so made by the said board of education.

17 The said commissioners of each ward shall, within fifteen days after their election, execute and deliver to the supervisors aforesaid, a bond with which such sureties as said supervisors shall approve, in the penalty of double the amount of public money appropriated to the use of the common schools of their respective wards, conditioned for the faithful performance of the duties of their office, and the proper application of all moneys coming in their hands for common school purposes. Such bond shall be filed by the said supervisors, in the office of the county clerk.

18 This act shall take effect immediately.

EARLY LEGISLATIVE REFERENCES TO FREE SCHOOLS

One of the first places in which the term " free school " is found in the legislative documents, is in the act of October 14, 1731, chapter 594, entitled "An act to encourage a public school in the city of New York for teaching Latin, Greek and mathematics."

And altho' the not rightly applying of a temporary salary heretofore allowed for a *Free School,* has been the chief Cause that an Encouragement for the like purpose has ever since been neglected; But in as much as the present Circumstances afford a better Prospect, and to the End our Youth may not be deprived of the Benefits before mentioned BE IT ENACTED by his Excellency the Governour the Council and the General Assembly, And it is hereby enacted by the Authority of the same That there shall be One Public School established and kept in the City of New York to teach Latin, Greek," and that the schoolmaster employed, " shall teach gratis and without any further reward or consideration from any person whatsoever, that what is allowed to him in this Act.

Twenty worthy pupils were to be selected from the various cities and counties to enjoy the benefits of this act. The schoolmaster was to receive 40 pounds a year for his services.

Act of April 8, 1801, Chapter 195

It was enacted that no payment shall thereafter be made to any of the county treasurers (under the act of encouragement of schools) passed the ninth day of April, 1795, until legislative provision shall be made on the subject.

Act of April 8, 1801, Chapter 189

The act directing certain moneys to be applied to the use of free schools in the city of New York. It directs the payment of an amount of money to various churches in the city of New York for conducting schools for the poor under the act for the encouragement of schools.

Act of April 18, 1843, Chapter 211

The act to establish free schools in the village of Poughkeepsie was passed to take effect immediately after the people of the village of Poughkeepsie had voted in favor.

Act of March 10, 1848, Chapter 81

Provides for the establishment of a free school in district 5 in the town of Flushing to be established when approved by a majority of the legal voters of said district.

Act of March 25, 1848, Chapter 138

Provides for a free school in district 4 in the town of Newton, Queens county, this act to take effect immediately.

Act of March 16, 1850, Chapter 60

An act to establish a free school in district 3 in the town of Newton.

Act of March 16, 1850, Chapter 66

Requiring the board of school commissioners in the city of Utica to prepare an estimate of the amount of money necessary to establish free schools in that city.

Act of March 18, 1850, Chapter 77

Providing for free schools in the village of Lockport.

Act of April 14, 1857, Chapter 171

Provides that the common schools of the city of Williamsburg shall be free to all children of said city between the ages of five and sixteen years inclusive, provided that a separate school or schools for colored children shall be maintained by the board of education. The said board shall prescribe the terms of admission to the evening schools and to the city academy, if any shall be established under this act, but they shall not make the payment of any money for entrance or tuition necessary for such admission.

Act of April 6, 1852, Chapter 156

Provides that every district or common school located in the village of Newburgh including the Newburgh High School and every school which may hereafter be located in the said village under this act, shall be free to all children between the ages of four and twenty-one years residing in the village.

Act of April 11, 1853, Chapter 151

Provides for free schools in the village of Waterloo.

Act of April 11, 1853, Chapter 171

Provides that school district 3 in the town of Cherry Valley, Otsego county, shall be free to all children between the ages of four and twenty-one years residing in that county.

Act of June 8, 1853, Chapter 344

Provides that the public schools in the town of Eastchester, Westchester county, shall be free to all children residing in the district.

Act of June 17, 1853, Chapter 365

Provides for free schools to be established in district 1 in the town of West Farms, Westchester county.

During the early period little educational legislation was enacted. Most of the legislations dealt with the transfer of " such moneys left over after the paupers were provided for " for the support of schools. Schools had originated in the arms of charity and in this period free education and pauperism were apparently closely allied. The following acts seem to illustrate this fact.

Act of March 21, 1791, Chapter 41

This act made it lawful for the overseers of the poor of the town of Clarmont to apply all moneys not needed for the relief of the poor to be used in the building and employment of a school teacher in that town.

Act of February 26, 1828, Chapter 44

The town of Edmeston relative to the appropriation of the surplus poor fund and likewise the chapter 151 of March 31, 1828, the act instructing the overseers of the poor in the town of Gouverneur in the county of St Lawrence to pay over such funds to the commission of common schools in that town. Similar act authorizing the overseers of the poor in the town of Saranac to pay over certain money in their hands to the commission of common schools passed February 5, 1829 (Chapter 23).

Act of April 18, 1829, Chapter 177

The overseers of the indigent of the town of Fort Edward are authorized to pay over $150 to the commission of highways and the remainder of the fund in their hands to the commissioners of the common schools.

Act of April 29, 1829, Chapter 299

Authorizing the overseers of the poor in the town of Pierpont to pay over to the commissioners of the common schools all the funds in their hands raised and collected for the support of the poor.

Act of February 22, 1830, Chapter 44

Instructing the overseers of the indigent in the town of DeKalb to turn over one thousand dollars out of the funds in their hands raised and collected for the support of the poor in that town.

Act of April 14, 1831, Chapter 125

Authorizing the application of the interest of the poor fund of the town of Macdonough to the support of the school fund.

Act of April 4, 1800, Chapter 101

Money appropriated to establish a school among the Oneida Indians living at Canasaraga.

" It is a somewhat curious fact that a free school for colored children was established in New York City before any free school for white children, in the true meaning of the words, existed. The first school for the latter was opened in 1801 by the Association of Women Friends for the Relief of the Poor (generally known as the Female Association), which had been organized in 1798 by a group of benevolent women connected with the Society of Friends. The necessity of a school was soon perceived, and in the year last mentioned it was decided to establish a school for the education of poor children whose parents belong to no religious society, and who, from some cause or other, can not be admitted into any of the charity schools of this city. The school was first attended by children of both sexes, but after a short trial the boys were discharged and only girls admitted."

Act of April 16, 1847, Chapter 74

An act authorizing the board of education of the city of New York to establish evening free schools for apprentices and others. This act provides for the organization and support of an evening school for the gratuitous education or instruction of apprentices and others whose daily avocations are such as to prevent their attending the public or ward schools now provided by law.

Act of April 11, 1848, Chapter 228

In relation to school district 12 in the towns of Milton and Ballston, Saratoga county, directs and empowers the trustees of the schools of these two villages to set apart from the school moneys appropriated to such district an amount necessary to provide instruction for the children under the age of sixteen who work in any manufacturing establishment in that district.

Act of April 20, 1830, Chapter 320

The method of an apportionment of school moneys changed so as to be according to population. It has been enacted that any person conceiving himself aggrieved in consequence of any ·decision made by any school district meeting, or by the trustees in refusing to admit any scholar gratuitously into any school that such may appeal to the superintendent of the common schools whose decision thereon shall be final.

"At the beginning of the nineteenth century the spirit of popular education was, so to speak, 'in the air,' and two events of far-reaching importance were about to take place; the enactment of a law providing the foundation for a permanent common school fund, and the establishment of the Free School Society in this city. These events render the year 1805 memorable in the educational history of the State."[1]

Chapter 15, Revised Statutes of 1827, on public instruction outlines the duties of the trustees of free school district (in relation to the payment by pupils)

"To exempt from the payment of the wages of teachers such poor persons within the district as they shall think proper.

"To certify such exemptions and deliver the certificate thereof to the clerk of the district.

"To ascertain for examination of the school lists kept by such teachers the number of days which each person not so exempted shall be liable to pay for instruction and the amount payable by each person."

Act of May 26, 1841, Chapter 260

"The trustees of any school district may exempt any poor person from the payment of the teacher's wages either in part or wholly and shall certify the whole amount of such exemption in any one quarter or term and the same shall be charged upon such district."

Act of April 8, 1844, Chapter 129

In this act a provision is made for the board of commissioners in the schools of Albany to provide books for poor pupils and to make provision for such pupils who can not pay tuition.

Act of April 8, 1844, Chapter 131

Fixes the rate of tuition fee for the schools of the city of Utica as not to exceed $2 a term.

New York Assembly Documents, 1844, Volume 2

From the annual report of the Superintendent of Common Schools, January 13, 1844, it is interesting to note the individual

---

[1] The New York Public School, by A. Emerson Palmer, page 15. Macmillan Company, 1905.

reports of the county superintendents in their attitudes toward the problem of free schools and private schools.

Act of April 25, 1831, Chapter 277

Provides that the superintendent of county poor houses which now are or hereafter may be established by law are hereby required to cause all county and town paupers over the age of five and under the age of sixteen years who now are or hereafter may be in said poor houses to be taught and educated in the same manner as children are now taught in the common schools of the State, at least one-fourth part of the time the said paupers shall remain in said poor houses.

Chapter 5

CONSTITUTIONAL CONVENTION (1846)

During the year 1846 the principle of free schools actually became a statewide issue. In this year a constitutional convention was held and the question arose as to whether the constitution should sanction free schools supported by taxes on property. Even before this convention opened, the press, the educational workers in the State and many prominent citizens were much interested in the movement to create a public sentiment which would urge upon the convention the adoption of such an amendment. Practically every educational organization had already passed resolutions advocating such a policy and in this year both political parties, the Whigs and Democrats, had adopted resolutions urging the amendment.

The following addresses, committee reports, proceedings of associations and newspaper articles are given for the purpose of showing the public attitude on the question as this general discussion reveals.

Support Free Schools

We would earnestly recommend to the public attention an article on another page, on the importance of supporting "*free schools*" in our land, from a patriot and veteran hero of the Revolution, which, as an argument, we have never seen surpassed. It glows with burning truth, and if there be in the statesmen of the present day a sufficiency of the fire of patriotism and philanthropy that animated the bosom of MARION, to be characterized by these hallowed terms, the torch of his reasoning will not be allowed to pass into forgetfulness, but will become a living principle, and influence their action in such a manner as will speedily bring to pass an amendment of our common school law that will secure impartial and sufficient instruction to every child in the community, as a permanent duty to the race, and the surest safeguard of the Republic.

For ourself, as an humble advocate of *Free Schools,* we feel eminently honored in being found in such exalted company, with such distinguished supporters of like opinions,— and while we rejoice that gradually the principle has been gaining hold of the people of the State, particularly in the dense population of cities, large villages, etc., we imagine our present law-makers could easily engraft upon and extend the principle to our whole state, without violence to any right, or the least disregard to the best interests of the people.

By the law of 1841, sec. 14, the trustees of district schools are authorized to exempt the indigent parents from paying tuition money, and tax the amount upon the property of the district, every quarter, or half yearly. The principle, then, is thereby established, that property is to be taxed for the education of poor children. There is also a previous provision in our school law, which required a tax upon the property of the towns equal to the amount of public money furnished by the State, " for the support of schools," which is devoted to the payment of teacher's wages, and applies to all the children in the schools,— so that all persons taught for the last thirty years in our common schools, were recipients of the moneys raised directly by tax for their education; and thus, there can be no boasting one over the other, in this respect.

But why all this complication, and diverse arrangement, and collection of these funds? Why adhere to the present system, when it is known to operate unequally, imperfectly, and without success in many districts,— and in other respects ineffectual, in comparison with the free school organizations, in our cities and large villages?

The fact is capable of daily demonstration, that the free school system is far superior, by its constant instruction to pupils in their early years — diffusing more knowledge in less time, than is acquired, as a general thing in our county districts,— and is less expensive in providing education for the children, either pro rata or per capita,— for it will be seen by the report of Dr. Reese, county superintendent of schools for New York, in 1844, that the entire expense of educating a child attending the schools of the Public School Society in that city, including tuition, books, stationery, fuel, insurance, etc., amounted to only *four dollars and forty cents per annum!* While at the same time, we are confident that every parent in the county of Westchester, who sent his child to a district school the whole of that year, and who paid the ordinary charge of the *rate bill;* paid more than that amount for him, besides having previously paid the annual tax levied " for the support of schools," books, etc., to say nothing of the tax for building the schoolhouse and the additional tax for the exempt children of the poor. . . .

We have canvassed this system in our own mind, and have watched its operation, until we are perfectly satisfied, that it is ineffective, unsuccessful, and unfitted to the complete and proper education of the masses, and we therefore earnestly desire the adoption of a more simple and salutary system of public instruction, which we believe can be adopted, without the slightest inconvenience, or serious dissatisfaction to the taxpayers of the State.

Our proposition, to which we respectfully invite the attention of the Legislature and the country press, is, so to amend the 14th section of the school law of 1841, that it shall read, " the trustees of each school district shall ascertain, after the payment of the public money devoted to the tuition of the pupils of such school, the amount due to the teacher, each year, and certify said amount to the town superintendent of schools, on or before the first day of December, and the said amount shall become a charge upon the town, and be assessed by the supervisor, in the same manner as other taxes for expenses of the town are levied, and to be paid to the town superintendent, and by him paid to the teacher in the same way that school moneys are now paid, by provisions of the law." Then, if the towns, at their annual meeting voted the " equal additional sum," as they are empowered to do, the balance levied as proposed above would be small; if they did not do so, it would be greater; but in no case equal to the present amount paid by taxpayers, who send to the school and pay a *rate bill,* besides the present taxes for those objects.

Let it not be urged that such tax would be unjust upon those who have educated their children, under the rate bill system, and have now no small children to participate in the tax; because, we have shown, that their children did participate in their proportion of the public money, raised as now, by tax, and if not to the extent now proposed, it was the fault of their stinted and shortsighted policy; and they only suffer in degree the evil of imperfect and unwise legislation, that ought to be abandoned for a more liberal and enlightened policy.

The illustrious Marion has said the evils of war were fastened upon his native State, because of the "lack of knowledge" in the inhabitants! Although we have not these particular evils hanging upon us at the present time, it will not be difficult to show that this State is also suffering large losses in persons and property through *ignorance and vice*. We know that all evils are not to be attributed to ignorance; yet, a great proportion of them may be avoided by a proper cultivation of the intellect and understanding. But our object is just now to show that ignorance is expensive. An intelligent gentleman has estimated that two hundred thousand dollars are paid annually in this country to lawyers,— the greater proportion of which comes of the want of knowledge in the clients, and a proper regard to the duties of life, and social intercourse. Here then, we have a tax vastly beyond all that is paid for education and all moral influences together; and shall we not then, in a word, abandon the ruinous practice of rearing members of the community, to become vicious and profitless citizens, and thus tax the prudent and prosperous portions of society ten fold for their support or correction afterwards?

We do most earnestly urge this *social reform* upon the attention of the community, and point them again to the truthful and thrilling arguments of the patriotic and devoted Marion, in their support.—*Westchester Herald, 1846.*

The following extract from Colonel Horry's "Life of General Marion" gives the remarks of General Marion to which reference is made in the above editorial:

I often went to see Marion. Our evenings were spent as might have been expected, between two old friends who had spent their better days together in scenes of honorable enterprise and danger. On the night of the last visit I ever made him, observing that the clock was going for ten, I asked him if it were not near his hour of rest.

"Oh no," said he, "we must not talk of bed yet. It is but seldom, you know that we meet. And as this may be our last, let us take all we can of it in chat. What do you think of the *times?*"

"Oh, glorious times" said I.

"Yes, thank God" replied he, "they are glorious times indeed, and fully equal to all that we had in hope when we drew our swords for independence. But I am afraid they won't last long."

I asked him why he thought so.

"Oh, knowledge, sir," said he, "is wanting! knowledge is wanting! Israel of old, you know, was *destroyed for lack of knowledge;* and all nations, all individuals, have come to naught from the same cause."

I told him I thought we were too happy to change so soon.

"Pshaw!" replied he, "that is nothing to the purpose. Happiness signifies nothing if it be not known and properly valued. Satan, we are told, was once an angel of light, but for want of duly considering his glorious state, he rebelled and lost all. And how many hundreds of young Carolinians have we not known, whose fathers left them all the means of happiness; elegant estates; handsome wives; and in short every blessing that the most luxurious could desire? Yet they could not rest, until by drinking and gambling, they had fooled away their fortunes, parted from their wives, and rendered themselves the veriest beggars and blackguards on earth.

"Now why was all this, but for *lack of knowledge?* For had those silly ones but known the evils of poverty, what a vile thing it is to wear a dirty shirt, a long beard and ragged coat; to go without dinner or to sponge for it among growling relations; or to be bespattered, or run over in the streets, by those who were once their fathers' overseers; I say had these poor boobies, in the days of their prosperity, known these things as they do now would they have squandered away the precious means of independence and pleasure, and have brought themselves to all this shame and sorrow? No, never, never, never.

"And so it is, most exactly, with nations. If those that are free and happy, did but know their blessings, do you think they would ever exchange them for slavery? If the Carthagenians, for example, in the days of their freedom and self-government, when they obeyed no laws, but that of their own making; paid no taxes but for their own benefit; and free as air, pursued their own interest as they liked; I say, that, if that once glorious and happy people, had known their blessings, would they have sacrificed them all, by their accursed factions to the Romans, to be ruled, they and their children, with a rod of iron, to be burthened like beasts, and crucified like malefactors? No, surely they would not.

"Well now to bring this home to ourselves. We fought for self-gevernment; God has pleased to give us one, better calculated perhaps to protect our rights, to foster our virtues, to call forth our energies, and to advance our condition nearer to perfection and happiness, than any government that was ever framed under the sun.

"But what signifies even this government, divine as it is if it be not known and prized as it deserves?"

I asked him how he thought this was best to be done.

"Why certainly," replied he, "by *free schools*."

I shook my head.

He observed it and asked me what I meant by that.

I told him I was afraid the legislature would look to their popularity and dread the expense.

He exclaimed. "God preserve our legislature from such 'penny wit and pound foolishness!' What sir? Keep a nation in ignorance rather than vote a little of their own money for education!" . . .

I sighed and told him I wished I had not broached the subject for it made me very sad.

"Yes," he replied, "it is enough to make anyone sad. But it cannot be helped but by a wiser course of things; for, if people will not do what will make them happy, God will surely chastise them; and this dreadful loss of public property, is one token of his displeasure at our neglect of public instruction. . . .

"The enormous sacrifice of public property, in the last war, being no more as before observed than the natural effect of public ignorance, ought to teach us that of all sins, there is none so hateful to God as national ignorance; that unfailing spring of *national ingratitude, rebellion, slavery and wretchedness!*

"But, if it be melancholy to think of so many elegant houses, rich furniture, fat cattle, and precious crops, destroyed for want of that patriotism, which a true knowledge of our interests would have inspired; then how much more melancholy, to think of those torrents of precious blood that were shed, those cruel slaughters and massacres, that took place among the citizens from the same cause! As proof that such hellish tragedies would never have been acted had our state but been enlightened, only let us look at the people of New England. From Britain their fathers had fled to America for religion's sake. Religion had taught them that God created men to be happy; that to be happy they must have virtue; that virtue is not to be attained without knowledge, nor knowledge without instruction, nor public instruction without *free schools,* nor free schools without legislative order.

"Among a people who fear God, the knowledge of duty, is the same as doing it. Believing it to be the first command of God 'let there be light,' and believing it to be the will of God that 'all should be instructed, from the least to the greatest,' these wise legislators, at once set about public instruction. They did not ask, how will my constituents like this? won't they turn me out? shall I not lose my three dollars per day? No! but fully persuaded that public instruction is God's will, because the people's good, they set about it like the true friends of the people.

"Now mark the happy consequence. When the war broke out, you heard of no division in New England, no toryism, nor any of its horrid effects; no houses in flames, kindled by the hands of fellow-citizens, no neighbors waylaying and shooting their neighbors, plundering their property, carrying off their stock, and aiding the British in the cursed work of American murder and subjugation. But on the contrary, with minds well informed of their rights and hearts glowing with love for themselves and posterity, they rose up against the enemy, firm and united, as a band of shepherds against the ravening wolves.

"And their valor in the field gave glorious proof how men will fight, when they know that their all is at stake. See Major Pitcairn, on the memorable 19th of April, 1775, marching from Boston, with one thousand British regulars, to burn the American stores at Concord. Though this heroic excursion was commenced under cover of night, the farmers soon took the alarm, and gathering around them with their fowling-pieces, presently knocked down one-fourth of their number and caused the rest to run, as, if, like the swine in the gospel, they had a *legion of devils at their backs.*

"Now with sorrowful eyes, let us look to our own State, where no pains were ever taken to enlighten the minds of the poor. There we have seen a people naturally as brave as the New Englanders, for *mere lack of knowledge of their blessings possessed or their dangers threatened,* suffer Lord Cornwallis, with only sixteen hundred men to chase General Greene upwards of three hundred miles! In fact, to scout him through the two great states of South and North Carolina as far as Guilford court house! And when Greene, joined at that place by two thousand, poor, illiterate militia men, determined at length to fight, what did he gain by them with all their numbers but disappointment and disgrace? For though posted very advantageously behind the corn field fences, they could not stand a single fire from the British, but in spite of their officers, broke and fled like base born slaves, leaving their loaded muskets sticking in the fence corners.

"But from this shameful sight, turn again to the land of *free schools;* to Bunker Hill. There behind a poor ditch of half a night's raising, you behold fifteen hundred militia men waiting the approach of three thousand British regulars, with a heavy train of artillery! With such odds against them, with such fearful odds in numbers, discipline, arms and martial fame, will they not shrink from the contest, and like their southern friends, jump up and run? Oh no! to a man, they have been taught to read; to a man, they have been instructed to know, and dearer than life to prize the blessings of *freedom.* Their bodies are lying behind ditches but their thoughts are on the wing, darting through eternity. The warning voice of God still rings in their ears. The hated forms of proud merciless kings, pass before their eyes. They look back to the days of old, and strengthen themselves as they think what their gallant forefathers dared for LIBERTY and for THEM. They looked forward to their own dear children, and yearn over the unoffending millions, now, in tearful eyes, looking up to them for protection. And shall this infinite host of deathless beings, created in God's own image and capable by *virtue and equal laws* of endless progression in glory and happiness; shall they be arrested from their high career, and from the free-born sons of God, be degraded into the slaves of man? Maddening at the accursed thought, they grasp their avenging firelocks and drawing their sights along the death-charged tubes, they long for the coming up of the British thousands. Three times the British thousands came up; and three times the dauntless yeoman waiting their near approach, received them with storms of thunder and lightning that shivered their ranks, and heaped the fields with their weltering carcases.

"In short, my dear sir, men will always fight for their government, according to their sense of its value. To value it aright, they must understand it. This they can not do without education. And a large portion of the citizens are poor and never can attain that inestimable blessing without the aid of government to bestow it freely upon them. And the more perfect the government, the greater the duty to make it well known. Selfish and oppressive governments indeed, as Christ observes, 'must hate the light and fear to come to it, because their deeds are evil.' But a fair and cheap government, like our Republic 'longs for the light, and rejoices to come to the light, that it may be manifested to be from God,' and well worth all the vigilance and valor that an enlightened nation can rally for its defense. And God knows, a good government can hardly ever be half anxious enough to give its citizens a thorough knowledge of its own excellencies. For as some of the most valuable truths, for lack of careful promulgation, have been lost, so the best governments on earth, if not duly known and prized, may be subverted. Ambitious demagogues will rise, and the people through ignorance and love of change, will follow them. Vast armies will be formed, and bloody battles fought. And after desolating their country with all the horrors of civil war, the guilty survivors will have to bend their necks to the iron yoke of some stern usuper; and like beasts of burden, to drag unpitied, those galling chains which they have riveted upon themselves for ever."

Professor Potter's Address

Prof. Potter, of Union College, addressed the school convention on Thursday evening. With the whole subject of education he is perfectly familiar, and probably feels as much interested in the improvement of schools as any other individual that could be named. He has done much for the advancement of popular education, and we trust he will long continue to labor in so important a field.

The professor spoke of the great effort that has been made, and is now making, to improve our common schools. Much has been done, but a great work is yet to be accomplished. He spoke of the claims of the system upon the public at large. It is important to the general welfare and prosperity of the people, that the entire population of the country be educated. He drew a comparison between the people of the United States, individually, as members of the great partnership company styled the "United States of America," and a common business co-partnership. In order for any business partnership to be prosperous there must be intelligence on the part of the individual partners. So, also, must there be intelligence on the part of the people who compose the great United States partnership. The question was, then, what course should be pursued in order that the people may become an intelligent and virtuous people? The answer is obvious: We must have schools — good common Schools.

The importance of free schools was strongly urged. The happy results of the free school system in this city, were cited as an instance. The number of scholars in the city schools had increased nearly, or quite one-half.

"The public," said Prof. P. "must either tax itself for knowledge, or be taxed for ignorance."

Good schools will have a powerful tendency to prevent the commission of crime. To the manufacturer it is of vast importance that the operatives in his employ should be intelligent. Facts, in all manufacturing districts go to show the great saving to the employer, whose operatives are intelligent.

One manufacturer in Massachusetts, by employing a more intelligent class of hands than he had been accustomed to, had increased the profits of his establishment one-twelfth.

Free Schools

A few petitions were forwarded to the last Legislature, asking that the district schools of the State be made free. The committee on colleges, academies and common schools in the Assembly, of which Mr. M. H. Brown was chairman, noticed the petitions and spoke of free schools as follows:

"There are petitions in the hands of the committee, asking that the 'common schools be made free schools;' that the education of the State be made a tax upon the property of the State. These petitions should be regarded with favor. They ask for that which would render our common school system perfect. While it would render the system more perfect, it would also render it more simple and obviate the objection to our common school laws that they are too complicated. Men of property, when they consider their true interests, will require that education in our primary schools be made free, in order that every child in the State may have the privilege of attending them. Such a provision would tax them, but that tax would be returned with ten fold interest. Property and life would be more valuable in the same ratio that the community should become more intelligent and virtuous. Money expended for the advancement of general education, is money wisely and safely as well as benevolently invested.

"While the committee believe that our common schools will never reach that state of perfection of which they are susceptible, until the "free system" is adopted, they also believe that every advance toward that desideratum in public instruction, will be effectually and permanently secured by being based in public favor. In a country where the will of the people is the only legitimate law giver, legislation will be powerless in the work of reformation, except its efforts be sustained by the strong arm of public opinion. It is not, therefore, safe to take legislative action in any instance affecting the State generally, unless it be founded on a strong, unequivocal and decided expression of the will of the people. The fact that petitions have been presented praying for so important an improvement in relation to our primary schools, constitutes a new era in the history of public instruction in this State. It is to be hoped that the attention of the people will be awakened on this subject and that we shall soon receive expressions decisive enough to warrant the favorable action of the Legislature. Argument is unnecessary for the purpose of showing the benefits of the system of "free schools." Our sister state of Massachusetts is an illustrious and enviable example of what the system is able to affect. No where in this western world are there better schools and a more intelligent community than in that State, whose name is associated with the landing of the pilgrims. That system would do as much for New York as it has done and is now doing for Massachusetts, and when the people call for it the Legislature will doubtless be prompt to answer the call."—*Teachers Advocate, February 4, 1846.*

Mr. J. J. Rockafellow, county superintendent of northern Allegany, in his annual report referred as follows to free schools:

" For two of the above maladies — incompetent teachers and short terms — I can think of no more speedy and effectual remedy, than the introduction of a system of free public schools.

ALONZO POTTER D.D. LL.D.
Bishop of Pennsylvania

"By this I mean no untried or uncertain system but such as has been in successful operation for the last few years, in several of our large cities and neighboring states. One that shall support our schools by *taxation* instead of *"Rate Bill."* Of late, I have taken occasion to bring this subject before the people, at every educational meeting of our country. It elicits much interest from the *patrons* of schools and, I think, meets with the approbation of a large *majority* of them. To this system there are doubtless some valid objections. But I think they are fully met by the consideration that it would secure longer terms and a still more efficient body of teachers. Many other strong considerations might be adduced in its favor, but this one alone, I deem sufficiently weighty to overbalance all objections that can be brought against the system. Now in our own country and also in many others — children are kept at school but a little more than seven months during the year and then left to suffer the consequences of a long intellectual famine. Were these same schools supported entirely by a tax upon property, we have every reason to believe that they would be kept open as many months in the year as practicable. Besides, no excuse could then be found for the employment of unqualified teachers because they are 'cheap.'"

On the score both of *equity and expediency,* it appears to me that the property of the State should educate the children of the State.

Mr Pierpont Potter, county superintendent of Queens county, in his annual report for 1846 wrote as follows:

"In my former reports, I have enumerated the obstacles which obstruct the prosperity of the common schools, and particularly in the village of Jamaica. The difficulties mentioned in those reports still continue. I know of no remedy but to make the *common schools free.* I am sometimes inclined to think that we have just about enough of the public money to create wrangling among the inhabitants. I hope that the day is not far distant when we shall be able to say — there is the common school and there is your tax — send your children to school or keep them home, there will be no difference in the expense. I have witnessed more than one instance under the present system, where one or two wealthy individuals, from some trifling offense, withdrew their children from the common school in the vicinity, and sent them either to a select or boarding school, which act so alarmed others in the district, that they withdrew their children through *fear of being compelled to pay a very high rate bill.* The result of all these evils was that those who had the patriotism and the firmness to adhere to the common school, were compelled to pay six or seven dollars per scholar for one quarter's tuition. Now, by having the common schools free, these evils could not occur. Make the common schools free, and then should ever so many wealthy pupils be withdrawn, no injury to the common school could arise as the *support* of the school would remain.

"The plan has been sufficiently tried in a sister state (Massachusetts) and the wisdom of the plan has been amply proved by the lapse of time. Indeed, I am convinced from four years experience as the County Superintendent, that our common schools must be Free, supported entirely at the public expense before they will or can answer the purpose for which they are designed."— *Teachers Advocate, April 22, 1846.*

State Convention for Revising the Constitution and the School System

Were there no higher motives than those of economy, to which an appeal for a free school system could be made, the question would hardly admit of doubt. There is a class in society who never decide on the merits of any proposition until influenced by metallic arguments; they never regard with favor the general good, whenever it conflicts, as they suppose, with their own private interest, and therefore, without any examination of this subject, stand arrayed against this, the noblest among the important reforms contemplated by the advocates of a new and better fundamental law for this State. There are those who oppose or view with callous indifference, this proposition, merely because they fear an increase of taxation. We therefore present a few statistics containing strong and impressive arguments for those of our fellow citizens who are willing to live the mere pensioners upon society — striving with a zeal that increases with each passing hour to garner up the emoluments afforded by a well-organized government without contributing to its support, and who aim at reaping a rich harvest from the progress of civilization without the least disposition to encourage those appliances by which society is to be elevated. These statistics enable us to form an estimate of the comparative expense of the *rate-bill* and the *free school system,* which will approximate to accuracy, when extended to the whole state; an estimate which will induce the mere worshipper of money to give support to this reform. We take the following from the Westchester Herald, which presents the subject, as far as it relates to the economy of the plan, in its true light." In the subjoined table "side by side, stand the present prevailing system of the *rate-bill,* for the support of schools, and the *free system of taxing property for their support,* and opening the door for all who will attend. Take from this table for instance, Albany, with her *rate-bill;* and Rochester, with her *free system;* in the first case two-sixths of the children are educated — in the other five-sixths of the children are educated. Again the average cost per scholar, is, of course, materially greater under the rate-bill, than under the free-school plan, as shown in the table, Albany paying $5.47 and Rochester paying from her property-tax, $3.99 for each child taught. Both cities, no doubt, have well-qualified teachers, and in sufficient numbers, while the children make excellent progress; yet it will be observed that the highest price of tuition money paid to their teachers in the two cities does not materially vary, considering the cost of living in these places.

"On the point of economy, therefore, as well as duty, we would respectfully urge upon the public attention the working of the free schools of this State, now sufficiently tested by experience — not saying at present anything of the advantages conferred upon the population of other states, where its principles are more generally practised upon, but simply presenting as has been said, the plea of economy, utility, and universal improvement."

Comparative Table of Statistics, in the Cities, etc., of this State

	Population	Children of school age	Number of the school lists	Average attendance	Cost per pupil on this average	Tax on each inhabitant	Amount received from school fund	Raised by tax	Total	Cost of school houses	Free schools which	Highest salary to male teacher	Highest salary to female teacher
New York....	371 102	80 000	59 385	19 467	$9 52	$0 40	$35 404	$150 014	$185 418	$750 000	Free	$1 000	$450
Brooklyn....	59 588	11 954	3 400	2 275	9 64	29	4 102	17 836	21 939	50 000	Free	700	300
Albany......	41 152	8 918	2 961	1 995	5 74	18	3 817	7 635	11 452	30 000	Rate	650	180
Buffalo.....	28 346	5 934	4 500	2 000	6 03	35	2 062	10 000	12 062	47 850	Free	600	200
Rochester...	25 207	5 890	4 946	3 274	3 99	40	2 286	10 700	12 986	42 050	Free	480	240
Troy........	21 781	3 600	890	604	9 94	17	1 700	3 700	5 400	14 000	Free	700	275
Utica.......	12 190	2 819	1 867	1 041	5 66	34	1 447	4 447	5 894		Rate	500	200
Schenectady.	6 555	1 614	467	310	4 12	09	640	640	1 280	700	Rate	260	108
Hudson......	5 557	1 400	650	475	7 04	48	642	2 700	3 342	3 000	Free	800	250
Syracuse.....	9 614	1 931	1 737	906	3 42	24	652	2 451	3 103	13 000	Rate	600	240
Geneva......	4 245	1 163	865	350	3 85	21	456	895	1 351	4 200	Rate	550	300

It will be seen by the above table that the amount per scholar where the free school system exists is nearly one-third less than that paid for no better instruction under the rate-bill system. This has been observed by the sound political economists of some places and has induced them to seek for such special legislation as would give them a local free school system. Wherever it has been adopted in this State and faithfully carried out, the people are unanimously in favor of it. We have never heard of a single objection to the system where it had been well worked. The only complaint in the city of Rochester arises from an oversight or mistaken policy of the board of education, by which a deficiency occured in raising a fund sufficient to sustain the schools during the whole year. To extricate themselves from this difficulty, the Board passed a resolution changing the commencement of the fiscal year from the 20th of May to the 1st of September, causing a vacation in the schools of three months. This is censured and is censurable, not because the beginning of the fiscal year was changed, but because the people's schools were to be closed during this period. This measure placed them back on the *pay system* and on that account is sincerely deprecated by a large majority of the citizens of our Queen City. They complain because they are deprived of the benefits of an admirable system for *three months* — an exigency which may never occur again. The very complaints growing out of the operations of the system in this city are strong arguments for its general adoption and vigorous support.

The Superintendent of Common Schools gives the following estimate of the whole annual expense of our schools, which he regards as a close approximation to accuracy .

Interest at 7 per cent on $3,115,590.55, the cost of schoolhouses etc., as returned by the marshals appointed to take the census.............................	$218 091 33
Fuel for 10,837 districts at $8 for each..	86 696 ..
Fee of collectors on $222,218 raised by tax at 3 per cent......................	6 666 54
Fees for collecting $458,127 on rate bills at 5 per cent........................	22 906 53
Repairs of schoolhouses, average $4 each.....................................	44 072 ..
Compensation of town superintendents and town officers, supervisors and town clerks, say...	25 500 ..
County superintendents of common schools..................................	28 000 ..
Total estimated expenses..	$431 902 22
Add amount actually expended as ascertained by the returns of 1844, including for libraries...	997 723 92
Making an aggregate expenditure of.......................................	$1 429 626 14

for the support of schools exclusive of books and stationery for the use of the scholars. Divide the above sum by 676,732, the number of scholars instructed, and the average cost for each child is $2.11.

The above estimate and statement is based on data, excluding New York, where the schools are all free, and the laws peculiar and local. It should be remembered that the average time the schools were taught the past year, is about eight months, and it is proper to observe that in order to have the tuition bills low, it is only needful that *all* the children of the district should attend the school promptly and diligently the whole term. Let those parents whose circumstances call for the exercise of exemptions be excused from paying, and a tax levied on the taxable property of the district, to meet the expense of the tuition of the exempted scholars; and the whole outlay for instruction and the contingent charges for supporting the present organization, will not much exceed two dollars for each child over five and under sixteen years of age; a less sum than it would cost to maintain a pupil at an academy or select and private school one quarter of the year."

It will be seen by the above estimate that, if a system could be adopted which would induce general attendance, the expense of educating each child would be far below the average cost, even in those places now under a free school system. It is the want of general attendance which increases the rate bills and makes the burdens onerous. Remove all these inducements to keep children from school, by making the property of the town support the schools, instead of those who send their children to them, and there will be the same motive in a pecuniary point of view, to induce *general attendance* which so often and so criminally prevents it. The terrors of a high rate bill will vanish and the people will sustain good schools at a less expense than is now paid for such as too many deem worthless, and which whether good or poor, do not meet the end of their creation, because large numbers are denied the enjoyment of their privileges.

Let the requisite amount be raised by direct taxation or by increasing the common school fund, from permanent revenues, so that it shall be sufficient to meet the deficiency raised by rate bills, and cheaper, more efficient and more extensive educational privileges will be given to the rising thousands, who are soon to control the affairs of the State, and whose influence for good upon our whole country and the world, will be strictly proportionate to the means employed to train them up for usefulness.—*Teachers Advocate, May 6, 1846*

State Convention for Revising the Constitution and the School System

From the tables and estimates in our last, it may be inferred that the expense of educating all the children of the State, under an energetic free school system, will not exceed that now paid for less than two-thirds of the number, under the present rate bill plan. We leave this view of the question, as a wise civil policy demands something more than a mere reduction of its expenses; it requires that an immense amount, now paid for the relief of pauperism, the punishment of criminals, and the support of standing armies, should be appropriated to a more delightful and humane work — one that brings blessings to society instead of curses, by the promotion of universal intelligence and virtue. All our punitory measures are designed to check and restrain vice; the machinery by which society is to be kept in a quiet and tranquil state, aims not at improvement; it is defective and expensive; it frequently hardens the offender, and entails upon the youth, far more vicious habits than those of their fathers, consequently will demand a larger number of officers, courts and prisons, to preserve the public peace. These appliances may be effectual, though at great expense, to restrain; but they can never improve society, for they do not contain the elements of human advancement.

It has been wisely remarked, that if "crime were regarded the greatest *luxury*, not one, indulged in by our citizens, is half so expensive." Even the most sharp sighted worldly policy dictates any expenditure, therefore, necessary to educate every child.

Some of the objections urged against the free school system by those who desire the advancement of society, are based upon the principle that "a thing is to be valued by its cost." That which is directly free of expense, will be unappreciated and neglected. The real worth and not the cost of a thing is, and should be made the true standard by which society should make its estimates. It is so in other matters and should be so in regard to education. But we have direct evidence of a contrary effect of the free school system. In the third annual report of the superintendent of the common schools of the city of Buffalo, for the year 1839, we find strong testimony in favor of the general attendance of the children and the respect of the people for the free schools. The following extract is proof that the privileges it affords will be appreciated, even when given without cost:

"The system now in operation, has thus far succeeded beyond the most sanguine hopes of its projectors and friends — its good effects are already apparent, from the desire to obtain admission into the schools, the prompt and constant attendance of their children, and their correct and orderly deportment while under the authority of the Teachers. Its general good effects upon the character of our active population, cannot but be in the highest degree beneficial, and the benefits to be hereafter derived from it, will be in exact proportion with the support and countenance which it may receive from the city authorities, and an enlightened community. The system adopted is the only one which can successfully bring home the benefits of education equally to all; and the only question is, whether the thousands of children in this city shall be educated by means of the free schools, or whether a large majority shall grow up in ignorance and vice, and thus become a source of expense under our criminal statutes."

The same superintendent, after four years official acquaintance with the workings of the system in that city, remarks in his report of 1844, that " public sentiment was never more united on any subject of local interest, than it now is upon the subject of our free school system. Its success has disarmed the opposition of open enemies, and the objections of doubtful friends, and nothing now remains but for the authorities by judicious and well considered additional departments, to bring our system of Free School education to a state of perfection and usefulness which will rival any other city within the borders of the Republic."

Experience abundantly proves the soundness of the policy, as tested in our own State, to be more economical, more efficient and better adapted to the wants of society, than any other which can be adopted. It tends to level upward children of different classes, and would soon banish the false and silly distinctions which the arrogant few would make, and thus implant sentiments suited to a free government. Mr Steele, in one of his reports, wisely says, " the sovereignty of the people is unquestioned, and the doctrine of universal suffrage is too firmly established to fear any curtailment of its privileges. The great importance of having universal education at all times co-equal with universal suffrage, must be obvious to every reflecting mind; and the doctrine that the property of the country should pay for the education of the people thereof, may justly be adopted as the only safe and true policy for the country to adopt. The property holder, paying the percentage upon his property required to disseminate universal education among the people, pays but a trifling premium for the insurance of the increased stability and protection of his property, and the permanence of the institutions under which it was accumulated."

No system of public instruction is worthy of legislative support which does not aim at spreading the blessing of knowledge and virtue to every child in the State. The greatest good to the greatest number, is the only maxim worthy the name of democracy. What more efficient way can there be of carrying this sound republican sentiment into practice, than by a liberal and wisely framed free school system.

The advance of political science in this country, is the result of experience in self-government. The object of our national policy is not so much to enrich and agrandize, as to ameliorate the sufferings, multiply the comforts, remove the evils, extend the privileges, and elevate the character of the man. A republic based upon any other than the universal diffusion of knowledge and virtue, cannot be made a government securing equal rights and protection to all its subjects. The first and highest aim, therefore, should be to adopt the most direct and efficient measures for the correct education of every child, whether born in affluence or cradled in poverty, in the same schools. A distinction in the character of our schools is the most powerful agency by which an invidious classification is made in the community, one that gives an adulatory regard for certain employments, and imposes a disrespect upon others, perhaps far more useful to society, and therefore in themselves the most honorable. Our system of instruction and school privileges, should, on this account, if no other, be uniform throughout the whole State, and so arranged as to embrace and educate side by side the children of all ranks and conditions. It should invite all to accept the invaluable boon of education, and not as now offer a pecuniary premium for nonattendance at school. The system of requiring to pay for time spent in school, and deducting for absences, is opening an account by which a premium is paid for ignorance, but if our schools were entirely free, the same premium would be paid for knowledge and virtue; it would be paid by the government as an investment to secure more useful and honorable citizens — an investment which alone can improve and exalt a nation of freemen. We therefore urge the importance and absolute necessity of a constitutional free school system, placed under such a plan of state supervision as we have suggested in a previous number. This, with our philosophical and admirable local supervision, will give it great efficiency and bring the blessings of knowledge to thousands now left to grow up in ignorance because our plan of education is not as universal as is the theory of our government.— *Teachers Advocate, May 13, 1846.*

We have already presented as indicative of public sentiment resolutions in favor of a free school system, which were adopted at primary meetings held in several of the different counties of the State, preparatory to the choice of delegates to the convention. The people still continue to give instruction on this question; their voice is heard in nearly every direction, urging this measure of reform with a zeal somewhat commensurate with the importance of the subject. A spirit of enquiry has gone abroad, and the answer comes sounding over hills and valleys, "*give us free schools.*"

In distant portions of the State exists a unanimity of sentiment seldom found on any other question of general interest.

At a convention of Whig delegates from the several towns in the county of Allegany, held at the court house in the village of Angelica, on Monday, April 6th, 1849, to nominate persons to represent them in the State Convention for revising the constitution, it was unanimously

Resolved, That as all our institutions are to be sustained and perpetuated by the intelligence of the mass, and as their influence must be exerted either for the weal or woe of our country, that we recommend to the favorable notice of the delegates to the state convention the necessity of making ample provisions for the maintenance and encouragement of a liberal system of common school education, securing to one and all the rudiments of an education entirely free from direct cost or charge, and that the present common school fund be increased for that purpose.

Such demonstrations of public sentiment indicate a soundness of policy well worthy of the Empire State, and evince that regard for the safety and perpetuity of our institutions which will be received as an earnest of fidelity and zeal in giving energy to the system.

There are other considerations besides the mere expressed will of the people, which we would present in favor of incorporating this system into the organic laws of the State. This will is predicated of something more than mere theory; it has the sanction of *successful experience* in Massachusetts and in portions of our own State. Soon after the organization of the government of Massachusetts, the principle of free schools was discussed thoroughly and adopted as a fundamental law. Provisions were made for the education of every child in the State, by the formation of districts, the erection of school houses, and direct taxation upon the property of each town. In addition to the establishment of free common schools, in which all the elementary branches of an English education were taught, a town high school was created, for the purpose of giving to all an opportunity to become instructed in the higher branches of education. In these high schools, no rate bills were made, but they were, like the common schools, free to all in the town. This system of academic instruction did not, however, work as well as was anticipated. This was occasioned by the difficulties growing out of the locality of these institutions. People residing at a distance from the high school became dissatisfied, as they could not avail themselves of its privileges without being subjected to an expense for board and other contingencies from which those in the immediate vicinity were entirely exempt. This was urged as an objection to the high school feature of the system but *never operated against the usefulness of its provisions for common school education.* Consequently in most towns the high schools have been abolished as free schools, while the free common school system was retained. The latter has been in operation more than *two hundred years,* gaining the confidence of the people by equalling the object of its creation.

Massachusetts is too deeply indebted to her Free School system, and has found too strong arguments in the increasing intelligence and virtue of her citizens, in favor of the plan, to admit even of an *attempt to remodel* their common school organization. The principles upon which it is based, are, and ever have been regarded as the only true basis for sound government.

Massachusetts stands unrivalled in the intelligence and enterprise with which all her varied interests have been promoted. The history of this State, from its first settlement to the present day, affords ample demonstration of the soundness of the views entertained by its early settlers, and prove to the world that learning and religion are not only the best safeguards of a commonwealth but also impart to it the elements of prosperity and happiness. Who can estimate the value of the free school system of Massachusetts? In the progress she has made in manufactures, and the application of scientific principles to the purposes of life, the citizens of our own State may find strong motives for the adoption of this principle of universal education. Our resources are far more abundant, yet we are many years behind the Bay State in rank and influence, mainly because we have not used the materials within our reach to the best advantage.

All sections of our country look to Massachusetts in matters pertaining to manufactures. The skill of her mechanics, her varied applications of science to the wants of man, and the inventive talents of her citizens, give to this, the Queen of the States, a controlling influence over our whole country. She is the standard by which to graduate the scale of American enterprize, infusing a noble and commanding zeal throughout the whole Union, which stimulates the inhabitants of remote places to greater efforts for their own elevation. In almost every village in this State and throughout the prairied West may be found the graduates of this free school system, diffusing in every direction the inestimable blessings it confers upon society. Massachusetts is too small to confine within her own borders, the priceless jewel of the progressive development of all that can benefit mankind . . . it is seen in every section of our country, in our cities, and along our coasts, in our commercial and manufacturing villages, among our farmers and in our courts, in all the appliances for the improvement of our race, from the District school, to the press; in whatever agency we employ to secure statesmen of the purest patriotism, clergymen of the noblest moral energy, and teachers of the loftiest intellect, we find no ordinary auxiliary in the authoritative voice of New England society. Whence comes this proud distinction of breathing an intellectual and moral breath into the organizations of other states, unless from the educational privileges so abundantly enjoyed by the sons and daughters of New England — privileges springing directly and solely out of the free school system. These splendid triumphs, achieved by the march of public opinion, are witnessed with gratification by our own citizens; they have caught the spirit and it is advancing, gathering momentum as it moves along; its reforming power is mingled with every question of public interest, sending forth appeals from all portions of the State, for an efficient system of common school education, which shall exert its benign influence upon every child in our territory; an influence omnipotent to check vice and immorality, and the dispenser of all the blessings conferred by civil and religious liberty to a people at once prepared to appreciate and preserve them.—*Teachers Advocate, April 29, 1846.*

Free Schools for Free Governments

Universal suffrage and universal ignorance would be a sad calamity to any country and bring in its train a legion of evils. The importance of having the people educated and virtuous, especially under a democratic form of government is generally admitted, though not carried into practice as fully as is necessary to preserve our institutions in their purity, and transmit them improved and enlarged to posterity.

This subject is receiving more attention, however, than is noticed by the mere casual observer. Amid the exciting topics of political reform, we find the subject of universal education peers aloft in its own peculiar grandeur. At several of the primary meetings the question of a constitutional *free school system* has been discussed. A voice from the people will, it is hoped, ring in the ears of those entrusted with the work of framing the new constitution, until this the noblest reform of the age shall be grafted upon it. This is not a party question. It should meet the concurrence of all parties, and we are happy to believe it does whenever and wherever it is carefully considered.

At the Jefferson County Whig constitutional convention assembled for the purpose of nominating candidates, a short time since, the following resolution was adopted:

Resolved, That as the prosperity of our free institutions depends upon the intelligence and love of order of the mass of the people, we recommend the most ample provision for the maintenance of an enlarged and liberal system of common school education, which shall secure *to every citizen* the rudiments of education wholly *free from cost or charge* — to which end, we recommend that the school fund be more liberally endowed from permanent sources of revenue.

At the Montgomery County Democratic convention, held on the 8th inst. in the village of Fonda, the subject of *free schools* was presented in the following resolutions, which were adopted unanimously:

Resolved, That, as a free and independent people, we are morally bound, in the reorganization of the fundamental law of the State, to keep in view steadfastly and singly, the best interests of the whole State, without regard to sectional interests, in order that the blessings and burdens of government may be equally distributed among all the citizens of the Commonwealth; thereby securing to ourselves its present benefits, and to posterity a valuable and unincumbered inheritance.

Securing a system of free schools so that the blessings of a thorough English education may be secured to the poor as well as the rich.

Onondaga county has taken a firm stand in reference to this question. In our first article on this subject may be found a strong resolution in favor of making provisions for our school system in the constitution, which was endorsed at a more recent meeting of delegates to represent the Democratic party, held at Camillus, on the 10th ult. We give the resolution:

Resolved, That we fully approve the resolutions adopted at the nominating convention of the 19th inst. and *particularly* the 9th resolution, recommending the *free school system,* and hail it as the first upon that subject coming from any political convention, and justly entitled to the consideration of all men as one of the most *beneficent,* if not the *greatest reforms of the age.*

This shows that the people of Onondaga county attach great importance to this question. The prevailing sentiment of the well informed and the humane in every section of the State, is in favor of a system which so eminently accords with the principles upon which our government is founded, and with the enlightened philanthrophy of this age and country.

Several of our public journals have spoken decidedly and correctly on this subject. Public opinion is rapidly forming in favor of a permanent and thoroughly-worked free school system. On the consideration of economy merely, without paying the least attention to the increased usefulness of the system — its influence in increasing the productiveness of the State, in developing all her resources and thus enriching her wealth, and last, though not least, its never-failing guaranty for the happiness and prosperity of the people — omitting these important considerations and placing the question on the basis of economy only, it is preeminently preferable to the one now in operation.

In proof of this we will submit a comparative table of school statistics in some of the cities and villages of the State — by which we shall establish the fact, not a mere estimation, but the fact that the amount paid per scholar, in those places adhering to the rate-bill system is about *one-third greater* than it is where the free school system is adopted. Now unless the rate-bill schools are *one-third better* than the free schools, there is an actual loss of that amount. Now it will not be contended that the *free schools* are inferior to any of the public schools in the State. Their teachers are as liberally paid, and we have yet to learn that the same amount of salary will not call into the free school service as high qualifications as it will for the rate bill schools.—*Teachers Advocate, April 22, 1846.*

We take it for granted that all who participate in the selection of delegates to the convention (the constitutional convention) expect that the educational wants of the state will be the first to occupy their attention.

It is gratifying to find that this subject is not, because so evidently important, entirely overlooked at our public meetings, preparatory to the choice of delegates.

At a Democratic convention, held March 19th, 1846, at the court house in the county of Onondaga, it was

Resolved, That we regard universal education through a system of common and free schools, as the great Democratic measure of the age — a measure without which Republican institutions can not be long sustained. To bestow upon every child in the state the best practical education, is the first and most indispensable duty of a Democratic government. We trust, therefore, that the convention will not fail to make ample provision for the accomplishment of this high purpose.

We hope that all our primary meetings will give an expression on this subject and that the press will enforce the necessity of engrafting a free school system upon our constitution.—*Teachers Advocate, April 1, 1846.*

COMMON SCHOOL STATE CONVENTION

The school men of this state held a convention in Albany on May 12, 1846, to discuss "the practicability and expediency of ingrafting the free school system upon our existing organization." The educational leaders of forty counties were represented in this gathering. It is also of interest to note that Horace Mann was among the noted educators, from outside the State, in attendance.

Common School State Convention

As reported by the District School Journal, Albany, July 1846

Our limits restrict us to a very brief notice of the proceedings of this body, which convened at the State Street Baptist Church in this city on the 12th of May last, and adjourned on the 15th, after a session of four days. A full and accurate report of the resolutions and debates, reports of committees, etc., has been given to the public through the columns of the Teachers Advocate; and we shall endeavor to find room from time to time, as we can, for such portions as we may deem of most interest to our readers. Several of the most eminent and distinguished educationists of the United States were present during nearly the entire session of the convention, and the subjects considered and discussed were exceedingly interesting and important. The Hon. Horace Mann, secretary of the board of education of Massachusetts; Horace Eaton, superintendent of common schools of Vermont; Theodore F. King, superintendent of New Jersey, and Nathan'el S. Benton, superintendent of New York, participated in the proceedings to a greater or less extent; and able and interesting addresses were delivered before the convention by each of them, with the exception of Dr King, who was compelled by illness to leave the city on the second day of the session.

The convention was called to order at 10 o'clock on Tuesday morning, (12th) by Dr Willard, of Albany, who on motion of Mr Wright, of Washington, took the chair temporarily — Mr Cooper, of Onondaga, editor of the Teachers Advocate, officiating as secretary.

On Wednesday morning, the convention took up the special order — the practicability and expediency of engrafting the free school system upon our existing organization, through the action of the state convention for the revisal of the constitution. Mr. Mann, being called upon for that purpose, gave a lucid and comprehensive exposition of the system of free schools, as it exists in Massachusetts.

Mr Mann's Speech

It would be ungracious in me to decline compliance with a request, so complimentary to myself, or rather to the state of Massachusetts, of which I am a public servant. I had not expected, however to be called upon, either at this time, or in this manner; and hence I must urge the excuse of being unprepared, so far as a man may ever permit himself to be found unprepared, on a question pertaining to the duties of his office.

Strange as it may seem, the subject of free schools, and of the right of a state to maintain them, is never agitated in Massachusetts. I recollect no public document in which this question is discussed; nor have I ever been present at a meeting where it was debated. It is a thing universally taken for granted and probably there is not a gentleman present, who has not thought more upon the subject than I have. If there be any such thing as innate ideas, we, in Massachusetts, are born with an innate idea of free schools; and a citizen with us would be as much surprised, at having a rate-bill presented to him for the attendance of his children at the district school, as he would if called upon to pay for enjoying the free light of the sun, or the common air of heaven. To argue this question, therefore, would seem almost like arguing a question respecting the existence of an instinct; you may prove with ever so much logical force

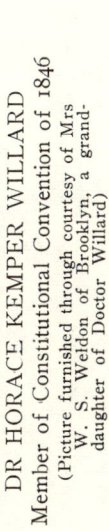

HORACE MANN

DR HORACE KEMPER WILLARD
Member of Constitutional Convention of 1846
(Picture furnished through courtesy of Mrs
W. S. Weldon of Brooklyn, a grand-
daughter of Doctor Willard)

that it does not exist, but when you have finished your demonstration, there it is.

In this State, however, and in most other states of our Union, and countries of the world, free schools are unknown. A fund may exist, a small tax may be levied upon property; but the residue of the cost of the school must be paid by those who send their children to it, and in proportion to the time of their attendance.

The resolution before us contemplates the prospective establishment of a system of free schools for the State of New York; and I acknowledge that when any new measure is propounded, the burden of proof rests upon those who ask for the change.

I will take up but a single point pertaining to this great subject, for, surrounded as I am, by gentlemen both willing and able to discuss it in all its bearings, I should deem myself inexcusable were I to anticipate, by a few cursory remarks, the points which ought to be presented and expounded in detail. I confine myself to a single point, namely; the obligation of a state, on the great principles of natural law and natural equity, to maintain free schools, for the universal education of its people; and I thank the convention for turning my attention to this point, which was never before so distinctly presented to my mind.

Shall the schools of a state be free? shall they be open to all? shall they invite and welcome all? shall they provide that amount and quality of instruction for all, which is indispensable to the welfare of the individual — to the brother, sister, father, mother — to the voter in municipal affairs; to the juror, witness and citizen; to one who by law, inherits a portion of the sovereignty of this great Republic? I propose to discuss the question, whether, according to the great, immutable principles of natural law and equity, this shall be done; or whether, on the other hand, each child shall be dependent for the education he may obtain, upon chance or charity or parental providence; and whether, if chance does not favor, nor charity smile, nor parents provide, the child shall be left without education, until he provides for himself. Sir, it appears to me that a child born in winter, may as well be left without warmth or shelter until he provides it for himself.

Were it not that the question of free schools involves the question of taxation, I suppose that but few would feel any objection against them; and still fewer, in the face of this community, and in the increasing light and liberality of the nineteenth century, would avow their objections. He must be a pretty bold man, who, at this day, in New England or New York, would resist the utmost diffusion of educational means. Such resistance, at the present time, strongly suggests the ideas of a distempered intellect and of hospital treatment. But free schools imply taxation: and it is a problem which no statesman has ever yet been able to solve, how to make taxes agreeable to all who pay them. Taxation has always been one of the characteristics of arbitrary power, hence, republicans are jealous of it. Taxation was one of the main causes for colonial resistance to the authority of Great Britain; and hence an aversion to it seems to run in our blood. I have always observed amongst our people, an exaggeration of ideas on this subject, a feeling in each individual, whatever the amount of the tax may be, that he will have to pay the whole of it. It is the hydrostatic paradox repeated, where the whole pressure bears upon each part. And hence it is, that those who will admit that a thorough, comprehensive and christian education — an education of all our faculties and susceptibilities of body and mind — is the equivalent of health and long life, of individual, social and national happiness, prosperity, and renown; nay, that education good or bad, is the synonyme of heaven and hell: I say, those who admit all this, still maintain that each family must pay for its own; they say, that come prosperity, or come adversity, to the individual or to the community, come honor or come infamy, come blessedness or come perdition, every man must pay for himself. The knot of this unwedgeable problem lies in the word pay. "Why should I who have no children," says one, "pay to educate yours?" "Why should I?" says another, "who have reared a family of children and educated them, now pay a second time, in order to educate yours; thus leaving a double burden?"

Now, in the first place, I am no apologist for unnecessary taxation. But it does not follow because despots make grievous exactions of their subjects, that citizens or voters will overtax themselves. The latter have the power of restriction in their own hands, and can pronounce a peremptory veto whenever they please.

Again, taxation for judicious and worthy objects, is not to be considered a burden, but only as the common condition of existence. We can not enjoy life, nor even subsist, without expenditure. Our daily food, our shelter, our raiment, are taxes — each man being his own assessor. In a wisely administered government, taxes are the fares which we pay in railroad cars — the price for being safely carried and well provided for, through the journey of life.

In the next place, it seems to me obvious that all objections to taxation for the support of free schools derive their plausibility from the fact that they are made by an individual, in his individual character — as an isolated, solitary being, having no relations with the community around him, having no ancestors to whom he himself is indebted, and as one, also, who is to leave no posterity having a claim upon him. In the midst of a populous community to which he is bound by innumerable ties, having had his own fortune and condition almost predetermined and foreordained by his predecessors, and being about to exert upon others as commanding an influence as has been exerted upon himself, the objector argues with us, just as he would argue, if there were only himself and his family on the western continent, and one other man and one other family on the eastern continent, and they and their families were the first and the last of the whole race. The arguments generally used by men against taxation for free schools are applicable only to such a case as this. Well, sir, if there were but one family in this hemisphere, and one other family in the other hemisphere, and if the head of one of these families should call upon the other to help educate his children, I admit that — except so far as good neighborhood might be concerned — there would be some soundness in such an objection; and I can conceive that the force of the appeal would be even more diminished, if a single family on a neighboring planet should make such an appeal to a single family on this planet. In self-defense, or in selfishness, one might say to the other, "What are your fortunes to me? You can neither molest nor assist me. Please to keep your own side of the oceanic or of the planetary spaces that divide us."

But is this the relation that we sustain towards each other? Has not every member of the community thousands around him, on whom he acts, and who are continually reacting upon him? Have we not all derived advantages from our ancestors, and are we not bound, as by an oath, to transmit these advantages, even in an improved condition, to our posterity? In this age of the world, in the present condition of society, no man can sink into his individuality, and sever the relations which bind him to society. The mind and heart must be enlarged, until they become coextensive with our enlarged relations. The individual no longer exists as an individual merely, but as a citizen among citizens; as a descendant of those who have gone before, as the ancestor of those who are to follow; and hence as the recipient of great blessings from the one, and the medium and transmitter of those blessings to the other. From these new relations new duties are evolved. Society must be preserved, and in order to preserve it, we must not look merely to what one family needs, but to what the whole community needs; not merely to what one generation needs, but to the wants of a succession of generations. To draw conclusions without considering these facts, is to leave out the most important part of our premises.

Now what is the fundamental, the paramount, indispensable need and necessity of a people? I say it is education, though deficient in everything else — though weak, impoverished, anarchical — yet education will give strength, competency and order; though abounding in everything that heart can desire, yet take away education, and all things will rush to ruin, as quickly as the solar system would return to chaos if gravitation and cohesion were destroyed. We need laws regulating all the rights of property, of person and of character. We need freedom of the press, freedom of speech, and freedom of conscience. For these purposes, we must have wise legislators; but we never shall have wise legislators with a foolish constituency.

If education then be the most important interest of society, it must be placed upon the most permanent and immovable basis that society can supply. It should not be founded upon the shifting sands of popular caprice or passion, or upon individual benevolence: but if there be a rock anywhere, it should be founded upon that rock.

What is the most permanent basis? — that which survives all changes, which retains its identity amid all vicissitudes. It is property — I mean the great, common, universal elements which constitute the basis of all property, the riches of the soil, the treasures of the sea, the light and warmth of the sun, the fertilizing clouds and streams and dews, the winds, the electric and vegetating agencies of nature. Individuals come and go, but these great bounties of heaven abide. Individual estates expand into opulence or shrink into poverty; but the munificence of heaven is as enduring as time.

We hear much said, not merely in courts of law, but in the marts of business and in the common speech of men, of the rights of property. Would it not be refreshing to hear something of the rights of men?

Have not men rights as well as property? Were men made for the property, or the property for men? It is of some consequence to know which is principal, and which is adjunct or accessory. As I read the sacred pages, men — not any one man, not any one generation — but the race, were to have "dominion" over all other created things.

Now I wish to examine, for a moment, this question; how much, what quality and description of ownership, any one man, or any one generation can have in the natural, substantive, enduring elements of wealth; in the soil; in metals and minerals; in precious stones, and in more precious coal and iron and granite; in the sun, the winds and the water. Has any one man, or any one generation, I ask, such an absolute ownership in these ingredients of all wealth, that his right is invaded when a portion of them is taken for the benefit of contemporaries and of posterity? I reply, certainly not. The earth and the fullness thereof were created for the race collectively. These were not created for Adam alone, nor for Noah alone, nor for the first discoverers or colonists who may have found or have peopled any part of the earth's ample domain. No! They were created for all, but to be possessed and enjoyed in succession. Each generation, subject to certain modifications for the encouragement of industry and frugality, has only a life lease in them. There are reasonable regulations in regard to the outgoing and incoming tenants — regulations which allow the incoming generations to anticipate a little, their full right to possession, and which also allow to the outgoing generations a brief control of their property after they are called to leave it. Let me illustrate this great principle of natural law by a reference to some of the unstable elements in regard to which the property of each individual is strongly qualified. Take the streams of water, or the winds for example. A stream as it descends from its sources to its mouth, is successively the property of all those through whose lands it passes. My neighbor who lives above me owned it yesterday, while it was passing through his lands; I own it today, while it is descending through mine, and the contiguous proprietor below will own it tomorrow while it is flowing through his, as it passes onward to the next. But the rights of each successive owner are not absolute and unqualified. They are limited by the rights of those who are entitled to subsequent possession. While a stream of water is passing through my demesnes, I can not corrupt it, so that it shall be valueless or offensive to the adjoining proprietor below. I cannot detain it, in its downward course, or divert it into some other direction so that it shall leave its channel dry. I may use it for various purposes — for agriculture, as in watering cattle or irrigating lands; for manufactures, as in turning wheels, etc.— but in all my uses of it, I must have regard to the rights of my neighbors lower down; so no two proprietors, nor any half dozen proprietors by conspiring together, can deprive an owner who lives below them all, of the ultimate rights which he has to the use of the stream in its descending course. So we see here, that a man has rights — rights of which he can not be divested without his own consent — in a stream of water, before it reaches the limits of his estate — at which latter point he may, somewhat emphatically call it his own. And in this sense, a man who lives at the outlet of a river, on the margin of the ocean, has certain unqualified rights in the fountains that well up from the earth at the distance of thousands **of miles.**

So it is with the ever-moving winds. No man has a permanent interest in the breezes that blow by him, and cool and refresh him as they blow. Every man has a temporary interest in them. From which quarter of the compass they may come, I have a right to use them as they are sweeping by; yet I must use them in reference to those other participants and coowners whom they are moving forward to bless. It is not lawful, therefore, for me to corrupt them; to load them with noxious gases or vapors, by which they will prove valueless or detrimental to him, whoever he may be, towards whom they are moving.

In one respect, the winds illustrate our relative rights and duties, even better than the streams. In the latter case, the rights are not only successive, but always in the same order of priority, those of the owner above necessarily preceding those of the owner below; and this order is unchangeable except by changing the ownership of the land itself to which the rights are appurtenant. But in the case of the winds which blow from every quarter of the heavens, I may have the prior right today, and with a change in their direction, my neighbor may have it tomorrow. If therefore today, when the wind is descending from me to him, I should usurp the right to use it to his detriment; tomorrow, when it is coming from him to me, he might inflict retributive usurpation upon me.

The light of the sun, too, is subject to the same benign and equitable laws. As this ethereal element passes by me, I have a right to bask in its beams, or to employ its quickening powers. But I have no right, even on my own land, to build up a wall mountain high, that shall eclipse the sun to my neighbor's eyes.

Now all these great principles of natural law to which I have adverted, are incorporated into, and constitute a part of the civil law of every civilized people; and they are obvious and simple illustrations of the great proprietary laws, by which individuals and generations hold their rights in the solid substance of the globe, and in the elements that move over its surface. As successive owners on a river's banks have equal rights to the waters that flow through their respective demesnes, subject only to the modification that the proprietors near the stream's source, must have precedence in the enjoyment of their rights over those lower down; so the rights of all the generations of mankind to the earth itself, to the streams that fertilize it, to the winds that bless it, and to the reviving light, are common rights, subject to similar modifications in regard to preceding and succeeding generations. They did not belong to our ancestors in perpetuity; they do not belong to us in perpetuity; and the right of the next generation in them will be limited and defeasible like ours. As we hold them subject to their claims, so will they hold them subject to the claims of their successors to the end of time. Yes, sir, the savage tribes that roam about the head springs of the Mississippi, have as good a right to ordain what use shall be made of its copious waters, when in their grand descent across a continent, they shall reach the shores of arts and civilization, as any of our predecessors had, or as we ourselves have, to say what shall be done in perpetuity, with the soil, the waters, the winds, the light, the great electrical and vegetative powers of nature, which on all hands must be allowed to constitute the indispensable elements of wealth.

I say then, that no man, however he may have acquired his property, has any natural right, any more than he has a moral one, to hold it, or to dispose of it, irrespective of the needs and claims of those, who, in the august procession of the generations, are to succeed him on this stage of existence. Holding his rights subject to their rights, he is bound to make provision for their highest wants.

Generation after generation comes from the creative energy of God. Each one stops for a brief period upon the earth, resting only as for a night, like migratory birds upon their passage, and then leave it forever to others, whose existence is as transitory as their own; and the flocks of water fowl which annually sweep across our latitudes in their passage to another clime, have as good a right to make a perpetual appropriation to their own use, of the lands over which they fly, as any one generation has to arrogate perpetual dominion and sovereignty for their own purposes, of that portion of the earth which it is their fortune to occupy during their brief temporal existence.

There is another consideration which bears upon this arrogant doctrine of absolute ownership or sovereignty. A man says, is not my property the result of my own earnings, or have I not inherited it by virtue of standing laws, from those who did earn it? I reply that this is not strictly true. For every unit that a man earns by his own labor or ingenuity, he receives hundreds and thousands from the All-bountiful giver. What would be the product of cotton plantations or wheat fields, did not heaven send down upon them its dews, its rains, its warmth and light? It is said that from 80 to 90 per cent of some of the great staple productions of agriculture come from the air and not from the earth. Hence those productions might more properly be called fruits of the atmosphere than of the soil. They are the perpetual riches which heaven sends to man, and the winds are made instrumental in equalizing the distribution. How much would the manufacturer earn were it not for the waters which God causes ceaselessly to flow; or for the mechanical force which He, and not we, has given to steam; and how would the commerce of the world be carried on, were it not for the great laws of nature, of electricity, of heat, of condensation, of rarefaction, which give birth to the winds, that, in conformity to His will, and not in obedience to any power of man, are continually traversing the earth?—These references show how much of the wealth, which men presumptuously call their own, because they claim to have earned it, is poured into their lap unasked and unthanked for, by the Being so infinite in his physical as well as his moral riches.

But the present wealth of the world has an additional element in it. Much of all that is capable of being earned by man, has been earned by our predecessors, and has come down to us from them in a consolidated and enduring form. We have not built all the houses in which we live, nor all the roads on which we travel, nor all the ships which we navigate. But even if we had, whence came all the arts and sciences, the discoveries and the inventions, without which, and without a common right to which, the valuation of the property of a whole nation would scarcely equal the inventory of a single man. Whence came a knowledge of agriculture without which we should have nothing to reap; or a knowledge of astronomy, without which we could not traverse the oceans; or a knowledge of chemistry and mechanical philosophy, without which the arts and trades cannot flourish? Most of these were prepared by those who have gone before us, some of them have come down from a remote antiquity. Surely all these boons and blessings belong as much to our posterity as to ourselves. They have not descended to us to be arrested and consumed here, or to be sequestrated from the ages to come.

These considerations limit still more extensively that absolutism of ownership which is so often claimed by the possessors of wealth.

But now we come to another stage in the argument. In regard to the wealth formed from the great substantive ingredients which are the property of all mankind, and which belong equally to successive generations, subject only to the condition that the use of one generation must necessarily precede that of another — in regard to this wealth, I say, at what time is it to be transferred from a preceding to a succeeding generation? — At what point are the latter to take possession of, or to derive benefit from it, and the earlier to relinquish it? Is each existing generation, and each individual of an existing generation, to hold fast to his possessions until death relaxes his grasp; or is something of the transfer and the benefit to be yielded beforehand? Is it not obvious that the latter is the true and the only alternative? If the incoming generation have no rights until the outgoing generation have retired, then is every individual that enters the world doomed to perish on the day he is born. According to the very constitution of things, each individual must derive sustenance and succor from society, and as soon as his eyes open to the light, or his lungs are inflated by the air. His wants can not be delayed until he himself can supply them. The demands of his nature must be answered, before he can provide for them; either by the performance of labor or by any exploits of skill. The infant must be fed before he can earn his bread; he must be clothed before he can prepare garments; and it is just as clear that he must be instructed before he can engage a teacher. Our laws do not allow a child to make a valid contract before he is twenty-one years of age; but any individual may supply a minor with necessaries, and such supply constitutes a legal claim against the parent, guardian, or other person, bound, as the law expresses it, to provide for him. Here then, the claims of the succeeding generation, not only upon the affection and care, but upon the property of the preceding one attach. God having given to the second generation as full and complete a right to the incomes and profits of the world — to the soil, to the sun's light and warmth, to the rain, to the chemical and vegetative laws by which the mysterious processes of nature are carried on,— God having given to the second generation, in their turn, as full and complete a right to all these, as he has given to the first; and to the third generation, as full and complete a right as to the second, and so on while the world stands, it necessarily follows that they must come into a partial and qualified possession of these rights, by the paramount law of nature, as soon as they are born. No human enactments can abolish or countervail this paramount and supreme law.

It is not at all in contravention of this view of the subject, that the adult portion of society takes upon itself the control and management of all existing property, until the rising generation have arrived at the age of majority. Nay, the object of their so doing is to preserve the rights of the generation which is still in its minority. Society, to this extent, is only a trustee, managing an estate for the benefit of the owner. This civil regulation, therefore, is only in furtherance of the great law we are expounding.

Coincident too, with this great law, is the wonderful provision that the

Creator has made for the care of offspring, in the affection of the parents. Heaven did not rely merely upon our perceptions of duty towards our offspring, and our fidelity in its performance. A powerful, all-mastering instinct of love was therefore implanted in the parental, and especially in the maternal breast, to anticipate the idea of duty, and to make duty a pleasure. For all those children who have been bereaved of parents, or who, worse than bereavement, have only monster-parents of intemperance, or cupidity, or any other form of vice — society is bound to be a parent, and to exercise the same rational care and providence that a wise father would exercise for his own children.

Another important consideration here meets us; which, however, instead of conflicting with, only confirms and commends the general argument. We find that previous and present possessors have laid their hand upon the whole earth. They have circumnavigated this planet; they have drawn lines across it, and have partitioned among themselves, not only the whole area or superficial contents, but have claimed it down to the centre, and up to the concave, a great inverted pyramid for each proprietor. They have said to each other, you protect me in the enjoyment of my claim, and I will protect you in the enjoyment of yours,— Thus they have combined together, and have created legislators, and judges, and executive officers, and organized armed bands to repel aggressions upon their claims. And so grasping and rapacious have mankind been, that they have taken more than they could use, more than they could perambulate and survey, more than they could see from the top of the highest mountain. There was some limit to their physical power of taking possession, but none to the exorbitancy of their desires. Like robbers, who divide their spoils before they know whether they shall find a victim, men have claimed a continent while still doubtful of its existence, and spread out their title from ocean to ocean, before their most adventurous pioneers had ever seen a shore of the realms they covered. The whole planet then, having been appropriated, there being no waste and open lands from which the new generations may be supplied as they come into existence, I say the new generations have the strongest conceivable claim upon their predecessors. They have more than a pre-emptive, they have a possessory right to some portion of that, all of which has been appropriated and taken up. A denial of this right by the present occupants is a breach of trust, a fraudulent misuse of their power. Economically, it is folly; morally, it is embezzlement and fraud.

I think we are now prepared to meet the question fully and directly. At what time, to what extent, and for what purpose, upon the great principles of natural law, is the incoming generation entitled to participate in the benefits of the world's wealth? In answer, their claim to a portion of it begins with the first breath they draw. The newborn infant must have sustenance and shelter and care. If the parents cannot supply these, society succeeds to the place of parents and must supply them. If at any period previous to the age of discretion, the parents are removed, or parental ability fails, society, at that point is bound to step in and fill the parent's place. To deny support and succor to any child, would be equivalent to a sentence of death — a capital execution of the infant, at which every soul shudders. But to preserve a child's life only, and then to stop, would be,— not the bestowment of a blessing or the performance of a duty, but the infliction of a curse. A child has interests far higher than those of mere physical existence. Better that the interests of the natural life should not be cared for, than that the higher interests of the character should be neglected. If a child has any claims to bread to keep him from perishing, he has far higher claims to knowledge to keep him from error, and its retinue of calamities. If a child has any claim to shelter — to protect him from the destroying elements, he has a far higher claim to be rescued from the infamy and perdition of vice and crime. If you will not legalize infanticide, you must supply sustenance. If you will not prepare madmen or incendiaries to destroy property and life, you must enlighten the intellect; if you will not invoke moral ruin, you must train up the young in the way they should go. In a word, you must educate the mind, as well as sustain the mere physical existence,— The time when this obligation attaches, corresponds with the age when the work can be most beneficially and efficaciously performed. As the right of sustenance then is of equal date with birth, the right to systematic intellectual and moral training begins, at least as early as when children are ordinarily sent to school. At that time, then, by the great and irrepealable law of nature, every child succeeds to so much more of the property of the community, as is necessary for his education. He is to receive this, not in the form of property, but in the form of education. This is another step in the transfer of the property of the present to a following generation. Probably this period of transfer, and the amount to be transferred at its arrival, may be modified by circumstances; and if so, the political institutions under which one is born, may have an important bearing upon the question. Certainly, in a republican government, the obligation of the predecessors, and consequently the right of the successors, extends to and embraces the means of such an amount of education as will fit each individual to perform the common duties of a citizen. It may go further than this point; certainly it cannot stop short of it.

The places and the processes where this transfer is to be provided for, and its amount determined, are the district school meeting, the town meeting, legislative halls, conventions for establishing or revising the fundamental laws of the State. If it be not done there, the community is faithless to its trust.

I bring my argument then to a close; and I present a test of its validity, which, as it seems to me, defies denial or evasion.

In obedience to the laws of God, and to the laws of all civilized nations, society is bound to protect natural life; and the natural life cannot be protected without the appropriation and use of a portion of the property which society possesses. We prohibit infanticide under penalty of death. We practice a refinement in this particular. The life of an infant is inviolable even before it is born; and he who feloniously takes it, is as subject to the extreme penalty of the law, as though he had cut down manhood in its vigor, or taken away a mother by violence from the midst of her maternal cares. But why preserve the natural life of a child — why preserve unborn embryos of life, if you do not intend to watch over and protect them, and expand them into usefulness and happiness? — You have no right — neither nature nor God confer any right, to inflict the curse of birth, the curse of ignorance, and vice, and poverty, and all the attendant unspeakable calamities upon any creature. You are brought, then, to this inevitable test. Either extinguish the natural life, or provide the means to make that life a blessing. Give us the right of infanticide, or give us free education.

Remarks of Mr Henry of Herkimer, Professor Thomson and Others on the Free School Resolution

Mr Mann was followed on the same side by Messrs Wilkins and Thomson of Rensselaer, Mack of Rochester, Willard of Albany, Dubois of Ulster, Cooper of Onondaga, Henry of Herkimer, and Thomson of Cayuga, who contended, in substance, that the time for engrafting the system of free schools upon our existing organization had fully come: that public sentiment in nearly every section of the State was prepared to sustain and adopt it; that its recognition as a part of our fundamental law, would not only relieve trustees and other officers of school districts of the oppressive and periodical burdens under which they are now compelled to labor in the assessment and collection of taxes and rate-bills — in their constant and almost unavoidable liability to vexatious and protracted litigation, without the possibility of adequate remuneration for their time and expenses, even if ultimately successful, and in the gratuitous devotion of so large a portion of their time, and frequently their means, to the fiscal affairs of their respective districts — but would bring within the fostering influences of the schools, hundreds, if not thousands, of indigent children, the claims of whose parents or guardians to exemption under the present system were either overlooked or disregarded, and who consequently were virtually deprived of those inestimable privileges, which the beneficence of the State designed to secure to every child within its borders, however humble the condition, or restricted the pecuniary means of his parents. The paramount duty and obligation of the State, thus to afford to each of its future citizens, without distinction or discrimination, the amplest facilities for a sound and comprehensive mental and moral education, were strongly insisted upon, and clearly and fully demonstrated; the superior advantages of the free school system, wherever it had been introduced within the State, as at Rochester, Buffalo, New York, Williamsburgh, Brooklyn, Poughkeepsie, Hudson, Utica and other places, pointed out and elucidated, and the importance of present action, in view of the pending re-organization of our frame of government, forcibly and eloquently urged.

Mr Henry remarked, that he cordially subscribed to the correctness of the views which have been so ably and eloquently presented by the learned gentleman upon his left (Gould Brown). He gave his full and unreserved assent to the definition of democracy which had just been given, namely, adequate provision for enabling citizens of every description to perfect themselves with the theory and practice of every department of duty. Catholic democracy rests satisfied with nothing short of the physical duty, moral and intellectual improvement, the proper development and discipline of the faculties of every individual of which the common wealth is composed. The right of the people to such an education, was asserted in every fundamental principle of a republic, and it had been this morning vindicated by the distinguished gentleman from Massachusetts (Hon. H. Mann), with an ability and eloquence which can not fail to carry conviction to every mind. When exposed to the destruction of fire and flood, was not property solely dependent upon manual labor for its preservation? When assailed by the mob, does not property rely upon the people for defense, even to the expense and sacrifice of life? When all that is held invaluable, dear and sacred, is endangered by foreign intrusion, on whom then is the chief reliance placed for security and protection? Can property, then, deny the means of education to the children of citizens who promptly perform these high and perilous duties? No, never. The right to be educated is clear and unquestionable, and it is the indispensable duty of property owners to furnish the necessary means for the enjoyment of this right.

But to "make haste slowly" is the great principle and duty of the enlightened and virtuous reformers. Present fully and truly to the consideration of the people all the facts in the case — give them sufficient time to deliberate, and doubt not for a moment they will come to a proper decision of the matter. He knew that many cities and towns were ready to make their schools perfectly free, but there were others not yet prepared to vote for such a measure. He believed very little additional legislation upon this subject to be called for at present. He thought that giving power to establish free schools to such cities and towns as desired it, and leaving all others to the provisions of the present law, was all that was practicable. Such a measure, he had no doubt, would meet the approbation and support of the people; and such was his confidence in the excellence and superiority of free schools, that he could not doubt that a few years' experiment upon the plan proposed, would seem firmly and immovably established in every town and city of the state.

Prof. J. B. Thomson, of Auburn, asked the indulgence of the convention for a few moments. In reply to the apprehensions expressed by the gentleman from Tompkins, lest some might regard the passage of the resolution as officious, as an infringement upon their privileges, he would say, it is always safe to do right. That it is right to support free schools, to make education free to all, has been clearly proved by the honorable gentleman from Massachusetts. If, therefore, it is right to establish free schools, it is right and safe for us to lend them our support, and at all time to express our opinion upon the subject. But he did not believe it would be regarded as a breach of privilege, or as travelling beyond the record, by any intelligent man, for this body to express their opinion upon this subject. He spoke, not as a school officer, but as one of the people, and therefore spoke with the more freedom and confidence: "Sir, we the people, desire our delegates, our servants, not only to think right, but to speak and act right.

"Though the right of every child to the privileges and blessings of education has been clearly established, he wished to submit another consideration upon this point. In the common transactions of life, if one man receives a favor, an actual good from his neighbor, it is a fundamental law of justice and right, that the recipient should reciprocate the favor, or return an equivalent for the good received.

"Now it is evident from observation and the history of the world, that education in its most comprehensive sense, the culture of the intellectual, and moral faculties of the young, by storing the public mind with knowledge and training it to habits of self-government, temperance and virtue, has a direct and powerful tendency to diminish the violations of law and the perpetration of crime. Hence, every man in the community receives a direct and palpable benefit by the diffusion of education. He has a more perfect security and enjoyment of his property, his person, his life, and his character, which is dearer than life. Now, sir, for this guaranty, this moral insurance of his possessions, his life and character, which he received from the better education of the whole body politic, I maintain, he is bound to pay, upon every principle of justice, as much as he is bound to pay for a policy of insurance on his houses or ships against the ravages of fire and the storms of the ocean. Indeed, the fires and ravages of incarnate depravity are oftentimes more to be dreaded than the raging of the physical elements.

"But there is another consideration in favor of free schools to which I would briefly advert; one, which in this calculating age may perhaps be more sensibly felt than the argument of right.

"I hold it would be a matter of public economy, as well as of sound wisdom and justice for the state to establish free schools, to send the benign influence of education like the sunlight, into every village, and hamlet, and family in the land.

"It has been already remarked, that the history of the world shows that crime decreases in proportion as education is diffused. In like manner, history shows that as ignorance prevails and the appetites and passions are suffered to go unchecked by the restraining and purifying power of education, transgressions and crimes increase in a duplicate rate. Now, to look after this increased number of transgressions of law, these disturbers of the peace, thieves, and robbers, and midnight assassins, and bring them to justice, obviously requires an increased number of police officers, of constables, and justices, and jurors, and judges. It also requires an increased number of jails and prisons. And who, I ask, is to build and support these jails and prisons, and pay the expenses of this long catalogue of peace officers? Surely no one can expect these rogues and villains themselves will pay the magistrates for the infliction of punishment. In this case, the old adage does not hold true; for they that dance do not pay the fiddler. No, sir, the state must foot the bill. Or rather I should say, this tax comes from your pocket and mine, and the pockets of our neighbors; for be it remembered, it is the people who pay the taxes to support the civil and criminal laws. And it requires no small tax to do it. In examining the supervisors' report of our county expenses the past year, I was astounded with the fact, that more money was raised to support this peace-keeping establishment, than was bestowed upon the common schools during the same time. This, it is presumed, is the case with most if not all the other sections of the state. For I am unwilling to admit that the intelligence and morals of the county of Cayuga, are inferior to those of her neighbors. Besides, sir, this estimate does not include the vast amount of time and money expended by individuals in law suits and arbitrations in order to obtain their just pecuniary dues, and to redress their injuries. Were these items included, the amount would be ten fold greater than that devoted to common schools. Who, therefore, will not agree with me in the position, that it would be a matter of economy for the state to establish at once a system of free schools? If half this sum were annually spent in diffusing knowledge and virtue through the community, who can tell how soon our jails would become tenantless, and our court houses fall into decay from disuse? And who would not more cheerfully pay a tax to train up an immortal spirit in the way it should go, than to bring old transgressors to punishment? Who will not say, it is better policy and sounder wisdom, to expend money to prevent crime, than it is to punish it after it is committed? Poor, poor indeed must be any consolation after my house is burnt, or the character of my child blasted forever, or its life destroyed — poor must be my consolation to know that the villain who perpetrated the deed is confined in prison, loaded with shackles, or that he is about to expiate his guilt upon the scaffold. Sir, in this case an ounce of prevention is worth a thousand pounds of cure. Again, I therefore ask, is it not most clearly a matter of state economy as well as wisdom and benevolence, to throw open the well-springs of education and invite all to drink freely of its waters?"

On the other hand, Messrs. Wright of Washington, Allen of Saratoga, Terhune of Greene, Robertson of Tompkins, and others, while conceding to its fullest extent, the principle that the schools throughout the State should be free — open to all without discrimination and without direct charge, and supported by the taxable property and resources of the community, doubted the expediency of a radical change in the existing organization, in this respect, at the present time — and contended that however sound in theory and desirable in practice, such a change might be, the public sentiment was not prepared for it — that its merits had not, as yet, been generally or sufficiently discussed; and that by insisting upon its adoption, under such circumstances, the most imminent danger might accrue to the system as it now exists. They contended that the whole subject might safely be referred to the good sense and sound judgment of the people and their representatives, who, in due season, would not fail to demand the adoption of the system of free schools, either as a substitute for, or an addition to, the existing organization.

The several propositions were, at the close of the debate on Wednesday morning, referred to a select committee, to digest and report a series of resolutions for the action of the convention.

On Thursday morning Mr Cooper, from the select committee to which had been referred the various resolutions and propositions relative to the adoption of the free school system, brought in a report which, after a renewed discussion by Messrs Mann of Massachusetts, Harrington, Valentine and Willard of Albany, Cooper of Onondaga, Robertson of Tompkins, Denman of Wyoming, and Wright of Washington, was amended, on the motion of the latter gentleman, and finally adopted by a majority of more than two-thirds of the county superintendents present, as follows:

Whereas, The system of free schools as adopted by Massachusetts and by several of the large cities and towns of this and other states, has been found by the practical experience of years to work well — securing a more general and punctual attendance of scholars — awakening a more widely extended and deeper interest in the minds of the great mass of the people in the success of our primary nurseries of education, thereby ensuring the elevation of the standard of common school instruction, and more widely diffusing the inestimable blessing of a sound and generous education; therefore,

Resolved, That this convention, fully impressed with the importance of the various considerations involved in this question of free schools, and believing that it is one that will sooner or later receive the approbation of all, do most respectfully commend the subject to the calm and dispassionate consideration of the sovereign people of this State, and to the favorable notice of the members of the convention about to assemble to revise the constitution of the State.

Resolved, That a certified copy of the above preamble and resolution be presented to the presiding officer of the convention referred to, with the request that the same may be laid before that honorable body for their consideration.

Thomas Weston Valentine

Thomas Weston Valentine was born in Northboro, Mass., February 16, 1818. He was educated in the schools of that town and at the Worcester Academy. He commenced teaching in Lancaster, Mass., in 1836. He later taught in his native town and in Pennsylvania and in 1842 removed to Albany, N. Y., where he was principal of a public school for eleven years. In 1853–4, he was superintendent of the Albany Orphan Asylum; was alderman in 1852–3–4; was editor of the *New York Teacher* for two years; and in 1855 became principal of Public School No. 19, Brooklyn, a school of over sixteen hundred pupils.

He was active in religious work and became a licensed laypreacher of the Baptist church. That he led a busy life is evidenced by his own statement as to the work accomplished in 1871: " His busiest season was in 1871, when his day school contained seventeen hundred pupils; his evening school (five evenings a week) fifty colored pupils; his Saturday evening Singing-School, twenty to forty — besides preparing three sermons a week for two different churches, nine miles apart and over fifty miles distant from his home — and all these duties, with the care of a family of seven, besides several boarders, and an occasional page of manuscript for this work (The Valentines in America) or letter to some newspaper, kept him rather busy."

Mr. Valentine was a zealous participator in the educational movements of his day. He was especially interested in promoting an *esprit de corps* among teachers. In 1838, he called and presided over the first convention of teachers ever held in Worcester county, Mass.

In 1844, he cooperated with Francis Dwight and others in obtaining from the Legislature of New York a better organization for the public schools of Albany; he was instrumental, in connection with other teachers of Albany, in calling the State Convention of Teachers in 1845, resulting in the organization of the State Teachers Association, the oldest of the kind in the country. In 1857, while President of the New York State Teachers Association, he made the first move which resulted in the formation in Philadelphia of the National Teachers Association, which became the National Education Association.

Henry Francis Harrington

Henry Francis Harrington, was born in Roxbury, Mass. August 15, 1814. He was educated in Phillips Academy, Exeter, N. H., and in Harvard College. After leaving college he spent a year as usher in the English High School of Boston and then became publisher and editor of a newspaper in Boston, a position for which he had an ardent inclination. The financial depression of 1837 and a serious illness compelled the abandonment of this work.

After a short season of labor in New York City as editor of a monthly periodical, during which time he was studying for the Unitarian ministry, Mr Harrington went south for his health and preached for several months in Savannah, Ga.

Returning to the north in the spring of 1841, he was for three years minister-at-large in the service of the Unitarian societies of Providence, R. I. He then founded successively a Unitarian society in Albany and Troy, N. Y., and Lawrence, Mass. In the last-named place he remained seven years and then moved to Cambridge, Mass., where he was pastor of a church for ten years.

In February 1865, he became superintendent of schools of New Bedford, Mass., and retained that position until his death in 1887. He was a progressive and efficient superintendent, whose reports were widely read. The memorial report issued after his death shows that he was much beloved and respected in the community which he served for such a long period of years.

James Bates Thomson

James Bates Thomson was born at Springfield, Vt., in 1803 and died in Brooklyn, N. Y., in 1883. He worked on his father's farm in summer and attended district school in winter until 1824, when he began to teach. He was graduated from Yale in 1834 and was principal of an academy at Nantucket, Mass., from 1835 to 1842. He married the daughter of William Coffin, a Nantucket sea captain, who later lived in Auburn, N. Y. Doctor Thomson, at the request of President Day of Yale, published an abridgment of Day's algebra for use in schools. In 1843 he assisted at the first teachers institute in New York State, such institute being organized in Ithaca by County Superintendent J. S. Denman and presided over by the Rev. Salem Town. For several years Doctor Thomson was actively engaged in organizing and extending teachers institutes and other similar gatherings. In 1845 he assisted in organizing the New York State Teachers Association and was elected its president. He received the degree of LL.D. from Hamilton College in 1853 and from the University of Tennessee in 1882. Mr Thomson attained considerable reputation as a conchologist. He published a very successful series of mathematical works, his arithmetical works alone having a sale of about 100,000 copies annually. His books include " School Algebra " (New Haven, 1843); a series of arithmetics (New York, 1845–52); and " Arithmetical Analysis " (1854).

Edward Cooper

The accounts of educational meetings held during the forties and early fifties show that Mr Edward Cooper was an active and consistent worker for free schools. While no biography and no picture of Mr Cooper are available, it appears that he lived in Westchester county and later removed to Onondaga county. He was the editor of the Teachers Advocate, the journal of the New York State Teachers Association, and later of the District School Journal.

COMMITTEE ON EDUCATION

The convention to amend the constitution met at Albany June 1, 1846. The following members were appointed on the "Committee on Education, Common Schools and the Appropriate Funds." which was also known as Committee No. 12: Henry Nicoll of New York, David Munro of Onondaga, John Bowdish of Montgomery, Andrew W. Young of Wyoming, George W. Tuthill of Orange, Dr Horace K. Willard of Albany, John H. Hunt of New York.

So far as possible, a brief biography and picture of each member of the committee is given.

Henry Nicoll

Henry Nicoll was a member of the Nicoll family, whose members have from time to time been prominent in the affairs of New York State. He was born in New York October 23, 1812 and was graduated from Columbia College in 1830. He studied law and became one of the leading lawyers of New York City. He was one of the active members of the constitutional convention of 1846, and served in Congress during the years 1847–49.

David Munro

David Munro settled in Camillus, Onondaga county, in 1808 and died May 10, 1866 at the age of eighty years. He served as post-

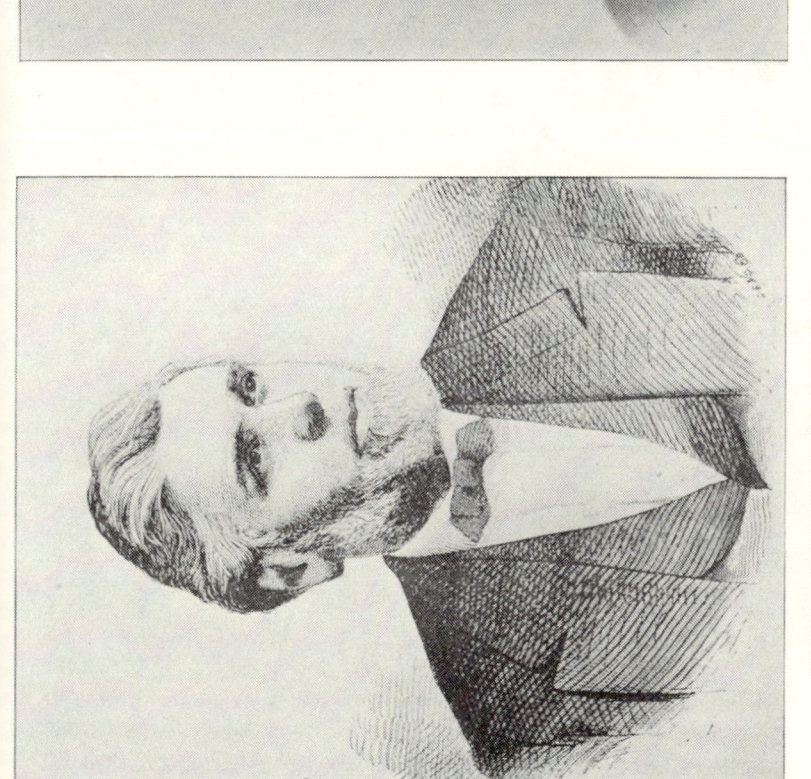

THOMAS WESTON VALENTINE
One of the founders of the New York State Teachers Association
(From "The Valentines in America," by Thomas Weston Valentine)

REV. HENRY F. HARRINGTON
Delegate to Common School State Convention of 1846
(Picture furnished through courtesy of Mr Allen P. Keith, superintendent of schools, New Bedford, Mass.)

DAVID MUNRO
Member of the Legislature in 1818, 1819, 1822, 1836, 1841, 1842; member of Constitutional Convention of 1846
(From "Onondaga's Centennial," edited by Dwight H. Bruce)

JAMES BATES THOMSON LL.D.
Author of a successful series of mathematical works and a prominent educator
(Picture from "New York State Teachers Association")

master of Camillus from 1811 until 1824. He was a justice of the peace for many years, long an associate judge of the court of common pleas, a member of the Legislature in 1818, 1819, 1822, 1836, 1841 and 1842, a presidential elector in 1836, and a member of the constitutional convention in 1846. He was a director in the old Bank of Salina and a director of the Salt Springs Bank from its incorporation until his decease. He had large landed interests in various parts of the county and was one of the foremost business men of his day. He married Abigail Carpenter in 1807.

John Bowdish

John Bowdish was born of Quaker parents at Charlestown, Montgomery county, in 1808. He worked on his father's farm and at the age of fifteen went to Albany, with fifty cents capital to start his business career. He accepted a position at fifty dollars a year, as a clerk. In 1829, he entered into partnership with Isaac Frost and opened a small store at Rural Grove. This business prospered and in time Mr Bowdish became sole proprietor.

In 1853 he became interested in banking and was one of the founders of the Sprakers Bank at Canajoharie and of the Mohawk River Bank of Fonda. In 1843, he was elected to the Legislature and in 1846 was chosen a member of the constitutional convention. In this convention he introduced a proposition for securing a constitutional system of free schools. The question was referred to the committee on education of which he was a member. In his History of Common Schools, S. S. Randall says, " Mr Bowdish made a powerful and eloquent appeal to the convention in behalf of free schools, in which he was sustained by Mr Nicoll of New York and others."

Mr Bowdish served as postmaster at Rural Grove for many years. He was a contributor in both prose and poetry to various papers and was much esteemed in his community as a successful business man and a public-spirited citizen.

Mr John Bowdish introduced a proposition for a constitutional system of free schools. In speaking in support of this measure, he said:

The welfare of a free government depends upon the virtue and intelligence of its subjects, the character and habits of its members; if true, we should make no distinction, the banner of education should be proudly unfurled " like the wild winds free," allowing all alike to enjoy its advantages. The child of the woodland cottage and princely mansion should, if possible, be educated together, that all may have an equal opportunity of rising to eminence and fame. It is a cardinal principle of republicanism that there is no royal road to distinction; it is held to be accessible to all. None are born to command nor to obey. In the order of nature, God has made no distinction; he has not provided for the poorer a coarser earth, a thinner air or a paler sky. The sun pours down its golden flood of light as cheerily on the poor man's home as on the rich man's palace. The cottager's children have as keen a sense of luxuriant nature as the pale sons of the wealthy. Neither has he stamped the imprint of a baser birth on the poor man's child than that of the rich, by which it may know with a certainty that its lot is to crawl, not to climb. Mind is immortal, it is imperial, it bears no mark of high or low, of rich or poor; it heeds no bounds of time or place, of rank or circumstances; it only needs liberty and learning to glide along in its course with the freedom of the rivulet that forms the mighty ocean. If properly cultivated, it will march on undisturbed until it reaches the summit of intellectual glory and usefulness.

At the close of his remarks, the proposition was adopted but later this action was rescinded.

Andrew W. Young

Andrew W. Young, a well-known author of works on the science of government and of several local histories, was born in Carlisle, Schoharie county, March 2, 1802. His educational opportunities comprised a few years' instruction at the common schools and a half term in Middlebury Academy at the age of nineteen. Several years earlier he had taught a term of school and teaching, with farm labor, was the employment of his youth. From the age of twenty-one, he was in the mercantile business for several years. In May 1830, he started the Warsaw Sentinel, and January 1, 1832, consolidated with the Republican Advocate, at Batavia, which he had bought. Three years later he sold out and entered on his labors for the diffusion of a knowledge of governmental administration. His works of this nature were "Science of Government" published at Warsaw, October 1835, "First Lessons in Civil Government" published in 1843 for use in this State and a similar work two years later for circulation in Ohio; "The American Statesman," a political history of the United States, published in 1855; the "Citizen's Manual" in 1858; "Government Class Report" in 1859; "National Economy" in 1860; and "First Book on Civil Government" in 1867. Mr Young was elected to the Assembly in 1845 and 1846 and a delegate to the constitutional convention in the latter year. He went to Warsaw in 1816, and after spending nearly the whole of forty years there, removed in 1855 to Ripley, Chautauqua county, and in 1868 to Red Wing,

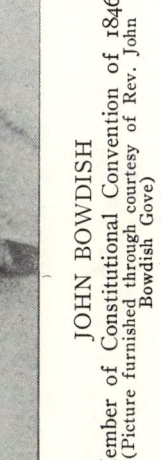

JOHN BOWDISH
Member of Constitutional Convention of 1846
(Picture furnished through courtesy of Rev. John Bowdish Gove)

ANDREW W. YOUNG
Member of Assembly, 1845 and 1846, and of the Constitutional Convention of 1846
(From "History of Wyoming County")

Minn. At the last named place his wife died and he soon after returned to Warsaw, establishing himself there about a year before his death, which occurred February 17, 1877. His local historical works are histories of Chautauqua county, N. Y. and Wayne county, Ind., and a history of Warsaw, N. Y.

Horace Kemper Willard[1]

Dr Horace Kemper Willard was born at Catskill, N. Y., in 1805. He studied medicine with Doctor Croswell and then went to Yale from which he was graduated at the age of twenty-one. He settled in Bloomfield, Delaware county, N. Y., where he married Miss Harriet Evelyn Merwin. In 1842 he took up the practice of medicine in the village of Knox, Albany county. Doctor Willard had a keen interest in educational affairs. In 1846 Doctor Willard took a prominent part in the common school state convention held at Albany. In that year he moved to Berne, Albany county, which was then a center of the antirent agitation. Retiring from the practice of his profession in 1863, he opened a drug store in Catskill. With his wife and five children he moved to Brooklyn in 1867, where later his wife died. In 1876, he married Miss Abigail St John. He died in 1882.

Doctor Willard is described as a man of sterling qualities and deep religious convictions — widely read and abreast of his profession. He was a member of the New York Medical Society.

John H. Hunt

John H. Hunt was born in 1804, and became a printer in New York City. At one time he was deputy collector of New York and was also a member of the constitutional convention of 1846.

Convention Journal

The following is the report of the journal of the Convention in relation to education:

On the 5th of June Mr Bowdish offered the following resolution:

Resolved, that the select committee just ordered be requested to inquire into the expediency of establishing a system of free schools and to report thereon for the consideration of the convention.

On the 15th of June Mr Robert Campbell jr of Steuben offered the following resolution:

Resolved, That it be referred to the committee on education, common schools and the appropriate funds to consider and report as to the propriety of constitutional provisions for the security of the common school,

---

Data furnished by Thomas E. Willard of Brooklyn, son of Dr H. K. Willard.

literature, deposit and other trust funds from conversion or destruction by the Legislature, and the establishment of such a system of common schools as will by taxation bestow the facilities of acquiring a good education upon every child in the state.

This resolution was adopted.

On the 18th of June Mr Henry Nicoll of New York offered the following resolution:

Resolved, That the comptroller be requested to furnish for the use of the convention a statement showing

1 The amount of the school fund, the character of the investments and the amount of money paid into the treasury and not invested. Also, a brief history of the changes made in the investment of the capital with a reference to the laws under which they were made, and the effect of these changes on the security or productiveness of the fund.

2 The same particulars in relation to the literature fund.

3 A statement of the present condition of the United States deposit fund, giving all the losses of capital, and specifying the counties in which the same have occurred. Also, the amount of the revenue derived annually from the fund, and the manner in which it is appropriated by existing laws, and showing the terms on which these moneys were deposited in the state treasury.

The resolution was adopted.

June 22, 1846, Mr Abel Huntington of Suffolk offered the following resolution:

Resolved, That the Secretary of State be requested to report to this convention, if any, what towns have been refused their distributive shares of the proceeds of the common school fund for nonconformity with the requisitions of the law regulating the distribution thereof.

The resolution was adopted.

On July 10 Mr Henry Nicoll of New York offered the following resolution:

Resolved, That the Secretary of the Regents of the University be requested to communicate to this convention the number of academies participating in the distribution of public moneys subsequent to the year 1834, with the aggregate amount of money distributed, and the aggregate number of pupils instructed in each year, and that he also state the amount of money distributed to the said academies or to any of them in each year for the purpose of educating common school teachers, with the number of pupils so educated each year.

Mr Arphaxed Loomis offered the following resolution:

Resolved, That it be referred to the committee on colleges, academies and common schools to inquire and report upon the expediency of securing by constitutional provision, that appropriations for colleges, academies and other institutions of learning shall be made on some just principles of proportion and forbidding special appropriations to particular institutions to the exclusion of others. Also to consider whether the office of Regents of the University may not be dispensed with without public detriment, and whether the present mode of appointing trustees of such institutions ought not to be abolished.

Both these resolutions were approved.

July 13 on motion of Mr William Penniman of Orleans it was resolved that Committee No. 7 be instructed to inquire into the expediency of abolishing the office of county superintendent of schools.

July 22d Mr Henry Nicoll of New York from Standing Committee No. 12 on "Education Common Schools and the Appropriate Funds" reported the **following proposed**

Article IX

1 *The proceeds of all lands belonging to this State except such parts thereof as may be reserved or appropriated to public use or ceded to the United States, which shall hereafter be sold or disposed of, together with the fund denominated the common school fund,* and all moneys heretofore appropriated by law to the use and benefit of the said fund, *shall be and remain a perpetual fund, the interest of which shall be inviolably appropriated and applied to the support of common schools throughout this State.*

2 It shall be the duty of the Legislature to pass such laws as may be necessary to keep at all times securely invested and to preserve from loss or waste all moneys arising from the sales of the said lands in the said first section mentioned, and all moneys now belonging, or which hereafter may belong, to the said common school fund.

3 The revenues accruing from the proportional share of the moneys of the United States received on deposit with this State, upon the terms specified in an act of Congress of the United States, entitled "An act to regulate the deposits of the public money, approved the 23d of June, 1836," after retaining as much thereof as may from time to time be necessary to make good any deficiency in the principal, shall hereafter be inviolably applied to the purposes of common school education, subject to the limitations and restrictions in the next succeeding sections contained.

4 All existing appropriations heretofore made by law, of portions of the said revenues in the preceding section mentioned, for terms of years which have not yet expired, shall continue to be made until the expiration of said terms of years and not afterwards.

5 The portion of the said revenues now directed by law to be annually paid over to the literature fund, shall be so paid in the year one thousand eight hundred and forty-seven, and not afterwards; and after that period all existing specific appropriations now directed by law to be paid out of the revenues of the literature fund, shall be paid out of the revenues in the said preceding third section mentioned, until otherwise ordered by the Legislature.

The committee further report, for the consideration of the convention, and recommend to be submitted to the people separately, the following additional section.

The Legislature shall, at its first session, after the adoption of this constitution, and from time to time thereafter, as shall be necessary, provide by law for the free education and instruction of every child between the ages of four and sixteen years, whose parents, guardians or employers shall be residents of the State, in the common schools now established, or which shall hereafter be established therein; the expense of such education and instruction, after applying the public funds as above provided, shall be defrayed by taxation, at the same time, and in the same manner, as may be provided by law for the liquidation of town and county charges.

Henry Nicoll, *Chairman*

October 1 Mr John Bowdish of Montgomery resolved,

That the convention will proceed to the consideration of the report of Committee No. 22 on education next after disposing of the report of Committee No. 4.

Mr Albert L. Baker of Washington moved to lay said resolution on the table. This motion was beaten by a vote of sixty against to thirty-four for.

The question was put as to whether the convention would agree to the resolution offered by Mr Bowdish, and it was carried by sixty-four ayes to twenty-nine nays.

October 8 Mr Henry Nicoll of New York offered the following resolution:

Resolved, That said Article 9 referred to on the date of (July 22) be referred to the Committee on Revision of the Articles of the Constitution with instruction to report the same instanter to the convention in the words following, to wit: [which is the same as given above].

On motion of Mr Nicoll, the first section of the said resolution was amended, by inserting after the word "States" in the 3d line, the words "and such as are contiguous to the salt springs."

In further proceeding upon the said resolution of Mr Nicoll, Mr Hoffman made a motion to lay the same upon the table.

Mr President put the question whether the convention would agree thereto, and it was determined in the affirmative. (Ayes 78, nays 22)

The ayes and nays being required by ten delegates,

Those who voted in the affirmative are

Mr Angel	Mr Harrison	Mr Ruggles
Mr Archer	Mr Hart	Mr Russell
Mr Avrault	Mr Hoffman	Mr St John
Mr F. F. Backus	Mr A. Huntington	Mr Sanford
Mr H. Backus	Mr Hyde	Mr Shaver
Mr Baker	Mr Kemble	Mr Shaw
Mr Bascom	Mr Kernan	Mr Sheldon
Mr Bergen	Mr Kingsley	Mr E. Spencer
Mr Brayton	Mr Kirkland	Mr W. H. Spencer
Mr Burr	Mr Loomis	Mr Stow
Mr Cambreleng	Mr Maxwell	Mr Strong
Mr R. Campbell, jr.	Mr Miller	Mr Taft
Mr Candee	Mr Morris	Mr Taggart
Mr Clyde	Mr Nellis	Mr Tallmadge
Mr Crooker	Mr Nicholas	Mr W. Taylor
Mr Dana	Mr O'Conor	Mr Tuthill
Mr Danforth	Mr Parish	Mr Warren
Mr Dodd	Mr Patterson	Mr Waterbury
Mr Dorlon	Mr Penniman	Mr White
Mr Dubois	Mr Perkins	Mr Witbeck
Mr Flanders	Mr Porter	Mr Wood
Mr Forsyth	Mr Powers	Mr Worden
Mr Gebhard	Mr President	Mr A. Wright
Mr Graham	Mr Rhoades	Mr W. B. Wright
Mr Greene	Mr Richmond	Mr Yawger
Mr Harris	Mr Riker	Mr Youngs 78

For the Negative

Mr Allen	Mr Mann	Mr Stanton
Mr Bowdish	Mr McNeil	Mr Stephens
Mr Brundage	Mr Marvin	Mr Swackhamer
Mr Conely	Mr Murphy	Mr Townsend
Mr Cornell	Mr Nicoll	Mr Vanschoonhoven
Mr Hotchkiss	Mr Salisbury	Mr Willard
Mr Hunt	Mr Shepard	Mr Young
Mr Kennedy		22

Thereupon,

The first and only section of said article 9, as reported by the committee on revision, was read in the words following, to wit:

Article IX

Section 1 The proceeds of all lands belonging to this State, except such parts thereof as may be reserved or appropriated to public use, or ceded to the United States, and such as are contiguous to the salt springs, which shall hereafter be sold or disposed of, together with the fund denominated the common school fund, shall be and remain a perpetual fund; the interest of which shall be inviolably appropriated and applied to the support of common schools throughout this State. Vide article on finances, Sec. 7.

Mr Hoffman made a motion that the convention should agree to strike out the said section, and insert in lieu thereof a section in the words following, to wit:

Section 1 The capital of the common school fund; the capital of the literature fund, and the capital of the United States deposite fund, shall be respectively preserved inviolate. The revenue of the said common school fund shall be applied to the support of common schools; the revenue of the said literature fund shall be applied to the support of academies, and the sum of twenty-five thousand dollars of the revenues of the United States deposite fund shall each year be appropriated to and made a part of the capital of the said common school fund.

Mr O'Conor made a motion to amend the said section offered by Mr Hoffman, by striking out the word "five," where it occurs between the words "twenty" and "thousand."

Mr President put the question whether the convention would agree to the said motion of Mr O'Conor, and it was determined in the negative. (Nays 66, ayes 35)

The ayes and nays being required by ten delegates,

Those who voted in the negative are

Mr F. F. Backus	Mr Hoffman	Mr Salisbury
Mr Bascom	Mr Hotchkiss	Mr Sheldon
Mr Bowdish	Mr Hunt	Mr E. Spencer
Mr Brayton	Mr A. Huntington	Mr W. H. Spencer
Mr Brundage	Mr Hutchinson	Mr Stanton
Mr Burr	Mr Kennedy	Mr Stephens
Mr Cambreleng	Mr Kernan	Mr Strong
Mr R. Campbell, jr.	Mr Kingsley	Mr Swackhamer
Mr Conely	Mr Loomis	Mr Taft
Mr Cook	Mr Mann	Mr Tallmadge
Mr Cornell	Mr McNeil	Mr J. J. Taylor
Mr Crooker	Mr Morris	Mr Tilden
Mr Cuddeback	Mr Munro	Mr Townsend
Mr Danforth	Mr Nellis	Mr Tuthill
Mr Dodd	Mr Nicoll	Mr VanSchoonhoven
Mr Dubois	Mr Powers	Mr Warren
Mr Flanders	Mr President	Mr Waterbury
Mr Gebhard	Mr Richmond	Mr Willard
Mr Graham	Mr Riker	Mr Witbeck
Mr Harris	Mr Ruggles	Mr W. Wright
Mr Harrison	Mr Russell	Mr Yawger
Mr Hart	Mr St John	Mr W. B. Wright 66

For the Affirmative

Mr Allen	Mr Kemble	Mr Rhoades
Mr Angel	Mr Kirkland	Mr Sanford
Mr Archer	Mr Marvin	Mr Shaver
Mr Ayrault	Mr Maxwell	Mr Shaw
Mr H. Backus	Mr Miller	Mr Stow
Mr Bergen	Mr Murphy	Mr Taggart
Mr Candee	Mr Nicholas	Mr W. Tayor
Mr Dana	Mr O'Conor	Mr White
Mr Dorlan	Mr Parish	Mr Wood
Mr Forsyth	Mr Patterson	Mr Young
Mr Greene	Mr Penniman	Mr Youngs
Mr Hyde	Mr Porter	35

Mr President put the question whether the convention would agree to the said motion of Mr Hoffman, to strike out and insert, and it was determined in the affirmative. (Ayes 104, nays 3)

The ayes and noes being required by ten delegates,
Those who voted in the affirmative are

Mr Allen	Mr Hyde	Mr Shaver
Mr Angel	Mr Jones	Mr Shaw
Mr Archer	Mr Kemble	Mr Sheldon
Mr Ayrault	Mr Kennedy	Mr Shepard
Mr F. F. Backus	Mr Kernan	Mr Smith
Mr H. Backus	Mr Kingsley	Mr E. Spencer
Mr Baker	Mr Kirkland	Mr W. H. Spencer
Mr Bascom	Mr Loomis	Mr Stanton
Mr Bergen	Mr Mann	Mr Stephens
Mr Bowdish	Mr McNeil	Mr Stow
Mr Brayton	Mr Marvin	Mr Strong
Mr Bruce	Mr Maxwell	Mr Swackhamer
Mr Burr	Mr Miller	Mr Taft
Mr Cambreleng	Mr Morris	Mr Taggart
Mr R. Campbell, Jr	Mr Munro	Mr Tallmadge
Mr Candee	Mr Murphy	Mr J. J. Taylor
Mr Clyde	Mr Nellis	Mr W. Taylor
Mr Conely	Mr Nicholas	Mr Tilden
Mr Cook	Mr Nicoll	Mr Townsend
Mr Cornell	Mr O'Conor	Mr Tuthill
Mr Crooker	Mr Parish	Mr Vanschoonhoven
Mr Dana	Mr Patterson	Mr Ward
Mr Danforth	Mr Penniman	Mr Warren
Mr Dorlan	Mr Perkins	Mr Waterbury
Mr Dubois	Mr Porter	Mr White
Mr Gebhard	Mr Powers	Mr Willard
Mr Graham	Mr President	Mr Witbeck
Mr Greene	Mr Rhoades	Mr Wood
Mr Harris	Mr Richmond	Mr Worden
Mr Harrison	Mr Riker	Mr A. Wright
Mr Hart	Mr Ruggles	Mr W. B. Wright
Mr Hoffman	Mr Russell	Mr Yawger
Mr Hunt	Mr St John	Mr Young
Mr A. Huntington	Mr Salisbury	Mr Youngs
Mr Hutchinson	Mr Sanford	104

For the Negative

Mr Brundage	Mr Cuddeback	Mr Hotchkiss	3

Mr Nicoll made a motion to insert a section, to be submitted to the people separately, in the words following, to wit:

The Legislature shall provide for the free education and instruction of every child of the State, in the common schools now established, or which shall hereafter be established therein.

Mr President put the question whether the convention would agree thereto, and it was determined in the affirmative. (Ayes 57, nays 52)

The ayes and nays being required by ten delegates,

Those who voted in the affirmative are

Mr Allen	Mr Cook	Mr Hutchinson
Mr Archer	Mr Cornell	Mr Jones
Mr F. F. Backus	Mr Dodd	Mr Kemble
Mr H. Backus	Mr Dorlan	Mr Kennedy
Mr Baker	Mr Dubois	Mr Kernan
Mr Bergen	Mr Forsyth	Mr Kirkland
Mr Bowdish	Mr Gebhard	Mr Loomis
Mr Cambreleng	Mr Harris	Mr Mann
Mr R. Campbell, jr	Mr Hotchkiss	Mr McNeil
Mr Conely	Mr E. Huntington	Mr Marvin

Mr Maxwell	Mr Shaver	Mr Tilden
Mr Miller	Mr Shepard	Mr Townsend
Mr Morris	Mr Smith	Mr Vanschoonhoven
Mr Murphy	Mr E. Spencer	Mr Warren
Mr Nellis	Mr Stephens	Mr White
Mr Nicoll	Mr Swackhamer	Mr Willard
Mr O'Conor	Mr Taft	Mr Worden
Mr Patterson	Mr Taggart	Mr Yawger
Mr Sanford	Mr J. J. Taylor	Mr Young — 57

For the Negative

Mr Angel	Mr Hunt	Mr Salisbury
Mr Ayrault	Mr A. Huntington	Mr Shaw
Mr Bascom	Mr Hyde	Mr Sheldon
Mr Brayton	Mr Kingsley	Mr W. H. Spencer
Mr Bruce	Mr Munro	Mr Stanton
Mr Brundage	Mr Nicholas	Mr Stow
Mr Burr	Mr Parish	Mr Strong
Mr Candee	Mr Penniman	Mr Tallmadge
Mr Crooker	Mr Perkins	Mr W. Taylor
Mr Cuddeback	Mr Porter	Mr Tuthill
Mr Dana	Mr Powers	Mr Ward
Mr Danforth	Mr President	Mr Waterbury
Mr Flanders	Mr Rhoades	Mr Witbeck
Mr Graham	Mr Richmond	Mr Wood
Mr Greene	Mr Riker	Mr W. Wright
Mr Harrison	Mr Ruggles	Mr W. B. Wright
Mr Hart	Mr Russell	Mr Youngs
Mr Hoffman	Mr St John	— 53

On motion of Mr Jones,

Ordered, That the last preceding section be referred to the committee on revision, with instructions to prepare the form of the ballot for carrying into effect its separate submission to the people.

Mr Danforth made a motion to reconsider the section for a separate submission to the people.

Ordered, That the same be laid upon the table.

Mr Ruggles made a motion that the convention should agree to a section in the words following, to wit:

The Legislature shall at the same time provide for raising the necessary taxes to carry into effect the provisions contained in the preceding section.

Mr Richmond made a motion to amend the said section, by inserting after the word "taxes," the words "in each school district."

Mr President put the question whether the convention would agree to the same, and it was determined in the affirmative.

Mr President then put the question whether the convention would agree to the said section offered by Mr Ruggles, as amended, and it was determined in the affirmative. (Ayes 80, nays 26)

The ayes and noes being required by ten delegates,

Those who voted in the affirmative are

Mr Angel	Mr Brayton	Mr R. Campbell, jr
Mr F. F. Backus	Mr Bruce	Mr Candee
Mr H. Backus	Mr Brundage	Mr Clyde
Mr Bascom	Mr Burr	Mr Cook
Mr Bergen	Mr Cambreleng	Mr Cornell

Mr Crooker	Mr Loomis	Mr Shepard
Mr Cuddeback	Mr Mann	Mr Smith
Mr Danforth	Mr McNeil	Mr Stanton
Mr Dodd	Mr Maxwell	Mr Stephens
Mr Dorlon	Mr Miller	Mr Stow
Mr Dubois	Mr Morris	Mr Strong
Mr Forsyth	Mr Munro	Mr Taft
Mr Gebhard	Mr Murphy	Mr Tallmadge
Mr Graham	Mr Nellis	Mr J. J. Taylor
Mr Greene	Mr Nicholas	Mr W. Taylor
Mr Hart	Mr Nicoll	Mr Tilden
Mr Hoffman	Mr O'Conor	Mr Townsend
Mr Hotchkiss	Mr Parish	Mr Tuthill
Mr Hunt	Mr Perkins	Mr Ward
Mr A. Huntington	Mr Porter	Mr Warren
Mr Hutchison	Mr Powers	Mr White
Mr Hyde	Mr Rhoades	Mr Willard
Mr Jones	Mr Richmond	Mr A. Wright
Mr Kemble	Mr Riker	Mr W. B. Wright
Mr Kennedy	Mr Ruggles	Mr Yawger
Mr Kernan	Mr Russell	Mr Youngs
Mr Kinsgley	Mr Sanford	80

For the Negative

Mr Allen	Mr Harrison	Mr E. Spencer
Mr Archer	Mr E. Huntington	Mr W. H. Spencer
Mr Ayrault	Mr Kirkland	Mr Swackhamer
Mr Baker	Mr Patterson	Mr Taggart
Mr Bowdish	Mr Penniman	Mr Vanschoonhoven
Mr Conely	Mr President	Mr Waterbury
Mr Dana	Mr St John	Mr Wood
Mr Flanders	Mr Salisbury	Mr Young
Mr Harris	Mr Shaw	26

On motion of Mr Ruggles,

Ordered, That the said last preceding section be submitted to the people, in connection with the section adopted on motion of Mr Nicoll.

And then the convention adjourned until 3½ o'clock p. m.

3½ O'CLOCK p. m.

The convention met pursuant to adjournment.

On motion of Mr Loomis,

Resolved, That article 9, be referred to a committee of one, with instructions to strike out the two last sections of the said article, and report the same, as amended, to the convention, instanter.

Debates were had thereon, and pending the same,

On motion of Mr ——— the call for the previous question was seconded by the convention, and the main question ordered to be put.

Mr President put the question whether the convention would agree to the said motion of Mr Loomis, and it was determined in the affirmative. (Ayes 61, nays 27)

The ayes and noes being required by ten delegates,

Those who voted in the affirmative are

Mr Allen	Mr Hart	Mr Riker
Mr Angel	Mr Hoffman	Mr Russell
Mr Ayrault	Mr Hunt	Mr St John
Mr Baker	Mr A. Huntington	Mr Salisbury
Mr Bascom	Mr Hyde	Mr Shaver
Mr Bergen	Mr Kernan	Mr Shaw
Mr Bull	Mr Kingsley	Mr Sheldon
Mr Burr	Mr Kirkland	Mr W. H. Spencer
Mr Cambreleng	Mr Loomis	Mr Stanton
Mr Candee	Mr Marvin	Mr Stetson
Mr Clyde	Mr Maxwell	Mr Strong
Mr Cook	Mr Miller	Mr Taggart
Mr Crooker	Mr Munro	Mr Tallmadge
Mr Cuddeback	Mr Nellis	Mr W. Taylor
Mr Dana	Mr Nicholas	Mr Ward
Mr Danforth	Mr O'Conor	Mr Waterbury
Mr Dodd	Mr Parish	Mr White
Mr Dubois	Mr Porter	Mr Wood
Mr Flanders	Mr Powers	Mr A. Wright
Mr Greene	Mr President	Mr Youngs
Mr Harrison		61

For the Negative

Mr Archer	Mr Hotchkiss	Mr Ruggles
Mr F. F. Backus	Mr Hutchinson	Mr Smith
Mr Bowdish	Mr Jones	Mr Stephens
Mr Brundage	Mr Mann	Mr Swackhamer
Mr R. Campbell, jr	Mr Morris	Mr Taft
Mr Conely	Mr Murphy	Mr J. J. Taylor
Mr Cornell	Mr Nicoll	Mr Townsend
Mr Dorlon	Mr Patterson	Mr Willard
Mr Forsyth	Mr Richmond	Mr Yawger 27

Ordered, That Mr Loomis, be the said committee.

Mr Loomis in pursuance of said instruction, reported said article to the convention, amended in compliance with the order of the convention.

Thereupon,

The article, as amended, was agreed to and ordered to be engrossed.

Editorial Comment on the Consideration of Free Schools by the Constitutional Convention

Here is a section reported by the committee on education to be submitted separately to the people for their approval or rejection, which we trust will receive a hearty "Yes" from three-fourths of our voters.

Remember, lovers of justice and intelligence, that a section providing for at least the nominal education of every child reared in the state and making the support of such education a part of the annual tax bill so that every common school shall be truly a free school is to come before you. Do not forget to vote "Yes" upon it. Here is the provision, *Section 6.*

The Legislature shall at its first session, after the adoption of this Constitution, and from time to time thereafter, as shall be necessary, provide for the free education and instruction of every child between the ages of four and sixteen years, whose parents, guardians or employers shall be residents of the State, in the common schools now established, or which shall hereafter be established therein; the expense of such education and instruction, after applying the public funds as above provided, shall be defrayed by taxation, at the same time, and in the same manner, as may be provided by law for the liquidation of town and county charges.

In the New York Weekly Tribune of August 24, the person who reported the Constitutional Convention for that paper said in regard to the Committee on Education:

Messrs. Tuthill and Willard have submitted minority reports from the Committee on Education. They both propose that the proceeds of State lands and the school funds shall form a permanent common school fund, and that the United States Deposit Fund shall be applied in the same way, and that the Legislature shall invest and secure the moneys. Messrs. Willard and Tuthill are opposed to universal education on Mr Nicoll's plan, the value of which no one can appreciate more than myself.— *Weekly New York Tribune, July 29, 1846.*

The School Fund

It will be seen in our report of the Conventional proceedings of Wednesday that a report was submitted by Mr Nicoll from committee no. 12 relating to the school fund. The report is contained in an article of six sections, the last of which the committee recommend should be submitted to the people separately. The particular articles of each section we presume would not be interesting to our readers. The school fund has become an important branch of the state property in which all are interested, and divested as it is of all political considerations, we trust the united wisdom of the Convention will carefully guard it from all improper application, and consider it in its true light, a sacred deposit for the benefit of the great cause of education.— *Kingston Democratic Journal, July 29, 1846.*

Constitutional Reform in Our Schools

Mr Editor:

Availing myself of your liberality in granting the use of your journal as a medium of free discussion of the many momentous subjects now before the assembled wisdom of this great State, I wish to call you and your readers attention to a proposition submitted to the Convention by the chairman of committee no. 12 on the subject of common schools, in the following terms:

The committee recommend the following to be submitted to the people separately, *Section 6.*

The Legislature shall, at its first session, after the adoption of this Constitution, and from time to time thereafter, as shall be necessary, provide by law for the free education and instruction of every child between the ages of four and sixteen years, whose parents, guardians or employers shall be residents of the State, in the common schools now established, or which shall hereafter be established therein; the expense of such education and instruction, after applying the public funds as above provided, shall be defrayed by taxation, at the same time, and in the same manner, as may be provided by law for the liquidation of town and county charges.

Henry Nicoll, Chairman

It will be seen that a new and startling principle is contained in the above section, one which is totally repugnant to a free, equal and democratic administration of law, and in direct conflict with the inherent and constitutional rights of every citizen.

This proposition contemplates the taxation of the community for the education of the children of those who are rich and able to educate their own children, as well as the education of the poor. The people have never expressed their dissent to being taxed for the purpose of educating the poor. They know that the permanency of our institutions depends upon the intelligence of the masses, and they willingly contribute to the expense of securing such intelligence under the idea that it is a simple performance of duty which every citizen owes to his country, and which is necessary for its long standing. It is upon this principle only that the people of a free country can be taxed even for the education of the poor. It is to advance their own interests by securing the country from that most formidable danger to republics, the ignorance and consequent turbulence of the masses; thus far, and no farther, can the principle be tolerated.

There is no danger that the children of the rich will grow up in ignorance and, therefore, the people cannot be called upon to provide for their education. By the rich are meant all those who are able to give their children a fair English education. Our present Constitution recognizes this principle by expressly providing that the property of the individual cannot be taken away from him without his consent, except for such purposes, and then only by giving adequate compensation. To allow the majority to say that the minority shall put out their property in the shape of taxes to defray the expense of the education of the children of others who are able to bear such expense, is a palpable blow at this well organized principle, and it is not the least odious because being submitted to the people it should meet the approval of the majority of them.

The school money should be devoted exclusively to the education of the poor, and if insufficient for that purpose, the deficiency should be supplied by a general State tax which would be more agreeable and popular with the people than the present system of petty and harassing district and neighborhood taxation. In the one case it all comes out of the public chest for the benefit of the needy, and in the other it seems to be merely the transferring of money from the pockets of one portion of the community into those of another. It is probable that the school fund united with the literature fund (which should be the case) would afford sufficient for this purpose without taxation, if it did not meet the absorbing touch of such useless offices as county and town superintendents, and waste in other ways before it finally reaches its destined object.

There is no force in the objection that it is invidious to make a distinction in this application between the rich and the poor. This objection never came from the side of the latter, but was kindly tendered by the advocates of the former. It is an old exploded and "obsolete idea" which obtained perhaps in more aristocratic times, but is wholly unworthy of the present. The time has gone by in this country for the honest poor man to be ashamed of his condition. It is no disgrace to be poor, but exceedingly inconvenient. Virtue is the best test of merit. To be just is always right, and justice demands that only those who need should fall under the public protection. But justice frowns upon compelling one man to pay toward the education of the children of his rich neighbor, or to go one step beyond his natural duty to his own offspring and to his country in contributing his share in behalf of the poor.

There is no subject in government more disagreeable than that of the call of the tax gatherer, and care should be taken that all who are made to contribute should feel the justice of their contributions. In any other event hard feelings and dissatisfaction are engendered against the laws, and the happiness of society deeply affected.

The proposition to submit this question to the votes of the people would be giving the sanction of the convention to any course which the electors might take, thereby destroying the moral feelings which the people might otherwise entertain against the injustice of the measure, leaving the majority free from those restraints to follow the dictates of their own interests to the subversion of the interests and the feelings of the minority. If it should be advisable to submit any proposition to the people, it should be that of educating the poor only, at the public expense, and of appropriating all school moneys to this object.

The chairman of the committee when reporting the above Section stated to the Convention that there was a difference of opinion in the committee with respect to it. No doubt differences of opinion existed among them upon at least some of the points mentioned above. The fact that the committee proposed to have it submitted to the people separately from the articles of the new Constitution affords evidence that they were not convinced of the entire propriety of the measure.

That the true principles of our government, and that right may prevail, in the settlement of this question is the fervent wish of at least ONE OF THE PEOPLE.—*Newburg Telegraph, August 6, 1846.*

The Convention — Free Schools

It will be perceived by the following report[1] of the committee on education and common schools, of the constitutional convention now in session in this city, that the free school system is proposed by them to be incorporated into the fundamental law of the State; and that the question of its adoption be submitted, separately, to the consideration of the people. We congratulate the friends of free education throughout the State, on this gratifying result; and we earnestly indulge the hope that the convention will sanction by a strong vote the enlightened principle adopted by the committee. As to its final adoption by an overwhelming majority of the people, on its presentation to them, disconnected from all other questions of policy or expediency, we can not permit ourselves to entertain a doubt. On this point the public sentiment, so far as our knowledge and information extend is strongly in favor of such an extension of the existing provisions of our common school system as shall embrace every child in the State. Inability to meet a heavy rate bill, at the expiration of each school term, must no longer be made the pretence for a virtual exclusion from the benefits of education, of hundreds and thousands of the children of indigent parents.

New York in this respect cannot longer afford to be behind her sister state of Massachusetts, where the free school principle has been thoroughly tested.

" Our Schools" observes the Hon. Horace Mann in his Seventh Annual Report, as secretary of the Massachusetts board of education " are perfectly

---

[1] For text of report, see Extract from Proceedings of the Convention.

free. A child would be as much astonished at being asked to pay any sum, however small for attending our common schools, as he would be if payment were demanded of him for walking in the public streets, for breathing the common air, or enjoying the warmth of the unappropriable sun. Massachusetts has the honor of establishing the first system of Free Schools in the world; and she projected a plan so elastic and expansive, in regard to the course of studies and the thoroughness of instruction, that it may be enlarged and perfected to meet any new wants of her citizens, to the end of time. Our system, too, is one and the same for both rich and poor; for as all human beings, in regard to their natural rights, stand upon a footing of equality before God, so, in this respect, the human has been copied from the divine plan of government, by placing all citizens on the same footing of equality before the law of the land."—*District School Journal, September, 1846.*

The constitutional convention reporter of the New York Tribune under date of September 26, 1846 gives the following under the heading " Train up a child in the way he should go."

Mr. Bowdish, who had never before spoken in the convention nor before a public body at any time in his life, rose and stated that he considered education as the grand foundation on which our republican institutions must be supported. Much had been done, but much yet remains to be done for the establishment of free schools where the children of the poor and of the rich might together receive instruction. He delivered an able, well-arranged address, which did credit both to his head and heart, containing true principles on which American freedom is to be perpetuated, and called the attention of the convention to a subject of vital importance but which is, I regret to see and say, too much neglected.

The noise made at times while he was speaking made it impossible for half the members to hear him, had they been so disposed, but I hope that his address will get into the public journals. He wished a settled system of education made permanent by the Constitution. He reminded members that millions of the children of the republic were uneducated, and that in 1840 it was found that over half a million of the whites over twenty years of age could neither read nor write. He proposed that report no. 12 on Education be considered tomorrow morning at ten, so that a plan might be matured whereby virtue and intelligence, patriotism and peace might take the place of ignorance and prejudice, and that the people be enabled to vote on the question whether or not all should obtain a good education, which, he considered, the best preventative of vice and crime.

Mr Baker moved to leave the resolution on the table. This was beaten by a vote of fifty-six to thirty-nine.

Mr Bowdish's resolution to take up the report on Education next was then carried by a vote of sixty-four to thirty.

I heartily congratulate the country on the success of this measure. Education — free and virtuous education — is the just inheritance of a land of equal rights and elective institutions. Ignorance, superstition and prejudice never can, never will stand on the same platform with intelligence, whether united with virtue or with vice.

The New York Weekly Tribune under date of October 14, 1846, reviews the amended constitution, and under the heading "Education and Schools" it states

I Funds. The capitals respectively of the school, literature and U. S. deposit funds are to be preserved inviolate, and their revenues to be duly appropriated. The sum of $25,000 per annum is to be taken from the revenue of the U. S. deposit fund and added to the capital of the school fund.

(The noble idea of having all our common schools free schools — that is, supported by a tax on property — failed, we perceive with sorrow.)

The New York Observer on October 17, 1846, said under the heading of the proposed Constitution:

"We do not intend to discuss its provisions . . . Several of the leading papers of this city have taken decided ground against the Constitution."

Free Schools

We continue to receive, from all quarters of the State, the most gratifying assurances of the popularity of this great measure of educational reform. Numerous and strong petitions for its adoption as a part of the constitution, have been forwarded to the convention; the Press has spoken freely and decidedly in its behalf; conventions and associations of teachers, school officers and friends of education have everywhere passed the most enthusiastic resolutions in its favor, and an intelligent and right-minded public sentiment has unequivocally sanctioned its introduction as a permanent part of our school system. While differences of opinion have existed in reference to the proposed diversion of the literature fund, and the increase of the common school appropriation from the State, on this great subject but one voice is heard from all who take an interest in the welfare and improvement of our institutions for public instruction, and the universal diffusion of knowledge. We rejoice that this is so: confident as we are that the final adoption of this much desired reform will conduce immeasurably to the elevation of our schools, the progress of light and truth, the dispersion of ignorance and error, and the permanent well being and happiness of the community.

Should the convention, as we earnestly trust it will, adopt the section reported by the committee, in reference to this proposition, we shall issue our November number immediately thereafter, and devote it entirely to the discussion and full elucidation of this great subject, in all its bearings, in order that the people, whose province it will then be to act upon it, may be enabled to judge of its merits with accuracy and discrimination: and we trust our example will be followed by every newspaper in the State. On the other hand, should the convention fail, for want of time, or otherwise, to incorporate this provision as a portion of the new constitution we shall still feel it our duty to continue to urge this subject upon the attention of the people, with a view to such action as may be practicable, through the medium of the Legislature.— *District School Journal, October 1846*

The Prospect Before Us

Now that the constitutional statesmen of our Commonwealth have deemed it inexpedient to engraft upon our fundamental institutions that system of free schools, by means of which our sister republic, Massachusetts, has attained so enviable a preeminence, and several of our most flourishing cities, including the metropolis, so decided an advance, in the great educational movement of the age, it becomes us to take a calm and dispassionate survey of the means of improvement and of effort which still remain. Our ample common school fund has been renewedly consecrated exclusively to the purposes for which it was originally designed. And adequate provision has been made, by constitutional enactment, for its progressive increase, to meet the probable wants of the future; while our academies are to receive the entire avails of the revenue arising from the U. S. deposit fund. Our excellent common school organization remains inviolate, and, we trust, inviolable.—*District School Journal, December 1846*

The interest in free schools continued after the defeat of that movement in 1846, as shown by the following:

The Support of Common Schools

Interest in the education of children is extending and deepening, we are happy to find, in the public mind in all parts of the State: And the support of the school system of this State, and its improvement occupies the minds of some of our best statesmen, and most enlightened philanthropists. So firm a hold has this subject upon the judgment of the people that, in the late Constitutional Convention, provision was not only made for the yearly increase of the Common School Fund, but a resolution for the separate submission of the question " shall the schools of our State be made FREE, by an additional tax upon the property thereof?" was adopted by that Body by a very liberal and decisive vote. But subsequently, the resolution was withdrawn, for reasons perhaps, but which have not yet satisfactorily appeared to the friends of the measure — One of our most enlightened and liberal minded citizens, in allusion to the withdrawal of the resolution, once adopted by the Convention, makes the following feeling and sensible reflections:

"It is indeed to be regretted that our late Convention for amending the Consitution, had not sanctioned the adoption by law of the Free School System throughout the State — This would have been simplified as well as equalized the present complicated machinery of our Common School establishment. The rich and poor, then, in our common public seminaries of learning, would stand where they ought to stand, on the same footing; and the special object of benevolence and of patriotism, originally contemplated and ever since cherished by our legislature, in regard to common Schools, would be certainly and effectually accomplished; for then, our poor, and all our poor, would be educated. But, we must wait and hope, and strive for a better state of things, in relation to this subject. At present the poor do not enjoy, nor does the operations of our school system secure them, that equal participation in the bounty of the State, to which they are entitled; much less, any special participation therein. Instead of being sought for and cheerfully admitted into our schools, as they should be, a large proportion of them are virtually excluded, and the money designed for their benefit, engrossed by others and applied to the use of those, who are able to pay for their own tuition. Thus, the great object of State benevolence, in this respect, is in part defeated."

The alternative which the friends of this cause have to adopt in the premises, is further action, and petition to the Legislature, which, we believe it is conceded, has full power to provide for such support of our common schools, as will secure the general education of all classes, especially of those whose parents are unable to provide the means to pay for their tuition; and it appears to us that the friends of *Free Schools* should still be active in their exertions to procure the passage of such law. There are at present about 11,000 district schools in this State, which report within their bounds 703,399 children, between the ages of 5 and 16; among whom are distributed annually from the funds of the State, 275,000 dollars, which, with an equal amount raised by the towns, in order to avail themselves of this amount, constitutes the whole amount of public money devoted to Teachers' wages in this State at 550,000 dollars. To this must be added, the amount paid by parents upon rate bills, which it is estimated may exceed this amount one-half, say 825,000 dollars which together forms an aggregate of 1,375,000 at present paid for instruction of about one-half of the pupils that should be in schools, while it is feared, as our correspondent intimates, a very great proportion of those absent, are the poor, who are not able to pay the rate-bill, and who do not receive their education, as a gratuity, under our present system, because of its complexity and difficulty of application.

Admitting the above positions to be correct, that but one half of the children reported attend these schools, for any period of the year, and we are confident this number does not average more than eight months' attendance; we shall have 301,133 under instruction, at an expense of $1,375,000 or $4.56 for each child taught for eight months in the year: besides all the expense for school houses, fuel, books, etc. without one half of the children drawn into the schools even for that period. While on the other hand, under the Free School System in the city of New York, a far greater proportion of the children attend for twelve months in the year, with improved modes of instruction and eminent Teachers, at an average expense of four dollars and forty cents each scholar, which amount includes not only the cost of tuition, but also of books repairs, fuel, apparatus, etc. In Rochester, moreover it has been found under the Free School System five-sixths of the children of the aforesaid age attend the schools, while in Albany, under the rate-bill system, not more than two-sixths were in attendance at the time, these facts were ascertained. Now, is it not a matter of economy as well as wisdom, to adopt that system which is the most efficient — most regular, constant, and least expense, for the accomplishment of the great desideratum, the general education of children of the State? In one case it cost four dollars and fifty-six cents for eight months' instruction to each child, without books, fuel, etc. in the other, four dollars and forty cents for twelve months' instruction for each child, including books, apparatus, fuel, etc. and reaching almost double the number of those whom it is the duty and the province of the State to provide for their education!

Let us look at the expense of constituting our Common Schools, Free Schools, by a tax upon the property thereof, which we believe to be the popular wish, could it be fairly tested; and which we conceive would not be seriously resisted by capitalists, and the wealthy portions of the community, when its importance and advantages were fully brought to bear upon their judgment and their liberality toward an unfortunate, yet innocent and deserving class of their fellow beings, and the future supporters of the social fabric society.

We have seen there are 11,000 Districts Schools in the State, which at an average of 250 dollars each per annum for Teacher's wages, would require the sum of $2,750,000. The public funds with the pay on rate-bills already provided, amount to $1,925,000. Balance of Teacher's wages to be raised, $825,000 or about three times the present amount of public money raised in the several towns for the support of the schools. And would this amount, or even the whole sum of $2,200,000 spread over the $617,000,000 of taxable property of the State, in any way oppress the tax payers, when by it they would secure the instruction of almost the entire juvenile population, in much less time than is now employed in parts of years, for the imperfect tuition of about half the number? In the cities, where Free Schools exist, a tolerable education is obtained by the scholars in attending from 7 to 12 years of age and they are then better prepared for trades, or other active employments while the pupils in our country schools seldom acquire a sufficient education under the present practice, up to 16 years of age, when the law excludes them from any further participation in the funds devoted to the cause of education.

Let this infallible truth be impressed upon the minds of our Legislators when contemplating this important subject, that children are the heritage and hope of the State; that their capacities of usefulness, support and defence. in after life, their activities, improvements, industry and production of labor and ingenuity, are to benefit the wealthy and other members of the community, even more than the parents that bore and sustained them in early infancy and childhood; and if by proper education, they become useful citizens, able defenders of the right in the cabinet and the field, the good results will unquestionably be felt in all parts of the Republic; and in this light, every child in the State has an irrefragable right and claim for an education in ordinary cases upon the property of the State. *Universal Education is the cheap defence of Nations.*— Teachers' Advocate, March 4, 1847

Rate Bill Exemptions

We are frequently told, when advocating a Free School System, that "the right to exempt a poor man's bill makes our present system as free as can be desired." Were it not that these exemptions tend to humiliate those who need encouragement there would be some force in the remark. The bare fact that a man's school bill is exempted is made the theme of reproachful conversation throughout the district and consequently induces those who need this provision of the law to keep their children from the school. In this, society depresses still lower that very class which sound policy dictates should receive its fostering care and protection. To extend the boon of education as a common charity is repugnant to the spirit of truly free Institutions.

These exemptions being taxable upon the district, are not made as freely as they should be — We know of many instances where the manner of offering to make them was such as to wound the spirit of a man and make their acceptance even worse than the bitings of poverty. School officers too often fear the illiberal spirit that frequently obtains in the district, and are deterred from obeying their own sense of justice and propriety by the expected frowns which the exemption will excite. If made a town charge it would be far better for those who receive the exemptions. There be less hesitancy in making and receiving them. A correspondent of the Poughkeepsie Telegraph has presented some facts on this subject that ought to make humanity blush. The editor of that paper has prefaced the communication in a pertinent and appropriate manner. We subjoin his remarks and communication.

We fear there are too many cases like the following in the administration of our complicated School Laws. Too many of the Trustees of districts are parsimonious. Liberal and enlightened men should always be chosen for these officers. — They should be men who will be willing to exempt any person in a district who will be distressed by paying the tuition of his children — men who will readily levy a tax upon a district whenever necessary — Men who will say that every child of persons of limited means, especially in winter must be in school. Such are the men who are wanted for the Trustees of School Districts. They will employ good Teachers, and exert themselves that the school may do good.— Ed. Telegraph.

Mr. Editor,— I wish to present a few facts through your columns to the public, with regard to our present school system. I feel very deeply the importance of making Education general; and I think there are some objections to the present system, inasmuch as it does not do this. I will not pretend to say but what the present law would make education general if its design was carried out according to the intentions of those who made it; but there are some things left discretionary with the officers of the district, which in many cases operate very injuriously upon the cause of Education. Quite a number of such cases have come within my own observation, and I will name a few only of them.

In one district which I am well acquainted, there are at the present time some six or eight children staying from school, because their parents are unable to pay their " school bills," and the trustees do not give them the benefit of the law as it was undoubtedly intended they should have.

Another case occurred in the northern part of the county. The individual was a poor mechanic. He had a large family, and wished to give his children as much education as possible. He sent them to school; but when the quarter ended, he was unable to pay only a part of his bill, yet the trustees refused to give him clear without he paid the whole bill. Consequently, a " Rate-bill " was made out, and the most useful articles he had for carrying on his trade, were taken and advertised for sale. On the first day of the sale, from some cause or other, I know not what, there were no purchasers present. But do you think these benevolent-hearted individuals were satisfied? Not they! The district had committed an important trust to their care, and they must not suffer a poor man to become a tax upon the district, so the day of sale was postponed! But these public spirited men were finally prevented from doing their work of benevolence, by an officer even higher in authority than themselves.

A teacher a few days ago, called upon a poor man and asked him why he had taken his children from school? He replied that he could not pay his school bill. The Teacher, more benevolent than his employers, (although he could not afford it) told him to send them to school, and what he did not pay or could not, he need not trouble himself about.

These are only a few of the great number of cases which has come within my observation, of a similar character. It is believed that schools are very often "broken up" by this course of conduct. There are some who are unable to pay the whole of their school bill, and knowing that they will be exacted (in many cases) to the uttermost farthing, they withdraw their children from the school. The school becomes small and is frequently discontinued until a ten dollar Teacher can be employed.

Yours,
H. D.

Poughkeepsie, Feb. 11th, 1847.

—Teachers' Advocate, April 1, 1847

The First Free School

The Waldenses, ancestors to the Vaudois, were the first people in Europe who made regulations as a community, that all the children of every degree should be taught the elementary branches of an education. For ages before the Scotch Parliament in 1494, made enactments which compelled the barons and substantial freeholders to send their sons to school, the Waldenses had taken care that all the children, including those of the poorest goatherds — should have access to some school free of expense. Their Teachers were their pastors, the two professions at that time being hardly separable. In other countries of Europe, learning was saved by the Priesthood from utter extinction for their own use and advantage; these saved it by accretion, but the Vaudois saved it by diffusion. Bernard of the 12th century, thus testifies with regard to them: "The rusticks and laymen in these valleys are taught to argue with and confute their betters upon subjects that they have had no business to meddle with; for they have schools every where in which the meanest of the people are allowed to attend."

New England has tried this free school system for almost two centuries. Its feasibility and utility has been there thoroughly tested — and the people are now convinced, both there and in our own state, that instead of the fool being taught but part of the year by a man called from the plough, or from behind the counter, that it ought to be taught the whole year by a regularly educated professional Teacher.—*Teachers' Advocate, July 9, 1847*

Press Comments

The following are some selections from the newspapers and periodicals commenting upon the constitutional convention:

From Report to Hon N. S. Benton from N. C. Blauvelt,[1] *County Superintendent Rockland County, October 22, 1845*

The want of education never was more visible to the people than at present. Its force is now just beginning to be felt. The excitement, which was so warmly agitated in this county during the last fall, has succeeded admirably in waking up the public mind to the importance of educating the people not only, but devising means for the accomplishment of so worthy an object. And were I called upon now to venture my opinion upon the probable conclusion to which the majority of the opposition have arrived, I could not but say, that they are favorable to the main features of our present system, in comparison with the system as administered at any period previous to its present organization.

It is not my object nor yet my wish to discuss the subject, yet I must here declare, that the public mind is rapidly verging towards a system of free schools, where a thorough English education shall be provided for every individual at the expense of the property of the people. It is the only system which is calculated effectually to secure a proper education to the masses, and under it a perfect and permanent safeguard to the free institutions of our country. That the scheme is practicable and salutary in the end to be attained, to wit, the affording of a proper education to all, a complete preparation for all the social and civil relations of life, I need only refer you to the public schools of the city of New York, whose character is not only daily progressing, but whose present condition will vie with that of any others in the state. The popular feeling of Rockland county is now on the side of free schools.—*District School Journal, August 1846*

Free Schools

At a recent state convention of county superintendents held at Albany, a resolution was adopted recommending the establishment of free public schools throughout the State. It was also resolved to bring the subjects in a special manner before the constitutional convention for its deliberate consideration.

The plan of adopting the system of making our public schools free to all,

---

[1] Nicholas C. Blauvelt was born July 22, 1814, near Spring Valley, and his childhood was passed on his father's farm. At a very early age he was sent to the district school and, having a natural aptitude for learning, he soon mastered the alphabet and astonished his parents by his proficiency. At the age of ten years he was taken to New York, and being placed in a select school taught by Isaac D. Cole, began the study of Latin. He remained there three months and was then sent to the New York High School, which was at that time considered the best in the city. When thirteen years old he was sent to the grammar school connected with Rutgers College, and in two years was prepared to enter college. By the advice of friends he remained in the school another year, joined the sophomore class and was graduated in 1833. It was the desire of his parents to have him enter the ministry, but not feeling prepared for that holy calling, he resolved to study medicine; but his parents objecting to this, he began teaching, and continued in this employment till 1841, when he was appointed by the board of supervisors to the office of county superintendent of common schools. In this position he remained three years. At the end of this time the office was abolished, and Mr Blauvelt resumed his former occupation, continuing to teach until 1852. In the fall of that year he was elected member of Assembly, where he served on the committee for colleges and common schools. In 1853 he established a mercantile business in Spring Valley, and continued it for ten or twelve years. In 1855 he was elected supervisor of the town of Ramapo, and was reelected the succeeding year. In 1863 he was elected school commissioner and held the office two terms, and was for fifteen years clerk of the board of supervisors. Deeply interested in the cause of education, he was instrumental in awakening the minds of his fellow citizens to the necessity of better school accommodation, and the result of his labors was the establishment of the union school of Spring Valley, and Mr Blauvelt was a member of the first board of education.

NICHOLAS BLAUVELT
(From "History of Rockland County" by Rev. David Cole)

is beginning to be talked of with much earnestness. The matter was most fully discussed by the enlightened educationists assembled in the recent convention. To establish free schools is of course to levy a tax for the amount it would require to sustain them, and we may very naturally look for the determined and persevering hostility to the measure from those not sufficiently patriotic to give up a tithe of their income for the public good. On the other hand, the poor, those in that happy medium possessing neither riches nor poverty, and those willing to make sacrifices for the common good, may be expected to advocate the plan.

For ourselves, we go in for the most perfect system of education, that which will most thoroughly and universally wake up the mind of the nation, and establish its morals, cost what it may. The money contributed to the thorough, intellectual and moral education of the poor, is like "bread cast upon the waters," to return again after many days. Men of property will do well not to condemn the plan of free public schools without canvassing the subject fairly. If we would sustain and increase the value of our property we must sustain the Republic, and if we would sustain the Republic, we must sustain schools for the people. If the system of free schools will more generally diffuse the blessings of education, then we hope to see it generally supported.—*Elmira Republican*

Prospects of a Free School System for the State

The friends of education will be highly gratified to learn that provisions will without doubt be made in the new Constitution for a system of Free Schools. The New York Morning News, in speaking of the Educational Committee, says:

Messrs Nicoll and Hunt of this city are on the Committee on Education, the former being Chairman; and if their associates are of kindred sentiments we may reasonably anticipate that the most enlightened and liberal provisions will be urged in relation to this vital and interesting subject.

The Committee is composed of Messrs Nicoll of New York, Munro of Onondaga, Bowdish of Montgomery, Young of Wyoming, Tuthill of Orange, Willard of Albany, and Hunt of New York.

We have no doubt of a report unanimously recommending a Free School System, liberally endowed and under an independent and efficient supervision. Mr Bowdish has already given ample evidence of sound and correct views on this subject. Judge Munro is a devoted friend of education and a representative of a *Free School County,* and hails from a town so alive to this great question, that its electors passed a resolution strongly recommending it as the great democratic measure of the age. The late State Convention of County Superintendents afforded an opportunity for Dr Willard to prove himself an able advocate for the system. His experience as County Superintendent has confirmed his opinions, and convinced him that an entire Free School System is the only one worthy of an entire Free People.— It was a source of gratification to us that his name was associated with that Committee, for we felt assured that the subject would be fully presented and fairly discussed. Of the other members of the Committee we have no personal knowledge, except that Mr Young is highly esteemed in his own County as a friend to education and as a man of sound judgment.

We therefore expect that this great subject will be fully and fairly discussed in the Committee, and that a strong report, unanimously recommending a Free School System under an independent and efficient supervision, as one of the amendments to the new Constitution.— *Teachers' Advocate, June 24, 1846*

Onondaga County Common School Association

A report was received from E. Cooper, chairman of the Committee on the Free Schools, which was adopted. The report was accompanied by the following resolutions, which were passed unanimously:

Whereas, Thorough and universal education is indispensably necessary to the support of a free Government, and is the only means of qualifying the mass of the people for developing the resources of the country, and for the full enjoyment of the blessings conferred by a well governed and intelligent republic, therefore

Resolved, That we regard a *free common school system,* with ample and permanent provisions for its support, as the great democratic measure of the age, demanded alike by the dictate of sound policy and the voice of a Heaven-born humanity; — a measure without which the integrity of our own free institutions cannot be preserved, and therefore should be provided for in the *fundamental law of the State.*— *Teachers' Advocate, July 15, 1846*

Free Schools

The Convention now in session at Albany, cannot, among the many subjects of their attention, select one of more importance in the amelioration of the masses and the perpetuity of free and economical government, than that of our future system of schools. In the progress of school reform, and in the devotion of ardent, zealous and able advocates of the cause, without distinction of party, New York is second to no State in the Union — pointing to her eleven thousand schools, she may well exclaim, as did the Roman matron, "these are my jewels." But perfection in human affairs has not, as yet, been attained; and we submit to the wisdom of the framers of our State Constitution, whether a system of Free Schools may not be devised, which will diffuse the light of intelligence to the remotest corners of our State, "dispensing its blessings like the dews of Heaven," upon which all, without distinction of caste or condition. The obstacles are not few which the poor now encounter in obtaining the simplest rudiments of book instruction, and the eminent men springing from that class, attain the object of their ambition, only through the exercise of unbending, indomitable resolution, which mankind rarely possess.

Such a system will constitute the only firm basis of social and political equality — the protection of property and the rights of persons, the preservation of good order, and obedience to the laws — the proper formation and limit of those laws; in short, the well being of community, and the successful issue of the experiment of self-government, demand that the means of education be proffered to the whole people.— *Teachers' Advocate, August 12, 1846*

The Free School System

Any individual at all conversant with the practical operation of the existing system, can readily refer to instances of frequent occurrence, where parents in comparatively indigent circumstances, but with large families of children of suitable age for common school instruction, are virtually compelled to keep their children at home, either from the capricious refusal of trustees to exempt them, wholly or in part, from the payment of their share of the rate bill, or from an unwillingness, growing out of an honest feeling of pride, to claim such exemption.

There is another mode, also, by which the expenses of the school are, in many instances, greatly enhanced by those who avail themselves of its privileges, and for which no adequate remedy can be devised under the present state of things. The term commences under the most flattering auspices, and the school is filled up with the children of the district. Soon, however, difficulties begin to be started — the teacher does not meet the expectation of some of his employers — the children first of one family and then another are gradually withdrawn — dissensions ensue — and before the term finally closes, the school has, perhaps, dwindled down to a mere fraction of its original size. Had the attendance been constant and regular, the rate bills would have been trifling — while under existing circumstances — circumstances over which those who have persisted in sending their children to school, could have exercised no possible control — the factions and discontented portion of the district who have virtually succeeded in breaking up the school, and paralyzing its capacity of usefulness, are charged in the rate bill only for the time they have actually sent — leaving those who have been the uniform and steady supporters of the school to pay a greatly augmented sum, and to sustain the chief burden of its maintenance. These are cases of frequent occurrence in the country districts; and their tendency is unfavorable in the extreme to the welfare and prosperity of the schools. A premium is, in fact, held out for their desertion: and amid the prevalence of district controversies and dissentions arising out of the local administration of the system, no readier or more effective mode presents itself to the respective combatants of annoying each other, than by thus skilfully transferring the pecuniary burden of the school to the shoulders of those who, while perhaps they may be the most desirous of availing themselves of the benefits of education thus placed within the reach of their children, are the least able to defray its increased expenses.

The only adequate remedy for these pervading evils is, we are convinced, to be found in the adoption of an enlightened system of Free Schools, to be supported at the public expense, from the public funds, and from the taxable property of the community generally.—*District School Journal, July 1846*

Teacher's Convention

Thursday, August 20, 9 A. M.

Called to order by J. W. Bulkeley, 1st Vice President.

Prayer by Rev. Mr Shepherd.

Minutes read and approved.

Mr Haywood, of Rensselaer co., presented a report on the School System, in which he took decided ground for free schools, and closed with the following resolution:

Resolved, That the school system of every Christian State should recognize the Bible as the standard of morals, the great source of truth.

Resolved, That we look with much interest to the action of the Constitutional Convention on the school system and we cordially approve that feature in the committee's report which would remove the tax on attendance and make the schools free. The people, we believe, are ready for the question.

These resolutions were adopted.

Mr Brittian offered the following resolution:

Resolved, That those Union Schools which sustain an Academical Department, should receive an appropriation from the Literature Fund in the same manner and on the same conditions as the regularly incorporated academies.

After an eloquent advocacy by Prof. Davis, Mr Freeman offered the following substitute:

Resolved, That the Union Schools, and all other literary institutions receiving aid from State, should be equally free to all and on the same terms as the Common Schools.— *Utica Daily Gazette, August 21, 1846*

Resolutions Adopted at First Annual Meeting of New York State Teachers Association, Utica, August 19, 1846

Resolved, That we fully and cordially approve of the propositions submitted by the committee on education, etc., to the State convention, now in session, for the establishment by law of a system of Free Schools, and for the free education of every child of the State, in the common schools now established, or hereafter to be established therein; and that we earnestly recommend its adoption by the Convention, and its sanction by the people, in the full conviction that the prosperity and well being of all our institutions, civil, social and religious, and that the welfare and happiness of the people, individually and collectively, are inseparably identified with the universal diffusion of sound knowledge and the inculcation of virtuous principles.

Resolved, That a copy of these resolutions, duly certified by the officers of this Association, be forwarded by the Secretaries to the President of the State Constitutional Convention, with a request that they be laid before that honorable body.

Free School System

Friend Cooper — It is with great pleasure that I have witnessed the presentation and advocacy of the system of Free Schools by the two Educational papers in this State.— The session of the Constitutional Convention makes this an appropriate period for the examination of this subject. The action of the recent State Convention of Co. Superintendents, was as favorable as could have been anticipated, or perhaps desired. I trust the subject will be considered by the Teachers' State Convention of this summer.

Although, Mr Editor, my peculiar field of labor is not in the cause of education, yet I can never forget the ties which my Teachers' life and associations have awakened; besides, it is the peculiar province of all who boast the honor of American citizenship to be connected with, and interested in, all that pertains to the education of the people. America is the country where the experiment of a thorough education of the masses is destined to be tried.

Strange, yet not stranger than true, that among the hundreds of nations that have sprung up, flourished and decayed; not one yet ever tested the results of a systematic and universal education of their people. New York has done much toward this object — is doing more — so has the land of the Pilgrims. But how far are we, although acknowledged to be taking the lead in educational enterprise and improvement, of any of our sister states, and consequently of the world, from the summit of *universal education*. And by education, I do not mean the "read, write and cipher" definition, but the philosophic one — the full and harmonious development of man's noble faculties, physical, intellectual and moral. Rome, cultivated in her early days, to considerable perfection, the physical of man — in her latter days, the intellectual; but the education of the moral faculties was never pursued to any great extent. The same may be said of Greece; in part of Egypt and the Saracens. But to a great extent, the beauties and unattainable perfections of the classic intellect of ancient days, exist only in the hereditary imagination of those so happy as to be able to appreciate them, and from the indistinctness and reverence with which we survey the Ancients, made venerable by the lapse of ages. Rome with all her glory — Greece, with all her fond and inspiring associations — Egpyt, once the centre of civilization and science; the Oriental nations, crowned with the honors of early Saracen literature — never dreamed of the untold and mighty effects of the Universal and thorough Education of the whole people.

We want no Helots as slaves, degraded, ignorant and down-trodden — but that all wearing the image of humanity, claiming likeness to their Grand Original, should be educated by the State. The degradation and moral depravity of any portion of community exerts its blighting influence, not only upon its unfortunate victims; but reacts with demoralizing tendencies upon the whole social fabric.

America seems marked out by the course of events as the appropriate land where improvements and reforms in Government, education and social organization are to be first tested. We are the most intelligent people on earth — the most active, enterprising and moral; why should we not solve the problems of man's progression with the greatest assurances of success. Our march is "onward and upward," he who dreams that the ultimatum of improvement in government, education and social policy are already attained, will soon be disappointed by the irresistably onward advance of the progressive energies of the American people. Republicanism is a great step from monarchy or any government of the few. And even now, in old England, the purpose is seriously made by one party to substitute a natural elective Aristocracy after the plan of the American Senate, for the hereditary House of Lords! With the increased democracy of our institutions should advance the equality and universality of education. With Universal Suffrage should be associated Universal Education.

It was a remark of the Revolutionary days, that education formed the basis of democratic freedom. It is a truth hallowed by its origin, and one we may well repeat and profit by; when through ignorance or general vice the masses of our people become degraded, O! where will be the glories of our democracy, the comparative perfection of our institutions? Wherein is the tyranny of a vicious mass of people preferable to that of a King? the pernicious effects are the same, except that the one possesses the power and inherent remedy of self-redress.

The genius of our institutions demands that the portals of education should be free as the air we breathe. Why is our government so much superior to the South American Republics? It consists only in the superiority of the people. And wherein does this superiority exist, as much as in the education of the people? O! if there is one boon I could obtain for my own dear land, if it could be purchased at the expense of toil, slavery, of life itself; it should be obtained, and America be blessed with Universal Education. This wild theory, this transcendentalism," I would purchase at any price. "Without it we are dead — or we live only to servitude "— with it we shall continue to be the guiding nation of the world — the peaceful missionaries of liberty, elevation and education — the transformers of the serfs and vassals of feudal ages to the noblemen of Nature —American Freemen. Ere long the announcement —" I am an American citizen," shall convey to the world not only the idea of an independent freeman, but of a refined, intelligent and educated man. Europe, Asia and Africa will look with wonder, admiration and awe, upon the beings that inhabit our land!

WILLIAM BARNES

Albany, June 24, 1846

— *Teachers' Advocate, July 15, 1846*

School System for a Free People

The following is the resolution appended to the excellent Report on the School System adopted by the State Teachers' Association, and published in our last:

Resolved, That we look with much interest to the action of the Constitutional Convention on the school system, and we cordially approve that feature in the Committee's report, which would remove the tax on attendance and make the schools free.

There is no doubt that the people are deeply interested in the action of the Convention in reference to this great question. A few days and their labors will be closed, but their work will be far from being finished, unless they make ample and permanent provisions for the free education of every child in the State, and place the workings of the system under the supervision of an officer whose whole attention shall be given to the subject — who will thus be enabled to study to improve its details and enlarge the benefits which are calculated to be effected by a liberal and thorough Common School organization.

In a State of the size and importance of New York, the school department should be independent and unembarrassed. Every thing connected with the educational interests of the people should be collected, and that which is calculated to perfect our system, whether in the details of its organization or in the means of bringing the mass to appreciate and avail themselves of its provisions, should be spread before the people.

It requires much wisdom, much experience, and a correct knowledge of mankind, to direct the educational interests of the people — it requires a sound and discriminating judgment to keep the mass united in their efforts, and a great amount of labor to keep the machinery of a thorough, however simple, school law in full force. There should be no confusion, no discrepancies in the decisions, no contradictions in the opinions advanced. A full and perfect record of the past should be kept to throw its light upon the requirements of the present. This cannot be done without a competent officer amply assisted in the duties of the department.

The office of the Secretary of State being strictly a political one, must be filled by the dominant party. A new incumbent is placed ex-officio, in charge of our common school interests, whenever one party triumphs over the rest. The evils of a frequent change at the head of the school department have not been as apparent as they would have been were it not that the deputy has held his post more permanently. He has kept the run of the business, understands what has been done, not so much from the meagre records of what has been transacted, as from his remembrance of what he has done, and his judgment direct him in regard to it, to what his memory may fail to recall. He would probably have decided an important question in this way, and therefore he is enabled to form some conception of what will render present decision consonant with a former one. Now we wish to be understood, not as censuring the State Superintendents, or the devoted and faithful deputy. The former have been removed by the fluctuations of party, almost as soon as they became acquainted with the details and manner of working the system — the latter has ruined his health in performing the labor — the real drudgery of the office, and yet there are no records of the important correspondence between the department and such of the 11,000 schools as have had occasion to apply to it for information and encouragement. Every commercial or manufacturing establishment of any business pretensions, keeps a copy of his own correspondence, but not so with the school department of the great State of New York, and simply because generous provisions have not been made to give it the means of doing its business in a safe and correct manner.

Should the present able and judicious officer be removed, and at the same time the devoted and experienced deputy, is there a man in the State capable of conducting the business of the department in such a manner as not to conflict with the past? The records of the department should be full and correct, and the experience of each year should be made to throw its rays upon the future. The only way to effect this, will be to divorce the school department from all the other departments of the government, to make the office of State Superintendent of schools independent and permanent to fill it with a man possessing educational, instead of political character, to give him a competent deputy and requisite number of clerks to transact with accuracy all the business of the department, and to make suitable provisions for a free intercourse with the people. To whom shall we look for the outline of a reform like this, unless to the Convention. How can we hope for their action on this important question, unless they cease their " much speaking " and " hobby riding."

We make this our last appeal, and we believe we present the sentiments and wishes of a large majority of those who will soon be called upon to give their approval or disapproval of the Constitution they have hoped their Convention would complete. The course taken on the separation of these important offices cannot be justified even by the Convention itself. It was presumed that the people had not investigated the question of separating the two offices, and of giving to that of Superintendent of Schools the dignity and permanency of being created by the Constitution, merely because it had not enlisted "hobby riders" in its favor. Unlike the judiciary question, it does not open the door for demagogues; but the interests of society and the permanency of our institutions require these provisions. The mass are beginning to demand it, and will not, it is hoped, accept a constitution which does not secure them an ample *free school system* whose supervision and management shall be unencumbered by the duties of a less important office of the government.—*Teachers' Advocate, October 1, 1846*

Views of Superintendents

It was by a narrow margin that the free schools failed to receive the constitutional sanction in 1846. Those interested in this great movement did not despair and we find N. S. Benton, Superintendent of Common Schools (December 31, 1847), making the following statements.

In his annual report to the Legislature, under date of January 12, 1847, Superintendent Benton makes the following statements:

In New York, Brooklyn, Rochester and Buffalo, these schools are free, and the charges for their support and for the erection and repairing of school houses, exceeding the public money annually apportioned, are defrayed by tax upon the real and personal property therein. . . .

No better plan of general organization and supervision, under a form of government depending entirely upon the popular will, has been or probably can be devised, capable of producing the astonishing results, annually exhibited in the documents accompanying the reports from this department for several years past; and while some are opposed, and others are in doubt, in respect to its great utility and efficiency, in arousing the active energies of a whole people, and directing those energies in the performance of an important duty, other States are assimilating their organizations to ours, and are modifying their laws to produce, if practicable, corresponding results. Why then should we abandon a system of inspection and superintendence so prolific of advantages and so esteemed? A review of the past and present condition of our public schools, can not fail to produce a strong conviction of their great usefulness; and no better system of instruction can be devised, to bring its benefits and its blessings within the reach of every one who may desire to embrace them, except schools entirely *free*. It provides instruction in all the elementary and useful branches of education, and in the common language of the country; and seeks to prepare the youth of the State for all the usual employments of life and to imbue them with a full knowledge of their duties and obligations, as citizens and constituent members of a great and growing community.

Extract from a report of Superintendent Benton under date of December 31, 1847:

The law requires that a school shall have been kept in a district four months in the preceding year by a licensed teacher to entitle it to an apportionment of school moneys; and schools are taught during what are now

WILLIAM BARNES

NATHANIEL S. BENTON
Secretary of State and Commissioner of Common Schools, 1845–47

called winter and summer terms, continuing from three to four, and some times five months each; and it certainly appears somewhat remarkable that, with all the advantages our system presents, not *one-seventh* of the children reported between five and sixteen years of age, attend the schools even six months.

The city of New York, with her admirable system of free schools, does not present to us this unfavorable and humiliating picture. In that city one-fourth of all the children reported attended school during the past year. There are other cities in the State where the schools are *free,* presenting the same favorable results. . . .

The Legislature have, heretofore, not been unmindful of the condition of these children; and by the 15th section of the act, chapter 260 of the Laws of 1841, schools for colored children may be established in any city or town in the State, which must be under the charge of the trustees of the districts in which they may be established. The Superintendent respectfully submits that as the act of 1847 provides for the establishement of *free* schools for this class of children, the object would be more successfully attained by applying the public bounty in aid of the schools already established, and which may be hereafter established under the provisions of the general school laws of the State, than it would be by continuing the appropriation in its present shape.

In our country, and more particularly in our State the government and the people are identical; and to treat this great trust fund as the property of the government separate from or independent of the constituency, would be violating a fundamental maxim of our institutions; and the appropriation of the net income of the fund to the maintenance of our public schools cannot justly be viewed in the light of a donation to the people. It is respectfully submitted that it would not be proper to consider a direct appropriation from the treasury to such an object a gratuity. If it be, then all our laws establishing free schools in cities and other localities are wrong in principle, and should be repealed.

Extract from a report of Superintendent Benton under date of December 31, 1847:

Free schools. These schools have been established by law in the cities of New York, Brooklyn, Buffalo, and Rochester, in the town of Williamsburgh and in the village of Poughkeepsie. The city of Albany, where a sum less than $200 was paid during the last year on rate bills, may be included among the *free* school cities. The official reports made to this office from the above places, do not afford data sufficiently correct and full to allow an accurate statement to be presented, showing the difference in the expense of tuition, in all these cities and localities, compared with other counties or the remaining portions of the same counties, in which free schools have been partially established.

A comparative statement cannot be presented, showing the whole expense incurred under our system, where the teachers' wages are partly paid by rate bills; because we have no means of ascertaining the amount of taxes raised in the districts, for the erection and repair of school houses, and the expenses of collecting those taxes and the rate bills for teachers' wages, which are very considerable and are legitimate items to be taken into consideration. Excluding the cities of Albany, Brooklyn, Buffalo, Hudson, New York, Rochester, Schenectady, Troy and Utica and the town of Williamsburgh, where the schools have been established and are conducted under the provisions of special and local laws, we have 10,801 school districts in which schools were taught in 1846, on an average of eight months; whole number of children taught during some part of the year in those districts, 631,787; number between 5 and 16 years of age, 571,859; and the whole amount of public money expended for teacher's wages, including the contributions by rate bills, was $859,441.10, averaging $1.36 for each pupil taught. In the city of New York, the average was $1.67 for twelve months tuition; in Brooklyn, $1.84; Buffalo, $1.51; Rochester, $1.80, and Williamsburgh, $1.85; showing the average expense, under the rate bill system, to be materially higher, taking into consideration the number of months schooling, than under the free school plan. According to the rate paid in the counties, a school taught twelve months would average $2.04 for each pupil. The extension of free schools in the State is progressing moderately; and laws are passed nearly every session of the Legislature, providing for their establishment in populous and wealthy villages; while the poorer and less populous districts, in the same towns, are left to struggle on, from year to year, in the best way they can — sustaining a school perhaps only four months in the year, to secure the next apportionment of the public moneys. Is this policy just?— is it right to discriminate in this manner, between the school children of the State? Why should ample provision be made for the children residing in particular localities, and others turned over to the naked bounties of the State; which, although munificent in the aggregate, are only sufficient to pay a few weeks tuition for each child? This great and essential question turns simply on the mode of taxation; by changing this and requiring the boards of supervisor, to raise upon the counties respectively, a sum equal to the amount apportioned from the treasury to each county for the support of schools, and upon the towns another sum equal to the apportionment of such town from the school fund, which would increase the local taxation upon the counties, not to exceed five-tenths of a mill on the valuation in any county, and our schools might be rendered nearly *free* to every child in the State.

This view may be illustrated by stating the actual results in two counties, irrespective of the sums apportioned and raised for the support of libraries.

Ontario county — In 1846, the amount of public money received and applied to the payment of teachers' wages, was.. $8,829 28
Amount paid on rate bills................................ 12,861 06

Whole sum paid for teachers' wages.................... $21,690 34

The whole number of children returned as having been taught some portion of the year, was 14,152, and the number reported between 5 and 16 years of age, was 11,466. By charging a fixed tuition fee of fifty cents each term, on the assumption that there will be two school terms in each district during the year, and take either of the above aggregates of children, and with the proposed charge, the following results will be obtained:

Whole amount appropriated by the State, after deducting one-fifth for library money	$3,596 64
Equal amount to be assessed on the county..................	3,596 64
Equal amount to be assessed on town.......................	3,596 64
	$10,789 92
Tuition fee of fifty cents on 11,466 children, assuming that this number will be entered at each winter and summer term	11,466 00
Aggregate of receipts to pay teachers' wages................	$22,255 92
Deduct amount actually paid as above......................	21,690 34
Leaving a surplus of......................................	$565 58

But if we take 14,152 as the number of children who will enter the schools at each term, the surplus would amount to $3,251.58. The corrected aggregate valuations in this county amounted in 1846 to $12,629,547.

Washington county — The amount of public money received and applied to the payment of teachers' wages during the same year, was... $7,344 49
Amount paid on rate bills.................................. 9,576 65

$16,921 14

Number of children taught some portion of the year, 12,814. Number of children between the school ages, 11,018

Whole amount of money appropriated by the State deducting one-fifth for library money...............................	$3,424 99
Equal amount to be assessed on county.....................	3,424 99
Equal amount to be assessed on towns......................	3,424 99
	$10,274 97
Tuition fee of fifty cents on 11,018 children, on the assumption before stated	11,018 00
Aggregate of receipts to pay teachers' wages................	$21,292 97
Deduct payments for teachers' wages in 1846...............	16,921 14
In this county there would be a surplus of....................	$4,371 83

which would be increased, if the tuition fee be charged or estimated on the number of children taught during the year.

The amount received and expended for teachers' wages in Ontario county was $1,736 more than the public money apportioned and the "equal sum" raised on the towns; and in Washington county, $494.51; and this excess was probably raised by voluntary taxes in the towns, in both cases. The average number of months' schooling appears to be the same in both counties. The corrected aggregate valuations in Washington, in 1846, stood at $6,173,997, which is about half of the amount given in Ontario.

The plan here suggested would secure, to a district containing 40 school children, an annual fund of at least $70.00 for the payment of teachers' wages, and it might with safety be estimated higher. It is simple, and avoids the necessity of issuing rate bills and saves the collector's fees on the warrant; as each pupil on entering the school will be required to pay a stipulated tuition fee in advance, as is now the practice in most of the academies in the State. It will secure a larger and more uniform attendance of scholars, and prevent the schools from being broken up by the withdrawal of children, under the apprehension that the rate bills will be unreasonably high, and remove many of the causes of contention and litigation in the districts, that exist under the present mode of providing compensation for teachers. The amount raised in the county, in the manner provided for levying State and county taxes, would subject at least $50,000,000 of corporate property to taxation for the benefit of the schools in the whole county, which is now enjoyed by the towns and cities, where those corporations are located or carry on business. Should this scheme be adopted, it will not be necessary to change or modify materially the present organization. The school moneys may be apportioned, as they now are, to the towns, on the ratio of population, and to the districts, according to the number of children residing in each. The school trustees should, however, be required to state in their annual reports, not only the names of the parents and guardians of children belonging to the district, but the number and names of such children in full, residing in the family of each inhabitant. They should also state the names of the school children, if any, in their district, that in their opinion ought to be exempted from the payment of the tuition fee; and these reports should be verified by the trustees, or at least two of them. It will probably be thought advisable to vest the power of apportioning these school moneys among the districts in some local board of the town, requiring such board to examine the trustees' reports and make the necessary inquiries as to any matters set forth in them, to correct any mistakes, and prevent duplicate returns of school children.

Excluding the city of New York, the estimates and computations contained in the statement below, show the results attainable by adopting the plan suggested.

Whole amount of public moneys apportioned to the remaining counties in 1846	$198,654 13
Proposed amount to be raised in counties.....................	198,654 13
Equal sum raised in the towns..............................	198,654 13
Aggregate amount of distribution.......................	$595,962 39
In the remaining 58 counties, there were 667,140 children taught in 1846, and assuming that each pays a tuition fee of 50 cents, a fund is raised of.......................................	333,570 00
Which added to the above makes a total of...............	$929,532 39
Whole amount of public money raised and expended for teachers' wages in 1846.......... $461,177 20	
Amount paid on rate bills same year............ 462,840 44	
	$924,017 64
	$5,514 75

It is perfectly safe to assume, that at least one half of the above number taught, attended the schools two terms, or were entered two terms, and would therefore be chargeable with the additional tuition or entrance fee of 50 cents, say.... $166,785 00

Excess produced $172,299 75

If we adopt the last method, in making the statements for Ontario and Washington counties, it will be found that in the former the amount paid for teachers' wages exceeds the fund produced $286.42; while in the latter the fund produced exceeds the amount actually paid $33.35. But this can not be material; *that is certain which can be made so;* and by defining the periods of the school terms and fixing the amount of the entrance or tuition fee, an adequate sum will be raised to sustain the schools an additional month in each year throughout the State.

Our fellow citizens have heretofore cheerfully acquiesced in the imposition of a tax to support the government and *sustain* the *credit* of the State, of more than *twice* the amount proposed to be raised in the plan suggested. What improvement, internal or external, is more worthy of the fostering care of the Legislature or of greater importance to the community, than the *mental* improvement of those who are soon to exercise all the privileges of citizens, and wield the destinies of the State. It would be an unjust impeachment of the patriotism and good sense of the people, to suppose they would not cheerfully embrace and cordially approve any reasonable measures which will reflect so much honor on the present, and confer such endearing benefits on the future.

The abundant provision made by the Constitution for the payment of the interest on and final extinguishment of *all* the General Fund and canal debt of the State, as well as for defraying the necessary expenses of the government, must remove all apprehension, if any was ever entertained, of a future tax being imposed for the support of government.

A powerful interest will be created in favor of the successful progress of our common schools; for those who contribute mainly to the increase of the proposed fund, will have children to educate, and will seek to do this out of the moneys they have already paid. The tuition fee will be so small for each scholar, that very few exemptions will be required; and the attendance " for four and less than six months," instead of being only 153,513 in the whole State, will be increased to three times that number. An annual tax of about seven-tenths of a mill on the valuations would, with the increased distributions from the Common School Fund, supply ample means to establish and support free schools, from six to eight months in every school district in the State.

Mr William A. Walker, County Superintendent of Common Schools for New York city in his report dated October 16, 1847, says:

Under another act of the last session the board of education are now about establishing a system of evening free schools " for the gratuitous education of apprentices and others, whose daily avocations prevent their attending the ward or public schools now provided by law." The beneficial provisions of this act are about being carried into effect, by the opening of five evening schools in different sections of the city, which will probably go into operation early in the coming month, under regulations and on a plan promising success, and with a course of study adapted to the peculiar wants of this class of pupils.

By January 1, 1848, free schools had been established in Buffalo. Brooklyn, Poughkeepsie, Rochester and Williamsburg and other cities were added to this list in that year, while the schools in the cities of Albany, Troy and Utica were substantially free. That is to say, approximately one-fourth of the schools of the State were now free.

Mr Benton was succeeded as Superintendent of Common Schools by Christopher Morgan, who assumed his duties January 31, 1848. His administration was distinguished by the great efforts made in the interest of common schools and their development. From the first he endeavored to accomplish two things, namely, the reestablishment of the county superintendent (abolished in 1846), and the establishment of free schools in the broadest sense. He embodies in his first annual report of 1849 both his views and the experience of the Department in reference to these great questions.

The Present System

The mode of supporting a school under the present system is as follows:
The Trustees employ a qualified teacher for stipulated wages. At the close of his term, they give him an order upon the town superintendent for such portion of the public money, as may have been voted by the district for the term, or in case no vote has been taken, for such portion as they think proper. But in no case can the trustees legally draw for more money than is due the teacher at the date of the order. If the public money is not sufficient to pay the teacher's wages, the trustees proceed to make out a rate-bill for the residue, charging each parent or guardian, according to the number of days' attendance of his children. Under the present law, the trustees have power to exempt indigent persons, and the amount exempted is a charge upon the district, and may be immediately collected by tax, or added to any tax thereafter levied. After the rate-bill is completed, thirty days' notice of its completion is given by the trustees, one of whom must be in attendance, on a day and place appointed in said notice, once a week for two successive weeks, to receive payment; and during the whole of the said thirty days any person may pay to either of the trustees, or to the teacher, the sum charged to him upon the rate-bill. At the expiration of the thirty days, if all the persons named in the rate-bill, have not voluntarily paid, the trustees put it, with their warrant, into the hands of the district collector, who has the same authority to collect it by levy and sale of goods and chattels, as a town collector.

The collector is also authorized to collect fees, not only upon the money paid to him, but upon that paid voluntarily to the trustees and teacher, and he is allowed thirty days to make his return to the trustees.

A more troublesome or vexatious system could not well be devised. A teacher having performed his contract, is yet obliged, unless the trustees advance the money, to wait thirty or sixty days for his pay. The first thirty days' delay under the notice is no advantage to any one. The time of the trustees is spent uselessly. Nothing is gained by payment to the trustees. Is there any other instance upon the statute book in which legislation compels a man to wait sixty days for his wages after he has completed his work? In the absence of any contract, the wages of the laborer are due and payable when his work is done. In the case of the teacher, the payment of his wages is postponed for sixty days after his school is closed, for payment from trustees can not be enforced until the time fixed by law for collection has expired.

A slight error in the apportionment of the rates, or in the legal forms of making it, subjects the trustees to a suit by any one of whom a few cents may have been illegally collected; and, unfortunately, there are not wanting in every town, persons ready to avail themselves of such errors.

The trustees can, if they choose, make out a tax for the amount of exemptions, and the collector is bound to collect it for the trifling fees, upon a five or ten dollar tax list.

A law has been passed, authorizing courts to deny costs to a plaintiff in a suit against trustees, and also authorizing boards of supervisors to order a tax to be assessed upon a district to refund costs and expenses incurred in suits by or against them, on account of the discharge of their official duties. But the law allows them nothing for their responsibility and labor, either in the discharge of their duties, or in the prosecutions, or defense of suits.

Now, a free school system may be devised that shall relieve trustees from the duty of making out rate-bills or tax lists in any case, and from all litigation arising therefrom, and which shall secure to the teacher his pay when his work is done.

It may be made applicable only to the towns, requiring the cities, however, to make their schools free, but leaving them to adopt such an organization as shall be suited to their peculiar wants.

Teachers complain of the rate-bill system, not only because it improperly withholds their wages, but because the trustees find great difficulty in exercising with fidelity, and at the same time satisfactorily, the power of exemption. While the cupidity of the taxpayer is excited, the pride of men of moderate means is aroused, and their sense of independence revolts at being certified and put upon the record as indigent persons.

The rate-bill system requires every person to pay in proportion to the attendance of his children. How strong then is the inducement of many parents, to wink at absence, and truancy, and how little are they inclined to second by parental authority the efforts of the teacher to enforce punctuality and regularity of attendance. The fact that the number of children attending school less than four months, uniformly exceeds the number attending a longer time, furnishes strong evidence for believing that the rate-bill system is the principal cause of the irregular attendance of scholars.

Letters have been addressed to the Superintendent from various parts of the State, urging him to recommend to the Legislature the free school system, and assuring him that the people are ready to sustain the legislature.

Free Schools

A free school is one whose doors are open to all who choose to enter.

In Connecticut, Vermont, Massachusetts, Rhode Island, New Hampshire and Maine, the common schools are nearly free; and in several of the cities and large villages of those States, as well as in some of our own, they are entirely so.

In Indiana the question has been recently submitted to the people, and a large majority decided in favor of free schools. Wisconsin has made early and ample provision for a system of free schools. Even in South Carolina, the schools are free to the free. I believe it is true, that in every state, county, town or village, where the question has been submitted to the decision of the people, they have been found in favor of the free system.

The system of free schools has been urged upon the attention of successive legislatures, but has been met by the assertion, and defeated on the alleged ground, that the people were not prepared for it. This may be true, but I have come to a different conclusion, from the fact that in the eleven localities in this State, where the matter has been submitted to the people, it has in every case met their approval.

The places in which the free schools are maintained, with the population of each in 1845, are as follows:

New York	371,223
Buffalo	29,773
Brooklyn	59,566
Syracuse	10,000
Rochester	25,265
Lansingburgh	4,000
Williamsburgh	11,338
Poughkeepsie	9,000
Flushing	3,918
Newtown	5,521
Bushwick	1,857
	531,453

The whole population of the State in 1845, was 2,604,495. It appears, therefore, that free schools are established in a portion of the State containing one-fifth of the entire population. If to the above we add the following places in which the schools are substantially free, although not by force of law, the above proportion will be increased to one-fourth:

Albany	41,139
Troy	21,709
Utica	12,190
	75,038

FREE SCHOOLS

Sustained by the foregoing statistics, it may be safe to presume, that so large a portion of the State having adopted the free system, and being satisfied with its operation, a majority of the other section of the State is prepared to approve it also.

When it is said that the people are not prepared for free schools, it is only another form of expressing a belief that they are opposed to taxation for their support. There is doubtless a respectable number of persons in every community, averse to taxation, not only for the support of schools, but for all the purposes of government. Still the Superintendent has an abiding confidence, that a majority of the legal voters, and a majority of the tax-payers in this State, would vote to support the schools by taxation. The annual reports of this department furnish reasons for this belief.

The money raised by the supervisors, equal to the amount appropriated from the funds of the State, is cheerfully voted and paid. In addition to this, many towns, at their annual meetings, vote to raise another sum, equal to that required to be raised by general laws. The aggregate sum thus voted in the State every year, is very large:

It was in 1847... $199,000 08
   do   1846... 155,974 20
   do   1845... 195,051 15
   do   1844... 191,473 93
   do   1843... 179,800 52

These sums were raised by the inhabitants of towns voluntarily, and under special laws inserted in the charters of cities and villages. It would appear from this, that the people are not opposed to taxation for free schools. The probable taxation, and the rate per cent necessary to support a free school system, can be ascertained by showing the actual expenses, in the cities and towns where it is established.

In the following table, the first column shows the valuation of the city of town in 1847; the second, the whole amount of school money from all sources; the third, the amount of public money appropriated to the city or town; the fourth, the amount actually raised in the city, or town, besides the public money; and the fifth, the rate of tax upon $100 of valuation:

	Valuation	School Money	Public Money	Amount of Tax	Rate on $100 val.
Albany	$11,387,376	$13,044 50	$4,331 50	$8,713 00	$0 07 5
Brooklyn	29,565,189	26,039 50	6,286 35	19,753 15	0 06 7
Buffalo	8,497,162	21,142 60	3,142 60	18,000 00	0 21 2
Bushwick	755,160	1,089 30	196 00	1,093 30	0 14 6
Flushing	2,398,135	1,593 03	413 60	1,179 43	0 05 0
Hudson	1,159,550	4,084 27	597 11	3,487 16	0 30 0
Newtown	1,989,175	3,743 77	582 75	2,763 54	0 15 0
New York	247,152,303	295,453 80	39,183 58	256,270 22	0 10 4
Poughkeepsie	3,499,191	5,470 66	1,244 58	4,226 08	0 12 0
Rochester	4,634,681	11,808 47	2,666 83	9,141 64	0 19 8
Utica	3,480,766	10,278 16	1,286 70	8,991 46	0 25 8
Williamsburgh ...	3,125,162	8,640 37	320 31	7,443 77	0 23 8

The amount paid on rate bills in Utica, $569.45, and in Albany, $67, is included in the school money for those places. In the other places the schools are free — or substantially so, very little being collected on rate bills in Troy, Lansingburgh, Poughkeepsie, Hudson and Flushing.

With this table, any one can tell what would be his tax for the support of schools in either of the places named. If he is a resident of New York, and is assessed $4,000, he pays a tax of $4.16. If assessed for $100,000, he pays $104. The sum raised in New York for school purposes, appears to be very large, but when it is apportioned upon the tax payers according to their property, it is a very light tax; and it would be light, even if it were doubled. If the common schools were what they should be, and a system of high schools were engrafted upon them, every child could be educated — the poor gratuitously — and the rich at a less expense than at private schools.

In the city of Brooklyn, the free schools are supported at the low rate of six dollars tax upon $10,000 of valuation. In the cities, the support of schools by a general tax, is but the association of all the citizens to effect an object in which all are mutually interested, and which can be better done by a combination of the means of all.

In order to show what would be the operation of the free school system in a town wholly agricultural, we will take the town of Duanesburgh, in Schenectady county, a town in which there is no considerable village, and which will serve as a fair example for the average of the agricultural towns. The valuation of Duanesburgh, in 1847, was $452,165. The amount of school money raised in the town was $346.94. The rate of taxation therefore, was a little more than seven cents and a half upon one hundred dollars of valuation. The amount received from the State was $346.94; the amount paid on rate bills was $987.16, and the amount raised in the town by rate bills and tax, $13,646.31, and the amount of exemptions was $30.31; the whole expense of the schools during the year, therefore, was $1,711.25. To raise this last sum by tax, would require a rate of thirty cents upon a hundred dollars. If then, each district were required to raise a tax equal to the amount apportioned to it by the town superintendent, the sum would be $1,387.76 for the town of Duanesburgh, and sufficient to support a school during eight months in a year in every district, that being the average time in that town. The continual increase of the common school fund would annually diminish the amount of taxation.

It is urged by the opponents of the system, that those who have property are taxed to educate their own, as well as the children of the poor; and that those who are blessed with property, but denied children, are also obliged to contribute something for the education of the indigent. Those who have omitted their duty, or are more fortunate than their neighbors in the possession of property, have no reason to complain of the trifling burthen which good fortune imposes upon them. Are property holders wronged or injured by this system of taxation?

Property is the creature of the law; its ownership is regulated by law; even the income of some kinds of property is limited by law. Human beings are property in South Carolina, and the taxes assessed upon them, and paid out of the earning of their labor, go to the support of free schools, while in this State there can be no property in man.

Land is property, and in civilized countries it constitutes the bulk of all property; yet it is not property in the absence of law. What idea of property in land has a Camanche Indian, or a Calmuck Tartar? To him the land is as free for his roaming, as the air for his breathing, or the water for his drink. The wild Bedouin will guard as his own, his tent, his camel, his wife; but his laws are the keenness of his scimetar, and the fleetness of his steed.

The security of property is one of the paramount objects of government; but how shall that security be attained? By the stern restraints and crushing force of military power? The experience of the last year, in Europe and America, has proven that there is greater security for persons and property in the general intelligence and education of the people, than in an overawing soldiery. Europe has been convulsed — cities have been the scenes of fearful and mortal strife — fields have been laid waste by contending armies — governments have been overthrown — revolution has followed revolution, uncertainty and insecurity are stamped upon all things — political changes have been effected only by civil war and commotion. The people of the United States have effected the choice of a Chief Magistrate, involving a change in the policy of the government; it was accomplished in a day, with the cheerful and peaceful acquiescence of the Union. These are the results of the intelligence and moral elevation of the American people.

There is a moral and intellectual power in the universal education of the people, which furnishes more abiding security for persons and property, than disciplined armies. Property must be taxed to support a soldiery; why should it not then contribute to a system of protection which may preclude the necessity of armies?

Crime and pauperism are too often the results of ignorance. The detection and punishment of the one, and the support of the other, are mainly effected by the imposition of taxes upon property.

Is it not wise, then, to establish a system of education, universal and complete, which may in a great measure, prevent the commission of crime, and avoid the evils of pauperism?

Joseph McKeen, county superintendent of Common Schools, for the city and county of New York, under date of November 1849, in speaking of free schools, discusses the free academy of the city, and the free evening schools as follows:

The Free Academy

This crowning institution of the free school system, in the city, is proceeding warily, admitting scholars semi-annually from the common schools only, and on rigid examinations. It is under the special supervision of a committee of the board of education, and although it is a free school, and most of the pupils within the legal school age, it is supported without any draft from the common school fund of the State, and is therefore not included in the numbers put down in this report.

Evening Schools

During the past year, there have been taught 15 evening free schools, in which were registered 6,976 scholars, of whom 3,451 were under 16 years of age. The schools were continued for 17 weeks, ending in February.

Of these 15 schools, 11 were for boys and 4 for girls. None of the pupils in these schools attended day schools. Of the whole number registered, 5,219 were males, and 1,757 females. Five hundred and eighty-one of them were over 21 years of age, and a large proportion of them foreigners by birth. . . .

Common school education is becoming the great and absorbing topic of the day. How knowledge may be increased and how universally diffused, are great questions which are now earnestly discussed by political economists and statesmen.

Moral and religious teachers have, in past years, been foremost in their advocacy of schools and learning; but statesmen now see that the time is at hand when opinions will be mightier than armies. It is therefore exceedingly important, that opinions should be founded on a basis of knowledge. Politicians are now doing their share for the general enlightenment of the world. Each well educated freeman now believes that there is truth in the adage that " knowledge is power." Universal education would put an end to many unnatural and oppressive inequalities in which some are raised to thrones without a virtue and others degraded to slavery without a crime. It is perhaps not surprising that it is now seen that universal education brings back those extremes of society to a general but elevated level; so that fictitious greatness is diminished and of course disturbed, while the squalidly ignorant are raised to the enjoyment of self respect. Education, in its civil and moral bearings upon men, as individuals, is unmeasured and immense. It diminishes crime, it increases knowledge, it multiplies fountains and resources of enjoyment, that the unlettered man can never know. Who, that realizes all this, can fail fervently to desire the union, the cooperation, the improvement, and the greater prosperity and success of the schools of the city. It is already the glory of these schools that they are free and perennial; and it is believed, that they are in general fully worthy of the public confidence and support.

The confluent tide of immigration, that sends thousands of poor children into our midst every year is increasing. Common sympathy and security require that the immigrant children should be speedily qualified for citizenship. In order for this, they must be assimilated or identified with us, and with our children, that we, as a nation, may stand a united and homogeneous people. Our permanence and security require this. Many of them are poor, and appeal to our humanity. If we leave them uneducated, our sin of omission will bring upon us, as a community, the retributive effects of insecurity of life and property, and an increase of our already enormous taxes for prisons and poor houses. We strive therefore to educate and elevate very one. We open the doors of the school-house, and we should compel them to come in: there is no other hope, either for them or for the country. The morals of our common christianity, in which we all agree, are inculcated in our common schools, and no sect has been allowed to enjoy any preference.

Extract concerning education from the Message of Governor John Young delivered to the Legislature in 1848:

Having discharged our whole duty to common schools, the higher institutions of learning must not be forgotten. Any abatement of the interest

JOHN YOUNG
Governor of New York, 1847–49

of the State in these institutions is to be felt almost exclusively by those, who, in their inquiries after knowledge, most require the paternal care of the State. By the fortunate sons of the affluent it is regarded with entire indifference, but to those who are the "artificers of their own fortune," rowing against a strong current, struggling with poverty and laboring with their hands to procure the means of cultivating their minds, it is matter of vital importance. The doctrine that would deny to these institutions any participation in the moneys, from time to time appropriated by the State to the cause of education, would strengthen the aristocracy of wealth by adding to it the aristocracy of letters.

The protection of property and the encouragement of its acquisition are among the important elements of civilization, but in legislating for a people whose institutions permit any boy, whatever his birth or condition, to aspire to the highest places of honor and usefulness, it is a manifest duty to enact such laws, relating to mental culture, as will place aspirants for honorable promotion upon a footing of equality.

While you should leave nothing undone to improve the character and enlarge the sphere of common schools, I feel assured that the ability of the State, in so far as it can be exerted without prejudice to other interests, will be put forth to furnish facilities for a higher order of attainments in literature and science.

Chapter 6
FREE SCHOOL BILL OF 1849

That the free school principles were actually being crystalized into a statewide movement is well illustrated by the following articles.

As early as 1844 the state convention of county superintendents held in Syracuse indorsed the following report of the committee on free schools:

Free Schools

Your committee on the subject of Free Schools would respectfully report, that every consideration of duty urges the recommendation and adoption of the most speedy and efficient measures for the support of public instruction. It has been ascertained from statistical sources, that more than seven-eighths of this entire community receive their education from common schools; hence it follows, as our schools are, so is the education of the people. When we turn our attention to that important subject, it is very natural for us to consider the condition of our common schools; and, if the system for the support of those schools is found defective, it then becomes our duty to suggest and devise a remedy. While it is admitted that our system of public instruction is a good one, and that the schools under it are making a steady progressive improvement, it is not to be supposed that the system is yet perfect or that the best measures have yet been adopted to perfect and secure an education for all the sons and daughters of our state. Although we have a fund, and an annual appropriation from that fund of two hundred and seventy-five thousand dollars, and an amount equal to that appropriation annually raised by tax for the support of our common schools, yet it is matter of fact, that even this amount is insufficient fully and satisfactorily to answer the object of the appropriation. There are children in the state of New York, and we have reason to believe, in almost every county in the state, who do not attend any school, for the very obvious reason, that their parents have not the means to pay their rate-bill; moreover the self-respect and pride of those parents forbid that they should be exonerated from such payment by the trustees. Nor is this all — without funds from some public source, sufficient to defray the entire expense of our schools; and that too in such a manner as to make them acceptable to the rich and available to the poor, we give rise to the private and select schools; thus creating a distinction in society, that ought not to exist in a community of freemen, who profess to believe in, and attempt to sustain the principles of republican liberty. The question then arises, how shall this evil be averted? Your committee are of opinion, that we should follow the example of many of our sister states; yea, more — that we should follow the noble example of some of the cities of our own state, New York, Poughkeepsie, Buffalo and Rochester, by adopting at once a system of school education that is free — thus affording the facilities for instruction to all, whether rich or poor. Will it be said that the Free School system imposes too heavy a tax on those who have no children to educate? Will it be said that it imposes too heavy a tax on the wealthy? As well might an objection be urged against raising a tax for other purposes; for defraying the expenses of our courts of justice in the trial of criminal causes, the support of the poor, and for levying taxes in time of war for the national defence. It is said that some of the most wealthy citizens of the city of New York, asked, and even petitioned the legislature for the passage of a law, to tax their property for the support of their public schools — thereby making them free for all whether rich or poor. In this they acted upon the principle, that it was unsafe to live in a community, where any portion of the rising generation are suffered to come upon the stage without an education, mental and moral. Ask the citizens and the superintendents of those cities where the free school system has been adopted, and where we are told that the experiment has been successfully and triumphantly tested. Are they willing to abandon it? No — they cling to it with an unyielding tenacity, as the only means of affording an education to all their children, and of securing protection to persons and property. Under all the circumstances of the case, your committee have come to the conclusion, that it is not only a duty but a wise policy to adopt the Free School system, throughout the length and breadth of the entire state, and that it should become a law: Therefore

Resolved, As the sense of this convention, that we are decidedly in favor of a Free School System; believing it better calculated to promote the interest and secure the permanency of our civil and religious institutions, than any other System that can be devised.

The following resolution was offered as a substitute:

Resolved, That the establishment of Free Schools throughout this state, be respectfully commended to the consideration of all of its citizens.

DAVID NAY, *Chairman*

Mr Nay was superintendent of Genesee county.

Views of Superintendents

Under date of October 10, 1844, I. F. Mack, superintendent of common schools for Rochester, says:

In the recent amendments to the school law of the State, providing for the establishment of "union schools," by which the means are in part furnished for at least a thorough English education, and brought to the door of every child; providing also for an efficient supervision of the schools by the appointment of county, and the election of town superintendents, there is doubtless presented to the minds of many a promise of future benefit. But in my view, while the superstructure has been framed in much wisdom, two fundamental evils exist in the system, through which it will ultimately fail of accomplishing its object.

To a man of wealth, residing in a village or densely settled neighborhood, the law offers little less than a bounty for the withdrawal of his patronage from the common, and conferring it upon the private school. In such event he is sure to pay but one rate bill, while by a different course he is liable to pay many. The loss of patronage results also in the loss of sympathy and interest, which to the common school are of vital importance.

Again, the poor man whose circumstances preclude the possibility of his paying rate bills, unwilling to become the marked object of charity, chooses the sad alternative of suffering his children to grow up in ignorance.

Upon the principle that "we most value what costs us most," schools supported by direct tax upon the property of the town, county, or State, would secure the interest and attention of men of wealth and influence; and the poor man, paying an annual tax of fifty cents, or, perhaps, no tax at all, would regard the school as his own, and the right to send the complement of children which often constitutes the "poor man's blessing," as most sacred. The child of the rich and of the poor would then meet, and each, forgetting the distinction which wealth creates, would mutually strive for the mastery. These are some of the benefits arising from the operation of the school system of this city. Indeed, no patriot can pass through the "free public schools" of Rochester without feeling his bosom swell with pleasing emotions a species of agrarianism is there exhibited which every lover of his country or his kind can heartily approve. That the education of any one is more important than that of another, is a principle founded only in pride and selfishness, and well may we doubt the sincerity of that vaunting politician who betrays his hypocrisy in his hostility to "free public schools."

Superintendent Mack, in his annual report of October 1, 1845, says:

The effect of Free Public Schools in a social point of view is most happy. All in them are taught to regard each other as members of the same community — having a common interest and a common country. Here the children of all classes learn to respect each other, and to regard the false distinctions and arrogant pretensions of the few as the fruit of depraved hearts or of improper education.

These schools are emphatically the nurseries of Republican habits, and of those sentiments and feelings, which are indispensable to the existence of a free government. Let us not so far listen to the cry of retrenchment on this subject as to reduce the amount raised for the support of the schools below a sum, which with due regard to economy, shall prove adequate to sustain them. If we would reduce the taxes of the city, let us begin somewhere else. Let us rather diminish our highway tax; for it is better by far that a well educated community travel over bad roads, than for an ignorant and consequently vicious one, to tread on marble. In this, *all* have a common interest. The peace, the safety of our city, requires the influence of the Public Schools.

The following editorial on free schools appeared in the District School Journal, Albany, August 1845:

There are encouraging symptoms in the manifestation of public opinion in various sections of the State tending to show that the ultimate adoption of the FREE SCHOOL SYSTEM, with the full and hearty concurrence of all classes of the community, is not so remote as its friends, in general, are disposed to apprehend. In addition to the able report of Mr Nay, of Genesee, made at the late state convention of county superintendents, which we take pleasure in laying before our readers in our paper of this month, several of the most leading and influential newspapers in different parts of the state, such as the New York Tribune, Westchester Herald, Onondaga Standard and others, have already taken decided and strong ground in favor of the proposed change. The *State Superintendent* has declared himself unequivocally in its favor; and is, we understand, engaged in the collection and preparation of a body of statistical evidence demonstrative not only of its entire practicability and general expediency, but of the numerous advantages, even in a pecuniary point of view, which its adoption is calculated to secure. Bishop Potter, whose eminent services in the cause of popular education, no less than his known practical good sense and sound discrimination, renders his name high authority on such a subject, openly took grounds for the ultimate adoption of this system, more than a year since, at the Rochester convention of county superintendents; and we have reason to believe that his views in this respect have been rather strengthened than weakened by subsequent developments. In short, the most influential and enlightened friends of education throughout the state, without, so far as our knowledge extends, a solitary exception, look forward to the time when this most desirable change can safely and harmoniously be effected, with the most undoubting confidence in its efficacy and beneficial results. The opportunity which the probable assembling of the Convention for the purpose of revising and re-constructing the entire fabric of our state government, will present for the full discussion of this great subject, in all its aspects, present and prospective, is eminently favorable to its early examination and settlement. In view of these facts we would respectfully but earnestly suggest to the friends of education in every section of the state to avail themselves of all suitable occasions at town and county conventions, teachers' associations and institutes, public lectures, etc., to present the question of the substitution for our existing system, that of *free schools,* to be supported and maintained by a general assessment on taxable property — to inform themselves thoroughly of the various facts which have a bearing directly or indirectly, on the subject; and to elicit, by resolutions or otherwise, so far as may be practicable, a general expression of the views, wishes and feelings of the community in this respect. The intelligent, efficient and decided co-operation of the people, without distinction of party or sect, is indispensable to the success of such a measure; and it is therefore of the utmost importance that it should be early, widely and faithfully canvassed. The several county superintendents especially will do well to ascertain fully the matured opinions of their constituents, in season to enable them to represent their views and wishes at the state convention in April next.

In his annual report, dated December 1845, O. G. Steele, superintendent of schools in Buffalo, writes as follows:

I think I am not mistaken in claiming for the city of Buffalo, the honor of being the first city in the State, which established entirely *Free Schools, and practically recognized the doctrine that the education of the children of the Republic, should be provided for by a tax upon its property; thus giving every family an equal right and an equal interest in their success and continued prosperity.* It is true that Free Schools existed in most of our large cities, but they were supported either by private munificence, or by benevolent societies, and were in effect, charity schools. In the city of New York, the

Free Schools were managed and controlled by the public school society, an institution established by benevolent individuals in the city of New York, under the auspices of DeWitt Clinton in 1805, and which has beyond doubt accomplished more for the cause of education than any other institution in the State.

The principle, however, of Free Education based upon the property of the city, and its management forming part of the city government, was not embraced in its organization, and it may well be doubted whether it would have been as successful, under any Legislative action, as it has been under that organization; when the time of its establishment, and the state of public feeling previous to 1840, is taken into account.

The principle is now generally recognized and acted upon in our principal cities, and I most sincerely trust that the time will soon arrive when it will be adopted as the law of the land, and *there is no reason for its adoption in cities that will not apply with equal force to every town and hamlet in the State.*

The subject of popular education has been for the last few years in constant agitation and discussion in all parts of the State, and vast improvement has been the consequence, not only in the condition of the schools themselves, and the details of their management, but in the state of the public mind; as might be expected an abundance of new theories have been broached, all doubtless springing from a sincere desire to advance the standard of education, but generally taking that practical directness and simplicity which is necessary in effecting the intended object. They have not, however, been without their value, in keeping the attention of the public directed to the subject and eliciting valuable suggestions from various quarters upon every detail of its extensive organization. From these various suggestions a general plan of state organization, having for its object a more complete dissemination of common school instruction, based upon the Free principle, and its expense provided for by the taxable property of the State should receive the attention of the friends of the cause, and some plan should be presented to the Legislature for its consideration. My own plan, I will briefly state, not that I suppose it perfect, or entitled to special consideration, but with a hope that some of its suggestions may awake attention in some influential quarter, which will give weight to any portion of it, which may be practical and valuable, and add such further suggestions as may be justified by experience and practical knowledge.

The basis of my plan is *free schools throughout the State,* the expense of which shall be maintained by tax upon the real and personal property of each town, and the management and direction of the schools of each town, to be under the control of the town authorities.

The school houses and furniture of each district to be provided by the local tax upon its taxable property and the current expenses to be raised in the same manner, yearly, or as often as may be necessary.

When any district neglects or refuses to provide the necessary school buildings and furniture, the town authorities ought to have power, and it should be their duty to order the necessary tax and to enforce its collection in the same manner that other town and county taxes are collected; and to direct the construction and furnishing of the school houses. The manner of appointing teachers, to be the same as now provided by law, but the wages of teachers to be paid from the town treasury, on the warrant of the Town Superintendents. *Rate bills to be entirely abolished.* The funds for the payment of teachers' wages to be raised yearly, and included in the regular town or county taxes, and should be sufficient to support a male teacher for six months of the year, and a female teacher for the remaining six months, at a reasonable rate of compensation.

Views of State Superintendents

N. F. Benton, Superintendent of Common Schools in the State of New York, in his report dated January 15, 1846, comments upon the unfortunate fact that there are so many children whose parents are unable to pay the rate bills, and the effect of this upon parents and children. He reports as follows:

The Superintendent feels compelled respectfully to call the attention of the Legislature to a very important provision of the existing laws, which he apprehends has, in practice, become almost a dead letter in many parts of the State. The marked difference between the whole number of children over five and under sixteen years of age reported by the trustees and the reported number under instruction for a period of less than four months, shows that a very considerable portion of the children of the State do not attend school for the term required to entitle a district to draw its share of the public money. The trustees of school districts are authorized, in the exercise of a sound discretion, to exempt from the payment of teachers' wages, any *indigent persons* in their districts, in part or wholly, and must certify such exemptions, and deliver the certificates thereof to the district clerk to be kept on file in his office; and such indigent persons as in the judgment of the trustees are unable to provide their proportion of *fuel* should be exempted from all liability to provide it, and from the payment of any tax therefor. The expense incurred by the exemptions from the payment of teachers' wages is made a charge upon *taxable property* in the district, and not exclusively upon those who contribute by rate bills to pay the balance of such wages; and in many districts the proportion to be paid by the latter would not be one dollar to ten assessed upon the property of those who do not send to the schools at all. By these beneficent provisions, the child of penury and the destitute orphan have been provided with ample means of instruction; and it now becomes a question of grave inquiry whether this law is faithfully and benignly executed. The right of the State to impose this condition, with the appropriations from the public treasury for the benefit of all, no one can question, and its benevolent features receive the commendation of every citizen of enlarged and philanthropic views. These exemptions were referred to a tribunal best acquainted with the conditions and pecuniary circumstances of the inhabitants of the districts, and this dispensing power, although addressed to the discretion of the trustees is, no doubt, to be exercised in every proper case, *without application* from those whose pecuniary circumstances rendered them unable to pay their portion of the rate bills. It might well have been supposed that the large appropriations annually made for the benefit of all, regarding neither condition in life, nor profession, would have produced a spirit of liberality in affording the means of education to the thousands of children, whose destitute situation rendered them the proper objects of this gratuity — a gratuity which, proffered by the high and solemn obligations of duty, should neither be misapplied nor withheld.

In the month of July last, the Superintendent made an effort to ascertain through the agency of the several town and county superintendents, the whole number of scholars exempted the last year, and the amount of the tax levied to pay teachers' wages in consequence of the exemptions. This effort failed entirely in eliciting the information sought for, as only twenty-four of the whole number of county superintendents in the State, responded in any manner to the call, and only twenty-two of the reports received, contained any information relating to the subject, and all without exception, were imperfect. . . .

The county superintendents generally concur in opinion that the foregoing provisions are not regarded to any extent by the trustees, and that certificates of exemption are seldom filed with the school district clerks, even when indigent parents are exempted from the payment of teachers' wages; while some of these officers remark that this enquiry for highly interesting information to be submitted to the Legislature, was considered by the school district officers as inquisitorial and obnoxious. We must have arrived at a very sublimated state of feeling in respect to private right and public duty, when any inquiry after facts which are, or should be, a matter of public record, and open to public inspection, shall be regarded as in the least offensive, or in any way objectionable.

What proportion of the whole number of children in the State are excluded from all participation in the benefit of our common schools, on account of the poverty of their parents or their own destination, cannot now be ascertained, and probably never will, however important these facts may be. The Superintendent believes that the number in the whole State, embracing our large cities, populous villages, and manufacturing towns, whose destitution entitles them to be placed upon the list of free scholars, according to the provisions of the existing laws, is much larger than has been generally supposed by accurate observers; and the lowest probable estimate we can make of that number is over forty-six thousand. The Superintendent will hereafter require of the trustees of school districts to state in their annual reports the whole number of exemptions certified by them during the year, "in part or wholly," of indigent persons within their districts, and the whole amount of such exemptions charged upon the district during the same year. This information will enable the department to communicate to the Legislature, from time to time, the extent to which the trustees exercise their authority in making exemptions, and will, it is believed, materially aid in forming plans for a more effectual remedy of the evils and inconveniences, it has hitherto been the policy of the State to overcome by the extension of its admirable system of public instruction. Among other obstacles to be encountered and successfully disposed of, is the reluctance of many parents to participate in the benefits now afforded, owing to the manner in which this bounty, as they call it, is bestowed. They say they will not send their children to the schools to be reproached for their poverty, and assailed with taunts that they are educated at the expense of their more fortunate neighbors. Those who entertain and express feelings of this sort, and would deny their offspring the greatest boon in the power of a parent to bestow, no doubt reason from false premises, and allow themselves to be influenced by motives as unkind towards the great mass of our fellow citizens as cruel towards their own children. . . .

The condition of this fund (the School Fund) and the permanent augmentation of it, so as to ensure a gradual and certain increase of the apportionments, commensurate with the increase of population and the public necessities, are subjects of vast importance to the State, and it is hoped will soon attract the earnest attention of the Legislature and the people. The entire support of the schools, by direct appropriations from the public treasury, is not now practicable, nor is it supposed to be desirable. But the State will have discharged its duty, when means sufficiently ample are provided to sustain our educational institutions, without rendering individual contributions either burdensome or vexatious; and the ratio of fifty cents to each child between five and sixteen years of age would probably secure every attainable advantage which legislative authority could well accomplish. The power conferred upon the inhabitants of the towns to impose a tax to a limited amount, for the support of schools, is not exerted, save in a very few instances, and the sums raised are in the aggregate, quite small. The non-exercise of this authority shows that the electors of the towns are not inclined to exert the taxing power, even where they might, and where it is obviously the interest of many of them to do so. Free schools have been established in many of our cities, by local laws applicable only to them; and why may not large and wealthy districts, in our populous villages, be placed upon the same footing? Here are found the largest number of persons who should be exempted, from their inability to pay the rate-bill for teachers' wages and here are congregated hundreds of children exposed to the contaminating influences of grogshop idleness and other vicious associations. A corrective may be found in the occupations of the school room, now closed against many of them; and it is believed that a law, guarded in its provisions, vesting in the taxable inhabitants of school districts which contain a certain number of children between the required ages, and a fixed amount in valuation of real and personal estate, to be ascertained from the last assessment roll of the town, the power to raise money by tax to be applied in the payment of teachers' wages would be acceptable, and carried into effect in a very considerable number of districts.

On March 4, 1846, at the meeting of the teachers and town superintendents of Ontario county held at Victor, the following resolution was adopted:

Resolved, That the taxable property of the State ought to educate the children of the State.

THE PASSAGE OF THE BILL (1849)

On March 25 of 1849, " an act establishing free schools throughout the State " was passed, its validity being conditioned on the approval of the people, to be decided in the election to be held in

November of that year. Governor Hamilton Fish in his annual message of January 2, 1849, states as follows:

The common school system of the State continues efficient in the discharge of this important object. The number of organized school districts, reported during the past year, was 10,621; and the number of children taught in the Common Schools during the year was 775,723, being an increase of 27,336 over the number reported the preceding year. The number of unincorporated and private schools reported was 1,785, in which 32,256 children were taught; making an aggregate of 807,979 children, who received instruction in the common and private schools of the State. The amount of public moneys paid for teachers' wages, during the year, was $639,008.00; and the amount paid on rate bills for teachers' wages was $466,674.44, being an aggregate of $1,105,682.44.

Intimately connected with the success of our institutions of learning is the establishment and support of libraries for the use of the public. The liberal and far-seeing policy of the law of 1838, provided for the formation and gradual increases of libraries in each of the School Districts of the State. During the past year $81,624.05 have been expended by the State for this object. Upwards of one million three hundred thousand volumes have already been distributed, carrying the means of mental culture into every portion of our widespread territory,— this beneficent legislation of the State, has recently been seconded by a signal example of individual liberality on the part of one, who, though not a native of our land, had realized in his own career the benefits of a full and fair participation in the privileges, which the liberal policy of our institutions extends to all, without regard to the place or the circumstances of birth. John Jacob Astor a native of Germany, who lately died at an advanced age, in the city of New York, by his will has devoted the large and, in this country, unprecedented amount of four hundred thousand dollars, to the foundation and perpetual support of a library for the free use of the public. The trustees to whom the management of this munificent donation has been committed, will, under the direction of the will, apply to the Legislature for an act of incorporation to render the management of the library and its funds safe and convenient. I cheerfully commend their application to your enlightened encouragement. The foundation of such an institution, with its treasures of learning, can not but be regarded as a striking event in the literary history of our State.

From the representations made to me, I am led to believe that the restoration of the office of County Superintendent would be productive of good to the school system. One of the injurious consequences of its abolition, as I am informed by the Department, is, that the reports for which it depended wholly on these officers are now greatly diminished in number, and that many of those received are so imperfect as to be of little value.

The report of the Executive Committee of the Normal School will show the condition of that most valuable agent in the cause of education. This school is doing a great and good work. It has ceased to be an experiment, and under its present judicious management, is growing in the confidence of its friends and attracting the interest of many who once doubted its practicability, or its usefulness.

OLIVER GRAY STEELE
Superintendent of schools in Buffalo, 1837-40
(From picture owned by The Buffalo Historical Society)

HAMILTON FISH
Governor of New York, 1849-51

The action of the Legislature in 1849 (taken from the legislative documents) is here presented.

The personnel of legislative committees to which the free school bill in the legislative session of 1849 was submitted was as follows:

Senate committee on literature — Hon. Thomas H. Bond, Oswego county; Hon. John T. Bush, Erie county; Hon. William M. Hawley, Steuben county.

Assembly committee on colleges, academies and common schools — Hon. James W. Beekman, New York county; Hon. James D. Button, Cayuga county; Hon. Gabriel P. Disosway, Richmond county; Hon. Alonzo Johnson, Chenango county; Hon. Robert H. Pruyn, Albany county.

Remarks of William M. Hawley, of Steuben, in Committee of the Whole, Senate, January 29, 1849, on the Bill to Establish Free Schools throughout the State

Mr Chairman.— I had the honor to introduce a bill similar to this at the last session of the Legislature, but on account of the mass of pressing business then before us, it received but little consideration. I have therefore felt it to be my duty to introduce it again.

To educate the rising generation and make them respectable and useful citizens, is a high and holy duty which we as faithful guardians of that sacred trust, are bound to perform. How or by what means it can be best accomplished are questions about which men may honestly differ.

From the examination I have been able to give the subject, I am satisfied that the only effectual way to secure that result, is to open the common schools to all, without distinction of rank or circumstances, make them entirely free, and bid every child in the State to come and partake freely, without money and without price. By the present law a portion of the expenses are paid by tax on property, and a portion by the public money.

Still there is some to be paid by those who send to school, and in proportion to the number of days their children attend; a large proportion of this is paid by a class of persons who work out by the day to procure the money, and are illy able to bear the expense. The consequence is, their children are not kept at school. Shall we in this enlightened age retain upon our statute books a provision which shall in any degree, deprive the rising generation of the full benefit of a common school education?

It is true that trustees have power to exempt from the payment of teachers' wages, such poor persons as are unable to pay their school bills. But this provision is too humiliating in its tendency to be productive of much good. Poor persons are not devoid of feeling, they have a sense of independence and self-respect as well as their more favored neighbors, and are unwilling to be pauperized to educate their children. The odium of this law is not unfrequently visited upon the heads of the poor unfortunate children. My heart has often been pained to see the tears trickling down their innocent cheeks because they had been twitted by their school fellows of obtaining their education as paupers. I have known them to refuse to attend school for that reason; and what parent, I ask, could have a heart to force his child to school under such circumstances?

But this is not the only objection to this law; we must bear in mind that all the exemptions on account of poverty, are to be paid by those who are not exempted. I have before stated, that a large proportion of these persons are scarcely able to pay their own bills, yet by the operation of this law, they are made to pay for educating the children of their neighbors a degree poorer than themselves. Can this be right? Is there an individual in this State so heartless as to desire the continuance of this cruel provision? I hope not.

Sir, I have conversed with many intelligent capitalists upon this subject, and I am happy to say that not one of them objected to the principle of free schools, provided the system should be made applicable to the whole State.

In preparing this bill, I deemed it advisable to provide for submitting it to the people for their approval at the ballot boxes, not because I am not prepared to adopt the measure at once, but because it proposes a great change in the manner of supporting schools. The people have a deep interest, not only in a pecuniary point of view, but in the ultimate success of the great system of common schools in this State, and for these reasons I desire to take their judgment upon it. I have no fears of the result, all experience has shown, that under our free institutions they are capable of looking to their own interests and welfare.

For these reasons I hope the motion of the honorable senator from the Ninth (Samuel I. Wilkins, Orange County) to strike out the section which provides for submitting it to the people will not prevail.

Sir, the honorable senator from the Sixth (William S. Johnson, New York) in advocating the adoption of the amendment, took occasion to attack the principle of the bill, and I feel called up to reply briefly to some of his remarks.

I understood the senator to say, that the State had already done enough for common schools, and that it was time to turn our attention to the academies, and do something for them, so that those who desired to educate their children above the common schools could do so.

Sir, I am no enemy to academies, I desire to see them flourish, and have no wish to deprive them of the benefit of the literature fund to which they are entitled. This bill does not propose in any manner to interfere with them. Let them prosper, and let those patronize them who desire to do so. This bill is designed to benefit a less favored class, who cannot attend acedemies, and who must of necessity be educated in the common schools or remain in ignorance.

Academies cannot be sustained in every school district, nor in every town. The time may possibly come, when one could be sustained in each county, but this generation cannot hope to see that day. If such were the case now, it would not obviate the necessity for this bill. There are many parents in the country, and I think more or less in every district, who can scarcely dress their children suitably to attend a district school, and are entirely unable to supply them with necessary board and clothing at an academy forty or fifty miles from home.

The honorable senator, snugly domiciled in the pampered city of New York, the great centre and seat of learning, where the schools are as free for his children as the water they drink and the air they breathe, seems to have forgotten that there are people out of that city who have children to educate.

Sir, I rejoice that in the narrow views entertained by that Senator, he stands solitary and alone. No heart in this hall beats in unison with his, and he is pre-eminently entitled to all the honor of his unenviable position. It is truly gratifying to know that the more liberal views of his honorable colleagues extend beyond the confines of the corporation, and that they have hearts for the necessities and privations of the rising generation, wherever they may be scattered among the hills and forests of the whole state.

The object of this bill is to elevate the standard of the only schools in which the great mass of young minds now opening into manhood must necessarily be taught, and make them capable of affording a good English education sufficient for the useful and necessary business transactions of life.

In order to do this, we must secure the patronage and influence of the wealthy. Let the great principle be established that property must educate the people, and our common schools will flourish. Tax men to pay common school teachers, and their children will be taught there. " Where a man's treasure is there will his heart be also " — comfortable houses will be provided, and competent teachers employed — the rich and poor will meet on a common level, be instructed in the same branches, and draw their moral and intellectual nourishment from the same fountain. Equality will be promoted, and the odious and increasing distinction between the rich and the poor will gradually disappear, and the unfortunate and downtrodden child of poverty will be elevated by association with those whom circumstances alone have made them their superiors.

The principle of free schools is ably and elaborately sustained by our worthy superintendent of common schools in his report now on our tables; much valuable statistical and other information is there given, showing the superior advantages of free schools in all cases where they have been established. The honorable senator from Dutchess (Alexander J. Coffin) has given us a history of the practical working of the free school in Poughkeepsie, and he gave it as his opinion, that the amount of money saved to the people by the improved condition of the morals and conduct of the youth, would more than balance the additional tax necessary to sustain the school, and it is worthy of consideration that in every city and village where free schools have been established, they are approved by the people.

The honorable senator from Saratoga (James M. Cook) took the same enlightened and liberal view of the subject, and in the course of his able remarks uttered the following beautiful and truthful sentence, " Good schools should be regarded as so many insurance offices scattered over the State; education is the safeguard of life and property."

Ignorance and idleness are but recruiting sergeants to jails and and other prisons, and in proportion to the advance of science and civilization, poverty and crime will disappear.

That property should educate the people, seems to me to be a proposition too plain and sound to be denied. Science and civilization protect it from destruction, make it useful and give it value. By education man is enabled to fathom the earth and explore the heavens; by it the great steam horse is driven along his iron track; by it the lightnings of heaven are tamed and sent along the telegraphic wires on errands for man. It develops and ennobles every high and holy feeling of our souls, which elevates us above the brutes that perish and allies us to God.

STATE OF NEW YORK
No. 14
IN ASSEMBLY, JAN. 11, 1849

REPORT

Of the Superintendent of Common Schools in answer to a Resolution of the Assembly

SECRETARY'S OFFICE
Department of Common Schools
Albany, January 10, 1849

Resolved, That the Superintendent of Common Schools be requested to transmit to this House, his opinion on the practicability of a law directing the distribution of the school moneys of each town in this State, among the several school districts where in the school houses of such districts are situated, without regard to the territory of which a district may be composed; except in cases where a town or district may have a local school fund, and in cases where a town may vote an additional sum for school purposes beyond what the law now requires to be raised; and excepting also the cases where a district may be composed in part of territory lying without the bounds of this State.

In answer to the above resolution, the Superintendent of Common Schools *Respectfully reports:*

The public money is first apportioned among the several counties, according to their population. The amount apportioned to a county is then divided among the towns in the same manner. But the town superintendent, in apportioning the money among the several school districts, uses as the basis of his calculations, not the population, but the number of children between the ages of five and sixteen years.

The trustees of joint districts report to the town superintendents of the several towns of whose territory the district may in part be formed, the number of children between the said ages in each of the several parts. The town superintendent, in making his distribution of the public money, allots to the part of a joint district in his town, its share, according to the number of children so reported.

This mode of distribution can operate unequally in only one way. It may happen that the part of a joint district in one town may contain no children between the said ages, and therefore, none of the money apportioned to the town can be apportioned to that district. And further, under the present mode of distribution, none of the money raised by the town, or the income of funds belonging to the town, will be apportioned to the part of a joint district in which there are no children between the ages of five and sixteen years.

But this inequality is not of so frequent occurence, or of such magnitude, as to need legislative remedy.

The main objection to the present mode of distribution is found in the labor imposed upon trustees of joint districts, of making two or more reports, and the trouble of town superintendents in distributing money to parts of districts.

WILLIAM M. HAWLEY
Senator from Steuben county, who introduced the free school act of 1849
(From Clayton's History of Steuben County)

CHRISTOPHER MORGAN
Secretary of State and Superintendent of Common Schools, 1848–52

The distribution is as fair and equal as could be hoped for under any law, the labor and trouble are unavoidable.

The resolution contemplates such a change in the law as to require trustees of joint districts to make but a single report to the town superintendent of the town in which the school house is situated, such town superintendent being authorized to apportion to the districts the share of the public money which the whole number of children between the ages of five and sixteen years would be entitled to draw.

This would simplify the reports, and save trustees much labor and perplexity.

The distribution, however, would, in almost every instance, be unequal and unjust. In one case, a district might draw public money more than sufficient to support a school, and in another, not enough to encourage the keeping of any school at all.

Let a joint district be composed of territory taken from two towns. Let the number of children in the district be one hundred between the ages of five and sixteen years, of whom ten reside in one town, and ninety in the other. Let the school house be in that part of the district in the town where the ten children reside. Let the latter town be thinly settled, and the other populous. Here is the case of ninety children, who have been included in the population, and who have therefore drawn money for the town in which they reside, being entitled only to their share of the smaller sum apportioned to a sparsely settled town. The small sum apportioned to the poorer town is distributed, also, to ninety children not living in it.

This may be called an extreme case, but there could not be perfect equality of distribution till the population of the two towns and the number of children in the two parts of the joint district are made exactly equal.

The principal cause of school district controversies, is the question of locating the sites of schoolhouses. A change of the law, as contemplated in the resolution, would multiply occasions for such disputes. Every joint district would be interested in having its schoolhouse situated in the most populous of the two or more towns, of whose territory it was in part formed. A district composed of the territory of the town of Guilderland and partly of that of Albany, would at once remove its schoolhouse within the limits of Albany.

A populous district might draw half the public money apportioned to a thinly settled town, while at the same time it would be entitled to none of the public money apportioned to the town in which the mass of its inhabitants resided.

While a change of the mode of distribution would relieve the town officers of much labor and perplexity, in the opinion of the undersigned, it would be inequitable, and therefore inexpedient.

Very respectfully
Your obedient servant
CHRISTOPHER MORGAN
Superintendent of Common Schools

To the Speaker of the Assembly

(In Senate, Friday, January 26)

The Committee of the Whole, Mr Lawrence in the chair, took up the bill to Establish Free Schools Throughout the State.

Mr Williams (of Tompkins county) moved to amend so as to put incorporated villages on a par with cities in this matter — the last under the bill being allowed to regulate the matter themselves.

Mr Cole (of Orleans county) opposed the amendment, Thomas Jefferson — and Mr C. believed every word he had written — said that "Cities and villages were ulcers on the body politic." This evil could only be obviated by general and universal education, and this Mr C. desired to attain. It was the only way to insure the faithful, competent and intelligent discharge of the duty, which every American citizen owed to his country. From his earliest opinion he had ever entertained the idea that we were the only people on earth prepared for a republican form of government, and the experience of twenty-five years had confirmed him in that opinion. Why was it? He thanked God that the pilgrim fathers who came over in the Mayflower,— for their blood flowed almost uncontaminated through his veins — when they landed at Plymouth Rock, were an educated people, who **brought with them the love of liberty,**— for they were all of the Roundhead genus. Those who came after them had helped to fight the battles of a great revolution in England and to sustain Whig principles. He was proud to say, that one of his ancestors was, during the whole of that time, in command of a regiment of Parliamentarians — and from him down every one of his descendants to this day held the same great Whig principles.

Bringing with them these principles, which held that the people were capable of self-government when educated for it — and carrying them out in the little democracies of their towns from that day to this — they had scattered broadcast over the land this system of common school education. Mr C. contrasted the conditions of the Southern States, where, as he said, these principles had not prevailed, with the Northern Free States — claiming for the latter the supremacy in morals, religion, politics, and in all that renders a nation happy, prosperous and great. In conclusion, Mr C. hoped that no Senator in favor of the bill would vote for the amendment.

Mr Martin (of Cattaraugus county) insisted that for all practical purposes, the common schools of the State were now free. The trustees of school districts had no power to exclude any child from a school whether the parent or guardian was able to pay for the teaching or not. But if the bill was necessary, he would make it also apply to cities. What was good for one was for the other?

Mr Fine (of St Lawrence county) suggested that this matter should be left to the people of the cities.

Mr Lawrence (of New York) said that in New York schools were entirely free.

Mr Fine said that, in his opinion, the common schools in villages should be rendered free.— Many children of the poor people were not sent to school because there was some little to pay, and although the trustees had the power to omit the amount, yet feelings of pride prevented the people from availing themselves of it. He hoped the villages would not be excepted from the operation of this bill. At an early period, Mr Clinton had recommended schools for the education of teachers; and after reflecting, he (Mr F.) thought the best schools for such purposes were the academies,— and he regretted the establishment of the State Normal school, which had tended to break down the academies.

Mr Geddes (of Onondaga county) said, under the present system, a man might send his child to school, and if the rates were not paid, they could take his bed from under him. He referred to the example of his own village, where, to induce poor people to send their children to school, the trustees had exempted them from taxation for schools. But this had created much complaint. He believed that every child should be educated — and he liked this bill in that it provided that each district should take care of its own school, inasmuch as by that, no district was liable to the effect of the blunders of another. He objected to that provision of it which did away with District Collectors, as creating an inconvenience to taxpayers. He expected that stockholders in companies who were to be taxed would object to this bill; but he would tell them it was better to pay it for that purpose than a larger sum for the support of police courts.

Mr Hawley (of Steuben county) sustained the provision obviating district collectors. Cities were included in this bill, and were to be governed by the city laws, which could not apply to the country. He denied that schools were free now throughout the State; he knew of instances where children who went free now, had felt themselves driven from school, because they were called paupers. He desired to remove all such stigmas, and to put everybody on a level — rich and poor, with respect to education. The object of the bill was to make property pay its share for the education of the people — without which property would be of no value.

Mr Williams's amendment was not understood. He believed villages were as capable to regulate their own schools as cities, and he desired to place them on the same footing. A general law should operate alike over the state.

Mr Coffin (of Dutchess county) said the first free school in the state was in the village of Poughkeepsie. Mr C. referred to the flourishing condition of the schools there — adding that there was but one school district under the direction of a board of education. He tho't some amendment should be made which would give the villages this power.

Mr Cook (of Saratoga county) said that capitalists generally were not and would not be opposed to this law. The money paid by them for common schools was precisely like the insurance they paid on their property — the same ends were sought and secured.

Mr Coffin said that although the free school system was a tax on Poughkeepsie of $4000 a year — yet the aggregate tax was not less than it was five years ago. There was as much gained on the one hand as lost on the other. It appeared to him that capitalists should be more willing to pay for education than for the punishment of crime.

There was some debate on the section relating to the manner of collecting the tax, when the committee rose and reported progress.

William M. Hawley

Born in Delaware county, February 13, 1802, William M. Hawley was the son of a farmer, who was able to afford his children but few educational advantages. William Hawley made the most of every opportunity that came to him and it is said that he had such a remarkable memory that he could repeat verbatim a large portion of any book, after reading it but once. Upon reaching his majority, he went to Allegany county, where he cleared a piece of land for tillage. In 1824, he was elected constable of the town of Almond and he took up the study of law. As he could not afford to devote his whole time to study, he studied at home, attended such sessions of court as he could in order to hear the trial of cases and after several years devoted to the work, he was admitted to the bar. He opened an office in Almond where he built up a practice of considerable importance. In 1837 he moved to Hornellsville, where he became one of the leading lawyers of that part of the State. In 1846 Governor Silas Wright appointed Mr Hawley first judge of Steuben county. In 1848 he was elected to the State Senate and was one of the prominent members of the sessions of 1848 and 1849.

He introduced a bill for free schools in the session of 1848 and, as this failed of enactment, he introduced in the session of 1849, the bill which later became the free school law of 1849.

Mr Hawley was a delegate to the convention which nominated Martin Van Buren for President and was one of the committee which drew up the resolutions, whose essential features were afterward adopted by the Republican party.

After retiring from the Senate, he devoted himself to the practice of his profession until his death in 1869.

John Fine

John Fine was born in New York, August 26, 1794. He entered Columbia College in 1805 and was graduated in 1809, at the age of 15, receiving the second honor, the English salutatory. Mr Fine studied law for five years in various law offices and then attended a course of law lectures of one year under Judges Reeve and Gould, at Litchfield, Conn. In 1815 he removed to St Lawrence county and formed a law partnership with Louis Hasbrouck, which continued until the death of the latter in 1834.

In the fall of 1824, Mr Fine was appointed first judge of the county and continued in this office by reappointment until 1839. In the fall of 1838, he was elected to Congress and for part of his term served on the committee on foreign affairs. In 1844, he was again appointed first judge of St Lawrence county and held that office until the adoption of the new constitution in 1847. During his service of over eighteen years on the bench, only three of his decisions were reversed. In 1848 he was elected to the State Senate and, while in that body, he introduced the bill enacted into law which gave married women control of their own property. In 1847 and 1849, Mr Fine ran unsuccessfully for election as judge of the Supreme Court. He was treasurer of St Lawrence county from 1821 to 1833.

Judge Fine received the degree of master of arts from Columbia College in 1812 and that of doctor of laws from Hamilton College in 1850. In 1852 he published a volume of lectures on law which showed the vast extent of his legal knowledge.

Frederick Stanley Martin

Frederick Stanley Martin, born in the county of Rutland, Vermont, on April 25, 1794, lived with his mother, a widow, until he was ten years of age, when he went to New Hartford, N. Y., to live with his uncle. At the age of sixteen, Mr Martin left his uncle's home to work in Whitehall. After an experience of six years as mercantile clerk, steward on a Lake Champlain steamer and sailor on a ship to England, Mr Martin in the fall of 1817 went to Canandaigua, which was then considered in "the far West." In the spring of 1818, he settled in Olean where he made his permanent home. In time Mr Martin became one of the wealthiest and most respected citizens of his community, having large property interests and being known as a clear-headed, substantial merchant.

Mr Martin was much interested in all public affairs of his time. He was the first president of the board of trustees of the Olean Academy. From 1826 until 1833 he was prominently identified with the state militia, holding the rank of major and later that of lieutenant colonel. In 1830 he received the unsolicited appointment of postmaster at Olean and held this position during the succeeding nine years. In 1840, Governor Seward appointed him "a judge of the county courts of Cattaraugus county" and he held this office for five years. In 1847 he was elected to the State Senate but was defeated in obtaining a renomination. His defeat was due to a political combination against him and the people of his assembly district were so incensed over the matter that at the assembly district convention held soon after, he was nominated by acclamation for the Assembly and later elected to that body. He had worked energetically for the Genesee Valley canal and in both the Senate and Assembly, he was a member of the important "canal" committee. In the fall of 1850, Mr Martin was elected to Congress and during his term supported the administration of President Fillmore.

James M. Cook

James M. Cook was born in Ballston Spa in 1807. His father was Judge Samuel Cook, who was a Master in Chancery in 1801; Examiner in Chancery in 1823; and one of the Judges of the Court of Common Pleas in 1820.

Mr Cook took up the study of law and was admitted to the bar. He was one of the organizers of the Ballston Spa Bank in 1838 and became its first president, serving in that capacity until 1856. In 1845 he purchased a cotton mill and later he became associated with his brother in an extensive cotton manufacturing business, which was later terminated by the scarcity of cotton due to the Civil War.

Mr Cook was prominent in public affairs. In the Constitutional Convention of 1846 and in the State Senate in which he served from 1847-1851, and again in 1863, he was one of the leaders of his party and known as a clear thinker, a ready speaker and an able debater. In 1851, he was declared elected State Treasurer and held that office from January 1, 1852 to November 2 of that year, when the contest brought by Benjamin Welch, Jr. was decided in favor of Mr Welch. Mr Cook was elected State Comptroller in 1853 and served for the years 1854 and 1855. In 1856, he was appointed Superintendent of the Banking Department and held that position until he resigned it in 1861.

In his own community, he was also honored, having served as President and Trustee of the Village of Ballston Spa during the years 1843-45. He was also supervisor for three years.

Mr Edward F. Gros in his " Centennial History of the Village of Ballston Spa " says that " The War of the Rebellion roused his (Mr Cook's) patriotism to an absorbing passion. To the enlistment and organization of troops, he gave both time and money. . . . In private life Mr Cook was a courtly gentleman, suave in manner, and a most entertaining conversationalist. A man of culture, fully informed on all matters of importance pertaining to the times in which he lived, he stood high in the public esteem, and was greatly respected wherever he was known."

Mr Cook died at Saratoga Springs in 1868.

John L. Lawrence

Honorable John L. Lawrence was a descendant of a family distinguished in the annals of both England and America. He was born in 1785, was graduated from Columbia University in 1803 and had a long and distinguished career as a lawyer, whose specialty

FREDERICK STANLEY MARTIN
State Senator, 1849
(From "Cattaraugus County," compiled by John Manley)

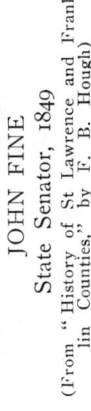

JOHN FINE
State Senator, 1849
(From "History of St Lawrence and Franklin Counties," by F. B. Hough)

JAMES M. COOK
State Senator, 1849
(From picture in "Centennial History of the
Village of Ballston S'a." Used by per-
mission of Mr Edward F. G

A. HYDE COLE
State Senator, 1849
(From "Pioneer History of Orleans County" by

JOHN L. LAWRENCE
Member of Senate, 1849
(From copyrighted picture in "Famous Families of New York"; used by courtesy of G. P. Putnam's Sons)

was banking and corporations. He was Secretary of Legation at Sweden, member of the Constitutional Convention of 1821, Assistant Register of the Court of Chancery, Presidential Elector, State Senator in 1848–49, City Comptroller, Assemblyman, Treasurer of Columbia University, first President of the Croton Aqueduct Commission, and United States Chargé d'Affaires at the Court of Sweden.

George Geddes

George Geddes was born at Fairmount, Onondaga county, in 1809. After receiving a good education, he studied law but never applied for admission to the bar. He preferred the profession of civil engineering and surveying. He became prominent in his profession and undertook many works of importance. He was an original member of the state survey commission. In 1848 he was elected to the State Senate and held office until 1851. He was the author of the general railway law under which the railroads of the State are incorporated. In 1881 he was a member of the commission to revise the tax laws and became well-known through his articles on the subject. He was a recognized authority on agriculture and owned a farm which twice received first prize at the State Fair for general excellent condition and productiveness. He was president of the State Agricultural Society and a frequent contributor to the New York Tribune, the Country Gentleman and other papers. He died in 1883.

Alexander J. Coffin

Senator Alexander J. Coffin was a prominent citizen of Poughkeepsie. He was a member of the committee that received Lafayette in 1824, was one of the first directors of the Poughkeepsie Bank organized in 1830 and was a member of the Board of Education. He was one of the organizers of the Republican party in Dutchess county.

John W. Tamblin

While John W. Tamblin of Evans Mills, Jefferson county, was a lawyer, he devoted more time to politics than to the practice of law. At one time, he edited a newspaper. He served in the Assembly for several years and was a member of the State Senate during the years 1849–1850.

Almeron Hyde Cole

Mr Cole was born at Lavanna, Cayuga county. N. Y., April 20, 1798. His parents removed to Auburn in 1807 and there he prepared for college and entered the Sophomore Class in Union College in 1815. Owing to changes in his family, he remained in college but two years.

He studied law with Judge Richardson, then first Judge of Cayuga county, and was admitted to the bar in his twenty-first year. After practicing law in Seneca Falls for a time, Mr Cole established himself at Albion. He served for 17 years as Justice of the Peace of the town of Barre and his counsel and advice were so highly valued by the people that he early became known by the title of "the counselor."

In November 1847, he was elected a member of the State Senate, where he served one term and declined a renomination. After leaving the Senate, he resumed the practice of law but later he closed his law office and devoted himself to the duties of executor of a large estate and to the management of a farm which he owned. He died October 14, 1859.

Legislative Summary

In Senate . . . The free school bill was also debated — no question.

Thursday, February 1, 1849

The same committee (of the whole), Mr Fuller in the chair, took up the bill to establish free schools throughout the State.

The section preserving the distinction between cities and the country was restored.

Mr S. H. P. Hall said the schools were now free and the only question here was between the two systems. He preferred the present system, and moved to strike out the section to submit it to the people.

Mr Cornwall denied that the schools were now accessible to all classes alike. He knew instances where school collectors had taken the bed of a family for the non-payment of the school rates. He hoped the motion would not prevail.

There was some further debate on this proposition, when the motion was adopted, and then the committee rose and reported the bill, and it was referred to a select committee to report complete.

References to Free School Law Taken from the Journal of the Assembly

Seventy-second Session

Mr Fish presented the petition of 520 citizens of Glen, Montgomery county, praying for an act establishing free schools, which was read and referred to the committee on colleges, academies and common schools.

January 10, 1849, p. 87

Mr Disoway presented a similar petition of the inhabitants of Richmond county, of which the same disposition was made.

January 22, 1849, p. 190

Mr W. S. Smith presented a petition of the board of education of the town of Flushing, praying for an amendment of the act to establish free schools in district 5, town of Flushing, which was read and referred to the committee on colleges, academies and common schools.

Mr Disoway presented two petitions of inhabitants of school district 7, town of Castletown, Richmond county, to establish free schools in the State, or if this be denied, to establish them in Richmond county, which was read and referred to the committee on colleges, academies and common schools.

January 25, 1849, p. 226

Mr Kidd presented a petition of sundry inhabitants of West Farms, Westchester county, praying for the establishment of free schools throughout the State, which was read and referred to the committee on colleges, academies and common schools.

January 26, 1849, p. 238

Mr Mowrey presented a similar petition of the inhabitants of Cambridge, Washington county, of which the same disposition was made.

January 27, 1849, p. 251

Mr Bagley presented a similar petition of the inhabitants of Jefferson county, of which the same disposition was made.

January 29, 1849, p. 258

Mr Boughton presented a similar petition of C. H. Greenleaf and 67 other inhabitants of Kings county, of which a same disposition was made.

February 3, 1849, p. 312

Mr W. S. Smith presented a similar petition of school district 12, in Oyster Bay, in Queens county, of which the same disposition was made.

February 5, 1849, p. 322

Mr Averill presented a similar petition of 80 inhabitants of Palatine, Montgomery county, of which a similar disposition was made.

February 6, 1849, p. 341

Mr W. H. Robertson presented a similar petition of the inhabitants of the village of Tarrytown, in the county of Westchester, of which the same disposition was made.

February 7, 1849, p. 363

Mr Wells presented a similar petition of Amos Hunt and others, inhabitants of Day and Edinburgh, Saratoga county, of which the same disposition was made.

February 8, 1849, p. 374

Messrs. Elwood and Hall presented three similar petitions of the inhabitants of Oneida and Tompkins counties, of which a same disposition was made.

February 8, 1849, p. 375

Mr Bush presented a similar petition of the inhabitants of Sullivan county of which the same disposition was made.

February 9, 1849, p. 388

Mr Averill presented the petition of sundry citizens of Fulton county for the establishment of free schools throughout the State, which was read and referred to the committee on colleges, academies and common schools.

February 9, 1849, p. 388

Mr W. H. Robertson presented a similar petition of the inhabitants of Sing Sing, Westchester county, of which the same disposition was made.

February 12, 1849, p. 418

Mr Nash presented a similar petition of 87 inhabitants of Chemung county of which the same disposition was made.

February 12, 1849, p. 418

Mr Roblee presented a similar petition of the inhabitants of Orleans county, of which the same disposition was made.

February 15, 1849, p. 468

Mr Kidd presented petitions of the inhabitants of Westchester county of which the same disposition was made.

February 16, 1849, p. 482

Messrs Speaker, Fish, Disoway and W. H. Robertson presented four several petitions of sundry inhabitants of the counties of Rensselaer, Richmond, Montgomery and Westchester, for the establishment of free schools throughout the State, which were referred to the committee on colleges, academies and schools.

February 19, 1849, p. 508

Mr Woodruff presented two petitions of sundry citizens of Dansville, against the establishment of a free union school in that village, and for the establishment of free schools throughout the State, which were read and referred to the committee on colleges, academies and common schools.

February 19, 1849, p. 509

Mr Fish presented a similar petition of the inhabitants of Montgomery county of which the same disposition was made.

February 21, 1849, p. 536

Mr Nash gave notice of his intention to ask leave to bring in a bill to establish free schools throughout the State.

February 24, 1849, p. 575

Mr Wheaton presented the memorial of the Onondaga county teacher's institute in favor of the establishment of free schools throughout the State, which was read and referred to the committee on colleges, academies and common schools.

Febaruary 26, 1849, p. 580

Mr Wheaton presented a petition of the sundry inhabitants of the county of Onondaga, praying for the establishment of free schools throughout the State, and a more effectual supervision and a further appropriation for teacher's institutes, which was read and referred to the committee on colleges, academies and common schools.

February 28, 1849, p. 612

Mr Pease presented the petition of sundry inhabitants of Jefferson county, for the establishment of free schools throughout the State, which was read and referred to the committee on colleges, academies and common schools.

February 28, 1849, p. 614

Mr Fish and Fox presented four petitions of sundry citizens of this State, praying for the establishment of free schools throughout the State, which as read and referred to the committee on colleges, academies and common schools.

March 6, 1849, p. 679

Mr Quackenboss presented similar petitions of the citizens of Steuben county, of which the same disposition was made.

March 7, 1849, p. 695

Mr Wheaton presented a similar petition of the sundry inhabitants of Jefferson county of which the same disposition was made.

March 10, 1849, p. 765

Mr Bogart presented the petition of John O'Blenis, of Rockland county, praying for the repeal of all laws relating to common schools, which was read and referred to the committee on colleges, academies and common schools.

March 13, 1849, p. 815

Mr Bogart presented a similar petition of the sundry inhabitants of Rockland county of which the same disposition was made.

March 14, 1849, p. 837

Mr W. S. Smith presented a similar petition of the sundry inhabitants of North Hempstead of which the same disposition was made.

March 15, 1849, p. 861

Mr W. H. Robertson presented a similar petition of the citizens of Westchester county, of which the same disposition was made.

March 17, 1849, p. 892

A message from the Senate was received and read, informing that they had passed without amendment the bill entitled as follows: "An act to amend an act to establish free schools in district number 5 in the town of Flushing passed March 10, 1848."

March 17, 1849, p. 900

The House then resolved itself into a committee of the whole on the special order of the day, it being the engrossed bill from the Senate, "An act establishing free schools throughout the State."

After some time spent thereon, Mr Speaker resumed the chair, and Mr Hale from said committee, reported progress and asked leave to sit again.

On motion of Mr Pruyn,

Resolved, That the engrossed bill from the Senate, "An act establishing free schools throughout the State," be made the special order for Monday evening at 7 o'clock."

March 17, 1849, p. 908

Messrs Pruyn, A. Robertson and Terry presented three petitions of sundry citizens of this State for the establishment of free schools throughout the State, which were read and referred to the committee of the whole when on the bill upon that subject.

March 19, 1849, p. 909

On motion of Mr Pruyn,
Resolved, That the special order of this evening, it being the bill entitled, "An act establishing free schools throughout the State," be postponed until evening at 7 o'clock"

March 19, 1849, p. 916

Mr W. H. Robertson presented the petition of sundry citizens of the town of Cortland, in the county of Westchester, for the establishment of free schools throughout the State, which was read and referred to the committee on colleges, academies and common schools.

March 20, 1849, p. 917

The House then resolved itself into a committee of the whole on the engrossed bill from the Senate, entitled, "An act establishing free schools throughout the State."

After some time spent thereon, Mr Thompson, from said committee, reported that the committee had gone through the bill, and agreed to the same without amendment, which report was agreed to.

By unanimous consent, The engrossed bill from the Senate, entitled, "An act establishing free schools throughout the State" was read a third time.

Mr Speaker put the question whether the House would agree to the final passage of the bill, and it was determined in the affirmative, a majority of all the members elected to the Assembly voting in favor thereof, and three-fifths of said members being present, as follows: Ayes 73, nays 7.

Those who voted in the affirmative are,

Mr Averill	Mr Graham	Mr W. H. Robertson
Mr Bailey	Mr Green	Mr Rounseville
Mr Beekman	Mr Hale	Mr Slocum
Mr Bellinger	Mr Hammond	Mr Smalley
Mr Boardman	Mr Hudson	Mr L. Ward Smith
Mr Bogart	Mr A. Johnson	Mr Stevens
Mr Boyce	Mr Kelsey	Mr Stevenson
Mr Brinkerhoff	Mr Kennedy	Mr Strevor
Mr Brewer	Mr Leavenworth	Mr Stryker
Mr Bush	Mr McKinney	Mr Sweet
Mr L. Butts	Mr Maine	Mr Terry
Mr Campbell	Mr Markel	Mr J. E. Thompson
Mr Clark	Mr Mersereau	Mr A. Tuttle
Mr Cornell	Mr Mowrey	Mr H. C. Tuthill
Mr Cross	Mr Nash	Mr Van Auken
Mr Elderkin	Mr Noble	Mr Van Order
Mr Fish	Mr Pardee	Mr Vincent
Mr Fiske	Mr Perley	Mr Ward
Mr Fitzhugh	Mr Picket	Mr Wheaton
Mr Fox	Mr Porter	Mr White
Mr Gates	Mr Preston	Mr Whittaker
Mr Gilbert	Mr Pruyn	Mr Wilcox
Mr Glass	Mr Quackenboss	Mr Woodruff
Mr Goff	Mr Robertson	Mr Young
Mr Gove		73

FREE SCHOOLS

Those who voted in the negative are,

Mr Buxton	Mr L. M. Gilbert	Mr Miller
Mr Culbert	Mr Hart	Mr Stewart
Mr Curtis		

7

Ordered, That the clerk return the said bill to the Senate, and inform them that the Assembly have passed same without amendment.

March 23, 1849, p. 1003

Mr W. S. Smith presented the petition of sundry citizens of Queens county, for the establishment of free schools throughout the State, which was read and laid on the table.

March 27, 1849, p. 1043

A message from the Senate was received and read, requesting the concurrence of the Assembly to the bill entitled, "An act to amend the act entitled, 'An act establishing free schools throughout the State,' passed March 26, 1849," which was read for the first time, and referred to the committee on colleges, academies and common schools.

March 27, 1849, p. 1055

Mr Bogart presented a petition of the citizens of Rockland county, for free schools throughout the State, which was read and laid on the table.

March 31, 1849, p. 1160

Mr Hart, from the select committee to which was referred the engrossed bill from the Senate, entitled, "An act in relation to the Fabius Select School in the county of Onondaga," to report complete, reported that the committee had gone through the said bill, and agreed to the same without amendment which report was agreed to.

Ordered, That the said bill be read the third time.

April 5, 1849, p. 1296

Mr Pruyn, from the committee on colleges, academies and common schools, to which was referred the engrossed bill from the Senate, entitled, "An act to amend an act entitled, 'An act establishing free schools throughout the State,' passed March 26, 1849," reported that the committee had examined the said bill, and saw no reason why the same should not be passed into a law.

Ordered, That said bill be read a third time.

April 5, 1849, p. 1297

The engrossed bill from the Senate, entitled, "An act to amend an act entitled, An act establishing free schools throughout the State, passed March 26, 1849," having been amended by unanimous consent.

The said bill was then read a third time.

Mr Speaker put the question whether the House would agree to the final passage of the bill, and it was determined in the affirmative, a majority of all the members elected to the Assembly voting in favor thereof as follows: Ayes 80, nays 6.

Ordered, That the clerk return the said bill to the Senate, and inform them that the Assembly have passed the same with the amendments therewith delivered.

Mr Averill moved the House reconsider its vote on the final passage of the bill.

Mr Speaker put the question whether the House would agree to the said motion of Mr Averill, and it was determined in the negative.

April 5, 1849, p. 1309

A message from the Senate was received and read, informing that they have concurred in the amendments of the House to the bill entitled, "An act to amend the act entitled, An act establishing free schools throughout the State,' passed March 26, 1849."

Ordered, That the clerk return the said bill to the Senate.

April 11, 1849, p. 1512

Chapter 140
An Act Establishng Free Schools Throughout the State
Passed March 26, 1849, " three fifths being present "

The People of the State of New York, represented in Senate and Assembly, do enact as follows:

1 Common schools in several school districts in this State shall be free to all persons residing in the district, over five, and under twenty-one years of age. Persons not residents of a district may be admitted into the schools kept therein, with the approbation, in writing, of the trustees thereof, or a majority of them.

2 It shall be the duty of the several boards of supervisors at their annual meeting, to cause to be levied and collected from their respective counties, in the same manner as county taxes, a sum equal to the amount of state school moneys apportioned to such counties and to apportion the same among the towns and cities in the same manner as the moneys received from the state are apportioned. They shall also cause to be levied and collected from each of the towns in their respective counties in the same manner as other town taxes, a sum equal to the amount of state school moneys apportioned to said towns respectively.

3 The trustees of each school district within thirty, and not less than fifteen days preceding the time for holding the district annual meeting in each year, shall prepare an estimate of the amount of money necessary to be raised in the district for the ensuing year, for the payment of the debts and expenses to be incurred by said district for fuel, furniture, school apparatus, repairs and insurance of school houses, contingent expenses, and teacher's wages, exclusive of the public money and the money required by the law to be raised by the county and towns, and the income of the local funds and shall cause printed or written notices to be posted for two weeks previous to said meeting upon the schoolhouse door, and in three or more of the public places in said district. The trustees shall present such estimate to such meeting and the voters present who are of full age, residing in such school district, and entitled to hold land in this State, who own or lease property in such district, subject to taxation for school purposes, or who shall have paid any district tax within two years preceding, or who owns any personal property liable to be taxed for school purposes in such dis-

trict, exceeding fifty dollars in value, exclusive of such as is exempt from executions and no others, shall vote thereon for each item separately, and so much of said estimate as shall be approved by a majority of the voters present, shall be levied and raised by tax on such district in the same manner as other district taxes are now by law levied and collected. District collectors shall in all cases, before entering upon the duties of their respective offices, give security to the satisfaction of the trustees, for the faithful discharge of their duties; and all moneys collected by them shall be paid to the trustees of their respective districts.

4 It shall be the duty of the collector, upon receiving his warrant, for two successive weeks, to receive such taxes as may be voluntary paid him; and in case the whole amount shall not be so paid in, the collector shall forthwith proceed to collect the same. He shall receive for his services, on all sums paid as aforesaid, one per cent, and upon all sums collected by him after the expiration of the time mentioned five per cent; and in case a levy and sale shall be necessarily made by such collector, he shall be entitled to traveling fees at the rate of six cents per mile, to be computed from the school house in such district.

5 If the trustees shall neglect to prepare the said estimate within the time herein limited, or shall neglect to post the required notice, it shall be lawful for the meeting to adjourn to such other time as will be sufficient to prepare the said estimate and give the said notice.

6 When the said voters of any district at their annual meeting shall refuse or neglect to raise by tax a sum of money which added to the public money, and the money raised by county and towns will support a school in said district for at least four months in a year, keep the school house in proper repair and furnish the necessary fuel, then it shall be the duty of said trustees to repair the school house, furnish the necessary fuel, and employ a teacher for four months, and the expense shall be levied and collected in the manner provided in the third section of this act.

7 Free and gratuitous education shall be given to each pupil, in each of the common, public, ward and district schools in the respective cities of this State, now incorporated or hereafter to be incorporated, including the schools of the public school society in the city of New York according to any law now in force in said cities. And by each city, where such free and gratuitous eduation is not already established, laws and ordinances may and shall without delay be passed providing for, and for securing and sustaining the system in each of their common public, ward and district schools.

8 All laws and parts of laws inconsistent with the provisions of this act, other than those relating to free schools in any cities in this state are hereby repealed.

9 In case any trustee or other school district officer shall use any money in his hands belonging to such district, and shall not apply the same as directed by law, he shall be deemed guilty of a misdemeanor and on conviction thereof shall be punished by fine, not exceeding five hundred dollars, or be imprisoned in a county jail not exceeding six months, or by both such fine and imprisonment.

10 The electors shall determine by ballot at the annual election to be held in November next, whether this act shall or shall not become a law.

11 It shall be the duty of the State Superintendent of common schools

to prepare and furnish to the several town clerks in this state, forms of the poll lists, returns and other necessary proceedings to carry into effect this act, and he shall also furnish, at the expense of the State, to each school district in the state five copies of this act and the forms prepared by him.

12 The ballots to be deposited in the ballot box shall be in the following form. Those cast in favor of the adoption of this act shall contain the following words:

SCHOOL

FOR THE NEW SCHOOL LAW

Those cast against this act shall contain the following words:

SCHOOL

AGAINST THE NEW SCHOOL LAW

And the ballots shall be folded so as to conceal all the words except the word School, which latter word shall not be concealed, but shall appear on the ballot as folded.

13 The inspectors of election in the several election districts shall furnish a separate ballot box into which shall be placed all the ballots given for or against the new school law. The inspectors shall canvass the ballots and make return thereof in the same manner as the votes given for the office of the governor and lieutenant governor are by law canvassed and returned.

14 In case a majority of all the votes in the State shall be cast against the new school law, this act shall be null and void; and in case all the votes in the state shall be cast for the new school law, then this act shall become a law, and shall take effect on the first day of January eighteen hundred and fifty.

References to Free School Law Taken from the Journal of the Senate

Seventy-second Session

In pursuance of the previous notice,

Mr Hawley asked for and obtained leave to introduce a bill entitled, "An act establishing free schools throughout the State," which was read for the first time, and by unanimous consent was also read the second time, and referred to the committee on literature.

January 5, 1849, p. 34

Mr Bond, from the committee on literature, to which was referred the bill introduced on notice by Mr Hawley, entitled "An act establishing free schools throughout the State," reported in favor of the passage of the same, which was committed to the committee of the whole.

January 9, 1849, p. 45

The Senate then resolved itself into a committee of the whole on the bill entitled, "An act establishing free schools throughout the State," and after some time spent thereon, Mr Fuller, from said committee, reported progress, and asked leave to sit again.

The President put the question upon granting such leave, and it was desided in the affirmative.

January 12, 1849, p. 55

The Senate then resolved itself into a committee of the whole on the bill entitled, "An act to establish free schools throughout the State," and after some time spent thereon, Mr Fuller, from said committee, reported progress, and asked for and obtained leave to sit again.

January 20, 1849, p. 94

On motion of Mr Hawley,

A substitute for said bill, being an act entitled, "An act establishing free schools throughout the State," was ordered printed and referred to said committee.

January 20, 1849, p. 95

The Senate then resolved itself into a committee of the whole on the bill entitled, "An act establishing free schools throughout the State," and after some time spent thereon, Mr Lawrence, from said committee, reported progress, and asked for and obtained leave to sit again.

January 26, 1849, p. 122

The Senate then resolved itself into a committee of the whole on the bill entitled, "An act establishing free schools throughout the State," and after some time spent thereon, Mr S. H. P. Hall, from said committee, reported progress, and asked for and obtained leave to sit again.

January 27, 1849, p. 127

The Senate then resolved itself into a committee of the whole on the bill entitled, "An act to establish free schools throughout the State," and after some time spent thereon, Mr Fuller, from said committee, reported progress, and asked for and obtained leave to sit again.

January 29, 1849, p. 130

The Senate then resolved itself into a committee of the whole on the bill entitled, "An act to establish free schools throughout the State," and after some time spent thereon, Mr Fuller, from said committee, reported in favor of the passage of the same.

On motion of Mr Cornwell, said bill was referred to a select committee consisting of Messrs Cornwell, Hawley and Lawrence, to consider and report complete.

February 1, 1849, p. 149

Mr Lawrence for the select committee, reported complete the bill entitled, "An act to establish free schools throughout the State,"

Ordered, That the question on agreeing with the report of the committee be laid on the table.

February 6, 1849, p. 165

The Senate then resolved itself into a committee of the whole on the bill entitled, "An act establishing free education throughout the State," and after some time spent thereon, Mr Bokee, from said committee, reported progress and asked for and obtained leave to sit again.

February 12, 1849, p. 200

The Senate then resolved itself into a committee of the whole on the bill entitled, "An act establishing free education throughout the State," and after some time spent thereon, Mr Bokee, from said committee, reported progress and asked for and obtained leave to sit again.

February 13, 1849, p. 204

Similar report was made by Mr Bokee on February 14, 1849. Same disposition.

February 16, 1849

The Senate then resolved itself into the committee of the whole on the bill entitled, "An act establishing free education throughout the State," and after some time spent thereon, Mr Bokee, from said committee, reported in favor of the passage of the same without amendment.

The question then being on agreeing to the report of the committee of the whole.

Mr. Johnson moved to amend the report by striking out of the second section all after the word "present" in the fourteenth line, and insert " shall be reported by the trustees to the town superintendent, and he shall lay such estimates before the board of supervisors of the county at their next annual meeting, and they shall consider the estimates from all the school districts of the county which shall be thus laid before them, and add to the sums of money, to be raised on each of the towns of the county, for defraying the necessary expenses thereof, such sums as they shall determine as necessary to raise on each town to effect the objects of this law, and the same shall be levied, collected and paid over as is directed by title second, chapter fifteen, of the first part of the Revised Statutes, and the acts amendatory thereof."

The President put the question upon agreeing to said motion, and it was decided in the negative, as follows:

For the affirmative

Mr Adams	Mr Frost	Mr Martin
Mr Bond	Mr Johnson	Mr Whallon
Mr Clark	Mr Lawrence	Mr Wilkin

For the negative

Mr Brownson	Mr Fine	Mr S. H. P. Hall
Mr Burch	Mr Floyd	Mr Hawley
Mr Coffin	Mr Fox	Mr Smith
Mr Cole	Mr Fuller	Mr Williams
Mr Colt	Mr Geddes	

Mr Johnson then moved to amend the report by adding at the end of the word "towns" in the 7th line of the second section the words, "But no district shall raise in any one year more than one mill on the dollar for the assessed value of the real and personal property of the district."

The President put the question upon agreeing to said motion, and it was decided in the negative, as follows:

For the affirmative

Mr Adams	Mr Frost	Mr Smith
Mr Bokee	Mr S. H. P. Hall	Mr Tamblin
Mr Clark	Mr Johnson	Mr Whallon
Mr Floyd	Mr Lawrence	Mr Wilkin

For the negative

Mr Bond	Mr Colt	Mr Geddes
Mr Brownson	Mr Fine	Mr Hawley
Mr Burch	Mr Fox	Mr Martin
Mr Coffin	Mr Fuller	Mr Williams
Mr Cole		

Mr Whallon moved to amend the report by adding after the word "towns" in the 7th line of the second section the words, "but no town shall raise a larger sum of money for the support of the common schools in any one year than they receive from the State."

The President put the question upon agreeing to said motion, and it was decided in the negative as follows:

For the affirmative

Mr Adams	Mr Frost	Mr Whallon
Mr Clark	Mr Johnson	Mr Wilkin
Mr Cole	Mr Martin	Mr Williams
Mr Fox	Mr Smith	

For the negative

Mr Bond	Mr Fine	Mr S. H. P. Hall
Mr Brownson	Mr Floyd	Mr Hawley
Mr Burch	Mr Fuller	Mr Lawrence
Mr Coffin	Mr Geddes	Mr Tamblin
Mr Colt		

On motion of Mr S. H. P. Hall,
Said bill was recommitted to the committee of the whole

February 16, 1849, p. 222

The Senate then resolved itself into a committee of the whole on the bill entitled, "An act to establish free education throughout the State," and after some time spent thereon, Mr Bokee, from said committee, reported progress, and asked for and obtained leave to sit again.

February 17, 1849, p. 229

The Senate then resolved itself into a committee of the whole on the bill entitled, "An act to establish free education throughout the State," and Mr Bokee, from said committee, reported that they had amended said bill by striking out the word "education" and inserting the word "schools."

February 17, 1849, p. 230

The Senate then resolved itself into the committee of the whole on the bill entitled, "An act to establish free schools throughout the State," and after some time spent thereon, Mr Bokee, from said committee, reported progress, and asked for and obtained leave to sit again.

March 2, 1849, p. 294

Similar report was made by Mr Floyd on March 5. Same disposition.

March 5, 1849, p. 309

The bill entitled, "An act establishing free schools throughout the State," being called up for consideration,
On motion of Mr Cornwell,
Ordered, That said bill be referred to a select committee consisting of Messrs Cornwell, Colt, Hawley, Johnson and Cook, to consider the report complete.

March 6, 1849, p. 312

Mr Colt, from select committee, reported complete, the bill entitled, "An act establishing free schools throughout the State,"

Ordered, That the said bill do have its third reading.

March 8, 1849, p. 320

The bill entitled, "An act establishing free schools throughout the State," coming up for its third reading.

On motion of Mr Colt, and by unanimous consent, the words " district libraries" were struck out of the sixth line of the third section.

Mr. Johnson moved to recommit this bill to the select committee who had reported the bill, to report complete

The President put the question upon agreeing to said motion, and it was decided in the affirmative as follows:

For the affirmative

Mr Adams	Mr Colt	Mr S. H. P. Hall
Mr Betts	Mr Cook	Mr W Hall
Mr Bond	Mr Cornwell	Mr Hawley
Mr Burch	Mr Fox	Mr Treadwell
Mr Cole	Mr Frost	

For the negative

| Mr Clark | Mr Floyd | Mr Martin |
| Mr Fine | | |

March 10, 1849, p. 338

Mr Cornwell from the select committee, reported complete the bill entitled, "An act to establish free schools throughout the State,"

On motion of Mr Geddes,

Ordered, That said report and bill be laid on the table.

On motion of Mr Geddes,

Ordered, That said bill be printed.

March 12, 1849, p. 346

On motion of Mr Cornwell,

The Senate then proceeded to consider the question on agreeing to the report of the select committee in the bill entitled, "An act authorizing free schools throughout the State,"

Mr Geddes moved to amend the report of the select committee by adding to the bill the following sections:

6 The electors shall determine by ballot at the annual election to be held in November, next, Shall or shall not become a law.

7 It shall be the duty of the state superintendent of common schools to prepare and furnish to the several town clerks in this state, forms of the poll lists, returns, and other necessary proceedings to carry into effect this act, and he shall also furnish, at the expense of the State, to each school district in the State five copies of the act, with the forms prepared by him.

8 The ballots to be deposited in the ballot box shall be in the following form. Those cast in favor of the adoption of this act shall contain the following words:

SCHOOL.

FOR THE NEW SCHOOL LAW.

Those cast against the adoption of the act shall contain the following words:

SCHOOL.

AGAINST THE NEW SCHOOL LAW.

And the ballots shall be so folded as to conceal all the words except the word school, which latter word shall not be concealed, but shall appear on the ballot as folded.

9 The inspectors of elections in the several election districts shall furnish a separate ballot box into which shall be placed all the ballots given for or against the new school law. The Inspectors shall canvass the ballots and make return thereof in the same manner as votes given for the office of governor and lieutenant-governor are by law canvassed and returned.

10 In case a majority of all the votes in the State shall be cast against free schools, this act shall be null and void; And in case a majority of the votes shall be cast in favor of the new school law, then this act shall become a law, and shall take effect on the first of January next.

The President put the question whether the Senate would agree to the amendment, and it was decided in the affirmative as follows:

For the affirmative

Mr Adams	Mr Cook	Mr Geddes
Mr Betts	Mr Fine	Mr S. H. P. Hall
Mr Bond	Mr Fox	Mr Treadwell
Mr Clark		

For the negative

Mr Burch	Mr Colt	Mr Johnson
Mr Bush	Mr Cornwell	Mr Wilkin
Mr Coffin	Mr Hawley	

The report of the committee was then agreed to, and the bill ordered to a third reading.

March 15, 1849, p. 369

The bill entitled, "An act establishing free schools throughout the State," was read the third time and passed, a majority of all the members elected to the Senate voting in favor thereof, and three fifths of all the members elected to the Senate being present on the final passage thereof, as follows:

For the affirmative

Mr Betts	Mr Colt	Mr Fuller
Mr Bond	Mr Cook	Mr Geddes
Mr Burch	Mr Cornwell	Mr S. H. P. Hall
Mr Bush	Mr Fine	Mr Hawley
Mr Clark	Mr Floyd	Mr Martin
Mr Coffin	Mr Fox	Mr Treadwell
Mr Cole	Mr Frost	Mr Wilkin

Ordered, That the clerk deliver said bill to the Assembly, and request their concurrence therein.

March 16, 1849, p. 377

A message was received from the Assembly, informing that they had passed the following bills without amendment: "An act to establish free schools throughout the State."

Ordered, That said bills be transmitted to the Governor.

March 24, 1849, p. 436

The same message was received from the Assembly on March 26. Same disposition.

Chapter 404

An act to amend an act entitled "An act establishing free schools throughout the State" passed March 26, 1849

Passed April 11, 1849, three-fifths being present

The People of the State of New-York, represented in Senate and Assembly, do enact as follows:

1 Section six of the act entitled "An act establishing free schools throughout the State," passed March 26, 1849, is hereby amended by striking out the word " second " in the last line of said section, and inserting the word " third " in lieu thereof, and the said section shall be amended accordingly in the printed copies of said act when published by the Secretary of State.

2 The fourteenth section of said act is amended by striking out therefrom all after the word " effect," and inserting in lieu thereof the word " immediately."

3 The trustees of any school district, or a majority of them, may at any time, after the adoption of this act by the people, and prior to the first annual meeting thereafter, if they deem it necessary, call a special meeting for the purpose mentioned in the third section of said act, and notice of the same shall be given at the same time and in the same manner as is required by said section in relation to the estimates therein mentioned.

4 This act shall take effect immediately.

Chapter 7

An act to amend " an act establishing free schools throughout the State," passed March 26, 1849

[Passed January 31, 1850, " three-fifths being present "]

The People of the State of New York, represented in Senate and Assembly, do enact as follows:

Section 1 The eighth section of the act entitled "An act establishing free schools throughout the State," is hereby amended, by inserting after the word " cities," the words " or villages," so that the said eighth section shall read, " all laws and parts of laws inconsistent with the provisions of this act, other than those relating to free schools in any cities or villages in this State, are hereby repealed."

§ 2 All the acts of the boards of education, or trustees of school districts, or of commissioners, and all other officers of school districts in villages, where free schools were established prior to the passage and approval of the act to amend the " Act establishing free schools throughout the State," passed March 26th, 1849, are hereby declared as valid and effectual as if the said act establishing free schools throughout the State had not been passed.

§ 3 This act shall take effect immediately.

Chapter 174, Laws of 1849
An act making appropriations for the support of common schools for the year 1849 and 1850

Passed March 30, 1849, "three-fifths being present"

The People of the State of New York, represented in Senate and Assembly, do enact as follows:

Section 1 The following sums are hereby appropriated to the objects hereinafter expressed to be paid out of the income of the several funds hereinafter designated in each of the years 1849 and 1850.

1 For the use of the common schools One hundred and twenty thousand dollars out of the revenue of the common school fund.

2 For the like purpose One hundred and ten thousand dollars out of the revenue of the United States Deposite Fund.

3 For the district school libraries the sum of Fifty-five thousand dollars out of the income of the said Deposite Fund; the said appropriation shall be paid on the conditions prescribed in the existing statutes of this State relating to common schools and according to the apportionment to be made by the State Superintendent.

Sec. 2 The treasurer shall pay on the warrant of the Comptroller out of the income of the United States Deposite or Literature Funds not otherwise appropriated to the trustees of one or more academies, as the Regents of the University shall designate, in each county in this State, the sum of Two hundred and fifty-dollars per year for the years One thousand eight hundred and fifty and One thousand eight hundred and fifty-one, provided such academy or academies shall have instructed in the science of common school teaching for at least four months during each of said years at least twenty individuals, but no such one county shall receive a larger sum than Two hundred and fifty dollars.

The vote by counties on the adoption of the free school plan in the elections of 1849 was as follows:

COUNTY	MAJORITY FOR FREE SCHOOLS	MAJORITY AGAINST FREE SCHOOLS
Albany	6 798	
Allegany	2 171	
Broome	1 030	
Cattaraugus	2 700	
Cayuga	2 373	
Chautauqua	2 098	
Chemung	1 897	
Chenango		432
Clinton	2 108	
Columbia	4 489	
Cortland	391	
Delaware	120	
Dutchess	6 327	
Erie	7 258	

COUNTY	MAJORITY FOR FREE SCHOOLS	MAJORITY AGAINST FREE SCHOOLS
Essex	1 779	
Franklin	1 378	
Fulton and Hamilton	1 137	
Genesee	1 504	
Greene	795	
Herkimer	1 932	
Jefferson	2 685	
Kings	8 390	
Lewis	755	
Livingston	2 060	
Madison	1 644	
Monroe	5 218	
Montgomery	3 437	
New York	19 739	
Niagara	972	
Oneida	4 595	
Onondaga	5 938	
Ontario	2 928	
Orange	2 160	
Orleans	1 470	
Oswego	3 124	
Otsego		10
Putnam	934	
Queens	2 256	
Rensselaer	6 276	
Richmond	1 415	
Rockland	703	
St Lawrence	2 451	
Saratoga	2 639	
Schenectady	2 000	
Schoharie	77	
Seneca	1 913	
Steuben	3 393	
Suffolk	1 541	
Sullivan	1 922	
Tioga		718
Ulster	4 506	
Warren	1 029	
Washington	1 811	
Wayne	1 658	
Westchester	3 572	
Wyoming	1 348	
Yates	1 651	
	158 181	1 240

EDITORIAL COMMENT ON THE FREE SCHOOL ACT OF 1849

Some of the newspaper articles published during the session of the Legislature and immediately after the passage of the free school act on March 26, 1849, were as follows:

Free Schools

In the senate of this state, on the 9th inst., Mr Bond reported favorably on the bill to establish free schools throughout this state. A proper bill to this effect, should pass the legislature without opposition. No public measure is of more public importance, or would promise more beneficial results.— *Schenectady Reflector, January 12, 1849*

Free Schools

The free school bill passed to its third reading in the Senate on the 15th inst., and bids fair to become a law. We hardly think so popular a measure will get swamped in the popular branch of the Legislature.— *Schenectady Reflector, March 23, 1849*

The Free School System is Urged

The free school system is urged upon the adoption of the State, by strong and weighty arguments. The experience of cities of the State, containing a population of over 600,000 shows the benefits of a system of free education. — *Utica Daily Gazette, January 13, 1849*

Free Schools

A bill is before the Legislature to establish free schools throughout the State — the expenses to be assessed upon the taxable property in each district. The sense of the people is to be taken before the act goes into operation — At the general election in November next, they are to vote upon the question, and if a majority of votes shall be cast for free schools, the new law will go into operation on the first day of September, 1850.—*Rochester Daily Democrat, January 29, 1849*

Free Schools

The first great care of our government, then, should be the education of the whole people. The simple but well-established fact that the number of voters in this country who are unable to read and write far exceeds the largest majority which has ever been claimed in the canvass for a President of the United States, is alone sufficient to startle the mind with apprehensions. That all our most important elections should be determined by the votes of persons who are utterly destitute of that degree of enlightenment which would enable them to execute their trust with fidelity to the best interest of their country, is indeed a fearful reflection, and one which calls loudly for the corrective influences of judicious legislation. Let the facilities of education, then be still farther increased. Let the plea of poverty no longer remain an excuse for ignorance, but let the door of the common school be thrown open free to all who will enter, and ignorance and vice will recede before the benign presence of knowledge and virtue, and our happy country will be secure in the intelligence of its people.

That the project of Free Schools will meet with opposition, is as certain as that men can be narrow-minded and selfish. That the interests of some, as it regards the immediate question of dollars and cents, will be found to clash with the principles upon which these schools must be conducted, is easily foreseen, but when a great national good is to be accomplished, the sordid calculations of the few should not be permitted to outweigh the urgent claims of the many. It is the misfortune of the poorer class to be abundantly blessed with children, while many of the wealthier class have comparatively few, and hence it will be argued that the tax for the support of Free Schools falls heaviest upon those who share the least in the benefits they dispense. Well, is not ignorance the " parent of vice? "— and is it not a wise economy to contribute of your substance for such a purpose, and to seek for protection in the intelligence and virtue of community, rather than to aid in supporting police officers, magistrates and prisons? How many thousand are at this moment, perhaps, expiating their offences against the lives and property of their fellows, who owe the first impulse of crime to ignorance, and who have persisted in vice until the penalty of the law has overtaken them — all for the want of early educational influences, which, perhaps, stern poverty denied them. Let, then, a single barrier no longer interpose between the humblest of our citizens and the Common Schools. Let the wholesome lessons, duties and habits of thought inculcated in these noble institutions, be as free to all as the air they breathe; and while we cannot doubt that the result will be satisfactory even in a pecuniary point of view, the influence upon the moral health of community will be far beyond the paltry estimate of dollars and cents.— *Montgomery Phœnix and Fort Plain Advertiser, February 1, 1849*

Common Schools

We acknowledged, a few days since, the receipt of Mr Morgan's report on the condition, prospects, etc., of our common schools. It is a subject which should interest every adult person in the State. When we look back and see what our forefathers were obliged to contend with — ignorance in its worst form — and compare their state with the present, when not a single man, woman, or child need be ignorant, we have cause for deep and heartfelt gratitude. Learning is now diffused through nearly every vein and channel of our land; and when the Legislature gives us *free* schools indeed, there will be no excuse for the neglect of the great advantages of education. Mr Morgan's report is very able, and his suggestions are not only worthy consideration, but immediate adoption. The matter of supervising the schools is admirably brought out, and we hope will have a proper effect upon all who desire an exact system and a faithful performance of duties. The District School Journal, in the hands of its able editor, has done, and is continuing to do, a good work. With such help the system must be improved and advanced in a ratio with the intelligence and growing necessities of the people. We commend the report to the careful perusal of our numerous readers.— *Syracuse Daily Star, February 9, 1849*

Free Schools

The Senate bill providing for free schools throughout the State passed the Assembly on Friday, precisely in the shape in which it passed the Senate. The bill has no doubt received the Executive sanction — but does not become operative until sanctioned by a majority of the popular vote at the ensuing general election.

That it will receive such sanction is scarcely to be doubted, if we may judge from the numerous petitions which have been presented at this and former sessions of the legislature. Whatever may be said of the details of the bill, the principle appears to be in accordance with the general sentiment. Nor is it to be imagined that a difference of opinion on minor points will prove an embarrassment to such as desire to see the primary schools open to all, free of charge.

We shall publish an official copy of the bill tomorrow — that our readers will be able to judge for themselves of the principle and details of this important measure.—*Albany Argus, March 26, 1849*

The Free School Law

We present to our readers today the "Free School Law" of our State. The Evening Journal in speaking of the passage of this Law says:

"The Act establishing Free Schools throughout the State, was passed through its third reading in the House, precisely as it came down from the Senate. It, therefore, now requires nothing but the signature of the Governor to become a law. Before, however, it can go into operation, it must receive the assent of the People, at the next general election. There is little doubt but that it will receive such assent; for it is not only in accordance with the sentiment of the great mass of the people, but it is as eminently just in principle, as it will be salutary in its results. There may be differences of opinion in regard to some of its details. But after the general principle shall have received the popular sanction, whatever defects are discovered in the details may be easily rectified.

We hazard nothing in predicting that through all time this law will be referred to as a noble monument of wisdom and munificence. The proposition of the first section of the act, that these schools should be "free to all," is sound and incontrovertible. That it has received the almost unanimous sanction of both Houses of the Legislature, is both commendable and gratifying. Its endorsement was due as well to the character of the State as to the spirit of the age. Our Common Schools should be what this law will make them, free as air. Their doors should be thrown wide open. The State can impart no richer legacy to her children, than a substantial common school education. It is the surest preventive of crime, and the best guarantee of good citizenship.— *Onondaga Standard, March 28, 1849*

Free Schools

The bill providing for free schools throughout the state, was passed in the House of Assembly, on Friday last, in precisely the shape in which it was transmitted by the Senate. Thus has this much desired measure become a law. The main features of the bill are as follows: It authorizes the levying of a county tax which shall be equal in amount to the sum apportioned by the state, and this is to be divided among the towns in the same manner as the school moneys from the state are divided. In addition to this, there shall be levied an amount, equal to the apportionment by the state, in each of the towns in the county, which is to be levied and collected the same as town taxes are raised. This county tax and the taxes levied in the towns, it will be seen, adds to the state bounty, a sum double its amount. An estimate is to be made in each school district of the amount necessary for school expenses in the district, such as for school apparatus, library, teacher's wages, furniture, fuel, etc., which estimate is to be exclusive of the public money, and the money to be raised by the county and town, due public notice of which shall be given, with a notice for a public meeting in the district; and such estimate, or so much thereof as shall be approved, shall be levied on the property in the district liable to be taxed. Should the voters of the district, neglect or refuse to raise such additional sum as would support the school for six months, the duty is devolved on the trustees of procuring a school to be kept for the period of four months, and raising the amount necessary to pay therefor, by tax. The schools are to be free to all over five, and under twenty-one years of age.

The act is not to go into effect until after its submission to the people of the state, at the ballot-boxes, in November next, when, if the result be favorable, it will go into operation.— *Schenectady Reflector, March 30, 1849*

Free School Law

An act establishing free schools throughout the State has passed the Legislature, which is to be submitted to the people at the next election for their approval. There can be no doubt that it will receive such approval. Public sentiment, if we have judged of it correctly, is ripe for a measure so just in principle and salutary in its results.

The details of the act can be improved, as experience points out its defects; and therefore we hope that a diversity of opinion in regard to its provisions will not prevent an almost unanimous assent to the great principles involved in the question of free education.

In our next number, we will give the law, together with the several acts relating to our school system passed by the Legislature of 1849 — a body distinguished for its enlightened views on the subject of education and its liberality and efficiency in its action upon this important subject.— *District School Journal, April 1, 1849*

Free Schools

We are enabled to publish this week the act of the Legislature, establishing free schools throughout the State. The question is to be referred to the people at the next annual election, and we cannot doubt that the cause of popular education will be sustained by their votes. New York is second to no other State in the Union in her efforts in behalf of public instruction, and by this noble act of opening the school houses to the youth of the State, she will build up a more lasting and beneficial monument than her boasted works of public improvement.— *Kingston Ulster Republican, April 4, 1849*

Memorial of the Onondaga County Teachers Institute to the Legislature, in Relation to Free Schools

To the Honorable the Legislature
of the State of New York

The undersigned having been appointed by the Onondaga County Teachers Institute, a committee to memorialize your honorable body for the establishment of a system of free schools throughout this State, respectfully invite attention to the following:

1 The duty of society to educate its younger members.

During the period when the young are most susceptible of impressions for good or evil — when the habits of their physical, intellectual and moral natures are forming for all future existence — they are wholly dependent upon the guidance of others. When they commence their earthly existence, they become members of community. They cannot be excluded from it. Facts warrant us in saying that if their early guidance is wrong, no earthly power can prevent them from being perpetual burdens to the body politic. But if they are properly guided during their most susceptible years, if right habits have been formed in them by their guardians, they then become valuable members of society.

The Creator has so ordered, that no member of society can suffer, without all participating: hence as a mere matter of self preservation, and of increased individual happiness, society is securing her own elevation by using the means within her reach to elevate the younger members. The older members are the natural guardians of the younger. They cannot escape from this duty. If we dislike our companions or our neighbors, we can form new associations, or remove to another locality; but when society receives an individual, she must do it even without her consent, and viper though he be, she must carry him in her bosom. The criminal statistics of the age furnish proof that ignorance and vice are the great disturbers of the public peace, and that they furnish the convicts of our prisons. How important then is it, that the young be trained to intelligence and virtue, if for no other reason, that the security of society shall be within herself more formidable than bolts and bars, or penal laws — the cheerful and intelligent co-operation of all, for the good of all.

The interests of society are best promoted by a thorough system of education. Those who are now responsible members are passing away, and others rising to fill their places and perform their duties. If they are better qualified to perform them as citizens and men than their predecessors, the commonwealth is the gainer; but if an inferior race follows, society is deteriorated, and it needs no spirit of prophecy to predict, that at no distant period our fair temple of Liberty will crumble to ruins.

2 The undersigned believe it to be a sound principle of political economy, that the value of property is increased in proportion to the security of the tenure by which it is held, and the facilities for its increase.

Let us then consider,

First, The security of property. In a civilized state men place the most value upon real estate, but among a barbarous or half civilized people the greatest value is set upon the necessaries of immediate existence, or immediate enjoyment. The Arab, the Mexican rancho, or even the wild American Indian, can conceive of but little value in the soil: his arms, his horse, and his ornaments, are to him most valuable, because they are most useful and best gratify his vanity. No man in his senses would buy real estate, with the liability at any moment of being deprived of it. And other things being equal, property will be very much influenced in its value by this feeling of security. In communities composed of the honest and the dishonest, the good and the bad, the value of property will depend much upon the relative proportion of the two classes. We may have the best of laws, but unless the moral sense of community is at least equally elevated, they will remain a dead letter upon the statute book, or at most but partially executed.

Second, The facilities for the increase of property. It seems to your memorialists evident, that in a country where there is but little security in the possession of property, and but few facilities for its increase, its value must be depressed. If we look for an example, Ireland, bleeding, famishing Ireland presents a mournful one. A writer in the Westminster Review thus speaks of her condition: "She is involved in a vicious circle of evils, which every day binds itself more tightly around her. The wretchedness of her people, caused by want of employment, makes them desperate, criminal and rebellious. And their despair, crime and rebellious spirit, scare away capital, deter the exertions of private enterprise, and thus perpetuate their non-employment and consequent misery." If the above extract be true, it seems to us to follow, that the insecurity of the times, and the liability of being deprived of capital, keeps every kind of property depressed. In France, too, men were deterred from private enterprise, on account of the instability of the times, thus forcing the provisional government to open the national workshops to keep the laboring multitudes from starvation. Facts warrant the statement, that, in those countries where the most general education prevails, there will be found most stability and security, and there the greatest facilities for the sure increase of property will be found; and there its value, other things being equal, will be most enhanced.

If the security of property is greatest, and also the facilities for its increase, in an educated community, it is manifestly the true interest of property holders to scatter broadcast over the land the seeds of knowledge. It will not be necessary for us to say, that indisputably the common school presents the most feasible means of accomplishing this object. Probably all the school education of at least five sixths of the rising generation will be acquired at these institutions. They should therefore be open to all, without distinction. They should be the common property of society, in which all the members should have an equal interest. But under their present management in this State (except a few cities and villages) the poor man must go and confess his poverty, and crave the privilege of sending his children to the common school, as the beggar craves a morsel of food. Is it strange that his dignity revolts at this?

All the operations of society are carried on, more or less, by means of money. The army, and all the operations of government, even to the mending of the highways, are supported by money drawn from the resources of the country, and not upon individuals as individuals. Prisons are built, and all the expenses of detecting, arresting, confining, trying and punishing criminals, are borne by the members of community in proportion to each one's pecuniary means. Our poor-houses are on the same footing, and are filled by imbeciles simply from ignorance. Why not, in justice to the young, support by the same equal and equitable tax the common school, which will prevent, in most instances, a life of crime, or a resort in after life to the poor-house? It is notorious, that the great body of the criminals in our prisons, and the paupers in our poor-houses, are of the lowest and most ignorant class. Shall that class go on widening and deepening by increase of itself, and by accessions from foreign lands? If so, the ship of State can hardly fail to flounder on the shoals of ignorance, or be dashed in pieces against the rocks of anarchy, unless prevented by more than human foresight.

3 Your memorialists have compiled the following statistics, showing the actual expense necessary to carry a system of free schools into successful operation throughout this State. And first, they would remark, that nearly one-fourth of the children in the State are now substantially enjoying all the privileges of free schools.

Hon. John C. Spencer, in his report to the Legislature, for 1839, estimated that the entire expense of schooling all the children in the State would average $3.35. The amount for tuition was only $1.77 per scholar.

We present the following estimates on the basis of Mr. Spencer's for the year 1847.

Interest on school houses and lands, for each of the 10,621 districts, at an average of $200 each..................	$127,452 00
Books and stationery for the 775,723 children, reported at $1 each	775,723 00
Fuel for each district, at $10 each.......................	106,210 00
Fees of collectors at 5 per cent, on local funds, local taxes and amounts raised by supervisors, $419,008................	20,950 40
Fees on rate bills, at 5 per cent, $466,674.44.............	23,333 72
Repairs of houses, at $5 each............................	53,105 00
Compensation of town superintendents (873), at an average of $50 each	43,650 00
Amount	$1,150,424 12
Amount paid teachers' wages...........................	1,105,682 34
Making an aggregate of............................	$2,256,106 46

expended in 1847, for school purposes.

Dividing this sum by the number of children reported as having actually attended school (775,723) and it gives an average cost per scholar, of $2.91. But the actual amount for instruction was $1,105,682.34, which, divided as before, gives for each scholar $1.42½. But of this sum only $466,674.44, was raised by rate bill, the balance of expenditure being now derived from the State, or by a property tax. This sum, divided as before, gives an average for each child of sixty cents; or taking the aggregate of taxable property in the State, for the year 1847, as reported by the Comptroller, at the sum of $632,699,993, and a tax of three-fourths of a mill per dollar, yields $474,529.99, which is more than sufficient to pay the rate bill of that year by

$7,950.55. In the city of Syracuse, it is estimated that a property tax of three-fifths of a mill per dollar will cover the tuition of pupils at the public schools.

In the report of Mr Randall, for the year 1840, it is stated, that in all the schools of Buffalo, public and private, previous to the free system, there were only 1,424 children, and that the amount paid for tuition was $19,094, being $13.41 per year for each scholar, or $3.35 per quarter. An estimate of the actual expense of yearly instruction of an equal number in the public schools, under the free system, showed an annual balance in favor of that system, of $11,254, or a saving of nearly two-thirds.

By comparing the estimate made by Mr Spencer, with the above, it will be seen that he estimates the expense of each pupil for a year, at $3.35; exactly the same as was paid in Buffalo for one quarter!

From the foregoing considerations, your memorialists would respectfully petition your honorable body, to give to the good people of the State of New York, at your present session, a system of free schools. And your memorialists will ever pray.

R. R. STETSON,
W. W. NEWMAN,
A. G. SALISBURY,
Committee.

Syracuse, February 24, 1849 —District School Journal, April 1, 1849

New York Free School Law

We are gratified to learn that this enlightened and benevolent project has at length received the legislative sanction, and now only awaits the ratification of the people to become the law of this State. We cannot for a moment doubt that that ratification will be accorded to it by a vote strongly indicative of the intelligence of the people, in relation to a subject which so vitally concerns themselves. The Press-by habit taught to give questions of public interest the closest scrutiny, and generally a faithful index of public sentiment — is almost unanimous in favor of the new system; and we shall be slow to believe that a few sordid worshippers of the "almighty dollar," can succeed in defeating a measure which presents the facilities of universal education, and which will do more towards suppressing crime, securing the rights of property, and promoting the moral health of community, than a dozen of other legislature enactments combined. We shall have more to say upon this subject, before the time of voting arrives. In the meantime, study the act, which will be found in another column.— *Fort Plain Weekly Radii, April 5, 1849*

The first section of the "Act establishing free-schools throughout the State," is as follows:

" Common-schools in the several school districts of this State shall be free to all persons residing in the district over five and under twenty-one years of age. Persons not residents of a district may be admitted into the schools kept therein, with the approbation in writing of the trustees thereof, or a majority of them."

"COMMON-SCHOOLS SHALL BE FREE TO ALL PERSONS RESIDING IN THE DISTRICT!" Worthy to be inscribed on columns

WILLIAM WATSON NEWMAN
(Picture furnished through courtesy of Mr C. W. Bardeen)

ALBERT GLEASON SALISBURY
(Picture furnished through courtesy of Mr C. W. Bardeen)

of marble in every town in the State. The act contains simple and intelligible rules of proceedings for the whole process, so as to guarantee a school in every district for at least four months in the year. The question of the adoption of this system is to be submitted to the people at the November election, and if a majority of votes shall be in its favor (which we cannot doubt) the law will take effect on the 1st of January, 1850. The provision includes the city of New York, which will then be on a par with the rest of the State. The effects of this law will be seen gloriously in 30 years, say by the census of 1880.— *The Independent, April 5, 1849*

We refer our readers to the new school law published to-day. Though long, its interest and importance will well repay perusal.

The system of "free schools" has long been the boast and glory of the New England States — and we rejoice that the legislature of the Empire State — Empire in all that constitutes commercial greatness, has now laid the foundation of her equal greatness in the wide field of education.

The details of the bill may not please every body; but these may be corrected as time and experience suggest. The principle of free schools, in its broadest and most universal scope, shall ever find an advocate in us.

Education, as we have before remarked, has been well defined by Burke to be "the cheap defense of nations." —- *Binghamton Daily Iris, April 17, 1849*

Free Schools — Schools in Lowell

Seeing by the prints that a bill for the establishment of free schools is before the New-York Legislature, I cannot forbear saying a word on a matter which lies so near my heart. Free Schools! Who can fully estimate the vast importance of these two words? Intelligence and happiness, not for the few but for the million. Make education free to the lowly as well as to the high-born, and you have nearly if not wholly swept away those false distinctions in society which in time will strike a death-blow at the very root to republicanism. For the past few years many educational movements have been made in New-York, and that much good has been the result none can doubt; but as well might a scholar expect to make good progress by commencing with the higher branches of an English education, and leaving first principles to be learned last, as New-York, permanently to improve her schools until this first great step has been taken. The great cry has been for better teachers, yet nevertheless, I firmly believe (and I do not speak this without an acquaintance with the subject,) that the supply has equalled the demand. That another body of persons can be found in New-York so self denying as her common school teachers I much doubt. With employers, in most cases, the question is not whether he or she be qualified for the responsible station of a teacher, but whether he can be obtained for a small compensation; nor do I believe this is from a want of liberality, nor yet from inability to appreciate the services of a good teacher, as many are ready to assert, but from necessity. The patronage of the wealthier portion of community is oftentimes wholly withdrawn from the humble district school, leaving it to be sustained by those who are illy able to bear the burden. And who that knows anything of a country population does not know that it is difficult for a large portion of the people to spare the few dollars necessary for the payment of the teacher. There is much said about teaching through a lofty missionary spirit, for the benefit of the race and not for money. Alas! for this beautiful theory teachers are not machines, which will operate by being daily wound up, but human beings, with frail bodies and physical wants like others of mankind. I think $40 per year a large average estimate for the female teacher of New-York. How can she be supported from such an income and still find means to furnish herself with books and necessary instruction beyond the most ordinary education? If well educated persons can be found who are willing to make teaching a profession under such a state of things, I should not hesitate to pronounce them deficient in energy, an ingredient all important in a teacher's composition; but I pass to speak of the schools in Lowell.

Free schools were established here under the present admirable and successful system, not without much opposition from capitalist whose pecuniary interests were liable to far less taxation under the old district system. When an appropriation of $6,000 for the building of the first Grammar School-house (some twenty years since,) was voted for by the School Committee, the measure was strongly opposed by Kirk Boott and others, but the house was built and a school was established, which soon became the pride and boast of the city; and to the gratification of the committee when, a short time after its establishment, Henry Clay and other distinguished gentlemen visited the city, they were conducted by Kirk Boott to this school, as an object of the first interest. There are three grades of schools, the Primary, Grammar and High Schools. Each grammar school is furnished with four teachers, and in addition to these, a writing and music master are in attendance two days in each week. Two hundred scholars are accommodated with ease; these are all seated in one room under the superintendence of the principal. The three female assistants are occupied the whole time in hearing recitations, having ten minutes only for a class, except in arithmetic, which occupies twenty. So one unacquainted with the perfect order which reigns in these schools, ten minutes would seem little more than sufficient time for the classes to get to and from the recitation room; yet much is accomplished in this short space of time, and nowhere can better scholars be found. A clock is placed in the school-room which strikes one every ten minutes, this is the signal for the scholars to take their places, and by the time one class is seated another is reciting. The great success of these schools is mostly attributable to the permanency of the teachers and the power given them. Some of the principals have taught the same school eighteen years, and many of the assistants have been employed seven or eight years. Changes are seldom made except from the resignation of the teachers, and even these are accepted with reluctance by the committee, who are solicitious to obtain well qualified teachers, and slow to part with them from slight causes. No child can be admitted to a grammar school without having first been examined by one of the teachers and pronounced qualified to enter some one of the classes; neither can he leave one school and enter another without a certificate from his teacher giving a good reason for his removal; and as the schools are free and under the control of a committee chosen by the people, the injudicious interference of parents is wholly precluded. I have gotten to the end of my sheet without having said hardly anything that was in my mind, but perhaps another time I shall be more successful; meanwhile may the legislators of my loved native State, establish Free Schools, and thus wreath for her a never failing garland.

E. D. P.

Lowell, Feb. 1849.— District School Journal, May 1, 1849

The Free School Principle

The providence of God has so ordered the vast and beneficent scheme of the Universe, that the substantial happiness and true welfare of every intelligent human being is dependent upon the degree in which those elements exist and are diffused around him: and consequently the greater and more beneficial the influence which he exerts in ameliorating the condition, supplying the wants and aiding the efforts of his fellow men the more abundant and ample will be his share of the resulting product. The voice of Christianity, of history and of experience alike proclaim this great and eternal truth: and no amount or combination of sordid selfishness intent on its own exclusive interest and coldly withdrawing itself from companionship with its kind can hope to accomplish its grovelling objects in contravention of those immutable principles upon which the broad superstructure of humanity itself is reared and sustained.

It is our design on this and subsequent occasions to advert more immediately to the great subject of education in its relation to the formation of character and the objects and pursuits of life — to illustrate its intimate connections with individual and social well-being — its importance as an indispensable agent of civilization and as the fundamental basis of all good government — and its relation with all that we are accustomed to value and to prize in the community which surrounds us.

The observation is frequently heard that here and there — in this or that community — and this or that neighborhood very little interest exists on the subject of education — very little attention is paid to it — and very little progress made. Nothing can be more erroneous or untrue. On every hand — in every locality — in every hamlet and settlement and in every household of the land, the work of education is in rapid and certain progress. From the cradle to the grave — in all the varieties and mutations of life — amid all its "chances and changes" — in the quiet and stillness of the family — in the ever widening circle of society with its numerous institutions, habits, manners, customs — in the crowded thoroughfares of commerce — the broad fields of labor — the spacious arena of politics — the brilliant circles of fashion and pleasure — and the retired walks of contemplation — no less than in the established seminaries of learning, the elementary or higher school, the academy, the college and the university — the education of the mind and of the heart is unceasingly in progress: and its results in all their magnitude and multiplicity are around and about us here and every where. To it we owe all that we are, have been or hope to be, here or hereafter; to it we are indebted for our happy homes, for the security for life, liberty, and the pursuit of happiness, which our invaluable institutions afford, and for the prodigious and accelerated advances of science in all its departments, of the arts in all their grandeur and utility, of legislation, in all its varied adaptations to our circumstances and wants, of political economy in all its comprehensiveness, and of christianity in all its beneficence. With or without our direct co-operation in any systematic plan for its extension and improvement, the great machinery of civilization is in constant and unintermitted revolution: and it only remains for us to determine its character and shape its results. If we neglect this duty, the work of education *still goes on*: but it is that education which alas! is all too rife, too potent and too efficacious already, in our midst — the education of the corrupted highways and bye-ways of the world — the education of those purlieus of vice, infamy and wretchedness which every where abound in most calamitous and fearful profusion. Around and about us on every hand are confiding ingenuous, hopeful and innocent youth — silently but powerfully appealing to our highest and noblest sympathies, for the proper development and direction of their expanding faculties — ready to travel with us in those paths of pleasantness and ways of peace which lead to wisdom and virtue and knowledge, but who, if we coldly and selfishly refuse to take them by the hand, will speedily and inevitably seek other guides and become apt proficients in that crowded school of vice and guilt and shame, whose skilful and hardened graduates fill our penitentiaries, disturb the quiet and the peace of our family fire side, and furnish the miserable and deluded victims of that fearful penalty which justice demands, and the laws exact of him who lifts his hand against his brother's blood! — *District School Journal, July 1849*

There is a paper published in Orange County, under the name, we believe, of the " Banner of Liberty," or some such high sounding title, which is engaged in a ferocious crusade against free schools, normal schools and popular education generally; and which seems apprehensive that the approaching triumph of the principle of Universal Education is destined to usher in all the evils of a despotic tyranny. Perhaps it may comfort the worthy editors to know that the warmest friends of education do not expect to bring within its pale, a greater proportion than ninety-nine out of every hundred of the whole population of the Republic ; an arrangement which will leave " ample verge and room enough," for himself and his friends for at least an entire generation.— *District School Journal, August, 1849*

The Free School System in Hudson

Not long since we had the pleasure of attending an exhibition of the children of the Public Schools of the city of Hudson, and of visiting, two of the largest schools, the one consisting of boys exclusively, under the charge of Mr Carver and Mrs Smith; and the other, consisting of girls, under the charge of Miss Nichols. The perfect order and discipline which appeared to prevail in these schools — each of them numbering some two hundred pupils — the exceeding neatness and beauty of their copy books — the marked superiority of their exercises in drawing, and the facility and promptness with which their simultaneous music, readings, and recitations were conducted — struck us as indicative, in all respects, of a system well conceived, judiciously administered, and widely and extensively beneficient in its effects. The public exercises at the Presbyterian Church, in which were gathered at least a thousand children, with their parents and friends, were interesting and instructive, and we needed no higher proof of the intrinsic excellency of the Free School System than was here presented. Two of the City Superintendents, J. W. Fairfield and Doct. Bronson, together with several eminent and distinguished Clergymen of the city and neighboring towns, were present and participated in the exercises of the day. The citizens of Hudson have, in our judgment, every reason to be proud of their excellent school system, and of the mode in which it is administered; and we hope to see their example copied, in due time, by every large town in the State.— *District School Journal, September 1849*

At the Whig State Convention the following resolution was offered by Mr Osgood, of Allegany and was adopted:

Resolved, That this Convention approves of the principles of the law passed at the last session of the Legislature, providing that the Common Schools of this State shall be free, and recommend that said law be sanctioned by the people at the ensuing election.— *Binghamton Republican, October 1, 1849*

To the Friends of Universal Education and Free Schools

The "Act establishing Free Schools throughout the State," passed at the last Session of the Legislature, is to be submitted for the approval or rejection of the electors of the State, at the ensuing November election. The importance and magnitude of the issue thus involved cannot fail of being duly appreciated by every enlightened mind; and the most ample means of information in reference to the principle and practical details of this great measure, should be within the reach of all.

With this view, we are requested to state the conductor of the District school journal has devoted, and will still continue to devote, the columns of that paper, until after the election, exclusively to that subject. In the August and September Nos. will be found a Circular Letter, addressed by the Hon. Horace Mann of Massachusetts, to several of the ablest and most experienced educators of the Union, in refernce to the intellectual, moral and social efforts capable of being produced by the adoption of a complete and enlightened system of Universal Education, based on the Free School System, together with the replies of the persons thus addressed. The publication of these letters will be continued in the October number, which will appear as early as the 20th inst.; and in the same number will be contained a masterly and able exposition of the principal arguments in favor of the adoption of the Free Schools System, from the pen of the Chief Superintendent of the schools of Upper Canada, . . . These arguments are chiefly based upon the practical operations of the system in Massachusetts, and such of the other States, cities or towns where it has been for any length of time in successful operation, and will be found to afford a perfect magazine of facts and illustrations in support of the proposed system. On the other hand, in order to afford the opponents of the system an opportunity of becoming acquainted with the arguments brought to bear against it, the same number will contain the recent manifesto of the New York Freeman's Journal, . . . a religious newspaper, devoted to the support of Catholic principles . . . against the adoption of the Free School System. The November No. of the Journal will be issued as early as the 15th of October, and will contain the views of the Editor, at considerable length, on this subject together with such other matter as may be deemed to have a practical bearing, on either side of the question.

The Journal is sent, at the expense of the State, to each of the eleven thousand School Districts, and is therefore acceptable to all who may desire information in reference to this interesting topic. Should an extra number of copies be required, they will be furnished on application to the editor,

S. S. Randall, Secretary's Office, in this city, at the rate of $2 per hundred for each number, or at $5 per hundred for the Aug., Sept., Oct. and Nov. numbers, where more than one hundred copies are ordered to one address.

Editors and publishers of papers throughout the State, favorable to the interests of education are respectfully requested to copy this notice.— *Binghamton Republican, October 5, 1849*

Free Schools — "Hear Both Sides"

The following article is taken from the "Freeman's Journal" of the city of New-York, of the date of Aug. 11. The Journal, although not perhaps the organ of the Roman Catholic Church in this country, is the most widely circulated newspaper advocating the tenets of that church.

The article is very speciously addressed to the prejudices and sectarian pride of the several Protestant denominations.

The conclusion to which the Editor would conduct his readers, although he does not express it, may be stated in two parts; 1st, that the state should make no public provision for the education of the people; and 2d, that all education should be under the direction of the church, or of the clergy of some denomination of christians.

We will not attempt to make an argument on this subject. We will, however, put this question to the people: "Are you willing to abandon and destroy your system of Common Schools, and commit the education of your children to the sectarian institutions, and private schools established and endowed by the various religious denominations?"

That is the question to be answered at the polls.

Compulsory "Free Schools"

At the election which is to take place on the first Tuesday of next November, the voters in the State of New-York are to be called upon to say whether the system of schools established by the State, and sustained by a compulsory tax on the citizens at large, is to be extended throughout the State. The taking cognomen of Free Schools has been given to this system, because it provides that every citizen, after being compelled to pay his part to the support of the school by law established, is to be as free to send his children to it as the Quaker or Baptist in England is free to attend the services of the Church by law established, for which he is duly tythed whether he goes to it or not. Did this free school system propose sufficient guarantees for a right and sound direction of education by the State, we should, nevertheless, be opposed to it, because it is unconstitutional, and every unconstitutional act must result sooner or later in embarrassments and evil; but the negation of sound principles of education implied in its very conception gives us stronger and multiplied reasons for opposing the measure.

The public sentiment of the community is with us in asserting the necessity of religion in the training of our youth. That sentiment may be unfortunately vague; it may and does differ lamentably in its conception of what is false and true in religion, but it nevertheless is pretty tolerably united in the profession of its belief that the influences of religion are necessary for the perpetuity of our political institutions, and for the well being of society.

But, in this country, the State very properly acknowledges its incompetency in matters religious. It can prescribe nothing in the premises; and does it all in simply protecting all religions in their legal rights. If then the State attempts to establish schools in the midst of conflicting religions, it can do so only by making practical negation of them all. Its schools must be independent of religion — void of it. If they be not so they will be a fraud upon its professions, and an injustice to whatever religions are disregarded. If they be honest and impartial, they must be as empty of religion as any broker's office in Wall Street.

Such irreligious schools are then in conflict with the professed public sentiment of the community; and there are but two ways that men attached to any religion can come to countenance them. The first way is by the hope which one or another sect may indulge of being able to control the system by its own influences. This is, however, a feeble reliance. The Presbyterians are the sect which have the most to hope in this way, because they are more politically active, and perhaps more intensely sectarian than any other. During the past four years they have succeeded in billeting one of their ministers, we believe, upon almost every public institution we know of,— from West Point to the Blind Asylum and the Alms House. And yet we know of no sect that has so repeatedly and publicly enforced the necessity of having their children educated in schools under their own supervision. They have good reasons for so doing, and we are persuaded that no one sect need hope to give efficient tone to the public schools of the State.

The other apology for professedly religious men in maintaining such schools, is, that in them nothing shall be taught but what is purely secular, and that the religious education of the children shall be confided to the Sunday instruction of the church, and to the conscience of the parents. If this be true, we must confess ourselves incapable of an abstraction sublime enough to comprehend it. What we do understand, what we see, what we hear from others who have better opportunities of seeing than we have, gives us the right and forces us to assert that in no community on the face of the earth have the religious needs of its children been in any such ways moderately provided for. We would by no means seem either to undervalue the Sunday instructions, or to excuse parents from the awful responsiblities of bringing up their children christianly. But it is precisely from those who have labored long and with the most zealous devotion in Sunday instruction that we hear it most earnestly asserted, that these exertions are, for the most part, fruitless, when for six days out of seven the children are subjected to the godless influence of godless schools. And on the other hand, it is precisely from those who appreciate most justly parental obligations, that we hear the bitterest lamentations, and the most doleful recitals of the effects of schools which unprotestantize the children of protestants at the expense of unchristianizing, and so far uncivilizing every body.

And even supposing schools are so constituted as to produce no effect directly injurious to religion, which is the utmost that can be asked; what delusion to suppose that the greater number of parents are in a condition to take charge of the daily religious training of the children? It is the lot of the larger portion of mankind to gain their daily bread by daily and harrassing toil; and those who are subjected to this, never have, and never will, as a general rule, attend to the religious training of their children; in fact, in some sense, their apology is good, they *cannot* do it. And among those who are better off in this world's goods who will venture to say that more disposition, or more moral capacity is to be found? Surely does it need to be argued out that, as a rule too general, school is necessary to fortify and protect children from the contagion of unhappy influences at home?

And, it is therefore, that the Catholic Church at first instituted daily schools, which are solely her creation. She instituted them as nurseries, first of religion and its doctrines, and virtues and discipline; and then, subordinately, of science under the guidance and direction of religion. To cut off these daily schools, which the Church established primarily for religious purposes, from the doctrine and discipline of religion for which they were instituted, and to devote them exclusively to secular education, is simply to bastardize the minds and hearts of youth, to substitute the opinions and arrogance of opinionated men for the traditions of christianity, to raise up a generation of infidels to succeed us, and to resolve all notions of religion into neatly dressed persons and tidily kept houses.

In the proposed measure of *free schools* for the State of New York, we see a system of wholesale oppression, an unconstitutional legislation to which we intend inviting the attention of the public who are to be interested. We shall do so in no spirit of party. The Methodists, Presbyterians, and every sect in the State, supposing them to believe their religion worth teaching, and capable of being taught to their children, have the same interest in the subject that we have. So has every class or community which may prefer choosing the kind of school and the teacher to which they shall commit their children, to having the whole thing arranged by the politicians. A State education is a curse near akin to a State religion. The men who shall pull the wires of political parties are as unfit to be entrusted with one as with the other. We have shown that this project is irreligious — impious would not be too strong a term — and we shall do what we can to show that it is the interest of the community at large to reject it.

Statements of the various misdoings of those in charge of the free schools in this city — the perversion and squandering of money — the inefficiency of instruction — the gross injustice practiced, apparently on system, in the appointment of teachers, etc. etc. etc., have been promised us from different quarters. We have been expecting to receive them for months past. Will the gentlemen who have spoken with us, and all others who have information of an exact and available kind, please to put us in possession of it? We give our readers in another column a morsel of the ordinary proceedings of the board of education.—*District School Journal, October 1849*

"A few days more and this important question is to be tested at the ballot box. Are the people prepared by reflection, and a thorough appreciation of the subject, to decide it in accordance with the spirit of the age, and with an intelligent regard for their own highest and best interests? We trust they are. To us the idea of a liberal system of education, adapted to the wants of the whole community, without discrimination, appears to be worthy of the first place in the public sentiment and regard; and that system should be free as the air we breathe, that every excuse for ignorance may be taken away, and the poorest may be on an equal footing with the richest in making their approach to the sources of education.

We are aware that this question has not received, and is not receiving, the attention which its importance demands. The political press is entirely absorbed with the great battle for the ascendancy and the spoils, and there is scarcely philanthropy and patriotism enough in the composition of the most pretending lovers of the dear people, to inspire even an incidental allusion to this subject. Its own merits are hence the advocates which must mainly commend it to the support of the people; and the great and beneficient idea which it involves — the salutary influence which its successful operations promises to exert upon the moral welfare and happiness of our people, surely invite the anxious consideration of every elector, and ought to incite him to its favorable remembrance at the ballot box.

The arguments aside from the view taken of the subject by Catholics — the reasons of whose jealousies are well understood and appreciated — against the establishment of Free Schools, in our opinion, are not sufficient to invoke and justify opposition. The rich miser who has no children to educate, has property to protect; and, to say the least, it ought to be a matter of no consideration to him, whether he be taxed to educate his neighbors and have his security in the general intelligence and virtue of his community, or to punish crimes which are the result of ignorance, and thus have his security only in the dread of law and its punishments. Does any one doubt that ninetenths of the crimes which are constantly perpetrating, and to procure the punishment of which a large item is annually added to our tax list, are the natural fruit of a defective education — of habits encouraged by idleness during that portion of life which should be wholly devoted to the District School, but which is neglected for the want of means and of the absence of early moral training? And who that does not doubt this — to say nothing of his duty as a lover of his race, and a friend of his country does not see in the Free School System, at least a partial remedy for vice and crime, and an element of merit which reaches beyond the paltry consideration of dollars and cents, while at the same time, even these are not sacrificed in its support? — *Canajoharie Weekly Radii, October 25, 1849*

At our approaching election the people of this State will give their decision for or against the law passed at the last Session of the Legislature providing for the establishment of Free Schools throughout the State. We trust the subject will receive an attentive consideration from all classes of society, as it involves interests of an enduring nature, and of vast consequences to the future welfare of the State.

We unhesitatingly declare ourselves, without a shadow of doubt, in favor of the law and its proposed policy. Its enlarged views, its democratic principles, its beneficient aims, and its ultimate blessings, are so great, that we give it a most sincere and hearty approval.— *Lowville Northern Journal, October 17, 1849*

Against Free Schools

The Poughkeepsie Eagle, a rabid whig journal, whom the Buffalo Express charges with opposition to the canal enlargement, offers its whig friends ballots AGAINST FREE SCHOOLS LAW. Opposition to internal improvement is followed by its counterpart OPPOSITION TO MENTAL IMPROVEMENT.— *Rochester Daily Advertiser, October 30, 1849*

Free Schools

The most important question to be decided at the ensuing election is that of the adoption or rejection of the law passed by the Legislature last winter, providing for the establishment of a general system of free schools throughout this State. We are of opinion, that with comparatively few exceptions, the people of the State are in favor of the law. But it has always been a hard matter to excite any amount of interest upon an abstract question of this character, and there is more danger that it will be lost by default, than from opposition.

In a country where the highest power lies in the hands of the people — where no other source of political sovereignty is recognized, education is one of the main pillars of the State. As a citizen of equal rights and duties with his fellows, each should thoroughly know the laws and institutions of his country, and understand the whole machinery of its government. The man properly educated is a good, a useful patriotic citizen. Our education hitherto has been very effective. It formerly was a work more surrounding circumstances than the effect of designed exertions. Until recently it has been regarded of that importance in its general bearing upon the destiny of man that it ought to be considered. We hold that society owes every child an education, and its first great duty towards its members is to provide the means of obtaining it. The aggregate property of all civil communities should be considered and held as a fund to provide the means of instruction for *all*. It is not only a measure of self-protection that this should be done, but a matter of high and indisputable *justice*. It is a plain principle of political economy relating to the greater interest of the *whole*. And more especially should it be so considered and acted upon in our country and among the masses. It is one of those reforms of the day, which has partially obtained, and which must not be suffered to rest until it has become general — become the prevailing principle in all the States. Free Education— based upon the property of the State, we should contend for, nor cease our exertions with anything short of it. A beginning has already been made. Free Schools have already been established and in successful operation upon a limited scale for a number of years past. Every where they have been tried they have gradually overcome all opposition, and established themselves in the public favor. Education is the birthright of every man in a civilized state. It is one of those inalienable rights which attach to him and of which he cannot be justly defrauded.

We know this proposition has its opponents, among those whose property will be called upon to bear the expense of a general and free system. But the first and essential object of all true government is the protection of the rights of the person. The rights of property are merely an incident — a circumstance arising out of the relation which the one bears to the other. Education, therefore, is one of those things which constitute a legitimate claim upon property.

Then, as a great equalizing principle — as a great moral agent — free education is an essential element of republican institutions. In fact, it is their very life blood — their moving principle, and in this view of the case, demands that it shall be enjoyed by all. And the public mind is fast settling down upon this plain and apparent truth. In the recent Convention which remodeled our State Constitution, it nearly triumphed, and became a part of the organic law. As it was, power was placed in the hands of the Legislature to adopt a general system of free schools throughout the State. A law was passed for this purpose last winter, but is to be acted upon at the ballot box in the coming election before it has vitality. All that is required for its success, is activity and agitation on the part of those who feel its importance, and take an active interest in its adoption. Let a work of agitation be commenced — one which will reach the public mind and obtain an expression, and the work is done. A blessing, rich with momentous results, has been conferred upon the present and future generations, and society has fulfilled one of its most plain and essential duties to its members and to itself.

To urge the importance of education, would be but to repeat truisms, to which we anticipate no dissentient voice. But it cannot, in the connection which it has been placed — in connection with a system of free schools — be too frequently and too earnestly urged upon the attention of all.— *Buffalo Commercial Advertiser, copied in District School Journal, October 1849*

Free Schools

We earnestly invite the attention of each one of our readers to the following masterly exposition of the advantages and benefits of the Free School System, from the pen of the Chief Superintendent of Schools of Upper Canada — a gentleman of the highest literary and moral qualifications, and an ardent and devoted friend of Popular Education. The whole subject is treated with a clearness, comprehensiveness and ability which cannot fail to commend it at once to the judgment of every reflecting mind; and we have no where met with so complete a summary of the main arguments relied upon by the friends of the Free School System, as is here presented. We hope it will be generally read and widely circulated.— *District School Journal, October 1849*

Address to the Inhabitants of Upper Canada, on the System of Free Schools: by the Chief Superintendent of Schools

I beg to invite the attention of the Public Press, of District Councillors and School Trustees, of Clergy and magistrates, and of all persons anxious for the education of all Canadian youth, to the principle on which the expense of promoting that object should be defrayed. The School Law authorises two methods, in addition to that of voluntary contribution; the method of rate-bill on parents sending children to school, and the method of assessment on the property of all, and thus securing to the children of all equal access to school instruction.— The discretionary power of adopting either method, is placed by law — where I think it ought to be placed — in the hands of the people themselves in each municipality. My present object is, simply to submit to your consideration the principal reasons which induce me to think that the one of these methods is better than the other, in order to secure to your children the advantages of a good education. The method which I believe you will find most efficient, has been thus defined: "A tax upon the property of all by the majority for the education of all."

I My first reason for commending this as the best method of providing for the education of your children is, that the people who have been educated under it for two hundred years, are distinguished for personal independence, general intelligence, great industry, economy and prosperity, and a wide diffusion of the comforts and enjoyments of domestic life. The truth of this remark in reference to the character and condition of the people of the New England States, will, I presume, be disputed by none. If their system of civil government be thought less favorable to the cultivation and exercise of some of the higher virtues than that which we enjoy, the efficacy of their school system is the more apparent under circumstances of comparative disadvantage. I will give the origin of this school system in the words of the English "Quarterly Journal of Education"—published under the superintendence of the society for the diffusion of useful knowledge, and at a time when Lord Brougham was Chairman, and Lord John Russell, Vice-Chairman of the Committee:

"The first hint of this system—the great principle of which is, that the property of all shall be taxed by the majority for the education of all—is to be found in the records of the city of Boston for the year 1635, when, at a public or 'body' meeting, a school-master was appointed 'for the teaching and nurturing of children among us,' and a portion of the public lands given him for his support. This, it should be remembered, was done within five years after the first peopling of that little peninsula, and before the humblest wants of its inhabitants were supplied; while their very subsistence from year to year, was uncertain; and when no man in the colony slept in his bed without apprehension from the savages, who not only everywhere crossed on their borders, but still dwelt in the midst of them.

"This was soon imitated in other villages and hamlets springing up in the wilderness. Winthrop, the earliest Governor of the colony, and the great patron of Free Schools, says in his journal under date of 1645, that divers Free Schools were erected in that year in other towns, and that in Boston it was determined to allow forever £50 a year to the master, with a house, and £30 to an usher. But thus far only the individual towns had acted. In 1647, however, the Colonial Assembly of Massachusetts made provisions, by law, that every town in which there were fifty families, should keep a Free School, in which reading and writing could be taught; and every town where there were one hundred families, should keep a school where youth could be prepared in Latin, Greek and Mathematics, for the College or University, which in 1638, had been established by the same authority at Cambridge. In 1656 and 1672, the colonies of Connecticut and New Haven, enacted similar laws; and from this time the system spread with the extending population of that part of America, until it became one of its settled and prominent characteristics, and has so continued to the present day."

I will now present the character of this system in the words of those who best understand it. That great American Statesman, Daniel Webster, received his early training in a Free School, and stated on one occasion, that had he as many children as old Priam himself, he would send them all to the Free School. Mr Webster, in his published speech on the Constitution of Massachusetts, expresses himself on the Free School system, in the following words:

"In this particular, New-England may be allowed to claim, I think, a merit of a peculiar character. She early adopted and has constantly maintained the principle, that it is the undoubted right, and the bounden duty of government, to provide for the instruction of all youth. That which is elsewhere left to chance, or to charity, we secure by law. For the purpose of public instruction, we hold every man subject to taxation in proportion to his property, and we look not to the question, whether he himself have, or have not, children to be benefited by the education for which he pays. We regard it as a wise and liberal system of police, by which property and life, and the peace of society are secured. We seek to prevent, in some measure, the extension of the penal code, by inspiring a salutary and conservative principle of virtue and knowledge in an early age. We hope to excite a feeling of respectability and a sense of character, by enlarging the capacity, and increasing the sphere of intellectual enjoyment. By general instruction, we seek, as far as possible, to purify the whole moral atmosphere; to keep good sentiments uppermost, and to turn the strong current of feeling and opinion, as well as the censures of the law, and the denunciations of religion, against immorality and crime. We hope for a security, beyond the law, and above the law, in the prevalence of enlightened and well-principled moral sentiment. We hope to continue and prolong the time, when, in the villages and farm-houses of New England, there may be undisturbed sleep within unbarred doors. And knowing that our government rests directly on the public will, that we may preserve it, we endeavor to give a safe and proper direction to that public will. We do not, indeed, expect all men to be philosophers or statesmen; but we confidently trust, and our expectation of the duration of our system of government rests on that trust, that by the diffusion of general knowledge and good and virtuous sentiments, the political fabric may be secure, as well against open violence and overthrow, as against the slow but sure undermining of licentiousness."

The Honorable Edward Everett,— late President of Harvard University, late Governor of the State of Massachusetts, and late American Ambassador to England — remarks as follows, in his Address on the "Advantage of Useful Knowledge to working men:"

"Think of the inestimable good conferred on all succeeding generations by the early settlers of America, who first established the system of Public Schools, where instruction should be furnished gratis, to all the children in the community. No such thing was before known in the world. There were Schools and Colleges supported by funds which had been bequeathed by charitable individuals; and in consequence, most of common Schools of this kind in Europe were regarded as establishments for the poor. So deeprooted is this idea, that when I have been applied to for information as to our Public Schools from those parts where no such system exists, I have frequently found it hard to obtain credit, when I have declared, that there was nothing disreputable in the public opinion here, in sending children to schools supported at the public charge. The idea of Free Schools for the whole people, when it first crossed the minds of our forefathers, was entirely original; and how much of the prosperity and happiness of their children and posterity has flowed from this living spring of public intelligence."

The following extracts from the Annual School Reports of 1847 and 1848, prepared by Secretary of the Massachusetts Board of Education, deserves special attention, as well for the beauty of their language as for the nobleness of the sentiments which they express:

"The present year (1847) completes the second century since the Free Schools of Massachusetts were first established. In 1647, when a few scattered and feeble settlements, almost buried in the depths of the forests, were all that constituted the Colony of Massachusetts, when the entire population consisted of twenty-one thousand souls; when the external means of the people were small, their dwellings humble, and their raiment and subsistence scanty and homely; when the whole valuation of all the colonial estates, both public and private, would hardly equal the inventory of many a private individual at the present day; when the fierce eye of the savage was nightly seen glaring from the edge of the surrounding wilderness, and no defence or succor was at hand; it was then, amid all these privations and dangers, that the Pilgrim Fathers conceived the magnificent idea of a Free and Universal Education for the people; and, amid all their poverty, they stinted themselves to still scantier pittance; amid all their toils, they imposed upon themselves still more burdensome labors; amid all their perils, they braved still greater dangers, that they might find the time and the means to reduce their grand conception to practice. Two divine ideas filled their great hearts,— their duty to God and to posterity. For the one, they built the Church; for the other, they opened the School. Religion and Knowledge!—two attributes of the same glorious and eternal truth,—and that truth, the only one on which immortal or mortal happiness can be securely founded.

"As an innovation upon all pre-existing policy and usages, the establishment of Free Schools was the boldest ever promulgated, since the commencement of the Christian Era. As a theory, it could have been refuted and silenced by a more formidable array of argument and experience than was ever marshalled against any other opinion of human origin. But time has ratified its soundness. Two centuries now proclaim it to be as wise as it was courageous, as beneficent as it was disinterested. It was one of those grand mental and moral experiments whose effects cannot be determined in a single generation. But now, according to the manner in which human life is computed, we are the sixth generation from its founders, and have we not reason to be grateful both to God and man for its unnumbered blessings? The sincerity of our gratitude must be tested by our efforts to perpetuate and improve what they established."—(Tenth Annual Report of the Board of Education, for 1847, pp. 107, 108.)

"The Massachusetts school system represents favorably the system of all the New England States. Not one of them has an element of prosperity or of permanence, of security against decay within, or the invasion of its rights from without, which ours does not possess. Our law requires that a school should be sustained in every town in the State,— even the smallest and the poorest not being excepted; and that this school shall be as open and free to all the children as the light of day, or the air of heaven. No child is met at the threshold of the school house door, to be asked for money, or whether his parents are native or foreign, whether or not they pay a tax, or what is their faith. The school-house is common property. All about it are enclosures and hedges, indicating private ownership and forbidding intrusion; but there is a spot which even rapacity dares not lay its finger upon. The most avaricious would as soon think of monopolizing the summer cloud, as it comes floating up from the west to shed its treasures upon the thirsty earth, as of monopolizing these fountains of knowledge. Public opinion,— that sovereign in representative governments,— is in harmony with the law. Not unfrequently there is some private opposition, and occasionally it avows itself and assumes an attitude of hostility; but perseverance on the part of the friends of progress always subdues it, and the success of their measures eventually shame it out of existence."—(Eleventh Annual Report, 1848, pp. 88, 89.)

"It is a gratifying circumstance that many of our sister States, convinced by our success, have followed our example; and at the present time, in the rich and populous County of Lancashire, in England, a movement is on foot, led on by some of the best men in the United Kingdom, whose object is to petition Parliament for a charter, empowering that county to establish a system of Free Schools, on a basis similar to ours."— (Ib. p. 24)

These extracts contain the testimony of the most competent witnesses as to the principles and efficiency of the Free School system; while the well known character of the New-England people, for self-reliance, economy, industry, morality, intelligence and general enterprise, is a sufficient illustration of the influence and tendency of the system, even under the admitted disadvantage of a defective Christianity and a peculiar form of government. What such a system of schools has accomplished in the less genial climate of New England under such circumstances, will it not accomplish in Upper Canada under more favorable circumstances? It is worthy of remark, that in no state or city where the Free School system has been fairly tried, has it ever been abandoned. The inhabitants of New-England who have tried it for two centuries, (and they are second to no people in their rigid notions of economy and individual rights,) regard it as the greatest blessing which their country enjoys, and her highest glory. Other cities, towns and states, are adopting the New-England system of supporting schools as fast as they become acquainted with its principles and operations.

2 This is also the most effectual method of providing the best, as well as the cheapest, school for the youth of each School Section. Our Schools are now often poor and feeble, because a large portion of the best educated inhabitants stand aloof from them, as unworthy of their support, as unfit to educate their children. Thus the Common Schools are frequently left to the care and support of the least instructed part of the population, and are then complained of as inferior in character and badly supported. The Free School system makes every man a supporter of the School according to his own property. All persons — and especially the more wealthy — who are thus identified with the School, will feel interested in it; they will be anxious that their contributions to the School should be as effective as possible, and that they themselves may derive all possible benefit from it. When all the inhabitants of a School Section thus become concerned in the School, its character and efficiency will inevitably be advanced. The more wealthy contributors will seek to make the School fit and efficient for the English education of their own children; the Trustees will be under no fears from the disinclination or opposition of particular individuals in employing a suitable teacher and stipulating his salary; and thus is the foundation laid for a good School, adapted to all the youth of the section. The character of the School will be as much advanced as the expense of it so individual parents will be diminished; the son of the poor man, equally with the son of the rich man, will drink from the stream of knowledge at the

common fountain, and will experience corresponding elevation of thought, sentiment, feeling and pursuit. Such a sight cannot fail to gladden the heart of Christian Humanity.

3 The Free School system is the true, and I think only effectual remedy for the pernicious and pauperising system which is at present incident to our Common Schools. Many children are now kept from School on the alleged grounds of parental poverty. How far this excuse is well founded, is immaterial to the question in hand; of the fact of the excuse itself, and of its wide spread blasing influence, there can be no doubt. Trustees of Schools are also invested with authority to exonerate poor parents, desirous of educating their children, from the payment of a School Rate-bill — an additional amount of Rate-bill being imposed on the more wealthy parents of children attending the school, in order to make up the deficiencies occasioned by the exemption of the poorer parents. Such parents are thus invested with the character of paupers; their children are educated as pauper children; while other parents, sooner than attach to themselves and children such a designation, will keep their children from the School altogether — thus entailing upon them the curse of ignorance, if not of idleness, in addition to the misfortune of poverty. Now, while one class of poor children are altogether deprived of the benefits of all education by a parental pride or indifference, the other class of them are educated as paupers or as ragged Scholars. Is it not likely that children educated under this character, will imbibe the spirit of it? If we would wish them to feel and act and rely upon themselves as free men when they grow up to manhood, let them be educated in that spirit when young. Such is the spirit of the Free School system. It banishes the very idea of pauperism from the School. No child comes there by sufferance; but every one comes there upon the ground of right. The poor man as well as the rich man pays for the support of the School according to his means; and the right of his son to the School is thus as legal as that of the rich man's son. It is true the poor man does not pay as large a tax in the abstract as his rich neighbor; but that does not the less entitle him to the protection of the law; nor should it less entitle him to the advantages provided by law for the education of his children. The grovelling and slavish spirit of pauperism becomes extinct in the atmosphere of the Free School. Pauperism and poor laws are unknown in Free-School countries; and a system of Free Schools would, in less than half a century, supercede their necessity in any country.

4 The system of Free Schools makes the best provision and furnishes the strongest inducements for the education of every youth in each School Section of the land. To compel the education of children by the terror of legal pains and penalties, is at variance with my ideas of the true method of promoting universal education; but to place before parents the strongest motives for educating their children, and to provide the best facilities for that purpose, is alike the dictate of sound policy and Christian patriotism. The Quarterly Rate-bill system holds out an inducement and temptation to a parent to keep his child from the School. The parents temptation and difficulty is increased in proportion to the number of children he has to educate. The Rate-bill is always sufficient to tempt the indifferent parent to keep his child or children from the School; it often compels the poor man to do so, or else to get them educated as paupers. In proportion to the small-

ness of the School will be the largeness of the Rate-bill on each of the few supporters of it, in order to make up the salary of the Teacher; and as the School diminishes in pupils will the Rate-bill increase on those that remain. The withdrawment of each pupil from the School lessens the resources of the Trustees to fulfil their engagement with the Teacher, and increases the temptation to others to remove their children also. Thus are Trustees often embarrassed and perplexed — Teachers deprived of the just fruits of their labors — good Teachers retiring and poor ones substituted — Schools often closed, and hundreds and thousands of children left without School instruction of any kind. Now, the Free-School system of supporting Schools puts an end to most of these evils. A rate being imposed upon each inhabitant of a School Section according to his means, provision is at once made for the education of every child in such section. Every parent feels that having paid his School-rate, whether little or much, he has paid what the law requires for that year's Common School education of all his children, and that they are all entitled by law to the benefits of the School. However poor a man may be, having paid what the law requires, he can claim the education of his children as a legal right, and not supplicate it as a cringing beggar. His children go to the School, not in the character and spirit of ragged pauperism, but in the ennobling spirit of conscious right, and on equal vantage ground with others. Each parent feeling that he has paid for the education of his children, naturally desires that they may have the benefit of it. While, therefore, the quarterly rate-bill per pupil is a temptation to each parent to keep his children from the School, the annual School rate upon property furnishes each parent with a corresponding inducement to send his children to School, relieving Trustees at the same time from all fear and uncertainty as to the means of providing for the Teacher's salary. It is not, therefore, surprising to find that wherever the Free School system has been tried in Upper Canada or elsewhere, the attendance of pupils at School has increased from fifty to three hundred per cent. The facilities thus provided for the education of each child in a School Section will leave the ignorant, careless, or unnatural parent without excuse for the educational neglect of his children. The finger of universal reproof and scorn pointed at him will soon prove more powerful than statute law, and without infringing any individual right, will morally compel him, in connection with higher considerations, to send his children to School. This is the system of "compulsory education" I wish to see every where in operation — the compulsion of provision for the universal education of children — the compulsion of their universal right to be educated — the compulsion of universal interest in the School — the compulsion of universal concentrated opinion in behalf of the education of every child in the land. Under such a system, in the course of ten years, an uneducated Canadian youth would be a monstrous phenomenon.

5 The system of Free Schools may also be commended upon the ground of its tendency to promote unity and mutual affection among the inhabitants of each School division. The imposition of quarterly rate-bills is a source of frequent neighborhood disputes and divisions. The imposition of an annual rate upon all the inhabitants of a School Section according to property puts an end to quarterly ratebill disputes and divisions, unites the feelings as well as the interests of all in one object, and tends to promote that

unity and mutual affection which a unity of object and a oneness of interest are calculated to create. The care and interest of one will be the care and interest of all — that is, to have the best School possible; — and the intellectual light of that School, like the material light of heaven, will freely beam upon every child in the School Section.

6 I think the system of Free School is, furthermore, most consonant with the true principles and ends of civil government. Can a more noble and economical provision be made for the security of life, liberty and property, than by removing and preventing the accumulation of that ignorance and its attendant vices which are the great sources of insecurity and danger, and the invariable pretext if not justification of despotism? Are any natural rights more fundamental and sacred than those of children to such an education as will fit them for their duties as citizens? If a parent is amenable to the laws who takes away a child's life by violence, or wilfully exposes it to starvation, does he less violate the inherent rights of the child in exposing it to moral and intellectual starvation? It is noble to recognize this inalienable right of infancy and youth by providing for them the means of the education to which they are entitled,— not as children of particular families, but as children of our race and country. And how perfectly does it harmonize with the true principles of civil government, for every man to support the laws and all institutions designed for the common good, according to his ability. This is the acknowledged principle of all just taxation; and it is the true principle of universal education. It links every man to his fellow-man in the obligations of the common interests; it wars with that greatest, meanest foe to all social advancement — the isolation of selfish individuality; and implants and nourishes the spirit of true patriotism by making each man feel that the welfare of the whole society is his welfare — that collective interests are first in order of importance and duty, and separate interests are second. And such relations and obligations have their counterpart in the spirit and injunctions of our Divine Christianity. There, while every man is required to bear his own burden according to his ability, the strong are to aid the weak, and the rich are to supply the deficiencies of the poor. This is the pervading feature and animating spirit of the Christian religion; and it is the basis of that system of supporting public Schools which demands the contribution of the poor man according to his penury and of the rich man according to his abundance.

7 But against this system of Free Schools, certain objections have been made; the principal of which I will briefly answer.

First objection: "The Common Schools are not fit to educate the children of the higher classes of society, and therefore these classes ought not to be taxed for the support of the Common Schools."

Answer — The argument of this object is the very cause of the evil on which the objection itself is founded. The unnatural and unpatriotic separation of the wealthier classes from the Common Schools, has caused its inefficiency and alleged degredation. Had the wealty classes been identified with the Common Schools equally with their poorer neighbors,— as is the case in Free School countries — the Common School would have been fit for the education of their children, and proportionably better than it now is for the education of the children of the more numerous common classes of society. In Free School cities and states, the Common Schools are acknowledged to be the best elementary Schools in such cities and states; so much so, that the Governor of the State of Massachusetts remarked at a late School celebration, that if he had the riches of an Astor, he would send all his children through the Common School to the highest institutions in the State. If the wealthy classes can support expensive Private Schools, their influence and exertions would elevate the Common School to an equality with, if not superiority over, any Private School, at less expense to themselves, and to the great benefit of their less affluent neighbors. The support of the education which is essential for the good of all, should be made obligatory upon all; and if all are combined in support of the Common School, it will soon be rendered fit for the English education of all. If persons do not choose to avail themselves of a public institution, that does not release them from the obligations of contributing to its support. It is also worthy of remark, that the Board of Trustees in each city and incorporated town in Upper Canada, has authority to establish Male and Female Primary, Secondary, and High Schools, adapted to the varied intellectual wants of each city and town; while in each country School Section, it requires the united means of intelligence of the whole population to establish and support one thoroughly good school.

Second objection: "It is unjust to tax persons for the support of a School which they do not patronize, and from which they derive no individual benefit."

Answer — If this objection be well founded, it puts an end to School-tax of every kind, and abolishes School and College endowments of every description; it annihilates all systems of public instruction, and leaves education and Schools to individual caprice and inclination. This doctrine was tried in the Belgian Netherlands after the revolt of Belgium from Holland in 1830; and in the course of five years, educational desolation spread throughout the Kingdom, and the Legislature had to interfere to prevent the population from sinking into semi-barbarism. But the principle of public tax for Schools has been avowed in every School Assessment which has ever been imposed by our Legislature, or by any District Council; the same principle is acted upon in the endowment of a Provincial University, for such endowment is as much public property as any part of the public annual revenue of the country. The principle has been avowed and acted upon by every Republican State of America, as well as by the Province of Canada and the countries of Europe. The only question is, as to the extent to which the principle should be applied — whether to raise a part or the whole of what is required to support the Public School. On this point it may be remarked, that if the principle be applied at all, it should be applied in that way and to that extent which will best promote the object contemplated — namely, the sound education of the people; and experience, as well as the nature of the case, shows, that the free system of supporting Schools is the most, and indeed the only, effectual means of promoting the universal education of the people.

I remark further on this second objection, that if it be sound, then must the institutions of government itself be abandoned. If a man can say, I am not to be taxed for the support of what I do not patronise, or from which I receive no individual benefit, then will many a man be exempted from contributing to support the administration of justice, for he does not patronise either the Civil or Criminal Courts; nor should he pay a tax for the erection and support of jails, for he seeks no benefit from them. Should it be said, that jails are necessary for the common safety and welfare, I answer, are they more so than Common Schools? Is a jail for the confinement and punishment of criminals more important to a community than a School for education in knowledge and virtue? In all good governments the interests of the majority are the rule of procedure; and in free governments the voice of the majority determines what shall be done by the whole population for the common interests, without reference to isolated individual cases of advantage or disadvantage, of inclination or disinclination. Does not the Common School involve the common interests; and the Free School system supposes a tax upon all by the majority for the education of all.

I observe again on this second objection, that what it assumes as fact is not true. It assumes that none are benefitted by the Common School but those who patronise it. This is lowest, narrowest and most selfish view of the subject, and indicates a mind the most contracted and grovelling. This view applied to a Provincial University, implies that no persons are benefitted by it except Graduates; applied to criminal jurisprudence and its requisite officers and prisons, it supposes that none are benefitted by them except those whose persons are rescued from the assaults of violence, or whose property is restored from the hands of theft; applied to canals, harbors, roads, &c., this view assumes that no persons derive any benefit from them except those who personally navigate or travel over them. The fact is, that whatever tends to diminish crime and lessen the expenses of criminal jurisprudence, enhances the value of a whole estate of a country or district; and is not this the tendency of good Common School education? And who has not witnessed the expenditure of more money in the detection, imprisonment and punishment of a single uneducated criminal, than would be necessary to educate in the Common School half a dozen children? Is it not better to spend money upon the child than upon the culprit — to prevent crime rather than punish it? Again, whatever adds to the security of property of all kinds increases its value; and does not the proper education of the people do so? Whatever also tends to develope the physical resources of a country, must add to the value of property; and is not this the tendency of the education of the people? Is not education in fact the power of the people to make all the resources of their country tributary to their interests and comforts? And is not this the most obvious and prominent distinguishing feature between an educated and uneducated people — the power of the former, and the powerlessness of the latter, to develope the resources of nature and providence, and make them subservient to human interests and enjoyments? Can this be done without increasing the value of property? I verily believe, that in the sound and universal education of the people, the balance of gain financially is on the side of the wealthier classes. If the poorer classes gain in intellectual power, and in the resources of individual and social happiness, the richer classes gain proportionately, I think more than proportionately, in the enhanced value of their property. As an illustration, take any two neighborhoods, equal in advantages of situation and natural fertility of soil — the one inhabited by an ignorant, and therefore unenterprising, grovelling, if not disorderly, population; the other peopled with a well-educated, and therefore enterprising, intelligent and industrious class of inhabitants. The difference in the value of all real estates in the two neighborhoods is ten if not an hundred-fold greater than the amount of school tax — that has ever been imposed upon it. And yet it is the School that makes the difference in the two neighborhoods; and the larger the field of experiments the more marked will be the difference. Hence in Free-School countries, where the experiment has been so tested as to become a system, there are no warmer advocates of it than men of the largest property and the greatest intelligence — the profoundest scholars and the ablest statesmen.

It has also been objected, that the lands of absentees ought not to be taxed for the support of Schools in the vicinity of such lands. I answered, the inhabitants of the School Sections in which such lands are situated are continually adding to the value of those lands by their labors and improvements, and are therefore entitled to some return, in the shape of a local School-tax, from such absentee landholders.

The objection that the Free School system is a pauperising system, has been sufficiently answered and exposed in a preceding part of this address. Such a term is only applicable to the present rate bill system, as I have shown; and the application of it to the Free School system is an exhibition of the sheerest ignorance of the subject, or a pitiful manœuvre of selfishness against the education of the working classes of the people. History is unanimous in the assertion, that the first race of New-England pilgrims were the best educated and most independent class of men that ever planted the standard of colonization in any new country. Yet among these men did the system of Free Schools originate; by their free and intelligent descendants has it been perpetuated and extended; their universal education has triumphed over the comparative barrenness of their soil and the severity of their climate, and made their States the metropolis of American manufacturers and mechanic arts, and the seat of the best Colleges and Schools in America. Nor is a page of their educational history disfigured with the narrative of a " Ragged School," or the anomaly of a pauper pupil.

I submit then the great question of Free Schools, or of universal education, (for I hold the two to be synonymous in fact,) to the grave consideration of the Canadian public. I think it properly appertains to the inhabitants of each School municipality to decide for themselves on this subject. I desire no further Legislative interference than to give the inhabitants of each School division the power of supporting their own School as they please. Of the result of their inquiries as to the best mode of supporting their School, I have no doubt; and in that result I read the brightest hope and the greatest wealth of future Canada.

[Signed]   E. RYERSON

Education Office,
Toronto, January, 1849

N. B. I have taken no notice of the objection founded upon the inequality and injustice of the assessment laws, in regard to Cities and Towns as well as country School Sections; as that objection lies against the assessment law, and not against the principle of the Free School system; and as, I trust, the imperfection of the assessment laws will be shortly remedied by Legislative enactment.

[*Signed*]   E. R.

— *Journal of Education for Upper Canada, January, 1849*

The Free School Act

We learn from the Oxford Times that the citizens of that village have had a large and intelligent meeting to discuss the merits of this act which is to be submitted to the people at the November Election. After ample discussion the act was approved by a large majority. This is a good step and should be followed in other places.—The act will no doubt become a law by a large majority of the voters of the state; and it will be a measure which will reflect a lasting honor on the Whig legislature which created it.— *Binghamton Republican, October 24, 1849*

The Free School Act

One of the most important questions to be decided by the people of this State is the Act establishing Free Schools throughout this State, which is to be submitted to them at the approaching election, for their adoption or rejection. The subject of Free Schools is one of such vital interest to the well-being of every community, and the importance of general education so universally conceded that we doubt the necessity of saying a word in favor of the adoption of the law in question, to those who so fully appreciate the benefits resulting from it, as the people of Cayuga county undoubtedly do. There may be those, however, even in so intelligent a community as this, who from various circumstances may underestimate the advantages of Free Schools, and perhaps even be opposed to them. Amongst this latter class may be those whose children have already been educated, or who have none to educate, whose property equally with those who have large families must be taxed. But we imagine there are very few comparatively, who are so fortunate as to have educated their children, or so unfortunate as to be destitute of them, and yet whom Providence has blessed with an abundance of this world's goods, that would not cheerfully contribute something from their abundance towards sustaining a system which shall place within the reach of the poor as well as the wealthy the inestimable blessings of Free Schools. We care not whether the rich ever avail themselves of the advantages of such a system or not. Still they are indirectly benefitted to a degree infinitely beyond the paltry sum they will be required to contribute towards its support. Even from mere selfish considerations they are more deeply interested in the subject of Universal Education than those for whose immediate benefit they are taxed. The stability of our government, the rights of property, the welfare of society and indeed the very existence of our free institutions depend upon the virtue of the people, and the people are virtuous just in proportion as they are enlightened.

But we doubt not that most of those to whom we have referred will cheerfully contribute their mite, towards an enlarged and liberal system of education from higher, and purer, and more patriotic movements than those of a selfish character. We believe there is benevolence and love of country enough amongst the wealthier portion of our population to aid not only with their money but with their whole influence to secure to the entire people of this State the great benefits contemplated by the enlightened act of last session. At any rate we sincerely hope that the act will receive the cordial and united support of all parties and sects, and of the rich as well as of the poor. Let it not be said that while the people of every New England State, of Pennsylvania, and of other States have secured to their children the blessings of Free Schools, the Empire State witholds them from hers.— *Editorial from Auburn Daily Advertiser, copied in District School Journal, November, 1849*

Free Schools

In most of the cities of the State the system of Free Schools has been in practical operation for several years and has been growing in popular favor with every day's experience. A large portion of the population are thus already subjected to the law, and their condition is not to be affected by the ratification or rejection of the act submitted to the people; the only question being whether it shall be extended to the rural districts. The objection which might perhaps have been anticipated from the large tax payers, to contributing to the education of the poor, has much less force in the country than in the cities, from the fact that much greater general equality of property exists in the former, and they hold very few persons who do not contribute to the payment of taxes. But in point of fact, and it is highly creditable to the property holders of the cities, very few indeed of them ever made the objection, although their real estate has borne heavy burdens for the immediate benefit of the children of the poor, who crowd the lanes and allies of the larger towns. Their enlightened self interest has taught them that it is better and cheaper to pay for the instruction than to pay for the ignorance of the children of poverty.

There is no reason to anticipate that the people of the agricultural districts will prove less sagacious — less generous they will prove, because the demand upon their generosity is so much less, from the comparative paucity of the non-paying recipients of public instruction. Indeed the collection of rate bills from those unable to pay them, and the exemption from payment of the few unable, in most rural districts, serves only to make an ungracious discrimination between different classes of the community, to remind the poor of their poverty, and to impress the idea that they are the objects of charity in each specific instance. The difference between the sum contributed under the present system and that which will be required to educate all without distinction, would rarely pay the expense wasted in the proceedings to designate those exempted from rate bills, and to collect them from their more fortunate neighbors. The practical management of common schools will be greatly simplified by the proposed change, and the reputation of the State abroad advanced by the formal recognition of the doctrine long established in her practice, that Education is a right as universal as personal freedom.— *Buffalo Commercial Advertiser, copied in District School Journal, November, 1849*

Vote for Free Schools

It should not escape the minds of voters that one of the most important questions presented to them this fall, is " for free schools " or " against free schools." In the city, we enjoy the advantages of education so generally that the question of free schools for the rest of the State will be very likely to receive little attention. But the want of a law, making education free to all is severely felt in the remote parts of the State and the generous supply of that want is demanded by our standing as republicans and civilized men. In some parts of our Union, free schools are universal and there may be seen the beneficial effects of such institutions in a law loving, industrious and happy people, who appreciate their advantages and reward the liberality of their government by their unexceptionable conduct.— *Utica Daily Gazette, November 5, 1849*

The Northern Journal under date of November 28, 1849, says under the following title

The Free School Law

We shall endeavor to answer the numerous questions about the result of this vote next week. The Utica Gazette gives the following:

Hard News from Buffalo.— Williamsburgh, Kings County, was unanimously in favor of the New School Law — not a vote being given against it in the village. Buffalo is beaten by three votes. In these days of close voting, this is a tremendous victory.— *Northern Journal, November 28, 1849*

This great measure — the making of the Schools of the State of New York free to all — has become a law by the overwhelming judgment of the people of the State. We rejoice most sincerely and fully at the successful result of this issue. Open every avenue to the education of the people — throw around them all the moral and religious influences which an enlightened and professedly Christian community can exert, and watch the rising generation with jealous care. The next age will achieve a national glory of peace and holy progress which the world has never witnessed.

The vote stands, for, 249,872; against, 91,951. Majority for the law, 157,921.— *Northern Journal, December 12, 1849*

The New School Law

Mr Editor:— Permit me to inquire through your paper whether the Legislature can rightfully alter, repeal or amend the Free School Act. It contains no reserve of authority by its terms, and the people in their original and sovereign capacity have adopted it. They are the Principal, and the Legislature are but the agent, and is it competent for the latter to alter or amend the proceedings of the former? The People previously voted for the New Constitution and adopted it, thereby placing that beyond the control of the Legislature. Now they have in like manner adopted the Free School Act; and is not this also placed beyond that control? It is a principle almost universal that the same authority is required to alter or amend as is required to make or to do an act. If this principle applies in this case, then is not the present " deformity," bearing the imposing name given to the Act, fixed upon us irremediably until the People shall themselves alter or repeal it?

Yours
H. C.

—*Rochester Daily Democrat, December 27, 1849*

Chapter 7

THE FIGHT FOR RESUBMISSION

In spite of the decisive popular verdict in the general election in November (1849) where the people expressed their approval of a free school law by a majority vote of 157,921 (249,872 ballots were cast for, and 91,571 against the bill) considerable hostility was encountered in the enforcement of the law. Superintendent Morgan in his report of 1850 comments upon the question as follows:

The adoption by the people of the "Act for the establishment of free schools throughout the State," and the consequent incorporation of its provisions into the statutes of the State as a portion of our common school system, constitutes a new and interesting era in the history and progress of that system. Every child between the ages of five and twenty-one, residing in the State, is entitled to free and gratuitous education in the common schools now established, or which may hereafter be established in pursuance of law, and the expense of such education beyond the annual appropriations from the revenue of the common school fund, and the amount required by law to be raised by the respective boards of supervisors upon the taxable property of the several towns and counties of the State, is to be provided by taxation upon the real and personal estate of the inhabitants of the respective school districts. Whatever difference of opinion may exist in reference to the particular mode of levying the tax thus authorized for the universal and free education of the youth of the State, the great principle that elementary instruction in our public schools, shall from henceforth, be free to all, without discrimination or restriction, has been definitely settled, and may be regarded as beyond the reach of controversy. The current of public opinion has long been tending towards this point, and in various sections of the State, including most of the cities and several of the large villages, ample provisions have, at different periods, been made for the free and gratuitous education of the young. Wherever the system has been put in operation, its results have signally vindicated the enlightened policy by which it was dictated and gladdened the hearts and excited the highest hopes of the philanthropist, the statesman and the Christian. It remains only that the efficient cooperation of the inhabitants and officers of the several school districts be secured in carrying into practical effect the provisions of the new system, to diffuse throughout every section of the State the inestimable blessings of a sound mental and moral education.

The late period in the year, at which the new law went into operation, has precluded the possibility of any action on the part of the board of supervisors of any proportion of the counties, in reference to the raising of the additional amount of public money required by the provisions for the support of the schools, during the ensuing year, and thereby an increased burden of taxation might at first view, seem to be cast upon the inhabitants of the several districts. In several of the counties, however, the necessary appropriation has been already made; and inasmuch as in the residue, the required amount, whether levied by the action of the board of supervisors and collected by the town collector, or raised by a district vote and levied by the trustees, will be equally apportioned upon the taxable property of those who are liable, and may, therefore, as well be paid in one form as the other, no permanent or serious inconvenience can possibly ensue. The transition from the former system to the new, will of course, be attended in its first stages with considerable difficulty and embarrassment; and it is to be apprehended, that in very many of the districts, the means of supporting the school for a longer period than four months will be withheld, either from the disinclination of a majority of the legal voters to impose an amount of taxation on themselves, beyond that which the law absolutely requires, without regard to the interests and welfare of the schools, or from mistaken views of the legal effect of their refusal to vote the requisite supplies for a longer period. In many sections of the State, the opinion is very prevalent that the omission of the board of supervisors to raise the additional amount of public money required by the new law, discharges the inhabitants of the respective districts from all obligations to proceed under the law: in others it is supposed that in the absence of any vote of the district authorizing a tax for the support of the schools, Trustees will be at liberty to raise the requisite amount on their own authority, for the maintenance of the schools for four months, and thereafter to resort to the system of rate bills. The necessity, also of providing by district taxation for the payment of the wages of teachers, falling due subsequently to the period when the new law went into operation, although for services in great part rendered previously, adds to the embarrassments, and increases the burdens of many districts. These, with various other difficulties, incident to the organization of a new and hitherto untried system, can scarcely fail of exerting an unfavorable influence upon its operation during the first year of its administration. The belief is, however, confidently entertained that as soon as these preliminary and unavoidable embarrassments are surmounted, the requisite amounts of public money duly raised in the several counties of the State, in accordance with the provisions of the new law, and the sound judgment of the inhabitants of the several districts brought to bear upon the policy, the objects and the design of the law, no obstacles will be interposed to its healthful and invigorating action. If experience shall discover defects in any of its provisions — and perfection is the attribute of no human institution, however carefully devised — the Legislature will, doubtless, promptly and cheerfully apply the necessary remedy. It is, however, due to the enlightened policy which dictated the law, and to the clear and unequivocal expression of the popular will which has sanctioned its enactments, that it should have a fair opportunity of developing its capabilities, as it has been adopted, before any material change in its features shall be attempted; and those of our fellow-citizens who, by their votes have given validity to its provisions as they exist, owe it to themselves, and to the cause of education, cordially and cheerfully to unite in carrying those provisions into effect in the mode best adapted to secure the most favorable results. Having by their united action at the polls, determined that henceforth the benefits and blessings of elementary education shall be freely placed at the disposal of every child of suitable age residing in the State, they are bound by every consideration of public duty and private obligation to render the invaluable boon thus conferred upon the rising generation, fully attainable and efficient. The necessity for any subsequent amendment or alteration of the law, if any such necessity should exist, can be adequately manifested only, by a faithful adherence in the first instance, to its provisions as they are; by which alone a fair test can be afforded of its practical utility.

If, however, it should be deemed expedient to make any alteration in the law, at the present session, the extension of the term of instruction from four to eight months, where the inhabitants refuse to vote the necessary estimates for the support of schools for that period, is respectfully recommended.

In view of the important principle engrafted by the new law upon our system of public instruction, it may not be inappropriate, in concluding this report, briefly to examine the object, aim and ends of that Common School education which has been secured to every future citizen of the State; what is its design and scope; and what it may reasonably be expected to accomplish in the suitable preparation of these who are to participate in its advantages, for the active duties and responsibilities of life. There is great danger, on the one hand, that the friends of popular education may place the standard of practicable attainment, in our Common Schools, too high, and expect from them more than under the most favorable auspices, they are capable of accomplishing; and on the other, that through the apathy and indifference of portions of the people, and a failure on the part of those most interested, to secure the highest attainable grade of ability in the employment of teachers, these elementary institutions may be left to languish and to fall behind the intellectual and moral requirements of the age. It must be kept in view that the Common School is, after all, but the portal to the great temple of education; that the foundations only, of knowledge, are here to be laid, and not the superstructure itself erected. But it should also be remembered that these foundations, if durably and comprehensively laid, may be made to support the noblest and most imposing fabric of human greatness; if defectively and wrongly, that the inevitable result will be a distorted, imperfect, or vicious character.

1 To enable our common schools adequately to accomplish the objects for which they are designed, it is in the first place indispensably requisite that they be furnished with teachers of the highest practicable grade of qualifications. To this end, teaching must itself be elevated to the rank of a science; and the work of elementary instruction be committed to the hands of those only who have prepared themselves for its proper performance by a thorough course of intellectual and moral culture. Normal schools, teachers institutes and academical departments, for the preparation of teachers, should be liberally encouraged and sustained, both by the Legislature and the people, as efficient instrumentalities for supplying this important course of instruction, and furnishing the schools of our State with competent teachers. To secure the services of these teachers, however, and to afford adequate encouragement to their increase, their compensation should be liberal, and their employment, so far as may be practicable, permanent and certain. In most of our school districts the practice has long prevailed of changing the teacher with nearly each successive term. This practice is injurious to all concerned. The teacher who is employed for one, or, at

most, two terms, of three or four months each, however well qualified he may be, and however desirous of promoting the advancement of the pupils committed to his charge, can rarely succeed in communicating the requisite amount of instruction in the various branches taught, in the mode he would desire, before the expiration of his term; nor can he be presumed to take that interest in the present attainments and future progress of his pupils which he would feel if he was more permanently connected with the school. His successor, in all probability, instead of carrying on the course of instruction he has commenced from the point where he left it, marks out for himself a new and different course; and with each new term of the school, the course of instruction is essentially changed, and much of the ground already gained required to be repeatedly gone over upon other and different principles. Much valuable time is thereby lost; needless expense incurred; and the systematic and regular growth of the expanding mind checked and retarded. By the employment, at a fair and liberal compensation, of a thoroughly qualified teacher for a term which shall enable him judiciously and comprehensively to lay the foundations of knowledge in the minds of those committed to his charge, and systematically to develop their faculties — passing from one branch of instruction to another, as he shall find his pupils prepared for the reception of additional attainments — a very large proportion of the time now comparatively wasted in desultory and aimless acquirements, would be gained to the parent and the child — the work of instruction would be far more thoroughly as well as speedily accomplished — and the teacher enabled to devote himself more assiduously and entirely to his important and responsible task, in the consciousness not only that his labors were well rewarded and properly appreciated, but also that his own welfare and reputation were indissolubly connected with the success of his undertaking.

2 A second indispensable requisite to the efficiency and success of our common schools, is the regular and constant attendance of every child not otherwise suitably provided with the opportunities and means of instruction. It should be the aim of the officers and inhabitants of each school district in the State, to make the common school, in every respect, equal, if not superior, to any other institution for elementary instruction, and thereby to secure, if possible, the attendance of every child of suitable age, and with it the personal interest and exertions of the parents. The means provided by the beneficence of the State and authorized and required to be raised by county, town and district taxation, are abundantly adequate to the accomplishment of this object; and there can be no good reason for the failure, in any instance, to place the district school upon a footing of equality, at least, with the most favored private or corporate institution of learning. Moreover it is most in accordance with the evident scope and design of all our republican institutions, that each of our future citizens shall participate equally, in all respects, in the facilities afforded by the laws for elementary instruction; and it is not to be disguised nor denied that the distinction heretofore existing between public and private schools — between the common and the select school, has operated injudiciously as well to the development of character as to the opportunities afforded to those in attendance upon them respectively, for future usefulness and success. The withdrawal from the common school of those children, whose parents have been in a condition to afford them

advantages of a higher kind than was there to be found, has tended to weaken, to a corresponding extent, the power and resources of the former, and to render it inadequate to the intellectual and moral wants of those who were left. Invidious distinctions thus made between the children of the rich and the poor, have been perpetuated; and the foundations of an aristacracy, not recognized by our institutions, and not in accordance with the public sentiment of the country, have been insensibly and probably undesignedly laid. This state of things should no longer be permitted to exist. Let each one of our common schools, now free to all, be made, in all respects, nurseries of knowledge and virtue; let teachers of the highest attainable grade of qualifications, be permanently placed in each; let all the influences which radiate from these elementary institutions upon the community at large, be of the purest and most healthful kind; and let all the children of the community, without discrimination or distinction, be there taught, side by side, and on a footing of the most perfect equality. Then shall we most completely realize the true theory of our free institutions — that " equality of privileges before the law " which lies at the foundation of our government, and which is the only equality the fathers and framers of our Constitution had in view. Then will an opportunity be afforded, for the free development, under the same favorable auspices, of the mental faculties, equally, of the most obscure child of poverty and misfortune, and the most favored inheritor of wealth and fortune; and then will the future aristocracy of our land consist only of that aristocracy of intellect and moral worth and power, before which all other distinctions " pale their ineffectual fires," and which all good men are prepared instinctively to reverence and respect.

3 The course of instruction in our common schools should be systematized, and as far as practicable, extended, so as to embrace within its scope all those branches of study necessary or desirable for completing a thorough English education. In every city and village school this should be deemed indispensably requisite. In the rural districts it can scarcely be expected to be accomplished to the same extent; although in very many of them, much may be done, under proper management, to carry forward the pupils from the lower to the higher branches in a much shorter period than has hitherto been found practicable. To this end, Trustees are recommended, in conjunction with the Teacher and other competent persons, to mark out a systematic course of instruction, embracing a period of at least five or six years, and comprehending all the branches of a good English education. A judicious and well-considered classification of the various pupils in attendance, should then be made, according to their respective attainments and capacities; and these pupils, after having thoroughly completed the elementary course, should successively be drafted into the more advanced classes, and their places supplied by others. This course of instruction should be steadily and faithfully pursued, however frequent may be the change of teachers, and should be varied only when found defective or incomplete. Wherever the resources of the district are unequal to a full development of the course thus marked out, the village, central or high school of the town should afford the means and the opportunity to the more advanced pupils of completing it. With the exception of the languages, and some of the higher branches of mathematics and chemical and astronomical science no sufficient reason is perceived why these more advanced common schools may not include within their range of

tuition all the studies now ordinarily pursued in our Academies and other incorporated Seminaries of learning. The employment of competent and well qualified female teachers, in the weaker districts, will probably be found not only the most economical, but the best and soundest policy — the more advanced scholars participating in the more extended advantages of the Central Town School.

Be this as it may, there can be no doubt of the practicability, as well as policy, of a thorough and complete course of instruction in such of the elementary branches as may be included within the plan and means of each district. Whatever is taught at all, should be well taught. The first principles of knowledge communicated to the learner should be firmly imbedded in the mind, and the foundation of the future superstructure be rendered adequate to any subsequent demand upon its stability and strength. Nothing should be permitted to be superficially or imperfectly passed over. The period of time intervening between the age at which the child is entitled to admission in the school and that at which he may be reasonably expected to leave it for some higher institution, is sufficiently long, if ordinarily improved, to embrace within its range a complete and exact mastery of all the elementary principles of human knowledge: and it is due to each one of the eight hundred thousand children for whom the State has so liberally and beneficially provided the means of education, that the opportunities thus afforded shall be improved to the best possible advantage by those to whom is committed the administration of this sacred trust.

4 In enumerating these various requisites to the success and improvement of the common schools of the State, it has been assumed that a sound and pure christian morality pervades all their teachings. The education of the heart must ever accompany and keep pace with that of the head. Correct principles, right motives and good habits must early be implanted in the youthful mind, and "grow with its growth and strengthen with its strength," and every influence which flows from the elementary school must be elevating and ennobling. Too much care cannot be taken by the inhabitants and officers of school districts, in excluding from the teacher's desk individuals of doubtful moral character, or in securing the services of those whose daily lessons and deportment shall inculcate and foster the great truths of humanity, integrity, conscientiousness and benevolence. To accomplish this, it is not necessary that the peculiar or sectarian views of any religious denomination should be taught, or even adverted to; nor is the Common School the proper place, in any point of view, to enforce the distinctions between the several religious sects. The foundations of character, usefulness and happiness may be laid in those enduring and comprehensive principles of christian ethics and morality which lie without and above the pale of mere theology; and this is the province of the common school, so far as its means are adequate and its jurisdiction extends.

If, therefore, the inhabitants and officers of the several school districts will avail themselves conscientiously and in good faith of the provisions so liberally made by the enlightened and comprehensive policy of the State for the support of elementary schools, they may reasonably look forward to results far surpassing the most sanguine expectations of these statesmen and philanthropists who have hitherto so indefatigably exerted themselves for the promotion of popular education. The coming generation will be prepared to enter upon the varied duties incumbent upon them with faculties unclouded by ignorance, and with principles and habits undebased by vice. The complicated machinery of civilization will move onward to the accomplishment of its majestic destiny, free from the incessant friction of selfish and sinister designs — the enormous expenditures now lavished upon the maintenance and support of criminal jurisprudence, prisons, penitentiaries and poor-houses; will be transferred to objects more in accordance with the spirit of the age — and we shall present the noble spectacle of an educated, enlightened, virtuous community, fulfilling a mission in the advancement of our common humanity, which has been assigned to no other people, in no other age — the practical realization of a free Republic, all whose institutions are based upon the intelligence and integrity of the people.

Press Comment

The opposition to the law brought up again the question of resubmitting to a popular vote the question of free schools. The attitude of the public and the public opinion as expressed through the press in regard to these matters is best illustrated by the following newspaper editorials and letters which appeared during the early part of 1850.

Common Schools

The great change that has taken place in these primary institutions, through the action of the people, has invested them with unusual importance. The people having sanctioned the law rendering the tuition free, the schools will move forward hereafter in a channel of greater usefulness and prosperity.

The Annual Report of the Superintendent of Common Schools — a very able document has just appeared. . . . The report discusses a variety of subjects connected with the schools. The Superintendent repudiates the idea that the people who have *voluntarily* in one year, made such ample provision for schools would shrink from the small additional amount of taxation imposed by the new law, making all the Schools Free. It is by no means certain that the burdens will be increased by the new law, but if they should be for a year or two they will be cheerfully borne. Like all new experiments the new law is destined to meet with opposition at first. It will work awkwardly for a while; but when all parts of the new machinery become properly adjusted, it will become one of the most popular measures ever sanctioned by the people. . . . The new free school law is commented upon at considerable length but as our readers are already acquainted with its main provisions, it is not necessary that we should occupy space with the details.

It is gratifying to know that in the men who have for the past two or three years been at the head of public affairs, the cause of education has had the warmest of friends, the superintendent, Hon. Christopher Morgan, and his able assistants, have exerted themselves diligently in favor of every measure calculated to further and promote the interests of the cause. They have their reward in the grateful hearts of the people.— *Rochester Daily Democrat, January, 5, 1850*

Free Schools Inimical to Despotism

The first free school ever established in Prussia was opened at Berlin by Dr Edder. It was closed by the authorities in a short time, and he was forbid to reopen it under pain of fine and imprisonment. We occasionally hear of opponents of free schools in this country. Let them profit by this lesson taught by despotic Prussia, and cherish those safeguards of freedom, the common schools.— *Rochester Daily Advertiser, January 24, 1850*

The Free School Law

We learn that much embarrassment is experienced, and much difficulty likely to ensue, in many of the school districts of this country, in consequence of the doubt and uncertainty attending some of the provisions of the new law, as applicable to the position in which the districts find themselves placed. The trouble grows out of the grossly stupid or careless manner in which the law was constructed, with reference to the situation of affairs at the time when it should go into operation. We speak not now of the principle of the law (that alone, without regard to the details, was passed upon by the voters,) but the law itself, as providing for putting in operation a new system of school education, is a disgrace to anything but the legislation of this State for the last two years — of that, it is a fair sample and average. It contains scarce a provision that is clear and explicit, and the two circulars issued by the Superintendent of Common Schools, designed to aid in its operation, seem only calclated to make " confusion worse confounded."

It would be interesting to notice the provisions of the law, the recommendations of the Superintendent of their various incongruities, in detail, but we have only time and space to allude to the present prominent difficulties that occur in the operation of the law. The first action under it was required to be taken by the board of supervisors at their annual meeting. They were required to levy upon the county a sum equal to the amount of the state school money apportioned to the county, upon each town a further sum equal to the state school money apportioned to the town; and on this required action of the Supervisors, is based the whole subsequent process of providing for the support of the schools by the districts, for the year. The supervisors of this (as well as other counties) not having levied the amounts required, in consequence of the inopportune time at which the law was made to take effect; their powers being limited to the annual meeting, and that having been held before notification of the adoption of the law was given, a deficiency of two-thirds the amount upon which the trustees are required to base their estimates and the districts their action, exists, and the question arises, how can it be supplied, and what can the districts legally do in the premises? The Superintendent, in his circular of Nov. 20, suggested that it could " be raised only by a loan, to be authorized at a special meeting of the board" (of supervisors,) "to be added to the amount to be levied on the county at the next annual meeting." It is perhaps sufficient to say of this, that the deacons of the several churches would be just as legally competent to authorize a loan and bind the county to a next year's tax to pay it. The Superintendent probably adopted the same conclusion, for on the 21st Dec. he issued another circular, dropping, tacitly, the project of a loan, and advising the districts that when the supervisors had omitted to act, the estimates prepared and submitted by the trustees, " must be based on the existing apportionment of the public money;" (that is, upon the amount of the state money alone,) and the balance requisite for the support of the schools for the year " can only be raised by a district tax." But is this position any more correct than that recommending a loan by the supervisors? Sec. 3 of the free school act, directs the trustees to prepare "an estimate of the amount of money necessary to be raised for the ensuing year — exclusive of the public money, and the money required by law to be raised by the counties and towns —" and so much of said estimate "as shall be approved by the majority of the voters of the district, in the manner prescribed, — "shall be levied and raised by tax on said district," etc. In case the district "refuse or neglect to raise by tax, a sum of money which, added to the public money, and the money raised by the county and towns, will support a school for at least four months," the trustees are authorized by section 6, to employ a teacher etc, and levy the expense, in the manner provided in sec. 3.

It will be seen that the estimate which the trustees are required to make, and the taxes authorized to be levied upon the districts, are all based upon the united amount of the state, county and town money apportioned to the district, and are, in each case, for the purpose of raising the necessary amount exclusive of the state, county and town money. Can the trustees then, adopt any other basis for their action? It is forcibly contended that they cannot— that the sums required by the law to be raised by the county and town, not having been raised, they cannot assume some unauthorized amount as the starting point, and levy a much larger tax upon the district than the law contemplates; — and that when the Supervisors did not levy the necessary amounts upon the counties and towns, the whole machinery of the system, as regards raising the necessary means in the districts for the school purposes, is suspended, until another annual meeting of the supervisors shall recur, or legislation shall furnish the necessary power to set it in motion. The opinions and constructions of the superintendent have no force, to confer powers, or legalize acts not authorized by the law itself. Under such circumstances, the district officers having the matter thrown upon their hands, should be well advised as to their course. Many consider the law unjust in operation, and doubtless resist the payment of taxes which are believed to be illegal. Indeed we have heard such a determination repeatedly expressed.

It is much to be regretted that a law effecting so vitally the interests of every neighborhood, should have been so loosely and shabbily made up — that there should not have been some man at the head of the school department, if not in the legislature, to impart to it some of the attributes of utility.— *Binghamton Democrat, January 31, 1850*

The Free School Law

The practical organization of the new system, throughout the several countries, towns and school districts of the state, is, at this time, the subject of very general interest. There are numerous and formidable embarrassments to contend with, in every direction — embarrassments unavoidably incidental to every radical change in previously existing systems — embarrassments growing out of the necessary imperfection of human legislalation, and that inability to forsee those numerous contingencies which experience only can bring to light. Thus far, however, we see no cause for discouragement or alarm. In all those counties — some twenty-five or thirty — where the additional amount of public money required by the new law has been raised by the board of supervisors, the system is already in full and beneficial operation. In the remaining counties, where the annual sessions of the board were concluded before the act took effect as a law, considerable opposition has been manifested, owing to the necessity of imposing a heavy additional amount of taxation on the districts to meet the deficiency of funds arising from the inability of the board of supervisors to act. The necessity, also, of providing for the expenses of the terms commencing previously to the time when the new law took effect, in addition to those hereafter to be contracted for, adds in many instances, to the pecuniary difficulties to be surmounted. The powers, duties and liabilities of trustees under the various provisions of the new law — the qualifications of voters at district meetings — the effect of the new provisions upon former enactments still remaining on the statute book — and the extent to which the latter are virtually repealed by the former as inconsistent and incompatible — these and numerous other important and difficult questions are daily submitted to the Department for its solution and advice — and the necessity for some additional, or at least explanatory legislative action is in many quarters insisted upon to enable the inhabitants and officers of the several districts to carry out the system in accordance with the views of its framers, and of the people by whom it has been sanctioned.

We have given in another column, such of the decisions and expositions of the Department under the new law, as may serve to remove some of the difficulties and embarrassments to which we have adverted — decisions and expositions made with great deliberation — upon a careful examination of the various provisions of both the new act and the former law — and generally after full and free consultation with both the late and present Attorney General, and in accordance with their views. It may reasonably, therefore, be presumed that school district officers will be safe in acting under these opinions, and that, in case of necessity, they will be sustained by the legal tribunals.

With reference to the necessity, probability, or expediency of further legislative enactments, declaratory or otherwise, at the present session, we concur generally in the views set forth in the annual report of the Superintendent, in another portion of our paper. Still we conceive that too much stress ought not to be laid upon the recent heavy vote of the people, adopting the new law. The primary object and intention of the voters was, unquestionably, to establish, beyond the reach of all future doubt and question, the great and fundamental principle of *free schools*. On this point there can be no controversy. The people either meant this, or they meant nothing. But the details necessary to carry out this principle, were not, we apprehend, generally intended to be definitively passed upon. These were regarded as of inferior importance — subject to such modifications, alterations and additions as the legislature might from time to time, deem it expedient, in conformity with the general wishes and views of their constituents, to adopt. Doubtless a much wiser and more judicious mode of carrying into practical operation the prominent principle sanctioned by the voters at the polls, than that which is provided by the existing law, might easily be devised: and we trust the legislature will not consider its powers in this respect, materially restricted by the popular vote adopting the act as submitted. They may, we think, safely rely upon the intelligence and practical good sense of their constituents to sustain them in the adoption of such alterations and improvements as experience may suggest, and sound wisdom and policy dictate: always taking care to keep in view the important principle clearly and definitively decreed by the people, that the schools shall be free to every child of the State. To contravene this principle in any mode, would be, in our judgment, little short of moral treason; it would be to stultify the great majority of our intelligent and respectable citizens: it would render us justly obnoxious to the sneers and reproaches of our fellow countrymen throughout the union; and put us back in the career of enlightened civilization, so far as to be beyond hope of recovery.

We are, therefore, for an uncompromising preservation of the *free school principle* in all its fullness and integrity, but at the same time in favor of such modifications of the existing system, as shall divest it of all its obnoxious or impracticable features. Hasty and inconsiderate legislation, in this important department, is, of course, to be deprecated, and if possible, avoided. Ample time should be given for the development of existing defects: different views and suggestions for improvement should be carefully collected and compared; neither the legislature nor the people should impatiently or unreflectingly rush forward in the work of reform: and whatever is done in this direction, should be carefully and deliberately matured, systematized, and simplified, in order, if possible, to avoid the necessity of future action, and to place our entire system of public instruction upon a permanent and satisfactory basis.

We shall take an opportunity again to recur to this subject in our next number; and to present such views for the consideration of the legislature and the people, as a somewhat extended survey of our educational interests, and of the practical working of the existing system, may dictate. Meantime it may be well to add that, aside from the recognition of the fundamental principle of the universal and free education of the youth of the State, we are committed to no theory, and wedded to no peculiar views. We desire only that such provision shall be made, as shall secure "the greatest good to the greatest number," and shall be most acceptable to the wishes and views of our fellow citizens generally, and we confidently count upon the cooperation of the enlightened friends of education throughout the the State, in securing this desirable result.—*District School Journal, February, 1850*

The New School Law

We have received a communication postmarked Trumansburg, Tompkins county, entirely anonymous in its character, over the common signature "Vox Populi" which is intended as an onslaught against the new school law. The communication is partly written and partly printed, and all without a responsible signature. It commences, "Print or not, as your sense of justice and of duty may dictate." Our sense of justice to ourselves, and duty to our neighbor has long since caused us to avow our determination to print no anonymous communications, and we see no good reason for deviating from a wholesome rule in this instance, to gratify some mistaken friend, who would fain have us believe that he exercises the "voice of the people," and that the expression at the ballot-box, last fall, was not genuine.

We are not ignorant of the fact that there are some candid opponents of the free school system, and there are many who believe the present law to be defective, but the great mass of the freemen of this State cherish the free school system as the key to their liberties — among the latter we are proud to be ranked; and while we might desire to modify the detail of the new law a little, we cannot for a moment desire to be found among that class of its opponents who assail the great principle of " Free Schools for a Free People." — *Rochester Daily Advertiser, February 14, 1850*

A bill has been introduced into the Senate of this State to refer the question of the repeal of the School Law to the decision of the people at the next election. We are sure the Legislature will be guilty of no such folly as the passing of it would involve. It is to be expected that the small minority which voted against the law, will be clamorous for its repeal, but such a decided expression as was given by the people of this State upon this question cannot be mistaken, and to unsettle the whole subject again would be an act of puerility of which we have no idea the Legislature will be guilty. We notice that quite a number of petitions are being sent to the Legislature for the repeal, but as they come from the small minority, it cannot be expected that the wishes of the great mass of the people will be delayed for this reason.— *Buffalo Commercial Advertiser, February 22, 1850*

Repeal of the Free School Act

A bill to repeal unconditionally, the free school act, has been reported in the Assembly, and referred to the committee of the whole. If there were any probability that the bill could become a law it would be but another specimen of the instability and uncertainty of legislation in the country. Less than a year since through the ballot box, upon an important question effecting the most vital interests of community. This decision was given in accordance with the enlightened spirit of the age, in a decisive majority in favor of free education, based upon the property of the State. But scarcely had the verdict of the people been rendered when efforts were commenced to procure the repeal of the law, thus enacted and thus sanctioned. The bill now reported to the Assembly, is the fruit of these efforts, but we have no idea that the body will so far stultify itself as to pass it. The friends of the beneficent measure of free education have made no efforts to sustain their action last fall, for they could have no idea that the Legislature would do so foolish a thing — one so much in opposition to the general sentiment of the State as to venture upon a repeal.

The great curse of this country, is first excessive legislation, and second, fickle and unstable legislation — a constant changing of laws. In our rapid progress, it is true, laws sooner become inapplicable to existing circumstances than in the staid and dormant nations of the old world. But even here, the constant change and amendment which we witness are conducive to any thing but the best interest of society. It is a peculiarity of the restless spirit of our people — the offspring of the aspiring ambition of young legislators, who seek to " make their mark " by some startling innovation under the specious title of reform — or to change the existing order of things, and not unfrequently by substituting crude and ill digested notions of their own.

We hope the general school law will escape the hands of the destroyer; but if defective, be so amended as to meet all the expectations of the people. It is one of those measures which form an era in our history — a measure

which is not of the present alone, but takes hold on the future through all coming time. It is but a practical recognition of one of the great duties of government, and as such commends itself to the enlightened patriotism of every citizen. Let it, then, be sustained, and perfected, that it may fulfill its mission in bestowing untold blessings upon succeeding generations.—
Buffalo Commercial Advertiser, March 29, 1850

Amendments to the Free School Law

The bill reported by the Senate committee on literature, to amend the free school law to which we alluded in our last, has been made the special order in the Senate for March 1st. It was prepared, as stated in the report, under the direction of the Secretary of State (the same officer designated by the Republican as the "distinguished whig Secretary") and its style and mode of expression would warrant the assertion that the original law was prepared under the same direction. They are very much "of a piece."

By the amendments proposed it is made the duty of the supervisors, at their annual meeting, to cause to be levied and collected, as a county tax, a sum twice the amount of the state school money apportioned to the county— and upon each town as a town tax, a sum equal to the state school money apportioned to the town — and such further sum as the electors, at the annual town meeting shall have directed to be raised.

If the district shall not raise by tax a sum which, added to the state, county and town money, apportioned to it will support a school for eight months, the trustees are required to have a school kept for eight months and levy the whole expense, for teachers' wages, fuel, repairs etc., by tax upon the district — and in such case the district shall not receive any share of the public money.

The Comptroller is authorized to loan to the supervisors from the school fund, the amount required to be raised by them, (in cases where it has not been raised), to be repaid, with interest, by a tax to be levied at the next annual meeting — towns and districts that have raised their proportions, to be exempted from the tax. The omission of the supervisors to raise the amount required, or to make the loan authorized, is not to invalidate the powers of the trustees or inhabitants of the districts, conferred by the original act, and all proceedings in the districts under that act are confirmed.

The office of town superintendent is abolished from the 1st of Nov. next, and a superintendent to be elected in each Assembly district, at a yearly salary of $500, one half to be paid by the county and one half from the school fund.

The supervisor of each town is to receive and disburse the school monies belonging to his town. The tax list to be delivered to the collector within thirty days after the expiration of each term. When collected, the collector is to pay the portion applicable to payment of teachers' wages to the town superintendent, (an officer abolished by a previous section,) and the residue to the trustees.

The foregoing contains the provisions, in substance, of the proposed law. We have not room at present for extended comments, but cannot suffer the occasion to pass without characterizing it as an attempt to remedy the deficiencies and imperfections of the law of the last year by a piece of patchwork equally defective and imperfect. The people have decided in favor of the principle of free schools; but if it is to be carried out in practice, a more liberal and enlightened policy than that to which the " distinguished whig Secretary" seems only capable of attaining, must be adopted. A just, liberal and equal system of taxation must be prescribed, and we think the whole amount necessary to be raised, should be levied as a state tax. The operation of the present law is so manifestly unjust and unequal, that it never can be administered without destroying entirely the usefulness of the district school system. That A. and B. can, by their votes, levy a portion of the expense of educating their children directly upon C., who is perhaps, less able to bear the burthen than themselves, is so revolting to every principle of equality and justice, that it will be resisted in a thousand ways, giving rise to animosites and dissensions in neighborhoods and districts, subversive, at once, of all hope of success in the schools. Incalculable mischief has already been done in this way by the present law, and the proposed amendments do not obviate the difficulty.

We hope the Legislature will reject the crudities of the Secretary and make a sensible and practical revision of the whole matter. If they cannot do that, they had better go back at once to the old system.— *Binghamton Democrat, February 28, 1850*

Amendments to the Free School Law

The Democrat, of last week, gave the substance of the free school act, reported by the Senate committee on literature, but not of the report of the committee accompanying it. The committee state that much opposition to the law has arisen from the reluctance of tax payers to vote the necessary money for the maintenance of free schools, and some districts have voted to reduce the time during which schools shall be kept open from 8 to 4 months, to save a small tax.

Rate bills are still liked because they fall upon parents and not upon property. Many parents under the old system, kept their children at home because they could not pay, and were not willing to confess themselves paupers to obtain free schooling. The State should make schools the right of every child. The constitution provides for the annual addition of $25,000 to the capital of the common school fund. The revenues of the canal will soon allow a surplus for schools. The rate bills for 1849 amounted to $489,696.63 — a similar sum has therefore to be raised, but which lessens every year until the School Fund becomes large enough to support the schools out of its incomes, without resort to taxation. The restoration of the office of a county or assembly district superintendent is recommended on the grounds that such office is needed as the medium of communication between the Department and the 900 towns and 11,000 school districts under its care. The territory is too large, the subdivisions and local officers too numerous, to allow of the necessary supervision. The expense would also be lessened over $15,000 a year!

Fifty-five out of fifty-nine counties in the State voted for the law, and a very large majority of votes was cast in its favor. The committee eloquently state the benefits of free education.

They say "At present we have but the alternative between prisons and schools; between a people educated, selfrespecting, selfrestraining, or an unreasoning populace, ignorant of the history of the past, or the learning of the present, ever ready to become the tools of a demagogue, and to act over again the massacre of St Bartholomew, or the reign of Terror."

By the amendments proposed it is made the duty of the supervisors, at their annual meeting, or at a special meeting, to cause to be levied and collected, as a county tax, a sum twice the amount of the state school money apportioned to the county — and upon each town as a town tax, a sum equal to the state school money apportioned to the town — and such further sum as the electors, at the annual town meeting shall have directed to be raised.

If the district shall not raise by a tax a sum which, added to the state, county and town money, apportioned to it, will support the school for eight months, the trustees are required to have a school kept for eight months and levy the whole expense, for teachers'wages, fuel, repairs, etc., by tax upon the district — and in such case the district shall not receive any share of the public money.

The Comptroller is authorized to loan to the supervisors from the school fund, the amount required to be raised by them (in cases where it has not been raised) to be repaid, with interest, by a tax to be levied at the next annual meeting — towns and districts that have raised their proportions, to be exempted from the tax. The omission of the supervisors to raise the amount required, or to make the loan authorized, is not to invalidate the powers of the trustees or inhabitants of the districts, conferred by the original act, and all proceedings in the districts under that act are confirmed.

The office of town superintendent is abolished from the first of November next, and a superintendent to be elected in each assembly district, at a yearly salary of $500, one-half to be paid by the county and one-half from the school fund.

The supervisor of each town is to receive and disburse the school monies belonging to his town. The tax list to be delivered to the collector within thirty days after the expiration of each term of school, and to include only the expense of such term. When collected, the collector is to pay the portion applicable to payment of teachers' wages to the town superintendent.

The bill has been discussed in committee of the whole in the Senate, and recommitted to the literature committe. We trust that all defects in the bill and system will be remedied, and such an act passed as will bear the scrutiny and receive the approbation of the people.

We have given the above digest of the report of the committee, merely for the information of our readers, that they may form and express what opinions and take such action as they please, on so interesting and important a subject.— *Binghamton Republican, March 6, 1850*

The New School Law

The opposition to this law is increasing daily, and we should not be surprised if it was repealed before the close of the present session of the Legislature.— *Plattsburgh Republican.*

A systematic effort has apparently been made throughout the State, to procure the repeal of this law; but we trust it will fail, at least, until there has been a further trial of the system. The law perhaps needs amendment in some essential particulars, and if so, it should be promptly done. Looking to the experience of other states, we see no serious obstacle to the establishment of a free school system in New York, that in all its details, will work to admiration, and give entire satisfaction to the people. The legislature, instead of repealing the law, should set themselves about the examination of its provisions, with the view of perfecting such amendments as seem to be required.— *Syracuse Daily Standard, March 7, 1850*

Free School Law

That this law is at this time far more unpopular than when it was voted upon and sanctioned by the people, will probably be readily conceded. The number of petitions which have been presented to the Legislature for its repeal and for its amendments, go far towards proving this; and yet we do not believe, should the proposition be carried into effect of again submitting it to the people, that the law would be rejected. The unprecedented majority by which the measure was established, was a verdict in favor of the main idea which it embraces, and was given without a thorough appreciation of the details of the bill. The opposition which since the election has arisen to the law, is a consequence of industrious efforts on the part of those pecuniarily most interested, to excite a prejudice against the leading principle itself by exaggerating the minor defects of that law; but we trust the popular mind is too enlightened not to perceive the difference between a great and beneficent idea, and the imperfections in the machinery with which it is proposed to carry that idea into effect. There are undoubtedly palpable defects in the free school law now in operation which demand an early correction; but we cannot unite in the clamor for its repeal before it shall have proved itself incapable of realizing the public expectation.— *Canajoharie Radii, March 21, 1850*

The Free School Law

Much complaint and dissatisfaction having been manifested by the people in almost every section of the state in relation to some of the provisions of the ".free school law" passed by the last legislature and a large number of petitions having been presented, praying for its repeal or modification, the subject was submitted to a select committee.

The committee have made their report, and we give below an abstract of the proposed amendments which we copy from the Argus of Saturday. It will be seen that it does away with the provision requiring a vote of the district on the raising of money for the support of the schools, which was producing much ill feeling and contention between neighbors and friends.

1st — It increases the amount of money to be distributed to districts, by requiring the boards of supervisors to lay and collect in their respective counties twice the amount such counties receive from the state school funds, instead of once as heretofore — and continue to raise the same amount to be raised on the towns as heretofore.

2nd — It provides for a more equal distribution of the monies — in order that weak districts, which are subject to almost as much expense to support a school, as other districts having a large amount of capital, and thereby producing a great inequality in taxation — by providing that two-fifths of the whole money shall be equally divided among the several school districts, and the remaining three-fifths, according to scholars attending school.

4th — It confines the public money in all cases to the payment of teachers' wages instead of repairs of schoolhouses and purchase of fuel etc., as in the act.

5th — It authorizes the trustees to levy and collect any deficiency for the payment of teachers' wages for the eight months on the taxable property of such district, without recourse to a vote of the district, thereby preventing the contention in district meeting, arising from allowing the district to vote the amount of money, and the length of time the school shall be kept in such district.

6th — It allows schools to be taught in the district at such other times as the schoolhouse shall not be required for free school purposes, and the expenses of such school to be paid by a rate bill on those attending such school.

7th — It authorizes the district to apply the library money to the payment of teachers' wages or continue the same for the purchase of books, as heretofore, in their discretion.— *Hudson Gazette, March 26, 1850*

The New School Law

It apears from the legislative reports, that one branch of the State Legislature has decided in favor of the policy of submitting this law again to the people. This, we are inclined to think, will not give general satisfaction. The policy is regarded by many as an unwise one, in almost any instance; and there are strong grounds in support of such an opinion. The objections which have been raised against the free school law, are not directed against the principle. We are glad to believe that the people favor such a benign measure. Objections are loudly urged against the details of the plan, the mode of assessment, etc. It is undoubtedly in the power of the Legislature to amend it in such particulars as is demanded by the general voice; but the evil will not be remedied by again submitting the question to the people. As it stands, we fear that it will be negatived by the popular vote, while a great majority not only recognize free schools as a good and beneficial measure, but would willingly support them, upon terms which would be equitable and just to all. In the Assembly, the vote was strong against resubmission, and it is not likely that such a proposition will be adopted. In the lower house, a plan of considerable importance, in this relation, has been nearly perfected. A bill is under discussion, taxing the State to the extent of $800,000, for the support of free schools. The bill has been pushed forward through nearly all the preliminary stages, and during its discussion, the most serious objection made to it, is that equality of taxation cannot be provided. The large districts will receive no more than smaller ones, while their expenses will be greater. This has been in a measure remedied, and there is a probability of the passage of the bill.— *Rochester Daily Democrat, April 4, 1850*

Free School Law

We have before us a "Report of the Select Committee on the petitions for the amendment or repeal of the Free School Law," made in Assembly, March 30th, 1850.

Although the report is signed by all the members, it would seem that a diversity of opinion existed in the committee as to the best mode of remedying the evils complained of. A portion of the committee were in favor of an unconditional repeal of the "free school law," another portion in favor of amending the law in several important particulars, while still another portion are in favor of submitting it again to the people. The committee say that, "already there have been presented over forty petitions for the amendment of the law, and over two hundred and fifty for its repeal."

They come from every corner of the State, from our villages, our secluded districts; from boards of supervisors — from town meetings, from "district meetings" from "public officers" and public meetings. "From the high and the low from the rich and the poor; those who voted for, and those who voted against it, all ask for important amendments or for its unconditional repeal, so that we shall be placed upon the platform of the old law, which has been occupied since 1812, with signal benefit to the State."

These petitions are signed by more than twenty thousand names — over seventeen thousand of which are for repeal. The committee argue that the people of this State are undoubtedly in favor of "free schools" in the abstract, but upon question of details there appears to be a great diversity of opinion, of which fact, we think the committee furnishes a striking example.

Free School Law

We gather from the report, that portions of the committee proposed at least three different bills for the consideration of the House, but of neither does the report furnish a copy.

What the ultimate action of the Legislature will be, it is difficult to determine. By the published proceedings it will be seen, that Mr. Burroughs' proposition has passed to levy a general tax upon the whole State, of a sum sufficient, with the present school fund, to make all the schools in the State free.

We do not think such a proposition would meet with general favor, or do we expect it can pass both houses and become a law at this late period in the session.

One opinion seems to be, that under the old system our schools were for all practical purposes free, and that under that system the gradual accumulation of the common school fund would in a few years amount to a sum sufficient to make them so in fact. Upon this point the committee hold the following language:

"Our common schools should and must be free; but we are not of opinion that the present law makes them so, however it be named; or rather that the principle of the present law is no more a free school one, than was the principle of the former. Under each system no one was excluded. Every one could then, as every one can now, find an open door, and a teacher to educate him."

The most prominent objection to the free school law, the committee say, "is the unequal rate of taxation" which it imposes — the taxable property in the districts or towns lying adjacent being in no equal proportion to the number of scholars. So that the greatest inequality exists in regard to taxation, ranging from 4 cents on one hundred dollars of valuation, to 36 cents.

In regard to the theory of taxation we find the following on page 23 of the report: "The State, as we have before affirmed, should provide the means for the common school education of all its children. The property of the State, in a 'fair, just, and equal proportion,' according to the different interest different persons may have in the subject, or the more immediate or remote benefits they may derive, should be made to support our schools founded for the general good of our children. The difficulty is, to determine what is this 'fair, just and equal proportion.' It is argued that there are two classes of persons instructed in our common schools — those who send to them and who are directly, and those who do not, and who are but indirectly interested in the subject. If this distinction is a correct one, then a result seems to follow — which is, that those who are directly interested should bear a greater proportion of the burthen than those who are but indirectly so, for the reason that while, like others, as members of the State, they have an indirect interest — as patrons of the schools, as parents of the pupils, there being educated, they have in addition to that indirect interest a direct one also."

The report goes on to show, that this principle has been recognized and approved not only by the people but by all those who have had the administration of our school laws in this State, and quote the opinions of N. S. Benton, State Supt. in 1846, John C. Spencer in 1840, and the views of Chancellor Kent, as sustaining the position that " Common School Establishments and education ought to rest in part upon local assessment and to be sustained and enforced by law according to the New England policy. That which costs nothing is lightly esteemed, and people generally will not take, or feel, much interest in common schools, unless they are taxed for their support."

In conclusion upon this branch of the subject, the report contains the following paragraph:

"In the state of Connecticut the large endowment of the public schools produced lassitude and neglect, and in many instances the funds were perverted to other purposes to such an extent that an entire change in the system became necessary. In cities, where there are large numbers who would not be instructed at all, if free schools were not provided, the evil must be encountered as being less in degree than that of total ignorance. But in country districts such destitution rarely exists, and when it does, provision is made by law for gratuitous instruction in each particular case."

"To this quotation it is not necessary for us to add a word: if it was true in 1840, it is equally so in 1850."

We fear the effect upon our common school system of too much legislative tinkering of the law by which it is regulated.— *Buffalo Commercial Advertiser, April 8, 1850*

Free Schools

Perhaps there exists no greater degree of popular delusion upon any subject than upon that which stands at the head of this article — much of the legislation on this subject, both municipal and general, has its origin in this delusion. And to this cause may be attributed in a great measure the almost unanimous vote in this State in favor of "free schools."

Probably not one in fifty of those who voted in favor of the law, ever saw it or knew anything of its provisions, or can tell now that the law is adopted and in force, whether the schools are any freer than they were before.

None were excluded on account of their inability to pay under the old system. And it is a matter of great doubt whether the expenses of maintaining the schools, which are not lessened, are as equitably apportioned or taxed under the new system as they were under the old. . . .

Although it was claimed, and it is now probably supposed by many, that the new law does not produce any change in this city, yet its practical effect will be, to compel this city to pay several thousand dollars annually towards the support of schools in the country towns in addition to the burdens of her own schools, which without any addition to their number must henceforward be about $30,000 annually. [Signed "A"] — *Buffalo Commercial Advertiser, January 11, 1850*

Your correspondent "A" in Saturday's paper, remarks:

"Although it was claimed, and it is now probably supposed by many, that the law does not produce any change in this city, yet its practical effect will be to compel this city to pay several thousand dollars annually towards the support of schools in the country towns in addition to the burdens of her own schools which without any addition to their number must henceforward be about $30,000 annually."

To show the fallacy of this statement, I will quote a section of the act reported from the committee on literature of the Senate, which there is no doubt will govern this matter: § 2 "It shall be the duty of the several boards of supervisors at their annual meetings, or at any special meeting duly convened (in pursuance of law) to cause to be levied and collected from their respective counties in the same manner as county taxes, a sum equal to twice the amount of state school moneys apportioned to such counties, and to apportion the same among the towns and cities in the same manner as the moneys received from the State are apportioned. They shall also cause to be levied and collected from each of the towns in their respective counties, in the same manner as other town taxes, a sum equal to the amount of state school moneys apportioned to said towns respectively, (and such further sum as the electors of each town shall have directed to be raised, at their annual town meetings, in pursuance of law).—*Buffalo Commercial Advertiser, February 11, 1850*

As your columns appear to be open for the discussion of the subject, I wish to make a few remarks upon the "popular delusion" alluded to by your correspondent A, of Saturday evening last.

He says "perhaps there exists no greater degree of popular delusion upon any subject, than upon that which stands at the head of this article." Probably not, Salem witchcraft was not a circumstance. It is a delusion that has been constantly and steadily increasing; shared in by the wisest, and greatest men of our State, since 1805–06, when the first permanent provision was made by the State for the support of common schools, till the present time, when the superior sagacity, and information of A has discovered that forty-nine-fiftieths of those who voted for the free school law, were sharing in the delusion and do not yet know whether the schools "are freer now than they were under the old law." It is somewhat interesting to see how this "delusion" has increased. In 1806, $57,757.24 was set apart as a fund, the annual interest of which was to be applied for the support of common schools throughout the State; but no distribution was to be made, till the revenue amounted to $50,000. In 1814, the first distribution was made; and the amount received by the districts from the State, was $48,376. The amount raised by the different counties, was $6,344.98, making $55,720.98 raised that year for common school purposes. From that first sympton the "delusion" steadily increased, till in the year 1849, when it seems to have attained its highest pitch — when a deluded Legislature laid before a deluded people, for their adoption or rejection, a law, making the blessing of a good education free to all — the amount received by the districts is $846,710.45 and in the same year was paid on rate bills by the great deluded $489,696.63, making a total of $1,336,397.08, squandered under the influence of this "popular delusion." But the crowning act of this "popular delusion" is, that by an "almost unanimous vote" the people refused to have the blessings of education measured by dollars and cents, any longer, but insist that like other of our good God's blessings — the air we breathe — the water we drink — they shall be free, and accessible to all who choose to partake. And permit me friend A to suggest that this "popular delusion" will continue till the original design of the founders of free schools in this city will be consummated by the establishment of a central school.

Thus much for the "popular delusion" part of the gentleman's communication. The balance will be attended to in due season.

Free Schools Again

It has been supposed by all sensible and practical men, that the question of Free Schools was definitely and effectually settled at the last general election. At any rate, the opinion is entertained by some plain republicans, that when a question of state policy long discussed by the people, passed upon by our State Legislature, submitted to the people, and after some six months' deliberate reflection, ratified by a majority of some 150,000, was somewhat comfortably put at rest.

Such has been the case with the free school question, and there has never been a question before the people of this State, more thoroughly discussed, more universally understood, or so intelligently voted upon as the present free school law.

The question was not one of party; no sect of politics or religion; no set of men claimed it as their measure. None of the ordinary means of electioneering were used in its behalf, and none were required. It was the spontaneous and free expression of the intelligence of the people, deliberately expressed as the most solemn duty which a free people are called upon to perform.

And yet with this state of facts fully before the people, and seemingly settled beyond the possibility of dispute, we have the whole subject gravely denounced as a "popular delusion" and that "not one in fifty knew what they were voting for."

Really, the people of this State must feel themselves highly complimented, and the voters of the city most particularly so. According to the views of this highly intelligent writer, the three noble spirits who voted against the free school law, were the only individuals who knew what they were about! Doubtless the writer himself is included in the charming trio, and I devoutly hope that these three righteous men will save our goodly city from the fate of Sodom and Gomorrah!

It would be an idle waste of time to meet any person, in an argument upon the propriety of free schools. With equal advantage might we discuss the propriety of the abolition of slavery, or imprisonment for debt in this State, or the restoration of the property qualification in voters. On either of these questions would the enterprising writer stand a better chance for retrogressive action than upon the question of free schools.

FRANKLIN

— *Buffalo Commercial Advertiser, February 12, 1850*

I wish to say a word in reply to that part of the communication of "A" which relates to the distribution of school moneys — although this is not connected in any way with the questions of the "Third D. Department." The present distribution is made under the census of the year 1845 — and is changed every five years at the time of the enumeration by the State and general government. In 1845, Buffalo contained 29,635 inhabitants, and the country 48,862. The census of the present year will show that there has been a much greater increase in the city than in the towns. In fact, when the last census of the city was taken, the increase was about 40%, while in the towns for five years it was only about 14%. The amount of moneys appropriated under the census of '45 was $8,600 to the county, of which $3,250 went to the city, so that the fears of "A" that several thousand dollars will be added to the expense of our schools without increasing them is but a "delusion."

By the way, I notice that in a second article "A" has consented to define what he means by "delusion." He says:

"Let me define what is meant by a "delusion" on the subject of free schools. It is a delusion to suppose that the schools are any more free than they were before the passage of the new law.

"It is a delusion to suppose that under that law the education of any more of the children and youths of the land will be secured, than under the old system.

"It is a delusion to suppose that free schools are to prove a panacea for all the evils of society, both political and moral.

"I might go on to enumerate a formidable list of delusions upon the subject apparent enough to everybody, but those who are wilfully or fanatically blind."

The first assertion I hold to be untrue in point of fact. Under the old law, all could go to school, to be sure, but there was a provision which made an inequality in the conditions. It required a confession of poverty, and thus caused those who availed themselves of it to appear among their fellows as special paupers. Under the new law no such invidious distinction exists, and who will contend that this does not render the schools more free in practice if not in theory. And how many there are who under the old law, would keep their children from school, rather than be compelled to appeal directly to their neighbors as for charity. While now all may cheerfully participate in a general fund. And this last fact answers his second proposition. All who have been observers of the working of the old school law, know within their personal acquaintance that its operation has had the effect to keep many from school. Having myself exercised the "birchen" authority, and "boarded round," a better opportunity has been given me for an acquaintance with the feelings of poor parents upon this subject than to "A" who, I would judge, was but little acquainted particularly with the workings of either the old system, or the new one as it exists in our city.

As to the third proposition, there is no one who contends that "free schools will be a panacea for all evils of society, both political and moral." But we do contend that free education, and its concomitants, are the most important "levers of civilization"— that the social, moral and political condition of a people where free schools are open to the mass is far in advance of those where but even partial means of education are provided. We need only look to the strong contrast which exists between different states of our Union as a proof of this, without referring to the countries of the old world where ignorance unbroken prevails, and where, as a consequence, political rights in the people are unknown, superstition and the animal vices exist, and where the arts of life are in a semibarbarous state — where the improvements which genius and science have introduced have not yet penetrated. It is a singular "delusion" of "A" that his opinion should be taken in opposition to that of all the good and great men who have interested themselves in the welfare of mankind — in opposition to the lights of experience, and the demonstrations of observation.

S

— *Buffalo Commercial Advertiser, February 15, 1850*

The New School Law

Mr Editor: As it is getting quite common to make inquires through the press, I trust you will not think I am intruding on your generosity if I should make some remarks upon the new school law — trusting the attention of the public will be called to the subject, as many of the districts are calling meetings to raise money to carry the new school law into effect. The superintendent has issued a circular to trustees and inhabitants of school districts, in which he says "an impression extensively prevails, throughout the state, as indicated by the daily correspondence of this Department, that the omission of the board of supervisors of the respective counties, to raise the additional amount of public money required by the new school law, dispenses with the necessity of preparing the estimates and voting the taxes required by that act, for the support of schools for the ensuing year, and in such cases resort may be had to the old rate bill system." He says:— "The superintendent deems it of the utmost importance that this erroneous impression should be removed. There is no other mode known to the law for the support of the schools of the State, subsequently to the period when the new law took effect (Nov. 30) than that which is prescribed by that law, and no rate bill can be legally made out under any circumstances for terms expiring after that date, or for any future school term."

I would ask what the Legislature meant when they said:

"Subdivision 14, sec. 82, chap. 480, laws of 1847, is hereby amended so as to read as follows:

"14. To deliver such rate bill with the warrant annexed, after the same shall have been made out and signed by them, to the collector of the district, who shall execute the same in like manner with other warrants directed by such trustees to such collector for the collection of district taxes, and the collector to whom such rate bill and warrant shall be delivered for collection, shall possess the same power, be entitled to the same fees, and subject to the same restrictions and liabilities, with their bail and sureties, as by this title is provided in proceedings to collect school district taxes."

Subdivisions 12th and 13th of the same section reads as follows:

"12. To ascertain by examination of the school list kept by such teachers, the number of days for which each person not so exempt shall be liable to pay for instruction and the amount payable by each person.

"13. To make out rate bill, containing the name of each person so liable, and the amount for which he is liable, and to annex thereto a warrant for the collection thereof."

Then follows subdivision 14th, which was amended by the new law as given above.— Amended April 11th, 1849.

Section 105, chap. 480, laws of 1847, is hereby amended so as to read as follows:

"When the necessary fuel for the school of any district shall not be provided by means of a tax on the inhabitants of the district or otherwise, it shall be the duty of the trustees of the district to provide the necessary fuel and levy a tax upon the inhabitants of the district to pay for the same."

The question is, how shall the trustees collect a bill for wood, where it was provided for at the annual meeting in October last, and voted by the meeting that it be paid by those sending to school? Cannot this be collected by a rate bill; if not, what can the word otherwise mean in the 105th section, as amended April 11th, 1849? Can the Legislature annul previous contracts?

Subdivision 8, sec. 82, chap. 480, laws of 1847, is hereby amended so as to read as follows:

"To pay the wages of such teachers when qualified, by giving them an order on the Town Superintendent for the public money belonging to their districts, so far as such moneys shall be sufficient for that purpose, and collect the residue of such wages from all persons liable therefor."

Should not the trustees give the teachers an order on the Town Superintendents, and then raise and collect the remainder from those who sent to school as formerly?

The section before amended reads as follows:

"To pay the wages of such teachers when qualified, out of the moneys which shall come into their hands from the town superintendent, so far as such moneys shall be sufficient for that purpose, and collect the residue of such wages, excepting such sums as may have been collected by the teachers, from all persons liable therefor."

All the alteration in the section as amended, if there is anything essential, is the direction for the trustees to give the teachers orders on the town superintendent. As this amendment was passed April 11th, 1849, and the new school law March 26, 1849, do not the amendments do away with the 1st and 3d sections of the new school law? as that was passed subsequently.

Have young men or women, over 21 years of age, a right to the common schools in one of the districts bordering on the city? A teacher thinks they ought to be turned out.

A FARMER

—*Rochester Daily Democrat, January 9, 1850*

Messrs Editors: As you have always been liberal in giving place in your columns for the discussion of all subjects relating to public interest, I take the liberty to offer some remarks on the new "free school law," as it is called.

It may seem to many to be quite out of place at this time to question the justice or expediency of this measure, since it has been passed upon and received such popular favor. But if this law is either *just* or *expedient* you will allow me to suggest a very important amendment.

It must be obvious that all are not alike able to provide suitable food and clothing for their children, and, therefore, cannot receive equal benefits from the free schools.

To relieve this difficulty I would recommend, that the Legislature be requested so to amend this statute as to give to the inhabitants of the several school districts power to raise such farther sums as the trustees of their respective districts may recommend to feed and clothe all over five and under twenty-one years of age, who may reside in the district, or may be admitted by the trustees to the benefits of the free schools, in the same manner as is now provided by law for teacher's wages, fuel, and other contingent expenses.

This at first may meet with opposition, but it is believed that it would be difficult to show any good reason why this amendment should not find favor as well as the law in question.

No parent can say he is not as much in duty bound to provide for and educate his children as he is to feed or clothe them; and if the public supply the latter want, he has so much the more for the former.

An important branch of parental education is to instruct children to be *frugal, industrious* and *honest;* without which a knowledge of letters or numbers are of no use. It cannot with truth be said that the free school system in its present form offers any aid to this kind of instruction, but raises formidable opposing barriers against it.

It may be that the *wisdom* of this *progressive* age will devise a more effective plan than has been named. One which would cover the whole ground, and thus supercede the necessity of a special act for the homestead exemption, or to make void all contracts for an amount equal to a homestead by, providing that all property in the state be equally divided annually.

No one will question or doubt the power of the Legislature to make such a law and submit it to the people; and they can respond to it with such *democratic unanimity* as to leave no doubt of its obligation, and in this way put on a level idleness with industry, extravagance with prudence, intemperance with sobriety — in short every species of vice with virtue.

FREE DEMOCRACY

— *Rochester Daily Democrat, February 4, 1850*

The New School Law

Messrs Editors: When there is an honest difference of opinion on any public measure, it is just and proper to discuss those measures, providing it is done with prudence and candor.

Previous to the adoption of the new school law, there was a general apathy in communities as to its effects, but now, when it has gone into operation, it has aroused their feelings and created discord and strife in former peaceable districts.

The undersigned, with hundreds of others, now believe the law to be unconstitutional, arbitrary, and unjust, and virtually destroying the principles of free government, and will be an injury to the schools by retarding instead of advancing education.

Free government is based on justice; laws are made to protect the rights of man against the caprice and cupidity of his fellow, to guard the weak against the strong, and defend the few from the encroachments of the many, and legislators are bound by the social contract to protect by law, the life, liberty, and property of every member of society.

But the new school law takes A's property without his consent and applies it to the benefit of B., which is unconstitutional, arbitrary, and unjust. Legislators have no right to license one man to infringe on the rights of his fellow, and it would be well if they never usurped the power.— And what are the great benefits that this new law will produce to sanction such injustice? Is it the education of the poor? No, for they were amply provided for under the old law. The state appropriation was amply sufficient to educate all the poor children in the state, if their parents were but willing to accept of it. What then was its object? Has it introduced any new system of instruction, or any improvement in moral discipline? Not any. Where then is the great boon to society? The name of free schools. A most glorious achievement. The schools of the Empire State are all free. Yes, made free by arbitrary taxation.

The cupidity of mankind prompts too many, to desire the property of their neighbors, and does not need any encouragement by legislation or popular applause. The youth, who is trained to think it right to take the earnings of his neighbor to pay his schooling, will easily palliate to his conscience for taking the fruits of his garden, or the contents of his granary. If B. takes A's money and purchases bread for his children, he is a felon and punished for the act, but if he pays for their schooling with it, it is a virtue sanctioned by law — which is weighing honesty by a very delicate ballance, and hair's breadth splitting of justice. Destroy the right of property, and civilization will cease to exist — agrarianism and force must become the order of the day.

But it will be an injury to the schools by lessening the inducements to industry and perseverance. One great hindrance to children's advancement in school, is the indifference of their parents. When there is no interest taken in the improvement of the child at home progress at school need not be expected; and remove the responsibility of paying, and you increase the indifference ten fold, for the love of money is the principal prompter to action with the bulk of mankind.

A cordial union of feeling and action is very essential to the advancement of any public measure, and none more so, than with the progress of schools. One faultfinding boy will contaminate a school and a few discontented members will ruin a district; and you cannot expect the friendly feeling nor cordial support of those who believe that they are unjustly compelled to give the fruits of their labors for the benefit of others.

But to conclude, the law is unconstitutional, arbitrary and unjust, imposing unnecessary taxation, which violates the right of property, and it will destroy the peace of society, by arousing the feelings of animosity of man against his fellow, and will deter the progress in learning by reducing the incentives to industry, without promoting any general good, and it ought to be immediately repealed.

WHEATLANDER

Wheatland, Feb. 4, 1850

— *Rochester Daily Democrat, February 7, 1850*

Messrs Editors: Having perceived several articles in recent numbers of the Democrat, adverse to the *principle* of the " free school law " especially the one signed " Wheatlander," will you permit a very humble individual, and a comparative stranger, to allow his thoughts on the subject to appear in your columns? Entertaining as he does, the same opinion as your worthy correspondent, that " when there is an honest difference of opinion on any public measure, it is quite proper to discuss those (that) measure, provided it is done with prudence and candor."

It is fair to presume, that previous to the enactment of any public measure, especially involving a principle of taxation among a free people, that that measure has been scrutinized and thoroughly discussed in the Legislature, whose immediate province it is to " protect the life, liberty and property of every member of the community." But as it is possible that even the wisest counsellors may propose and adopt measures too hastily, it is both just and proper that their proceedings should be submitted to the *test of experience,* and the ordeal of public opinion; and I claim, on behalf of the " new school law," the *former,* and with regard to the *latter,* it has hitherto been sanctioned by the public vote; and if " Wheatlander " be a true Republican, I presume he acknowledges the correctness of the sentiment, " Vox Populi Vox Dei." Be that as it may, I will endeavor briefly to examine the sentiments advanced by him.

I am at issue with " Wheatlander " in his belief that this law is " unconstitutional, arbitrary, unjust, and virtually destroying the principles of free government, and will be an injury to the schools by retarding instead of advancing education." Were those my sentiments, I certainly should denounce the measure, in terms even stronger than he has; but, with all due deference to his acute reasonings, I differ from him in toto, as to the principle, and he will pardon me when I question the patriotism of his principles. I maintain that the law *is constitutional,* because power is given to the Legislature by the constitution itself to devise and propose such measures as, in its judgment, may appear best calculated to promote the welfare of the people and the perpetuity of the Union. In the present instance there would have been nothing unconstitutional if the law had been allowed to go into operation without previously subjecting it to a general vote; and if there be any arbitrariness in it the constitution alone is chargeable therewith; and I think the skill of your correspondent would be put to a very severe test to improve that constitution. I hope "Wheatlander" and myself may both behold the day when every good measure shall be carried into effect without taxation, according to the laws of nature and sound reasoning, but, until that is the case, we must be content to allow the imposition of taxes, as the least of two evils.

Admitting, then, that taxation is justifiable in some circumstances surely it must follow that to tax for the promotion of education is more just than for other purposes; especially as the education of the people is the great bulwark of liberty and prosperity.

Your correspondent goes on to remark that "Free government is based on justice, laws are made to protect the rights of man against his fellow, to guard the weak against the strong, and defend the *few* against the encroachments of the *many;* and legislators are bound by the *social* compact to protect by law the life, liberty and property of every member of a community." The sentiments embodied in the last quotation lead me strongly to suspect that "Wheatlander" must have received his political education under the auspices of a foreign despot, or under kingly authority, inasmuch as the law-makers in such countries make the laws to "defend the *few* against the *many;*" this is so purely aristocratic, that it must be obvious that an impartial reader could come to no other conclusion. Fortunately, however, *this* government is bound by the "social compact to protect the interests of the many against the encroachments of the few," thus imposing a salutary check to avarice and "cupidity" so very agreeable to anti-republican governments. Whatever may be the opinion of the "hundreds" who think with your correspondent, I have the satisfaction of knowing that his "hundreds" are opposed by millions in this free and happy country.

I have yet to be convinced how it is that the "new school law" *takes* A's property, *without his consent,* and applies it for the benefit of B. Of course no individual would willingly consent to have money *forced* from his pocket; but *it is not so* in the present instance (unless indeed all taxation is direct robbery,) for the *people have taxed themselves;* and in this, as in all other cases, the consent of the minority can be lawfully and justly claimed to the acts of the majority; invert this order, and you immediately put an end to the principles now governing the intelligent world; and I, moreover, firmly believe, that every landowner will, by the operation of this law, enhance rather than decrease the value of his property. It may not be the immediate, but it must be the ultimate result.

That economy should be rigidly observed in the administration of all laws, I willingly admit; and if there are any funds now available to further the interests of the "free school law," those who have charge of such funds are bound by honor and honesty to see that they are properly applied; this would materially diminish the amount to be raised. If the report of the Superintendent of Common Schools is to be credited, an enormous amount belonging to the school fund is misapplied or bearing no interest in this State. I submit to "Wheatlander" that he would be rendering a greater service towards subduing the "discord and strife in peaceable districts," by directing his attention to this subject, and obtaining the co-operation of the aggrieved "hundreds." And by turning that fund into its legitimate channel, with the usual state appropriations, there would then be probably little, if anything, to raise in addition; in which case our common schools would be free indeed.

Another popular argument against this law is, that it gives education as a capital to be used wherever and whenever its possessor pleases; and that its tendency is to encourage parents in idleness and children in vicious habits, and unlawful pursuits. With respect to the former objection, I maintain that government sustains a relation to the people analogous to that which a parent sustains to his family; who is required by nature to provide for every animal want of his offspring to the utmost of his physical strength: and the principles of our common humanity are outraged by that parent who discharges not that moral obligation. In like manner the guardians of the public mind and morals, are bound by the same laws to provide the means for training the rising generations in those principles absolutely necessary to the maintenance of a government dependent upon the popular will: and are called upon to levy a tax upon the only *available capital*, which is land, to meet the expenses incurred by the discharge of their appointed duty.

The land of the country is the great capital of the Nation, and, while its possessors are to be protected in their lawful share, there is no other legitimate source from which taxes can be so unobjectionably derived: and whilst it is freely admitted that the purchasers of land have a lawful claim, and are entitled to the most interest they can derive therefrom; that interest would be not only greatly augmented by a more careful cultivation, but would easily yield more abundantly, if the knowledge which sound education imparts be assiduously applied. Now, if this education be freely given to the enduring sons of toil whilst it gives *them* a capital in knowledge, cannot fail to afford the most reasonable and ample return in actual profit to the land owner!

Unfortunately there are many parents who alike dishonor their character, their country and their God, by setting a pernicious example of idleness, extravagance and dissipation. To counteract this influence and implant more worthy motives in the breasts of the children of such parents, it becomes the duty of every good citizen, and much more that of an enlightened Government, to provide for the strengthening and perpetuity of those institutions, wherein is set before youth the benefits resulting from intellectual pursuits.

Again, there are thousands of poor but industrious men in this country, whose hard earnings are scarcely sufficient to supply the daily bread of their children; and yet those children have an undoubted claim upon the great storehouse of wisdom, who are hourly begging to be supplied with mental food, which food can be amply obtained from the common schools. Shall not their mental desires be satisfied, since, by the sweat of their father's brow the land yields plenteously? Forbid it every generous feeling! This earth was given to the children of men, and there is land enough, and to spare, to supply all the bodily and mental wants of the human family. But alas! The cloven foot of aristocracy begins to tread this land of freedom! That hydra-headed monster *monoply* is making fearful strides; his hideous figure is observable on the right and on the left; in the east and in the west; in the north and in the south; and he has planted the print of his feet even in the tracks of our Pilgrim Fathers! And instead of the cry those worthies raised as a watchword to posterity, "The Bible and the spelling book for our children" our ears are pained to hear the cry of avarice and ambition — "Land! more land!" Forgetful of the admonition, "They that would be rich, fall into temptation and a snare."

Such are the observations which a comparative stranger has made since he has been among you; and he hopes he may be pardoned for expressing the fear that the institutions of the country are in danger from the rapid strides which proud aristocracy is making, and for suggesting to all who entertain similar sentiments with "Wheatlander" the propriety of pausing and seriously reflecting upon the motives by which they may possibly be influenced in their opposition, to a measure, which, upon mature reflection will not appear so dangerous and unjust as they imagine, and turn their thoughts and energies to those efforts calculated to strengthen the institutions of the country; by the subversion of the foundations of ignorance.

The desire to remove erroneous sentiments, and to assist in promoting sound education, I wish you, Messrs Editors, to receive as an apology for the length of this article.

WEST BRIGHTONIAN
— *Rochester Daily Democrat, March 6, 1850*

The Free School Law

Messrs Editors: I was in hopes that the usurpations of power which the Legislature exercised last session, by giving the law-making power to the people, was the result of oversight, caused by an over anxious desire to do good; but it is with sincere regret that we are compelled to believe that it originated in a design to change the fundamental principles of the government, for I see that Mr. Mann has introduced a bill to again test the school law by a popular vote.

Our government is a representative one. The framers of the constitution, profiting by the experience of ancient Greece, vested the law-making power with the representatives of the people, and what right has the Legislature to change it to the popular voice? Are they invested with absolute power to form any kind of government that suits their caprice? If our government is a popular one; if the law-making power exists directly with the people, what call is there for a Legislature? any one who chooses may propose laws, and the popular voice sanction them by a majority vote, and it must become the law of the land. But, I repeat, what right has the Legislature to change the fundamental principles of the government? when and how were they clothed with absolute power to enable them to alter the constitution at pleasure? But the self-creating power of an absolute power is but a small part of the mischief that this usurpation will inflict on society.

What are the legitimate ends of government but to protect the rights of man? and what are those rights that have to be protected? *Life, liberty* and *property,* and of those, property requires the most guardianship, for the cupidity and avarice of man are constantly making inroads on the possessions of his neighbor. Why are laws made for the collection of debts? Why are statute books filled with acts to punish fraud, theft, forgery, and a hundred various shades of man's encroachments on the property of his fellow? what are the principal cases that occupy our courts of justice? what is it that gives the principal employment to our hundreds of lawyers, but the violation of the rights of property?

It is much to be regretted that our legislature does not realize the great evil that it does the morals of community in encouraging their cupidity by a popular vote. Of all the acts of popular government, there are none so ruinous to the principles of honesty as to sanction taxation by the popular voice. Thousands of voters are not tax-payers, but will profit themselves by the violations of their neighbor's rights; *and it does not appear to be realized that a righteous cause does not justify unjust means.*

It is fallacious to think that a popular vote, no matter how large the majority, can create right. If all the State should vote that James should divide his farm among his neighbors, in ten, five or one acre lots, or even one foot parcels, it would not make it just. They might have the power, but I would rather say that they might by force compel him to do it, and the law of force will be the order of the day.

TRUTH

—*Rochester Daily Democrat, March 14, 1850*

The New School Law

Messrs Editors: I have read several articles of late in your excellent paper, relative to the new school law. The subject is one of such vast importance that I think you will pardon me for troubling you again with another upon that most important subject. All agree in this: that education is a great blessing to all, and that every child should have an opportunity to acquire a good common school education. But there are different opinions in regard to the best method of effecting the object sought for. Mr. Young, author of **the Science of Government**, published in 1847 a new edition, adapted to the new constitution and to the laws of 1847, says: "Thus we see how wisely the government has provided for the education of the people. The poorest child need not remain ignorant. If all the youth in our country would improve the means they have of becoming well educated, and make a good use of their learning, how greatly would the people share in the blessings of a republican government." If Mr. Young is correct, and I think he is, why the necessity of this change? Under the old law the schools were conducted harmoniously, and were in a flourishing condition; but what are their condition now?— Some have four months' schooling where they formerly had ten, and some have none. Hatred and malice have taken the place of peace and harmony. Can the district schools prosper under such circumstances? All must say no. Why then keep up this system. But what says the Senate committee on this subject? They say there is complaint that the school law of this State, by repeated alterations and amendments, has become voluminous and complicated almost beyond comprehension — so much so as to require gradually revising, simplifying and abridging, is by no means unjust, and such a course is recommended by that committee. They say that much of the opposition to the new school law has arisen from reluctance of the taxpayers to vote the necessary money for the maintenance of the free schools. This is true; and why is it, when the law received a large majority of the votes cast in the State, and that some seven-eighths of the inhabitants of school districts where petitions have been circulated have signed to repeal the law? It is because experience has shown the inequality and the unjustness in its practical application. It causes many people to pay for schooling their neighbor's children who are wealthy, own large farms, and free from debt, while they, many of them, are young men who have by industry and economy labored hard to accumulate a little property (as the old saying is, "for a wet day") and purchased farms, paid the little they had accumulated, and gave mortgages for one-half, and some for three-fourths of the purchase money; then go to work, labor night and day, deprive themselves of luxuries and the comforts of life, and need every shilling they can earn to make their payments, and yet must be taxed for the full amount of these farms to pay for schooling the children of those who have their farms paid for, have elegant buildings, and are enjoying all the luxuries and comforts of life, ride in their carriages and live in splendor.

Nearly one-half of the taxpayers in the district where I live are similarly situated, and there are many such cases in every district so far as my knowledge extends. This is the cause why the appropriations are voted down. These same persons are willing to pay for schooling the children of poor men, but not for those who are not worth twice or thrice as much as they are. We were satisfied with the old law, it was good enough. It is an old saying that it is best to let well enough alone. The Legislature may make laws that will allow our neighbors to put their hands into our pockets and take out our money, but it will take a higher power to make them reconciled to it and friendly towards each other. The committee say that the rate-bills are still regarded with favor, because they fall not upon the property of a district but upon the parents who have children to send to school. They say many parents, however, under the old system kept their children at home because they could not afford to pay, and because they were not willing to confess their pauperism which alone entitled them to free schooling. This is getting to be quite an argument with those who are in favor of free schools and is one newly manufactured. I am in my sixtieth year, have lived in different towns and counties in the State, have brought up and educated a family of children, and have had much to do with the district schools, but I never heard a poor man say he would keep his children at home for that reason, but when they have been urged to send their children to school, I have frequently heard them say they had nothing for them to carry for their dinners, or that their clothing was not such as they desired, and others were indifferent as to their education. If the Legislature should remedy this, there would many more attend the schools.

The committee, in order to show the benefits of free schools, states a case of murder. I will give their words. They say, already the farmer exposed to the midnight murderer, who (as has just occurred in New Jersey) climbs by an upper window into his house, and slaughters wife and husband in their bed chamber. That murderer was an untaught stranger, who came, unblessed by a free school, to our shores, and revenged himself upon a prosperity he envied by robbery and outrage. One of the members of that committee is a resident of Rochester. Why did he not state a case in his own city, which occurred recently; and whether that man was an untaught stranger, and unblessed by a free school? What was it but the skill and the science he possessed, that saved him from the severity of the law? Why not mentioned the case that occurred in Boston; was not that man unblessed by free schools? Is free schools a sure guarantee against crime? The committee would have us think so; but it is not so. If a man's inclination is to commit crime, education will enable him to carry it out more effectually, and elude the vigilance of the law; but if he is inclined to do good, education will make him a more useful man. Why does not this committee, who have so much sympathy for the poor, tell us how the public money is expended; and whether the schools could not be made free by that fund, if rightly appropriated.

And why the colleges receive from three to four thousand dollars each from the public money?—Geneva College receives $4,000 yearly—the students in that college number 37, more than $108 to each one, and probably others about the same. Are they poor men's sons? judge for yourselves! While our common school children draw from the State, and some, twice that amount, so they draw from the State less than fifty cents. Why is this so? Taxpayers, look to it.

These are the amendments submitted to the Senate by the committee on literature:

§ 2 It shall be the duty of the several boards of supervisors at their annual meetings, or at any special meeting duly convened, (in pursuance to law,) to cause to be levied and collected from their respective counties, in the same manner as county taxes, a sum equal to twice the amount of state school moneys apportioned to such counties, and to apportion the same among the towns and cities in the same manner as the moneys received from the State are apportioned. They shall also cause to be levied and collected from each of the towns in their respective counties in the same manner as other town taxes, a sum equal to the amount of state school moneys apportioned to said towns respectively, (and such further sum as the electors of each town shall have directed to be raised at their annual town meeting, in pursuance of law.)

§ 2 The sixth section of the aforesaid is hereby amended so as to read as **follows:**

§ 6 When the said voters of any district at their annual meeting, (or at a special meeting called for that purpose in pursuance of law) shall refuse or neglect to raise by tax a sum of money, which added to the sum apportioned to said district by the State, and the money raised by the board of supervisors, under the second section of this act, will support a school in said district for at least eight months of the year, keep the school house in proper repair, and furnish the necessary fuel, and employ a teacher, or teachers, for **eight months,** and the whole expense shall be levied and collected in the manner provided in the third section of this act; and no district so refusing or neglecting to make provision as required by this act, for the proper support of a school for at least eight months in a year, shall receive any share of the public money.

§ 3 The Comptroller is hereby authorized to loan from the common school fund to the supervisors of any county in which the amount required by the second section of the act hereby amended shall not have been raised, a sum equal to such amount, on the production of a certified copy of the resolution of such board to apply for such loan: And it shall be the duty of such board, at its first annual session thereafter, to levy and collect upon the taxable property of the county, in the same manner as other county taxes are levied and collected, an amount sufficient to repay said loan, with interest, and when collected it shall be the duty of the county treasurer to pay over the same to **the Comptroller;** but such towns or districts in said county as shall have duly raised their share of the amounts required by law, shall not be subject to the levy and collection of the county tax as hereinbefore provided.

§ 4 The omission of the board of supervisors of any county to raise the additional amount required by the second section of the act hereby amended, at their last annual meeting, or to direct the loan hereinbefore provided for, to be made, shall not be construed in any manner to affect or invalidate the duties and powers conferred and imposed upon the trustees and inhabitants of the several school districts by the third and succeeding sections of said act: And all proceedings heretofore had in the several districts, under and in pursuance of the sections aforesaid, are hereby confirmed.

If the above amendments should become a law we shall have some thirty-five thousand dollars for school purposes to be collected next fall. Look out and prepare for the collector.

A FARMER

— *Rochester Daily Advertiser, February 19, 1850*

Chapter 8

THE ACT OF RESUBMISSION, 1850

To meet this verulent hostility against the free school measure, the Legislature passed a bill to resubmit the question to a popular vote. The following is a detailed account of the action of the Legislature in 1850 as taken from the Assembly and Senate documents.

Governor Fish in his annual message of 1850 makes the following reference to the establishment of free schools:

The adoption by the people at the last annual election, of the act to establish free schools throughout the State, will effect a most important change in the system of common school education. Under this law, the common schools are to be free to all persons over five and under twenty-one years of age. On the first day of July last, there were 11,191 organized school districts in the State; being an increase of 570 over the number reported last year; and the number of children taught in the common schools during the year, was 778,309, being an increase of 2586 over the preceding year. There are 1893 unincorporated and private schools in the State, comprising 72,785 pupils. The aggregate amount of public money received by the several common school districts from all sources, during the year, was $846,710.45. Of this sum, $626,456.69 have been apportioned for the payment of teachers' wages. In addition to which, $489,696.63 were raised in the several districts on rate bills for the same object, making an aggregate of $1,143,401.16 expended for teachers' wages during the year ending January 1st, 1849.

1850
In Senate

Jan. 8 (Doc. 67) Petition praying amendment to new school law to revive free school law of village of Poughkeepsie, referred to Committee on Literature

Jan. 12 " Mr Beekman of Committee on Literature, to which was referred a petition for that purpose, reported a bill entitled "AN Act to amend an Act Establishing Free Schools Throughout the State, passed March 26, 1849. Read, by unanimous consent read second time and referred to Committee of the Whole.

Jan. 14 " Debated in Committee of Whole (Details of debate not given in material copied)

Jan. 15 " Debated in Committee of Whole (Details of debate not given in material copied)

Jan. 24 " Resolutions of Board of Supervisors of Allegany Co. presented, asking for law to legalize their proceedings and amend free school law, Referred to Committee on Literature

Jan. 30 (Doc. 67) Mr. Miller of Committee on Literature reported favorably on bill with amendments, Committed to Committee of the Whole.
Bill ordered engrossed for third reading.
Bill read and passed.
See Document 64 for copy of bill

Jan. 31 " Message from Assembly that bill had been passed without amendment. Bill sent to Governor.

Feb. 1 " Mr. Beekman from Committee on Literature, to which was referred petition for that purpose, reported in writing and introduced a bill entitled "An Act *further* to amend 'An Act establishing free schools throughout the State, passed March 26, 1849.'" Read twice and referred to Committee of the Whole.
(See Document 42 for report and proposed bill)

March 1 " Considered in Committee of Whole and held in Committee.

March 2 " Considered in the Committee of the Whole

March 9 " On motion of Mr Beekman resolved that bill be made special order for Tuesday, March 12

March 13 " In Committee of the Whole, two bills were considered The bill to further amend, etc.
"An Act to submit to the people at the next annual election the question of the repeal of the act establishing free schools throughout the State, passed March 26,"

April 1 " Both bills discussed in Committee of Whole. Second bill amended by striking out words "except New York City." Second bill referred to select committee. First bill held in Committee of the Whole.
(The resubmission bill Doc. 44 was passed April 10. No record of Senate action from April 1 to April 10 copied)

1850

In Assembly

Jan. 12 (Doc. 67) Mr Lesley, in pursuance of previous notice, asked for and obtained leave to introduce a bill entitled "An Act to amend an act establishing free schools throughout the State, passed March 26, 1849."
Read twice and referred to committee on colleges, academies and common schools.
(Bill with same title introduced in Senate Mr Beekman same day)

Jan. 15 " Mr Ward introduced a bill entitled "An act to amend an act entitled an Act establishing free schools throughout the State so as to equalize the tax and to require eight months school." Read twice and referred to committee on colleges, academies and common schools.

Jan. 30 (Doc. 67) Message received from Senate asking concurrence in bill entitled "An Act to amend an act establishing free schools throughout the State, passed March 26, 1849" Bill read third time and passed by vote of 92 to 0. Bill ordered returned to Senate.

Feb. 14 " Resolution offered upholding free school principle and requesting appointment of commission to frame new plan to provide free schools and to simplify common school law. Resolution laid on table.

March 2 " The Attorney General submitted an opinion on constitutionality of free school law (Doc. 41)

March 16 " Mr McLean gave notice that he would introduce a bill to submit to people at the next annual election, the question of repeal of the act establishing free schools throughout the State, excluding cities and villages from voting thereon which had free schools under special charters previous to the adoption of the recent free school law.

March 18 " Mr McLean introduced a bill entitled "An act to submit to the people at the next annual election the question of the repeal of the act establishing free schools throughout the State. Referred to select committee.

March 22 " Mr Robinson of select committee to which had been referred sundry petitions, resolutions, etc. introduced bill entitled "An act further to amend the act establishing free schools, passed March 26, 1849" Referred to Committee of the Whole. Made special order for March 27.

1850

In Senate

March 26 " Ordered that said bill (?) be engrossed for third reading

Mr. Kingsley, from minority of select committee, to which was referred sundry petitions, remonstrances, reported and introduced a bill entitled "An act to repeal Chapter 140 and Chapter 404 of the Laws of 1849." Read twice and referred to Committee of the Whole.

Mr. Kingsley from the select committee to which was referred the bill entitled "An act to submit to the people at the next annual election the question of repeal of the act establishing free schools throughout the State" reported that the committee had made amendments to the bill and saw no reason why it should not be passed as amended. Referred to Committee of the Whole.

March 27 (Doc. 67) Considered in Committee of the Whole
> An act further to amend the act establishing free schools throughout the State, passed March 26, 1849
> (Resubmission act Doc. 44 passed April 10. Nothing copied between April 1 and April 10)
> During the session of 1850, there are records in the Assembly Journal of the receipt of two or three hundred petitions asking for repeal or modification of free school law. Six remonstrances against repeal of law received from Montgomery, Warren and Livingston counties.
> See Doc. 54 Petition from Pompey

April 1 " Considered in Committee of the Whole
> "An act making appropriations for the support of common schools for the year one thousand eight hundred and fifty-one and one thousand eight hundred and fifty-two.
> An act to provide for the support of common schools.
> An act further to amend the act establishing free schools throughout the State, passed March 26, 1849
> An act to submit to the people at the next annual election the question of the repeal of the act establishing free schools throughout the State.

References to the Repeal of the Free School Act

From the Journal of the Assembly of the State of New York; 73d session, 1850

The petition of sundry inhabitants of the county of Oneida, praying for the repeal of the free school law, was read and referred to the committee on colleges, academies and common schools.

Jan. 25, 1850, p. 203

The petition of sundry inhabitants of the county of Tompkins, praying for a repeal of the common school law, was read and referred to the committee on colleges, academies and common schools.

Feb. 8, 1850, p. 311

Four several petitions of sundry inhabitants of the counties of Oswego, Niagara and Monroe, praying for the repeal of the free school law, were read and referred to the committee on colleges, academies and common schools.

Feb. 11, 1850, p. 328

Three several petitions of sundry inhabitants of the counties of Monroe and Rockland praying for the repeal of the free school law, were read and referred to the committee on colleges, academies and common schools.

Feb. 9, 1850, p. 319

Five several petitions of sundry inhabitants of the counties of Albany, Jefferson, Oneida, Otsego and Saratoga, praying for a repeal or modification of the free school law, were read and referred to the committee on colleges, academies and common schools.

Feb. 12, 1850. p. 340

Three sundry petitions of sundry inhabitants of the counties of Niagara, Montgomery and Tompkins for a repeal of the free school law, were read and referred to the committee on colleges, academies and common schools.

Feb. 13, 1850, p. 352

Six several petitions of sundry inhabitants of the counties of Herkimer, Queens, Dutchess, Rockland and Columbia praying for a repeal or modification of the new school law, were read and referred to the committee on colleges, academies and common schools.

Feb. 14, 1850, p. 360

Petitions Praying for the Repeal or Modification of the Free School Law

Date (1850)	The petition of sundry inhabitants of the county of	Praying for	Page
Feb. 15	Putnam	Repeal	381
Feb. 19	Orleans and Niagara	Repeal	395
Feb. 21	Five petitions. Suffolk, Greene, Monroe and Ontario (and the remonstrance of Warren against repeal) noted below	Repeal	410
Feb. 23	Thirteen petitions. Steuben, Orange, Onondaga, Tompkins, Wayne, Rockland, Otsego, Cortland and Oneida	Repeal	426
Feb. 26	Seven petitions. Dutchess, Tompkins, Saratoga, Rockland, Oneida and Orange	Repeal or modification	460
Feb. 27	Seven petitions. Livingston, Wayne, Cortland, Rockland, Genesee, Columbia and Tompkins (remonstrance from Livingston co.)	Repeal	482
Feb. 28	Thirteen petitions. Otsego, Orange, Cortland, Seneca, St Lawrence, Tompkins, Monroe, Yates and Suffolk	Repeal or modification	494
Mar. 6	Eight petitions. Orange, Cortland, Saratoga, Tioga and Oswego	Repeal or modification	594

All were read and referred to the committee on colleges, academies and common schools.

Mar. 7	Thirty petitions. Montgomery, Wyoming, Albany, Oswego, Schoharie, Cortland, Oneida, Monroe, Yates, Oswego and Tompkins	Modification or repeal	611
Mar. 8	Sixteen petitions. Livingston, Genesee, Seneca, Monroe, Tompkins, Oswego, Chemung, Wyoming, Broome, Orange, Otsego and Wayne	Repeal or modification	635
Mar. 9	Eighteen petitions. Queens, Cayuga, Madison, Saratoga, Greene, Oswego, Allegany, Otsego, Seneca and Herkimer	Repeal	639

Date (1850)	The petition of sundry inhabitants of the county of	Praying for	Page
Mar. 11	Fifty-six petitions................. Seneca, Wayne, Genesee, Livingston, Cayuga, Broome, Greene, Jefferson, Monroe, Otsego, Richmond and Niagara	Repeal or modification.	653
Mar. 13	Ten petitions..................... Albany, Livingston, Monroe, Broome, Otsego, Saratoga and Washington	Repeal.............	677
Mar. 14	Twelve petitions.................. Wyoming, Tompkins, Cayuga, Wayne, Onondaga, Saratoga and Orange	Repeal or modification.	695

All the above were read and referred to the select committee on that subject.

The following petitions, except pages 766 and 775, were read to the select committee on that subject:

Mar. 15	Six petitions..................... Orange, Steuben, Oneida, Seneca, Cortland and Saratoga	Repeal or modification.	726
Mar. 16	By unanimous consent............. Mr McLean gave notice that he would, at an early day, introduce a bill to submit to the people at the next annual election, the question of the repeal of the act establishing free schools throughout the state, excluding cities and villages from voting thereon which had free schools under special charters previous to the adoption of the recent free school law	....	766
Mar. 18	Ten petitions..................... Schoharie, Wayne, Tompkins, Suffolk, Rockland and Cortland	Repeal or modification.	768
Mar. 18	In pursuance of previous notice, Mr McLean asked for and obtained leave to introduce a bill entitled, " An act to submit to the people at the next annual election the question of the repeal of the act establishing free schools throughout the State," which was read the first time, and by unanimous consent was also read the second time, and referred to a select committee	....	775
Mar. 19	Ten petitions..................... Livingston, Saratoga, Monroe, Wayne, Greene, Otsego, Cayuga and Chautauqua	Repeal or alteration...	778
Mar. 20	Five petitions.................... Delaware, Livingston, Otsego and Ulster	Repeal.............	806

The following two petitions were read and referred to the select committee on that subject:

FREE SCHOOLS 271

Date (1850)	The petition of sundry inhabitants of the county of	Praying for	Page
Mar. 21	Twelve petitions................... Wyoming, Washington, Ulster, Seneca, Saratoga, Queens, Steuben, Otsego, Orange and Suffolk	Repeal or alteration...	821
Mar. 22	Fourteen petitions................. Washington, Greene, Orange, Wayne, Oswego, Sullivan, Oneida and Clinton	Repeal or modification.	828
Mar. 22	By unanimous consent............................		829

Mr Robinson, from the select committee, to which were referred sundry petitions, resolutions, &c., in relation to the new school law, reported and asked and obtained leave to bring a bill entitled " An act further to amend the act establishing free schools, passed March 26, 1849," which was read the first time, and by unanimous consent was also read a second time, and committed to the committee of the whole.

Mr Robinson moved that said bill be made the special order for consideration on Wednesday next, March 27th, at 11 o'clock, a. m.

Mr Speaker put the question whether the House would agree to the said motion of Mr Robinson, and it was determined in the affirmative, two-thirds voting in favor thereof.

| Mar. 26 | Twenty-four petitions............... Saratoga, Dutchess, Chemung, Livingston, Columbia, Washington, Sullivan, Oswego, Delaware, Jefferson, Niagara, Steuben, Orange, Broome, St Lawrence and Wayne | Repeal or modification. | 910 |

The above (March 26, 1850) was read and referred to the select committee on that subject:

| Mar. 26 | Ordered, That the said bill be engrossed for a third reading.... | | 919 |

Mr Kingsley, from the minority of the select committee, to which was referred sundry petitions and remonstrances in relation to free school law, reported and asked and obtained leave to bring in a bill entitled, " An act to repeal chapter 140 and chapter 404 of the laws of 1849," which was read the first time, and by unanimous consent was also read the second time, and committed to the committee of the whole.

Mr Kingsley, from the select committee, to which was referred the bill entitled, " An act to submit to the people at the next annual election the question of repeal of the act establishing free schools throughout the State," reported that the committee had examined said bill, and made sundry amendments thereto, and saw no reason why the same, as amended, should not be passed into a law.

Ordered, That said bill be committeed to the committee of the whole.

| Mar. 27 | Four petitions..................... Dutchess, Wyoming and Madison (Four remonstrances from Montgomery and Warren against the same) | Repeal............. | 960 |
| Mar. 30 | Twelve petitions................... Madison, Broome, Albany, Washington, Orange, Cattaraugus, Ulster, Cayuga and Tompkins | Repeal or modification. | 1034 |

The two petitions above were read and referred to the select committee on that subject.

The House then resolved itself into a committee of the whole on the bills entitled as follows:

"An act making appropriations for the support of common schools for the year one thousand eight hundred and fifty-one and one thousand eight hundred and fifty-two."

"An act to provide for the support of common schools."

"An act further to amend the act establishing free schools throughout the State, passed March 26, 1849."

"An act to submit to the people at the next annual election the question of the repeal of the act establishing free schools throughout the State."

And after some time spent thereon, the hour of two o'clock having arrived, Mr Speaker resumed the chair, and the House took a recess.

Apr. 1, 1850, p. 1069

Remonstrances against the Repeal of the Free School Law

". . . and the remonstrance of sundry inhabitants of the county of Warren against the repeal of said law " p. 410

". . . and the remonstrance of sundry inhabitants of the county of Livingston against the same (the repeal of the new school law) " p. 482

". . . and four several remonstrances of sundry inhabitants of the counties of Montgomery and Warren against the same (the repeal of the free school law)" was read and referred to the committee of the whole p. 960

All the above were read and referred to the committee on colleges, academies and common schools.

References to the Amendment of the Free School Act

Jan.	8	Mr. Geddes presented the petition of A. J. Coffin for an amendment of the new school law that will revive the free school law of the village of Poughkeepsie, which was referred to the committee on literature.	39
Jan.	12	Mr Beekman, from the committee on literature, to which was referred a petition for that purpose, reported a bill entitled, "An act to amend an act establishing free schools throughout the State, passed March 26, 1849," which was read the first time, and by unanimous consent was also read a second time, and committed to a committee of the whole.	62
Jan.	15	The Senate then resolved itself into a committee of the whole on the bill entitled, "An act to amend an act establishing free schools throughout the State, passed March 26, 1849," and after some time spent thereon, Mr Curtis, from said committee, reported progress, and asked for and obtained leave to sit again. On motion of Mr Crolius, The Senate then adjourned until 11 o'clock tomorrow morning. (Was debated in com. of whole on Jan. 14)	70

Jan.	24	Mr Robinson presented the resolutions of the board of supervisors of Allegany co., for a law to legalize their proceedings and to amend the free school law, which were referred to the committee on literature.	110
Jan.	30	Mr Miller, from the committee on literature, to which was referred the bill entitled, "An act to amend 'An act authorizing free schools throughout the State,' passed March 26, 1849," reported in favor of the passage of the same with amendments, which was committed to the committee of the whole.	140
Jan.	30	Mr Cook moved that the bill entitled, "An act to amend 'An act establishing free schools throughout the State,' passed March 26, 1849," be engrossed for a third reading.	141
Jan.	30	Mr Carroll, from the committee on engrossed bills, reported as correctly engrossed the bill entitled, "An act to amend an act establishing free schools throughout the State, passed March 26, 1849."	142

Ordered, That the said bill do have its third reading.

The bill entitled, "An act to amend an act establishing free schools throughout the State, passed March 26, 1849," was read the third time and passed, a majority of all the members elected to the Senate voting in favor thereof, and three-fifths of said members being present on the final passage thereof, as follows:

For the affirmative:

Mr Beekman	Mr Curtis	Mr Skinner
Mr Brandreth	Mr Dart	Mr Stanton
Mr Brown	Mr Dimmick	Mr Stone
Mr Carroll	Mr Fox	Mr Tuttle
Mr Colt	Mr Johnson	Mr Upham
Mr Cook	Mr Mann	Mr Williams
Mr Crolius	Mr Miller	Mr Owen
Mr Cross	Mr Morgan	Mr Robinson

(See Doc. 64 copy of bill.)

Jan.	31	A message was received from the Assembly, informing that they had passed, without amendment, the bill entitled, "An act to amend an act establishing free schools throughout the State, passed March 26, 1849."	146

Ordered, That the Clerk deliver said bill to the Governor.

Feb.	1	Mr Beekman, from the committee on literature, to which was referred the petition for that purpose, reported in writing, and introduced a bill entitled, "An act further to amend 'An act establishing free schools throughout the State,' passed March 26, 1849," which was read the first time, and by unanimous consent was also read the second time, and committed to the committee of the whole.	149

| Feb. 25 | The President presented the petition of inhabitants of Chautauqua county for an amendment of the free school law, which was referred to the committee of the whole having in charge the bill on that subject. | 248 |
| March 1 | The Senate then resolved itself into a committee of the whole on the special order for the day, being the bills entitled as follows: | 279 |

"An act further to amend the act establishing free schools throughout the State, passed March 26, 1849."

And after some time spent on said first mentioned bill, Mr Johnson, from said committee, reported progress, and asked and obtained leave to sit again.

Mr Carroll moved that the committee of the whole be discharged from the further consideration of the said bill, and that the same be recommitted to the committee on literature.

The President put the question whether the Senate would agree to said motion, and it was decided in the affirmative.

| March 2 | The Senate then resolved itself into a committee of the whole on the bill entitled, "An act establishing free schools throughout the State, passed March 26, 1849," and after some time spent thereon, Mr. Johnson, from said committee, reported progress and asked for and obtained leave to sit again. | 291 |
| March 9 | On motion of Mr Beekman, | 338 |

Resolved, That Senate bill No. 156, being "An act further to amend 'An act establishing free schools throughout the State,' passed March 26, 1849," be made the special order for Tuesday next, March 12, immediately after executive session.

| March 13 | The Senate then resolved itself into a committee of the whole on the following bills: | 353 |

"An act further to amend 'An act establishing free schools throughout the State,' passed March 26, 1849."

"An act to submit to the people at the next annual election the question of the repeal of the act establishing free schools throughout the State."

And after some time spent thereon, Mr Brown, from said committee, reported progress on the three first mentioned bills, and asked for and obtained leave to sit again.

Mr Brown, from the same committee, reported said last mentioned bill to the Senate without amendment.

The President put the question whether the Senate would agree to said report, and it was decided in the affirmative.

Ordered, That said bill be engrossed for a third reading.

| April 1 | The Senate then resolved itself into a committee of the whole on the following bills: | 549 |

"An act further to amend an act establishing free schools throughout the State."

"An act to submit to the people at the next annual election the question of the repeal of the act establishing free schools throughout the State."

And after some time spent thereon, Mr Johnson, from said committee, reported progress on said first and third mentioned bills, and asked and obtained leave to sit again.

Mr Johnson, from the same committee, reported in favor of the passage of said second mentioned bill with amendments.

Mr Stanton moved that report of the committee on said second mentioned bill be laid on the table.

The President put the question whether the Senate would agree to said motion, and it was decided in the negative.

Mr Dart moved to amend said report by striking out from the second section of said bill the words " execept the city of New York."

The President put the question whether the Senate would agree to the said amendment, and it was decided in the affirmative, as follows:

For the affirmative

Mr Colt	Mr Dimmick	Mr Owen
Mr Cook	Mr Fox	Mr Robinson
Mr Crook	Mr Johnson	Mr Skinner
Mr Cross	Mr Mann	Mr Stanton
Mr Dart	Mr Miller	Mr Stone
	Mr Tuttle — 16	

For the negative

Mr Beekman	Mr Brown	Mr Curtis
	Mr Williams — 4	

The President then put the question whether the Senate would agree to the report of the committee of the whole, and it was decided in the affirmative.

Mr Cook moved that said bill be referred to a select committee to report complete.

Ordered, That said motion be referred to the select committee of eight.

References to the Amendment of the Free School Law

From the Journal of the Assembly of the State of New York; 73d session, 1850

In pursuance of previous notice, Mr Lesley asked for and obtained leave to introduce a bill entitled, "An act to amend an act establishing free schools throughout the state, passed March 26, 1849," which was read the first time, and by unanimous consent was read a second time, and referred to the committee on colleges, academies and common schools.

Jan. 12, 1850, p. 109

In pursuance of previous notice, Mr Ward asked for and obtained leave to introduce a bill entitled, "An act to amend an act entitled, 'An act establishing free schools throughout the state so as to equalize the tax, and to require eight months schools," which was read the first time, and by unanimous consent was also read a second time, and referred to the committee on colleges, academies and common schools.

Jan 15, 1850, p. 124

The petition of the board of education of the city of Troy, praying for an amendment of the free school law, was read and referred to the committee on colleges, academies and common scnools.

Jan. 22, 1850, p. 181

The petition of sundry inhabitants of the county of Rockland praying for a modification of the free school law, was read and referred to the committee on colleges, academies and common schools.

Jan. 26, 1850, p. 213

Two several petitions of sundry inhabitants of the counties of Westchester and Albany, praying for an amendment of the free school law, were read and referred to the committee on colleges, academies and common schools.

Jan. 29, 1850, p. 224

A message from the Senate was received and read, requesting the concurrence of the Assembly to the bill entitled, "An act to amend an act establishing free schools throughout the State, passed March 26, 1849."

By unanimous consent,

Ordered, That said bill be read a third time.

Mr Speaker put the question whether the house would agree to the final passage of said bill, and it was determined in the affirmative, a majority of all the members elected to the Senate voting in favor thereof, as follows:

Ayes 92

Noes 00

Ordered, That the Clerk return the said bill to the Senate, and inform them that the Assembly have passed the same without amendment.

Jan. 30, 1850, p. 245

The following petitions praying for the amendment or modification of the free school law were read and referred to the committee on colleges, academies and common schools:

Jan. 31, 1850 Two petitions, Cortland and Rockland counties.........	247
Feb. 1, 1850 Petition, Saratoga	255
Feb. 2, 1850 Two petitions, Chautauqua	262
Feb. 4, 1850 Two petitions, Oneida and Rockland counties............	275
Feb. 25, 1850 Four petitions, Tompkins, Wayne, Allegany and Jefferson counties	442

References to the Establishment of Free Schools

Taken from the
Journal of the Assembly of the State of New York, 73d Session

Mr. Fullerton offered for the consideration of the House, the following preamble and resolutions, to wit:

Whereas, The law passed by the last Legislature, known as the "free school law" has proved imperfect in its details, unequal in its operation, and entirely inadequate in its effect its intended purpose and is now the subject of general dissatisfaction and complaint; and whereas, our whole common schools system, has by excessive legislation, by repeated alteration and amendment become unnecessarily voluminous and complicated, difficult to comprehend and execute; and whereas, in the opinion of this Legislature a law establishing free schools upon just and equitable principles, and a thorough revision and abridgement of our common school laws would be in accordance with the will of our constituents, the spirit of the age, and the interests and policy of the State. Therefore,

Resolved, That in view of the importance of the subject and the time required to perfect the same, it is the opinion of this body that a commission should be established to consist of three members to be appointed by the governor whose duty it shall be to devise and prepare a bill providing for establishing and supporting free schools, throughout the State upon just and equitable principles, and thoroughly to revise, abridge and simplify the common school system and law of the State and report the same to the next Legislature.

Resolved, That the committee on colleges, academies and common schools, are hereby instructed to prepare and report to this House, a bill providing for and establishing such commission.

Ordered, That the said resolutions be laid on the table.

Feb. 14, 1850, p. 365

The House then resolved itself into a committee of the whole on the bill entitled as follows:

"An act further to amend the act establishing free schools throughout the State, passed March 26, 1849.

Mar. 27, 1850, p. 967

Report of the committee on literature in relation to petitions for the amendments to the act establishing free schools throughout the State

In Senate, February 1, 1850

The committee on literature, to which was referred various petitions, praying for amendments to the act establishing free schools throughout the State, passed March 26, 1849, report

That it is evident from the memorials submitted to them that the present laws require, in some particulars, a careful revision to make them accomplish fully the ends of their enactment.

The complaint of a meeting of citizens of Orange county "that the school laws of this State, by repeated alterations and amendments have become voluminous and complicated almost beyond comprehension, so much so as to require radically revising, simplifying and abridging," is by no means unjust; and the first step towards the permanent establishment of the free school system, this committee recommend a revision and simplification of the school laws by the Secretary of State.

It has become apparent, however, that much of the opposition to the new school law has arisen from a reluctance on the part of the taxpayers to the vote necessary money for the due maintenance of the free schools. Some districts have even voted to diminish the number of months during which their schools shall be kept open from eight months to four, content to give their children half the teaching which the law intended, rather than submit to the smallest tax.

Rate bills are still regarded with favor, because they fall, not upon the property of a district, but upon the parents who have children to send to school. Many parents, however, under the old system, kept their children at home, because they could not afford to pay, and because they were not willing to confess the pauperism which alone entitled them to free schooling. It should be the aim of the State to make admission to its schools the absolute right of the child of every citizen, a right which it shall be no meanness in the rich man to enjoy, nor degradation to the poor man to claim.

By the ninth article of the constitution provision is made for the annual addition of $25,000 to the capital of the Common School Fund. The revenues of the canals will soon allow a portion to be devoted to the support of the schools, beyond what is required for interest, repairs and accumulation. The rate bills for 1849 amounted to $489,696.63; and we have therefore to provide for raising a similar amount, which lessens every year until our school fund becomes large enough to support the schools out of its incomes, without resort to taxation. The Governor of this State again recommends the restoration of the office of county superintendent, which he had advised in his message of last year.

In his annual report of 1849, the State Superintendent presented strong testimony to show that the office of county superintendent had been unwisely dispensed with. His predecessors, without exception, disapproved of the abolishment of the office, and were right in insisting that such an officer is needed, as the medium of communication between the department and the 900 towns and 11,000 school districts under its care. "The territory is too large," says the State Superintendent, "its subdivisions too many, its relations too diverse, the local officers too numerous, and the interval between the department and them too wide to permit that actual and minute supervision which is necessary to an efficient administration of the school laws."

The chief objection in the minds of those unacquainted with the subject to the plan proposed by the State Superintendent, was probably the expense. By the present system, the nine hundred town superintendents, at a compensation averaging $75 a year each, cost the State $67,500; or to be accurate, as the number of towns in 1849 was 873, the cost was $65,475. Deducting from the 128 Assembly districts those embraced within cities having Boards of Education or city superintendents, not more than 100 will remain as the number to furnish superintendents in the way proposed by the Secretary of State, and set forth in the act herewith submitted to the Senate. At $500 each, the cost would be but $50,000, a positive saving of more than $15,000, while the system would give to the schools the constant supervision of competent men, paid for their whole time, and proud of an honorable office. The benefits of such a change cannot be easily overrated. The vast array of school districts spread all over the State would be quickened into rivalry and good discipine. Reports would be more readily and correctly returned to the Department of State, and new energy everywhere infused. The present organization is like that of an army without officers between the corporal and the staff, its regiments without colonels, its companies without captains. This would be deemed but a sorry simplification of the art of

War; yet almost such is the condition of our school system. This Committee, therefore, recommended that the suggestions of the State Superintendent, confirmed by another year's experience, be favorably considered and acted upon.

The objection to restoring the office of county superintendent is simply that a county is often too large to permit the proper care of all its schools by one person. Assembly districts furnish more convenient divisions of territory.

The free school law has received a very large majority of the votes cast in this State in its favor. Fifty-five counties voted for the law, and only four against it. Such an expression of the public will is not to be disregarded.

Thoroughly persuaded that free education is of the last importance to the welfare of the State, the committee on literature do not hesitate to recommend that full provision by the towns or districts according to law, for the maintenance of free schools, during at least eight months of the year, shall be the condition on which, and on which only they shall receive any portion of the public school fund.

The benefits of free education are not now for the first time to be doubted. Nothing valuable comes without toil and cost. Our hopes of political freedom, of personal security, of unforced conscience, all hold by the anchor of faith in the intelligence of the people. France has the opportunity of freedom, but not the people of which freemen are made; nor the schools which rear good citizens.

The day is coming, we already see its dawning in our own State, when education shall be by all held as necessary as food; and whenever the reign of peace on earth shall begin, with the sword will also be laid aside the shackles of the convict, and our prisons shall be turned into colleges and free schools. At present we have but the alternative of prisons or schools; between a people educated, self-respecting, self-restraining, or an unreasoning populace, ignorant of the history of the past or of the learning of the present, ever ready to become the tools of a demagogue and to act over again the massacre of St Bartholomew or the Reign of Terror.

Already the farmer is exposed to the midnight murderer, who (as has just occurred in New Jersey) climbs by an upper window into his house, and slaughters wife and husband in their bed-chamber. That murderer was an untaught stranger, who came, unblessed by a free school, to our shores, and revenged himself upon a prosperity he envied, by robbery and outrage. Almost three hundred thousand strangers, like him untaught in such schools as ours, land every year at the single port of New York. Shall we not protect ourselves against their children, if we cannot against them? Between the standing army of school masters, and the armed police; between the spelling book and the bayonet, there is no difficulty now in choosing. Let us seize the opportunity; let us insist upon upholding our schools, and New York will sustain as proud a reputation for the best free education, as she now does for the best system of prison discipline.

The committee submit the Senate the following act, prepared under the direction of the Secretary of State as the Superintendent of Common Schools.

All which is respectfully submitted.

JAMES W. BEEKMAN
SAMUEL MILLER

AN ACT

Further to amend the act establishing free schools throughout the State, passed March 26, 1849.

The people of the State of New York, represented in Senate and Assembly, do enact as follows:

§ 1 The second section of the act entitled "An act establishing free schools throughout the State," is hereby amended so as to read as follows:

§ 2 It shall be the duty of the several boards of supervisors, at their annual meetings, or at any special meeting duly convened (in pursuance of law,) to cause to be levied and collected from their respective counties, in the same manner as county taxes, a sum equal to twice the amount of State school moneys apportioned to such counties, and to apportion the same among the towns and cities in the same manner as the moneys received from the State are apportioned. They shall also cause to be levied and collected from each of the towns in their respective counties in the same manner as other town taxes, a sum equal to the amount of State school moneys apportioned to said towns respectively, (and such further sum as the electors of each town shall have directed to be raised, at their annual town meeting, in pursuance of the law).

§ 2 The sixth section of the act aforesaid is hereby amended so as to read as follows:

§ 6 When the said voters of any district at their annual meeting, (or at a special meeting called for that purpose in pursuance of the law,) shall refuse or neglect to raise by tax a sum of money, which added (to the sum apportioned to said district by the State), and the money raised by the board of supervisors, under the second section of this act, will support a school in said district for at least eight months in a year, keep the school house in proper repair, and furnish the necessary fuel, then it shall be the duty of said trustees to repair the school house, purchase the necessary fuel, employ a teacher, or teachers, for eight months, and the whole expense shall be levied and collected in the manner provided in the third section of this act; and no district so refusing and neglecting to make provision as required by this act, for the proper support of a school for at least eight months in a year, shall receive any share of the public money.

§ 3 The Comptroller is hereby authorized to loan from the Common School Fund to the supervisors of any county in which the amount required by the second section of the act hereby amended shall not have been raised, a sum equal to such amount, on the production of a certified copy of the resolution of such board to apply for such loan; and it shall be the duty of such board, at its annual session thereafter, to levy and collect upon the taxable property of the county, in the same manner as other county taxes are levied and collected, an amount sufficient to repay said loan, with interest, and when collected it shall be the duty of the county treasurer to pay over the same to the Comptroller but such towns and districts in said county as shall have duly raised their share of the amount required by law, shall not be subject to the levy and collection of the county tax as hereinbefore provided.

§ 4 The omission of the board of supervisors of any county to raise the additional amount required by the second section of the act hereby amended, at their last annual meeting, or to direct the loan herein before provided for, to be made, shall not be construed in any manner to affect or invalidate the duties and powers conferred and imposed upon the trustees and inhabitants of the several school districts by the third and succeeding sections of said act: And all proceedings heretofore had in the several distrcts, under and in pursuance of the sections aforesaid are hereby confirmed.

§ 5 The office of town superintendent is hereby abolished on and after the first Monday of November next.

§ 6 There shall in each Assembly district, except in those cities or villages which now have or shall hereafter have, a city superintendent or board of education, a superintendent called the Assembly Superintendent; he shall be elected by the people, and shall hold his office for three years. He shall receive an annual salary of $500, one-half of which shall be a county charge, and the other half shall be paid from the unappropriated revenue of the Common School Fund. He shall perform all the duties now required by law from town superintendents except the receipt and disbursement of monies.

§ 7 It shall be the duty of the supervisor of each town to receive and disburse the school monies belonging to his town.

§ 8 Assembly superintendents shall have appellate jurisdiction over all school district controversies, subject to review by the State Superintendent.

§ 9 The tax list and warrant for the collection of the respective amounts required to be raised under this act by the inhabitants or trustees of the several districts, shall be made out and delivered to the collector within thirty days after the expiration of the respective terms of schools provided for, and shall embrace only such portions of the amount so raised as are required to meet the actual expenses of such terms. When collected it shall be the duty of the collector to pay over such portion of the moneys raised as may be applicable to the payment of teachers' wages to the town superintendent of the town in which the school house of the district is situated, subject to the order of a majority of the trustees in favor of such duly qualified teacher as may have been employed by them; and the residue of the amount so raised shall be paid over to the trustees, to be by them expended in pursuance of the vote of the district, or for the purposes specified in this act.

§ 10 Section 16 of chap. 382 of the Laws of 1849, is hereby so amended as to read as follows:

§ 16 Sections fifteen, eighty-three, one hundred and six, one hundred and seven and one hundred and eight, of chapter four hundred and eighty, Laws of eighteen hundred and forty-seven, and section three, chapter two hundred and fifty-eight, Laws of eighteen hundred and forty-seven, are hereby repealed.

§ 11 It shall be the duty of the Superintendent of Common Schools to cause to be prepared, published and forwarded to the officers of the several school districts of the State, and to each town clerk, and to each county clerk, a copy of the Revised Statutes relating to common schools, as amended by the several acts subsequently passed, with such digest, forms, instructions and expositions as he may deem expedient, for the use of the inhabitants and officers of the several districts, counties and towns aforesaid.

§ 12 All acts and parts of acts inconsistent with the provisions of this act are hereby repealed.

§ 13 This act shall take effect immediately.

Report of the Attorney General in Answer to a Resolution of the Assembly

In Assembly, March 2, 1850

Attorney General's Office
Albany, March 2, 1850

To the Assembly:

I have the honor to acknowledge the receipt of the resolution of the Assembly of the 23d of February last, requesting me to communicate my opinion in relation to the constitutionality of the law passed March 26, 1849, entitled "An act establishing free schools throughout the State," and in answer thereto I respectfully submit the following as the result of my examination of the question.

I am not aware that there is any provision of the constitution which is in conflict with this law, nor do I know on what ground those who affirm that the law is unconstitutional, rest their argument.

If it be said that the Legislature cannot enact a law depending on a condition to give it force as a law, I answer that the legislative power is not thus restricted by any clause of the constitution. Not a session of the Legislature passes without the enactment of some law depending on some condition for its vitality. Almost every law conferring corporate powers and privileges is obnoxious to this objection, as are also most of the statutes for individual benefit or relief. To A is granted a particular thing, on condition that he pays a particular sum of money; he pays, and the act becomes operative. To B is granted the privilege of doing a particular act, on condition that the consent in writing of such a judge or such a court is first obtained; the consent is obtained, and the act becomes operative. It was thought advisable at one period of our history to enlarge the Erie canal. An act was therefore passed directing the enlargement, provided the Canal Board should be of opinion that the public interests demanded it. The law was conditional. The Canal Board were of opinion that the public welfare would be promoted by the enlargement; and that the opinion gave effect to the law. But cases exist precisely analogous to this. The charter of the city of New York was passed by the Legislature, but whether it should take effect as a law or not was made to depend on the result of a vote of the electors of the city. So of the law providing New York with the Croton water, and so of the law providing the city of Albany with pure and wholesome water.

The powers of the Legislature under the constitution of 1821, were substantially the same as under the present constitution, and laws were enacted under it depending on the happening of subsequent events to give them effect, or in other words, referring it to the people to determine by ballot at an election whether the act should become a law. Such was the license law of 1845, and the law providing for the constitutional convention is a signal instance of this kind of legislation. Many of the acts above alluded to have passed under judicial examination and construction, but nobody, lawyer or judge, has ever doubted their constitutionality to my knowledge. If this law is unconstitutional, then the law providing for the late State convention was equally so, and for the same reason; but it will be found a difficult task to assign any good reason in support of the proposition that either of them is unconstitutional.

This is not the case of a delegation of authority by the Legislature to any other body to legislate for it or for the people, nor is it a delegation of power to the people at large to legislate. All the functions of legislative authority are exhausted on the bill before it passes from the law making power. All the forms required by the constitution or the rules of legislation to reduce the subject of the form of law, are applied to it. Its details are perfected, its provisions completed, and in its perfected form it passes both Houses by a constitutional vote, and receives the executive sanction. Whether it shall become operative as a law or not depends on a contingency, but nothing is to be added to or taken from it, nor are its provisions to be changed or modified by any other power. The contingency happened on which the vitality of the law depended, and then the law which the Legislature made became the law of the land.

It may be urged that the constitution by requiring certain acts of the Legislature to be submitted to the people, before they become binding as laws, negatives the idea that any other law can be thus submitted. But it must be borne in mind that these provisions are restrictive of the power of the Legislature. They take away a power which the Legislature would possess without them, but do not at all prevent the Legislature from doing in every instance what they require it to do in the particular instance. Can there be a doubt that in the absence of these restrictions it would be competent for the Legislature to submit every bill creating a State debt to the people for their sanction before it should become a law? The Legislature is but an agent of the people, and I think it may with great propriety and in perfect keeping with the constitution, submit every act making great and important changes in laws of general interest, to the sovereign authority for its approval. I cannot see that by so doing it would transcend its constitutional limit.

I have no doubt of the constitutionality of this law.

Respectfully submitted.

L. S. CHATFIELD
Attorney-General

Petition of inhabitants of Pompey for the repeal of the free school act

In Assembly, March 30, 1850

To the Legislature of the State of New York:

The petition of the subscribers, inhabitants of the town of Pompey, respectfully showeth:

That your petitioners pray your honorable body to repeal at once and unconditionally, the act entitled "An act establishing free schools throughout the State," and the act amending the same.

We find a general opinion prevailing that the law was unconstitutionally passed, being in contravention of the 1st section of the 3d article of the Constitution. That our government is in form a representative government, and that the Senate and Assembly, in whom the legislative power is vested, are bound to assume the responsibility of finally deciding as well as proposing every law. The exceptions in a subsequent article requiring certain laws to be submitted to the people, is an exclusion of all other cases. We hold that, but in those excepted cases, you have no more right to transfer to the great body of the voters a legislative power vested in yourselves, than you have to transfer the pardoning power from the Governor to the town meetings.

Again, the act in question is held to be a violation of the 13th section of the 7th article of the Constitution. We have no doubt that if this law had been framed in accordance with that section, it would have been defeated in its passage through the Legislature; but when it was seen that it was not to be a law by the act of the Legislature, no one seemed to have taken the trouble to mature the bill, or spend a thought upon the proper provisions in such a law.

We are aware that the courts may, in due time, annul a law which violates the Constitution; but they cannot act until a case arises, is matured and regularly brought before them. The Legislature can act at once, and it is better that an unconstitutional law be obliterated from the statute book, than that it should remain to entrap the unwary.

We find the act to be troublesome, irritating, and every way injurious. It produces strifes, jealousies, divisions and animosities in every district, and bids fair to disappoint the hopes of the friends of " general education."

We have no doubt that the law was passed under a delusion; certainly under a great misapprehension. It could not well be otherwise; the great body of the voters had not read the act, and few that had, had studied its operation, and not expecting that the title of the act was a cheat and a lie, they gave it their vote, expecting that the schools would be supported from the public funds, without imposing the burthen of rate bills or taxation. The pretended grievances urged for the passage of this law, we believe, were imaginary and fictitious. But by repeated reiteration it came to be believed by some that there really were cases where individuals suffered so intensely by being recognized as exempted from the rate bills for inability to pay; that the whole system of our common schools must be turned into chaos; that these oversensitive individuals may be relieved from such intolerable sufferings. By this law they are relieved by being authorized to put their hands into their neighbors' pockets at discretion.

Under our former system if there was any law that would exclude a child from school — but from choice we have never stumbled upon it; certainly we never had known one excluded — but if there was any such law, how simple a matter to repeal it. The relief afforded under that system to parents, by charging the erection and maintenance of the school house and appurtenances upon the property of the district, and by the aid derived from the public school moneys in paying teachers' wages, so reduced the expense to the parent that the remnant of teachers' wages, when collected in the form of a rate bill, was neither considered as a tax, nor felt to be a burthen; and hence it operated with as much general success and harmony as could be expected of an institution in which so many individuals were required to cooperate. But when the new school law comes to be tried ,and its ramifying power of taxation seen and felt, and a tax to be rated by one set of men and paid in great part by another in the school district, then the people are compelled to study out, and made to see and feel the mischiefs entailed upon the community by this law.

A law somewhat upon this plan may possibly be the best for cities and large villages; but in the country, the cases of individual injustice arising under it, that are constantly presenting themselves, preclude all hope that it will or can be acquiesced in by the people of the country. Business, capital, profitable employment, concentrate in cities and large villages; banks, insurance companies, railroad, and other accumulations, are there to yield their princely contributions to the tax-gatherer. But in the country there are no overgrown fortunes. A few individuals in a school district in the country are better off than their neighbors, but generally with debts and expenses in proportion. A case of frequent occurrence in the country is where a man has struggled through life, from poverty up to competency, and then exhausted and embarrassed himself by educating and setting out in life his own children, and is now visited by this law, in every form of taxation, to school the children of his more thriftless neighbors. It will be difficult to convince such a man that such taxation is either honest or just. But he is not the only individual who will clearly see and keenly feel the injustice of taxing one man for another's benefit. Every candid and fair-minded man sympathises with the man so oppressed, and is indignant at the power which inflicts the oppression.

In many districts, the numerical majority of the district will pay from one-fifth to one-quarter of the tax they vote, and sometimes a still smaller proportion. When they vote the highest possible tax upon their neighbors who have no children to send to the common school, do we expect that the tax payers are to be lulled by the song that it is the act of the law — that it is the principle of our government that the majority should govern?

Let us illustrate that principle by supposing a case. The leaders of a political party, seeing by the turning of the tides that their hopes will soon be shipwrecked, cast about for the means to extend their influence and secure their power. They find it necessary to increase their votes; and deeming the poor the most easily brought over, they enact that the poor man, who in the street shall meet his neighbor that may be better off, may present a pistol to his breast, and say to him, " You, sir, have been industrious, frugal, and painstaking, and hence you are able to educate your children; while I have been idle, careless and profligate. Now, sir, the power is mine; surrender to me your purse or your life, that my children may be as well educated as yours."

We startle at the morality of such legislation, and feel convinced of the one great moral to be deducted from the American Revolution, that neither the omnipotence of the British Parliament, nor the omnipotence of any other legislative body, can sanctify injustice or oppression. No American statesman, who has read the history of his own country, should need to be convinced that the most certain mode of securing the ready and cheerful acquiescence of the people to a government of laws is, that the laws themselves be framed in a spirit of fairness, or justice, and uprightness.

We also enter our protest and remonstrance against the project of establishing the office of county superintendents or Assembly district superintendents. We are sick of all that sort of improvement which consists in change. Such appointments will be mere party appointments, and very likely to be conferred upon the man who cannot spell words of over two syllables. We have found by experience that every new law is very likely to be a book of riddles.

Dated, Pompey, Onondaga county,
    February 19, 1850

Report of the select committee on the petitions for the amendment or repeal of the free school law

Assembly document 150, March 26, 1850

Mr Kingsley, from the select committee appointed to take into consideration the petitions for the repeal and amendment of the free school law, in behalf of the majority and minority of said committee, makes the following report:

That the said committee entered upon the discharge of its important and arduous duties, with an unfeigned diffidence, in their own powers, to do justice to the subject assigned to their care. They have endeavored, however, to discharge their duty. In deliberating upon the subject, they have felt the responsibility of their position; that feeling has sometimes pressed upon them with a power almost overwhelming, and they have been tempted to give up the work in despair. It is not strange that this is so, for how can they help realising that they are acting upon a subject of the utmost importance to ourselves, our present and all future generations. Our common schools are now, as they ever must be, the great nursing places of our heroes and statesmen; the places in which are to be formed our future rulers; where our wise and learned men are to receive the rudiments of their education, and where the great mass, the laboring and hardy yeomanry of our land, are to receive the whole of theirs. If we look around us, we find but very few indeed, who have ever gone further than the old log school-house, near by their fathers' farm or the better one in their native village, in its pleasant spot, and hallowed by youthful associations. There, the greater part of our population is educated; there, habits of thought and of moral feeling are formed; and there too the mind receives impressions which are everlasting; and have a controlling influence upon the action of the man through all his life. A few go thence to the academy, and a smaller portion still, at last complete their scholastic course at our colleges. But they go there with impressions received at the common school; and as the man is there made, such is he in his future life.

And not only are our sons there educated, but our daughters also; those who are to be the mothers of future generations. They must there be fitted for the arduous duties and the responsibilities of their life, as our sons for theirs; and there they, also, must form those habits of thought and feeling, those principles of action, which are not only to govern them, but are to be enstamped, also, upon the minds of their sons and daughters; who are, in their turn, to succeed them.

Who can estimate a mother's influence, or a sister's power, over the heart and conduct of a son or a brother? Silently and unperceived they do their work; the character is formed; the individual knows it not; yet, after years reveal the fact, and show him how much of a blessing or a curse have been the influence of his mother, the power of his sister, and the effect of those other impressions received at the school-house in his boyhood days; when his mind and character were fresh and easily moulded, and he receiving the rudiments of his moral, mental and physical education.

How important then, in view of its ultimate consequences, is the common school, and how careful should we be that it perform its appropriate work, unchecked and untrammeled, receiving the cordial and hearty support of the whole body of the population! This last indeed is a necessary condition for the full and complete success of the system. If it is looked upon with a suspicious eye, or opposed, by even a small portion of those affected by it; if jealousies, complaints, ill-feeling and ill-will, are caused by its practical operation, (however unjust those feelings may be in the abstract) then it fails of accomplishing its object, and instead of a blessing, it may become a curse.

Our State early recognized the importance of engrafting upon its policy a good common school system, one by which all, even the poorest, might receive an education which would fit them for the transaction of the business of life, would prepare them for discharging well their part as members of a free independent State; nay more, would fit them to be freemen. In 1795, so soon after our country had achieved its independence, an act was passed by which the sum of $50,000 was appropriated annually for five years, among the several towns in the State, a sum equal to that thus granted, being directed to be raised by the towns for an additional aid to their common schools. In 1805, a permanent fund for their support was raised, which was increased by subsequent legislative appropriations, until, in 1812, the system in operation till within the past year, was established, under the direction of a State superintendent of common schools, which office was afterwards attached to that of Secretary of State. That system prospered to an eminent degree; the people approved of it, and sustained it well; it was their pride, and our citizens removing to the far west, the glorious land of promise, would point their neighbors, the inhabitants of their new home, with pride and admiration to the glorious common school system of their "own native Empire State," and earnestly recommend it to them for their adoption. And why should they not? It gave a good English education to every one of whatever nation he was born, or under whatever sky; it asked not if he was rich or poor, but opened its school house door to the son of poverty as well as to the heir of riches; the State, acknowledging its duty and obligation, from its own abundant resources gave a part of the funds, the towns supplied an equal portion, and what was lacking, those who enjoyed its benefits gladly paid.

Nor were the new states reluctant to follow the example thus commended to their approbation and imitation. Ohio, Indiana, Illinois, Missouri, Kentucky, Tennessee, Mississippi, Louisiana, Georgia, Michigan and Alabama, gladly followed in our lead, established systems similar to ours, and provided the necessary means for carrying them into full and complete operation. Nor is this all. A self denying and christian spirit impelled a few, a noble few, to leave homes and kindred, and on a beautiful cluster of islands in the far-off Pacific to plant the standard of the cross, and to call around it the benighted and degraded there. They had with them, first of all, the bible; they next had the recollection of their common schools at home, and remembering their happy influences on the character of the people, they established similar schools there, and they have found them a most powerful auxiliary in their noble work; the intellect is awakened, cultivated and expanded; and as a natural consequence, the moral nature of the man is made tender and prepared to receive with approbation, the teachings of a pure and holy religion. He learns to look with disgust and abhorrence upon his idolatrous worship, and to love that divine system which the missionary brings.

The beneficent results of our system upon our own population can not be doubted or denied. Go where we will, we find the school house and the school master. Go also where we will, we find an honest, a laboring and an intelligent population. On every side are pleasant houses, cultivated farms, happy villages, and all the marks of thrift and industry. Enter the humble school house, and an interesting sight is before you. Instead of roving about the streets or highways learning idleness, dissipation and vice, are gathered those who are hereafter to be our rulers, our wise men and our statesmen. They are not learning that which will make them a curse to the world; they are not contracting habits which will work their own and others ruin, they are not preparing for a life of crime, but they are fitting themselves to act well their part as citizens of a great and free nation, worthy of the highest honors it may have in its power to bestow. Our observation shows us, that with the general diffusion of practical knowledge among the masses, idleness, sensual indulgence, and crime decrease, and give way to industry, honesty and virtue. True, however well educated and refined a nation may be, however knowledge may be disseminated among the masses, idleness and crime with their attendant evils are not entirely done away; all past experience proves this; but the same experience also proves, that it is among an ignorant and degraded people, that we are to look for the greatest degrees of vicious indulgence, the most atrocious crimes, the most regardless sloth, and in fine, for a general prevalence of all those vices, and those degrees of wickedness which so degrade and debase our human nature, and which, if universally prevalent, would make of this world, a modal lazar house, instead of the beautiful and pleasant one that it should be. Indeed, it cannot be denied, our experience has given the remark the force of an axiom, that a general diffusion of knowledge among the masses, has a tendency to elevate them and increase the general amount of virtue and consequent happiness in their midst, while its absence produces a contrary and disastrous effect.

It is not strange then that, as a consequence of the common school system of which we are speaking, near by our school houses we find the church erected, in which, during one day in seven, a happy, intelligent and contented congregation is found, with sincere hearts, worshipping a divinity whose precepts are pure and holy, whose requirements are not heavy, and whose rewards are glorious;— that we find our young men emerging from the portals of " the poor man's college," and occupying positions of eminence and renown; that we follow them through the higher institutions of learning which the State also provides for and watches over, until they graduate at our universities, and soon become our great men, and those whom we love and delight to honor; that we find them the eloquent defenders of the rights of man at the bar of justice; merchants whose sails whiten the seas of Indian lands, and bring back rich freights and princely cargoes; teachers of a world-wide renown, preparing their students for the stations they and others now occupy; or filling the pulpit and pointing their hearers, rapt with their words of persuasion and eloquence, to the better country which is before them, and all, everywhere, diffusing knowledge, refinement and happiness in their pathways, a blessing to those by whom they are surrounded; a blessing also to the world at large.

While thus our common school system makes us wiser and better men, while it thus diffuses the blessings of knowledge and intelligence into every hamlet and secluded district, it also makes our people a happier one. It does this by expanding the scope and grasp of the mind, cultivating its better powers and faculties, and bringing the moral attributes of man into a more full and perfect action. The degrading, ignorant and vicious have their enjoyment, it is true, but it is of a mere sensual and fleeting character; while to the educated mind, new and lasting sources of pleasure are opened; the whole of creation to his intelligent vision is one of beauty and enjoyment; his powers of appreciating and enjoying what is before him, are enlarged and increased, and where before one faculty ministered to his happiness, a thousand now are brought into life and activity; he feels himself a new man, and in a new world. Nor is it thus only with the individual members of a state, but the great whole — the entire of the population has its happiness increased, so that it is universally true, that wherever we find a nation where the people generally are educated and intelligent, that nation is a contented and a happy one also. Who would prefer the wild freedom of the savage and his joys, to the mild restraint, comfort and enjoyment of his enlightened neighbor?

Other benefits arising from a general diffusion of knowledge, might be mentioned here, but we forbear. We have endeavored to show that such a diffusion increases the prosperity, virtue and happiness of a nation; and it is from this position that we derive an important point in our argument, which is: — The obligation of a state to provide for this general dissemination of knowledge among its people.

Governments are formed for certain and specific purposes. In a state of nature, each one is free to do what and as he chooses. But he enters into a compact with others, by which a government is formed; some natural rights are yielded for the general good of all, and in consideration of certain benefits, which the government seek and require, and which the ruler or rulers agree shall be accordingly conferred upon them. Among these are, that the members shall be protected in their persons and property; another and more important one at the present is, that the government shall so conduct itself — that the State, through its Legislatures or other constituted agents, shall make such laws, and adopt such a course of policy, as shall confer the greatest amount of happiness upon its members; and shall give them the greatest degree of prosperity consistent with the general good of all. We have already shown, that a good common school system produces and effects these results, and we therefore conclude, that it is the highest interest of the State, its most imperative duty, to establish and maintain such a system, and by all necessary rules, laws and regulations, to give it life and a full and complete operation. And not this alone — it has not only to pass laws, but it must furnish, or provide for, the means also. The wealth of a nation belongs to the individuals of that nation; when it is necessary to promote the general good, that wealth should be applied to effectuate that end, not with a lavish, not with a penurious hand, but in such a manner as most effectually to accomplish the object desired. The schools thus provided, being for the common benefits of the State, should be supported by the State; not directly it may be, but at least indirectly; that is, that in some way or other, the property of the State, in a fair, just and equal proportion according to the different interests different persons may have in the subject, or the more immediate or remote benefits they may derive from the sums thus appropriated, should be made to support the schools so established for the general good of all. They should also be free to all. Such schools the State is bound to provide; schools which are open to all, whence no one shall be excluded, whatever his race, or comparative situation in life; but whose doors shall open as gladly to one as to another, and where all shall be on a perfect equality. We claim not that the State should so bestow its means as to give to every one, freely, a collegiate or even an academic education; but only that it is bound by every consideration of utility and justice, to furnish the means for the common education of every child within its boundaries — that it should give to every one an opportunity for so improving the powers which Nature's God has given him, that he may be enabled to discharge the ordinary duties of life with ease and correctly, and prepared also to proceed farther and farther into the great ocean of science which lays before him. Else the State has not performed all its duty; it has not done all in its power to increase the virtue, safety, prosperity, and happiness of its people, and in so far, is a debtor to those who made it.

As we have before remarked our State early in its existence as an independent one, discovered this great truth, and setting itself to work accordingly in 1795, made an appropriation of $500,000 annually for five years, the people of the towns raising a corresponding amount, and which sums were applied to the support of common schools. For some reason or other, it appears that but $149,250 were actually paid during this time, and that from the year 1801, when the last of said payments was made, to 1814, nothing whatever was paid by the State for common school purposes. But although nothing was paid, the State was not unmindful of its obligation in the premises; and in 1805 an act was passed, appropriating 500,000 acres of land " to raise a fund for the encouragement of common schools," which fund was to be a permanent one; the Surveyor General to sell the land, the Comptroller to loan the principal derived from such sale and the accruing interest, until the whole interest should amount to $50,000 annually, after which the interest was to be distributed among the common schools in such a manner as the Legislature should direct, and which investment was the foundation of the present school fund.

In 1810, another act was passed, which providing for the payment of the salaries of the clerks of the Supreme Court from their fees, directed that the surplus of those fees, after such salaries were paid, should be appropriated to the common school fund. It was several years, however, before a surplus was realized, and the act itself was repealed in 1821, some $78,000 having been received from the operations of the act.

The next step in the perfecting of the system, was the appointment by the Governor in 1811, under a power conferred in the supply bill of that year, of three commissioners, to report a system for the organization, regulation and establishment of common schools, to the next Legislature. This commission discharged its duty in the making of a report, accompanied by a bill of the Legislature of 1812, and on the 19th of June of that year, a law was perfected and passed which was the basis of our common school system until within a very short time, and which system so many are anxious that we should now restore.

This law of 1812 was but the basis of our old system, and in succeeding years, it was very essentially modified and changed. It provided that a State Superintendent should be appointed, and that the public money should be apportioned to such towns only as should voluntarily raise an equal amount by a tax. In 1814, this feature was changed, and the supervisors were directed annually to raise, by a tax on several towns, a sum equal to that received by them from the State. Other amendments were made from time to time, up to 1821, when the duties of the office of State Superintendent were transferred to the Secretary of State.

In 1814, the first appropriation from the proceeds of the common school fund established in 1805, was made. It was the bare pittance of $48,376 only; but it was the germ of a mightier sum which was thereafter to be realized from the wise foresight of our fathers in their liberal appropriation — an appropriation then comparatively worthless, but which it was foreseen, as the result has proved true, would in the end be of a great and commanding value. This fund has, in various ways, at different times been increased until now, when we have a capital belonging to our common school fund of $2,244,000, protected and assured to us by the guarantees of the Constitution as a fund for common school purposes, set apart inviolate and forever. From this fund, which must gradually yet surely from the provisions of the same Constitution, increase, we now annually distribute $285,000 and more, which sum, increasing as the fund itself has enlarged, will each year make our schools more and more perfectly and practically "free."

This is a magnificent sum for a State to set apart for a purpose like this. It is not for war; it is not for the destruction of human life; it is not for the forging of the instruments of battle, or the building of armed navies, that these millions are devoted; but for the education and cultivation of immortal minds, and to render them wiser, better, and happier than they would otherwise be; for the teaching of those lessons which will one day beat the sword into the plough-share and the spear into the pruning hook; for the inculcation of those principles which are yet to cover the earth with the blessings of peace, and imbue its inhabitants with a feeling of good will each towards the other.

This sum has not been appropriated in vain. Each succeeding year has seen a greater, and a still greater number of pupils flocking into the schools thus fostered and nourished by the care of the State, until within the past year, an army of nearly 800,000 children has there received the rudiments — it may be, the whole — of that education which is so necessary and so well adapted to render each of them happy, prosperous, and industrious, the better fitted for the stations of importance in life which, as citizens of a great republic, they may hereafter — many of them, at least — be called upon to fill.

But, it is not in this manner alone that the State has endeavored to discharge the duty incumbent upon it, of educating and improving its population. It has set apart another fund, the annual income of which is applied to the purchasing and keeping up of a suitable miscellaneous library in each of the school districts of the State. It was a wise, a laudable, and a benevolent policy which instigated this measure, and one the influence of which cannot even be fully estimated, and least of all cannot be during the generation in which it originated. The kings of the old world have collected at their capitals vast numbers of books, rare, valuable and costly. They are carefully kept in splendid buildings, which are adorned with all the embellishments of art. To the wise, the curious enquirer, the wealthy, or the noble, they are open; but to the illiterate, the poor, or the ignoble, from their location, and the ban of prejudice or custom, they are forbidden places, and their volumes, emphatically, " sealed books." Of what use to the peasant of Normandy or the sunny plains of Languedoc are all the treasures deposited in the libraries of the French capital? Of what use to the serf of Russia, or to the laborer of England, are the libraries at St. Petersburgh or London? Of what use are any of the libraries of Europe to the great mass of the surrounding population? None! To the vast majority, they might as well be buried in the depths of the sea, or scattered to the four winds of heaven, as to be where they are.

The State of New York has done better and more wisely than the kingdoms of the old world. While, like them, she has gathered her splendid library at her Capitol, which contains, as it should, books of rare and costly value, many of which are valuable to only a few, she has heeded the wants, not of a portion only of her population, but those of the whole of it. In every district through all her State, she has placed a library of such books as her farmers, her mechanics, her merchants, her apprentices her whole people, old or young, need. That library is open for all; no one is excluded of debarred from its privileges; but each one finds, at home, a library for his own and his neighbors' use.

Viewed in this light, the spectacle which New York presents is a proud and glorious one. She has divided the State into eleven thousand five hundred districts of convenient size; in every one of these she has caused to be erected a school house, helped to pay the teacher who has taught there, and side by side with the school house has placed a library such as the population reads. The spectacle truly is one which may challenge the admiration of the world.

Your committee ask pardon for this seeming digression. We should not have alluded to our library system but we could not forbear, when speaking of what has been done for the cause of popular education, to refer to this point also, and for the further reason that some of your petitioners have asked, that the fund now applied for the purchase of libraries may be devoted to a different purpose.

It may not be amiss, for the proper understanding of some portions of the subsequent part of our report, for us here to briefly mention the leading features of the common school system in operation up to the passage of the free school law.

By that system the State annually distributed to the several towns of the State, their proportionate share of the revenues of the Common School Fund. The boards of supervisors, at their annual meetings caused to be levied, on each of the towns in their counties, a sum equal in amount to that received from the State, and such further sum as the electors of the town might have directed; these sums, (with the addition of that received by some towns and from local and other funds, and amounting, in all the

State, to an annual average of $20,000) made the public money of the town, which was divided among the several school districts of the town in proportion to the number of children therein, over five and under sixteen years of age, according to the last report of the district trustees. Schools were to be kept during four months in each year, and for such longer time as the trustees should determine, and the amount remaining due for teachers' wages, after deducting the public money, was raised by rate-bills from those sending to school, they being taxed for that purpose in proportion to the number of days their children had attended the school.

As we have before remarked, this system worked well. Minor defects were from time to time discovered in it, which were rectified as fast and as well as possible, but no material alterations were made in it from the time of its institution in 1812, except those before mentioned, until within a very recent period.

Within a few years, however, in some of our cities and large villages, a different system was adopted and with great success. We allude to what is now called the "free school system." It is very different from the other, dispensing with the rate-bill entirely, and raising the amount left unpaid for the expenses of the district, after deducting the public money, by a direct tax upon the property of the district. The advantage of it is that no one is deterred from sending his children to school through fear of the rate-bill, which he is too poor to pay, or from a pride which forbids him to ask an exemption from its burthens, though such an exemption was provided for the benefit of such persons. In our large cities, which are crowded with the children of foreigners and others, the system worked, and ever must work, advantageously from the large number of those who draw public money and the greater comparative cheapness of supporting schools in such places, than in the sparse and thinly settled country districts.

A defect in the old system, of a grave and serious character, was that many who really ought to have been exempted from any and all the burthens of common schools, either from the inattention or remissness of the district trustees, or a pride on their part for which they would not claim it, were not exempted, and were deterred from sending their children to school. In 1845, the State Superintendent made an effort to learn, from the reports of subordinate school officers, the number of children who were, for these reasons, kept from our schools. The returns upon this head were very imperfect, but enough was returned to authorize the opinion that, in all the State, over 46,000 children were thus deprived of a participation in the benefits of our common schools. This was a serious evil; these children were to be provided for, we would have been unjust to have left them practically unable to enter those schools which the State and its citizens had provided for their benefit as well as for that of any other children.

The free school laws in the cities, and to which we have just referred, had been found very useful in bringing in this class of children. The opinion began to prevail, that the system would operate equally well in the country, and would bring in those children there, whose parents were unable or unwilling, as the law then was, to send them to school. Petitions for that purpose were sent in to the Legislature of 1849; the State Superintendent of that year recommended the plan, and, accordingly, a general free school law was prepared and submitted to the people, at the general election in that year, for their adoption or rejection. It is useless to say that the law was adopted by a majority of thousands, of hundreds of thousands; and thus, in a day, that system of common schools, which had been in existence since 1812, was laid away, and a new one, and to a great extent untried, substituted in its place. Though the provisions of this law are known and familiar to us all, it may not be improper for us to refer briefly to its leading features. In the first place, it provided that, " Common schools in the several school districts in this State shall be free to all persons residing in the district over five and under twenty-one years of age;" and that non-residents might be admitted, on such terms as the trustees should impose. It next provided that, in addition to the amount of public money before raised, there should be collected, by a tax levied on the counties, a sum equal to that received by the counties from the State; making an increase of fifty per cent upon the amount theretofore raised by a tax; the whole amount so raised to be dividede among the districts in the same manner as by the previous law. Then came the third section of the act, which, taking that power from the trustees, in whose hands it had before been, gave to the inhabitants of the district the voting of what the common school expenses of the district for the succeeding year should be; and the amount they fixed, after deducting the public money, was to be raised, by a tax upon the property of the district liable to taxation. As a safe guard against the contingency that the inhabitants might refuse or neglect, in some cases, to make the necessary appropriations, the trustees were authorised to raise, by tax as before, an amount sufficient, after deducting the public money to support a school four months in the year. So that, as in the old law, a school was required to be kept that length of time, let what would happen.

This law has now been in operation some four months only, and yet we are already daily receiving petitions for its amendment, or its total and entire repeal. Already there have been presented over forty petitions for its amendment, and over two hundred and fifty for its repeal. They come from every corner of the State; from our villages; our secluded districts; from our boards of supervisors; our town meetings; from the high and low; the rich and poor; those who voted for, and those who voted against it; all ages, conditions and classes, are here, and respectfully ask us, either to make essential and important amendments to the law, or, by its repeal, to place us where we were before, upon the platform we had occupied since 1812. In this manner, and for these purposes, some twenty thousand names, of which over two thousand are for amendments, and over seventeen thousand are for repeal, have been presented to us; and we are called upon, by every consideration of duty and interest, to listen to these complaints, and grant such relief as it may be in our power to bestow.

It is not strange, that the change from the rate-bill to the new system should be accompanied with evils, difficulties and embarrassments. That was to be expected, but no one could have calculated, judging from the workings of the free system in our cities and villages, that its operations, in the country, would be so disastrous to the best interests of our schools, as the result has shown. For years, the average length of time that schools have been taught, has been eight months throughout the State; now, your committee hazards nothing in saying, that it will not average more than five or six months, and were it not for the necessity imposed by law, that schools shall be kept up for four months in the year, the average would reach even less than five months; and the time in which our schools are kept open, would thus be reduced nearly one-half, whereas now, as it is, this term is reduced at least one-third from its usual average before. Not only are our schools thus closed for a portion of the year, during which they were before taught, but this diminution is accompanied by much ill-feeling on the part of those who were intended to be benefited by the act in question; indeed, it cannot be denied, that as the law now is, it is condemned by the whole and united voice of the people of the State, who, in great numbers, as it were, have come to us, and petitioned that we repeal it from our statute books, or else make such amendments to it as shall make it more acceptable to them, and, as they claim, and we believe, more beneficial to the cause of common schools. Among these petitioners we recognize names of high standing and influence, men of experience and judgment, men of wealth and indigence, men of all classes and situations of life; and believing as we do, that no system, however perfect in itself, can be of benefit, when opposed by those interested in it, we feel ourselves bound to do what we can to allay the existing excitement, and to suggest such amendments or alterations as shall bring back our common schools to their former healthful action, their former hold upon the affections and esteem of our people. And in order that we may recommend such amendments or alterations as will best accomplish this end, it is proper to examine into the principal causes of complaint now made against the law, that, like wise physicians understanding the disease, its location, and its causes, we may be able to apply the proper remedy.

The most prominent objection, and your committee is constrained to say, that in their opinion it is a valid one, is the unequal rate of taxation in different counties, towns and districts even, which is caused by the practical working of the present law. No doubt can be entertained that this taxation is most unequal and should be corrected. The public money is distributed into the several school districts of the town, in proportion to the number of children therein of a certain age. Now, in the large districts there being a great number of these children, more money is received than in the smaller ones, the proportion being in some instances as great as from 1 to 3, or even 5; that is to say, while one district may receive $25 of public money, another one in the same town, and it may be an adjoining one, receives $75, $100 or even $150, while it is evident to every one, that the expense of the several schools differ but comparatively in a small degree. A house has to be built in each, fuel furnished, teacher boarded, and teacher hired, so that the expenses of the smaller one are nearly as great as those of the larger school, though the amount of their public money is so very much different in amount. And again, in the larger districts, there is more property, usually, than in the smaller, and the consequence is, that when the tax is levied upon the district, to collect the amount remaining due for teachers' wages, &c., the amount raised in the smaller in proportion to its valuation is very much greater than in the larger district.

A very few examples may be introduced, well authenticated, which will more completely show the present operation of the system, as far as regards this subject.

In Queens county, we are told by petitioners from there, the following are the amounts of taxable property in several of the towns, the number of children, and the amount per cent paid for the school tax, viz:

	Taxable property		Scholars tax
Roslyn	$160,000	over	200 has to raise 36¢ on $100
Great Neck	311,000	over	92 has to raise 12¢ on 100
Flower Hill	195,000	over	98 has to raise 12¢ on 100
Cow Bay	———	over	79 has to raise 4¢ on 100

Again: in Cortland county, in one district, where the assessment of property is about $12,500, it has been found necessary to keep up a school eight months, to raise $67 on the taxable property of the district; while on the other hand, in another district where a school is kept ten months, with much higher wages to teachers than in the other, they have to raise but $63, by a district tax, upon the property of the district, which is assessed at from $100,000 to $150,000.

Again: in many of the districts, such is the disparity between the valuation and number of children, that the district, where it receives its apportionment of the public money, receives $10 to $50 less than the amount actually paid by it upon the tax.

Other instances have come to the knowledge of your committee, but we will not take time to mention them; those we have given, are not extreme ones, or such as rarely occur; from the nature of the case, they must be frequent and universal, and present a strong argument against the details, at least of the present law.

Another objection, and one which goes further than the last, is that it is not right for the State to raise money by a tax, for this purpose to any greater extent than it did under the old law. The objection opposes the present system of taxation itself, without regard to any particular inequality which may result from it. In regard to this objection, your committee are partially apart. In one view of the case, if the amount could be raised directly by a State tax, they would recommend that it should be so collected; as that can not be done, a diversity of views arises, in regard to the practical operations of a system of county taxation, in lieu of a State one, which with other matters caused us to disagree, and has its influence in preventing us from making a unanimous report.

Another objection to the law is the power conferred in the third section of the act, which leaves it in the power of the districts to vote down the estimates of the trustees, and in effect, to prevent the school from being kept longer than the four months which the law prescribes. This provision leaves it in the power of disaffected individuals, who may happen to obtain a majority in their district, to shut up their school for eight months in the year, a power which we think should not be left to the vacillating mind or excitement of a public meeting, but which should be restored to the trustees, who are freely chosen by the voters of the district, as capable and qualified to act for the rest in the entire management of their common schools, or else be definitely fixed by the legislature itself. Your committee are unanimously of the opinion, that had this provision been left out of the law of 1849, many of the bad defects of the free system, would have been avoided, and there would be more harmony in our common school operations than now exists. The practical effect of the provision was to array one class against another, and create divisions, dissensions and ill will in a cause which of all others, should receive the united, hearty and cordial support of all.

Another objection, and one to which we have before referred, is, the operation of the present law, in diminishing the length of time in which our common schools are taught. A bare reference to the petitions for the repeal of the law will abundantly show, that this objection is founded upon the truth. It is a lamentable fact, that in many, and your committee is of the opinion, that in a majority of the districts in the State, either no school has been voted or that the trustees are tied up to a four, five or six month's school. At least it cannot be denied or disputed, that the average length of time, during which schools will be taught in 1850, will be much under the average of 1849, or of any of the preceding years. This fact should have a great influence upon our action. It is our duty, our imperative duty, to so regulate our common school system, that our schools be not diminished in usefulness, or shortened in their terms, and if our laws are such as to diminish their usefulness, in any respect, or to close them up, for a period when the interests of our children demand they should be open; then we should apply a corrective, either in the total repeal of those laws, or the enactment of such amendments as will accomplish the object desired. We should do something to heal this difficulty, and to bring back our schools to the situation which they occupied but a few short months ago, from which they have so suddenly, so unfortunately fallen.

Many other objections are urged by your numerous petitioners, for which they claim that the law should be repealed. Time, however, will not permit us to do farther than to barely refer to them. It is claimed that it is not the duty of the government to support common schools by compulsory taxation; that it is a law of nature that a parent should take care of the education of his children, while the law, in effect, takes it from him and gives it to the State; that minors are taxed for their property, without their consent; that old men, who have, by their industry, accumulated property and educated their own children in such a manner as they thought best, are now taxed for the education of children of others; that the law, though intended for the benefit of the poor man, works against him, as it in many instances shuts up the school against his children for eight months in the year; that the old law afforded all needed help to the poor, and was a voluntary, while this is a compulsory one; that the law is unconstitutional, or if not, is unjust and cannot be sustained; that it helps the vicious and indolent only; that a tax might as well be levied and collected for the benefit of religious and charitable societies, with a thousand other objections which we will not mention, as they are of a minor character and should not have a controlling influence in a matter of the great importance which this possesses; and in regard to the objection which we have just specified, it will be seen, by a glance, that many are equally applicable to the old as to the new law, and indeed, if valid here, would be equally valid against taxation for any purpose whatever.

With this view of the case, your committee are unanimously of the opinion, that something should be done to relieve those who are really suffering under the present law, to relieve the interests of our common schools from the incubus which lays upon them. Of the necessity of this, there can be no doubt; the difficulty and it is a great one, is to apply proper and appropriate means for the accomplishment of the object so ardently desired. In common with every one, we have but one wish, one aim in the matter; and that is, to so remedy the evils under which we are now laboring, as to place our common schools on a proper, sure and lasting basis, a basis upon which they may accomplish their mission as the mental and moral nurseries of those who are to succeed us.

On the one hand a majority of your committee have come to the conclusion that the law can be so amended as to remove the difficulties now in the way, and to the entire satisfaction of the people. On the other hand, the minority after giving the subject as careful and attentive a consideration as they can do, have not been able to acquiesce in this conclusion, and, accordingly, must dissent therefrom. Believing as the majority does, that the law can be properly amended, they have prepared, and herewith submit, a bill for that purpose. Its provisions are brief, but such as they think calculated to remove all just grounds of complaints, and to restore our common schools to their former high standing and prosperity, and also open and free to all. They have thought it their duty, in view of the overwhelming majority in favor of free schools, at the last election, to amend the law, rather than repeal; to cure its infirmities rather than to take away its existence. They do not pretend or imagine that, even with these amendments, it will be a perfect law; but they cannot but think, that it will be greatly improved by them, that our people will be satisfied, and wait for time and experience, and future legislation to make such further amendments as may be found necessary.

The main features of the amendments proposed by the majority of your committee, with the reasons for them, may be here briefly stated.

Carrying out the principle laid down in the former part of this report, **that the property of the State should pay for the common school education** of its children, and realizing the great inequality which now exists in the necessity for raising so much from the districts, your committee have proposed to raise an additional amount by direct taxation: were it possible, under the provisions of the Constitution, they would recommend that this be a State tax; as it is not, they have adopted the next best plan, and propose to raise the additional sum by direct taxation upon the respective counties; they accordingly provide, in the second section of their bill, that there shall be levied upon the counties a sum amounting to twice that received from the State, instead of an equal sum, as now, and the same upon the towns as under the present law. They also provide in section 10 of their bill, that the library money may be also applied for the support of teachers' wages, if a majority of the legal voters of the district shall so direct. By a calculation based upon the public and other moneys of the past year, and the current expenses for teachers' wages &c., during the same time it is found that, if the public moneys are the same this year as that, and teachers' wages, &c., also the same, the additional sum now proposed to be raised on the counties, joined to the library money, will so nearly pay all the usual common school expenses of the year as to leave but an average sum of three dollars to be raised in each district of the State—

a sum really trifling and unimportant. But your committee are aware that according to the present system of apportioning the public moneys among the several districts, if this additional sum which they propose is raised, some districts will receive much more than they may need, even to keep up a school during the whole year; while the poorer districts, those which most need help, will receive but a comparatively small pittance, and will languish under the burthens of taxation, and, as a necessary consequence, will gradually become extinct, or their schools useless.

To prevent this consequence, your committee have proposed, in the fifth section of their bill, to introduce an entirely new system of apportionment, and one which they think will, at the first glance, commend itself to the approbation of everyone. By its provisions, two-fifths of the public money of the town, applicable to teachers' wages, are to be equally divided among its several districts, and the remainder in proportion to the number of children in the districts attending school for four months or more during the preceding year. The advantages of this proposition are, that it will give a greater proportionate amount of money to the smaller and poorer districts, and thereby lessen their burthens, while, at the same time, by dividing a certain share of the money, in a proportion based upon the number of scholars actually attending school, it will offer to parents and others an inducement to get all their children into their schools, as the more in actual attendance, the more the district receives of the bounty of the State. By this section, then, we aim to make a more perfect distribution of our public money, and to call a greater number into attendance as pupils in our common schools; results which should be desired by everyone — which no one will oppose.

Experience has shown that the present provision requiring schools to be kept only four months in each year, is much too short; and your committee have therefore, after much thought and deliberation, concluded to require that they shall be kept at least eight months in the year, or be debarred from a participation in the public moneys. As this, however, might sometimes work injustice, they have given to the town superintendent authority to lessen this time, for a proper cause to be shown him. This provision, with its guard, the majority think a good one, and one which will have a beneficial effect; they therefore most cordially recommend it for your adoption.

Another feature of their proposed bill, and one which not only the majority, but the minority of your committee also, think an important and salutary one, is, that they propose to strike out the third and fifth sections of the present free school act. We have before referred to these sections, as containing some of the most objectionable features of the present law, as they have put it in the power of a majority of each district to reduce the time their schools are kept to a very small one, and one much too limited for the best interests of their children. But they have done more than this; their practical operation has sown dissension and discord in many a district, where before were peace and harmony, and inflicted a wound upon the cause of popular education by estranging those who were formerly friends, which, under the most skilful management, it will take years to heal. Your committee, thinking it better to entirely take this power from the vacillating opinions and views of a district meeting, have struck those sections from their proposed bill, and, as before remarked, fixed the time by statute in which schools are to be kept, subject to necessary alterations by the town superintendent.

The majority of your committee have proposed other amendments; as, if schools are kept longer than eight months, that any sum to be raised for the increased time, shall be collected by a rate bill; that each district may direct how the fuel shall be procured, and how the teacher boarded; that the expenses of the districts shall not exceed a certain sum; with others, the necessity or object of which will be apparent without any explanation on our part, and we, therefore, leave them without any further remark, respectfully submitting them for the approval, or, at least, for the kind and favorable consideration of the House.

In preparing these amendments they have had much trouble and difficulty. The field is a new one, and it must remain for actual experiment to test the utility or the inutility of the bill they have framed. That it will, if passed, be of benefit to our common schools, and harmonize the conflicting feelings now existing, is their sincere belief, and they, accordingly, as sincerely desire that it may be adopted.

It is with much diffidence and embarrassment that the minority of your committee has felt itself compelled to dissent from the conclusions of the majority. In doing so, they are governed by a sincere desire to act only for the best interests of our common schools, and to restore them to their former high standing, their former usefulness, and their former position in the regards of our people. The subject is a delicate one; it is one of the utmost importance, and we would not rashly propose to go back, for the present, at least, to our former system. We, however, are constrained to think, that in the present crisis, no other course is open before us; that no other plan will satisfy our people, or remove the deep and all pervading feeling of hostility which exists against our present law; that amend it as we may, it will still be the system of which they so heartily disapprove now, of which, we fear, they would as heartily disapprove hereafter.

It is beyond a doubt, that the people do disapprove of the details, at least of the present law. Its operation has had a withering and blasting effect. Is it not then, reasonable to believe, that, although the law be amended, and its more repulsive provisions stricken out, if it still retain any of its old features, it will, notwithstanding all its amendments, be unpopular with the people. We think that it is; and, thinking so, cannot turn a deaf ear to the thousands of petitioners, who have asked its unconditional repeal. They ask this, that they may return for the present, at least, to their old and well-tried system, well satisfied as they are, that it is not always well to change from a good and available plan to one untried and unknown. The free school system promised well; the name had in it a charm; it was pleasant to the ear of the poor man; it sounded musically to him as he thought of the benefits it would confer on his children around him; the man of moderate means and the one of wealth were as charmed as he; all thought not of its possible evils, but they looked only at its probable benefits, and the good it had done in the crowded city; and the result was, that a majority, counting by its hundred and tens of thousands, spoke in favor of the law. A few months only, and the feeling is changed; the poor man finds, as the law commences its workings, that his children are deprived even of a part of their former privileges, for the school house door is now closed at times when it was opened before, and there are stern feelings rising in the breast of the rich man against him, as one of whose children he is obliged to educate by compulsion, which he is loth to do; the man of moderate wealth, the man of great wealth, and the one who has educated his own family according to the means with which he was blessed, now find their taxes increased, their poor neighbors educating their children upon the funds the law has wrung from them; and they imbibe a stern prejudice against it in all its aspects, provisions and features. The minority are constrained to believe, that amend that law as we may, it will be looked upon with an unfavorable eye, and regarded by all with unconquerable feelings of aversion.

But the minority of your committee leaving, for the present, their general objections to the proposed amendments, and to which they propose to again refer before they conclude, have some serious objections to several of the particular amendments which are proposed in the bill submitted by the majority, and they wish, as briefly as may be, to refer to them.

One of the sections of the bill so proposed, provides, that the library money may, in the discretion of the voters in the district, be applied for the payment of teachers' wages. To this proposition, your minority can never agree. The library fund should be a sacred one, never to be diverted. It does not now, nor did it ever, belong to the Common School Fund; and that fund has no right to it, more than it has to any other of the funds of the State: If given then, to that fund, as it practically is, under the provisions of this section, it is given without consideration, and to the destruction of one of the most valuable and important of all our common school interests. We do not claim that our library system is perfect; or that it has, in all respects worked according to the intentions of its originators; but we do claim in all sincerity that it has done and is doing, an incalculable amount of good, an amount not yet fully perceived, but which after years will more completely and satisfactorily develop. Who can estimate the value of the influence it exerts in giving our young men a taste for reading? Who can tell the amount of its influence in forming the youthful mind? Who can now, or ever, sum up all its benefits? However convenient or proper, then, it might be in individual instances, to apply this fund to the support of common schools, (and such cases there are) your minority cannot consent that it be diverted from its original purpose. The system is now defective; granted; shall we then away with it? No! the defects are not inherent in the system itself; let us then remove and remedy these defects, but preserve the rest.

Another feature of the proposed bill to which the minority cannot assent is the provision, that if schools are kept for a longer time than eight months in the year, the deficiency shall be raised, as formerly by a rate-bill. This, in point of principle, though it may not be of great practical importance, your minority deem very objectionable. If there is anything in the free school principle, then this provision is wrong; if there is not, then there is no reason why we should not immediately return to the old rate-bill system, and no necessity for a free school law, or these great and extensive increases of taxation which the majority bill proposes.

Another objectionable view of the case is, that the taxation proposed by the majority will be very unequal. It may not be as unequal as now, for the greater part of that which the present law raises in the several districts will be levied on the country. But it must be obvious, that even to raise the tax in this manner great inequality of taxation must ensue. The relative number of children and amount of taxable property in the several counties is very far from being uniform; the same property is assessed at different rates in different counties, and most of all, under our present assessment laws, property owned in one county is frequently taxed in another. This is particularly the case in some of the interior counties; the surplus property of men of wealth in several of these is invested in banks, railroad stock, incorporated companies for manufacturing purposes, etc., etc. in other counties than their own; and however proper it may be, in ordinary cases, for that property to be taxed in the county in which it is invested, we think it would be unjust in a tax such as this bill proposes. If the property of the county is to be taxed for the benefit of the common schools therein, then all the property owned in the county should then be taxed, else great inequality and positive injustice must arise, in one county being deprived of its fair share of capital to the benefit of another.

Indeed, the minority of your committee think that in the absence of power to provide for the support of our common schools by a State tax, there is no system of taxation that can be devised proposing to raise all the funds necessary by a direct tax aside from rate bills, that can operate otherwise than in an unequal and unjust manner.

There may be other objections to particular provisions in the proposed bill, but the minority, leaving them, will return to others of a more general character.

We think that, in theory at least, it is proposed to raise too much by general taxation. Upon this point the minority would speak with great diffidence, and all due regard for the opinions of those who think differently than we do. But this is a question of vital consequence, and one to which we should all earnestly look. The State, as we have before affirmed, should provide the means for the common school education of all its children. The property of the State in a "fair, just and equal proportion" according to the different interests different persons may have in the subject, or the more immediate or remote benefits they may derive, should be made to support our schools founded for the general good of all our children. The difficulty is to determine what is this "fair, just and equal proportion." Upon this question the minority may well hesitate in giving an opinion, for it is one of great doubt, and, we had almost said, one impossible to answer. They however cannot help recognizing the principle, that there are two classes of persons who are interested in our common schools: those who send to them and who are directly, and those who do not and who are but indirectly, interested in the subject. If this distinction is a correct one, then a result seems to follow, which is, that those who are directly interested should bear a greater proportion of the burden than those who are but indirectly so, for the reason that while, like the others, as members of the State, they have an indirect interest; as patrons of the schools, as parents of the pupils there being educated, they have, in addition to that indirect interest, a direct one also.

We therefore come to the conclusion, that while the property of State should bear a proportionate share of the expense of our schools, those who send to them should also do the same; though this may not be an universal principle, or always a controlling one.

This principle has been approved by others before us. In 1846, N. S. Benton, in his annual report to the Legislature as State Superintendent, uses the following language: "The State will have discharged its duty when means sufficiently ample are provided to sustain our educational institutions, without rendering individual contributions either burdensome or vexatious." That in his opinion the State had already discharged this duty, is evident; for in a former part of the same report, after speaking of the law as it then was in this respect, and the bountiful provisions it had made, he concludes that "by these beneficent provisions, the child of penury and the destitute orphans have been provided with ample means of instruction, and it now becomes a question of grave inquiry whether this law is faithfully and benignly executed," was one of the principle reasons why a resort to the free school system was first proposed and recommended to our people.

Another view of this subject is, that parents, if they are directly taxed for the support of their schools, will naturally feel more interested in them, than if all the money comes from a general fund to which they have contributed, it is true, but only in an indirect manner. It is their school; they pay for it; they have a direct interest in it. This view is also sustained by others; Chancellor Kent, (Com. vol. 2, p. 196, n. a.) speaking of this subject, says, "Common school establishments and education ought to rest in part upon local assessment, and to be sustained and enforced by law according to the New England policy. That which costs nothing, is lightly estimated, and people generally, will not take or feel much interest in common schools, unless they are taxed for their support." The Hon. John C. Spencer, also, in his annual report as State Superintendent in 1840, makes use of similar language, which we trust we shall be pardoned for quoting in extenso, as it is so clear, lucid, and directly to the purpose. He says, "While public beneficence is bestowed in such a degree as to stimulate individual enterprise, it performs its proper office; when it exceeds that limit, it tempts to reliance upon its aid, and necessarily relaxes the exertions of those who receive it. The spirit of our institutions is hostile to such dependence; it requires that the citizens should exercise a constant vigilance over their own institutions as the surest means of preserving them. A direct pecuniary contribution to the maintenance of schools identifies them with the feelings of the people, and secures their faithful and economical management. A reference to the free schools and other institutions of learning in England, which have been over-loaded by endowments, will exhibit not only the jobbing speculation which has perverted them from the noble object for which they were designed, but will show that when the government and wealthy individuals have contributed the most, the people have done the least, either in money or effort; and that, instead of being nurseries of education for the whole, they have been almost exclusively appropriated to the benefit of the few. The consequence has been, that while some most accomplished scholars have been produced, the education of the mass has been neglected. These schools were not of the people; they did not establish them, nor did they contribute to their support; and of course they regarded them as things in which they had little or no interest.

"In the State of Connecticut, the large endowment of the public schools produced lassitude and neglect, and in many instances the funds were perverted to other purposes, to such an extent, that an entire change in the system became necessary. In the cities where there are large numbers, who would not be instructed at all, if free schools were not provided, the evil must be encouraged as being less in degree than that of total ignorance. But in country districts such destitution rarely exists, and when it does, provision is made by law for gratuitous instruction in each particular case."

To this quotation it is not necessary for us to add a word; if it was true in 1840, it is equally so in 1850.

Again, another objection is, that the law is compulsory; the money is collected by a peremptory tax; no provision is made for the inhabitants of a district to exempt and pay for the education of a poor man's family, living in their midst; the strong arm of the law says they must do it. We grant, that to a certain extent the money should be raised as is proposed by this bill; but we think that all of it should not be raised in this manner. Such is also the opinion of John A. Dix, who in his report as State Superintendent in 1838, used the following language: "The common school system of this State has been carried to its present high degree of excellence, principally by persuasion, by appeals to the interest of the inhabitants of school districts; and it is believed that the improvements of which schools are susceptible, may be secured by a continuation of the same policy. To change a system of measures which has worked so well, for compulsory ENACTMENTS, would be unwise; nor is it deemed advisable to impose on the inhabitants of school districts any further burdens, unless the measure is accompanied by an additional contribution of pecuniary aid."

The law is not only compulsory in its taxation, but it is also so in regard to the length of time during which our schools shall be taught. This is found a necessary provision in the proposed bill, and to the minority it speaks volumes against it. Under the old law, which required a four months school only, the average throughout the State was one of eight months. A change is made, and a compulsory system is adopted in place of a voluntary one, and even with the amendments, which are to make way with and remove all objections, it is found necessary, from fear that the term will be shortened, to require, absolutely that an eight months school shall be kept, or the public money will be withheld. Before, such a school was willingly kept. Does it not argue that "there's something rotten in Denmark," some serious defect in a system which finds it necessary to prescribe a longer term than before? It seems to us that it does. Give the people such a law as they approve, and, our word for it, their own interest will prompt them to keep up their schools for a reasonable and proper length of time.

Another objection we have against the bill, is the great increase of taxation which will result if it is passed. Taking the amount the past year paid from the common school fund, as an average amount for succeeding years, and it will be seen that that sum being $285,000, the counties will raise twice that amount, that is, $570,000, and the towns the half of that being another

$285,000; thus making the gross amount of town and county taxes each year, $885,000, being $570,000 more than under the old law. Now, under the old law, the deficiency to be raised by taxation was raised by rate-bills, and the amount was willingly paid by those sending to school. This fact we all know; the proposition is to raise it by a county tax. The minority has already given its opinion, that this will work unequally and unjustly; they have now to add, that in their opinion, it will be met with the decided disapprobation of our taxpayers. Their petitions show that they complain of the great increase of taxes; that the real estate of the land is already over-burthened; that it will operate unequally and oppressively upon tenants, mortgagors, or purchasers by contract of land; that a poor man, owning a small farm, his own children educated already, will have to contribute to the education of the children of his wealthy neighbor: all these, and other complaints are made, and this minority cannot but think with some justice also. But we base an objection upon another ground still: admitting, as they may safely do, that, in the abstract, it were just to impose this additional tax, still it would be unwise and impolitic to do it, from the general disapprobation with which it would be regarded. It cannot be doubted that great opposition will be made to such a tax, and that the system which requires it, will be viewed with a general disfavor, and repugnance. If this is so, the law cannot have a good effect; our common schools cannot prosper. To flourish, they must be established in the affections of our people; they must not be met with opposition, or ill-will, our districts must not be the arenas of personal strife, and animosities; for as surely as they are, so surely will the cause of popular education languish to decay; so surely will rank grass and weeds grow around our school-house doors, so surely will our common school system be numbered " among the things that were," being wounded and killed by the lavish kindness of its friends. From such a result may we be mercifully spared.

Other objections throng to our minds, "thick as leaves in Vallambrosa," but we forbear to mention them. Enough, it seems to us, has been said, and we therefore leave this part of the subject, with the remark that these reasons have influenced us to think that the present law should be unconditionally repealed. To this conclusion we have come with great reluctance; but it is one from which our better convictions, our sincere desire for the prosperity of our common schools, will not permit us to escape. If we err, it is not from the heart.

But we are asked, Are you opposed to free schools? Our answer is an emphatic negative. Our common schools should and must be free; but we are not of the opinioin that the present law makes them so, however it may be named; or rather, that the principle of the present law is no more a free school one, than was the principle of the former. Under each system no one was excluded; every one could then, as every one now, find an open door, and a teacher to educate him. The only real difference in the two (there being practically an apparent one, in the looseness of the exemption under the old system,) is that in the one, the money was raised by a rate-bill, in the other by a direct tax; in each instance the property of the district pays the amount, though in different proportions. Both, then, may be called free-school systems, if we correctly understand the term, and apply it to a system which provides that a certain amount shall be raised by a tax, (and it must be immaterial upon what principle that tax is levied) and then all children shall share in its benefits.

But we opine, that a free school system, as the people now understand it, as they understood it at our last election, means something different from this, that it means one which is sustained directly by the State, without any individual taxation whatever, except in a small degree, as we will presently mention. Such a system, the minority are desirous of having. At the present it may be an impossibility; but "there's a good time coming," and we hope, at a day not far distant, that a system like this will be ours.

But for the present, the minority of your committee think that there is no other course for us to adopt, but to return to the old rate-bill system. They have endeavored to examine the subject in all its bearings and aspects, and the more they look at it, the more are they convinced that this is the only available plan, the only one which can bring about the results we all so ardently desire.

The minority would not be understood in any part of their argument, to take decisive grounds against the support of our common schools by the bounty of the State. But they do think, judging from the experience of Connecticut, and for the additional reasons mentioned in the extracts which we have just made, that it will never be wise to entirely dispense with the rate-bill system. We, as just mentioned, are in favor of a free school law, by which the State shall furnish all the means, except a very small portion, to be raised in a proper manner from those sending to school. But the minority also think it not well, to pass from the rate-bill system to this, with too great rapidity. It should be a gradual change, and one for which the people will all be prepared; which will not come upon them unawares, but which is foreseen, expected and desired. Through such a change we are now passing. By the provisions of our constitution, the sum of $25,000 is annually added to our common school fund; from the silent operations of this gradual increase, year after year the fund is enlarged, and year after year a greater sum is divided among our schools. In four years, one hundred thousand are added to the fund; the interest of that is divided among the towns, they raising a corresponding sum, and thus we find our capital, in effect, every fourth year increased $200,000. Nor is this all; large quantities of land belonging to the State, and which have been totally unproductive, are a part of our common school fund. It is a source of gratulation to every one, that these lands are now becoming productive, and will undoubtedly, in a few years, yield a large increase, to be added to the productive capital of that fund. Especially is this the case, in respect to the lands in Essex, Hamilton and other northern counties. With a commendable liberality, the State has lately made, and is even now making, appropriations for the improvement of that part of her possessions, the effect of which will be, to improve those wild regions, and as a natural consequence, to increase the value to a surprising amount, of the lands there which she owns. Not only their nominal but their actual value also will be increased, and large additions, from their sales, must be made to the common school fund.

The effect of all this will be, that in a few years from these and other sources, a fund will be raised, the annual income of which will be sufficient for the entire support of our common schools; then they will be free indeed; they will be so practically and truly; unequal taxation will be unknown; complaints will be merged into blessings and we will have the best, yea, as we have already had the very best system of common school education in the world. For that time, let us all devoutly hope!

But it may be said, that we are abandoning the position taken, that the rate bill system should not be entirely laid aside. To this we answer, that from the gradual increase of this fund, our people will become habituated to the free-school plan; gradually, yet surely, it will take the place of the other; and then if it works, as the same plan did in Connecticut, to diminish the influence and beneficial effects of our schools, by diminishing the interest of the people in them, a corrective may easily be applied, and the danger avoided.

But your committee, will bring their report, already too extended, to a close. They have endeavored to show the necessity and importance of a common school system, and the duty of the State to maintain it, by providing the necessary means for carrying it into operation; they have also attempted to show what the State has done in the discharge of this duty and the reasons for the change made in the system; they have tried to show, also, that the new system is an imperfect one, and requires material alterations, or to be repealed. The majority of your committee have proposed amendments, and give their reasons for them; the minority, compelled to dissent, have given their reasons also, and bring in a bill for the repeal of the law. Aware, also, that many are of the opinion, in view of the overwhelming majority in favor of the law, at our last election, that we should not repeal it, but should re-submit the question to them; and a bill for that purpose having been submitted to the house by one of the members from Livingston (Mr McLean) the minority instead of reporting against the same, think it proper to report it for the consideration of the house, with their own bill for repeal. In this manner, the whole question will be brought before the committee of the whole, and the merits of the different propositions, to amend, repeal, or re-submit to the people, can have a full, and fair, and free discussion.

The members of your committee deeply regret their inability to do justice to the subject committed to their charge. They are now compelled to make their report, for the shortness of the time left to the close of the session, forbids them to longer delay. In submitting this report, they are painfully conscious of its many imperfections, the crude, unpolished and indigested manner in which it is written. As it is, however, they submit it to the House for its indulgent and favorable consideration.

Let what will be the action of this Legislature in regard to this momentous question, your committee earnestly hope that it will be for the benefit of our common schools; that, by us, their interests may be protected and nourished, their prosperity increased, and their means of usefulness enlarged and extended; that whatever system be finally adopted, it will be one loved of the people; a system whose roots will enter deeply into the hearts and affections of our people, whose kindly shade will extend over all the State, its grateful protection and shelter; then will we all pray:

"Lord, ever let it flourish; Lord, ever keep its verdure green!"

C. ROBINSON	H. BREWER, *Chairman*
JOHN OVERHISER	LEWIS KINGSLEY
BENJ. J. COWLES	DAVID SILL
T. O. BISHOP	*Minority*
IRA E. IRISH	
Majority	

Report of a majority of the committee on literature on " a bill to provide for the support of common schools."

In Senate, April 9, 1850

Mr Beekman, from a majority of the committee on literature to which was referred the engrossed bill from the Assembly entitled an act to provide for the support of common schools, report,

That after carefully considering the provisions of the act submitted to them, they have come to the conclusion that it ought not to become a law for the following reasons.

The Assembly bill proposes to repeal the free school law absolutely, by repealing in § 7 chapters 140 and 404 of the Session Laws of 1849, and by restoring and reviving all laws repealed by said chapters 140 and 404.

That a measure deliberately adopted by the suffrages of the people of this State, at a popular election in which fifty-five counties voted aye, and but four counties voted no, and the clear majority in its favor was no less than one hundred and fifty-eight thousand, should be quietly repealed by a subordinate section of a law bearing another title, is certainly rather hasty, and perhaps unconstitutional legislation.

The free school law of 1849 has not worked equally well in all parts of the State. From the 11,000 school districts, some three hundred petitions have come up to the Legislature praying amendment or repeal. Nineteen twentieths of the school districts have sent no petitions, and eight-tenths have made no complaint even by letter, on any subject whatever.

The committee on literature, early in the session, after a full conference with the department of common schools, in the office of the Secretary of State, reported certain amendments, which were, after some debate, laid over until the lapse of time rendered new amendments necessary. Those were made and duly reported on the 1st March. (Senate Bill No. 156). But a bill introduced on notice by Senator Mann, on the 2d March, (No. 161), entitled " an act to submit to the people at the next annual election the question of the repeal of the act establishing free schools throughout the State," found more favor with the Senate, and finally passed that body.

This measure proposed no amendments; submitted the imperfect free school law of 1849 with all those defects which experience had developed, untouched, to the popular vote; and it would almost seem with the purpose of defeating the law by aid of the disgust felt for one or two of its subordinate clauses.

The Assembly, however, has struck out an independent line of legislation on the subject of schools. It is now proposed to raise by tax eight hundred thousand dollars, and to pay over that sum when raised to the county treasurers, subject to the order of the State Superintendent of Common Schools. This officer is directed, on or before the first day of January in each year, to apportion and divide this $800,000 among the several school districts, parts of districts and neighborhood, in their several towns and wards, by dividing one-fourth of the whole amount of public money equally among the several districts. In towns where there are parts of districts and separate neighborhoods the distribution of the one-fourth to be made as follows: divide the one-fourth by the number of districts, parts of districts and separate neighborhoods, each whole district to be entitled to the sum so ascertained, and each part of district to be entitled to such proportion of such sum as the number of children between five and sixteen therein bears to the number in the part of the said district in the adjoining town, and each separate neighborhood to be entitled to such proportion of said sum as the number of children therein between said ages bears to the average number in the district in said town, and apportioning the remaining three-fourths in the mode now prescribed by law, and said moneys shall be applied exclusively to the payment of teachers' wages.

§ 5 Repeals so much of the Revised Statutes as requires supervisors to raise by tax on each town a sum equal to the amount of school money apportioned to such towns, and provides for its collection and payment, and all subsequent provisions of law incompatible with the act passed by the Assembly.

§ 8 Excepts from the operation of the act all special acts relating to schools in any of the incorporated cities or villages of this State, save only that all cities and villages shall be subject to the tax necessary to raise the sum of $800,000, mentioned in the first section of the bill.

No provision is made for the submission of this question to the people, as by Senator Mann's bill, and the Senate is called to pass absolutely upon the repeal of the free school law by simple enactment, after having just decided that they would not do so, but would refer the question again to the popular vote.

One of the most interesting questions that have been discussed in both Houses during the present session, has been the just and uniform assessment of property for the purpose of taxation. Although elaborate bills have been presented to the respective branches of the Legislature, no final action has been had in either; and it is probable that should this school bill become a law, the levy of $800,000 which it directs, will be carried out under the present unequal system of valuation.

All the cities in the State would, by its unjust operation, be compelled to raise several times as much school money as they could receive. While many counties would derive a large sum over and above what they would raise by taxation (in some cases several thousands) all which money would be drawn from the cities, villages or neighborhood, where capital happened to be accumulated. The effect of the measure upon the city of New York is well set forth in the following statement, prepared by Hon. Mr Waters, a member of the New York delegation in Assembly.

Statement, showing the operation of Mr Burroughs' school bill in the city and county of New York

The bill proposes to raise $800,000 by tax, apportioned among the several counties of the State in proportion to the assessed value of the real and personal estate therein.

By the last returns, the whole assessment of the State was, in round numbers...	$665,000,000 00
And the assessment of the city and county of New York was.	254,000,000 00
or rather more than 38 per cent.	
The city and county of New York would therefore pay 38 per cent of the $800,000 tax, or......................	304,000 00

The distribution of the proceeds of this tax is to be as follows, viz.:

One-fourth, according to the number of school districts; each district, large or small, receiving an equal proportion.

Three-fourths, according to the number of scholars, being the ratio adopted in the distribution of the school fund.

The whole State contains upwards of......................	11,000 districts
The city and county of New York.........................	194 do
or about one-sixtieth of the number.	

But on reference to the distribution of school moneys, last year, it will be seen that the city and county of New York have rather more than one-seventh of the scholars.

It follows that the districts in the city average more than eight times as many scholars as the districts in the country, and yet are to receive the same amount only of the first distribution.

This amount will be one-sixtieth of $200,000, or, in round numbers, to make allowance for fractions........................	$3,500 00
The remaining $600,000 will be divided in proportion to the number of scholars, of which New York has 14 per cent, making.	84,000 00
Total amount returned to the city and county of New York....	$87,500 00
The city and county of New York thus pays...................	$304,000 00
And receives	87,000 00
Leaving a balance, contributed by her to the support of schools in the country, from which she receives no benefit whatever..	$216,500 00

It will also be borne in mind, that in the country a lot can be purchased and a schoolhouse built for from $500 to $1,000; while in New York the cost ranges from $25,000 to $40,000.

That the same teacher can be had in the country for $200 a year, who in the city would command $700 — a difference owing chiefly to the increased cost of living.

It is not, therefore, out of the way to say that it costs from three to four times as much to educate a child in New York city as in the country, and therefore to make the distribution equal and fair, the whole amount raised by the city, should be expended there; or in other words, the city should be exempted from the operation of the law.

The city expended last year for schools		$376,000
The amount to be raised by this bill	$304,000	
Add her share of school fund, say	41,000	
		345,000
Deducting this leaves a balance of		$31,000

Showing that the whole moneys raised under this bill, with the school moneys added, will be $31,000 less than the actual expenditures of last year.

Further, it is to be remembered that the rate of assessment is vastly greater in the city than in the country. An additional objection to the bill is, that it leaves in force all the local laws imposing special taxes on the cities and villages for school purposes.

New York city by local law is compelled to raise:

1. The amount of school money distributed	$41,000
2. One-twentieth of one per cent	127,000
Add the amount levied by this bill,	304,000
Making a fixed yearly tax of	$472,000
Now deduct from this the amount which goes to the country exclusively	216,500
Leaves for New York City	$255,500
But the amount expended last year was	$376,000
Deduct the above amount	255,500
Leaves	$120,500
Which the city must raise in addition, in order to maintain her schools in the same condition as last year, add	
Fixed yearly taxes above	472,000
Annual burden on the city of New York	$592,500

from $216,500 of which she received no benefit, and from the residue about one-fourth of the benefit which the country gets from the same amount. One effect, as Mr. Walters, shows, will be to compel the city of New York to raise very nearly $600,000 in order to sustain its present schools, for which they now pay $376,000; leaving a net contribution towards the support of country schools of $216,500.

The same objection will be raised by every city in the State.

By passing this bill, counties which received more than they contributed, would have a direct interest in preventing any change in the present laws of assessment for taxation. What is now difficult might then be impossible; and the discontent of the people might take a direction against the sacred cause of education, for whose sake the detested tax was levied.

Grave objections exist to a school system in which the residents of districts and neighborhoods have nothing to do with self-taxation. Town-meetings are time-honored auxiliaries of freedom. Your committee, in recommending town taxation and district taxation in certain cases, expressly desire to keep alive a local interest in each particular school.

"The school system of New York," says Mr Flagg, then Superintendent, "has been formed by combining the advantages of the different plans of supporting common schools, which prevail in the New England states. Our system happily combines the principles of a state fund and a town tax. Enough is apportioned from the State treasury to invite and encourage the coöperation of districts and towns; and not so much as to induce the inhabitants to believe that they have nothing more to do than to hire a teacher to absorb the public money.

The free school law of 1849 was aimed against rate-bills. It obliged districts to tax themselves heavily and as has been found, unequally. The amendments twice submitted by this committee were intended to equalize this taxation, and by throwing the weight of it upon the towns, to take away many of the causes of discontent. The Assembly bill, however, now under consideration, aims to support schools by a general tax to a limited extent, while it retains the rate bill to make up the deficiency, and unconditionally repeals the Free School Law of 1849, and all other statutes which are inconsistent with the act proposed, thus accomplishing no good thing for education while enforcing upon a grand scale the very same unequal taxation which is made the chief ground of complaint against the present law.

Districts now pay unequal portions of school money. This bill arrays *counties* against each other, and bribes those counties which contain no cities or villages to persist in injustice towards their neighbors. Your committee therefore intercede once more for the preservation of the Free Schools, and recommend that the Assembly bill now reported, be not passed by the Senate.

All of which is respectfully submitted.

JAMES W. BEEKMAN,
SAMUEL MILLER.

Albany, April 9, 1850

Resubmission Law

An act to submit to the people at the next annual election the question of the repeal of the act establishing Free Schools throughout the State.

Passed April 10, 1850. (Chapter 378)

The People of the State of New York, represented in Senate and Assembly, do enact as follows:

§ 1 The electors of this State shall determine by ballot, at the annual election to be held in November next, whether the Act entitled "An Act establishing Free Schools throughout the State," passed March 26th, 1849, and the Act entitled "An Act to amend an Act" entitled "An Act establishing Free Schools, throughout the State," passed April 11th, 1849, shall be repealed.

§ 2 It shall be the duty of the State Superintendent of Common Schools, to prepare and furnish to the several town clerks in this State, forms of the poll lists, returns and other necessary proceedings, to carry into effect this act, and he shall also furnish, at the expense of the State, to each School district in this State, five copies of this act, with the forms prepared by him.

§ 3 The ballots to be deposited in the ballotbox, shall be in the following form:

Those cast in favor of the adoption of such repeal shall contain the following words:

SCHOOL

" For the repeal of the new School law."

Those cast against such repeal, shall contain the following words:

SCHOOL

"Against the repeal of the new School law."

And the ballots shall be so folded as to conceal all the words, except the word

" SCHOOL "

Which latter head shall not be concealed, but shall appear on the ballot, as folded.

§ 4 The inspectors of election in the several election districts, shall furnish a separate ballotbox, into which shall be placed all the ballots given for, or against the repeal of the new school law. The inspectors shall canvass the ballots and make return thereof, in the same manner as votes given for, the office of Governor, and Lieutenant Governor, are by law canvassed and returned, and the Board of State Canvassers, shall ascertain, declare and certify the result in the same manner as they are required to do, in respect to the votes given for Governor.

§ 5 In case a majority of all the votes given in the state shall be cast against the repeal of the new school law, then such law shall remain in force, as if this act had not been passed. And in case a majority of all the votes given in the State shall be cast for the repeal of the new school law, then the act establishing free schools throughout the State, passed March 26th 1849, and the act amending the same, passed April 11, 1849, shall be repealed, and such repeal shall take effect ten days after the result shall be ascertained and certified by the Board of State Canvassers.

§ 6 In case the act mentioned in the first section of this act shall be repealed as aforesaid then all the acts which were repealed by the act entitled "An Act establishing free schools," passed March 26th, 1849, shall be revived and enforced in the same manner as if the aforesaid act, passed March 26th, 1849, had never been passed.

§ 7. The repeal of the "Act establishing Free Schools throughout the State," passed March 26th, 1849, shall not affect any act done, or right accrued or established, or any prosecution, suit or proceeding, had or commenced in any civil case previous to the term when such repeal shall take effect, but every such act, right and proceeding shall remain as valid as if the act so repealed had remained in force.

Chapter 9
THE CAMPAIGN BEFORE THE NOVEMBER ELECTION IN 1850

The passage of the resubmission bill by the Legislature immediately started campaigns by those both who favored the repeal and those who favored the free school prinicple. The spirit of these campaigns can best be understood by a careful reading of the resolutions, extracts fro mletters and newspaper clippings.

Monroe County Teachers' Association

Mr N. A. Woodward, from a select committee, reported a series of resolutions in relation to the free school law recently enacted by the people of this State, which after a protracted discussion, was adopted, as follows:

Resolved, That we still consider the passage of the free school law by the people of this State, as a step of real progress in the cause of education.

Resolved, That by bringing into our schools during the past winter a large number of scholars who would not otherwise have attended, and by an increased punctuality on the part of scholars, the free school law has in these respects, at least, fully answered the expectations of its advocates.

Resolved, That we are decidedly in favor of the free school principle, and believe the same is true of nine-tenths of the voters in western New York.

Resolved, That we consider the details of that law objectionable, particularly that part of it which makes the length of time schools are to be taught, and the amount of funds devoted to school purposes dependent upon a vote of the several districts, as the tendency of such provision is to produce inequality of taxation, hostility to schools, and cause dissension, back-biting and strife, throughout every neighborhood in the State.

Resolved, That in our opinion public sentiment in western New York demanded the amendment and not the repeal or the reenactment of the present free school law.

Resolved, That we consider the jeopardizing of the free school principle, before it has had a fair trial, by submitting so soon again to the people, a law that, although highly objectionable in detail, was passed by an overwhelming majority, as a hitherto unheard of species of demagagueism, and deserving the censure of every friend of education and free government in the land.— *Rochester Daily Democrat, April 23, 1850*

Secretary's Office

Address of W. L. Crandal before the Onondaga County Teachers Institute, April 20, 1850

Shall New York Have Free Schools?

The electors of the State will determine this question by their votes in November next. That vote, if in favor of free schools, will settle the question forever: If against, which God forbid! a contest will have been commenced, never to rest until the triumphant recognition of the great and glorious principle, that the property of a state should educate the children of a state.

No other question relating to the internal polity of the State of New York, can equal this in magnitude. The Erie canal — a magnificent work — has signalized New York throughout the civilized world. But great as is that work — splendid and beneficent as it is in its results upon the happiness of man — how it pales before the blazing light of the proposition, that the education of ALL the children of the State, upon terms of perfect equality, shall be provided for by law! Whose mind is capacious enough to take in at one view the height and depth, the length and breadth of such a proposition! It will develop intellectual and moral wealth from the ranks of the poor, and moral wealth from the ranks of the rich, compared with which the Erie canal is a bauble. Both are good, both invaluable, both great; but the soul of man ranks higher than the clay which encases it.

On which side of the free school question, do you suppose the man of giant mind, of noble sympathies, of wise and profound forecast— of whose memory the Erie canal is an imperishable monument — would be found today, could he reappear in our midst? Think you De Witt Clinton, were he to step forth from the voiceless abode of the dead, would cast a ballot at the coming election, "For the repeal of the new school law?" No citizen of the State of New York, who knows aught of her glorious history, who has any self-respect, or the capacity to appreciate the man of whom Martin Van Buren said we might almost envy him the honors of the tomb, would for a moment profess a doubt as to what that vote would be. So far from a vote for the repeal of that law, who can doubt, that if his spirit could take cognizance of affairs in this State, he would gladly, were it in his power to do so, resign the high and honorable distinction of Father of the Erie Canal, for that of Father of a Free School System for the State of New York?

An affirmative vote on this question — a vote against repeal — will make New York an empire in moral greatness, and will secure to the State, in intellectual and moral wealth, results as astonishing as those produced by the Erie canal in its physical resources. It will show to the world, and to all future ages, that if, in 1850, the "lion and the lamb" do not lie down together in the State of New York, the children of the rich and of the poor sit upon the same bench at school, the rights of the one distinctly recognized as exactly equal to the rights of the other.

A portion of the professed friends of free schools, in the Senate and Assembly, have betrayed the cause of the 800,000 children of New York, in obedience to the behests of some soulless corporations, and the united phalanx of Shylocks in the State. They have compelled these children — through their friends — to defend the dearest interest of their lives under the terrible pressure of a false issue, wickedly, cruelly made up. Surely, if the Incarnate Son of God had dwelt upon the earth in 1850, he never would have said, "What man is there of you, whom if his son ask bread will he give him a stone? Or if he ask a fish, will he give him a serpent?" In the attempt to betray the holy cause of free schools into the hands of its enemies, the members of the Senate and Assembly — who profess to be the friends of that cause — almost literally realized that which our Saviour was content to state hypothetically.

This betrayal consists in compelling the cause of these 800,000 children to rest for success upon adoption of a law, the details of which may almost be said to meet the views of none. What an ordeal, through which these recreant men have compelled a great and holy principle to pass! But though thus enveloped in the thick blackness of falsehood, the clear sunlight of Truth will break through all, like the dancing beams of the morning, reveal every feature of the great and beautiful principle for which we contend, in all its fair and just proportions.

This most extraordinary position of the question of *Free Schools,* induces us to address you. We shall

First, give you a brief statement of the old school system of this State in its leading features.

Second, give a similar statement of the present system.

Third, as far as we can command the facts, give you a statement of the changes in the present law which the friends of free schools proposed in the Legislature, and which, in the Assembly, they passed.

Fourth, this will reveal the character and extent of the treachery of those professed friends of free schools in the Senate and Assembly, who voted to submit the present law to the people at the coming election. And

Lastly, we shall present some considerations, which we trust will measurably place this question in its true attitude before the people.

The Old System

The main features of the late common school system of this State, were as follows:

1 The interest on the common school fund was annually divided among the counties in proportion to their population as compared with the whole State — and then redivided among all the towns and cities upon the same ratio.

2 An amount precisely equal to the sum thus received by the town, was required to be raised by the town as a tax upon all its real and personal property.

3 This was the extent of the public money under this system, except as derived from local funds.

4 This money was applicable to the payment of the wages of teachers, qualified according to the requirements of law, and to no other object except libraries.

5 The money thus raised by a town, added to the amount received by it from the State, was distributed to the districts, as follows:

" In proportion to the number of children, *in each,* over the age of five years, and under the age of sixteen years, as the same shall have appeared from the last annual report of their respective trustees " (of the school districts).— See Revised Statutes.

Hence the amount of money received by any school district, depended solely on the number of children the previous year residing in it, over the age of five years and under the age of sixteen years.

6 The balance over and above the money thus received by the district, requisite for the payment of teachers, was assessed upon all the children in attendance upon the school, in proportion to the number of days each had attended.

7 The *indigent* were to be exempted from payment. When a term commenced, it was the duty of the trustees to investigate and settle satisfactorily in their own minds the pecuniary condition of all in the district who had children of school age — so far as the question as to whether they were or were not able to pay their share of the teacher's wages was involved.

If they determined that a family was not able to pay for the tuition of its children, that fact was to be certified by the trustees, and the certificate filed in the office of the district clerk.

If a family, in their opinion, was able to pay one-third, that was certified in the same manner — if one-half, that was likewise certified — and so on through the Districts, until all the individual cases of exemption, in whole or in part, were duly certified by the Trustees, and duly recorded in the office of the clerk of the district.

When the term closed, bills for the payment of the teacher's wages were made out against all who had attended, on the pro rata principle; but in collection, the exemptions theretofore certified by the trustees, were observed.

So it might happen, although $100 might be due on the teacher's wages, and though bills to precisely that amount were made out, that only $80 would be collected. The balance would be advanced to the teacher from the pockets of the trustees, and made a charge upon the district — all in accordance with the provisions of the following section of the Revised Statutes:

"The trustees of any school district may exempt any *indigent person* from the payment of the teacher's wages, either in part or wholly, and shall certify the whole amount of such exemption in any one quarter or term, and the same shall be a charge upon such district."

8 The right to vote at district meetings was limited to citizens who had paid a rate bill within one year, or had paid district taxes within two years, or who owned personal property to the value of $50, liable to taxation for district purposes, over and above property exempt from execution.

9 The expense of building, repairing and furnishing schoolhouses, et cetera, was defrayed by assessment upon the property of the district.

10 The town superintendent of common schools was not authorized to pay over public money to any school district, until in possession of a certificate from the trustees thereof, that within the year a school had been kept four months by a teacher duly qualified.

Such were the leading features of the common school system of this State, as existing on the 6th day of November, 1849 — the day on which the people adopted a new one, by majority of 157,921.

We come now to an exposition of the main features of

The Present System

1 Money received from the State, precisely as under the old system.

2 Money raised by town assessment, precisely the same as before.

3 This is not all the public money under this system. A sum precisely equal to that received by the county from the state fund, is raised by county tax, and distributed to the towns on the ratio by which the state money is distributed.

So that under the present system each district is to receive its proportion of three times the amount apportioned by the State, instead of twice the amount as under the old.

4 The money thus provided is distributed to the districts precisely as under the old system.

5 The money thus received by the district is applicable only to the payment of the teacher and for library.

6 The balance over and above the money thus received by the dis-

trict, requisite for the payment of teachers' wages, is assessed upon the real and personal property of the district not by law exempt from taxation.

7 No official census, certificate, or record, of those persons in the district, having children of school age, who are indigent wholly or in part. But the schools of the State are declared open and free to every human being to be found within its borders, who is over five and under twenty-one years of age. Here we discovered the two systems to be in character as wide as the poles asunder.

8 The right to vote at district meetings, the same under both systems — except, that of course no mention is made of the "payment of a rate bill," as qualification under the present.

9 The cost of building, repairing and furnishing schoolhouses, et cetera, defrayed in the same manner as under the old system.

10 School to be kept four months by a duly qualified teacher, or the district not entitled to any portion of the public money.

It may be remarked that all provisions relating to the gospel and school fund, remain unchanged.

The law establishing the present system passed the Legislature on the 26th of March, 1849, and provided that it should be voted on by the people of the State at the next annual election, and that the ballots used, should be of the following form:

SCHOOL.
" FOR THE NEW SCHOOL LAW."

SCHOOL.
"AGAINST THE NEW SCHOOL LAW."

The word school to be folded outside, and to serve only as a label.

It will be seen that the only financial changes made by the adoption of the new system, are these:

1st. A sum is now raised by the county equal to that apportioned to it by the State. No such sum was raised before.

2d. The amount of deficiency in the public money to pay teachers' wages, is now supplied by assessment upon the property of the district liable to taxation. Before, the amount was assessed upon the children in attendance.

In other words, a county tax is now raised, where none was raised before — and the rate bill or tax per pupil, which before existed, is abolished.

We have thus, at some trifling cost of labor, stated the main features of the two systems. Both can be understood almost at a glance, though there is one feature of the present system which we shall hereafter subject to the test of an elucidation in detail. We now propose, as the next step in the argument, to present some of the changes desired in the present law by the steadfast friends of free schools.

For these, we shall refer to some of the amendments presented or passed, in the Senate and Assembly, at the recent session of our Legislature. They will sufficiently indicate that which we believe to be true, namely, that the free school law, *in its present shape,* has few, if any friends; by which we mean, that there are few friends of free schools who do not desire to see the law amended.

For this purpose, we will, on the present occasion, cite but two legislative acts in proof: one in the Senate, and one in the Assembly. We will take the report of the committee on literature of the Senate, and the bill which passed the Assembly.

Look at the report of the committee on literature. It was signed by James W. Beekman, of New York, and Samuel Miller of Rochester. The report accompanying the bill is a clear and eloquent paper, and opens with this frank and emphatic declaration:

"It is evident, from the memorials submitted to the committee, that the present laws require, in some particulars, a careful revision to make them accomplish fully the ends of their enactment."

In reference to one feature of the old system, they say:

"Many parents kept their children home because they could not afford to pay, and because they were *not willing to confess the pauperism* which alone entitled them to free schooling."

Again, as to the future, they say:

"The revenues of the canals will soon allow a portion to be devoted to the support of schools. The rate bills for 1849 amounted to $489,696.63; and we have therefore to provide for raising a similar amount, which lessens every year until our school fund becomes large enough to support the schools out of its incomes, without a resort to taxation."

And near the close of the report, we have this terse and beautiful passage, which deserves to be printed in letters of gold:

"The benefits of free education are not now for the first time to be doubted. Nothing valuable comes without toil and cost. Our hopes of political freedom, of personal security, of unforced conscience, are held by the anchor of faith in the intelligence of the people. France has the opportunity of freedom, but not the people of which freemen are made; nor the *schools* which rear good citizens."

Now for the bill which accompanied the report, and which was submitted to the Senate. Of all its numerous and valuable amendments, we shall state but a portion. It abolished the office of town superintendent, and provided for assembly district superintendents, to be elective — half of the salary to be paid by the county, and half out of unappropriated school monies. But the amendments of this bill were these:

1 That each county should raise by county tax double the amount received from the State, instead of once the amount as now provided.

2 That schools be taught eight months in the year, in order to entitle the district to any public money, instead of four.

The effect of the first of these amendments would be to make the amount received by each district one quarter larger than it now is — and of course, by so much lessen the amount to be raised by the district. As the law now stands, the sum of $23,046.94 is annually distributed to the several districts of the county, which sum under the operation of this proposed amendment, would be increased to $30,715.92. There are 299 schoolhouses in this county. If divided equally among them, it would give a little over $100 to each, instead of a little over $75, as at present.

This bill did not pass the Senate, and for a sufficient reason. The history of this whole matter, for this year, leaves one fact standing out in bold relief: That the people of this State are now cursed with a Senate, a majority of whom, at heart, are opposed to free schools. If such were not the case, would not some form of amendment, as in the case of the Assembly, have passed the body? Is there a Senator professing to be friendly to free schools, who voted for this resubmission, and yet who will declare that the present law is the highest attainable point of perfection on this subject? Not a man of them all has the hardihood to take such an attitude before the public. For, if the law is perfect, why did you vote to resubmit? On what pretext do you vote to resubmit a law which you say is perfect? A law which just five months before was adopted by 158,000 majority — by a vote of almost three to one — when only about 15,000 petitioned for repeal or modification, and not a soul for its resubmission! It would, indeed, be a curious and interesting spectacle, to see a Senator of this State, who has the nerve to stand up before any audience, and take the position that the present law is as good a one as can be made.

But if driven — as driven he must be — from holding a position which thus on its face destroys itself, and, hotly pursued by those whose sacred cause he has betrayed, he seeks shelter under the assumption that the present law is imperfect, and ought to be amended — what then is his attitude? Does he not thus avow his willingness to cast the principle of free schools into the sea of popular opinion, and, instead of furnishing a life-buoy, to hang about it the weight of the unjust and hence unpopular details with which that just principle is now surrounded? Does he not also avow that he is friendly to free schools, but is willing to compel their friends — the friends of the principle on which free education rests — to go into battle for the defence of those schools and that principle, with their arms pinioned? "And Joab said to Amasa, Art thou in health my brother? And Joab took Amasa by the beard with his right hand to kiss him. Therefore Amasa took no heed to the sword that was in Joab's hand: so he smote him therewith in the fifth rib."

Such is the interesting dilemma in which Senators, who profess to be the friends of free education but voted to resubmit this law, have placed themselves.

Why did not such Senators *insist* that if the free school question were again to be submitted, it must be in some one of the forms proposed by its known and reliable friends. Why not *insist,* in any and every event, under any and all circumstances, upon such amendments? Then, if resubmitted, it would go to the people upon a true, and not as now, upon a false issue. Then, if amended by the Legislature, the people would quietly have tested the wisdom of the amendments in practice. Then, if not amended or resubmitted, the amendments proposed, would have been of record, and would have constituted rallying points in the further efforts of the friends of progress and reform.

We have spoken thus of the Senate separately, as an act of justice. It was there, in that select, small, and preeminently deliberative body, that this resubmission law — which in whatever aspect it can be viewed, is a cheat and a fraud — was introduced by Mr Mann, of Utica, and coolly passed some weeks before the close of the session.

We shall give but one more example in illustration of the position, that the real friends of free schools desire the amendment of the present law. It is the action of the Assembly. The following letter, from one of the most intelligent and reliable friends of free education in this State, places this question in its true light. There is other information in the letter, which is equally interesting and instructive, and may surprise some who have not had occasion to observe the machinery in legislation, by which the poor — the honest sons of toil — are so often defrauded of their rights. Here is the letter, which we give entire:

Secretary's Office,
Albany, April 17, 1850

DEAR SIR: Yours of the 15th reached me last evening. I avail myself of the earliest opportunity of complying with your request, so far as I am able to do so.

I send you enclosed, a copy of the act passed at midnight of the last day of the session, by a majority of one vote of the whole number elected, and which even had not the formality of reading except by its title.

I understand the whole number of petitioners for the repeal or modification of the free school law, was about 15,000: and I am not aware of a single petition for a resubmission of that law to the people.

The whole number of votes cast in November last in favor of the law was 249,872; against it, 91,951 — majority 157,921. Three counties only gave majorities against it — Chenango, Tompkins and Otsego — the aggregate of which amounted to about 1,200.

I have not been able to obtain a copy of the bill which passed the Assembly. Its purport was, to raise a state tax of $800,000 annually upon the real and personal property of the State, to be appropriated to the gratuitous education of the children of the State in common schools for a period not less than eight months during the year.

Mr. E. W. Curtis, of your county, is familiar with the practical details of the bill — having assiduously labored to secure its passage.

You may at all times freely command my service in behalf of free schools.

Yours truly
S. S. RANDALL

W. L. Crandal, Esq., Syracuse

This letter was in reply to enquiries addressed on Monday last to Mr Randall, upon the points noticed in his letter; and although not designed for publication, we regard it as containing precisely the sort of information the public wish for, and therefore give it. It completes the web in which one class of submission legislators are entangled.

What Change Is Demanded

The fact that the real, reliable *friends* of free education, desire a change in the present law, is now established by competent proof.

The only remaining point to settle, is the *principle* upon which the change should be made. To our minds, that is perfectly clear. The law, in its practical working, should, to the highest degree of perfection we can look for in human institutions, clearly illustrate the principle on which it is founded.

That principle is, that the property of a state, should educate the children of a state. This settled, it follows that the benefits of the system being equally enjoyed, its expenses should be equally shared.

Does the existing law violate this principle of equity, which is but another name for justice? In other words, if an attempt was actually made, in the formation of the present law, to carry out that principle, was the attempt successful? Is the law such, that it cannot be greatly improved, if, indeed, it cannot be made entirely satisfactory to every man in the State whose only objection, is, not to free schools, but to the inequality of the present law?

We propose, in a few words, to show

First — That the present law, in its practical operation is not equal.

Second — That the great feature of the amendments of the committee of the Senate, and of the bill which passed the Assembly, is, in each case, to destroy this inequality, and to illustrate our motto: Equality of Benefits — Equality of Burdens.

By recurring to our statement of the main features of the existing school law, it will be seen that each county receives a portion of the common school fund, in the ratio of its population as compared with the whole State, and that this money is apportioned to the several towns on precisely the same principle. That the board of supervisors then direct each town to raise, by town tax, an amount equal to that thus received. And that the same board raise by county tax an amount equal to the aggregate received by the county from the State, and this is apportioned to the towns upon the ratio already mentioned.

There is but one step more between the collection and the application of the money. That step is its *distribution to the districts*. And though the last step, it is very far from being the least. It is this which has caused

"This great commotion,
The country through"

which has frightened Senators from their propriety — which caused 15,000 persons, out of the 92,000 who voted against it on its passage, to petition for a repeal or modification of the law. This would not frighten such men as lived in the times that "tried men's souls," it is true; but the people now are compelled to take up with such material as they have, and they must not be surprised if occasionally they enlist a soldier, who, tho' he struts mightily when filling his cartridge-box and burnishing his musket, breaks the lines and abandons the field, at the first onset by the enemy.

To return. We have now traced the state, county and town money, combined, into the hands of the town superintendent of common schools, who is by law charged with the duty of its distribution to the districts — which is the last step before it reaches the hands of the teachers. Upon what basis or ratio does the superintendent make this distribution? Upon that of population? No. In proportion to the amount of taxable property in the district? No. In the proportion of the relative aggregate school attendance in each district, during the last year? No. In proportion to the number of months a school was taught the previous year? No. In proportion to the number of indigent children exempted from the payment of the rate bill? No. Not one of all these enters into the ratio upon which, by law, he is required to make the distribution. But he is required to distribute the money to all the districts in his town, in proportion — so says the law — to the number of children between the ages of five and sixteen residing in each district the previous year.

As we have no actual case before us, showing the practical operation of this plan of district distribution, we will suppose one which will not fail to illustrate the principle involved.

During the year ending 1st July 1849, the number of children taught in the common schools of this county, was 23,873. The amount of money received by the districts in that year from State, county and town was

SAMUEL S. RANDALL
Deputy Superintendent of Common Schools, editor of the "District School Journal" and later superintendent of schools of New York City. An active and indefatigable advocate of free schools.
(Picture from Barnard's Journal of Education)

$23,036.94, or nearly a dollar for every pupil taught in 1849. If Mr Beekman's Senate bill were to be adopted, the amount distributed would be $30,715.92, or about a dollar and a quarter per child.

Now we will suppose that in district no. 1 in the town of Fabius, there are 20 children between the ages of 5 and 16. In district no. 2, adjoining, there are 80, or 4 times as many. Does it not follow that district no. 2 annually draws — as the term is — four times as much of the money provided by the State, county and town, as district no. 1? In this supposed case, one district draws $20, the other $80.

No man of ordinary sense will deny that if the State undertake to educate its children, all those children are entitled to equal facilities for the acquirement of an education. Now, the children of no. 1 in Fabius, need and desire as good a school education as those of no. 2. The public good requires thorough and sound education in one district, precisely as much as in any other district. And if this principle be carried out, the cost of teachers in district no. 1 will be the same — or so nearly the same as to make the difference unworthy of mention — as in district no. 2, with four times the amount of money from the public.

It will therefore be seen, that if, under the present law, this equality of expense be incurred, in the supposed case — and it is a case which may exist substantially in every town of the State — $60 more must be annually raised by district no. 1, for the support of a school than by district no. 2.

Now let us suppose further, that the taxable property of the one district is equal to that of the other. That Mr A in one, and Mr B in the other are each assessed in the sum of $10,000, and that neither have children. Suppose that the taxable property of each district amounts to $50,000 — each of these men will pay one-fifth of the taxes of his district. Now, one-fifth of the $60 which No. 1 is compelled to raise over and above what is raised by no. 2, is $12 — and therefore Mr A pays annually $12 more for the support of schools than is paid by Mr B, who has the same amount of property; while the benefit in one case is precisely the same as in the other.

Is this a law which confers equal benefits, and imposes equal burdens? Is this a law which any Senator or Assemblyman dare say to the public, he wholly approves? Is this a law which anyone who voted for the resubmission, will have the courage to say could not have been improved by the Legislature? Is this a law which an honest friend of free schools would submit to a vote, the result of which involves the success of the great principle? These questions may all be answered by an emphatic — No! The thousands upon thousands of the honest, laborious, intelligent poor of this State, have asked for no such legislation as this — legislation which is a stalking compound of deception, fraud and cowardice.

We use this language and this argument, to vindicate the cause of truth — the cause of justice and humanity. The poor — "God help them!" — are not heard in our halls of legislation. "As a sheep before her shearers is dumb," so the voice of the poor is not heard there. But at the ballot-box they can be heard. Its potential voice — if we do not misjudge — will, in November next, sound in the ears of their betrayers like the "rushing of mighty waters." That terrible ballot,

"Falls as snow-flakes on the sod —
But executes a freeman's will
As lightning does the will of God."

The fabled thunder of Jove was a whisper compared with the American ballot; and that son of toil in New York, who is so regardless of his relations and obligations to God and man, as to stifle its utterance in behalf of free education to the children of the people, at the coming election, deserves to have his memory perish forever from the minds even of those who owe to him their being.

If any incarnate fiend in human form, attempts to oppress — to dictate the vote of a poor man on this question — let him be met as the tigress meets the assailant of her offspring. Tell him that by choice, by nature and by law, you are the protector of the rights and interests of the young immortals placed under your charge; that for their safekeeping, you have a responsibility infinitely higher than any which man can impose; that sooner shall your "right hand forget her cunning," than drop a ballot not duly indorsed — "AGAINST THE REPEAL of the New School Law."

Equality

From the facts shown, it appears to us that there can exist but one objection to the present law, on the part of those in favor of the principle of free schools, viz: That the burdens it imposes are not equally distributed.

Now let us see whether the friends of free schools are worthy of trust, in their profession of a desire to remove this inequality of burdens. If they are, then it is perfectly safe to vote "Against the Repeal of the New School Law."

"Actions speak louder than words." Look first at the Senate bill, by Messrs Beeman and Miller, from the committee on literature. They are men who have no superiors in the Senate, for intelligence, high character and philanthropy. Their bill proposed to double the county tax. This would give to each district one-quarter more money than it now receives. Each district would then have to raise one-quarter less money than it now does, to maintain a suitable school. The bill provided for eight months school in each district — precisely the average in the county of Onondaga, in 1849. The amount proposed by this bill to be raised by general tax may not be enough. But it is the principle of this amendment at which we are to look. The extent of its application, could be determined satisfactorily by experience.

Now look at the Assembly bill — not a mere proposition of a committee, but a bill which passed by what may be termed an overwhelming vote, as will be seen by the following letter:

Albany, April 18, 1850

DEAR SIR: The vote in the Assembly on the final passage of the bill introduced by Mr Burroughs, was 69 to 30.

Yours truly
S. S. RANDALL

W. L. Crandal, Esq., Clerk Board of Education, Syracuse"

That bill — so triumphantly passed — was sent to the Senate several days prior to the adjournment of the Legislature. And what were its provisions? Were they calculated to relieve the districts, to promote equality in burdens and benefits? It provided for raising annually $800,000 by a state tax — $200,000 to be divided equally among the 11,191 school districts of the State. The amount of money paid by them all, in 1849, on rate bills, was only

$489,696.63. And the amount received by the districts, applicable to teachers' wages, was $653,704.53.

Thus it is, that ALL the propositions emanating from the reliable friends of free education, point in the same direction: to the relief of districts — to equality — to justice — to having the cost and the benefit go hand in hand.

Are we not, then, justified by the undeniable and established facts of the case, in appealing to every man, who believes the children of the poor ought to be educated; that the official earmark upon the poor by trustees is a disgrace to the age; that a pauper aristocracy in our schools as provided by the old system is hostile to the genius of our institutions; who believe that the children of the poor are not more highly blest by a system of free education than are the children of the rich; who believe that by the operation of such a system, the lesson of respect for others learned by the children of the rich, is no less valuable than the sense of self-respect the children of the poor are allowed to imbibe. We say, are we not justified in frankly and candidly asking all such men, of whatever age or occupation or circumstances in life, if the friends of free schools have not just as much encouragement, just as much hope, *in the future,* in voting for the present law at the coming election, as they would have, if this Legislature had been as honest as all future Legislatures will doubtless find it for their interest to be, and had made the proper amendments before a resubmission, as they will be made after the great principle has been again triumphantly sustained by the people?

Rights of Children

The children of a state own so much of the property of a state as is necessary to educate them for a prompt and enlightened discharge of the duties required of them as citizens — the degree of that education clearly depending upon the state of society. To the use of so much property, for that object, they have an imprescriptible, indefeasible right. Those who hold the property of a state, do so, to this extent, as stewards of the Almighty, for these children. When this office is faithfully, zealously and cheerfully executed by men of wealth, it becomes a truly noble one. Men who thus hold wealth are an ornament, a blessing to their race — the almoners of God's bounty. Thus exercised, the talent to accumulate wealth takes rank among the most valuable and honorable with which man is endowed. Men who have wealth will make their own election as to the manner in which they will discharge the sacred trust with which they are invested — sacred, so far as fitting the generation succeeding them for their high duties, is concerned. It is proper — as free moral agents — that they should do so, because by one course their own happiness will be increased, and by the other diminished. But we demand — and the people of this county and State will demand — that the children shall have their own. We protest, and they will protest, against the monstrous injustice, the stupendous wrong, of a denial. The right of society to so much of the property of a state as is needful to imprison or hang the thief, the seducer, or the murderer, is unquestioned. It is raised by a general tax, and nobody questions. But where shall we find a mind so deformed as to maintain that the rich alone are interested in the vindication of injured innocence or purity, which is thus secured at the expense of property — by a general tax upon property? If not, why are the expenses incurred in the punishment of these crimes, and in the means used to prevent depredations upon *all,* by a similar assessment upon the property of all, answer this question at their leisure.

Again: Who denies the *right* of every child in the state, not otherwise provided for, to so much of the property of a state, as is necessary to feed, clothe and shelter him? And yet — " Tell it not in Gath, publish it not in the streets of Askelon "— there are actually to be found men who deny the right of every child to have his mind, by the same instrumentality, invested with the beautiful habiliments of knowledge — to have the curtains withdrawn from his darkened soul — unless it shall have been " certified " by a board of trustees, and duly recorded, that his father or his mother, as the case may be, is a pauper! Amazing infatuation!— that invests the mind of man with less dignity, value and consideration, than the crumbling clay curiously fashioned for its temporary dwelling.

Generation succeeds generation, each fed, clothed and sheltered from the productions of the earth, and following each other in the order of accession, each takes up an abode within its bosom. The common mother of us all furnishes to the teeming multitudes of each generation temples for the indwelling of their spiritual nature, and which it receives back again when that nature has no further use for them. By what authority can a portion only of those at any one time upon the face of the earth, claim exclusive title to the benefits accruing from the common bounties of Providence? Let those who claim this monopoly prove title by exhibiting a charter from Him who has been their owner from the period before time was. Whose are the earth, the water, the air, the sun which vivifies all? Are the inappreciable benefits resulting from these munificent endowments to be monopolized by any portion of the existing race, or are they, in fitting harmony with the spirit of the Parent of us all, to be employed, so far as is necessary, in fitting the generation soon to assume all the active responsibilities of life, for an intelligent fulfilment of all their relations to man and to their Creator?

Who Produces Wealth?

It is the laborer. It is the laborer who produces the wealth of a state. The wealth of a state, consists of whatever can be appropriated to relieve the necessities, or to contribute to the happiness of mankind, and in the means of securing the production of those things which contribute to these ends. Who hewed down your forests? Who built your roads and bridges? Who built the dwellings of the country — its hovels and its palaces — its store-houses and public edifices? Who constructed the Erie canal? Who built your railroads? Who built the vessels which bring to your shores the products of very clime in exchange for those of your own? Who produced our daily food? Who produced the raiment with which we are clothed — from the brogan to the gossamery lace about a fashionable lady's neck? Who produced the gold and silver in your pockets, and in the vaults of your banks? To all this there is but one answer — the *laborer.* All these things are produced by the " sweat of the brow," and in no other way. These, are the taxable wealth of a state.

Who Pays the Taxes?

The *laborer.* No man has produced any more wealth than has been the result of the application of his physical powers, or of his mental powers in such a way as to "make two blades of grass grow where one grew before." We shall not here go into a general argument as to who are producers and who are not; we shall be perfectly understood without this; and shall therefore only add, that all men are producers, who labor either with the hands or head, for that which tends to the comfort, the happiness or the improvement of society. The mechanic whose ingenuity produces a machine which will do the work of a thousand men, is a laborer, and a producer of wealth, in a greatly multiplied sense of the term.

The Corollary

Labor, therefore, is entitled to the education of all its children, upon the same platform with the children of those whose peculiar sagacity, in a peculiar channel of thought and action, enables them to accumulate an extraordinary share of the profits of labor. No one will dispute our conclusion, who does not question our premises.

Labor, then, is the great source of the wealth all about us, which is represented in dollars and cents on the tax lists. If we find who do the labor of a state, we at the same time find who produce the wealth of a state. Look about you, and see who do it. Now, have the men whose names stand opposite the highest figures upon the tax lists, performed the labor — that labor which alone produces wealth — necessary for the production of the wealth thus represented? If not, do they, in fact, pay the so much talked of tax which goes to educate the children of the laborer? The men who, in obedience to laws, which no one questions, own this wealth, have accumulated it, not produced it: they have, by skill in business, forecast, judgment, accumulated more property than they could possibly have produced; and their title to it, when honestly acquired, none but the base call in question. But the title to so much of that property as is necessary to fit, by a proper education, the children of those who earned it by their toil, for the various responsibilities of society, never became vested in those who hold it. So much property is held by all, for the benefit of all. Its title is imprescriptibly vested in those children; it is registered in heaven; and no ingenuity of craft, no subtlety of avarice, no stretch of audacity, can subvert it. We take this property — the child is educated with it — and to the modern Shylock who questions our procedure, we quietly reply — "This bond doth give thee here no jot of blood."

The Cruelties of a Free School System

But alas! an appeal is made to our humanity — and this appeal we recognize and obey. We are told that the man worth $10,000, $15,000, $25,000, $50,000, or even $100,000, and who has no children, is assessed on his property to aid in defraying the school expenses of those who have! Was such oppression and inhumanity ever before heard of in the long history of mankind? — always "saving and excepting" the bloody code of Draco? When that great poet of nature — that man of mighty heart — the immortal Burns — told the world, that

> "Man's inhumanity to man
> Makes countless thousands mourn"

little did he dream that it was in reserve for some future bard to render tame and spiritless this outpouring of universal sympathy by singing the "inhumanities" of a free school system! Could the heroes of Independence Hall, of the 4th of July, 1776, be made aware of such a system of oppression as this, might we not expect that their bones would turn in their graves? And could they be again endowed with an earthly form and consciousness, that they would blush and hang their heads for very shame, to think that, when compared with the oppressions of our time, they had made so much ado over the aggressions of the British government? Think of it — just stepping upon the threshold of the last half of the nineteenth century — a man who has wealth in his possession, and no children, is called upon by the laws to contribute his mite toward the school education of the children of those whose toil earned that very wealth!

Poor, childless, soulless, rich man! — if such an one there be in this county. Your soul shut out forever from those perennial joys that spring from the artless, innocent, confiding love of children: You would deprive yourself of the privilege and luxury of doing good when it lies in your power to do it: You would deprive yourself, while living, of the heart's incense of thousands, and of their daily and hourly blessings on your memory after you have gone to your final account. When you are determined to do all this to yourself, what shall we, what can we, say? Shall we say of you, that you have sundered every sympathy of a soul tuned by its Giver in such glorious harmony? — that you are a stranger to all the qualities which distinguish humanity, save that one which with the relentless energy of despair, binds you, hugs you, to the only god of your devotion — the almighty dollar?

But if there are such beings in our county — which we will not believe till we have proof of the fact — walking erect, and in features bearing a resemblance to the "human face divine," we most sincerely commiserate their condition. What! cut off from the sympathies of their fellow men sympathies in as perfect harmony as the "music of the spheres!" We have not prostituted the language, by calling them men — for "God said, Let us make man in our image, after our likeness." A man is not merely a thing with two legs, walking erect, with the power and disposition to make money. Such is not a true portrait it is a wretched caricature. A man is a being endowed with sympathies as wide as the race to which he belongs; with an intellect which can appreciate and admire the immensity and beneficence of the Creator's works; a being who can comprehend, and attempt to fulfil, the obligations which his own exalted attitude in the scale of being, and his destiny, so clearly impose: loving and being loved, doing and receiving good, he goes on his way rejoicing in the numberless blessings with which his path is strewed. Such is an outline of a man. But if such specimens could be found in our community as were first referred to — which we emphatically deny — what a pity it is, that — glued all over with hard dollars, forming a shield as impenetrable as the hide of a rhinoceros — they could not colonize to some dear, delightful spot of earth, beyond the clamor of the irrepressible sympathies of our nature! Or, like Tantalus, condemned to live in the midst of these sources of the most exquisite enjoyment, but, isolated by this shield, forever debarred the privilege of tasting them.

Was the old System Well Enough?

We are told — though rarely — that "things were well enough under the old system." Not so. It was not "well enough" that the children of the poor, to the estimated number of 60,000 in the State, were kept from school by their inability to pay. It was not "well enough" that at school, a portion of the children on a bench should sit as paupers, and the balance as "paying subscribers." It is declared in Holy Writ that "The race is not to the swift, nor the battle to the strong, nor yet riches to men of understanding; for time and chance happeneth to all." The experience of all ages corroborates these truths. This united testimony proves that the possession of wealth is not even prima facie evidence that the man possesses brains; nor is the want of it, similar proof that he is destitute of them. "Time and chance happeneth to all," says the wise and inspired writer. It may happen — it is not at all unlikely to happen — that in the very next generation, this business of trustee "certifying" may change hands. People who now, "in the lust of the eye and the pride of life," say in their hearts that it is "well enough" to have the parents of these children annually certified as paupers, would do well to remember that "Pride goeth before destruction, and a haughty spirit before a fall;" and that nothing is more likely to occur, than that the children of those who they now so complacently "certify" and record as paupers, will perform the same grateful office for their own offspring in the second generation.

It was not "well enough" that the amount of exemption in the county of Onondaga should have been $325.61, in 1849 — a few pennies over one dollar for each schoolhouse in the county! Will any man who can read and write and cypher, say that this was "well enough?" Six hundred and twenty-four children exempted that year, and $325.61 paid for their tuition — or about 52 cents apiece paid for the annual tuition of each of the exempted pupils of this county. We ask the wealthy and intelligent and large-minded men of the county of Onondaga, in all sincerity and earnestness, if that was "well enough"? — if they can afford to have such a state of things surround the families they are rearing? For who can doubt that under such a state of things, many hundreds were kept from attendance at all, by the fact of their inability to pay? The two facts here brought to light — the number of children exempted, and the paltry and wholly insufficient amount paid for their tuition — are enough to consign the old system to redemptionless perdition in the minds of all intelligent, thinking men. The age in which we live is emphatically an age of progress; and the ideas which were "well enough" for 25 years ago, are not necessarily well enough for the present, or for the future. The ideas to prevail in the last half of the nineteenth century, are entirely distinct and in advance of the ideas which prevailed in the first half. The philosophy which will surely prevail in the former, will be, that the thorough education of the children of those without property, is as important to them individually, and to society, as the education of the children of those who have property. And also, that the earmark of indigence does not necessarily indicate a brainless man or woman — or a man or woman destitute of the highest mental and moral elevation, cultivation and refinement. A change of philosophy requires a corresponding change of practice; and as the last day, when wealth will be regarded — even prima facie — as a badge of honor, and correlatively, poverty as one of disgrace and occasion for contumely, will soon be numbered among "the things that were," — and as the day is fast approaching when intellectual and moral worth will maintain their rightful supremacy among men, so the dawning of that change in society demands a corresponding change in legislation — as laws, in this country, except when the people are temporarily betrayed, are a mere transcript of the social organization.

Fifty-two cents per annum, paid in Onondaga county for the tuition of each of its exempted pupils! The simple fact, stamps enduring disgrace upon the old system.

Again: It is not "well enough" that the children of those who are more largely endowed with a share of this world's goods should have their tender and impressible minds imbued with the odious distinctions which the old system created. Sound philosophy and an enlightened humanity declare this is not "well enough." Horrible as are the results of a system of slavery upon the enslaved, it can hardly with truth be said that it debases them in a more appalling ratio than it does the enslavers. Perforce, it shuts out the light of knowledge and of heaven's truth from the minds of the enslaved; but the practical tendency of the system is to secure the active exercise and development — and the consequent supremacy — of the worst passions and the meanest sentiments of the enslavers. So upon the benches of our common schools, under the old system. In the minds of the children of the rich and of the poor, that system nourishes and stimulates to a premature and fatal growth, the worst and the meanest sentiments of our nature — contempt and envy — hate and disrespect. That child is as effectually degraded who is educated not to look upon the intrinsic qualities of any human being as the true test of respect and regard, as he whose education and circumstances lead to a loss of his own self-respect. For it is not too much to say — it is a principle too plain and self-evident to be controverted — that he who is so trained as not to make inherent qualities and virtues and acquirements the test of dignity and character in others, will not make them such in his own case: And therefore, the result to those among the rich or wealthy who insist that "certified" indigence shall be the test of a school education free of expense, is inevitably to impress upon the minds of their own children a standard for the estimation of character, which can not fail deplorably to degrade them in the scale of moral excellence. No boon of higher value can be extended to the children of the rich than to provide that they sit day by day and year by year upon the same benches with those of the humble poor, upon terms of the most absolute equality of rights and privileges. It is educating them for the highest happiness; for, turn the subject which way we will, whether the fact be acknowledged or denied, the truth remains as irreversible as any other law of nature, that no man knows aught of real happiness, who is a stranger to the sympathies of his fellow men. Riches, not so used as to secure that sympathy, never yet conferred happiness upon a human being. And those sympathies must be of an elevated, not of a degrading cast. If man — made in the image of his God — become so degraded, so fallen from the integrity of his nature, that his only pleasure is derived from hugging gold to his bosom, and yielding it the oblation of his morning and evening orisons, he makes no nearer approach to a realization of the true dignity and happiness of a human being, than does the fallen spirit, who, for a fancied independence of another sort, took up an abode in the regions of darkness and despair, in exchange for the society of angels. The laws written by the Creator upon the constitution of man, declare in plain, intelligible langage, that his highest happiness shall forever, in all states of his being consist in the supremacy of his moral sentiments. The pride, the arrogance, the selfishness of the human mind, are ever, under the most favorable circumstances, sufficiently active to require that they be held in constant check; and if so kept in childhood, they will never fail to attain an adequate development in maturity. This is the concurrent testimony of all good and truly great men in all ages of the world; it is the reiterated lesson of revelation. If, then, by a system of free schools, we can nourish and develop *equality of feeling* — naturally resulting from this equality of position — and that feeling can be thus daily inwrought with the very web and woof of their minds and characters, a blessing is conferred upon the children of the wealthy, which, in any other form, it is utterly beyond the power of money to bestow. Like the dews of heaven, and as silently and insensibly, free schools dispense their blessings with the same beneficence and the same munificence, alike upon the children of the rich and of the poor.

Upon even a brief examination, therefore, of the principles and tendencies of the old system, we are constrained to declare, that it is not " well enough " for the present age.

The Dollar Argument

Under this head, we shall content ourselves with stating the proposition, that, as a mere question of dollars and cents, the Empire State, at the end of ten years, would be the richer for the adoption of a thorough, liberal and enlightened system of free education. " There is that withholdeth more than is meet, but it tendeth to poverty."

Value of Education

It is not in the power of any pen or of any tongue, to portray the contrast between an educated and an uneducated mind. Mental activity is a law of human happiness. By mental activity, we mean a due exercise of all the faculties. This can never be attained, while the intellect is uninstructed in the wonderful facts and laws of nature. When this work has been properly commenced in childhood and youth, the field of mental activity — delightful, unceasing activity — is limitless. To the uneducated mind, all this is comparatively a blank. Nature, to such a one, is almost an unwritten page — is not vocal with praise of the wisdom, order and beauty of the Creator's works — in a word, is a drear, tenantless waste. But ask the man or woman of mature years — however meagre may be the resources of wealth at command — whose mind is well stored, if he or she would exchange the results of school discipline of mind and instruction, for any farm or any township in Onondaga, and the answer, in all cases except where there is moral debasement, would be a decided negative. If, then, the value of an education can not be estimated by one who possesses it, would it not, if possessed, be as great a prize to another who has not been able to obtain it? By education, we mean the exercise, discipline and development of all the faculties: securing to the individual, at maturity, the power of successful self-education. If the worth of this can not be computed in dollars and cents, in houses and lands, by its truly fortunate possessors, what folly and injustice for society to withhold the mere rust of wealth, requisite to confer the boon upon all who desire it.

In Conclusion

"*Agitate! Agitate! Agitate!*"— should be the motto of every friend of free schools. We are told by the highest authority, that our Senators did not think it wise to submit the law properly amended, for a vote, for fear the people would not understand the amendments! Scatter facts and correct principles broadcast, and prove to the world that this imputation is a slander: that the people are capable not only of comprehending truth, but can detect it even through the mazes of falsehood with which in this case it has been enveloped by those Senators. Let it be made apparent as the noonday sun, that the only way to manifest a friendship for *free schools,* at the ballot box, is to vote "Against the Repeal of the New School Law." Sustain the law by a triumphant vote, and it will be amended to the satisfaction of all who hold to the great and glorious principle, that the property of a state should educate the children of a state. On this point there is no room for doubt. The enemies of free schools will be as deeply interested as their friends, in making the law what it should be. The enemies of free education have triumphed, in securing the submission, at this election, of a law in a form not desired by the friends of that cause. Let it be their last triumph. Sustain the law — save the *principle* — and we thereby press them into the work of putting the law into the best possible shape. Their interest will then urge them in that direction.

The reputation, honor, influence, future glory, and permanent prosperity and progress of New York, are involved in the decision of this question. Let young men, whose interests and hopes are identified with this noble State, vindicate her fame and character at this crisis. This cause will triumph. Truth is more mighty than error. Humanity, even in this age of silver and gold, is more mighty than blind selfishness. Let the victory be resplendent. Let it be, for all future time, the proudest record to be found in the archives of the Empire State. But above all, let Onondaga win the banner in this contest. We have men of wealth who will take the lead in the cause of free education. They are noble men, and merit large reward for their good and powerful influence. Public sentiment on education has been gradually advancing and ripening in this county, for several years. It is comparatively sound. There is no county in the State in advance of her in the cause of universal education. Let not any considerable number of votes against free schools at this election, place upon so fair a page an ineffaceable blot, and cast a mildew upon the moral influence she now possesses. In the name of a just, honorable, manly pride, we appeal to our people to avert such a result. Let our county — so privileged in position and native resources — be second to none in a work to which all in a few years will point with exultation.

We again say: *Agitate! Organize!* These are the mottoes of truth; silence and stealth the countersigns of error. Let the watchfires of *free education to all the people,* be lighted upon every hill-top and in every valley; let the shouts of its friends echo and reecho from every hamlet; let it be declared by all the people of Onondaga, that the immortal mind of man is of more value than the few shillings requisite to secure its illumination. And let the cheering watchwords at the election, be —" *a vote against the repeal of the new school law,*" and "A contest which never ends, but in glorious triumph!"

To all we say, let not the plaintive wail go up to heaven from thousands upon thousands of children in this State, in November next, that the great State of New York shuts the doors of her schoolhouses in the faces of the poor, and the light of knowledge from their souls. Let not the trying alternative be placed before the poor, intelligent, refined and high-souled mothers of this State, to be certified as paupers, or have their children deprived of the inestimable blessing of a school education. Let this cup of bitter agony pass from them. How will they breathe "freer and deeper," when, at the close of that election, the shout goes up from the glad voices of their children, "*Our school is free!*"

Mr. E. C. Pomeroy submitted and read the following resolutions:

1 *Resolved,* That this institute is in favor of free schools.

2 *Resolved,* That the property of a state, should educate the children of a state.

3 *Resolved,* That as the system of free education we advocate, confers equal benefits, its burdens also should be equal.

4 *Resolved,* That we are in favor of such amendments of the present law, as shall eradicate the inequalities of the system.

5 *Resolved,* That a vote of the people at the coming election in favor of a repeal of the new school law, would be construed by the opponents of free education, as a verdict against the principle of free schools.

6 *Resolved,* That it is duty of the friends of free education, to vote "*Against the repeal of the new school law.*"

7 *Resolved,* That we heartily approve the call for a *convention of the town superintendents* of this county, to meet at the city hall, in Syracuse, on Tuesday, the 4th day of June next; and we earnestly invite the friends of free education to be present with them on that occasion.

8 *Resolved,* That we cordially respond to the call for a *state convention of the friends of free schools,* to be held in Syracuse on Wednesday, the 12th of June next.

9 *Resolved,* That we recommend a county and state organization in behalf of the cause of free education, which shall include every school district.

10 *Resolved,* That the following gentlemen, residents of Syracuse, are respectfully invited to meet pursuant to call, and act for the time being upon matters relating to state and county organization, to wit:

Alfred H. Hovey	James Noxon
Dudley P. Phelps	Amos Westcott
P. H. Agan	John McCarthy
Daniel McDougall	Charles Andrews
R. H. Gardner	C. B. Scott
Chas. P. Williston	S. F. Smith
J. W. Barker	E. T. Hayden
George Goodrich	C. A. Wheaton
Chas. B. Sedgwick	John W. Jones
George Kellogg	Lewis J. Gillet
J. M. Winchell	Daniel Gott, Jr.
P. Montgomery	James Johonnot

11 *Resolved,* That we look with confidence for a continued support of the cause of free schools by the press of this State in the present important crisis.

12 *Resolved,* That the newspapers of this county are requested to publish the address of the institute, and the accompanying resolutions.

After remarks by several members of the institute, the address and resolutions, were unaimously adopted.

Convention of Town Superintendents of Onondaga — Free Schools

At a convention of the town superintendents of common schools of the county of Onondaga, held at the city hall, Syracuse, on Wednesday, April 17, 1850, pursuant to notice — W. L. Crandall, as superintendent of the county, took the chair, as required by the regulations of the secretary of state, and Samuel D. Luce, of Manlius, was chosen secretary.

On motion of Mr Noyes, of Otisco, the following resolution was unanimously adopted:

Resolved, That the several town superintendents of common schools of the county of Onondaga, are requested to meet at the city hall in Syracuse, on *Tuesday, the 4th day of June next,* to take into consideration the action required by the resubmission of the free school law to a vote of the people.

The following resolutions were offered:

Resolved, That this convention is in favor of free schools.

Resolved, That whatever may be the defects, in detail, of the present free school law, we shall vote to retain it, as the only means of manifesting our friendship for the glorious principles, that the property of a state should educate the children of a state — trusting to the future for all desired amendments.

Resolved, That we recommend that a *state convention of the friends of free schools* be held at the city hall, in the city of Syracuse, on Wednesday, the 12th day of June next, at 10 o'clock a. m., with a view to organized effort in sustaining the honor and permanent welfare of New York, which are involved in the decision of this question.

Resolved, That the papers of this county, the Albany Argus, Evening Journal, Atlas and State Register, be requested to copy these proceedings, and that the other newspapers of the State, friendly to free schools, are invited to copy them, or at least the resolution recommending a state convention.

These resolutions called out considerable conversation, in which Messrs Wells of Pompey, Luce of Manlius, Frisbie of Clay, Noyes of Otisco, and several others participated. The resolutions were unanimously adopted.

Whereupon, the convention adjourned to Tuesday, *the 4th day of June next, at the city hall,* at 10 o'clock a. m.

W. L. Crandall, *Chairman*
Samuel D. Luce, *Secretary*

— *Syracuse Post Standard, April 19, 1850*

The Free School Clarion and " Free School Pepper Corns "

William L. Crandall of Syracuse was an ardent worker for the cause of free schools and in July 1850 announcement was made that a weekly paper called " The Free School Clarion " would be issued for the express purpose of creating sentiment to oppose the repeal of the free school act at the election of 1850. The following documents give the material available in relation to the Free School Clarion and also include the articles called "Free School Pepper Corns" which were undoubtedly written by Mr Crandall.

While no biography of Mr Crandall has been found, there are occasional references to him in newspapers and other documents which give us meagre data in reference to him. He was undoubtedly one of the strongest and most able supporters of the principle that the schools of the State should be free to all the children of the State. In a letter from Deputy State Superintendent S. S. Randall of 1850, he addresses Mr. Crandall as "Clerk, Board of Education, Syracuse." He was chairman of a convention of town superintendents of Onondaga county in April 1850 and the Syracuse Daily Standard refers to him as "superintendent of the county town." In the many conventions and local meeting held during the years 1846-51 by the friends of free schools, Mr. Crandall took a prominent part. Between the holding of the state free school convention of July 1850 and the election of that year, when the people voted on the resubmission bill, Kinny and Masters, publishers of the Syracuse Daily Star, authorized Mr Crandall to issue a publication called "The Free School Clarion" to stimulate interest in the free school movement. In the comments on this publication in the Binghamton Democrat, Mr. Crandall is referred to as "an able editor." He was editor at various times of the Syracuse Journal, the Onondaga Standard and the Onondaga Democrat.

Free School Pepper-Corns[1]

No. IV

We are told by those who say the old system was "well enough" that that system provided for the school education of those not able to pay tuition — and therefore, that it fulfilled all the obligations of society on this head.

In 1849, there were 778,000 children taught in the common schools of this State.

And 16,900 were exempted from paying rate bills! — and for them 62 cents apiece was paid that year by the "property of the State" for tuition!

What a humbug to pretend that the old system provided suitable school education for those not able to pay!

Does any man, with either a grain of practical knowledge or of common sense, believe that out of the 850,000 children of school age in this State, only 16,900 are unable to pay for their tuition?

By *unable* to pay for their tuition, I mean upon whom the payment of it is *unreasonably onerous*. The man — a day laborer, a carpenter, mason, blacksmith, shoemaker, tailor, printer — of whatever occupation he may be — who

---
[1] These articles were undoubtedly written by Mr W. L. Crandall.

has a half dozen children of school age, all of whom he must shelter, feed, clothe, pay their bills in sickness, and pay his own expenses out of the earnings of his daily toil, has a *right* to the aid of his next neighbor worth $5000 or $10,000 who has not a child to shelter or sustain in sickness or in health — or even if he has an equal number, but has this superabundance of property compared with the other. Upon the former school tuition is an unreasonable tax.

Think of 62 cents a year, for the exempted poor, by the great State of New York! "Oh, shame! where is thy blush?" upon the cheek of the man who can pretend that the old system was "well enough" for a day like the present, when the maxim is, that a "man's a man" and that money is *not* manhood.

Peter Ploughshare
— *Syracuse Daily Star, May 10, 1850*

No. V

Is it more important to the individual, or to society, that the child of a rich man should be educated, than it is that the child of a poor man should be educated?

Peter Ploughshare
— *Syracuse Daily Star, May 11, 1850*

No. VI

No man will *openly* maintain that a good education is *more important* to the child of a rich man, than to the child of a poor man.

It being, then, *universally* conceded, that it is of the utmost importance to society that *all* should be well educated, who is prepared to deny that *all* should be educated upon the *same platform?*

By this I mean, that public provision should be made for the thorough education of *all*. If any choose to employ private teachers, that is all well enough. They are entitled to do so. But it is not only infamous and blackhearted to require that a child be officially registered as a pauper, before he can have free schooling, but it is in the teeth of the best interests of society. It is calculated to degrade those thus certified; to lessen their self-respect; to lower the tone of their ambition; to diminish their enterprise; to crush their hopes; to excite the spirit of envy and hate.

These are among the legitimate fruits of the plan of *certified juvenile pauperism* provided for under the old school system.

It is behind the age.

You can not find a man, permitted to walk in respectable circles, who is so selfish and degraded, as to deny that those *absolutely unable* to pay, should be exempted. How can this be done, under the old system, except by the brand of pauperism? A hard-working man, with half a dozen children, feeds, clothes, shelters them, pays their doctors bills, and by the most unremitting toil, and the most rigid economy and frugality — by providing the rudest raiment and the coarsest fare, such as the rich would disdain — he is able to *keep the family under one roof,* and meet his payments — yet he, a man who is a man in the noblest sense of the term, an honest man, who does something for the benefit of his race, is to be publicly recorded as a *pauper,* or shoulder the additional burthen of paying for the tuition of all those children! And a fusty bachelor, with a soul just large enough to comprehend the dimensions of his pile of dollars, or a miserable miser gloating over his thousands, will talk to you of the *injustice* of their paying for the tuition of those children!

PETER PLOUGHSHARE
— *Syracuse Daily Star, May 13, 1850*

No. VII

It is objected, that education does not improve the *moral character* of a people; that there are more educated than uneducated rascals; that the criminal list swells with the diffusion of education.

I have listened to this objection to free schools, from the lips of a lawyer and politician, within the three weeks past.

I never heard it, however, from the lips of a man who was not educated. This is a very significant fact.

For the sake of the argument, we will grant the premises of this class of objectors! The answer is this: It is conceded that education gives a man more power, in whatever direction he exercises his talents. Now, if the effect of education is to develop rascality, we respectfully insist that no privileged class shall enjoy a monopoly of this article; that all shall have a fair start. We insist upon equality. We object to one child being fitted to cheat, while the balance must tamely submit to be cheated.

If education is calculated to make men scoundrels, there is no good reason why only a small number should be educated. If this assumption be true, education makes of one portion of society, beasts of prey, and the remainder victims. We propose that all be thoroughly educated. Then Turk will meet Turk — Greek meet Greek. An equipoise will be established. It will be "diamond cut diamond," and therefore no cutting can be done. The several individuals of society will be like two positive or two negative magnetic poles; being kindred and equal to each other, they mutually repel and leave matters in *statu quo*. So here. If all have equal acquirements, so far all will have equal power: one can not harm the other: and we would thus, on the assumption of my objector, by the thorough education of all, at least establish negatively a system of practical morality.

PETER PLOUGHSHARE
— *Syracuse Daily Star, May 14, 1850*

No. VIII

The people of this State are to decide by their votes in November next, whether or not New York shall have free schools.

Upon this question, every citizen of the State has a vote.

The act submitting the present free school law to a vote of the people the coming November, is a piece of the most cold-blooded, heartless villainy, ever perpetrated by the Legislature of this State.

This is strong language, if true; if untrue, it is very weak. In the course of one or two dozen numbers, I shall give facts which will enable every one to judge for himself.

PETER PLOUGHSHARE
— *Syracuse Daily Star, May 15, 1850*

No. IX

In 1846, when it had been determined that a new constitution should be framed for New York, an effort was made to incorporate in it a free school provision.

A state convention of county superintendents was held in Albany, in May, 1846, which was attended by Horace Mann, Gov. Eaton, of Vermont, and other able and distinguished men — all of whom advocated free schools. S. S. Randall, the able and zealous deputy state superintendent, presided over the convention. The convention resolved in favor of free schools, and resolved to memorialize the constitutional convention.

The constitutional convention did adopt an article providing for free schools; but, just prior to the adjournment, struck it out.

PETER PLOUGHSHARE
—*Syracuse Daily Star, May 16, 1850*

No. X

The hopes of the friends of free education in this State, were dashed in an instant, by this one rash and extraordinary act of the constitutional convention. It astonished everybody, and has never been explained.

During the winter of 1849, a vigorous movement in behalf of free schools, was made in the Legislature. It resulted in the passage of the present school law of the State. The act provided that it should be passed upon by the people at the election in November, and that if more ballots were cast for than against it, it should become a law.

The vote stood 249,872 for the new school law; 91,951 against it; making the majority for the new law, 157,921.

Such is, in brief, the history of free school legislation in this State, up to the 1st January, 1850, when the present Legislature assembled at Albany.

PETER PLOUGHSHARE
—*Syracuse Daily Star, May 17, 1850*

No. XI

We have now brought the free school legislation of the State up to the time of the meeting of the present Legislature in January last.

That body assembled just two months after the people had ratified the present law by 158,000 majority.

What are we to understand by that expression of the popular will? What were the members of the Legislature to understand by it? — and what should have been the action of honest men upon that understanding?

It is this: The 249,872 who voted " For the New School Law " are to be set down as so many men unqualifiedly in favor of the principle, that " the property of a state should educate the children of such state." Had they been opposed to this principle, they would not have voted for the law. Exceptions are possible; but they can be proven only by establishing the stupidity of the voter who constitutes the exception.

As to the 91,951 who voted last November *against* the law, it can not be assumed safely that they were *all* opposed to this principle. Their hostility, in some cases, may have sprung from objections to the details of the present law.

Take any view which reason can sanction, and the expression by the people *for* the principle, was overwhelming.

PETER PLOUGHSHARE
— *Syracuse Daily Star, May 18, 1850*

No. XII

In my last number, I brought the history of free school legislation down to the meeting of the Legislature on the first of January last.

It was shown, that on the 6th of November previous, the people of the State had adopted the present law by 158,000 majority.

Now, what was the language of that vote to the Legislature? Was it not that by a vote of almost three to one, the people desired the present law?

Well, what was the next step? It appears that when the law went into effect, some of its practical details were found to be of a character to disappoint most of those who voted for the law.

There were 92,000 who voted against the law; and during the last session 15,000 petitioners to the Legislature, requested the repeal or modification of the law.

Now, which was to be taken as the true and real expression of the wish of the people of this State? Was the 158,000 majority at an election, or was the expressed wish of 15,000 by petition, to be taken as that expression?

If they say the 158,000 majority, then *why* did not they permit the law to remain unaltered?

If they say the 15,000 petitioners gave the true expression, *why*, in the name of common sense, did they not obey it? Why did not they repeal or modify the law, as requested?

Will one of those recreant Senators stand up and tell the people *why* he did not either obey the 158,000 majority, or else the 15,000 who petitioned? Or, in other words, why he disobeyed both?

Not one of them will tell. Not one dare tell. Not one of them all, has the moral courage to tell. For no man who had not the courage to let that law remain, or to insist on its modification, or to vote for its repeal, has the courage, after he has deliberately betrayed 800,000 children, to stand up and give the reasons of that betrayal.

In my next I will give a glance at the *reasons* why this betrayal is unparalleled in moral turpitude by any other act in the history of legislation in this State.

PETER PLOUGHSHARE
— *Syracuse Daily Star, May 28, 1850*

To the Press of the State

It will be seen that every newspaper in the State is requested to copy the following notice. A more reasonable request could not well be made. It will be complied with. We do not believe there is a paper in the State, which will not promptly and cheerfully publish this call.

It will be seen that the opponents of free schools, are invited to discuss the question. The convention will be a strong one. Strong men have already promised to be there. It will be a pleasant and interesting occasion:

Free School State Convention

To the People of New York:

The question whether the State of New York shall, or shall not, have *free schools,* is to be decided at the polls in November next. It is a question of great moment. Its decision involves vast results. It will affect to an extent not fully appreciated, the physical, intellectual, social and moral interests of the State. In a word, the Empire State is to be dishonored, or to be elevated, by that vote.

This question must be discussed. Organization is indispensable. We therefore join in the call for a *state convention* of the friends of free schools, to be held at Syracuse on *Wednesday, the 12th day of June next,* at 10 o'clock a. m. We invite the opponents of free schools to present their views of the question in debate.

Invitations will be extended to quite a number of the most able and distinguished friends of universal education, in this and other states.

We respectfully ask of every editor of a newspaper in this State, at least one early insertion of this call, and such notice as he shall deem fitting.

A. H. Hovey	Wm. Jackson
Daniel Pratt	Amos Westcott
Dudley P. Phelps	John W. Barker
Charles B. Sedgwick	Charles A. Wheaton
John McCarthy	Joseph A. Allen
Wm. H. Hoyt	Q. A. Johnson
John W. Jones	Lewis J. Gillet
P. Montgomery	George C. Kellogg
Daniel McDougall	James Jahonnot
J. M. Winchell	E. C. Pomeroy
P. H. Agan	Charles P. Williston
S. F. Smith	C. B. Scott
R. H. Gardner	W. L. Crandall

Committee

Syracuse, May 17, 1850

— *Syracuse Daily Star, May 18, 1850*

That the signers of the call for the free school convention were representative citizens of Syracuse is indicated by the following items in relation to them:

Alfred H. Hovey — Mayor of Syracuse in 1850

Daniel Pratt — Judge of the Supreme Court in 1850 and later became Attorney General of the State

Dudley P. Phelps — A leading attorney who later became county treasurer

Charles B. Sedgwick — One of the attorneys who drafted the original charter for Syracuse; later was elected to Congress

Dr William H. Hoyt — A prominent physician

Patrick H. Agan — One of the founders of the Syracuse Standard and its political editor for twenty years; county treasurer and postmaster

S. F. Smith — Postmaster of Syracuse; at one time proprietor of the Syracuse Standard
Roland H. Gardner — District attorney in 1850
William Jackson — At one time postmaster of Syracuse
Dr Amos Westcott — A civil engineer, who later qualified as a physician and dentist. At one time mayor of Syracuse
John W. Barker — Director of Third National Bank; member of the Onondaga Creek Commission
Charles A. Wheaton — A prominent citizen at one time president of the board of education
Joseph A. Allen — A well-known teacher of this time
Charles Williston — At one time mayor of Syracuse
William L. Crandall — Editor at different times of the Syracuse Journal, the Onondaga Standard and the Onondaga Democrat; published the Free School Clarion

Shall New York Have Free Schools?

This is a question of great moment, and it is one which the people of this State will be called to vote upon in November. At the first thought, it is impossible to suppose there could be any other than a most emphatic affirmative response to such a question. Yet it is feared unless the friends of education are energetic and alive to this subject, that it will be defeated through negligence, rather than from an organized or formidable opposition. The future great moral, social, political, and pecuniary interests of New York are more directly involved in the issue of this question, than in almost any other ever presented for the consideration of its citizens. We are glad to notice that a free school state convention has been called at Syracuse, to be held on the 12th of June. The subject will be alluded to more in detail hereafter.— *Oswego Times. From Syracuse Daily Star, May 23, 1850*

Free School State Convention
Postponement
To Wednesday, 10th day of July

To the People of New York:

Correspondence with warm friends of free schools in different sections of the State, has induced the committee, in accordance with the views of those gentlemen, and to enable some to attend, to postpone the day of holding the New York free school state convention, at Syracuse, to *Wednesday, the tenth of July next, at 10 o'clock, a. m.*

The *Albany Argus, Evening Journal, Albany Atlas,* and *Albany State Register,* are respectfully requested to give this notice, entire, an immediate insertion in their columns, in order to bring it before their exchanges throughout every county in the State; and to insert it in their semiweekly and weekly editions.

All other editors in the State — whether friendly to a free school system, or opposed to it — are also respectfully requested to give this notice an insertion — that all who desire to participate in the doings of that gathering, may have due notice thereof.

A. H. Hovey	Wm. Jackson
Daniel Pratt	Amos Westcott
Dudley P. Phelps	John W. Barker
Charles B. Sedgwick	Charles A. Wheaton
John McCarthy	Joseph A. Allen
Wm. H. Hoyt	Q. A. Johnson
John W. Jones	Lewis J. Gillet
P. Montgomery	George C. Kellogg
Daniel McDougall	James Jahonnot
J. M. Winchell	E. C. Pomeroy
P. H. Agan	Charles P. Williston
S. F. Smith	C. B. Scott
R. H. Gardner	W. L. Crandall

Committee

Syracuse, May 30, 1850

— *Syracuse Daily Star, May 31, 1850*

N. Y. Free School State Convention
Circular

Syracuse, May 18, 1850

Dear Sir:

As you are doubtless well aware, the Legislature of the State of New York, at its recent session, passed an act resubmitting the present free school law to a vote of the people at the state election to be held in November next.

The free school law was passed by the Legislature at the session of 1849. It contained a provision, that it should be voted on by the people of the then next state election — and that the act should become a law, provided a majority of all the votes cast on the question should be in its favor. The vote stood 249,872 for the new law; 91,951 against it; majority for the law, 157,921.

The present law went into operation about the middle of November last; and on the 10th of April, the Legislature passed the act to resubmit it! About 15,000 petitioned for a repeal *or* modification of the law, and none for resubmission!

The friends of free education are greatly embarrassed by this action of the Legislature. It was frankly conceded by the real friends of free schools, in the Legislature, that the present law is not such as they desire. The same position is taken by the enlightened friends of the cause out of the Legislature. The law has been demonstrated by practical experience, to be unequal in its distribution of benefits and burdens. Why should such a law be submitted to a vote? — a law which neither the enemies nor the friends of free schools any longer desire?

In other words, the Legislature have submitted to a vote of the people, a law the details of which the friends of free schools do not approve. But the fate of the great principle for which we contend, that "*The Property of a State should Educate the Children of a State,*" is involved in the fate of that law. The burden cast by the Legislature upon the friends of free education — the outrage perpetrated by this resubmission, upon the dearest interest of the poor — is seen at a glance. Like one of old, they compel us to "make brick without straw."

It is under these circumstances, we appeal to you to lend the weight of your character, talents and counsel, to the cause of free education in this State, at this moment of its greatest peril, by attendance upon the *state convention* of the friends of *free* schools, to be held at Syracuse, on Wednesday, the 10th of July next, at 10 o'clock a. m. This invitation will be extended to quite a number of able and distinguished friends of universal education in this and other states, and to some opponents of free schools.

You are respectfully requested to furnish us your reply at the earliest practicable moment. And allow us to appeal to you, on behalf of the value of the interests involved, that that answer be an acceptance.

Very respectfully
Your obedient servants

(Signed by the Syracuse Free School Committee — A. H. Hovey, Chairman, W L. Crandall, Secretary.)

— *Syracuse Daily Star, May 31, 1850*

Free School Notice

"The friends of free schools in the second assembly district of this county, are requested to meet in convention on Saturday, the 8th of June, at the home of T. W. Bingham, in the village of Canajoharie, for the purpose of appointing delegates to attend the state free school convention, to be held at Syracuse on the 12th of June. It is hoped the friends of free schools of the several towns in this district, will see that the towns are fully represented.

"Fort Plain, May 25, 1850."

We cheerfully give place to the above, and avail ourself of the opportunity to urge the friends of free schools to be up and doing. We have not the remotest idea that the present free school act will be repudiated by the people, if a proper attention is given to the subject; but we wish to see it sustained by even a larger majority than before, and trust to the wisdom of a future Legislature to correct the imperfections which have emboldened its enemies to clamor for its repeal. Let the friends of the system beware, for a verdict against this act will be claimed as a verdict against the principle itself, and it will require the labor of years to secure the passage of another act.— *Canajoharie Radii, May 30, 1850*

Free School Convention

On the 17th of April last, the county convention of town superintendents of common schools of this county, resolved that they would hold a convention *this day*, to take into consideration the free school question, as presented by the Legislature.

The convention will meet at the city hall, this morning, at 10 o'clock. The friends and the enemies of free schools are invited to attend and to express their sentiments touching the question.— *Syracuse Daily Star. June 4, 1850*

County Convention of Town Superintendents

At a convention of the town superintendents of common schools of the county of Onondaga, held at the city hall, in Syracuse, on Tuesday, the 4th day of June, 1850, A. H. Wells, of Pompey, was called to the chair, and S. D. Luce of Fayetteville, chosen secretary.

On motion, Mr Noyes, of Otisco, Mr Truesdell, of Camillus, and Mr Crandall, of Syracuse, were appointed a committee on county organization

After considerable conversation, as to the condition of the question, the convention took a recess till 2 o'clock.

Afternoon Session

The majority of the committee — consisting of Messrs Noyes and Crandall — submitted a written report, upon the necessity of organization, and a plan to carry it out.

The committee unanimously reported a series of resolutions.

Whereupon, on motion of Mr Truesdell, the resolutions were unanimously adopted.

An animated discussion was then had upon a motion to adopt the report of a majority of the committee, which lasted several hours, in which Messrs Truesdell, Crandall, Rexford, C. Andrews, Noyes, S. E. Andrews, Truair, and E. C. Pomeroy took part, when, after some amendments, the report of the majority of the committee, was unanimously adopted, as follows:

The committee on county organization, beg leave respectfully to report

That the necessity of a *thorough organization,* arises from the fact that the Legislature has presented the free school question to the people of the State, under a false issue. That false issue, is all *against* the cause of free schools.

The House of Assembly passed a bill, by a vote of 69 to 30, for raising by a tax upon the property of the whole State, the sum of $800,000 per annum, to be divided among the school districts of the State.

It will be seen by this, that 69 members of the Assembly were in favor of a bountiful provision by the State, for the free education of all the children of the State, upon terms of equality. With this, or some other law, providing for the free education of all the children of the State, at the expense of the State, and bearing equally upon all, an overwhelming majority of the people would be pleased. It is the *principle which will be adopted.* In voting for — and in resustaining — the *present* law, the friends of free schools intend to secure eventually a system which shall bear equally upon all the property of the State.

But what did the Senate do? Some weeks before the close of the session, that body passed the bill resubmitting the present law, to a vote at the next election. That body steadily *refused* to pass any amendments. All the *friends* of free schools in the Senate and Assembly, were in favor of *amendments.* Petitions were sent in, in favor of amendments. What did all this argue? Did it not show, conclusively, that the friends and enemies of free schools, in and out of the Legislature, desired to have the *present law* altered? Certainly. Why, then, should they have submitted such a law to a vote of the people? What did those Senators — those who voted for resubmission — *mean* by voting to resubmit this law? What end did they expect to have attained by it? The friends of free schools, in the action, had declared themselves dissatisfied with *this* law. There were petitions from the people to have it *amended* by the Legislature. But there were *no* petitions to have the law remain as it was. What, then, was to be the language of a vote by the people on this law? Senators knew that the people, if they voted to sustain the law, would wish — the first thing — to have it amended. They knew that a vote "For the New Free School Law" would not be a vote to *keep* the present law on the statute book. And they knew, also, that a vote *against* sustaining the present law would be construed by the enemies of free schools, as *against the principles of free schools.*

Now, did they not well know, that the manner in which the question was placed by them before the people of the State, was likely to induce *some* who were in favor of educating the children of the State by the property of the State to vote no, on account of their objections to the present law?

This matter is so plain, that no answer is needed. But *action* is needed, to *save the principle* from the assaults of ignorance, prejudice, and mammon! And this action cannot be successful, without *county and town organization.*

For this purpose we recommend that an *executive committee* be appointed to consist of three, to be located at Syracuse.

That one man be appointed in each town, to correspond for the town with the executive committee.

That town associations of the friends of free education be organized in every town, with a view to discussion of the free school question in all its aspects.

The hope of the friends of free education in this State, lies in the *dissemination of facts and correct views* of the question, and of the arguments and appeals which naturally spring from these facts. The heart of the people is right; and the pride of every true son of New York, should lead him to look with scorn upon the idea of one retrograde step by this great State — an empire in itself, and an example to the Union and the world — upon a question which more than any other than can be named, involves its honor and reputation, not only at home, but with all the civilized communities of the globe.

Resolutions

1 *Resolved,* That we are in favor of free schools.

2 *Resolved,* That the property of a state should educate the children of a state; and that such a system is the cheapest insurance ever paid by property for the security of life, personal rights, and of property itself.

3 *Resolved,* That we are in favor of paying the tuition of the children of the State, by a tax upon the property of the whole State.

4 *Resolved,* That taxable property is produced by labor; and that therefore, the laborers of the State, who earn its property, but who do not generally accumulate much of it, are entitled to the education of their children by the property thus earned.

5 *Resolved,* That the friends of free schools in every town and neighborhood of the county, should make arrangements for holding meetings, and securing addresses and discussions upon the subject of free schools, prior to the coming election.

Executive Committee

On motion of Mr Truesdell, Messrs Hiram Putnam, Steuben Rexford, and W. L. Crandall, were appointed the executive committee.

Town Committees

In pursuance of the recommendation of the report on county organization, the following committees of one, were appointed:

Camillus	D. C. LeRoy
Elbridge	Dr Williams
Van Buren	Chauncey Goodrich
Lysander	H. G. McGonegal
Clay	D. G. Frisbie
Cicero	C. C. Newcomb
Onondaga	Norman Green
Pompey	A H. Wells
Otisco	Benjamin J. Cowles
Spafford	Town Superintendent
Salina	Dr. C. S. Sterling
Geddes	E. W. Curtis
Manlius	S. D. Luce
DeWitt	Thomas H. Wands
Tully	Myron Wheaton
Lafayette	Mr Goodell, Town Supt.
Skaneateles	Mr Hammond, Town Supt.
Fabius	S. C. Harris
Marcellus	Dr Cowles

On motion, *Resolved,* That the proceedings be published in the newspapers of this county, and that S. E. Andrews, T. S Truair, and W L. Crandall, be a publishing committee

Whereupon, the convention adjourned to Wednesday, the 10th day of July, at 10 o'clock a. m.— the day and hour of the state convention.

A. H. WELLS, *Chairman*

S. D. LUCE, *Secretary*

—Syracuse Daily Star, June 10, 185

Free School State Convention
Letter from Bishop Potter

Philadelphia, May 29, 1850

MY DEAR SIR:

Your letter of the 21st inst. reached me when I was so much engaged in duties of pressing necessity, that I have been obliged to postpone a reply. I regret that an indispensable engagement in the city of New York, for the 13th of June — made some time since — will deprive me of the pleasure of being present at your proposed convention. If I had not unlimited confidence in the good feeling of my former fellow citizens, I should doubt whether they would relish the active participation by one from another state in public questions of such great and all absorbing interest. Did my engagements permit, however, I should be much inclined to put their magnanimity to the test. Since I left your State, I have not bestowed much reflection upon the subject of free schools, nor have I examined the provisions of your late law providing for their establishment. But as advised at present, I should say to all the friends of universal education, stand by the fundamental principle of that law, but promptly correct all its defects.

To charge the property of the State with the expense of educating its children, seems to me to be as much for the interest of capital as for labor. It is a recognition by the State, too, of its highest and most solemn duties. It is the readiest way of rendering schools both accessible and acceptable to all; and it will entitle the Legislature to assert a power which may be requisite — the power of exacting the attendance at schools of certain children who most need but are least likely to receive, the nursing care which good schools alone can give. In recognizing this principle, New York has done herself great honor. Long may it be before she renounces it.

In great haste
I am, dear sir
Yours, most truly
ALONZO POTTER[1]

Replies

The following replies have thus far been received. The reader will bear in mind, that it is quite probable some who could not be here on the 12th of June, will be here on the 10th of July:

From Gov. Seward
"Washington, May 24, 1850

GENTLEMEN:

If the nature of my duties here were such as to allow me to be absent from Congress, I would most cheerfully and gratefully accept your invitation to attend the free school state convention.

But I could not do so with propriety, nor perhaps without hazarding too important public interests.

I pray to be assured, that I regard the principle upon which you insist, as one of vast importance to the public welfare and the best interests of mankind; and that I sincerely hope that the deliberations of the convention, may result in the adoption of such details of administration as may com-

---

[1] The Rt. Rev. Alonzo Potter D.D. LL.D., the first president of the American Association for the Advancement of Education, was born of parents who were from Rhode Island, in Dutchess county, New York, in 1800 and died in San Francisco, Cal., July 4, 1865. After attending the common schools of his town until he was fourteen, he received his college preparation in an academy in Poughkeepsie and was graduated from Union College in 1818.
He then commenced teaching in Philadelphia and was the following year called to Union College as tutor. He held the chair of mathematics and natural philosophy from 1821 to 1826, when he became rector of St. Paul's Church in Boston. In 1831, on solicitation of his father-in-law, President Nott of Union College, he returned to the college as its vice president, which office he held until 1845, when he was elected bishop of the diocese of Pennsylvania.
As a college officer and teacher, he was said to have no superior in the thoroughness of his instruction. It is also said that no man of his day did more to promote the cause of popular education and religious philanthrophy. He was the adviser of the state department at Albany and was prominent in all movements for the improvement of the schools. He was the author of several educational works and a much sought-for speaker and counselor at all county, state and national school conventions.

mend the principle to the general favor of the people of our great and flourishing State.

I am, with great respect
Your humble servant
WILLIAM H. SEWARD

A. H. Hovey, W. L. Crandall, and others, committee."

From J. A. McMaster
OFFICE OF THE FREEMAN'S JOURNAL
New York, May 23, 1850

GENTLEMAN:

I this morning received a copy of the circular you have addressed, calling for a state convention at Syracuse to consider the new law for free schools.

I suppose that it is as one of the earliest and most constant opponents of the New Law that you have had the courtesy to invite me; and in appreciation of that courtesy, I make haste to accept the invitation. I will be in Syracuse on the 12th proximo, if not unavoidably prevented, for the purpose of hearing what the friends of the law have to say; and, perhaps, if agreeable to you and to them, to state in few and simple terms the grounds of my objections to it.

I remain, very respectfully, Yours, &c.

J. A. MCMASTER

To Messrs. Hovey, Crandall, and others, Committee, Syracuse.

From Horace Greely

The only letter yet received from Mr. Greely, is a private one to a member of the Committee. We take a sentence or two:

New York, May 27, 1850

FRIEND C—:

You have not given time enough for the assembling of a fit convention. I must be up in the interior of the State in July, and cannot well come in June — *But I think I shall.* But you need time to bring together the best men in the State. Dr Nott should be there," &c., &c. "I will do my part, but I wish you had been a little more behind as to time."

Yours
HORACE GREELEY

(Other letters received, are of the same tenor as regards the *time* of holding the convention — hence the change to the 10th of July.)

Aurora, May 25, 1850

A. H. Hovey, and others, Committee:

GENTLEMEN.—Your cicular was duly received, and in compliance with your request, I hasten to send you my reply.

The object for which the convention is called, is one of momentous interest to the educational cause of the State. No action, however, under existing circumstances, can, in my opinion, arrest the rejection of the law next November. The action of the Legislature on the subject, was, to say the least, weak and cowardly. The true course would have been to hold on, and from time to time *alter* and *amend*, as experience should suggest, till all the workings were made to harmonize in a system, equitable and satisfactory. Instead of throwing it back upon the people with its imperfections, they could and should have amended them, according to their judgment, and by no means have exposed a child of so much promise to be strangled at its birth.

That the property of the State should educate the children of the State, I hold to be sound doctrine; and I had hopes something at least approximating that point, would have been reached at the last session. I entertain no doubt that the carrying out a measure of that kind, would, ultimately, contribute more to the property of the interests of the State, in the aggregate, than any single law now on our statute books. What can any state or country be or do, without educated mind?

It is, in my judgment, the *duty* of the State to educate the children of the State. No system of popular education can be perfected, so effectually to secure a general diffusion of knowledge among all classes, in any other way. For years, I have advocated the cause of free schools; and to me, it seems, if there were no higher considerations brought into account than political economy even, the measure would command undivided support.

I shall be on business in New York at the time of your meeting, and of of course deprived of the pleasure of attendance.

Respectfully, yours, &c.,
SALEM TOWN

(The attendance of this veteran in the cause of universal education, will probably now be secured).

Albany, May 29, 1850

GENTLEMEN:

It will afford me the utmost gratification to attend the proposed state convention of the friends of free schools, to be held in your city, in accordance with your very obliging invitation. And most happy should I be to meet on that interesting occasion, all those of our fellow-citizens of every sect and party, who would open the avenues of universal education broadly and freely to every child of the State, in all coming time; who have the intellect to perceive and the heart to appreciate the vast importance of such a measure upon all the political, social, industrial, moral and religious interests of the community, and the determination to devote all their energies to the accomplishment and full practical realization of this great undertaking.

I earnestly trust that every Christian, every patriot, every philanthropist, will feel himself called upon by every consideration which can appeal to his nobler nature, to avail himself of every proper instrumentality to secure to the eight hundred thousand children and future citizens of the State, the incalculable blessings of a sound physical, mental and moral education.

Such an opportunity may never occur again. If neglected now, in all human probability, to the great majority of the responsible actors of the present generation it never will again occur. The crisis is one of most momentous interest. Upon its results depends the present and future welfare of millions of immortal beings, whose imploring voices are audible only to the quickened ear of faith. As we shall now determine, generations yet unborn will, in long succession, "rise up and call us blessed," or require the retribution of solemn obligations neglected and disregarded. The question before us is one which soars infinitely above and beyond all the petty struggles of personal and political ambition — all the ephemeral interests of the passing hour — and fixes its high regards upon the future — the permanent and the lasting welfare of humanity. In all its aspects, it is one which demands the concentrated energy of every higher and nobler faculty of our being; and no man who richly appreciates the duty incumbent upon him as an intelligent and responsible actor on the great theatre of Christian civilization, can be indifferent to the momentous struggle impending between the supporters and the opponents of *universal education in schools free to all.*

Very truly and respectfully
Your obedient servant
SAM'L RANDALL

Messrs. Hovey, Crandall, and others, Committee, Syracuse.

Cortland-Village, May 25, 1850

GENTLEMEN:

I received last evening, your circular of May 18th, inviting me to attend a state convention on the subject of the free school law, to be held in Syracuse on the 12th proximo. If I can arrange my business so as to render it practicable, it will give me pleasure to be present, and to take a part in the deliberations on the important subject the convention is called to discuss.

Very respectfully, your ob't serv't,
HENRY S. RANDALL

A. H. Hovey, and others, Committee.

From Bradford R. Wood

Albany, 29th May, 1850

GENTLEMEN:

I regret that such is the health of my family, I cannot be with you on the 12th of June next. I heartily respond to the views contained in your circular, and cordially reciprocate your feelings in regard to popular education, and trust you will devise a system of free school instruction obviating the objections to the present law, and yet meeting the wants and rights of every child in the State.

I am, very respectfully
Your obedient serv't,
BRADFORD R. WOOD

To Messrs. A. Hovey, Daniel Pratt, D. P. Phelps, C. B. Sedgwick, and others, Committee.

— Syracuse Daily Star, June 17, 1850

Free School State Convention
Further Replies

The following constitute all the further replies to this date, the 12th of June, instant:

From Horace Greeley

Washington, June 6, 1850

DEAR SIR:

Your second letter, reminding me that I am among those invited to attend the free school state convention at Syracuse next month, has reached me this morning.

REV. SALEM TOWN

HORACE GREELEY

Though obliged to spend the present week in this city, I had resolved to leave very unseasonably and at great inconvenience, in order to be present at the convention on the day originally named. I did not suppose any formal acceptance requisite, since I need no other invitation than the general one addressed to all friends of free schools. The postponement of the meeting, however, will greatly diminish the personal inconvenience of attending, but was not needed to fix my resolution. I shall attend of course, if life and health permit, and hope at least to show my good will meantime by exhorting and entreating other friends to do so. Deeming of vital importance the maintenance of the principle that all the children shall receive a good common school education without regard to the pecuniary ability of their parents to defray the expense — to their intellectual capacity to appreciate its value — or to their moral virtue to deprive themselves of sensual gratifications to secure to their children so priceless an acquisition — I will try to do my best in the contest which our late Legislature so causelessly thrust upon us.

If I shared the apprehensions of many friends of free schools, I should doubtless labor in the cause with more efficiency; but I have so unhesitating a conviction that the principle of free education will be sustained by at least one hundred thousand majority, that I have not yet been thoroughly enlisted in the canvass. I feel very sure that you may set down the Commercial Emporium as safe for thirty thousand majority on the right side, and if forty thousand shall seem to be needed, they can be had, and ten thousand more within five miles of our city hall. We have *tried* free schools, our way — tried them fully and fairly — and know what we vote for. You may trust us; and any open opposition can but serve to swell our majority.

Yours

HORACE GREELEY

To W. L. Crandall, of Committee, &c.

From James O. Brayman

OFFICE COMMERCIAL ADVERTISER

Buffalo, May 28, 1850

GENTS:

I received, a day or two since, a circular from Syracuse, calling a state convention in that city of the friends of free schools, with a view of taking some action to secure the success of the principle involved in sustaining the present law upon the subject, which has been resubmittetd by the Legislature to the people. Constant business engagements will undoubtedly prevent my attendance upon the occasion, but I avail myself of this mode of expressing to you my strongest sympathy with the objects of the convention, and my deep and abiding interest in the cause of free education. Agreeing with you that friends of the *principle,* are compelled, by what I cannot but regard as the unwise action of the Legislature, to make an issue upon a defective and objectionable law, yet this should not, in my view, discourage us, but only nerve our hearts the stronger to do battle in this glorious cause, for the reason, that its opponents have, by a combination of circumstances, been placed upon the "vantage ground." We should be content with nothing short of a full recognition of the duty of the Government, to provide for the free education of all by a tax upon the property of the State; nor cease our efforts until free schools become incorporated into our political system, as the settled policy of the State.

The decision which is to be made in November, will have an important and perhaps a conclusive bearing upon the subject for years to come. It is therefore vitally essential that the whole subject, in all its relations and connections, be thoroughly canvassed — that light be shed abroad among the people — that the issue be made, not so much with those who oppose the existing law, as with those who oppose the general principle of free education. The idea that the *friends* of the measure will go for the amendment and perfection of the law, must be made to occupy a prominent position in all that is said and done.

We, in Buffalo, have tried the free school system for nearly fifteen years, and so much has it commended itself to the favor of our citizens, that but *three* of all the voters in the city could be found to cast their suffrages against extending its benefits and blessings to the State at large. Such, I doubt not, will be the result, when a system equally unobjectionable, shall become fairly and fully in operation throughout the State.

I regard the convention to be held in your city as one of the most important that has assembled in this State for years. In its object, how immeasurably higher is it than those political Conventions which annually recur — calling forth a heated interest from all classes of our citizens. I trust, therefore, that it will command that consideration from our people which its importance merits, and that the great and good, the patriotic and the philanthropic, from every section of the State, may be present to participate in its deliberations, and to give tone and efficiency to its resolves.

Yours in haste,
JAS. O. BRAYMAN

A. H. Hovey, Esq., and others, Com.

From John V. L. Pruyn

Albany, June 5, 1850

GENTLEMEN:

In acknowledging the receipt of your invitation to attend the free school state convention, to be held at Syracuse, in July, I desire to express my decided approval of the *principle* of the free school law, and my earnest hope that it may receive a fair trial. A Republican government cannot be permanently sustained unless the people are educated. The rights of the masses will not be respected unless they are in a position to assert them, and that position can only be attained by education. Nor can property be effectually protected, except by the strong barrier which moral education builds up in its defense, teaching men their duty to others, as well as to themselves.

The people of our State having by a very strong vote approved the free school law, which approval has gone forth to the world as proof of their discernment and patriotism, it would be discreditable to the honor and reputation of the State to abandon the principle before it had been fairly tried. Proper self-respect, and a due regard for consistency, should prevent this. This subject is not so new or novel that we should be alarmed at it. We know what it is and what it proposes, and let us see if we cannot work out its end. In my opinion, it needs but to be thoroughly understood, to secure a larger vote from the people now, than it did before. Defects in the details of the law, can easily be remedied by legislation.

I shall endeavor to attend the convention, but cannot be at all certain at this time that I can do so. Hoping that your efforts will be productive of the good results intended, I remain, with great respect,

Yours, &c., &c.,

JOHN V. L. PRUYN[1]

A. H. Hovey, W. L. Crandall, and others, Committee.

From Senator Beekman

New York, June 11, 1850

W. L. Crandall, Esq., Secretary, &c.,

DEAR SIR:

I replied to the invitation with which the committee have honored me, some time since, by a letter to yourself, in which I was able to give only a conditional acceptance. The postponement, however, of the convention to the 10th of July, will, I hope, enable me to be present.

Free education I regard as the corner stone of our political institutions. Without schools, *ballots* would be but instruments of mischief. The mingling of children of various religious creeds in common schools, goes far to promote peace and good will, and to prevent the growth of bigotry. Let us sustain, then, by all means, our free school system. The law of 1849 can be so amended as to be unobjectionable. The *principle* never was wrong.

Very sincerely yours

JAMES W. BEEKMAN[1]

To the Committee on the Free School Convention.

—*Syracuse Daily Star, June 16, 1850*

---

[1] John Van Schaick Lansing Pruyn was born in Albany, N. Y., in 1811 and was a member of a Holland-Dutch family that had been identified with the life of Albany and the colony of New York for over two centuries. He attended the Albany Academy, studied law and was admitted to the bar. Much of his earlier practice was in the court of chancery in which he appeared with marked success. He was identified with large business and philanthropic interests. In 1853, his relations to the railway system of New York State became so great that he was obliged to relinquish his law practice. He was a director and counsel of the Mohawk & Hudson Railroad Company, which built the first railroad in the State, if not in the United States. He was also connected with other roads forming a system extending from Albany and Troy to Buffalo and which later were consolidated into the New York Central Company. Mr Pruyn drew the consolidation agreement in connection with the formation of the New York Central Company, and was a director and general counsel for the new company for many years. He was one of the original trustees of the Mutual Life Insurance Company and an officer in other large corporations.

In 1861 he was elected a State Senator. He was a member of the commission to build the new Capitol and he laid the first cornerstone of that building. He served in Congress for two terms.

In 1844, he was appointed a Regent of the University of the State of New York and served for 33 years, 15 of which he was Chancellor of the University. He was also trustee of the State Normal College at Albany and of St. Stephen's College at Annandale, N. Y. He died in 1877.

[1] James W. Beekman was born November 22, 1815 and died January 15, 1877. He married Miss Milledollar, the daughter of the president of Rutgers College. Mr Beekman was graduated from Columbia in 1834 and was later admitted to the bar. He traveled extensively and upon his return to this country made the voyage in one of the first ocean steamships. He was a member of the Assembly in 1848 and of the State Senate in 1849–51. He was an active member of the Legislature and carried through the bill that created Central Park in New York City. He was interested in public matters in New York City and at various times served as a trustee of the medical department of Columbia University and as trustee of the college proper, as vice president of the New York Historical Society, as vice president of the New York Hospital, as trustee of the Women's Hospital, and as trustee of the New York Dispensary. He was a strong supporter of the free school movement.

Free School State Convention
Further Replies

We insert today, the replies of Hon. Christopher Morgan, present Secretary of State and Superintendent of Common Schools; of Hon. Horace Mann; and of Hon. Halsey R. Wing, recently first judge of Warren county.

From Christopher Morgan

Secretary's Office
Albany, June 18, 1850

Gentlemen:

I have received your circular inviting me to attend the free school state convention to be held at Syracuse.

It will afford me pleasure to unite with the friends of free schools, for my earnest advocacy of the principle has brought upon me no inconsiderable degree of reproach.

It is in my judgment the bounden duty of the State to provide the means for educating every child within its limits.

Universal education will not only diminish vice and poverty, but will add greatly to the social enjoyment of mankind.

The present law is defective, and its operation unequal — sometimes oppressive. If, however, the principle of free schools is maintained by the people, as I trust it will be, the law may be so amended as to obviate the objections so strenuously urged by its opponents.

Although differing with a large and respectable portion of our electors, I must continue to urge upon the consideration of the people a system of free and universal education.

Very respectfully
Your obedient servant
CHRISTOPHER MORGAN

Messrs A. H. Hovey, W. L. Crandall, and others, Committee.

From Horace Mann

House of Representatives
Washington, June 19, 1850

W. L. Crandall, Esq.,

Dear Sir:

Should I go over from Macedonia to help you, who shall take care of Macedonia? Important primary, holy even, as we have been accustomed to regard education, yet there is a work to be done which precedes education; which does not look immediately to its *perfectures,* but to its existence. This preliminary, this antecedent work, I, among others, am set here to do.

It is likely that the day appointed for your convention will be the very time when we shall be in the "thick of the fight." I wish I were as confident of victory for us, as I am for you: for I cannot believe it possible that New York will annul the noble vote she has just given; degrade her character and disinherit her offspring of the noblest patrimony, by an abandonment of the cause of free schools.

I received your address, which I read with pleasure and instruction. I also had a letter from Mr May, which I should have found time — or made it — to answer, had I not seen the postponement announced. I have been so much engrossed with duties, that I could attend to only those which were most imperative.

I hope you are all in that state of mind, when both hope and fear become the most powerful of impulses. Work, as though you hoped to gain everything; work, as though you feared to lose everything.

Very truly and sincerely,

Yours, &c., &c.,

HORACE MANN

From Halsey R. Wing

Glens Falls, *21st June, 1850*

GENTLEMEN:

I have received your circular inviting me to attend the "State Convention of the friends of Free Schools," to be holden at Syracuse on the 10th day of July. I thank you for the courtesy, and reply, that if my business engagements permit, I shall deem it a most agreeable duty to be present as one of "the friends" of this great and philanthropic cause which is to elicit this demonstration.

I do not permit myself to doubt for a moment the early and firm establishment of the noble *principle* for which we contend. True, the temporizing and disingenuous act of the present Legislature, has loaded this principle with the many and grievous defects of the new school law: and thus the friends of resubmission — with a clever adroitness which might perhaps be creditable to the small cunning of some petty smuggler — have contrived to cover up, and, so far as their *wishes* were potent, to crush the truth of that principle beneath the weight of those odious defects. But they evidently overlooked both the poetry and reality of the line —

"Truth crush'd to earth, shall rise again."

The property of our citizens is protected by the virtue and intelligence of the people; and it would be a gross reflection on the justice and patriotism of those citizens, to assume that they will not cheerfully impose upon their property the light charge required to supply adequate means for rearing, in virtue and intelligence, the very children who, in a few short years, will themselves be the people.

The proposed convention, will, I presume, devise some plan of action by which the voters will be enabled to "*see through*" the Legislative legerdemain, which hopes to defeat a conceded, and, standing alone, invincible good, by its unfortunate, though unnecessary, association with admitted evils.

With the question fairly understood by the people, I confidently anticipate that, at the coming election, they will triumphantly sustain the present school law, with all its faulty details, for the sake of the glorious principle which pervades it,— and, at the same time, see to it, that men are returned to the next Legislature, who will so *amend* the law as to **make** it *right* and *satisfactory*.

Respectfully
Yours, &c.
H. R. WING[1]

Messrs. Hovey, Crandal, and others, Committee.
— *Syracuse Daily Star, June 27, 1850*

Free School State Convention
Railroad Rates

The committee of arrangements for the free school state convention to be held in this city on the 10th of July next, are authorized by the several railroad companies between Albany and Buffalo to say that tickets will be sold for that convention — good for one passage each way,— up to and including the 12th — not afterwards — for one fare. Persons wishing to avail themselves of this reduction will be required, when applying at the various stations for tickets, to show their letters of appointment or invitation, or to be reputably introduced.

Free School State Convention
Meeting of Ladies

At a meeting of the ladies of Syracuse, interested in the free school question, at the house of *Mrs Stephen Smith*, on Monday evening, June 24th, 1850, *Mrs L. Wallace* was called upon to preside, and *L. Savage* to act as secretary.

The following resolutions were unanimously adopted:

Resolved, That we approve of the plan of universal education in *schools free to all*.

Resolved, That we cordially invite the attendance of ladies upon this convention, as we deem this eminently a question upon which woman's influence should be felt.

Resolved, That we hereby tender the hospitalities of the city to all ladies who attend the convention, and to their companions or escort.

Resolved, That the following ladies are hereby appointed a committee to carry into effect the foregoing resolution; and that the ladies of the city are requested to communicate with any members of the committee, in reference to the necessary arrangements for the entertainment of all:

Mrs E. W. Leavenworth	Mrs H. Loomis
" John Wilkinson	" Lyman Clary
" Wm. Jackson	" L. Stevens
" R. M. Pelton	" John F. Wyman
" —— Pierson	" Stephen Smith
" Hervey Sheldon	" Joseph Seymour
" J. B. Huntington	" —— Craves
" E. F. Wallace	" Phillips
" Charles Rust	

— *Syracuse Daily Standard, June 28, 1850*

---

[1] Halsey Rogers Wing was born in Sandy Hill, N. Y., and was educated in the schools of Fort Edward, the Lenox (Mass.) Academy, Yale University and Middlebury College. After being admitted to the bar, he practised in Albany county, Brockport and Buffalo and finally settled in Glens Falls in 1841. In 1843 he was appointed county superintendent of common schools and 1845 first judge of the county. In 1851 he became identified with various large business interests and gradually withdrew from the practice of the law. He was a strong supporter of all educational movements in his community and was identified with various associations for the advancement of the interests of Glens Falls. He died in 1870.

HALSEY ROGERS WING

Free School Meeting

There was a meeting of citizens at the council chamber last evening, for the purpose of appointing delegates to the free school state convention, to be held in Syracuse, on the 10th inst., and to transact such other business as might be deemed expedient, relating to the subject of free schools.— Hon. O. Allen in the chair, and Jas. O. Brayman, secretary.

On the motion of O. G. Steele,

Resolved, That a committee of five be appointed to name a list of delegates to the state convention, and to present resolutions for the consideration of the meeting.

The chair appointed as such a committee, O. G. Steele,[1] D. Bowen, Ald. H. Park, Ald. M. P. Bush, and D. F. Lee.

While the Committee were out the chairman gave a history of the action of the Legislature upon the subject of free schools last winter.

The committee returned and reported the following list of resolutions, and delegates, which report was unanimously adopted.

Resolved, That the stability and perpetuity of our republican institutions depend upon universal education and general intelligence.

Resolved, That we hold it to be the bounden duty of the State to provide by law for the establishment of free schools within its jurisdiction, supported by taxation upon its real and personal estate.

Resolved, That the children of the State are entitled to a sufficient education to qualify them to perform intelligently their duties as citizens of a republican government — and this can only be accomplished by a system of common school education, which shall be free to all, and for the benefit of all.

Resolved, That we are in favor of giving the present law a united and energetic support, and thus secure the establishment of the great principle of free education. We look upon the existing law as a vast improvement upon the old rate-bill system, and desire that the law shall have a fair trial, and remain subject to improvements and amendments as experience may show to be necessary.

Resolved, As citizens of Buffalo we look with pride upon our free school system, as now permanently established by law and rejoice that it has reached a point of stability and efficiency which has extinguished all doubts in regard to policy.

Resolved, That the same public evils which required the establishment of free schools in this city 12 years ago, exist in a greater or less degree in the

---

[1] Mr Frank Severance, Secretary of the Buffalo Historical Society, furnishes the following data in relation to Oliver Gray Steele:

Mr. Steele was born in New Haven, Conn., December 16, 1805. After attending the public school until he was twelve years of age, he went to New York City where he served for two years as a message boy. He then returned to Connecticut, where he learned the bookbinding trade. In May 1827, he went to Buffalo and in 1830 established himself as a bookseller and bookbinder. He married Miss Sarah E. Hull and both he and his wife became identified with all movements for progress in Buffalo. Mr Steele was prominent in civic affairs, serving as a fireman in the volunteer force and as alderman. He prospered in a business way and became secretary and manager of the Buffalo Gas Light Company and also secretary and later president of the Buffalo Water Work Company.

Previous to 1837, there were but seven public schools in Buffalo and these were inadequately housed and equipped and attended only by the children of the poorest classes in the city. In 1837 a system of free public schools was inaugurated. It seemed difficult to get anyone to serve as superintendent but Mr. Steele became interested in the schools and accepted the position. He served for three years and was paid the munificent salary of $75 a year. He always manifested a keen interest in educational matters and was a founder of the Buffalo State Normal School and a member of its governing board. He was also a founder of the Buffalo Academy of Fine Arts and at one time its president. He died November 11, 1879.

entire State, and the same remedy which has proved so effectual in the city will be equally so when applied to the country at large.

Resolved, That we highly approve of the proposed free school state convention to be held at Syracuse on the 10th inst. and recommend the following men as delegates to represent this city upon that occasion.

— *Buffalo Commercial Advertiser, July 6, 1850*

Prospectus of the Free School Clarion
"Knowledge is Power"

The voters of New York are to determine, in November, whether they will, or whether they will not, have *schools free to all*. It is a momentous question. It involves the pecuniary, intellectual, social and moral interests of New York — its greatness in the future — for "*knowledge is power.*" At this age, to be destitute of knowledge, is to be destitute of power. Shall, then, this boom — this blessing — be extended to *all* the children of the State, on equal terms? Shall the State say to all the children within its borders, "Ho! every one that thirsteth; whoever will let him partake of the water of knowledge, without money and without price?" Will New York augment its power in this way? That is the question to be decided in November.

By a fraud unequalled in the annals of New York legislation, this question is presented to the people under a *false issue*. The enemies of free schools outnumbered or outwitted the friends of free schools in the Legislature; and they have resubmitted to a vote of the people, for approval or rejection, a law which they know should be amended. The men who voted for that resubmission, hoped to *crush* free schools. They have the vantage ground-- the same as a defendant in a case would have who was permitted to draw the declaration. But their meshes of falsehood can be broken. Their well arranged design can be foiled. But it can be done only by the dissemination of opinions, facts, and arguments. For this purpose we shall publish the "*Free School Clarion.*"

It will be edited by the subscriber.

The effective aid and cooperation of some of the ablest minds of the State have been secured. All points involved in this mighty question — a question which throws all other topics of legislation in the shade — will be thoroughly discussed. Through its columns, the sincere opponents of free schools, will be heard.

The *Free School Clarion* will be issued on or about the 10th of July, 1850 — will be printed on good type and good paper, on these terms:

Single copy	25c
Four copies, one address	$1.00
Ten " " "	2.00
Fifteen " " "	3.00
Twenty-five " " "	5.00
Fifty " " "	8.00

It will be issued weekly, in *quarto form,* and one no. will be issued after the election, giving the returns, and such suggestions as shall naturally arise from the result.

Address   W. L. CRANDALL
Syracuse, July 2, 1850.

— *Syracuse Daily Star, July 10, 1850*

Free School Convention

This body met at Market Hall at 10 o'clock yesterday morning, and was called to order by Mr Winchell, of Onondaga, on whose motion S. S. Randall of Albany, was called to the chair. Mr Rick, of Erie, was appointed secretary.

Upon taking the chair, Mr Randall made some very eloquent and appropriate remarks.

On motion of E. Curtiss, of Onondaga, a committee of seven was appointed to report permanent officers for the convention. The chair named as such committee Messrs Curtiss, of Onondaga; Beekman, of N. Y.; Steele, of Erie; Holley, of Wyoming; Coburn, of Tioga; Phelps, of Albany; and Woolworth, of Cortland.

On motion of Mr Steele, of Erie,

Resolved, That a committee of seven be appointed to draw up and present a report and resolutions, expressive of the sense of this convention on the subject of free school education.

The chair named as such committee, Messrs Greely, of N. Y.; Randall, of Cortland; Steele, of Erie; May, of Onondaga; Beekman, of N. Y.; Coburn, of Tioga; Phelps, of Albany; Sedgwick, of Onondaga, and Leggett, of Westchester.

On motion of O. B. Pierce, of Oneida, the convention took a recess until 12 o'clock, to complete its organization.

Afternoon Session.

At 12 o'clock M., the convention met pursuant to adjournment. The committee on organization reported as follows:

President: Christopher Morgan.

Vice Presidents: J. C. Carey of New York, W. H. Leggett of Westchester, Asabel Stone of Madison, Rev. H. Mandeville of Albany, O. G. Steele of Erie, H. Putnam of Onondaga, W. F. Cady of Oswego, and C. R. Coburn of Tioga.

Secretaries: Wm. L. Crandall, of Onondaga, W. K. Viele of Erie, D. C. Bloomer of Seneca, Wm. F. Phelps of Albany.

On motion, it was *Resolved,* That the gentlemen present be requested to report the names of persons in attendance from their respective counties, on the reassembling of the convention.

The chairman of the committee on resolutions reported the following, which was unanimously adopted:

Resolved, That this convention has learned with profound regret of the sudden and unexpected death of the President of the United States, and that in token of respect for his memory we do now adjourn until 2 o'clock P. M.

2 o'clock P. M.

The convention was called to order by the chairman pro tem, and the Blakely family being present, were called for, and favored the convention with an appropriate " free school song." A prayer was offered by Rev. G. H. Warner, of Buffalo. The president was conducted to the chair by Messrs Woolworth and Cary.

Upon taking the chair, Mr Morgan submitted some very appropriate remarks, alluding in a feeling manner to the news of the death of President

Taylor, and expressing himself the uncompromising advocate of universal education.

Mr Sedgwick, the chairman of the committee on resolutions, reported the following:

1st. *Resolved,* That the proposition before this convention and this State is not that our present system of common schools, with all of its provisions and details, is perfect, but that this law should be maintained in so far as it provides that all of our common schools *be free to all the children of the State.*

2d. *Resolved,* That the principle upheld by this convention, the principle which should be fixed and established in the political economy of this State is that the property of State should educate the children of the State, or in the words of the first section of the act, that common schools, in the several districts of the State, should be free to all persons in the districts, under 21 years of age.

3d. *Resolved,* That the true welfare of the State is to be attained not wholly by highways and canals, by asylums and penitentiaries, by police and standing armies, but by the development of the physical, intellectual and moral energies of the people, therefore if the former should be sustained at the public expense, much more should the thorough education of the whole people be amply provided for from the same source.

The foregoing resolutions were ably discussed by Mr Bloss, of Rochester, and Rev. Mr Waldo, of Ontario.

4th. *Resolved,* That the emphatic vote of the people at the last election in favor of the act establishing free schools throughout the State, was clearly indicative of the sanction and approval of the principle which directed the enactment of that law, and that no defects in the subordinate details of the provisions there made for the universal education of the children of the State will warrant or justify the abandonment of the principle or the total repeal of the law.

Discussed by Rev. Mr May, of Onondaga, Starr, of Monroe, Mandeville, of Albany, Lord, of Ohio, and Waldo, of Cortland.

5th. *Resolved,* That we pledge ourselves to use all proper means and influence in our power individually and collectively to procure the renewed sanction of the people to the great principle of free schools as the only sure and effectual Palladium of their liberty, happiness and prosperity — as the best safeguard of their rights and the surest preservative of those noble institutions handed down to us by the framers and fathers of our Republic.

6th. *Resolved,* That the friends of free schools be requested to procure the publication of the address and resolutions of this convention in all the newspapers of the several counties throughout the State.

7th. *Resolved,* That it be recommended by the friends of free schools in each county to hold a convention at their county seat on the first Monday of October next, or some more convenient day, for the purpose of organizing and preparing for the election.

Pending the adoption of the 4th resolution, Mr Greeley, of N. Y., being loudly called for, came forward, but instead of discussing the resolution, asked leave to present a report which had been prepared by the committee. Leave being granted, Mr G. read a very able report, pointed, argumentative and convincing, taking decided and incontrovertible grounds in favor of free and universal education, which was received with great applause.

Mr Thompson, of Erie, spoke in opposition to the law, but expressed himself in favor of the principle of free schools.

The Blakely family were then called for, and entertained the convention with another " free school song."

Mr McMaster, of New York, spoke in opposition to the resolutions and in opposition to the principle of free schools, denying the right of the State to assume the education of the people.

Mr Bloss, of Monroe, here introduced the following resolution:

Resolved, That we most cordially invite the people of this State, and recommend to the next Legislature such an amendment of the act of 1849, establishing free schools, as will make the expense of supporting such schools, over and above the annual revenue of the common school fund, a charge upon the real and personal property of the State, equitably assessed, according to a just and fair valuation of such property, and that we recommend the circulation throughout the State, of a memorial to the next Legislature to this effect.

The question on the adoption of Mr Greeley's report was then taken, and it was unanimously adopted.

Adjourned, to meet at 7 o'clock P. M.

—*Syracuse Daily Standard, July 11, 1850*

Free School Convention

The convention met at 7 o'clock. The president in the chair. The Blakelys were introduced and favored the convention with one of their fine performances.

Mr Bascomb, of Seneca, obtained the floor and spoke at much length and ability against free schools. Eight o'clock having arrived, he concluded his remarks.

Mr Randall having been appointed to lecture at that hour, he was introduced, and commenced by saying that he had pledged himself to answer all objections that might be raised against free schools. That pledge he should redeem, but as he had been requested to lecture on a certain subject, his remarks, which were in writing, were prepared with special reference to the subject, and he should therefore be compelled to forego the pleasure of replying to his eloquent and honorable friend until the coming day. He then proceeded with his address a very able and learned production, addressed to the parents, teachers and pupils of the city of Syracuse.

At the conclusion of Mr Randall's remarks, Mr Greeley was loudly called for, who remarked that as other business would take him from the city in the morning, he would say what he had on the subject at that time. He proceeded to reply to Mr McMaster of New York, who spoke during the afternoon session, and ended with some most convincing arguments in favor of free schools and universal education.

The president announced his inability to remain longer with the convention, owing to pressing official duties, and called one of the vice presidents to the chair, and on taking leave, made a most powerful, eloquent and unanswerable appeal in favor of the free school system, expressing his entire conviction of its final triumph in the Empire State.

Adjourned to meet next day at 8 o'clock A. M.

Second Day

Morning Session

The convention was principally occupied yesterday morning in discussing resolutions and principles introduced the day previous. The series of resolutions presented by the committee of seven, and published in our paper yesterday, were adopted, and many interesting remarks made by members of the convention. Mr Randall said that an average of 10 scholars to each district, making an average of over 100,000 had attended the common schools of this State during the past year, more than during any previous year.

The bill for submitting the free school law to the people this fall, was passed by the Assembly at the last hour of the session without its having been read. Petitions were thrown in from all parts of the State against the law, while its friends made no effort in its behalf.

Much was said of the inequality of the law in reference to taxation; but all agreed that this was the law of assessment, and not the free school law. It was warmly contested that the property within the State should be equally taxed for the support of "free schools," and thereby prevent crime, as well as for the punishment of criminals, and that the friends of free schools do not propose to increase taxation, but to change the appropriation of it. A committee was appointed to propose a plan for thoroughly carrying on the principles of this convention.

The following additional resolutions were passed by the convention:

No. 6. *Resolved,* That we are opposed to the old school law, because its operation was contrary to the principles of democratic government. While it professed to be liberal, it gave the avaricious parent an excuse for keeping his children from the school; while it should have furnished intellectual aliment free to all the children of the State, it virtually drove thousands from the schoolhouse, by wounding their pride and branding them as paupers; while it should have discriminated between the right of the child to public beneficence and that of the parent, it often treated unkindly and blasted the hopes of the former, on account of the improvidence or misfortunes of the latter; while it was far better than no system of public education, it did not supply the wants of the rising generation, who were calling for "light, more light still."

No. 7. *Resolved,* That we will most cordially unite with the people of this State and recommend to the next legislature, such amendment of the act of 1848, establishing free schools, as shall make the expenses of supporting such schools over and above the annual revenue of the common school fund, a charge upon the real and personal property in the State, county and town equitably assessed according to a fair and just valuation of such property; and make such other amendments of the law of 1849, as they in their wisdom shall seem to be best; and we recommend that a memorial be circulated in each district of the State, embodying such alterations as to the inhabitants of each district may seem desirable.

—*Syracuse Daily Standard, July 12, 1850*

Free School Convention
Second Day

Afternoon Session

Convention assembled at 2 o'clock, and was called to order by chairman.

Mr Winchell, from the committee on organizing a plan for disseminating information among the voters of the State, to prepare them for the free school issue in November next, reported as follows:

" That they consider a complete and thorough organization, essential to the success of the free school measure, and propose the following plan for consideration:

The appointment of four classes of executive committees.

1 A state central committee to be appointed by this convention, consisting of seven persons, residents of the city of Syracuse.

2 A subcommittee of five in each county, to be appointed by the central committee, and to reside in the shire-town of said county.

3 Another committee of three in each town, to be appointed by the respective county committees, and to reside in the principal village of said town.

4 A district committee of three, in each school district, to be appointed by the respective town committees.

It shall be the duty of these committees to procure and direct the operations of public speakers, to lecture, if possible, in every school district in the State; to publish and circulate all documents tending to the general enlightenment, and to devise and execute such other measures as will, in their estimation, promote the same great object.

It is desired that the Committees in furtherance of this plan, receive and solicit donations in their respective territories; and keep an accurate account of receipts and expenditures, to be reported in some public journal immediately after election.

The district committees shall record the names of all voters in their respective districts, as early as the first of October, and report to the county committees through the town committees, the prospective result of the election, that the former may be advised what sections stand most in need of efficient aid. In like manner and for the same purpose shall the county committees report to the central committee, as early as the 15th of Oct.

To effectively carry out this plan, we earnestly recommend the greatest care in the appointment of the committees, especially that for the State; as on the thorough execution of the measure, its usefulness must entirely depend. They would suggest that where municipal and other civil officers, including postmasters, are *known* to be qualified for these duties, they receive the preference; and that no man shall be made chairman of any committee unless known to possess energy and zeal.

This report was taken up for consideration by sections, and was finally unanimously adopted.

On motion, the aid and cooperation of the press throughout the State was respectfully requested to contribute their influence in the furtherance of the principles of free schools.

The chairman appointed the following gentlemen, residents of Syracuse, as the state central committee: Messrs Chas. P. Sedgwick, Harvey Baldwin, Wm. Jackson, D. P. Phelps, J. M. Winchell, and A. G. Salisbury

Messrs McMasters of N. Y., Prof. Baerman of Troy, Beekman and Whitney of New York, Baldwin of Syracuse, addressed the convention eloquently, pro. and con. on the subject of free schools.

The following resolution, offered by Mr Crandall of Syracuse, was unanimously adopted:

Resolved, That this convention recommend to the several towns of this State, the formation of town associations to secure the discussion of the free school question.

Votes of thanks were tendered the officers of the convention, the city of Syracuse, and its citizens.

When at six o'clock the convention adjourned, sine die.

— *Syracuse Daily Standard, July 12, 1850*

Free School Clarion

We have hitherto neglected to notice the prospectus of a paper to be called the " Free School Clarion," about to be issued from the office of the *Star,* in this city. The paper is to be conducted by W. L. Crandall, Esq., and to be devoted exclusively to the advocacy of free schools, and to sustaining the present law as the surest method of preserving the principle in this State. In the hands of Mr C. the paper will prove an efficient publication, as he is now devoted to that subject, having wholly withdrawn from politics.

— *Syracuse Daily Standard, July 8, 1850*

Kinney & Masters of Syracuse will issue on the 10th inst., a weekly paper, with the above title, to be published until after the election. It will strenuously advocate free schools, and will offer a hearing through its columns to sincere opponents. W. L. Crandall, Esq., is to be editor. . . .

Mr Crandall is a devoted friend of free education, and will throw all his energies into the campaign, in advocacy of the cause. But he nevertheless proposes to open the columns of the Clarion to the discussion of the whole subject, allowing the friends and the foes of the principle involved to be heard. It should, therefore, have a general circulation, that when the question shall be decided, there shall not be, as now, the plea that the people did not understand the subject. Information should be spread abroad — every voter should be brought to exercise his thoughts in the investigation of the whole question in all its hearings and relations. The friends of free schools owe it to themselves and to the cause to contribute the means to send the Clarion into every part of the State.

— *Buffalo Commercial Advertiser, July 9, 1850*

The question of free schools is to form no inconsiderable element in the coming election in this State Its full and free discussion, before the people, is desirable. The Free School Clarion published at Syracuse, discusses the subject on both sides, and is exclusively devoted to it. As a matter of general intelligence, therefore, we insert below the prospectus:

Shall, or shall not, New York have free schools? This question is to be decided by the electors of this State, at the polls in November next. It is admitted by all that the question is one of importance and absorbing **importance.**

Yet this question has never been discussed before the people of New York. It was not discussed in 1849. It was never discussed within the borders of the State, except at the state superintendents' convention, in 1846, and at the state free school convention at Syracuse, which adjourned yesterday. No county or town or neighborhood meetings have been held, at which the principle, the right, the policy, the economy, or the superiority of free schools was discussed. The press of the State has not discussed it. The pulpit has not discussed it. In no form have the important facts and arguments which control this great question, been presented to the people at large.

The object of the Free School Clarion is to meet this state of the case. It will contain a full account of the history of the common school system; its organization; its results. It will also give every view that the great minds of the State can present, for and against free schools. It will contain all the reasons why the change should be made; why the late system does not meet the demands of the present age. In our opinion, the Clarion will be found most valuable for preservation, as furnishing interesting matter not to be found in any existing publication. It is almost superfluous to say, that this information and argument are indispensable to the right decision of this cause at the election.

Each number will contain an able article written by some opponent of free schools. Opponents, as well as friends, will read the Clarion with interest, both sides will be presented. The object is, to have the question understood.

The free school state convention, held at Syracuse on the 10th and 11th of July inst., which was the largest and ablest school convention ever held in New York, if not in the Union — unanimously adopted the following resolution, offered by S. S. Randall, of Albany:

Resolved, That we approve of the establishment of the Free School Clarion, at the city of Syracuse, for the purpose of disseminating as widely as possible information in reference to the address, adopted at the Onondaga county teachers' institute at its last session, and the address of Charles B. Sedgwick, Esq., at a previous session of the institute, among the friends of free schools throughout the State.

The first number of the Clarion was issued on the 10th of July. The second will contain the address of the convention from the pen of Horace Greeley, and the resolutions.

— *Buffalo Commercial Advertiser, July 29, 1850*

This paper will be published at Syracuse until the 1st of November, and will be devoted to the free school question, with reference to the vote of the people at the next election.

It will advocate the principle, that the property of the State should educate the children of the State. It does not approve the manner in which the present school law carries out that principle. But it will maintain that the honor and reputation of New York demands that the people sustain the principle by sustaining the law, and then compel amendments by the Legislature.

All these points will be fully discussed, and some of them by the best minds in the country. The policy of the free schools will be thoroughly presented. How can this great question be intelligently decided, unless thoroughly examined?

The Clarion has another distinct feature. Each number *will contain an able article written by some opponent of free schools*. Opponents, as well as friends, will read the Clarion with interest, for both sides will be presented. The object is to have the question understood.

Every intelligent individual, therefor, who wishes to secure the leading facts, ideas and arguments, pro and con, upon this great question — and in a form convenient for preservation, can now do so for a trifling sum.

— *Albany Argus, August 2, 1850*

The Free School Law

The citizens of Buffalo, friendly to the principle of free schools throughout the State and in favor of sustaining it at the coming election, are requested to meet at the common council chamber on Wednesday evening, October 30, to effect such organization as will bring out a full expression of public sentiment at the polls.

                    O. G. Steele
                    N. H. Gardner
                    H. K. Viele
                    S. S. Jewett
                    Harrison Park
                              Committee for the County of Erie

— *Buffalo Commercial Advertiser, October 29, 1850*

Free Schools

On Wednesday evening, 30th of October, in response to the call, a meeting of citizens was convened in the city council chamber, for the purpose of concerting measures for securing a full vote favorable to a law for the support and maintenance of free schools throughout the State. Organization was effected by the choice of Wm. Lovering, president, Patrick Short and John A. Welmer, vice presidents, and Wm. Treat, secretary.

The object of the meeting having been briefly stated, a motion of Mr O. G. Steele, was sustained, suggesting a committee on resolutions, and a committee on nominations of a vigilance committee, be appointed by the chair.

For a committee on resolutions the president appointed Messrs V. M. Rice, O. G. Steele, and F. C. Brunch.

The committee on resolutions submitted the following with the accompanying preamble, which, on motion, were accepted and adapted.

Whereas, by an act of the Legislature the question of free schools, has been again submitted to a vote of the electors of this State — and whereas, through the influence of the enemies of a system of education which embraces alike the rich and the poor, the children of the laboring man and those of the capitalist, its resubmission was effected before the operations of the law could be tested — and whereas, we have fully tested the benefits of such a system in this city, and believe it to be of vital importance to the security of property and to the hopes and welfare of the children throughout the State — and, whereas, it has become " a fixed fact," that under the operation of the new law, there were added to the schools over one hundred thousand children — a mighty band for weal or woe! — and, whereas, it will be competent for the Legislature to make such amendments to the present law as experience may show to be necessary — and, whereas, in the opinion of this meeting, a vote of the people against repeal, will finally settle the principle of schools, free to all, and bear the highest testimonal of our earnest, desire for the welfare of the country and the perpetuity of its free institutions by intelligent freemen, therefore,

Resolved, That we will make it our business upon the day appointed to test the question, not only to vote against the repeal of the new school law ourselves, but to urge our fellow citizens to do likewise.

The following names of persons were submitted by report of committee to constitute a vigilance committeee and their report adapted.

— *Buffalo Commercial Advertiser, October 31, 1850*

Form of the Ballot

SCHOOL
For the Repeal of the New School Law

SCHOOL
Against the Repeal of the New School Law

The ballot must be so folded as to conceal all the words except the word "School" which must appear on the ballot as folded.

— *Rochester Daily Democrat, October 8, 1850*

The Mechanics on Free Schools

An Address

Adopted by the annual convention of Mechanics' Mutual Protections of the State of New York, held at Syracuse, Aug. 15, 1850;

With the request that every paper in the State of New York friendly to free schools give it an insertion.

Fellow mechanics! Workers of whatever name or occupation! Citizens of every class of this great Empire State.

We are called to act, at our coming election, upon one of the greatest questions, if not the most momentous one, that ever did or ever can agitate a free people. Shall or shall we not have schools free to all children of the commonwealth, of whatever condition or calling?

It being a question, whose decision will not only effect the interests of those now on the stage of action, but will continue to radiate its good or evil effects in an increased ratio of power upon those who are to rise up in our places, to guide the ship of State, and hold in trust the charter of human liberty, it is our duty to act with that consideration which shall result in the accomplishment of the greatest good. To this end, we should suffer no prejudices to bias our judgments, no personal piques to warp our feelings — no mercenary motive to thwart our generous impulses — but rather consider the subject calmly in all its bearings, then rise above all selfish feelings, and act wholly for the good of our Race and for those who are yet too young to feel, know and act for themselves.

Believing, then, that the establishment of a system of free schools is called for by right and justice, this convention should not shrink from urging upon every citizen of this State who believes that the child should be " trained up in the way he should go," that " knowledge is power," to put his shoulder to the work and help to triumphantly sustain the decision once made by the people, that our schools should be free.

There is no one, probably, among all the opponents of the measure, that will deny the great and inestimable worth of a good education, or that republican institutions can never live and thrive among an ignorant people. They all admit these truths, yet many of them will deny any right to Government to diffuse intelligence among its subjects. They seem to forget it is to Government they are indebted for their success, and their right to acquire and hold property — that it is the intelligence of the people that makes their rights respected.

Property is aquired by labor — by sweating and toiling. It is the strong sinews and muscles that fill the coffers of the world. It is by the intelligence and industry of its people that a nation prospers and grows rich. If that industry is guided by knowledge, the rise of the nation to power and renown, is just in proportion to the perfection of their knowledge. The truth of this is seen in the striking contrasts that are found wherever ignorance of knowledge is enthroned, and is strongly exhibited between the Scotchman and the Hottentot, the European and the Indian, the Englishman and the Australian, or the people of the United States and the people of Mexico.

If a nation's wealth is wrought out by the toil of its subjects — if its greatness is built up by those subjects — it must follow that it owes them reciprocal obligations. It should accrue to them the greatest amount of good possible in all things concerning their temporal affairs, and open to them such streams of light as shall tend to enlarge their mental powers and increase their comforts and pleasures, thereby improving their condition in all respects, while at the same time it would build a bulwark of defense in the hearts of its subjects that no enemy could break down.

In the words of one of education's most able champions, " The State in its sovereign capacity has the deepest interest in this matter." If it would spread the means of intelligence and self-culture over its entire surface, making them diffusive as sunshine, causing them to penetrate into every hamlet and dwelling, and like the vernal sun quickening into life the seeds of usefulness and worth, wherever the prodigal hand of Virtue may have scattered them; it would call into existence an order of men who would improve its arts, impart wisdom to its counsels, and extend the beneficent sphere of its charities. Not for its own sake only, should it assume this work. It is a corollary from the axioms of its constitution that every child born within its borders, should be enlightened. In its paternal character it is bound, even to those who can make no requital. Sacredly is it bound to develop all the existing capacities, and to secure the utmost attainable well-being of that vast crowd and throng of men who, without being known during life beyond the neighboring hills — without leaving any proud name behind them after death, still by their lifelong industry, fill up, as it were, drop by drop, the mighty stream of the country's prosperity.

There is not a barbarous nation that has any specific established government, but makes ample provision for the comparatively superior education of its heir of sovereignty. How much more needful then, that *all* should be prepared for their responsibilities where all are born to the right to hold and exercise controlling power!

It is the State and property holders who reap the increased value that honest industry gives to everything.

The poor day-laborer receives only a stipulated pittance of four, six, or ten shillings for his day's toil, which with the vicissitudes that surround him, is too often barely enough to keep together the body and soul of those dependent on his hands for support. Now his toil, combined with that of his fellows, may have the effect to increase the value of the property in the vicinity, five, ten, fifteen, or even one hundred per cent; yet does he receive any of the pecuniary benefit? It falls to the lot of the property holders and tends to increase the disparity, and is even too often used to augment the poor man's misery.

This being the case, and no one can truly deny it who will look at the facts as they exist — it is but justice that property, inasmuch as it is the creation of the State, gathered by the hand of toil, and held in trust by its citizens for their present use, to be transmitted to coming generations, should be used by the State to enoble and elevate those, by giving to all people the means of that light and knowledge which shall enable them rightly to understand their responsibilities and duties as sentient beings and citizens of a common republic.

Let the opposers of free schools make a thorough and candid examination of all of our jails, prisons and other places of criminal punishment — let him look into the records of our courts, and see what a startling disparity is exhibited between the uneducated and those possessing a common school education. Let him sit down with an unbiased mind and contemplate, even in his own circle of acquaintance, the great difference in the capacity of those of equal natural abilities who are educated, and those who are not. Let him sum the advantages that would accrue to himself, to themselves and to the community, were they possessed of the knowledge to be acquired in a well conducted common school. Let him go into a neighborhood where the mass are illiterate, ignorant and superstitious (for superstition as well as crime always goes hand in hand with ignorance) and mark how Discord holds revel — how crime stalks about and property is held at low value. Let him visit it again and find the place occupied by intelligent citizens and mark the change. Thrift and order now bear sway, while property has doubled and trebled in value. Let him make these and other legitimate fruits of a truly enlightened people, and he will no longer oppose the spread of that knowledge which must flow from a well supported system of free schools.

There are many who oppose the present law and yet are in favor of a free system. They object to some details of this law, preferring others instead. Now it can not be expected that any law, especially one of so great magnitude, can at its inception be made perfect and satisfactory to all. It is not in the constitution of human law givers. Let the law be made as it will, it can not suit in every particular all those who are favorable to the principle involved. Why, then, should those who are friends of education wrangle about small points and details, and thus lose the good we all so much prize?

There are those who are deadly opposed to the dissemination of knowledge, who will battle against any and every system that can be devised to dissipate the darkness of ignorance. It is with such characters we clasp hands as " hail fellows well met " when we conclude to throw our influence in the present crisis against the present law. And a defeat at the coming election would be hailed by them as an emphatic quietus, now and forever, on the subject of free schools in this State.

It is in view, then, of the welfare and progress of untold numbers, and of our future prosperity as a people, that we would most earnestly urge upon every friend of universal education reform, to lay aside his prejudices, and give the cause a hearty support.

Then may we have the opportunity to give the law a fair test, correct its defects, and eventually make it what the wants of the people demand. It has not yet had a fair trial. It was met on the very threshold of its adoption by the most virulent opposition. Every means was resorted to by a portion of its opponents that could be devised, to render it odious and burdensome, and thus set the wavering against it, and make its strongest friends doubt its expediency. In part they have succeeded — so far as to induce our Legislature again to refer it to the People.

And now let the people thunder back to the Legislature their displeasure in such tones as shall teach our servants not again to put in jeopardy the will of such a vast majority as last November bade our schools be free.

T. E. Wetmore
Wm. McAvoy of Rochester
J. A. Haneschuck of N. Y.
R. Sparks
Chas. Sentell of Waterloo
Committee

— *Journal of Education and Teachers Advocate, September 16, 1850*

The National Educational Convention
(Held at Philadelphia, Pa., August 28–31, 1850)

The 3d day's proceedings commenced, Mr Henry, of Washington, in the chair, with the discussion of the annexed resolution, submitted by Mr McElligott, of New York, upon which sprung up the most interesting and animated debate of the session.

The resolution is as follows, viz:

Resolved, As the judgment of this convention, that a due regard to mere political interests, no less than the higher obligations of Christian duty, requires of every state to provide, by general tax or otherwise, a system of free schools, accessible to every child of suitable age within its limits, and affording to all equal advantages for a sound and efficient course of instruction, physical, moral and intellectual.

The resolution was discussed by J. W. Bulkley, of New York; G. F. Thayer, of Mass.; Dr Cutter of Mass.; Joel B. Sutherland, of Penn.; Mr Steckman of Ohio; Mr Burleigh of Baltimore; Mr Pennypacker of Penn.; Nathan Nathans of Philadelphia; James N. McElligott of New York; Henry Hazen of New York; Mr Ryerson, Superintendent of Public Instruction of Upper Canada; Mr Forbes of Mass.; Henry Barnard of Conn.;

Mr Green of Massachusetts; Mr Rainey of Cincinnati; Mr Hamill of New Jersey; Bishop Potter of Penn.; Mr Lee of New York; Dr Elder of Philadelphia; Mr Clark of Louisiana; Professor Rogers of Virginia; Mr Newbury of Michigan; Rev. Washburn of New York; Jos. Cowperwaithe of Philadelphia; Mr Ludlow, of Philadelphia.

The debate was upon the question whether the convention should recommend *free schools,* as distinguished from schools generally; and also whether there should be a general tax. Several amendments were offered, and voted down. Another discussion was upon the question whether the schools should be styled "public" or "free schools." An amendment by striking out the latter words and inserting "public' was voted down.

Mr Barnard, of Connecticut, offered an amendment as a substitute, designed to get over the difficulty, which was also voted down.

Bishop Potter, of Pennsylvania, offered a substitute, which was voted down.

The original resolution was finally adopted, by a vote nearly unanimous.
— *Journal of Education and Teachers Advocate, September 16, 1850*

Free Schools

Mr Editor: I had the pleasure last evening of attending a meeting of the inhabitants of the fifth ward, in this village, held at the schoolhouse. A. W. Jackson, Esq., was called to the chair, and Col. Smith offered the following resolution, which, after a very animated discussion pro and con, was adopted by an overwhelming majority:

Resolved, That we are in favor of free schools as the best safeguards of our free government; and that as the best means of securing them, we will vote for the present free school law at the coming election, and will use our influence to have it so amended by the next Legislature, that the taxes for the support of the schools shall be more equitably assessed upon the property in the State.

Would it not be a good plan for the friends of free schools to hold meetings in their respective school districts throughout the county, and give the subject a thorough discussion?

Broome county did well on that question last fall; but I hope she will make a cleaner sweep this time, and give so large a majority for free schools that our representative in the Legislature, whoever he may be, will not deem it necessary to ask his constituents *again* if they meant what they said when they voted for free schools

Fourth Ward
— *Binghamton Republican, September 24, 1850*

Education by Law

Mr Editor

The most benevolent and philanthropic minds of the age are pleading earnestly in behalf of the thorough education of the people; for upon this depends everything great and good to the human family. If this be the fact, let all who think of voting against the free school law, reflect that their opposition springs from a lack of proper love for their fellow men. If any one desires to be good, and to pursue the noblest life, keep this fact before him, that the thoughts of the wisest are the most truthful, and the feelings of the purest are the most correct. If, then, an individual finds himself inclined against the course of the best men, let him reflect that he is not as good as he should be. It is dangerous for a man to vote against the free education of the people, for that is a question of such momentous moral consequences, that our regard for it springs from our love for man, and our opposition to it, is due to our selfishness and our hatred of our fellow men! To him therefore, who votes against the law will be imputed baseness of character, and so will all the good and true of the State and world regard it.

The people *must* be educated. Some parents are too poor to educate their children, and many who are not poor are too base to do so. Shall the children of the poor be held accountable for their parents' poverty — shall we say to them, "you are to blame for having poor parents?" God forbid! Shall we say to the children of base parents, 'you are guilty of your parents' folly, and it is good enough for you to be bred in ignorance?' God forbid!

We know that all poverty, vice, crime, and misery result from ignorance. It has starved millions in Europe; it has impoverished 25,000,000 out of 30,000,000 of the population of Great Britain. It has kept the old world in despotism and superstition. It has filled the jails, poor houses, penitentiaries, hospitals and asylums of this country. It has thrown 20,000 of the people of the city of New York, into damp and filthy cellars, where they eat, sleep and lodge in darkness and away from fresh air. It has built all our cities against the laws of health, and they are slaughter houses of humanity. Forty thousand people in Cincinnati, where I reside, get scarcely a fresh breath of air during the whole year. Ignorance has done all this, and ten thousand times more injury to the human family.

All evils are to be removed by education, and he who votes against the development of the young, votes for all the vices, crime, poverty and woe of the world.

If the law be imperfect, let it be amended by the legislature; but let not the the system of free schools be voted down.

Yours &c,
L. A. HINE

— *Syracuse Daily Standard, July 8, 1850*

"The question before the people is not schools or no schools as I have frequently had occasion to remind its advocate. W."

I quote from memory, but think this the spirit, if not verbatim, of "W's" language. And I take the position that to many children (and the children more than any one else are interested), in effect the question is — "schools or no schools?"

Under the operation of the old law, poor parents dreaded the rate bill, and many were too proud to send their sons and daughters to school under the sanction of a law which counted them paupers. The effect was, that a great many thousands were kept out of the common schools. To them the doors, leading to light and hope, were virtually closed. For them there were "no schools."

Under the encouraging operation of the new school law most of these children have been gathered in. For them there are now " schools."

In most of the districts where there is a population made of persons engaged in different occupations, the increase of the number of children brought into the schools has been beyond anticipation. It has ranged from 12 to 100 scholars.

No man can know how hard it was for many to pay a rate bill, unless he has been the father of a large family of children, which he has supported by his daily toil. By the time a parent thus situated has paid his rent, bought his wood, his flour, butter, pork or beef, tea, clothes, shoes, (if he can afford one-half of these articles) for himself, wife and 5 or 9 children, he can have but little left, saying nothing of church rent) with which to pay a rate bill. Neither can a selfish, spiritless man, appreciate the feelings of a noble father when he knew, that if his children went to school at all, they must go as paupers. Away with praise for a law which pressed thus upon man's dignity, upon his self-respect.

Sustain the present law and let the children know and feel that to drink at the fountain of knowledge is their right, that henceforth they may partake freely, and their children after them and so on from generation to generation far into a better future, and a shout of joy and gladness shall arise from the fullness of their young hearts, making the hills and the valleys of the Empire State ring for very joy.

"A good time's coming boys
Wait a little longer."

—*Buffalo Commercial Advertiser, August 23, 1850*

Public Education

The reference of the free school law back to the people of this State for their decision at the coming election has given rise to considerable discussion, not only upon the merits of the law itself, but also upon the subject of education in its general bearing upon society. Strange as it may appear, there is a class in the community, who contend that the child should be restricted to the common English branches, while another, and we believe and trust, the larger class claim that every child should have the opportunity of reaching the highest attainments.

That a liberal system of instruction is best calculated to ensure permanency to republican institutions, there would seem to be no chance for more than one opinion. Our government is one of equal rights, intended, as far as government can do it, to promote an equalization of gifts and blessings, and so far as education can be made a gift of the government, it should be universal. In its quality and character, it should not stop short of the utmost expansion of the mind.

The constitutions of our nation and state governments place all men upon an equality in the right to vote, and it is but a natural and necessary accompaniment of that right that their intellectual advantages should be equalized. To give a man power, and then to deny him that intelligence which is indispensable to enable him to exercise it understandingly, is to confer not only a useless but a fatal gift. The elective franchise conferred upon a body of men incapable of reasoning or reflecting, would destroy the government it was intended to support. When we say we believe in the capacity of men for self-government, we always pay them the compliment of supposing them to be enlightened. An ignorant man may have the right to vote, but the most rampant demagogue could not believe in his capacity, and it is only safe to allow him this privilege upon the principle that the intelligent will govern the ignorant, and render subordinate that portion of the community, although entitled only to equal privilege and power. The only equitable and safe principle is to render as far as practicable all parts alike intelligent.

So far has the principle of the necessity of education in a free government been admitted, that in every State all parties have united in establishing systems of instruction. These systems have been limited at first by lack of pecuniary means, but have expanded with the increasing wealth of the country, until even our common schools have become the means of a wide range of instruction.

Our educational as well as our political system is intended to break down all inequalities and place men upon the same platform of duties, honors and advantages. The public school system should not be degraded by the preservation of better systems for the rich and privileged, which tend to classify society, and keep up those invidious distinctions, which it should be the aim of a government like ours to overthrow. The rich as well as the poor should be proud to partake of it, and when it reaches such perfection that those who would be separatists can have no excuse for seeking a more liberal education elsewhere, it will be a day of true rejoicing to all the friends of rational progress in liberty.

— *Syracuse Daily Standard, July 9, 1850*

We are aware that not a few of our readers are opposed to the present free school law, if not to free schools under any circumstances. We are aware, too, that they claim to be reasonable men, and hence ought not to refuse to listen to what may be said in defence of the principle, while its friends profess a willingness to allow due weight to all that may be said against it. As for ourselves, we believe it to be a righteous provision — one which is in accordance with the spirit of rational reform which marks the present century — and, when properly regulated, one which is capable of working out enduring benefits to the country. We do not say this particularly in reference to the present act — which in our opinion is imperfect in several of its provisions, and, perhaps in some particulars, unequal and oppressive — but we speak of the principle itself — believing at the same time that the law sought to be repealed is in the main wise and liberal, and as near perfection as an average of laws equally complicated and important. The machinery which regulates our common schools, has ever been most difficult of such an adjustment as would secure its highest efficiency; and hence legislation upon this subject has been varied and frequent, and a long series of years has scarcely been able to perfect the system as established under the old law. Is it reasonable, then, to look for perfection in the first draft of a law which makes such important changes in the whole system, and to condemn all the provisions of that law because a few of them need amendment and modification? We cannot so regard it. The friends of reform were a long time engaged in procuring the passage of an act establishing free schools in this State, and they had a right to ask and expect at least a fair trial of such act, before its provisions were bitterly assailed and before a clamor should be raised for its repeal. The act again submitting it to the people — almost immediately after they had sustained it by an overwhelming majority — was an insult to their intelligence and stability; and we shall be disappointed if their verdict is not an emphatic repetition of their former decision. Amendment and not repeal is what the public sentiment requires; and we doubt very much whether the intelligent voters of the Empire State are so soon ready to do an act defeating their own interests and demonstrating their inconsistency.

As to the idea itself of having our primary institutions of learning free to all who will avail themselves of the important benefits which they confer, it appears to us there should be but one opinion. Indeed, we much mistake the temper of the times, if so beneficent a reform has been agitated merely for the purpose of an early and more effective defeat. The interests of a people must ever be deeply involved in the character and success of the provisions which may be made for the education of the rising generation, and in the means employed to secure the benefits of such education to the largest possible number. In the intelligence and virtue of the people must ever be the strongest guaranty of the stability of a republic; and that man who does most to disseminate the principles of morality and truth, to bring all the youths of the land under a salutary mental and moral discipline, and thus labors to enlighten and elevate the common understanding, he is the greatest benefactor, and deserves most of the people he is faithfully serving. And in aspiring thus to deserve well of one's country, it becomes a question of interest how the great object is best accomplished without imposing undue burdens upon those not naturally compelled to bear them, and how far individuals are morally under obligations to make sacrifice, if need be, for the general good. Free schools, we are told, demand too many of these, but the experience of other States is a conclusive answer to the objection, and the reflection which we have been able to bestow upon the subject produce the conviction that the advantage which the individual derives from the general benefits more than counterbalances the petty sacrifices which he may be called upon to make. More anon.

— *Canajoharie Radii* (editorial), *June 6, 1850*[1]

Free Schools

The importance of the subject of education — the interest which must attach itself to the means which are proposed to elevate its standard, and to secure its universal dissemination — are surely a sufficient apology for

---

[1] James Arkell, manufacturer. was a descendant of Sir Hugh De Aracle and of Sir George Rooke, names famous in English history. He was born October 16, 1829, in Berkshire, England, emigrated with his parents to America, and settled on a tarm near Canajoharie, N. Y. He early developed literary taste and while yet a boy began lecturing. He was for many years manager and proprietor of the Canajoharie Radii, and in 1859 he and Adam Smith embarked in the manufacture of paper sacks, which has since developed into a very large and lucrative business. Mr. Arkell was a staunch Republican. He was State Senator and a power in the councils of his party. He was a ready and eloquent speaker and a powerful writer on political and financial affairs. He included among his friends many of the eminent statesmen of his day and was a frequent and welcome visitor to General Grant in his last illness. He was the chief promotor and owner of the Mt. McGregor Railroad and for some years the principal proprietor of the Albany Evening Journal. In 1853 he married Sarah H. Bartlett, who was born in 1835 at Philmont, and is a daughter of Ebenezer Bartlettt of Massachusetts.

frequent discussion and reflection. Especially is that system which proposes to make free to every child in the State the important blessing of education, worthy of our most serious consideration; nor do we see the propriety of permitting a difference of opinion to arrest an unreserved expression of our sentiments on the subjects. The moral and intellectual training of the rising generation — of the future defenders of the liberties which we cherish, of the mothers of the heroes and statesmen who are to become the hope and the pride of another day — is a subject of momentous importance; and it becomes us as it became our fathers, and will become our children, to guard well the institutions committed to our and their charge, and so to modify and improve them as to meet the wants of a progressing age, and to make them the strongest safe-guards of the blessings which are our, and will be their, inheritance.

It is a trite saying, but one which bears repetition well, that in the virtue and intelligence of a people, is the guaranty of their liberties and happiness. He, then, who devotes his energies most successfully to the cause of education — to the perfection of that system whose exclusive object is the mental and moral elevation of the youth of our land, is most of a patriot and philanthropist, and deserves most of his country. His services may not at all times be appreciated — he has frequently to combat the supposed interest, and the prejudice of community, in defending his cherished theory, and becomes discouraged at the indifference which on almost every hand greets a question which he justly regards as of the most vital importance. But experience, that truthful teacher, must eventually assert its prerogative of decision — must make manifest whatever of merit may be contained in the systems he advocates — and ultimate triumph will be his rich reward. Let, then, the advocate of a liberal education take courage, nor heed the interested clamors around him.

Whether a well-regulated system of free schools is the one best calculated to secure the great object of the popular intelligence and virtue, can hardly be regarded as an unsolved problem, since in every instance where it has been tried it has worked well. Unfortunately the law establishing free schools in this State, bears upon it the mark of the enemies of the principle itself; and its admitted imperfections have been industrially magnified and harped upon, until some suppose, however vainly, that the idea of free schools is unpopular, and will be discarded by the people. The present law, most unfairly we think, is made the criterion of the capacity of the system which it pretends to establish; and it is our firm conviction that it is amendment and not repeal which the popular sentiment requires, and which will be most wise and beneficent. With the law then we have at present nothing to do — we go for the leading principle — believing that the law should be and will be made acceptable by judicious alterations as suggested by experience.

And what are the objections to free schools? They are not numerous; and as some of them are ably met by the address adopted at the recent convention, we will quote from that document:

Whoever among you has had patience to follow an opponent of the law through his devious course of reasoning, well knows that his citadel is the assumption that it is wrong to tax one man to educate another's children,

JAMES ARKELL
Owner of the Canajoharie Radii during the struggle
for free schools
(Picture furnished through courtesy of Mr
Warren Scott, editor, Canajoharie Radii)

unless it be the children of absolute paupers. This assumption, if conceded, is fatal not to free schools merely, but to any common schools whatever. If elementary education be properly and only a parental duty, then the State should leave it wholly to the voluntary and unobserved efforts and combinations of parents. Then the taxation of a district to build a schoolhouse, is usurpation and extortion. Then all the laws which have been passed, making compulsory provision for common schools, or intended to increase their efficiency, are impertinent, agrarian and confiscating. Yet few of our opponents will venture to take this or any other ground of radical hostility to the free school principle. The difference between their position and ours is mainly one of degree. We abide constantly by the principles on which only can any public provision for education be justified; they stop half way, and in so doing, condemn their own course in coming so far.

To the assertion that it is wrong to tax A to provide instruction for the children of B, we reply that we would tax both A and B, for school purposes, each in proportion to his ability, not as parents but as possessors of property, and because property is deeply interested in the education of all. There is no farm, no bank, no mill, no shop (unless it be a grog-shop) which is not more valuable and more profitable to its owner if located among a well educated, than if surrounded by an ignorant population. Simply as a matter of interest, we hold it the duty of property to itself to provide education for all. Not therefore, as the children of A, or of B, but as children of New York, her future cultivators, artisans, instructors, citizens, electors and rulers, we plead for the education of all at the cost for the benefit of all. In a community where a single vote cast in ignorance may involve the country in war, in aggression and untold calamities, property cannot afford that there be any considerable proportion of ignorant voters nor ignorant mothers of voters. To whomsoever shall urge the duty to B to educate his children in spite of his relative poverty, we say, urge upon him that duty to the extent of your powers of persuasion, and we will second you as well as we may.

After the State has done all in its power, there will still remain enough for every father to do in the way of educating and disciplining his children. But this rudimentary intellectual culture of the common school is an undertaking not of individual parents, but of the community — the State, and the State alone should provide therefore as it provides for its other institutions. It has very wisely declined the care of public worship, which in other countries forms a very important portion of its duties and the public burdens, and has nobly assumed the charge of popular education, which other governments too generally repudiate. Having thus resolved that B's children shall be educated, not for his sake, but in furtherance of its own policy, and in deference to its own safety, the State would do wrong to tax his property to defray the cost of this safeguard to property. The common schools of New York are to her what their respective standing armies are to Russia and Austria; and it would be as fair to support the latter by a head-tax as the former. The child of indigence who attends the district school is discharging a public duty, and should be as welcome there as the heir of affluence and social distinction. He should be made to feel that his due training and development are the subject of general solicitude. Property can better afford to educate four children in the schoolhouse than one in the street. The teacher, when fairly remunerated, as he too often is not, is a far less expensive functionary than the sheriff, the district attorney or the judge. One burglar or thief costs more to the community than all the teachers of an average township. The statistics of our state prisons prove that at least three-fourths of our criminals are drawn from that one-fourth of our population which has enjoyed the least educational advantages — mainly no such advantages at all. Let our common schools be abolished tomorrow, and property would soon be taxed many times their annual cost in the shape of robberies, riots and depredations. For every teacher dismissed, a new deputy sheriff, constable or policemen would be required. And the dismissal from our schools of those children of poor but not abject parents whom the free school law has called into them, would be identical in principle with the destruction of the schools altogether. A large portion of our children would be educated if there were no common schools, but these, we know, would not be.

But we are asked why a citizen who has worked, and saved, and thrived, should pay for schooling the children of his neighbor, who has drank, and frolicked and squandered, till he has little or nothing left. We answer, he should do it in order that these needy and disgraced children may not become what their father is, and so, very probably, in time a public burden as criminals or paupers. The children of the drunkard and reprobate have a hard enough lot, without being surrendered to his judgment and self-denial for the measure of their education. If they are to have no more instruction than he shall see fit and feel able to pay for, a kind Heaven must regard them with sad compassion, and man ought not utterly to leave them uncared for and subjected to such moral and intellectual influences only as their desolate homes must afford. To stake the education of our State's future rulers and mothers on such parents' ideas of their own ability and their children's moral needs, is madness — is treason to the common weal. They will be quite enough detained even from free schools by supposed inability to clothe or spare them; but to cast into the wrong scale a dead weight of paternal appetite and avarice, in the form of rate-bills, is to consign them heartlessly to intellectual darkness and moral perdition.

And in truth the argument for taxing in equal amounts the improvidently destitute and the frugally affluent father of a family for school purposes, is precisely as strong for taxing them in equal amounts to build courthouses, support paupers, diffuse justice, or for any other purpose whatever. Nay, it is even stronger; for the drinking, thriftless, idle parent, is far more likely to bring expense on the community, in the shape of crime, to be punished, or pauperism to be supported, than his thrifty and temperate neighbor, and, according to our adversaries' logic, he should pay more taxes on his log cabin and patch of weedy garden, than that neighbor on his spacious mansion and bounteous farm. The former will probably turn off two paupers to one from the latter, and should be assessed in a pauper rate bill, accordingly. And his argument from parental misconduct against the justice of free schools is of a piece with the rest.

—Canajoharie Radii, July 25, 1850

Free Schools

Are the friends of free schools aware that a vigorous effort is being made to defeat them at the November election? Several papers have been established for the express purpose of preparing the people to vote against the system — meetings are held, and every exertion is put forth to carry their point — and unless these exertions are met by a corresponding effort on the part of its friends, large as was the majority in its favor, the system may be defeated. Should it unfortunately be defeated, bear in mind that it will be the result of apathy and indifference; and years may elapse before another opportunity is afforded to establish this great and benevolent principle. Be up and doing, then. Canvass your districts — enlighten the popular mind on the subject, and there will be no danger. Do not permit your opponents successfully to confound the defects in the details of the present law with the principle itself — they are up to this trick, and if successful, they will claim the result as a verdict against free schools however established. The following is from the pen of S. S. Randall, Dept. Supt. of Com. Schools, and we invite to it the serious attention of the reader:

"I sincerely trust the friends of universal education will leave no effort untried to sustain this noble principle. Upon their faithful exertions everything will depend. It is from apathy alone that we have anything to fear. The official returns of the Department will show an accession during the present year of upward of one hundred thousand children to our common schools beyond the number heretofore embraced. This fact alone should be decisive of the contest; and I could wish it were generally known and understood. The intellectual and moral culture of 100,000 souls, it does seem to me should outweigh every paltry consideration of mere pecuniary interest. Every true friend to the lasting welfare and permanent improvement of his kind, should rally to the rescue of this vast army of immortal beings from ignorance and its disastrous results. By our action this fall we virtually exclude from, or admit to, the blessings of education, one hundred thousand of the youth of our State."

Where are the clergy, and Christians of every denominations at this momentous crisis? Every pulpit in the land should resound on this great theme in tones which should carry conviction to the most unthinking and selfish. "Inasmuch as ye have done it to one of the least of these, my brethren ye have done it unto me," and here are one hundred thousand "little ones" appealing to us for the bread of life.

— *Canajoharie Radii, October 3, 1850*

The School Laws

One of the most important questions to be passed upon by the people at the coming election, is that submitted to them by the Legislature, in reference to the repeal of the act of March 1849, called the "Free School Law." The law alluded to, it was discovered, when it became necessary to carry it into effect, was entirely unsuited to the purposes for which it was designated, and under the specious exterior of a measure to make the common schools of the State free to all, was better calculated to disorganize the districts, and in the end, destroy the usefulness of the system. Petitions,

almost without number, poured in upon the Legislature at its last session, asking the amendment or repeal of the law; but the law-givers dodged alike all questions of amendment and repeal, and passed an act submitting it to the people, to decide by ballot, whether or not the law should be repealed. The Legislature, having failed to do its duty, the people are called on to act, and in a manner, too, the least calculated to give a definite and correct expression to their opinions and wishes. They can only vote for or against the repeal of the law. If the repeal succeeds the old system is revived, and continues in force as it was before the passage of the law of 1849, until it shall be amended or a new one again substituted. If the vote shall be against the repeal, the only direct effect is to approve and establish the law as it is. The matters involved in the question are in the highest degree important, as well in regard to the interests of education, which should receive the first attention, as to the rights of individuals and communities. That they may receive proper consideration, as far as depends, on us, we propose to devote a reasonable space from time to time to such communications and selections as shall fairly present the various arguments; and for that purpose, we solicit well written original articles of moderate length from those who are disposed to give the subject their attention. We publish this week the resolutions of the mass meeting at Hampton, Oneida co., which are moderate in tone and take ground in favor of repeal.
— *Binghamton Democrat, September 12, 1850*

Important Fact

The Deputy Superintendent of Common Schools, S. S. Randall, Esq., states in an official letter from the department, dated the 28th ultimo, " that the returns received during the present year thus far, show an accession of upwards of one hundred thousand children to our common schools, beyond the number heretofore embraced.
— *Binghamton Republican, September 26, 1850*

A Free School Mass Convention

Mr Stuart: With a commendable zeal and interest in the well-being of the common schools of our county, our town superintendent, and others having immediate charge of the schools in this village, have made preparations for holding a teachers' institute in this place during the ensuing two weeks, commencing on Monday next. It is hoped, that this effort to prepare and improve teachers for their arduous duties, will be met with commensurate zeal and interest on the part of teachers, and the public at large; that the movers in this object will not only have the assistance of those capable of instruction, but that they will be aided by the countenance of our citizens, both male and female.

And, as the time is approaching when the fate of the free schools is to be decided, at the ballot box — when the people are to decide whether a landed aristocracy shall blot out the people's luminaries, or whether they shall be free to all — it has been suggested that, some time during the session of the institute, a mass convention of the friends of free schools, be holden, that the people of Broome may be heard on this question, prior to its final decision. I would suggest that Thursday, the 24th inst, be designated as the

day for holding said convention, and if the proper persons for calling such convention, shall see proper to do so, it is to be hoped that every friend of the cause will be on hand, and that those who are opposed to the question will also be there, to hear what is said on the occasion, and to advance such arguments as they may have in support of their side of the question.
— *Binghamton Republican, October 11, 1850*

The Anti-Free School Movements

Every day shows that the opponents of this law are in danger of becoming enemies to the principle of free schools, and if the law is repealed, it will be next to impossible to pass another, even on a better foundation. The true way to remedy the evil complained of, is to amend the law, instead of repealing it.

The Free School Clarion, published at Syracuse, thus defines the position of those who are in favor of keeping our present law, and making it better.

"To vote down the law would be childish, if the majority are in favor of any law for free schools. It would be saying that the State of New York have not wisdom enough to make a free school law to satisfy themselves. For, if the law is bad — as it is — then amend it. To vote down a law would be saying we are incapable of amending it. This would appear childish to the whole civilized world, and, after accomplished, to those who did it.

"Our position is this: In favor of schools absolutely free to all; property to pay the tuition therein; and in favor of amending the present law, so that the requisite amount over the public money shall be assessed upon the property of the whole State."

The N. Y. Independent says in relation to the proposed publication of a newspaper to advocate the views of opponents of the law, "think of it — a paper established in the State of New York, in the year 1850, to put down free schools! Tell it not in Austria. The Pope will of course know all about it through Bishop Hughes."
— *Utica Daily Gazette, September 2, 1850*

Free Schools — Mr Randall

The Syracuse Journal of May 18, published a portion of our remarks of week before last, on the free school law, and appends to them the following among other remarks of the same tenor:

"The free soil organ at Cortland, has a strange way of manifesting its sympathies for freedom. It is death to the free school law. We understand it is the special organ of Henry S. Randall, the defeated Secretary of State. Public rumor has it, that the above article, and others of the like kind, are got up by him, to show what *he* would have done, had he prevailed over Secretary Morgan. It is not unlikely that Mr Randall may be the candidate for the same office, the second time, or some other state officer, as he is becoming the lion of the party.

"It looks strange at Syracuse, that he should select opposition to "free schools" as his hobby to ride on. We can tell him, that the hobby can't enter the course in Onondaga. We doubt whether there can fifty men be found in Syracuse to go against *free schools*. His popularity even among Hunkers, will fail him, if he rides such a hobby. We cannot believe that the voters of the State will hesitate a moment, to declare by the most decisive vote ever taken on any occasion, that education is a public interest, and that "the children of the State shall be educated upon the property of the State."

We give the above as a *specimen* of the warfare waged against the gentleman whose name stands at the head of this article, by certain whig presses. Their *motives* for so doing, we leave all to judge for themselves. They are sufficiently apparent.

Where the Journal got its "public rumor" that we are the "special organ" of Mr Randall, or that we speak for him on the subject of free school law, we are at a loss to know. At all events, it is utterly untrue. We neither claim nor possess any authority to speak for him on this or any other matter. He is in no wise responsible for anything that appears in our columns. We do not even know what course he will pursue in relation to the free school law.

Early in our publication of the Democrat, we were requested by Mr Randall neither to republish the encomiums which were being from time to time lavished on him by the democratic presses of the State, nor reply to any attack from whig quarters. Hitherto we have rigidly observed his request. In the present instance, we felt that justice both to ourselves and to him, demanded the expression we have made.

— *Cortland Democrat, from Syracuse Daily Standard, May 28, 1850*

Below are printed various letters to newspapers in opposition to free schools and the answers to some of them:

The Free School Law — Opposition to It

We publish below a call of citizens of the county, for a mass meeting to be held at Hampton, Aug. 22d (tomorrow) in opposition to the provisions of the free school law. We owe an apology to the gentlemen concerned, for having omitted its publication till so late a date, but as we gave orders two weeks since for its insertion, we supposed till yesterday that they had been complied with. Our apology is that the illness of the publisher, and the absence of two persons connected with the paper, have thrown so many duties upon the editor, the omission was overlooked, in the press of business.

We the undersigned, tax payers and others opposed to the provisions of the so called free school law, do hereby unite with our fellow citizens throughout the county in recommending a *mass meeting*, at Hampton on Thursday, August 22, 1850, at 11 o'clock, a. m., of all such persons as are opposed to the unequal, unjust and oppressive features of said act; and to take such measures as the meeting, when convened, shall think advisable, to express our decided disapprobation by a vigorous and united rally at the polls of the ensuing election in opposition to this odious measure.

Speakers will attend and address the meeting. A general attendance is respectfully requested.

[Signed by 285 persons.]

— *Utica Daily Gazette, August 21, 1850*

The Free School Law

It has excited considerable surprise that a law, which was adopted by a vote so nearly unanimous that its opposers were hardly worth the counting, was assailed almost immediately upon its going into operation, by the most determined opposition and that now, a vote nearly equal to that by which it was adopted, is ready to be cast for its abolition. The popular vote by which the law was adopted has placed it out of the power of the Legislature to amend or modify, and although there are features in it which all approve, it is thought impracticable to reject some and retain others, and the opponents of certain sections are obliged to advocate the repeal of the entire act. That the law is defective and objectionable, is sufficiently evidenced by the storm of opposition that manifested itself, immediately after its provisions went into operation. It is a little curious, however that parties with different interests unite in opposing the law. Thus the country voters oppose it because it imposes a tax upon them disproportionate to their population, and they are jealous of the cities. The cities incline to think their situation rather worse than that of the country. Taxation is at the bottom of the fault-finding and probably as much is chargeable to unequal and unjust assessments, as to anything else.

At the meeting to be held to-day at Hampton, the opponents of the law will make a clear representation of their views, and it will be interesting to all who are concerned in this question (and who is not?) to hear a lucid exposition of the defects, which practical experience has discovered in the existing act.

—*Utica Daily Gazette, August 22, 1850*

Mass Meetings of the Opponents of the Present Free School Law

Pursuant to call a meeting of the citizens of Oneida county, opposed to the present free school law, assembled in the Presbyterian Church, at Hampton yesterday, Aug. 22, 1850, and on motion of Hon. Pomeroy Jones, Hon. Truman Enos was called to the chair, and P. A. Hall chosen secretary.

On motion of Hiram Shays, a committee of five was appointed by the chair to report permanent officers for the convention. The following gentlemen were appointed such committee. Hiram Shays, of New Hartford, David Moulton of Floyd, Pomeroy Jones of Westmoreland, Henry White of Utica, and Henry T. Utley of Rome.

Pending the action of this committee, the meeting adjourned for one hour, at the expiration of which time, it reorganised and the committee reported, through their chairman as follows:

President — George Bristol, of Kirkland.

Vice Presidents — Arnold Mason, of New Hartford, Henry White of Utica, Horace Adams of Rome, John Curry of Trenton.

Secretaries — Michael McQuade of Utica, Philip A. Hale of Floyd.

On motion of J. A. Stebbins, a committee of six was appointed by the chair to report resolutions for the consideration of the meeting, as follows:

Hiram Shays, David Pixley, John D. Leland, Hector Roberts, John French and Squire Utley.

On motion of Pomeroy Jones, a committee of seven was appointed by the chair to draft an address to the electors of the county and State, expressive of the views of the meeting. Chair appointed Hon. P. Jones, Henry T. Utley,

Arnold Mason, Ephraim Palmer, —— Kimball, Michael McQuade, and Hiram Denio.

During the absence of the committees, David Moulton, of Floyd, addressed the meeting at length. This distinguished advocate of retrenchment, and eloquent orator, descanted at length on his poor farm in the northwest corner of Floyd, on the obnoxious character of the law under consideration, on the fact that the only strenuous advocates of the law were editors and clergy (who will always, we hope, be found ready to write and speak in the favor of general and free education,) on the absurdity of men, who possessed no property — though we suppose he will allow some of them the possession of brains — making themselves prominent in this matter, and concluded that "the time had arrived" when the people should take the question into their own hands. He spoke sneeringly of "such men as Eton Comstock, J. P. Fitch, and O. B. Pierce," who are in favor of free education. He said, on concluding his address, that he had been severe on editors, but we hope that will not stand in the way of our neighbor of the Observer, when he is called on in the fall to say, that "Mr Moulton is every way worthy the support of enlightened and liberal Democrats." In the whole course of the speech, no word was spoken of the job taken by the member from Floyd last spring to repair the county house, which we learn has not turned out so fortunately nor progressed so rapidly as he then promised, in the fervor of his rage for economy. We have great respect for the opinions and motives of many gentlemen engaged in this movement of opposition to free schools, but we cannot avoid the conclusion that Mr Moulton wants to run for Congress.

Hon. Fortune C. White, formerly of this county who was present at the meeting, followed in a few remarks in opposition to the law. He strongly objected to the course of Legislatures, in making laws and sending them to the people for endorsement. It was shirking responsibility and but half doing business. He denounced the unequal system of taxation as enforced by this law. If we are to have free schools and be taxed for them, let the taxes be raised and thrown into a central treasury, whence they shall be distributed in due and just proportion. This is a question for the farmers to decide. The district wranglings, the lawsuits, the ill feeling and confusion caused already by its operation, are evidence that it is a bad and imperfect law. It should and will be opposed and repealed, and although he came as a looker on, he was glad of an opportunity to raise his voice in aid of this movement.

The com. on resolutions reported through their chairman the following:
Preamble and Resolutions

Whereas, The act of the Legislature of this State entitled "an act establishing free schools throughout the State" passed April 26, 1849, and providing for the raising of taxes for the support of common schools as follows:

First, Requiring the board of supervisors to levy upon each county a tax equal to the amount of state school moneys appropriated to such county.

Second, Also requiring the board of supervisors of each county at the same time to levy upon each town in the county, a tax equal to the amount of state school moneys appropriated to such town.

Third, Submitting to the voters of each school district the right to levy and raise by tax upon the property situate in each district, such additional sum annually as the trustees of each district think proper to designate.

And whereas, The said Legislature in and by said act, submitted to the people of this State, the question whether the said act should or should not become a law, and a majority of the electors who voted upon the subject, having voted in favor thereof, and the Legislature of 1850 having doubts whether a fair and full expression of the opinions of the electors of this State had been given upon this subject, again submitted to the electors of this State, the question whether the said act shall or shall not continue to be a law of this State, to be determined at the approaching election.

Now, therefore, This meeting deem it of vital importance to the interests of our common schools, as well as to the rights of our citizens, in the enjoyment of their property that this subject should be fully, freely and fairly discussed and understood by every elector, before voting upon a law in many respects the most important of any which has come from a legislative body, this meeting having attentively considered the subject, do adopt the following resolutions:

1st. *Resolved,* That every tax levied upon property for the support of common schools, should be general and equal throughout the State and the amount fixed upon by some general and inflexible rule and not dependent upon the fluctuating opinions from year to year of counties, cities, towns and districts.

2d. *Resolved,* That the school law of 1849 in its provisions for such complicated and multifarious modes of taxation, in its provisions for a struggle at every school district meeting for high or low taxes as may suit the fancy or caprice, generosity or parsimony of the voters for the time being, has introduced a new and unwholesome element into our common school system, calculated to engender strife and bitter contention in every district and wholly subversive of the prosperity of these invaluable nurseries of learning, virtue, and liberty.

3d. *Resolved,* That the act of 1849, appears to be based upon the hypothesis that where learning is most needed, there the district will be the most willing to vote the largest tax, but experience shows this is a gross error. It is to the well educated that the community look for the most efficient support of our common schools.

4th. *Resolved,* That should the law of 1849, be sustained by another vote of the electors of this State, future Legislatures will feel less authorized to change it in any respect, or remedy its gross defects than the Legislature of 1850 did. Hence it is the duty of every elector to vote against the law in order that future Legislatures may be untrammelled upon this important subject.

5th. *Resolved,* That we approve of our representative system of government, and that it is a violation of the principles of that system and of the constitution of this State for our Legislature to shrink from the responsibilities which that constitution imposes upon them, by asking the people to pass laws, which they themselves fear to enact.

6th. *Resolved,* That we would hail with delight a return to the former school law, under which our common schools had become eminently successful and whose beneficial effects were seen and felt throughout the entire

State; deeming it far more just and equitable and better calculated to produce the results desired by the friends of education, than the present one and sufficiently free for all practical purposes; and we hereby pledge ourselves to the friends of that law, to do our whole duty at the polls in favor of such returns.

7th. *Resolved*, That all the papers of this county be respectfully requested to publish the proceedings of this meeting and that the Albany Argus, Evening Journal, State Register, and Atlas and all the other papers in the State be requested to copy the same.

Resolved, That a corresponding committee of five be appointed in the county to take charge of the matter and that to that committee be entrusted the question of starting a newspaper, to be devoted to opposition of the free school law, until after election. David Moulton of Floyd, John French of New Hartford, Michael McQuade of Utica, Squire Utley of Western, and Henry Bristol of Kirkland were appointed such committee.

Convention then adjourned.

— *Utica Daily Gazette, August 23, 1850*

The Anti-Free School Convention

Strange as this heading may sound, it is a fact that a convention of this character was held last week at Utica. Among other measures, it is proposed to start a newspaper to oppose free education. This is a step backwards for which we did not suppose any respectable number of people in any state would be prepared.

Bost. Atlas

The convention was held at Hampton, nine mile from Utica, although we believe one of our daily papers glories in its concurrence in the sentiments of the meeting. It may perhaps be proper to say that the opposition is to the existing law rather than to the principle, but many well meaning people confound the two, and in opposing the law, become bitter enemies to the principle. And to do justice to our neighbors, they are not so much enemies to the law, as in favor of publishing a paper to oppose it.— *Utica Daily Gazette, August 30, 1850*

Anti-Free School Convention

The opponents of our free school system are invited to meet in convention at Jefferson, Chemung county, on the 24th instant, at 1 p. m. The call is signed by H. D. Barto, of Trumansburg, and 29 others.— *Buffalo Commercial Advertiser, August 19, 1850*

Free School Law

We have received the first number of a paper entitled the " Independent Freeman," published at Jefferson, Chemung county, and devoted to the repeal of the present free school law. It is a handsome sheet, and the number before us evinces considerable ability. Terms, $1.50 per annum; for clubs, a less price.— *Syracuse Daily Standard, June 15, 1850*

DEAR MR EDITOR:

I notice in your paper of May 8th, some comments upon what is termed the new free school law, and an invitation to your readers in the country who feel an interest in the success of our school system, to give you their views on the subject. I feel a deep interest in the subject, but am not accustomed to writing for publication. But when a man imbued with pure republican principles, as I profess to be, sees such great injustice practiced in our halls of legislation as was enacted in the passage of the free school act, it is time, although at the sacrifice of some personal feeling, for him to give his views, such as they are, to be used or not, as you think proper.

First the free school law, as it is termed, is in my opinion, unconstitutional. It is unequal and unjust in its operation. It does not really benefit that class of the community for whose advantage it was intended; but is really more oppressive upon that class of community which the advocates of the system harp so much about, " the poor."

When the law came before the people in the fall of '49, it was something new. There was something captivating in the title. The people did not understand it, and did not stop to consider how, or in what manner it was going to work — the justice or injustice of it. The idea that the schools would be free, was enough. The people were all to be educated to become teachers, and graduate, men and women were to become learned, virtuous and honest, vice and crime were to cease, our jails, poor houses and houses for correction, were to be vacated at once, the poor be made rich, the ignorant wise, all without any other agency than that of the free schools. But, as you say, the practical operation of the law the last year brought its details more under the observation of the people, who before knew but little more of the law than its title. So at the election, every man must go for the free school law, not stopping to consider who was to pay the expense; and you may think it a hard accusation, but it is nevertheless true, that some did not know that it was going to cost anything; others were heard to say they did not care where the money to pay the expense came from, so that they could get themselves or their children educated and warmed, while at the school room without expense to themselves.

The constitution is intended to give equal protection to the rights and privileges of every man and forbids the taking of the accumulation of one man's labor and economy for the use and comfort of another, equally able to provide for himself.— Yet this free school law does it, because it requires A, who has by industry and economy obtained a little property, to support him in his old age or infirm years, and has perhaps, reared and educated a large family of children, without any aid from the State, to contribute two, three, five, or ten dollars, annually to pay for the education of the children of B — and for the purchase of fuel to keep them warm and comfortable while in the schoolroom. There are numbers of young men (or those who call themselves so) in almost every school district who are healthy and able to work, and can always find employment enough and earn money enough to pay for attending balls, exhibitions and places of public amusement, but when it comes to paying a school bill they are not able — they have not the money to do it. " This Mr A, he's worth a thousand or two dollars, he's able to pay it for me, let him do it." — *Buffalo Commercial Advertiser, June 8, 1850*

Free Education

I was highly pleased to see in your paper of Saturday, a communication in reference to the free school law. Discussion is what is needed. Your correspondent well asserts the importance of the question — its absorbing importance. He invokes discussion and begs that your paper be his medium. On these points, I agree with him fully. No question of equal magnitude was ever before submitted to the people of this State. Not only are the merits of the question at issue, but, from the peculiar circumstances with which it is environed, the honor and reputation of the principle of free education by the people of this State, would be a subject of comment and amazement by the educated minds of all civilized countries. To Ohio and Michigan, it would come like a thunderclap in clear sky. New York owes it to her own discernment and patriotism, to the common sense and pride of her people, to the Union and to mankind, not to place herself in an attitude to be thus reproached.

Upon these points, your correspondent and myself agree. First, the importance of the subject. The necessity of discussion. And lastly, opposition to the present free school law. But here we part. I am in favor of the education of every child in the State, by the property of the State. I hold that the property necessary for that purpose, belongs, by imprescriptible right, to those children. To withhold it from them, is to deny a right — is to commit a wrong. The reasons for these two opinions, I shall not give today, as I have another point alluded to below. I wish to pay my respects to the old system. If we vote down the present law, we instantly go to the old. That is not "well enough," as it appears to me.— S. S. Randall, the able and eloquent Deputy State Superintendent, has had the matter investigated, and the reports of 30 counties convince him that in those counties, or half the State, not less than fifty thousand children stay from school on account of the old system. New York cannot afford it. No, no; the old system is behind the intelligence of the present age, which teaches us that it is better to pay the same amount of taxation for schools, than to sheriffs, jailors, judges, district attornies, jurymen, constables, etc., etc. To one object or to the other, the taxes will be applied. Which gives the greatest security to property? — to life? — to personal right? Let my friend, your correspondent, tell us.

Let me not be misunderstood. My opinion is, that the property of the whole State should educate the children of the whole State. This would make benefits and the burdens equal. It would effectually remove the inequalities which are now justly complained of. I shall vote for the present law, next fall, merely to manifest my friendship for the principle of free education. But are we asked to go back to the old system? — *Buffalo Commercial Advertiser, June 12, 1850*

To the County Committees and Electors of the State of New York

At the approaching election the question of free school education is to be decided at the ballot box. Believing that the existing system is eminently condusive to the diffusion of sound principles of knowledge, and intimately connected with the morality and prosperity of the State, the undersigned earnestly solicit the attention of the various county committees, irrespective of party to the following suggestions:

1 That the county committees, and the friends of free schools provide and distribute in the several townships the necessary tickets.

2 That on the day of election, school tickets be abundantly furnished at the time with the local political tickets, in every election district.

Vigilance in carrying out these recommendations cannot fail to sustain triumphantly the principles of free school education; and the existing laws that embody it, can be perfected, if necessary, by future legislation.

October 24, 1850

H. H. Martin[1]	Franklin Townsend[7]
E. B. O'Callaghan[2]	Watts Sherman[8]
Caleb S. Woodhull[3]	Friend Humphrey[9]
Wm. F. Havemeyer[4]	Bradford R. Wood[10]
James Harper[5]	Luther Bradish[11]
E. C. Benedict[6]	Robert Kelly[12]

— *Rochester Daily Democrat, October 26, 1850*

---

[1] Henry H. Martin was born in Avon in 1809. He was educated in the Albany Academy and at Union College. He served as private secretary to Governor Throop and Governor Marcy and later formed a law partnership with John V. L. Pruyn of Albany. He became cashier and later president of the Albany Savings Bank and held the latter position until his death in 1886. He was also identified with various other financial institutions.

[2] Edmund Bailey O'Callaghan was born February 29, 1797, in Mallow, near Cork, Ireland. After receiving a liberal education at home, he went to Paris for two years, where he studied medicine. Looking to the New World as offering great opportunities, Doctor O'Callaghan came to Quebec in 1823, completed his studies and was admitted to the practice of medicine in 1827. While in Quebec, he took a prominent part in the Catholic emancipation movement. Later moving to Montreal, he became active in the political opposition to the government. He became editor of the "Vindicator," a popular organ, and was elected to the provincial parliament. His activities led to such feeling against him that in 1853, the members of one of the tory clubs wrecked his newspaper office. He opposed the use of arms but, when the struggle between the government and the opposition reached the point where force seemed unavoidable, he fought on the opposition side. After the government victory, he fled to the United States, with a reward for his capture offered by the Canadian government. It is said that, in his later years, Doctor O'Callahan avoided all reference to his Canadian experiences. It is known that, although the government offered pardon to those who had fought against it, he made no attempt to have the ban lifted in his case nor did he ever revisit Canada.

Doctor O'Callaghan took up the practice of medicine in Albany, N. Y., and soon made friends among the prominent people of the State. He edited an industrial paper called the "Northern Light." When the antirent troubles were attracting attention, he took up the study of the Dutch language so that he might obtain more complete information as to the rights of the patroons. Astonished to find the vast amount of information contained in the untranslated Dutch documents in the possession of the State and of private owners, Doctor O'Callaghan began a systematic study of the history of the colony, which resulted in the publication of his "History of New Netherland" in two volumes. In its depth of research and freshness of style, this work was a revelation to the public and to students; but, while it gave the author a wide reputation, it was published at a loss to him. The interest aroused by the book led to the State sending Mr. John Brodhead to England, France and Holland to collect material relating to American history and especially to that of the State of New York. Doctor O'Callaghan was called upon to edit this work, which resulted in a publication of eleven volumes.

With his reputation as a historian soundly established, Doctor O'Callaghan wrote, edited and compiled many other works, a number of them being based upon documents found in the colonial archives of the office of the Secretary of State. Among these were the Journals of the Legislative Councils, a Calendar of State Papers, Lists of Land Grants, Revolutionary Papers, etc.

Having been invited to compile and edit the early documents in the possession of New York City, Doctor O'Callaghan moved to that city. After completing the extensive work, to Doctor O'Callaghan's great distress, politics interfered and the books were not published. Soon after he was taken ill and after an illness of over two years, he died on May 29, 1880, surrounded by the extensive library of American history which he had collected.

[3] Caleb Smith Woodhull, a descendant of Richard Woodhull, patentee of Brookhaven, L. I., was born February 26, 1792 at Miller's Place, L. I. He entered Yale College in 1808, at the age of fifteen and was graduated with the honors of his class in 1811.

He was a private in the War of 1812, being a member of the militia in New York City, which was charged with the safety of the city. He continued his connection with the militia until 1830.

In 1817 he was admitted to the bar in New York City. He was elected a member of the common council of New York City in 1836 and held that office for eight years. In 1849, he was elected mayor of New York and held that office until January 1851.

Our Free School Law

As we are soon to be called upon to do for ourselves what we have elected and paid others to do for us that is, to legislate upon the school law; and as we cannot discuss the subject by talking to each other across the hall, as those could do and should have done who were delegated for that purpose, we must confer with each other by the only means left us, either through the press or by the trouble and expense of public meetings.

Every person of intelligence, and with proper social feeling, is fully aware of the value and importance of an educated compared with an uneducated people.

In discussing the present school law, its friends seem to assume that they are exclusively the champions of free schools, and everybody is denounced as opposed to free schools and even opposed to educating our children at all, and especially our poorer children if we dare to call in question the wisdom or the fitness of the present law, either as a whole or in its detail. This is

---

During his term as mayor, Jenny Lind visited New York and he became her sole adviser as to her many charities during her stay in New York. Mr Woodhull died at Miller's Place, July 16, 1866.
He is described "as a man of broad political outlook and possessed not only the unshaken confidence and esteem of his friends but the high regards of his political opponents as well. his sound judgment, integrity and talents made him a man of great usefulness in his generation."

[4] William F. Havemeyer was born in New York City, February 12, 1804. At the age of fifteen he entered Columbia College, and was graduated in 1823. In 1828 he commenced business as a sugar refiner and prospered in the business until he retired in 1848. The reputation he had earned as a man of sound judgment, ability and integrity secured for him the distinction of a presidential elector in 1844.
In 1845 he was elected mayor of New York City and his administration of municipal affairs was so satisfactory that in 1848 he was again chosen for the same office. Mr Havemeyer was the first president of the board known as the "Commissioners of Emigration," and in that position was influential in reforming many of the wrongs and abuses to which emigrants had been subjected by swindling agents and runners. In 1851 he was elected to the presidency of the Bank of North America and filled that position for ten years.
After retiring from his second term of office, Mr Havemeyer steadily declined any further special honors until the fall of 1872, when he was again nominated for the office of mayor. He was elected to this office, and served until his death on November 30, 1874.

[5] James Harper, publisher, founder of the house of Harper & Brothers, was born at Newtown, L. I., April 13, 1795. His father was Joseph Harper, who was a farmer at Newtown. The father of Joseph Harper, James Harper, was an Englishman, one of the earliest American Methodists who came to this country. He settled as a schoolmaster at Newtown, about 1740. Joseph Harper married Elizabeth Kollyer, who is described as having been "a woman of vigorous and superior character, of a cheerful piety and kindly humor." James was their eldest child, and when sixteen years of age he and his brother John were apprenticed to two printers in New York. They were both well-trained boys, with sound principles, while James was also possessed of great personal strength, and both were noted for their regular and correct habits. In the office were James served his apprenticeship, Thurlow Weed was a fellow-workman, and the two there formed a friendship which lasted through life. James soon became a noted pressman. The two brothers were thrifty, and when they had served their apprenticeship, they were in possession of a small capital, which represented their joint savings. To this was added something from their father's means, and they started a business of their own, a small printing office in Dover street, New York. Here they printed books to order, their first work being completed in August 1817, when they delivered 2000 copies of Seneca's "Morals." Their next book was Mair's "Introduction to Latin Syntax;" and in April 1818, thy printed 500 copies of Locke's "Essay upon the Human Understanding;" and upon this volume appeared, for the first time, the imprint of J. & J. Harper as publishers. From this small beginning and by exercising care and judgment in all their undertakings, the young firm soon grew to eminence in publishing. The placing of two younger brothers, Joseph Wesley and Fletcher, as apprentices to the firm, was in due time followed by their admission as partners, when the name was changed to Harper & Brothers. James Harper sustained throughout his life his devotion to the cause of temperance and religion. He was remarkable for his spirit of toleration and for the kindly way in which he excused the faults and aberations of others. In politics he was a Whig as long as that party lasted, and in 1844 was elected mayor of the city of New York, a position in which he gained the respect of all who had occasion to come in contact with him. He was frequently asked to be a candidate for other important offices, but always declined, preferring to devote himself to his business. He died in New York, March 25, 1869.

not right. It would be strange indeed if the thousands of men in this State, who had devoted portions of their own life to teaching, and all their lives to promoting the interests of education, should know nothing of the matter, while official station alone should confer all the wisdom upon a few.

I start with the assertion that I would open the door of the schoolhouse to every child in the State, whatever may be his or her condition, and further that the property and productive industry of the State should sustain the schools. In the next place I assert that our old school system which we have been about forty years in maturing, is, in its financial provisions, with trifling exceptions, the best that has yet been devised in any country; and the wisest step we can take is to get back to it as soon as we can.

[6] Erastus Cornelius Benedict, at one time Chancellor of the Board of Regents, was born in Branford, Conn., March 19, 1800. The family was descended from one of the name who landed in Massachusetts Bay in 1838 and they were people of standing in their communities. Mr Benedict's father was a Presbyterian minister and he was in charge consecutively of churches at New Windsor, Franklin and Chatham, New York. Erastus was therefore brought up in New York State. At eighteen he entered the sophomore class at Williams College and was graduated therefrom in 1821. He served as principal of an academy at Jamestown and of one at Newburgh but in 1823 commenced the study of law with Judge Samuel R. Betts and was admitted to the bar in 1824. He served two years as deputy clerk of the United States District Court and then took up his law practice, devoting himself to admiralty law with such success that he became the leading lawyer of New York in this branch of practice. In 1850 he published "The American Admiralty, its Jurisdiction and Practice" which became a standard authority on this subject.

Mr Benedict was also much interested in literary work and in the promotion of education. In 1860 he published "A Run Through Europe," the result of a six months' vacation. He was deeply interested in mediaeval Latin poetry and translated "The Hymn of Hildebert" and other sacred poems. In 1840 he delivered the annual address before the alumni of Williams College. In 1879 he read in London, before the International Association for Codifying the Law of Nations, a paper on "Liability for Collisions as Sea." At the fifty-ninth anniversary of the New York Historical Society, he read a paper in vindication of the Pilgrim Fathers from the unwarranted attacks made upon them. In July 1878, on opening the Convocation as Chancellor, he delivered an address of great learning and suggestiveness.

Mr Benedict early became interested in public affairs of his city and State. He was a member of the common council in 1840. In 1848 and again in 1864, he was elected to the Assembly of the State of New York and, in 1872, to the Senate. He was a member of the board of Education of New York City from 1850 to 1863 and for several years its president. He was elected a Regent of the University of the State of New York in 1855, in 1872 was elected Vice Chancellor of that body and in 1878 was made Chancellor. His honorary degree of doctor of laws was conferred upon him by Williams College, of which he was for many years a trustee. He died in New York, October 22, 1880 in his eighty-first year.

[7] Franklin Townsend was born in Albany, September 28, 1821, the son of Isaah Townsend, who was a prominent business man of Albany. He was educated at the Albany Boys Academy. In 1852 he married Miss Anna Josephine King. Mr Townsend was an iron founder and banker and became one of the leading business men of Albany serving as vice president of the Albany Savings Bank and president of the New York State National Bank. He had also a keen interest in public affairs and was elected to the board of aldermen and to the board of supervisors. Later he served in the Assembly and for nearly nine years he was Adjutant General of New York State. He died September 11, 1898.

[8] Watts Sherman was born February 22, 1809. He was for many years cashier of the Albany City Bank, and at the time of his death in February 1865, was a member of the firm of Duncan, Sherman & Co. of New York City. He commenced his business career as teller of the Ontario County Bank at Canadaigua and was cashier of the Livingston County Bank at Geneseo, before going to Albany in 1834. He removed to New York in 1851. Mr Sherman was known as a man of the strictest integrity in his business life. His home in New York was a center of social life and was frequented by the most cultured people of New York and by the distinguished foreigners who visited New York during the lifetime of Mr Sherman and that of his brilliant wife.

[9] Friend Humphrey was born at Simsbury, Conn., March 8, 1787. His father died when he was about four years old and his mother gave him such opportunities for an education as were offered at that time. At the age of fourteen, he went to live with Judge Burt, a tanner of New Hartford, Conn., who agreed to teach him his trade. A few years later he removed to Lansingburg, N. Y., with the family of Mr Burt. About 1811 Mr Humphrey married Hannah Hinman of Lansingburg, who died in 1822. About 1825 he married Julia Ann Hoyt of Utica, who lived until 1851.

When twenty-four years of age, Mr Humphrey moved to Albany and engaged in the tanning and leather and hides businesses. He became one of the leading dealers of the State and was often employed by other dealers to buy for them as they valued his expert judgment.

Our public school fund in this State has a capital of $5,000,000, producing an annual income of $280,000, which is distributed annually amongst the several school districts to which is added a like sum raised by direct taxation upon the real and personal property of the towns and counties in the State, amounting to $560,000; the residue for the support of the schools has been collected by a rate bill of those sending to school who were able to pay,

---

Mr Humphrey held the office of alderman from 1819 to 1832, and was also supervisor for several terms. He was elected Representative in 1828. He was elected to the State Senate in 1839. He helw the office om mayor of Albany in 1843-45, ad in 1849-50.

Having a keen interest in the affairs of Albany, Mr Humphrey was one of the incorporators and a member of the first board of directors of the Merchants Insurance Company, a trustee of the old Albany Savings Bank, a member of the first board of trustees of the Albany Medical College and a governor of the Albaay Hospital.

[10] Bradford Ripley Wood, lawyer and diplomat, was born at Westbury, Conn., September 30, 1800, son of Samuel and Rebecca (Lyon) Wood. His grandfather, the Rev. Samuel Wood, (1724-77) was a Congregational clergyman who served as chaplain of the 5th Connecticut regiment in the Revolution, was taken prisoner at the capture of Fort Washington, November 16, 1776, and died on the British prison ship Asia. His great-grandfather, David Wood, was the son of Daniel Wood, a farmer.

Bradford R. Wood was graduated at Union College in 1824. He taught school, lectured on temperance, education and patriotism; studied law under Robert Lansing of Watertown, N. Y., and Harmanus Bleecker of Albany and was admitted to the bar in 1827. At various times he was in partnership with J. V. N. Yates, Arthur Southwick, Jacob I. Werner, and Clinton Deforest. He was president of the Albany Young Men's Temperance Society in 1832 and of the Albany City Temperance Society in 1851. In 1841 he was made a life member of the Young Men's Association, and in 1850 was one of the founders of the First Congregational Church of Albany, of which he was a trustee for many years. During 1863-83 he was vice president of the American Home Missionary Society. He was a member of the 29th Congress (1845-1847), as a Democrat, when he opposed the admission of Texas as a slave state. In 1861 he became United States minister to Denmark and established a warm friendship between Denmark and the federal government during the four years he held the office. Upon his return to the United States he was made a commissioner to deepen New York harbor. He was a member of the American Geographical and Statistical Society, honorary president of the African Institute of Paris, and he received the honorary degree of LL.D. from Williams College in 1870. Though a Democrat for many years, he was always opposed to slavery, and in 1855 became one of the founders of the Republican Party in New York State. He was married August 24, 1834, to Eliza, widow of Joseph W. Clark and daughter of Thomas Gould, of Albany, and had six sons and two daughters. He died in Albany September 26, 1889.

[11] Luther Bradish was born September 15, 1783, in Cummington, Mass. In 1804 he was graduated from Williams College, which institution later conferred upon him the degree of LL.D. He entered upon the profession of law in New York City but shortly thereafter made an extended tour through the West Indies, South America and the British Isles. He returned to this country and served as a volunteer in the War of 1812. In 1820 he went to Europe for the purpose of studying conditions in the Levant with a view to formulating a plan upon which the United States might enter into relations with Turkey. He crossed the ocean in a United States ship-of-war which joined a squadron of ships and made a tour of the Mediterranean. Having made an exhaustive study of conditions in the Near East, Mr Bradish submitted his report to the government and with this as a basis the desired relations with Turkey were established. Mr Bradish remained abroad six years, visiting the Near East, Egypt, Russia and in fact every country in Europe.

Upon his return to New York in 1827, he was elected a member of the Assembly and held this office from 1827 to 1830 and again from 1835 to 1838. In 1838 he was made Speaker of the Assembly and in 1838 and again in 1840 he was elected Lieutenant Governor of the State of New York. In 1842 he was the Whig candidate for Governor but was not elected.

Mr Bradish had a deep interest in educational, charitable and reformatory questions. He served on boards of trustees of many charitable institutions and was president of the New York Historical Society and president of the American Bible Society.

Mr Bradish was married twice, his first wife being Miss Helen Elizabeth Gibbs of Newport, R. I., and his second Miss Mary Eliza Hart of New York City. Mr Bradish died August 30, 1863.

[12] Robert Kelly was born in 1808. He was graduated from Columbia College in 1826 and engaged in commercial business amassing a large fortune. He retired from business in 1836. He was said to have had a mastery of eight languages. Being much interested in public affairs, he held at various times the following positions: Chamberlain of New York City, president of the House of Refuge, vice president of the Merchants' Clerks Savings Bank, director of the Mechanics' Bank, director of the United States Trust Company, trustee of the Clinton Hall Association, trustee of the New York Society Library, Chairman of the Democratic city committee, Democratic state committeeman, trustee of New York, Madison and Rochester Universities. From the last named institution he received the degree of LL.D. Mr Kelly was a member of the board of Education of New York City from 1847-1850, during part of which time he was its president. In March 1856 he was elected a member of the Board of Regents of the University of the State of New York but his death in April 1856 cut short his work on this board.

EDMUND BAILEY O'CALLAGHAN, MD. LL.D.
(From picture owned by The Albany Institute and Historical and Art Society)

HENRY H. MARTIN

WILLIAM F. HAVEMEYER
Mayor of New York City, 1845–46, 1848–49 and 1873–74

CALEB WOODHULL
Mayor of New York, 1849–51

JAMES HARPER
One of the founders of Harper & Brothers, publishers; mayor of New York City, 1844-45
(From National Cyclopedia of American Biography)

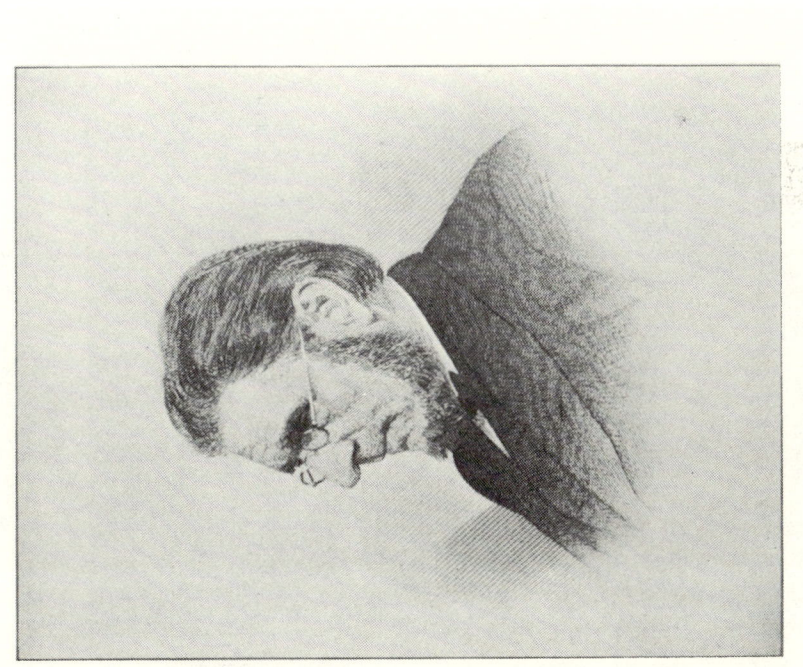

ERASTUS C. BENEDICT
Elected Regent of The University of the State of New York in 1855, Vice Chancellor of that body in 1872 and Chancellor in 1878
(From "Public Service of the State of New York" by Chadbourne and Moore)

FRIEND HUMPHREY
Mayor of Albany, 1843-45, 1849-50
(From "Albany Chronicles"; used through the courtesy of Mr Cuyler Reynolds, the compiler)

FRANKLIN TOWNSEND
Member of Assembly; Adjutant General of New York State, 1869-73, 1875-79
(From picture in "Albany Chronicles"; used by permission of Mr Cuyler Reynolds, the compiler)

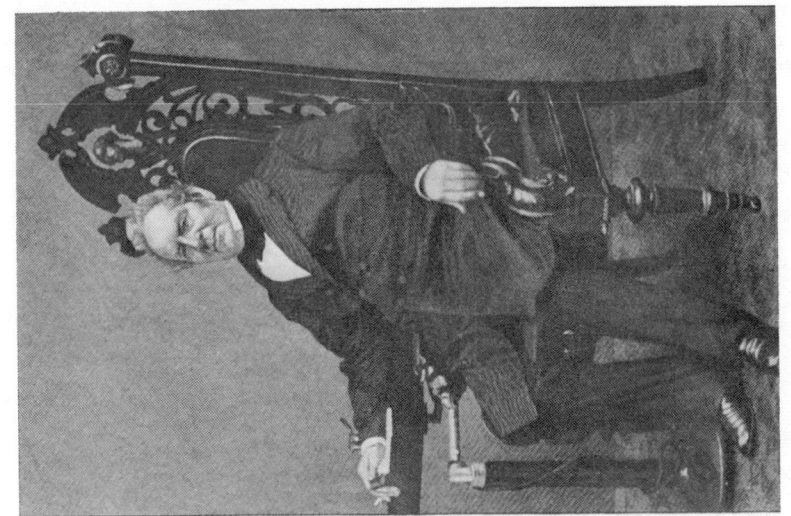

LUTHER BRADISH
Member of Assembly, 1827-30 and 1835-38;
Lieutenant Governor, 1838-42
(From The Electric Magazine)

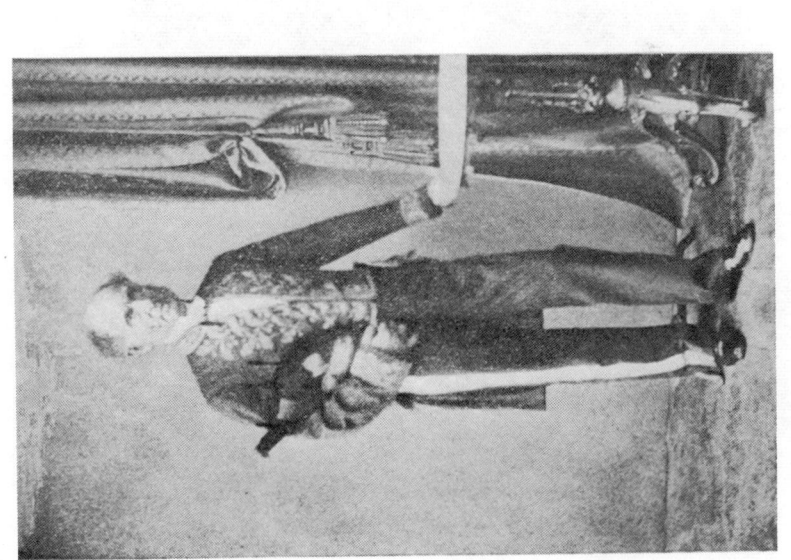

BRADFORD RIPLEY WOOD
Member of the Twenty-ninth Congress; Minister
to Denmark, 1861-65
(From picture owned by Miss Charlotte
Clark, Albany, N. Y.)

ROBERT KELLY
(From picture owned by the city of New York)

and those who are not had their bills paid by a tax on the district or out of the public money. That law should be so amended as to make it imperative upon the trustees to pay the tuition of all indigent children in the district out of the public fund. This would not take more than from one-tenth to one-fourth of that fund in any district. Let the rest be apportioned as now. If the trustees should act oppressively let an appeal lie to the district, where the poor children will always be safe.

But it is objected that this makes paupers of the poor children. I ask, paupers to whom? — Answer — to the State. What does the present law make of them but paupers? And paupers, too, upon the earnings of their neighbors, instead of upon the state fund which nobody feels. In which of these two conditions would they be most likely to be reminded of their dependence?

The horror of being educated out of the public fund has not shocked the sensibilities of some of the most splendid men to be found in one of our most honorable professions, who did not suffer from being educated as "pious young men;" and why should we suppose the sensibilities of the indigent children in our school districts more acute?

The present free school law has no advantages over the old in this respect but on the contrary one of the strongest objections to it is that it *compels* a large class of industrious and respectable people to pauperize their children who are able and desirous to educate them themselves. There are thousands of men in the State whose names are not on the assessors' book or if on at all, are there for very small amounts, whose weekly and monthly earnings are more than those of their farmer neighbors who are high on those books, and of course have the schools to support. These nontaxpaying men, if they send to the school at all, are obliged to send as paupers, which they have no desire to do, and which, if they have the feelings and spirit of men, they would not do if they could help themselves.

To illustrate: here is a school district in the country with sixty scholars. The valuation of the property in the district is sixty thousand dollars. Now any one sending to this school who is not on the assessors' list at all, or who is there for less than $1000 on each scholar he sends to school, sends as a pauper on his taxpaying neighbor. This is talked of between parents and children and our social harmony is suffering a thousand times more from it than from all the good that can ever come of the system.

Another source of social disturbance is that the people of the district are compelled by this law to come together once a year and vote for the term of their school. Experience has shown that this brings us conflict between the taxpaying and the nontaxpaying classes. Experience has also shown that in hundreds of instances where under the old law, a school had been taught from eight to twelve months in the year, the term has been voted down for four months. On the other hand, where the taxpayers have been out voted and compelled, against their wills to educate their neighbor's children, hatred and ill feeling has been ingendered, neighbors who have hitherto lived on friendly terms, have not done so since the last winter school meeting, and the nontaxpayers have in some instances found that they have won a dear victory, for they find they want other things of their taxpaying neighbors besides payment of their school bill. This should have been foreseen. For if we set one class of our people by law to war upon another, it would be strange if they would not war back again; and if we pass laws to set the weak to war against the strong, it does not require a wise man to foretell the result in the end.

I believe all can see that we can not get on with the law as it now is. I can not believe the last Legislature sent us this law expecting we would enact it again, when they all very well knew it would be practically so mischievous in its effects upon society and so destructive of our common schools. I think I do not misunderstand them when I suppose that as their predecessors had sent this strange law to the people, which they had as strangely passed because labeled free schools, they could do no less than send it to us again after we had taken off the label and seen what it covered, that we might and would repeal it. I consider this law "an impracticable abstraction;" as self-destructive as it is, should the people unfortunately recredit it, its friends will insist upon its inviolability, because twice sanctioned by the people its defects are to be as much sanctioned as its excellences, if it has any, for we are not permitted to discriminate and repeal part and sanction part. If we repeal it, we fall back upon the old law, under which we have prospered so well, and whose defect we can easily cure. If we reaffirm it, we fasten it upon us with all its deformities for years to come.

Mr Beekman of our State senate, in a speech last winter evincing much research, although intended in favor of this new law, furnished one of the strongest arguments I have seen against it and in favor of the old system.

He gave the educational statistics of several of the countries in Europe, and of several of our states here, showing that the proportion of the population attending schools here was much greater than in Europe, and then showed this undeniable fact in favor of our old system, to wit: That in New England and Ohio, under their free school system sustained by direct taxation, one in four of the population attended common schools whilst in this State, under the old law, one in three and one-tenth attended school; showing that under our old system we were just ten per cent better than they are in New England, under their free school by direct taxation, which they have been a century in maturing. And now we are cooly asked to retrograde that ten per cent to improve our condition. I do not know why we should do so except it be from sheer love of direct taxation. This would be rather a new doctrine, and should not be popular. It certainly has not been hitherto.

All direct taxation is odious and should not be resorted to except from pressing necessity. Although fully provided for in the constitution of the United States, the general government has never dared to resort to it to meet the ordinary expenses of government, and the taxpayers of this State are not prepared to submit to its increase to an extent from four to eight mills on a dollar until they are satisfied of its absolute necessity and of its justice.

No system of direct taxation has yet been devised for this State which is not extremely unequal in its burdens. Personal property and especially in the hands of large capitalists, has never been reached so as to bear anything like its share in taxation while real estate is always shown up at full length to the assessor's eye. This disparity is most sensibly felt, and especially by our agricultural population. That class of our people especially feel most sensibly the injustice of that system of double taxation, which occurs whenever property is under mortgage. The mortgagee is taxed to the amount of the mortgage as personal property and the mortgagor is again taxed for the farm or property mortgaged as owner. The mortgagee is the actual owner of the farm to the amount of the mortgage and so far as he is liable to taxation for it nobody else should be. If a man owns stock in a corporation the corporation alone is taxed for it. He is not taxed again as stockholder.

A very large proportion of the farms in this State are under mortgage to a greater or less extent, the purchase money on a sale is seldom fully paid down. The purchaser often goes in debt for half or more of it, and expects with severe labor and severe economy to keep down his interest and little by little to wear away the principal. Such a man under present free school law is frequently compelled, whether he has children of his own to educate or not to educate those of his neighbor who is much wealthier than himself and whose property or whose income is not taxed. Such a man is made to feel and keenly to feel a sense of injustice and in many instances of oppression in this law of his country. He is made to feel as no honest, industrious man so commendably striving to better his condition and to better his country should be made to feel. And would you countenance the man who under the sanction of the law would appropriate the earnings of such a neighbor and those of his family to educate his own children that he might lay up his own earnings or spend them for his own gratification? Or would you countenance the man who would take the earnings of such a man to educate his children, that he himself might spend his time in idleness and his means in profligacy, even if he was mean spirited enough to pauperize his children and throw them upon his taxpaying neighbor who although taxpayer, lives by his own hard labor and that of his family.

Let us repeal this new law that is so unjust and is working and always will work so much mischief to society and to our common schools and get back to that old system which has been matured by the wisdom of forty years, and under which we were ten per cent of New England herself and much more than that in advance of any other country. We will greet the old system as an old friend under whose countenance we have done so well. Where it is not perfect, we will make it so. Our schools will then be free as water. Those who are able to educate their children will do it as they should do, and they will see that their money is well laid out; and those who are not able, have an ample public fund for it without taxing their neighbors.

If any children are found in the streets untaught, make it the duty of the trustees to place them in the schools upon the public fund; our schools will then be practically free; our odious system of direct taxation will not be aggravated and the asperities and ill blood which one year's operation under this unfortunate law have engendered will in time wear away and we shall outgrow the evils which it has cast upon us.

AN OLD SCHOOLMASTER
—*Albany Argus, August 31, 1850*

Having presented the principal points of objection to the free school law and shown where it differs from the old, it only remains to urge upon the voters of the State of New York to examine the subject in the light of an enlarged and liberal patriotism, and act in view of the real questions at issue, which are these. Is the new law preferable to the old? Is it more in accordance with the spirit of our republican institutions? Will it diffuse more widely and more equally the benefits of Education? Will the expenses be more equitably apportioned? And finally, will the aggregate practical benefits to be derived from the adoption of the new be greater than those we have actually derived from the old system? Having settled these questions in his own mind, let every voter in the State come forward and deposit his for or against the change — let no man be deferred from a free expression of his honest convictions by the fear of being denounced as an " enemy to free schools." For if the positions assumed and attempted to be sustained by facts, and arguments which every unprejudiced reader can appreciate for himself are true, the schools under the old system are more practically " free schools " than under the new. The question to be decided is the adoption of the new, and partially untried system, to which there are great and apparently insurmountable objections, or a return to the old well tried system with which the people were satisfied.

Let no man be deceived in regard to the real question at issue, or the result inevitably to follow the adoption of the new law. The idea that subsequent legislation can remedy all defects is entirely fallacious. Yield up to the strong arm of the law the control of your common schools; and the power to tax your property for their entire support; and you yield a power you can never recover. " Revolutions never go backwards." The next step will be to popularize your churches; make their teachings conform to some popular standard from which all sectarianism is excluded; and then levy the expense of their support by a compulsory tax upon " the property of the State." This would be " Church and State " with a vengeance. Yet it is but one step beyond where the " free school law " carries us. Who doubts that the same appliances brought to bear upon this question, by demagogues and fanatics (perhaps of another class,) would produce a popular vote in favor of such a law.

It is said that it is unfair to connect the operation of unequal and unjust taxation with the adoption of the new " free school law," whereas this is one of the principal objections to it. No system of compulsory taxation can be devised that will not operate unequally and unjustly that entirely excludes the rate bills. The strength and popularity of our school system, like that of our system of government, consists in the fact that it is dependent for its support upon the people — that the power of the support and control is diffused over the entire mass, and not concentrated in the government. Every State has a right to regulate its own internal affairs without the knows the power, and feels the responsibility of his position, will be the strength and perpetuity of our institutions.

When the government becomes strong, and the people weak and powerless, then farewell to our liberties. Our forefathers wisely considered this, and left nothing for the law to do, which could be better done without. They wanted no hordes of public officers to do that which they could do themselves. This is a fundamental principle of our republican government. Every state has a right to regulate its own internal affairs without the interference of any other State. Each county in the State has the same right to regulate its own local affairs — every town the same right, and every school district the same right.

What may be considered very proper in regard to the local domestic relations of one State, county, town or district, may be considered far otherwise in another. There is no such equality of circumstances, opinions or feelings, existing as will justify the universal application of a law or principle indiscriminately, and that government which leaves nothing to the opinions, desires, wishes, or discretion of the people to individuals or communities is a despotism.

We must take society as it is and not as we would have it. It is unreasonable to suppose that we can ever make the entire mass of community equally wealthy, learned or virtuous, unless we destroy all motive to the acquisition of either wealth, learning or virtue, and reduce all to the level of the lowest, which seems to be the desire and determination of modern theorists as well as the tendency of modern legislation.

There is no universal panacea for poverty, ignorance and vice. The world is and always has been full of these evils and will continue to be, as long as it is inhabited by the fallen race of Adam.

Plant a schoolhouse upon every square mile of our territory, multiply teachers until the number is sufficient to furnish one for every house, appropriate the entire property of the State for their support, and you have accomplished but little towards making our entire population either learned or virtuous. W.

— *Buffalo Commercial Advertiser, September 11, 1850*

Free Schools

An effort is being made to induce the electors of this city to vote for the free school law. Is this right? We have a free school system of our own, established by ourselves and supported by a direct assessment upon the property of our citizens. When the question of free schools in our city came to be voted upon, what would we have thought of the propriety of permitting the inhabitants of the country towns to vote upon the question and decide it for us? The answer is obvious. We would have condemned it as an unjust and impertinent interference with a matter belonging exclusively to ourselves. Yet there is a disposition on the part of some of our citizens to perpetrate a like indignity upon our neighbors in the country towns.

So far as I am informed the inhabitants in the rural districts are opposed to the law establishing free schools, and if it be voted down, it will be because the inhabitants of the cities outvote them.

We have in Buffalo our system of free schools, and although it is obnoxious to very many objections, yet there are, no doubt, preponderating reasons why it should be sustained. In populous towns, there are great numbers of children whose parents are destitute of any desire to do anything for their moral and intellectual culture, as they are of the means of accomplishing it. With the facilities which the public schools afford their more virtuous neighbors by a little effort may secure to such children the benefits of education. Besides this class there is another which we may denominate the laboring unfortunate poor, who have the desire but not the means to educate their children.

In the country, however, these cases are exceedingly rare, and whenever they occur, the law as it has stood for years has invested a discretionary power in the district trustees to omit all such persons on their tax list.

The law now proposed to be forced upon the people, in effect proposes to compel a man, who has already at his own expense educated a family of eight children, and has only two left to be educated, to pay just as much for the tuition of those two as his neighbor of equal property does for that of his entire family, consisting (if you please) of 12 children. To illustrate still further the injustice of the law, let us state a case which actually exists: There is a widow in the town of Alden, whose husband has left her with a small farm of fifty acres, and one child to be educated. The income from this farm does not exceed one hundred and twenty-five dollars per annum. Near her, in the same school district, lives a mechanic who is not the owner of any real estate, but has an annual income from his business of at least five hundred dollars. He has five children who attend the district school. The widow's little farm is taxed to support the school. The mechanic pays not a cent. What say you, brother city voters, if we vote at all, shall we vote for the law? R.

—*Buffalo Commercial Advertiser, November 4, 1850*

The Free School Question

Mr Editor — I have been much amused at lamentations of the free school law, and somewhat vexed with the benevolent, milk-and-water style in which it has been attempted to reconcile them to its operations, by portraying the glorious objects to which their money is to be applied.

Now, I claim to be one of the honest, huge-fisted democracy in favor of speaking out plain, and would not resort to duplicity even to promote a good cause, especially when we have strength to carry our points by main force. That learning is an excellent thing to its possessor, and not without value to community, is unquestionable. But if our object was only the education of the children of the State, we should effect it by simply requiring the parent to discharge his duty to his own offspring, merely aiding on our part such as from poverty or other causes, as might need assistance. We are, however, looking far beyond this.

I would therefore advise the unhappy tax-payers to reserve their groans for a tighter pinch, for they may rest assured the " occasion will offer." Having tasted blood, we confess we like it, and shall call for more. It is a delightful circumstance, this being legally (and therefore honestly) entitled to put our hand in our neighbor's pocket, and abstract his wealth therefrom. No matter whether it is acquired on his part by luck or hard labor, it counts the same to us.

This year we commence the operation by taking their money ostensibly to establish free schools; not because education is thereby promoted, but for the reason that it forms a magnificent hobby, on which benevolent greenhorns can ride so nicely. Next year we must make a draft to clothe our children and render their appearance at school respectable — the next that they may be well fed. Philanthropy will no longer permit that the good living of the children shall be in any manner dependant upon the industry of the parents, excepting, of course, the children of aristocratic property-holders. Then after that — but I will not anticipate farther. Worthy and benevolent objects will present themselves as long as the money holds out.

In addition to the direct advantages to those who have nothing, and are too independent to work, resulting from the adoption of this policy, there will be incidental benefits of no slight importance. The money will be better spent. For won't we, the independent people, know better how to agreeably make disbursements (that being our business) than can those whose time is employed in toil and labor.

The inordinate desire for gain, the constant struggle to amass wealth, is an admitted evil of great magnitude. We will apply a sovereign remedy to this, by removing all incentives to exertion and accumulation.

We will thus change the direction of the golden current, and hasten on the golden age, when the idle and the thriftless shall be supported in luxury, and the toiling economist be made to exclaim in all sincerity, "blessed be nothing."

PEOPLE

— Rochester Daily Democrat, August 20, 1850

Free Schools

MESSRS. EDITORS — We noticed in your journal of August 20, an article signed "People," in which the author, without presenting any arguments against the free schools system, treated its advocates and doctrines with that ironical "nonchalance" which one might reasonably suppose would belong to the "huge-fisted democracy" of which he owns himself a member. It is true, that this, like all other important questions, has its two sides. Each side has its advocates and friends, who will not be found unwilling to meet their opponents, with strong reasons for the grounds which they occupy and attempt to maintain. But in this, like other questions, let the strongest reasoning and the weightiest arguments prevail.

If the opponents of free schools can show the benefits to be derived from a common school system which shall be wholly individual in its character, as to the advantages it offers for educating the children of the State, to be greater than a system which secures to all, irrespective of caste or condition, then let us see them, that we may act accordingly. What should be the objects of a common school? To educate those whose purses are long enough to pay for it? To educate the rich and influential? No! these are not the ones who need the common school. To them the door of higher institutions is always open, and the hand of science and art is always ready to welcome. But to those less affluent and to the extreme poor, is the common school a boon of no small value. Nor is education a matter wholly individual and personal.

The children of a state are the property of the state, and as such should be educated to subserve the interests of the state. The parents will still find enough to do in the intellectual and moral training of his children, after the state has done its part. But suppose the parents happen to be of that class (of which there are many) who entirely neglect the culture, moral and mental, of their children; but who by their precept and example are constantly exerting an example directly tending to make them members of society as worthless as themselves. What then? Why the children, not the authors of their shame, must be told that they, having had the misforune to be born under an inauspicious star, are singled out from their more fortunate neighbors, and branded as paupers, to be educated at public expense, and jeered at by their associates as the dependents of charity. Where is the child who would not feel the shame, whose cheek would not burn with blushes at being thus exposed a victim to a cruel fate? It is not the parent himself who alone receives the benefit in the education of his child, especially if he belongs to the class we have just described. He can feel no paternal pride in beholding his offspring mount the ladder of success, while he is unwilling to strain a nerve to aid him in his aspirings for knowledge and the means of usefulness. Who then receives the benefit? Is it the child? If so, is not the money well expended, even though it be a tax on the wealth of the childless lordling? To what better use could it be **applied?**

But it may be said that we have no right to appropriate the property of one individual to the direct and sole benefit of another. True; but is the education of the pauper child his own exclusive good? Is not community, of which he is a component part, likewise benefited? If so, then the taxed property goes to benefit the people at large — the State; and it is on this principle that all taxation is founded. Why is it that property is taxed for the erection of poorhouses and penitentiaries? Is it alone for the good of their occupants, or is it to serve the interests of the community and guard its safety? Which is the best philosophy to support paupers and criminals at a public charge, and leave their children to follow in their footsteps of sin and shame, so that when the first generation shall have paid the penalty of their crimes, a second may be prepared to fill their places, or to give their children, whose minds are calling for " light more light still," the means to store them with a fund of useful knowledge, and thus prepare them for the future members of this great and free Republic. Not like " People " with his " huge-fisted democracy " close the portals to wisdom, and let the benighted mind grovel on till at last it, too, finds a home in the prison or asylum — but with a hand of true benevolence, prompted by a heart swelling with noble purposes, open the gates to the temple of knowledge — bid the outcast and unfortunate enter, and with the torch of truth explore its profoundest depths.

While it is not denied that the " free school act " of last year was very defective in many of its details, which might be amended or repealed, it seems to us that no sage political economist or true-hearted philanthropist will question the soundness of the *principle* of free schools. Let our common schools be State institutions insomuch as the general diffusion of knowledge tends to diminish the the expenses of the State by the enlightment of its citizens, and like other institutions, let individual wealth bear its " pro rata " share of the burden. Then will come that " golden age " when " People " with the " toiling economist " will say " blessed are all things."

E.

— *Rochester Daily Democrat, September 1850*

Against Free Schools

The following letter in opposition to free schools we received a few days since, and cheerfully give publicity to the same, *verbatim et literatim.* Its arguments are *most potent,* and should come to the knowledge and *understanding* of every voter in the State before the ides of November.

Here it is:

To the Edetor of the Syracuse Star:

DEAR SIR:

I did suppose after such A total failour to git A Convention on the subject of free schooles, there would be at least alittle Relaxation in zeal on your part, but one would think that you ware weddid to the presant unjust Law, and, sir, it is not from anavirtion to Free Schools in the taxpayors that I expect to see the welth in mass rise and show to the law making power, that they had better try Again under this law, if a mejority of voters happen to be not taxpayers, then they will blead the few to Death, and perhaps in the next Destrict, being composed of difrant Meterals, will voate the least posable some, thus you see that the Law is unequal in its baring, I would goe A Law after this sort and amfulley in belief that such A Law would receive A haretey Approoval at the Ballet Box, say add to the presant schoole fund the united states Deposits and supply the Defishancey with states stockes baring 6 or 7 purcent to Runfor A term of years say 25 and those Bonds would make the Basis for Banking to be secuered or paid down and the Money invested as the other funds are and to meet the yearley intrest on such Bonds and levey A yearley tax on the people till the Revenew of the Canal has Redeamed itself to gather with those Bonds, if that fails then resort to taxation and distribet to the schooles under the olde Law under such a just Modosopperandi all would approve.

C. W ———.

P. S. if you insert this correct the orthogerphy.

—*Syracuse Daily Star, August 2, 1850*

Free School Law — A Fact

At the annual meeting of school district no. 14 in Marcellus and Skaneateles, on the 7th inst., held for the choice of district officers, and to provide for the support of schools for the year, at which an unusually large number was present, the meeting was called to order, and organized, and after discussing the necessity of good schools, and the blessings they confer on our children and the country, and the oppressive, unjust, and *unequal* effects of the present free school law on the district,— The meeting was by a unanimous vote adjourned to the first Monday in October, 1851, without choosing an officer, or making any provision for a *public* school — choosing rather to keep private school entirely at their own expense, for small children through the summer, (as they did last year) and send the larger ones out of the district, as they may be able, which they find costs them only about half as much as it would to keep a public *" free school"* eight months in a year, under the present law.

This district is a small one, and because we are so unfortunate as not to be blest with many children, or much property, we are virtually deprived of *any* school for our poor, after paying two or three taxes (town, county and state) to support the falsely so-called "*free* schools" in the state, we can well afford to lose all that for the benefit of others, and school our own children at our own private expense rather than maintain a *free* school under this law, while schools in some large districts are fully maintained by the public money which has been paid in by us and others. Is this equality? The *effect* of this law is unjust and unequal, and we protest against it. We hear of many other districts taking the same or a similar course, to avoid the unjust effects of this law; and many a poor child in the state will be deprived of *any* schooling, after paying heavy taxes to support that fraudulent act, with a popular name, got up by a venal Legislature, to gain a little political capital that they might be able to ride that hobby, and retain their ill-deserved seats for another year. The popular vote given for that act last year, proves the liberality as well as the gullibility of the people; and the general condemnation of the law the first year, as shown by the numerous petitions to the Legislature for its repeal or amendment, and the action of the legislature upon those petitions, prove the desire of the people to get rid of the law and cowardice on the part of the legislature, in sending the law, *unaltered,* back to the people to be voted on again.

A Citizen of the District
—*Syracuse Daily Standard, October 12, 1850*

Relation of Education to Crime

Mr S. S. Randall states that an examination of the official returns made to the Secretary of State by the sheriffs of the several counties, of the convictions had in the several courts of record throughout the State, and in the courts of special sessions in the respective cities from the year 1840 to 1848, both inclusive, comprising a period of nine years, gives the following results: The whole number of persons returned as having been convicted of crimes in the several counties and cities of the State, during the period referred to, was 27,949; of these, 1132 were returned as having received a "common education," 414 as having a "tolerably good education," and 128 only as "well educated." Of the remaining 26,225, about half were able merely to read and write. The residue were destitute of *any* education whatever.—*Syracuse Daily Standard, July 4, 1850.*

The Law and its Operation

Mr W. S. Crandall, a member of the free school committee, and editor of the Clarion, in order to defend the position of the Syracuse convention, and to repel the assertions of the Son of New England, has called to his aid Mr S. S. Randall, with his statements in relation to the education of state convicts, and given in a publication in the Livingston Union. He makes out that in 28,000 convicts, only about 1714 were educated, and that of the residue, 26,225, about half could barely read and write; therefore, no objection should be made against the new law, or against allowing one part of the electors to take such sum of money as they please from their neighbors, under pretences of education; and as conscientious scruples may exist as to the justice of such a course, so the Syracuse convention wisely provided that moral and religious culture had nothing to do with free school education.— This official statement says, '*about half these 26,225, could barely read and write,*' and there is no evidence but that these 26,225 have all attended our schools; they have all had the opportunity of attending, either our common schools, or the free schools, which have long existed in our cities, free school advocates speak of children attending school, and call it education when nothing but a careless attempt at teaching is made, and those attempts have been made without instruction or learning. There are many children now to be found who have attended school for six, eight, or ten years, that can barely read and write. That crime and expenditure of money had taken place, as stated in No. 3, I had the proof to sustain the statement; as to the degeneracy of most of the common schools, I furnished that proof also, as given in the School Journal. I retract nothing that is contained in No. 3 or any other No. I will give what I before stated; a part of the report of the Rev. Mr. Dunning, chaplain of the Mt Pleasant prison. He says, Jan. 8, 1848,—

"A large proportion of our convicts are between the ages of sixteen and twenty-five. Many of these were detected in, and punished for, their first violation of the laws; others had progressed farther in vicious and criminal courses, but never, till within the prison's walls, had stopped for reflection. Many of this class are well educated, and belong to highly respectable families.

(*Signed*)   HALSEY DUNNING
"*Chaplain, &c.*"

Extract from the last message of Gov. Seward

"According to reports at the State Department, there have been four hundred and ninety-seven convictions of felons, including six capital cases, and about four thousand convictions of misdemeanors and minor offences, showing an increase of greater proportion. . . . Although more than four thousand persons are annually confined in our county jails. Those penitentiaries often exhibit scenes revolting to humanity, and many a youthful prisoner, instead of being subjected to a salutary discipline, becomes more depraved. I indulge a hope that this interesting subject, so often fruitlessly submitted to the Legislature, will receive your enlightened consideration."

Extract from the last Message of Governor Fish

"The Western House of Refuge for Juvenile Delinquents was in readiness in August last for the reception of persons committed thereto. I made an order, designating the counties which send juvenile delinquents to this house; it has now thirty-one inmates. The building, as now completed, affords accommodation for one hundred; three more wings can be added — each can accommodate one hundred inmates. . . . It will be seen from the rapidity with which the house is filling up, that its capacity will soon be exhausted, and another wing will be required, the cost of which will be ten or twelve thousand dollars. The past summer, the male department of the House of Refuge in the city of New York, has become so crowded, that its managers issued a notice that no more boys could be received. The whole number of children received in this house from its establishment to December 12, 1849, was 4690. At the latter date, there were 334 in the house; without more extensive accommodations, this number is larger than is consistent with a proper classification of the children, which is necessary for reformation, rather than punishment of crime, from which parental influence and good advice, kindly administered, might have restrained them. Should the Legislature determine to enlarge the Western House of Refuge, it will be advisable to transfer to that establishment from New York."

I will give one more extract from the Message of Governor Seward. " It will be shown to you that 20,000 children in the city of New York, of suitable age, are not at all instructed in the public schools, while the whole number in all the residue of the State, not taught in common schools, does not exceed 9000. . . . In our general system, trustees chosen by tax-paying citizens, levy taxes, build houses, employ and pay teachers, govern schools. . . . In the public school system of the city, 100 are trustees and instructors, and by continued consent of the common councils, are the dispensers of 35,000 dollars school fund of the State, and $95,000 derived from tax upon real and personal estates of the city. They build houses, appoint and remove teachers, fix their compensation, and prescribe the moral, religious, and intellectual instruction, their powers are effective and far-reaching, and are not derived from the community whose children are educated, and whose property is taxed, and who hold in fee the public school edifices, valued at $800,000. As neglected children of both sexes, who are found in hordes upon the wharfs and in corners of the streets, surrounded by evil associates, disturbing the public peace, committing petty depredations, and going from bad to worse, until their course terminates in high crimes and infamy; such presentment was made by a grand jury on a recent occasion."

Such is an official statement of the condition of the free schools of the city of New York, and a picture of what they will be throughout the State, under the present law, where the parent is suspended from the supervision and responsibility of educating his children, his parental affection becomes subverted, and the child is left in a state of orphanage. By a reference to the State Legislation at the last session, to provide prisons for the rapid accumulation of juvenile delinquents, we find 12,000 dollars appropriated to erect another wing to the Western House of Refuge, sufficient for 100 delinquents. For the support of the Society for the Reformation of Juvenile Delinquents of New York City, 8000 dollars.

To each of the three Dispensaries (under state charters) for delinquents each, $500

To enlarge the Clinton Prison, $20,000

For Sing Sing Prison, $9000. For Croton water, $4000. For building work-shop, $20,000.

For the Orphan Asylum of Prince Street, $5000.

For a new penitentiary in Onondaga, for offences under felony, juvenile delinquents under 16 years of age, for disorderly persons by order of justices of the peace.

The foregoing sketch of the moral condition of the youth of our State, especially in New York City, where free schools have existed for more than 30 years, and under the heavy taxation that has been imposed upon the people of this State since 1815, together with the large state funds in aid of schools, shows that neither the morals of the people of the State, nor the habits of our youth are improved since 1815. Before that time schools were supported wholly by voluntary contribution; with this exposition, the two systems and their effects can be contrasted; having seen the operation of both, we can safely judge of them. The comparison of the state of crime in article no 3, between the rural counties and those densely populated, shows a far better state of morals in the rural countries and the deportment, regulation and progress of these schools are also in much better condition, which can readily be ascribed to the feeble state of the districts requiring the special care and attention of the parents; as it cost them more they made it worth more too. — In this age of experiments it appears that the editor of the Clarion has taken a position which he no doubt expects to distinguish himself under his insignia of popular education; he says he is delighted to see opposers of the new school express their aristocratic sentiments. When I resist your attempts to plunder my pockets and apply the booty to your own indefinite term of popular education, and repudiate the doctrine of applying it to cultivate the moral sense or to religious culture, call me by any name you please that is not characteristic of your doctrine. If the common courts continue and you get a majority of the electors to support the law and it should be as operative in Syracuse as free schools are in New York, perhaps your penitentiary would get a large share of inmates. As example has strong influence it may occur that rooms may be wanted in the state building at Onondaga for some of our lads for while the fathers are voting money out of their neighbors pocket to school the boys, they are inventing keys and have obtained access to many of the desks and stores of a certain village in Livingstone county.

On examination of the juvenile penitentiary of this State, it does appear that in early life, no business industrious employment, had been required of them by their parents; and if sent to school, were left to the chances of their own inclinations, whether to apply themselves to study, or to join in the vicious examples of most children in populous places. Go to the House of Refuge — examine the early habits of the Youth! All were addicted to profanity — all but one using tobacco, — most of them to intemperance, and all of them unrestrained by parental influence. It is found that the youth strictly educated to industry, and kept in the retirements of life, and wholly dependent on private education, however limited, are seldom, if ever, found in a penitentiary. The brute recognizes the law of nature, they feed and protect their young until they come to maturity; and shall *man* throw off natural affection, and give over to the State those whom God hath given him, or abandon them to the vices of unrestrained nature!

I would suggest a subject of inquiry for the Clarion editor, and wish his answer.— What has occasioned that state of morals in Onondaga that requires a penitentiary to take charge of children under 16, and whether the town of Marcellus, or any part of that county, still retains the principles, habits, and morals of their first settlers,— such as Judge Bradley, Drs Beach and Chapman, Deacon Rice, Mrs Bellamy, Smith, Tarl, Lawrence, and others of their associates — and did *they* maintain schools, morality and religion?

So far as the principle of the free school law has gone into effect in the country, especially in some of the more populous places, we find their morals, being neglected by parents, soon partake of the character of the children of the city of New York where grand jurors present them as public nuisances, notwithstanding free schools have existed there for 30 years.

A Son of New England
—*Rochester Daily Advertiser, October 8, 1850*

The Free School Act

A case has recently been decided by Judge Shankland, in the Supreme Court of the State, which is of some considerable importance. It was that of Henry D. Bartoo vs. David W. Himrod, and others, school trustees, in Tompkins county. The action was brought for taking and selling property under a warrant issued by virtue of the provisions of what is called the new school law. A special verdict was taken by the plaintiff at the last Tompkins circuit, held by Hon. W. H. Shankland, and the question of the constitutionality of the law reserved. He has now directed a judgment for the plaintiff for the following reasons:

I base my decision of this cause on the broad ground that the act establishing free schools throughout the State, passed March 26, 1849, is unconstitutional; because instead of the Legislature passing the law definitely themselves, they have attempted to delegate their constitutional power in this respect to the people in their primary assemblies. The 10th and 14th sections of the act expressly refers the question, whether the act becomes a law or not, to the people at the polls.

The reasons why this can not be constitutionally done are fully given in the case of Parker vs. the Commonwealth, 6 Barr, Rep. 515–16, the reasoning in which case, so far is applicable to this case, and fully approved.— *Buffalo Commercial Advertiser, October 21, 1850.*

Free Schools

We hope the majority sustaining the free schools, will be found satisfactory to the Legislature soon to assemble, and to the people of the State even though it may fall short of 100,000. The great principle being now settled, the law is open for amendment. The objectionable features of it, and we have always thought there were such, may be so altered as to become acceptable to every liberalized sane man who has property to be protected, or children to be educated.

We have all along seen that the hastily drawn, and ill devised provisions of the law were in many respects objectionable; and the premature way in which it was sprung, by its enemies, upon the people, before the necessary means were procured for carrying out its details, jeopardized the popularity and stability of the whole system. Our fears were that the whole matter had become so essentially mystified, that the people would in disgust or in despair, abandon the whole matter.

Before the election we felt assured that a vast majority of the people of this State were in favor of Free Schools, that they sincerely desired that the whole people might be educated and qualified for citizenship. Yet still there was a lingering fear in our mind that the whole subject was getting so beset with collateral issues as to endanger the great principle of the freedom of knowledge. We rejoice that that matter is now settled. While the people have almost with one voice agreed that the present law is imperfect and unequal in its provisions, yet they would rather take it with its radicable evils than to run the risk of placing themselves in a false position because of these feelings of opposition to curable faults.

We congratulate the good people of the State upon these decisions. And we pray the legislature that they correct the errors in the law, making it a subject of prominent interest to see that provisions are made to educate, in all the common school branches, every child in the State.— *Journal of Education, December 1, 1850.*

Free Schools

We copy today, by request, and with pleasure, the view of an esteemed and sound democratic farmer of western New York, on a subject of the free-school law — which is again to be submitted to the people at the next election.

His objections to the law, it will be seen, are not and do not apply to the principle itself — but to the inequality which it bears upon localities, under the present system of assessment and taxation. It, in fact, brings home, by familiar illustrations, a truth which has been long left, that our system of taxation is unequal and requires thorough revision and amendment. The free-school principle, in itself, finds few, if any, opponents. In carrying out this principle, recourse was necessarily had to the present system of taxation, and it may be said with truth that the only opposition which the principle has ever met with, has grown out of its connection with a system of assessment which however equal in theory, experience has shown to be practically the reverse.

That this was the real difficulty, was apparent enough at the last session of the legislature. The discussions show very clearly, that it would be idle to attempt the establishment of Free Schools, with the prospect of permanency and the public acquiescence, until some plan should be devised and put in operation which shall distribute the burthen equally over the property of the state. And hence the effort, long continued and perserveringly pressed, by the friends of free schools, in advance of any action on the existing school law, to equalize taxation.

This effort having proved abortive, the efforts to amend the law failed also. It was finally determined to resubmit the question to the people; and it goes again to that tribunal, unfortunately for the principle, as we think, connected with a system of taxation which is the subject of general discontent. How far this connection of a popular with an unpopular principle, will operate to embarrass the former, is obvious from the strictures on the latter which we copy. They are entitled, from their source, as well as from their temperate manner, to consideration, and will no doubt receive it at the hands of the farming population to whom and for whom he has a right to speak.— *Albany Argus (editorial), July 29, 1850.*

The School Law

(From the Batavia Spirit of the Times)

By an act passed last winter, the electors of the State are again required to vote for or against the new school law. I did not vote upon the question at the last election, because I did then and still do deny the power of the

Legislature to throw back upon its constituency the duties of the legislation. By the constitution the powers of the legislation are exclusively vested in the Legislature, with the exception of the power to create a debt in certain cases and the required vote of the people on proposed amendments of the constitution. The members of the Legislature in the Senate and Assembly convened, are the agents of the people, assembled to perform their duty under the constitution. I contend that they have no right to flinch from the responsibilities of their station — to throw back upon their principals, the people, the duties which they have undertaken to perform and are paid for performing.

This act of the Legislature should not be countenanced as a precedent. If followed hereafter, it may be productive of much evil — instead of having one law referred to us at each election hereafter, we may have twenty. It is easy to see the social discord, confusion and anarchy that the practice of transferring legislation to the people under this precedent, would, in a short time produce.

Again — the constitution declares that a majority of the members of the Legislature elected, (not of the quorum voting,) shall be necessary to the passage of any law. Upon this principle that the majority shall rule, a majority of all of the voters residing in the States and not of those who may come to the polls and vote, should be required to sanction the present law. If vitality is given to the present law by the act of the people and not of the Legislature, then I assert that a majority of the whole people entitled to vote, whether if they vote or not, should be required, to render the law valid and morally binding upon the whole people of the State.

But it was not my intention when I commenced this article to say anything upon the subject of this novel course of legislation. I may refer to it again in a subsequent article.

The law submitted declares two principles — first, that schools shall be free. Second, it prescribes a principle or plan of taxation for their support, exceedingly unequal and oppressive in its operation, and the elector is forced to vote for or against the whole law. If he resides in a farming community and is honestly in favor of free schools he cannot go for this principle without putting his neck in a yoke, which, upon the least reflection, no man of spirit and intelligence, would for one moment consent to wear.

The injustice of the law, after one year's experience under it, is so generally known, that I need say little in regard to its operation. It is well understood that it bears heavily upon the agricultural towns as compared with cities and villages. It is everywhere unequal and unjust. In a village near me is a school district in which are located three banks and a section of a railroad. The amount of taxable property in this district is, say one million of dollars — in an adjoining district the amount of taxable property is about one-tenth of that sum. In the same town are two adjoining districts. In the one are say fifty scholars and $80,000 taxable property; and in the other twenty-five scholars and $40,000 taxable property. The inhabitants of the latter district with half the means of the former, are subject to the same yearly expenses for maintaining a school.

These are not singular instances of the inequality produced by this law, but similar instances I venture to affirm may be found in every town in the State.

This school law seems to have been framed in analogy to the poor laws of Great Britain, and for a long period adopted in this country, and which require the parishes and towns to support their own poor.

I shall not stop here to discuss the injustice of these poor laws. Even if they could be relied on as a precedent for the new school law. It is well known that after the revolution in the hurry to settle the new government we adopted many of the unequal and unjust laws of England, laws originally made under the most despotic kings of that country, and maintained by the aristocracy through a long course of years for the purpose of relieving the wealthy and noble of the land from the taxes and burthens of the government. Our forefathers adopted these laws from necessity and for the present, very much as our puritanical forefathers adopted the laws of God — until they had time to make better.

But there is no just analogy between these poor laws and the school law, excepting so far as to require the towns and districts to educate in their schools the children of the poor, and a provision to this effect has always been contained in our school law. But when the State commands that all its children, the rich as well as the poor shall be educated, it is just that the tax for that purpose should be a charge upon all the taxable property of the State, as much as the expenses for arming and training the militia, or for any other general object.

Shall we vote for this law under the impression that the Legislature will, hereafter, amend it and make it more just and equitable? Let us not deceive ourselves on this score. The history of the law so far, although short, is instructive. Many thousands undoubtedly, voted for this law at the last election, under the expectation that the Legislature, at its next session would amend it. But what was the result? The proposition to graduate the tax for the support of free schools upon the whole property of the State, was distinctly submitted in the assembly by Mr. Burroughs, a member from the county of Orleans, and enforced with much spirit and ability, but that body refused to entertain the proposition. It was opposed by members from the large towns, and I believe by the whole delegation from the city of New York. That great city will not consent that her taxable property amounting to nearly three hundred millions of dollars, should go into a common fund, with the other taxable property of the State, for the purpose of educating all the children of the State.

It was said by Mr. Jefferson that great cities were great sores upon the body corporate. That all cities and villages are so to a certain extent, cannot be denied. They are like civil government itself — necessary evils. I certainly do not wish to excite a prejudice on the part of the country, against cities and villages. But I wish to say, distinctly, to the laboring farmers in the rural districts of the state, that, in my judgment, it will be a long time before we shall obtain any important amendment of this school law should it again be sanctioned by the popular vote.

Communities of men as well as individuals, are very apt to regard their own interests when taxes are assessed by the State. That the present school law favors the capitalists who mostly congregate in the cities and villages at the expense of the farming community, is evident. The law is favorable to them, and their combined opposition to any future amendment may be expected.

Associated wealth, it has been said by some, is the dynasty of modern states. The truth of this saying is fully exemplified in the history and present condition of the civil governments on the other side of the Atlantic. It remains to be seen whether the same influence shall dictate to us and control the destinies of this country.

The national government, we expect, will continue its indirect and unequal system of taxation, but under the state administration we have been led to hope that the burthens of government would be more justly distributed.

There are doubtless many in the state who will vote for this school law with a proviso, that is, provided the legislature will hereafter amend it as proposed by Mr Burroughs last winter. But, I repeat, let no one be deceived with the expectation of any such amendment. We shall be told, by those whose interest it is to maintain the present law, that it has been twice sanctioned by the approval of the people, and that the legislature have really no more power than they would have over a fundamental law or amendment of the constitution which has been thus sanctioned. With what propriety can we again be asked to vote for this law, with the prospect of an amendment, when the last act of the Legislature before sending the law to us a second time, was, to refuse the very amendment. If the legislature really desire the vote of the people on free schools why did they not submit that distinct proposition only?

I conclude, therefore, that the only proper and safe course, at the next election, will be to vote against this law, and let our agents or servants in the Legislature understand that if they want us to assume the responsibility of legislation for them that they have — the privilege of voting upon distinct propositions, separately — that they shall not be allowed to compel us to vote for a bad law in the whole, for the privileging of approving one good principle contained in it.

The proposition is insulting. It proceeds upon the idea of the hobby riding demigogue that the people, like children, will swallow almost anything, if some sweet or pleasant thing is mixed with it.

I have ever considered a just and equal system of taxation in a free country — a system carefully graduated upon capital and not upon labor, as more important to the cause of freedom and humanity than any other consideration. The subject should command our increasing vigilance.

A Farmer
—*Albany Argus, August 2, 1850*

Free School Principle

To the Editors of the Argus:

I have just risen from the perusal of an article in your paper of Monday last, from the Batavia " Spirit of the Times," in favor of the unconditional repeal of the existing free school law, and which purports to express, and I doubt not, does express the views of an esteemed and sound democratic farmer of western New York, on this subject. Believing, as I do that many of the positions assumed in that article are untenable and unsound and that the conclusions of the writer are unwise and unjust, I respectfully ask the favor of a small space in your columns for the purpose of pointing out what I deem to be the radical defects of the reasoning employed, and the inferences deduced.

I cheerfully concur with the writer of the article in question, in his view relative to the inexpediency and impropriety, if not the unconstitutionality of thus calling upon the people, in mass, to sanction or repudiate a law. I will not say that a law thus sanctioned is of no validity. Such a declaration can properly emanate only from our highest judicial tribunal. But in my judgment, this mode of legislation could never have been contemplated by the framers of our constitution; and its only effect is to transfer the legislative power and authority from the arena properly and specifically assigned to another and quite incongruous tribunal. I regret that the precedent should ever have been established; and sincerely trust that the present will be the last occasion we shall have for its use. As to the majority requisite to give validity to the popular expression in a case of this kind, I do not know that we are justifiable in laying down any positive rules. A majority of all those voting may, perhaps, fairly be regarded as sufficient for this purpose.

But to the merits of the question before us. I understand the writer of the article under review, to occupy a position antagonistical to the existing law, and not to the principle of free schools; and the whole drift of his argument is to the effect that the friends of this great principle have no assurance, and can have none, that a verdict against the repeal of the present law, will secure the adoption of such amendments and modifications of that law as will serve to render its provisions generally acceptable to the people. It strikes me on the other hand, that they have the strongest possible assurances of which the case will admit.

The details of the present law are universally condemned. I do not know of a single individual who desires to retain it, as a whole, upon the statute book for a single hour after a meeting of the legislature. It is defective in many very important respects: and none more pertinaciously urged upon the last legislature, the duty of amending it in these respects than the most active and efficient friends of the principle contained in the first section. We are all, therefore, agreed upon this point; and if the only question to be determined by the electors at the polls was, whether this law, as it is, should stand or fall, I apprehend there would be very little difference of opinion. The representatives of every assembly district in the state cannot therefore if they would, mistake the will of their constituents in this respect. And if those constituents prefer any particular mode in which this obnoxious law should be amended, they have only to indicate their will, and if necessary, require pledges in advance from the candidates at the polls.

But what will be the effect of a repeal of the existing law, as a whole? Does "A Farmer" suppose for one moment that a law embodying the principle of free schools, would, in that event, be likely to pass either the present, or any succeeding legislation, for a quarter of a century to come? I venture to say there is not an intelligent individual in the state, who entertains such an idea. The rejection of the present law, imperfect and highly objectional as it is, insures therefore, the total defeat of the free school principle, beyond the hope of resurrection; while its renewed sanction by the people recognizing and preserving the principle leaves it open to such amendments and modifications as shall be demanded by public sentiment from every section of the state.

It is not the fault of the friends of free schools that so embarrassing an issue has been forced upon them. They demanded distinct and specific amendments to the act of 1849; the assembly by a heavy and strong vote adopted these amendments; the Senate laid them upon their table; and at the close of the session, the two houses, being unable to agree, determined, in the absence of a single petition to that effect, and directly in disregard of public sentiment strongly expressed to resubmit the present law. The people literally asked for bread and the legislature gave them stones!

Now what, under such circumstances is the plain path of duty for the friends of education and free schools? Shall they, after years of toiling, patient, earnest effort to secure the recognition and adoption of this great measure, and when success is already fairly within their grasp, turn their back upon the cherished object of their labor, simply because it is not in all respects what they would have it; or shall they fix their regards firmly and unwaveringly upon the Principle, and determine to sustain and perpetuate that, at all hazards? If this can only be accomplished by sustaining the present law, then it should be sustained, and the legislature called upon to apply the necessary corrective.

The opponents of free schools will rally in one compact mass in favor of the repeal of the present law well aware that success on this issue will prove the death blow to the entire system. Many of them will profess great devotion to the principle, and endeavor to disguise their real hostility to it by a war of posts against the details of the act of 1849. Will the friends of universal education allow themselves to be duped by this shallow devise, and be found shoulder to shoulder with their opponents in prostrating the hopes and paralizing the energy of the advocates and supporters of free schools? I trust not. Let it be remembered that this issue is not whether the existing law shall remain on the statute book, but whether the State of New York, having determined by an overwhelming majority, that her 10,000 schools shall henceforth be free to every child within her border, that determination shall be reversed or triumphantly sustained. It is idle to talk about imperfections and efficiency of any particular system while the principle itself is in controversy. Once settled that, and an enlightened legislature, coming fresh from the people, will have no difficulty in adjusting details. If my democratic friend from Batavia, will declare himself opposed to the principle of free schools, he will be promptly and fairly met; and at all events, his right to advise those who think with him, as to the course most proper to be pursued by them for the accomplishment of the object they have in view, will not be contemplated. If, on the other hand, he is in reality a friend of free schools, he has in my humble judgment taken the most effectual means to secure the defeat of the very measure he approves. Every vote given, at the approaching election for the repeal of the new school law is, in effect, if not in intention, a vote against the principle of universal education: while, on the other hand, every vote cast " against the repeal of that act " is a vote in favor of that principle.

In common I doubt not, with the vast majority of the friends of free schools I am opposed to the details of the existing law, and desire and expect to see it amended and essentially modified; but I shall, nevertheless, vote against its repeal, in the full confidence that an enlightened legislature will carry out the clearly expressed wishes of the people in such a mode as will prove generally satisfactory.

A Friend to Education

— *Albany Argus, August 3, 1850*

The Senate bill repealing the free school law passed the House on the last night of the session, by 67 ayes to 22 nays. The House bill, providing for raising a general tax of $800,000 upon the State, had been previously lost in the Senate. We regard this as extremely unfortunate legislation. The action was based upon the petition of some 17,000 of those who voted against the proposition last fall, and in the face of 160,000 majority in its favor. This unstable, changing policy, has a tendency to destroy all confidence in legislative action, and in the permanency of all laws. There is one redeeming feature about it, however, the whole question is to be again submitted to the people.— *Buffalo Commercial Advertiser, April 12, 1850*

The Free School Law

The act to submit to the people, at the next annual election, the repeal of the act establishing free schools throughout the State, provides:

1 To submit the question of repeal or no repeal to the people, in November next.

2 Requires the State Superintendent to furnish each town clerk with one copy, and each school district with five copies of the law, with blank forms, poll lists, &c.

3 A separate box is to be provided to the tickets, which are to be "School — against the repeal of the new School Law." The tickets to be canvassed by state canvassers, same as votes for Governor, &c.

4 If the act is repealed, then all the acts repealed by the law are to become in force. But no suits, &c., which may have grown out of the law, are to be affected.— *Rochester Daily Democrat, April 13, 1850*

The School Law

The great anxiety which has prevailed to know what the Legislature would do to repair the breaches and remedy the defects in the school law of the last session, will hardly be satisfied with the knowledge that nothing has been done, except to send the question of its repeal to the people, to be voted on at the next election. Our wise Legislature have figured in this matter very much like the renowned hero, who

"with forty thousand men,
Marched up the hill and then marched down again."

This we apprehend, will be found a very inconvenient and unsatisfactory way of legislating. The vote of the pepole can only apply to the particular question, and in the particular form proposed.— Last year they adopted a law because of a principle it was supposed to contain, taking it for granted that the congregated wisdom of the great whig party, including "the distinguished whig Secretary of State" was competent to pass a law for the attainment of a simple, plain object; but instead of "free schools," it opened upon the system a very Pandora's box of evils. The present Legislature lacking the ability to find the appropriate remedy or the courage to apply it, have waived all responsibility, and the people, after suffering in their dearest interests all the effects of political and legislative charlatanry, will, in time, have the privilege of saying whether they will continue the evils they are experiencing, or return to the old system. They have no means of amendment, or middle choice. The question is the law as they have found it, or not the law.—*Binghamton Democrat, April 18, 1850*

Free School Law

The following is the vote upon the repeal of the free school law, in the several towns in this county as officially announced:

	For Repeal	Against
Aurora	317	198
Amherst	134	208
Alden	209	146
Brandt	145	23
Boston	169	86
Black Rock	107	564
Concord	348	143
Clarence	199	119
Collins	321	334
Colden	45	92
Cheektowaga	56	5
Evans	202	103
Eden	325	142
Hamburgh	300	218
Holland	183	65
Lancaster	109	156
Newstead	289	142
Sardinia	230	77
Tonawanda	220	243
Wales	252	117
Buffalo — 1st ward	110	479
2d ward	38	838
3d ward	105	458
4th ward	174	1017
5th ward	30	544
Total	4672	6445
		4672
Majority against repeal		1773

It will be seen that 15 of the 20 country towns gave majorities in favor of repeal.

The majority vote by counties for and against the free school law is shown in the following table:

County	For Free Schools	Against Free Schools
Albany	5 272	
Allegany		1 626
Broome		175
Cattaraugus		979
Cayuga		230
Chautauqua		1 630
Chemung		180
Chenango		2 470
Clinton		70
Columbia	1 828	
Cortland		1 997
Delaware		2 028
Dutchess	3 923	
Erie	1 743	
Essex		579
Franklin		443
Fulton and Hamilton		973
Genesee		1 132
Greene		1 379
Herkimer		50
Jefferson		2 106
Kings	10 076	
Lewis		964
Livingston		1 051
Madison		642
Monroe		68
Montgomery	1 042	
New York	37 827	

	For Free Schools	Against Free Schools
Niagara		1 292
Oneida		897
Onondaga	1 926	
Ontario		742
Orange		909
Orleans		1 312
Oswego		471
Otsego		1 720
Putnam		114
Queens	508	
Rensselaer	3 806	
Richmond	861	
Rockland	112	
St Lawrence		1 069
Saratoga		1 134
Schenectady	52	
Schoharie		2 548
Seneca	303	
Steuben		1 361
Suffolk		368
Sullivan		273
Tioga		1 654
Tompkins		2 517
Ulster	237	
Warren		704
Washington		1 008
Wayne		2 137
Westchester	2 272	
Wyoming		1 545
Yates		661
Total	71 912	46 874

The majority against repeal, 25,038.

—*Buffalo Commercial Advertiser, November 22, 1850*

The Free School Law Sustained
(From the Albany Journal)

We have, at length, the official vote on this exciting topic from fifty two of the fifty nine counties in the State, showing a majority of upwards of *thirty two thousand* against the repeal of the law. The remaining seven counties will probably reduce this majority somewhat; but it may safely be stated at from twenty-five to **thirty thousand.**

In view of the numerous embarassments which surround this question — the misconception to a very considerable extent, of the issue involved — and the fact that very few of the conductors of the political press throughout the State felt themselves called upon to interfere in the discussion, on the one side or the other,— this result must be deemed decisive by the public sentiment in favor of the principle of free schools. We trust the Legislature will so modify the existing law, as to render its details acceptable to all parties.

We are requested by the State Superintendent to state for the benefit of officers and inhabitants of school districts generally, that in his opinion and that of the Attorney General, who has been consulted on this subject, the late decision of Judge Shankland, of the Supreme Court, adverse to the constitutionality of the existing law, is conclusive only as between the parties to the suit before him; and that until such judgment is, in some way affirmed by the Court of Appeals, the law must be deemed constitutional and valid to all intents and purposes. Both the Superintendent and the Attorney General are decidedly of opinion that the law was constitutionally enacted; and that there is no probability that the Court of Appeals, should the question ever come before that tribunal, will otherwise decide. —*Binghamton Republican, November 19, 1850*

Free Schools

It appears from so much of the returns as have reached us, that the people of the State have decided against the repeal of the present free school act by a pretty large majority. The city of New York alone giving some 38,000 in favor of the law and only a few hundred against it. The most of the cities have voted in favor of the law, and opposition generally has come from the "rural districts." The resubmission to the people of this law, so short a time after its emphatic sanction by them, was a most silly piece of business and their verdict is such as we had a right to expect from their general intelligence. They are not apt in so marked a manner to stultify themselves, and have shown themselves capable of distinguishing between a principle, and a defect in the machinery which applies it. And now that the law has been sustained let it be thoroughly tried, and let judicious legislation remedy the imperfections which may be developed by experience. Ten years hence and few will be willing to acknowledge that they ever opposed it." — *Canajoharie Radii, November 14, 1850*

The Free School Law

The New York Courier and Enquirer has the following remarks upon the subject of the school law and its affirmance by the vote of the cities of the State:

This city alone, it will be remembered, gave a majority of 30,000 against the repeal of the law; and if the aggregate majority is no greater than the Journal supposes, it is clear that the cities have decided the question. And yet the cities are not affected in the least by the law, while it is believed by many to bear oppressively upon the country districts. Such a result is very much to be deprecated, as it will inevitably feed and increase that jealousy of the country districts towards the city, which is always strong enough, and from which nothing but evil can result. It will be remembered that a proposition was brought forward last winter, and carried through the Assembly, to pay the entire expenses of the free schools through the State, out of the general fund. This would have the effect of making New York City support her own free schools and at the same time contribute over $200,000 annually towards supporting the free schools of the rural districts. This bill was prevented from becoming a law by the passage of the law submitting the whole subject again to the people. And if now the free school law shall have been kept in force by the cities, and against the wishes of the country districts, the effort will undoubtedly be renewed to put it upon a basis which shall throw a large proportion of the expense upon property in the cities: — and the chances of its success are decidedly increased by the recent canvass.

The adjustment of this vexed question, upon a basis which shall at once promote the cause of universal education, and relieve the people from unjust and unequal taxation, will be one of the most important and difficult duties of the Legislature at its coming session.—*Buffalo Commercial Advertiser, November 20, 1850*

Joseph McKeen, superintendent of common schools for the city and county of New York in his report dated November 1, 1850, says under the heading

Free Schools

It is commonly expected of a New England superintendent of schools, when the subject of free schools is under consideration, that he will run off into an eulogy upon the pilgrims, Massachusetts, and the fathers who settled these Eastern States. I have often thought that these eulogiums were more faithful to the filial reverence which is due to the good men who were our ancestors, than to the veritable history of the early days of the common schools. As a son of New England, I claim to know something of their educational institutions. Their colleges and higher seminaries of learning have always been among the best in this country, and they have contributed in a great degree to make and sustain a respect among the people for learning. Common schools have been taught from time immemorial in the district school houses, for about three months in the winter, by students, and by young men of various callings, who were but partially educated, and that partial education having but little if any reference to teaching. A long vacation ensued, and the school passed into the hands of some young woman, who tried her skill for the first time in the line of instruction. In this way a school was kept for half the year, without much of professional skill or system about it. But it was so much better than no school; so much better than was done in some other parts of the country, that sons, "to the manor born," have written and published laudatory chronicles of the teachers, until they are now almost fulsome. The truth is, there is to this day no perfected system of common school education in this country. That of the State of New York is probably the best, and that is very far from being what it ought to be.

It is, perhaps, not so important that the school should be absolutely free, as that it should embrace within its salutary influences the instruction of the whole youthful population. In some countries, as in Prussia, it has been found that assessing a small school tax upon every child of the school age, (from 7 to 14,) whether the child attend school or not, produced a larger average attendance than a school entirely free, leaving the attendance voluntary and optional. Seven years of every child is said to be due to the school.

It is the opinion of the Hon. H. Barnard, the able superintendent of Connecticut, and many others, that paying a small sum makes parents have a higher appreciation of the school, and they are more likely to send their children regularly to it, than if the school were made absolutely free. We cannot fail to feel respect for this desire of a people to pay for what they use, and to use it all the more freely because they pay for it. A system of taxation, to be perfectly equitable, ought to be so distributed among the various interests of the community which are to be benefited by it, as to draw from each a return for the good received. The doctrine that the property of the State must pay for the education of the children of the State, is a sort of admitted truism, which is susceptible, however, of sundry explanations. To say that one man has a right to another man's money, to educate the children of the former, or for any other purpose, is not true; but for the State to say that property shall be taxed for the benefit of the community in which it is, and to increase the security of the property itself, is true beyond all dispute.

There is no one item, in all our catalogue of public burdens, which ought to be hailed with so much tolerance and favor as that which goes to educate the youthful population. Education prevents and diminishes crime, gives security to property, lessens the expense of poor-rates, hospitals, prisons, and police establishments. It dispels the gloomy superstitions of ignorance; it evokes the innate energies of genius; it quickens and defines human enjoyments; and it subordinates the mightly physical agencies of nature, which it finds out and applies to the service and comfort of man.

A liberal policy would then seem to commend itself to every good citizen in behalf of this beneficent instrumentality. It is the behest of wisdom that the common elements of necessary knowledge be made universally free. This is the common sentiment of the people of New York. The light of Heaven and the pure water from the mountain are free, for both man and beast, in all parts of the country where the works of God remain undisturbed. In this crowded city, the princely tax payers delight humbly to imitate the munificence of Heaven; and we see, when night comes on, a bright artificial light in all our streets; the pure gushing waters are in the free hydrants at the corners; and the free schools are telling, day and night, in all parts of the city. No rich man sleeps the worse for his liberality; and every poor man loves his county the more by reason of its unsurpassed privileges.

Chapter 10

THE FREE SCHOOL LAW OF 1851

The question of the repeal of the law of 1849 was defeated in the election of November of 1850 by a 25,000 majority. Superintendent Morgan in his annual report of 1851 comments as follows upon the educational situation:

The history of the past year, in reference to this great enterprise, has been one of mingled triumph and disaster. The principle incorporated in the "Act for the establishment of free schools throughout the State," has been again subjected to the test of public opinion. In their almost unanimous approval of that *principle* in the canvass of 1849, the electors very generally overlooked the specific details of the bill submitted to their sanction, confiding in the disposition of the Legislature to modify such of its features as might be practically objectionable. Serious obstacles to the successful operation of the law presented themselves almost upon the threshold of its administration. The boards of supervisors in more than one-half the counties of the State, had adjourned their annual sessions before the act took effect, without making the appropriations required by its provisions, leaving the several school districts to sustain a most unequal and oppressive burden of taxation for the support of their schools.

Inequalities in the valuations of taxable property contributed, in many localities, greatly to aggravate this burden, and a spirit of opposition to the new law, inflamed by its determined opponents, manifested itself at the primary district meetings, and too often resulted in the entire rejection of the estimates prepared by the trustees and the limitation of the term of school to the lowest possible period authorized by law. Appeals were assiduously made to the cupidity of the heavy tax payers — their interests sought to be arrayed against that of their less favored brethren, and against the interests of their children; their passions stimulated by the real inequalities as well as fancied injustice of the burdens imposed by the new law, were readily enlisted against every attempt to carry it into operation. Numerous petitions were sent to the Legislature, praying for its repeal or for such amendments as might render it more generally acceptable.

It was obvious that the law was liable to just and serious objections, and that it did not meet with that general approval which was necessary to ensure its success. Under these circumstances, the friends of the new system were among the first to concede the defects of the bill, and while urging the preservation of the fundamental *principle* which it involved, were anxiously solicitous so to modify the details of the measure, as to obviate all its obnoxious features. At their suggestion and with their co-operation, bills were introduced into both branches of the Legislature, providing for a general and equitable system of State or county taxation, for the purpose of rendering the common schools free to all, dispensing with the necessity of a district assessment, out of which the principal embarrassment had originated. In the Assembly the measures thus proposed were approved by a large majority; the Senate did not concur in the action of the house, but sent to the house a bill proposing a re-submission of the law to the people. At the close of the session, and when it became evident that no modification of the obnoxious law could be obtained, this bill received the assent of the house.

By adoption of this measure, the friends of free schools found themselves in a very embarrassing position. They were compelled either to give their votes and influence in favor of the continuance of a law, some of the distinctive features of which were at variance both with their wishes and judgment, or, by sanctioning its repeal, hazard the principle which had been deliberately adopted by the Legislature and approved by the emphatic expression of the public will. The issue thus presented could not fail of being greatly misapprehended. While the electors secured the renewed triumph of the principle involved, there can be no doubt that thousands of votes were cast for the *repeal* of the law by citizens who desired only its amendment, and who could have recorded their suffrages in favor of a system of free schools properly guarded, had the form of the ballot permitted them to do so.

It remains then for the Legislature to give efficacy to this renewed expression of the popular will, by the enactment of a law which shall definitely engraft the free school principle upon our existing system of primary education, and at the same time remove all just cause of complaint as to the inequality of taxation. District taxation has been found to be unjust, unequal, and oppressive. It should therefore at once be abandoned, so far as the ordinary support of the schools is concerned. The funds necessary for the payment of teachers' wages, in addition to the amount received from the state treasury, should be provided either by a state tax equitably levied on real and personal property according to a fixed and uniform standard of valuation, by a county and town tax levied and assessed in the same manner, or by such a combination of these three modes as might be deemed most expedient and judicious.

The common schools of the State should be declared free to every resident of the respective districts, of the proper age to participate in their benefits; and their support should be made a charge upon the whole property either of the State at large, or of the respective counties and towns in which they are situated.

The bill which passed the Assembly at its last session, provided for the levying of an annual tax of $800,000 on the real and personal property of the State according to the assessed valuation of such property, and for the distribution of the aggregate amount so to be raised, among the several counties and towns of the State, according to the number of children, of proper school age, residing in each. This sum, together with the amount annually apportioned from the revenue of the common school fund, would, it was supposed, be sufficient for the support of the several schools of the State during an average period of eight months in each year. The whole amount expended for teachers' wages, during the year 1849, was $1,322,696.24, to which is to be added an aggregate amount of $110,000 for library purposes, making in the whole $1,432,696.24. The Superintendent, however, entertains no doubt that the amount proposed to be raised by the bill referred to, in conjunction with the state appropriation, the revenue from which is rapidly and steadily increasing, will be amply adequate to the payment of

FREE SCHOOLS 421

teachers' wages for the average length of time during which the schools have heretofore been taught, and to the annual and adequate replenishment of the libraries and necessary apparatus in the schools.

Under the present defectively administered system of assessment however, such a tax will operate very unequally in different sections of the State. The standard of valuation both of real and personal property, varies, as, is well known, in nearly every county of the State; while in some, it is estimated at its fair and full market value, in others it is assessed at three-fourths, two-thirds and sometimes as low as one half its actual value. If, therefore, the existing standard of valuation is to be made the basis of the apportionment of the proposed tax, it is manifest that a very unjust and oppressive burden will be cast upon those counties where the assessment is in strict accordance with the provisions of law, for the benefit of those sections in which its requirements are valued by an arbitrary standard of valuation.

The distribution of money when raised, serves likewise to render this disproportion still more manifest, that being based upon the population according to the last preceding census of the respective counties. To exhibit the practical operation of this system, a table has been constructed under the direction of the department, and is appended to the present report, (see appendix,) by which it will be seen that the city of New York with a population of 371,223, according to the last census, and a valuation of real and personal property amounting in the aggregate to $254,192,527, *contributes* $505,295.33 annually as her proportion of the proposed State tax, while she will be entitled to *receive* only $114,025.33 as her share of its proceeds; the county of Dutchess with a population of 55,124 and a valuation of $19,390,632 contributes $23,288.92 and receives only $16,931.96; the county of Kings with a population of 78,691 and a valuation of about $40,000,000 contributes $47,940.21 and receives only $24,170.83, a diminution of nearly *one-half;* the county of Westchester with a population of 47,578 and a valuation of $20,018,964, contributes $24,043.57 and receives only $14,613.12; and the counties of Livingston, Ontario, and Queens, each receive a considerably less amount than they contribute. On the other hand, every other county in the State, receives an equal or a greater amount than it is called upon to contribute. The county of Allegany with a population of 40,000 and a valuation of $3,797,486, raises $4569.93 and receives *nearly three times* that amount, or $12,312.25; the county of Chenango with a population nearly the same and a valuation of $10,786,131, raises $5159.22 and receives $12,255.73; the county of Delaware with a population of 37,000 and a valuation of $3,737,810, raises $4489.26 and receives $11,361.89; the county of Greene with a population of 32,000 and a valuation of $2,746,933, raises $3300.00 and receives $9815.95; the county of Jefferson with a population of 65,000 and a valuation of $7,200,881, raises $8648.54 and receives $19,965.17; the county of St Lawrence with a population of 62,354 and a valuation of $3,587,629, raises $4308.88 and receives $19,152.73, between four and five times more than she contributes; the county of Schoharie with a population of 32,488 and a valuation of $1,817,804, raises $2183.25 and receives $9979.06, an excess of nearly *five times* the amount contributed; and the counties of Steuben, Tompkins and Ulster, receive from twice to three times the amount contributed by each. These discrepancies it is obvious, in a great measure, grow out of the existing inequalities in the respective standards of valuation adopted in the several counties; and should the Legislature deem it expedient to charge the annual support of the schools, over and above the revenue of the school fund, upon the taxable property of the State, and to retain the existing mode of distribution, the necessity of devising some mode by which the standard of valuation should be as nearly as practicable uniform throughout the State, will be apparent. If this can be accomplished, or if the distribution of the funds raised were directed to be made upon the same basis with the apportionment of the tax, there can be no doubt, in the judgment of the Superintendent, that a state tax for the support of our common schools will prove the simplest, most efficient and beneficial mode of providing for the object in view: the establishment and maintenance of a system of free school education, in accordance with the expressed wishes of inhabitants of the State.

If, however, this were found impracticable, the same result may be obtained by requiring the board of supervisors of each county of the State to raise *twice* the amount apportioned to the county, as a county tax, and levy an equal amount as a town tax, in the mode prescribed by the existing law, which requires only an *equal* amount to be levied as a county and town tax respectively. This provision would simply increase the amount of school money now by law required to be raised, one-third, while it would entirely dispense with district taxation, for the current support of the schools. Inequalities in the standard of valuation adopted by the respective counties, would in this case prove unjust and burdensome to none; as the existing law has made complete provision for the adjustment of such inequalities in the case of joint districts formed from parts of two or more counties or towns. The whole amount of taxable property of each county would contribute in equal and fair proportions to the support of the schools located within its territory; and the angry dissensions growing out of the necessity of district taxation, the fruitful source of nearly all the opposition which has been made to the existing law, would be averted.

In apportioning the public money, and the money raised by a county or state tax among the several school districts, the Superintendent is of opinion that some more effectual provision than now exists, should be made for the smaller and weaker districts, upon whom the burden of supporting a school for any considerable length of time during the year, is peculiarly oppressive. If a specified amount, say for instance fifty dollars, were required to be apportioned to every duly organized district whose report for the preceding year shall be found in accordance with law, leaving the balance to be apportioned according to the number of children between the ages of four and twenty-one years residing in the district, the necessary encouragement would be afforded to every district, however limited its means, or however sparse its population, while ample resources would be left for the larger and more populous districts. The several districts being thus furnished with adequate funds for the maintenance of efficient schools during an average period of eight months in each year, the trustees should be peremptorily required to expend the moneys thus placed at their disposal, in the employment of suitably qualified teachers for such a length of time as those means may justify.

Such an arrangement would, it is believed, prove almost universally acceptable to the people of the State. The principle involved has repeatedly received the sanction of public sentiment. It is in accordance with the enlightened spirit of the age. It is the only system compatible with the genius and spirit of our republican institutions. It is not a novelty, now for the first time, sought to be engrafted upon our legislation, but a principle recognized and carried in to practical operation in our sister state of Massachusetts from the earliest period of its colonial history — identified with her greatness and prosperity, her influence and her wealth, and transplanted from her soil to that of some of the younger states of the Union.

In each of our own cities, and in many of our larger villages it has been established and successfully sustained by the general approval of their citizens; and wherever it has obtained a foothold, it has never been abandoned. It is only requisite to adjust the details of the system, equitably and fairly, to commend it to the approbation of every good citizen as the noblest palladium and most effectual support of our free institutions.

The existing law has excited a degree of opposition which was not anticipated, but it is believed that it has grown out of the defects of the law, rather than from any prevailing hostility to the principle of free schools.

No law can be successfully and prosperously administered under our government, which does not receive the general approval of the people. It is the earnest desire, therefore, of the Superintendent, that the present law should be so amended as to produce greater equality — to remove all reasonable ground of complaint, and to render our great system of education more efficient and useful.

The idea of universal education is the grand central idea of the age. Upon this broad and comprehensive basis, all the experience of the past, all the crowding phenomena of the present, and all our hopes and aspiration for the future, must rest. Our forefathers have transmitted to us a noble inheritance of national, intellectual, moral and religious freedom. They have confided our destiny as a people to our own hands. Upon our individual and combined intelligence, virtue, and patriotism, rests the solution of the great problem of self-government. We should be untrue to ourselves, untrue to the memory of our statesmen and patriots, untrue to the cause of liberty, of civilization and humanity, if we neglected the assiduous cultivation of those means, by which alone we can secure the realization of the hopes we have excited. Those means are the *universal education of our future citizens,* without discrimination or distinction. Wherever in our midst, a human being exists, with capacities and faculties to be developed, improved, cultivated and directed, the avenues of knowledge should be freely opened and every facility affored to their unrestricted entrance. Ignorance should no more be countenanced than vice and crime. The one leads almost inevitably to the other. Banish ignorance, and in its stead introduce intelligence, science, knowledge and increasing wisdom and enlightenment, and you remove in most cases, all those incentives to idleness, vice and crime, which now produce such a frightful harvest of retribution, misery and wretchedness. Educate every child, "to the top of his faculties," and you not only secure the community against the depredations of the ignorant, and the criminal, but you bestow upon it, instead, productive artisans, good citizens, upright jurors and magistrates, enlightened statesmen, scientific discoverers and inventors, and the dispensers of a pervading influence in favor of honesty, virtue and true goodness. Educate every child physically, morally and intellectually, from the age of four to twenty-one, and many of your prisons, penitentiaries and almshouses will be converted into schools of industry and temples of science; and the immense amount now contributed for their maintenance and support will be diverted into far more profitable channels. Educate every child — not superficially — not partially — but thoroughly — develope equally and healthfully every faculty of his nature — every capability of his being — and you infuse a new and invigorating element into the very life blood of civilization — an element which will diffuse itself throughout every vein and artery of the social and political system, purifying, strengthening and regenerating all its impulses, elevating its aspirations, and clothing it with a power equal to every demand upon its vast energies and resources.

These are some of the results which must follow in the train of a wisely matured and judiciously organized system of universal education. They are not imaginary, but sober inductions from well authenticated facts — deliberate conclusions from established principles, sanctioned by the concurrent testimony of experienced educators and eminent statesmen and philanthropists. If names are needed to enforce the lesson they teach, those of Washington and Franklin and Hamilton and Jefferson and Clinton, with a long array of patriots and statesmen, may be cited. If facts are required to illustrate the connection between ignorance and crime, let the official return of convictions in the several courts of the State for the last ten years be examined, and the instructive lesson be heeded. Out of nearly 28,000 persons convicted of crime, but 128 had enjoyed the benefits of a *good* common school education; 414 only had what the returning officers characterize as a "tolerable" share of learning; and of the residue, about one-half could either read or write. Let similar statistics be gathered from the wretched inmates of our poor-house establishments, and similar results would undoubtedly be developed. Is it not therefore incomparably better, as a mere prudential question of political economy, to provide ample means for the education of the whole community, and to bring those means within the reach of every child, than to impose a much larger tax for the protection of that community against the depredations of the ignorant, the idle, and the vicious, and for the support of the imbecile, the thoughtless, and intemperate?

Every consideration connected with the present and future welfare of the community — every dictate of an enlightened humanity — every impulse of an enlarged and comprehensive spirit of philanthropy, combine in favor of the adoption of this great principle. Public sentiment has declared in its favor. The new states which, within the past few years, have been added to the Confederacy, have adopted it as the basis of their system of public instruction; and the older States, as one by one they are reconstructing their fundamental laws and constitutions, are engrafting the same principle upon their institutions. Shall New York, in this noble enterprise of education, retrace her steps? Shall she disappoint the high hopes and expectations she has excited, by receding from the advanced position she now occupies in the van of educational improvement? Her past career, in all those elements which go to make up the essential wealth and greatness of a people, has been one of progress and uninterrupted expansion. Her far-seeing legisla-

HENRY S. RANDALL
Secretary of State and Superintendent of Common Schools, 1852–54

tors and statesmen, uninfluenced by the scepticism of the timid, the ignorant, and the faithless, and unawed by the denunciations of the hostile, prosecuted that great work of internal improvement which will forever illustrate the pride and glory of her political history. The rich results of the experiment thus boldly ventured upon have vindicated their wisdom. Is the development of the intellectual and moral resources of her millions of future citizens an object of less interest, demanding a less devoted consecration of the energies of her people, and worthy of a less firm and uncompromising perseverance?

Disregarding the feeling of the present hour, and looking only to the future, will the consciousness of having laid the foundation for the universal education of our people be a less pleasing subject of contemplation than that of having aided in replenishing the coffers of their weatlh?

In conclusion the Superintendent can not feel that he has fully met the responsibility devolved upon him by his official relations to the schools of the State, were he to fail in again urging upon the Legislature the definite adoption of this beneficent measure. Let its details be so adjusted as to bear equally upon all, oppressively upon none. Let every discordant element of strife and passion be removed from the councils of the districts, let the necessary assessment for the great object in view, be diffused over the vast aggregate of the wealth and property of the State. Then let teachers, worthy of the name, teachers intellectually and morally qualified for the discharge of their high and responsible duties, dispense the benefits and riches of education, equally and impartially, to the eight hundred thousand children who annually congregate within the district school room.

The children of the rich and the poor, the high and the low, the native and the foreigner, will then participate alike in the inexhaustible treasures of intellect, they will commence their career upon a footing of equality, under the fostering guardianship of the State, and will gradually ripen into enlightened and useful citizens, prepared for all the varied duties of life and for the full enjoyment of all the blessings incident to humanity.

The issues which the friends of free schools had raised had for a compromise the law of 1851. There seemed to be an apparent willingness on the part of those interested to stand by and see what good might come out of the law as it now stood. This attitude is best illustrated from the extract from the annual report of Henry S. Randall, Superintendent of Common Schools, submitted December 31, 1853:

In the annual report from this Department, last year, the undersigned presented several plans for the improvement of our common school system; but, for reasons then assigned, he did not ask, nor subsequently attempt to procure immediate legislative action on, beyond a few of these which were considered of pressing necessity, and which would not materially affect the structure of the system. The reasons assigned for this course were, that our school laws had been so often changed during the last few years, that a proper opportunity was not given to test their actual merits or defects, and to provide the best remedies for the latter, where clearly found to exist; that a system kept thus unsettled, could not acquire vigor and adapt itself to the diversified circumstances of a widespread population; that the local officers charged with its administration, numbering nearly sixty thousand, and usually chosen with little reference, to their familiarity with the nice construction of statutes, were confused and discouraged by these incessant changes, and hence discharged their duties not only with a want of accuracy, but with a want of zeal still more fatal to the prosperity of our schools.

Another reason was assigned for a pause in school legislation. Some of the most prominent and probably objectionable features of the present law, were adopted as a compromise between the parties to the bitter controversy which grew out of the enactment of the free school law of 1849. This controversy had proved so disastrous, not only to the immediate prosperity of the schools, but to that concert of feeling and action among the inhabitants of districts, on which the future success of the schools depended, that a reagitation of the topics involved in it was not deemed expedient, until time had somewhat mitigated past asperities, and given opportunity for that calm reflection which could not fail to teach sensible men the folly of periling interests so high and dear, by like causes in future.

The preceding considerations not only prevented the undersigned from urging plans of change immediately, the ultimate utility of which he considered unquestionable, but from mentioning others which have elicited much popular discussion and advocacy, but in regard to the present or abstract expediency of which, or in regard to the precise details for safely and wisely carrying out which, his own views were not fully matured. Practicing the same caution which he urged on the Legislature, he preferred, as then avowed, to bring to his aid the observation and experience of another year, before making propositions in regard to which any of the above doubts were entertained, subjects of official recommendation or censure.

The question now arises, has the proper period yet arrived for any material revision of our school laws? Have existing defects proved so serious as to demand it? If so, has sufficient time been given for experience to add its suggestion to those of sound theory, in indicating the appropriate remedies? Have the fires of controversy so far died away, as to permit that unanimity of purpose and effort which are indispensable to success?

On the whole, the undersigned is disposed to answer these questions affirmatively; to assume that the time has arrived when sound conservatism lies in action. Existing defects, as will presently be shown, are deep seated, and are exerting widely pernicious influences. A three years' lull in school legislation has afforded a reasonable opportunity for examination. The final decision by the court of last resort that the free school law of 1849 is unconstitutional, has to great extent, ended the heart-burnings which its enactment engendered. No accumulation of great and doubtful questions of State policy, it would now appear, will press upon the Legislature to engross its time and attention. A Superintendent comes into office, to act as the official aider and adviser of the Legislature, who is not called upon to express opinions on an imperfectly tried past, or on freshly broached theories of the future; nor will his action be necessarily cramped by the ultraism and the jealousies of excited school factions. On all of these accounts the period would seem to be as propitious for action, as any which the difficult and not very flexible circumstances which invest the subject will permit to occur. And if a revision is entered upon, expediency would seem to require that it be made as complete, even to minor details, as practicable, both to the end that all the parts of the system may be made to harmonize, and to avoid the necessity of the those speedy amendments which will continue to keep the system unsettled.

The parts of the school system which require revision are those connected with its pecuniary structure, and those which determine its success in its first main object of educating the young. They will be examined in this order.

The $800,000 School Tax

Attention was called last year to the obvious fact that if a tax yielding a fixed amount met the wants of the schools, and justly determined the proportion in which the property of the State, as such, should contribute to the support of popular education, in any given year, it certainly could not fulfil these conditions five years afterwards, when both population and property had largely advanced. The increase of population would necessarily diminish the allowance to each scholar, and the increase of property would diminish the percentum of its burthen. The gradual exemption of wealth at the expense of a corresponding depression of popular education, is a policy which will find few advocates. As one of the compromises which followed the repeal of the free school law of 1849, an immediate disturbance of this provision was not recommended last year; but it is obvious that no revision of the school system would be complete, or would obtain general acquiescence beyond a short period, which should fail to change a basis of taxation, which, for this specific purpose, is so unsound in theory and so pernicious in practice.

A mill tax on the property of the State was recommended last year as the proper ultimate substitute for the present one. It was recommended by a previous Superintendent, and it seems to be the rate of state taxation for school purposes, generally fixed upon by the investigating friends of popular education, as the one best calculated to do justice to all interests. The wealth of the State has virtually acquiesced in its property by assenting to the present tax, which when it was imposed, exceeded a mill on the dollar of the assessed value of the property of the State. Its adoption would probably be accepted by all parties as a final disposition of the subject.

Distribution of the School Moneys

The distribution of the public school moneys in a manner to confer an equal share of their benefits on localities and individuals, has been found attended with great difficulty. Prior to 1849, the proceeds of the school fund and an equal sum raised by the towns, were ultimately divided among the towns on basis of population, and among the school districts on the basis of the pupils returned as residing in them. This plan of distribution operated greatly to the advantage of populous and wealthy districts, over districts differently situated in these particulars. The expense of a small or a large school of the same grade, does not greatly vary. In thinly populated regions, a district not too large to admit of convenient access to the schoolhouse, would necessarily include but a small population, and consequently, but a small number of scholars; and the same causes which lead to the limitation of population, generally lead to the limitation of wealth. A distribution based on the number of pupils, would give to such a district a comparatively small amount of money; would consequently lead to the imposition of more onerous rate bills and the latter would fall where there was the least ability to pay them. Yet this system was long acquiesced in. Both the law and public sentiment recognized the cost of education as mainly a personal burthen, which every man was required to incur for his own offspring. Following out the same idea, it was not felt that the Legislature had a right to attempt to equalize the burdens of education, as between localities or individuals, by adopting any peculiar system of distributing the public moneys specifically designed to attain that end; but rather that it was bound to give every scholar his pro rata share of those moneys, and leave parents to provide what was further necessary as best they might.

A different theory as to where rested the responsibility of educating the people; began to prevail. As ignorance is the parent of crime and civil disorder, it was claimed that a free government was bound to provide for its own stability, and wealth to pay for its own security, by assuming the burthen of popular education. It was insisted that after using the revenues set apart by the government for that purpose, the common schools of the State ought to be supported by a direct tax on property. This principle, to its fullest extent, was engrafted into our laws in 1849. This wholly changed the theory on which a proper distribution of the school moneys rested. If the property of the State is required to support the education of the State, it follows, that the benefit received by it being everywhere the same, its burthens should in like manner be the same. And another important principle came into operation. When the State determined that education should be supported by public contribution, it gave to every citizen a common and equal right to the benefits accruing therefrom. The spirit and theory of the law was, not to aid parents in educating their offspring by dividing a particular sum of money between them, but that the State should assume the whole expense of such education, and raise whatever sum was necessary therefor. Every child was equally entitled to an *education,* whether residing in the heart of the city of New York, or on the hills of Hamilton county. But wholly overlooking the principles on which it was based, the " free school act " of 1849, substantially retained the previously existing plan of distribution: to counties and towns on the basis of population, to school districts on that of enumerated pupils. Not only was the cardinal theory of the law thus violated, but the unequal effects of such a distribution, when applied to such increased sums of money, became vastly more apparent than under the old law. In the densely populated districts of cities and villages, the schools received more than was sufficient for their support from the avails of the school fund and from county and town taxes, while in the thinly inhabited country districts, it was necessary to resort to additional and onerous district taxes (which had now taken the place of rate bills) to make up deficiencies. It sometimes happened that this additional district tax reached several mills on the dollar; thus making a practical difference of two or three hundred per centum in the taxation of adjacent and not unfrequently adjoining property, to attain an object from which the benefits derived were equal, and the duty of contributing to the attainment of which was consequently equal.

Results so flagrantly unjust, could not long be tolerated. The rural regions crushed by the operation of the law, through their representatives, repealed it. The agricultural population of the State have ever shown that they prize the blessing of universal education, and are willing to make as many sacrifices to secure it, as the inhabitants of cities. They demonstrated this by patiently paying more in proportion to their property, than the latter, to educate their children, for a period of more than fifty years anterior to 1849. It was the *structure* and not the *principle* of the free school law of 1849, which gave to the popular vote on it so well defined a local classification. The country cordially united with the cities in passing the school act of 1851, which was intended to recognise the same main principle, that the property of the State shall educate the children of the State.

The act of 1851 distributes two-thirds of all the public money, on the previously established basis. But to guard against the local inequalities before produced, it provides that one-third of the public money, (excepting library money) shall be divided by districts; in other words, that every district in the State, wholly irrespective of its number of pupils, shall receive an equal share from it. This has effectually relieved the country districts. It is strenuously urged in many quarters that it has done more than this — that it has turned the scale in the opposite direction, and made the burthen of supporting schools lighter both to property and persons, in the country, than in the cities and villages. In proof of this, such statistics as the following are pointed to: The number of pupils (between four and twenty-one), reported in the city of New York, in 1850, was 120,812. These were included in 215 districts, making 561 pupils for each district. The share which each district in the State received from the equally divided one-third of the public moneys, was $29.85; and consequently all the New York schools received from this source $6417.75. The six counties of Allegany, Madison, Oswego, Otsego, St. Lawrence, and Steuben, did not report quite an equal number of pupils, viz., 120,124. But these were arranged in 1914 districts, and their share in the one-third division, was $57,132.90. New York contributed $255,670.80 toward the $800,000 State school tax; the above named counties contributed $55,667.75. New York, over and above that portion of its contribution to the state tax which was disbursed within its own limits, paid an excess to support education in other counties, of $129,971.91. In the six counties named, there was no excess over their own disbursements, but a deficiency of $54,027.38 to be made up from the excesses in other counties. All the pupils in the city of Utica were included in one district and, consequently, received but one share from the distribution by districts. Yet Utica included more pupils, and paid more taxes than half a dozen of the country towns in the same county, which, perhaps, received nearly a hundred such shares. Examples like the above, are to be found throughout the State.

Striking, and at first view, seemingly unjust as are these results, no valid objection can be made to the provision of law which produces them, providing it produces the concurrent results of everywhere equal taxation, and everywhere equal facilities for education. If the doctrine maintains that the property of the State, as such, shall support public education, no sound reason can be assigned why its aggregation in cities shall relieve it from paying as much on the dollar for that object, as is paid by the more thinly diffused wealth of the country; or why, as has been sometimes urged, county lines should limit its disbursement. If the doctrine maintains that the wealthy individual, though he have no children, shall aid poorer neighbor in paying for schools, no sound reason can be assigned why the wealthy county or neighborhood shall not aid the poorer one for the same end. It is no greater hardship for New York to aid Oneida, than it is for the city of Utica, in that county, to aid one of its poorer towns, and the hardship is greater in neither case than it is to tax any one individual for the benefit of another. The only theory on which a state tax for education can be defended at all, is that education is a common concern and interest, as much as the support of government; and who thinks of claiming that the sums raised by tax for the latter purpose, shall be exclusively disbursed in the counties where they are collected? That education is a common concern and interest, in practice, no one will dispute. The vice and crime which it is intended to prevent, are hedged in by no county or town lines. The burglar who marauds, or the incendiary who lays in ashes, the wealth of cities, may come from the country. If ignorance and demoralization contaminate the purity of elections in one election district of a city, the corrupt vote of that district may control results which will be felt for generations on every farm and in every hamlet of the State. Government must abandon the theory that it is its province to educate the people, or it is bound, so far as laws can reasonably accomplish it, to make the burthens and benefits of any system which it employs for this object, alike throughout every square mile and between every individual within its borders.

But while wealth can justly claim no exemption or privilege from its aggregation in localities, it would be equally dishonest and short sighted to take advantage of numbers to rob it, anywhere, of an equal share of those benefits to which it so largely contributes. Owing to the fact that, under special laws, the moneys necessary to defray the expense of schools, beyond the public moneys, are usually raised in cities by city taxes, while in the country the rate bill system was restored by the act of 1851, it is difficult to present numerical or other definite statistics, to show the amount of such extra cost as between city and country districts. But, from the best sources of information, within his possession, it is the opinion of the undersigned that this is now greater, and necessarily greater, in the former than in the latter. In other words, he believes that the one-third equal distribution by districts, more than protects the country, and inflicts an unequal burthen on the city districts. Incidentally, it is productive of another evil. No one familiar with the subject of education need be informed of the superior advantages in point of economy, classification, and effective action, which large schools possess, where the density of population admits of them, over small schools. A distribution which gives as much from one-third of the public moneys to a school of fifty scholars, as to one of a thousand, necessarily operates as a penalty on the formation of large schools; indeed, it directly encourages and promotes subdivision. Efforts are constantly made to divide districts now scarcely strong enough to support good schools, where one of the prominent inducing motives must be unquestionably looked for in this provision of law, or at least, which never would have been thought of but for this provision. Boards of education act independently in these matters; and when such provisions are made by town superintendents, unless their acts are appealed from, the evil cannot be arrested by this department. Many such are undoubtedly made, without a shadow of reason or sound policy to justify them.

The necessary measures to place the distribution of the public school moneys on a just and equal footing, demand the serious attention of the Legislature. A recurrence to the plan of division by inhabitants and by pupils, in force prior to 1851, would seem to be out of the question, as it produced far greater pecuniary inequalities than are produced by the present one, and its effects were even more disastrous proportionably, to popular education, because they fell on the localities and individuals where there was the least ability to meet them. The undersigned suggests that the distribution of one-third of the public moneys by districts (with the same exception as now, of library moneys) be continued in force, but that for the purposes of such distribution, every district containing . . . pupils, shall for every additional pupil, receive another and the same share of the public moneys as a separate school district. The undersigned has not had opportunity to make the comparisons which would furnish accurate data to fill the above blanks. If properly filled, the present inequalities would be corrected, and that discrimination which the law now practically makes against large schools, removed in the most effectual manner. They should be filled with numbers low enough to afford a just measure of relief to city and village districts, but still sufficiently high to prevent the legitimate objects of the one-third equal distribution from being defeated. The propriety of such a measure, in the abstract, has already been distinctly acquiesced in by the Legislature. That body, with great unanimity, passed an act on the 18th day of June last, which provided that " union free schools," formed by the consolidation of two or more districts, should continue to receive, for five years, the same sum from the one-third of the public moneys divided by districts, to which the districts composing them would have been entitled had they remained unconsolidated. To encourage this most useful class of schools, often established and kept up under great inconveniences to attendance, it is recommended that the above provision in their favor be made permanent. The large city schools, whether formed by consolidation of districts or not, are substantially union schools. They have the same system of classification, as regards teachers and pupils, and the higher branches of learning are also taught in them. To apply the same rule to them that has already been applied to union schools, with the exception of allowing a fixed number of pupils to represent a district, would seem to be a measure not only commended by justice, so far as themselves are concerned, but it is believed that it will afford the safest means for fairly adjusting the pecuniary burthens of our school system.

The undersigned has discussed the above subject at considerable length, because he has felt that it is the great and difficult one pertaining to the financial structure of our school system. It involves an adjustment of rights and duties between powerful and antagonizing monetary, and unfortunately, sectional interests. To guard against that excited popular controversy, ever so hurtful to our schools, it is necessary that this question be approached in a spirit of great candor and caution. He is usually held excusable who asserts, even to the extreme, the interests of his locality. But that man cannot be held excusable, who to attain a local advantage, would take one step to impair the love and confidence of our whole people in that great and beneficent institution, established by the wisdom of our forefathers, the influences of which should enter every house, to surround its firesides with intelligence; to cooperate with religion in laying the foundations of private and public virtue; and to protect and preserve the State by training up generations of men worthy to discharge that duty. . . .

He again recommends that the school districts of the State be divided into as many academy districts as there are now, or may hereafter be academies; that each academy be required to annually receive from the common schools in its district, and gratuitously educate a pupil for every $——— received from the State; and that colleges be required to receive pupils from such free departments in a prescribed number of academies, on the same footing. The pupils from the district schools should, probably, be selected by town superintendents; the basis of selection being a certain grade of educational qualification, ability as manifested by a rapid progress in learning, and general merit.

The entire feasibility of carrying the above plan into successful practice, fortunately does not rest on conjecture. The New York Free Academy receives its pupils on the basis above recommended, from the common schools of the city, and it educates them gratuitously. Its doors are as open to the poor as to the rich. It has been in operation several years, and no difficulties are found in carrying out the arrangements made necessary by its peculiarity of organization. On account of the principle adopted in their selection, its pupils, representing every social and pecuniary stratum of society, present a uniformly high grade of scholarship and ability, which it would be almost impossible to find in an academy receiving pupils in the ordinary method. So marked has been its success and so auspicions the results of the plan, that the hope expressed by the undersigned, last year, that a college organized on the same basis, would be soon established in New York, is likely to be realized. The time is probably not far distant, when free academies, required to receive their pupils exclusively on the ground of educational qualifications and merit, will be founded in all the principal cities of the State. A free college, with the same tests of admission, already exists, the "Hobart Free College," at Geneva. The undersigned has obtained a knowledge of its affairs from official sources, and here, too, the plan advocated meets with deserved success. . . .

It was shown, last year, that the distribution of the public moneys to academies and colleges in the method above proposed, would result as favorably to them, pecuniarily, as the present one. In another and equally important particular, it would materially promote their interests. It is useless to attempt to disguise the fact that the donations of the public funds to these institutions, as now constituted, are regarded with jealousy and aversion by a not inconsiderable portion of the community. Unmistakable manifestations of this feeling have been witnessed in our legislative halls and elsewhere. Is it wonderful, under the circumstances, that it should be so? Demagogues, mistaking the sources of this feeling, have denounced the higher institutions of learning; and superficial observers have mistaken their railings for embodiments of popular sentiment. But the body of the people entertain no such views. They know too well that we owe our existence, as a nation, to high popular and individual intelligence, more than to the sword,

They do not forget the solemn voice of the Father of his country, pleading for higher as well as lower institutions of learning. They do not need to be reminded, that the great statesman who went farthest in the doctrine of human equality — who did most to obliterate every vestige of artisocracy, privllege and rank — desired it to be recorded in his epitaph, as one of the three crowning acts of his life, that he was the founder of the University of Virginia. No part of the people of New York, would contribute to the overthrow of those seats of learning, where their own Clintons Livingstons, Jays and Hamiltons, had the talents nurtured and disciplined, which laid the foundations of the State, developed its physical resources, and started it onward in its career of prosperity and greatness. But a large portion of its citizens demand, and have a right to demand, that where they give they shall also receive — that the doctrine of an absolute and practical equality in privileges, which the onward march of public sentiment has introduced into one class of our public schools, shall prevail in all our public schools, so far as they are sustained by the State. This done, all vestige of antagonism between the higher and lower ones, is at once swept away. Indeed, the poor man will feel that he has a deeper interest in sustaining the academies and colleges, than the rich man, because he can alone obtain, through them, those advantages for his offspring, which the money of the other could buy from other sources. He will toil on through life unrepiningly, when he knows that by the justice of a parental government, the avenues to wealth, preferment and renown, are made as open to his children as to those of the most fortunate or most favored citizen of the land. The winter cold and the scorching heat will be welcome to him, his plain food and lowly pallet will be sweet to him, greater privations if necessary will be cheerfully endured by him, when he reflects that his son, if gifted for the task, may be prepared to go forth like the son of the small New Hampshire farmer, to see wealth and power bow down about him; to have senates and nations hang on his words; to leave the impress of his mind on the arts, institutions and literature of a people, and on the destinies of a race. And that son will not only weep like Webster, when he remembers the sacrifices of a noble parent, but with gratitude for what he owes to the just beneficence of his country.

Press Comment

The serious opposition to the school law that had " obvious and universally conceded defects " continued. The friends of the free school principle began to realize that some plan must be devised whereby the best in the law might be preserved and still appease the opposition. This movement is best illustrated in the following editorials that appeared in the "Journal of Education and Teachers Advocate " and in other periodicals of that day.

[Journal of Education and Teachers' Advocate, Tuesday, Dec. 1, 1850. p. 372] (Editorial)

Free Schools

We hope the majority sustaining the free schools, will be found satisfactory to the Legislature soon to assemble, and to the people of the State even though it may fall short of 100,000. The great principle being now settled, the law is open for amendment. The objectionable features of it, and we have always thought there were such, may be so altered as to become acceptable to every *liberalized* sane man who has property to be protected, or children to be educated.

We have all along seen that the hastily drawn, and ill devised provisions of the law were in many respects objectionable; and the premature way in which it was sprung, by its enemies, upon the people, before the necessary means were procured for carrying out its details, jeopardized the popularity and stability of the whole system. Our fears were that the whole matter had become so essentially mystified, that the people would in disgust or in despair, abandon the whole matter.

Before the election we felt assured that a vast majority of the people of this State were in favor of free schools, that they sincerely desired that the whole people might be educated and qualified for citizenship. Yet still there was a lingering fear in our mind that the whole subject was getting so beset with collateral issues as to endanger the great principle of the freedom of knowledge. We rejoice that *that* matter is now settled. While the people have almost with one voice agreed that the present law is imperfect and unequal in its provisions, yet they would rather take it with its radical evils than to run the risk of placing themselves in a false position because of this feeling of opposition to curable faults.

We congratulate the good people of the State upon these decisions. And we pray the Legislature that they correct the errors in the law, making it a subject of prominent interest to see that provisions are made to educate, in all the common school branches, every child in the State.—*Journal of Education and Teachers Advocate, December 1, 1850*

Memorial on Free Schools

By Westchester County Board of Supervisors

To the Legislature of the State of New York:

The board of supervisors of the county of Westchester, in their collective and individual capacity, would respectfully present the following views on the subject of amending the law in relation to free schools.

That they regard the recent action of those electors who voted for the repeal of the school law, as arising more from the peculiar features and unjust and unequal operation of the law, than from any inherent opposition to the principles of general education; and therefore most earnestly and respectfully urge upon your honorable body, such amendments to the new school law as will remove well founded objections, and secure a fair and equitable taxation of the property of the State for the accomplishment of this important feature of republican government, and render the Law acceptable to the body of the people.

Local and frequent taxations are always onerous and unsatisfactory to the people;— and your memorialists, would in view of this fact, urge that your honorable body pass and enact a law taking the property of the State for the support of free schools throughout the State; and the present system of direct taxation and raising money in the several school districts for school purposes be abolished; and we recommend the formation of a board of county education in the several counties of the State, similar to the city of New York.—*Journal of Education, January 1, 1851*

Free Schools

The Hon. Henry A. Wise of Accomac, Va., recently delivered an address at Northapmton, Virginia, on Popular Education from which the following is extracted.

"The rich bachelor, or man who has no children and much property, should be taxed most of all, if any distinction of persons at all were made. He who has wealth and no children, needs the protection of the state and the community in which he lives *for the security of his person and of his property*, and he has selfishly evaded (the bachelor I mean) the burthens in society of supporting a wife and family of children — the highest duty of a good citizen. He wants virtue and wants knowledge in all around him to guard his possessions, and ought he not to pay his part of the expenses of the guards? The free schools are the guards of all persons and property where they exist, and without knowledge and virtue among the people, the state, with all its powers, can not support people and property. Has the churlish miser a suit pending involving thousands of his hoarded gold? Who is to be the jury to try the fate of his dollars? Can they read, and write and cipher? Does the bachelor sue for injury to his character? Do the juries where he lives value reputation? Does he want a piece of work done requiring skill? Are mechanics where he lives men of skill, well instructed in their business? The free schools would give him juries capable of constructing his will when he dies, and a mechanic skilled enough to construct his coffin, or, it might be, a divine to preach his funeral sermon!"—*Journal of Education, January 1, 1851*

The School Law

The subject of greatest importance to be brought before the Legislature at the coming session is undoubtedly that of the new school law. No other, touches the interests of every neighborhood in its pecuniary, social, moral, and intellectual elements so nearly or will be watched with half the anxiety. The law, after having been handled like a football between the Legislature and the people for the last two years comes back from the late vote of the people, instead of being settled, in more "questionable shape" than ever. The nominal majority against repeal is shown by the official canvass to be 25,139; but this result is produced by the vote of New York and other cities which have their separate and independent school systems, and are entirely exempt from the operations of this law. The city of New York alone gives 37,827 majority against repeal, while the vote in other cities similarly situated in reference to the law adds several thousands to the majority. If the vote of the cities where the law does not apply had been rejected, as it manifestly should have been, and only those portions of the State allowed to vote which were to be affected by the law, the majority for repeal would have been nearly as large as it is now the other way.

That the law in its present shape can not be executed, without destroying the usefulness of the common school system, is apparent. The plan of taxation under it, and which is, practically, to be exercised by one neighbor against another, for his own benefit, is too unequal to be tolerated; and those who claim the most for the vote at the late election, only regard it as an approval of the principle of free schools, and admit the necessity of a radical change in the law; and if the principle, as it is called, is to be carried out by taxation, it can only be done by a general tax upon the whole property of the State. This, it seems to us, is the least that the Legislature can think of doing, and the vote in the cities on the question may be fairly taken as an evidence of their wish to make common cause in a work they regard as so desirable for the country and their willingness to submit to the necessary burdens. But the country members will no doubt, almost to a man, regard themselves instructed, by the unmistakable vote of most of the counties where the law was designed to operate, in favor of an unconditional repeal, and the restoration of the old system; and before they adopt any other plan than that declared as the will of their constituents, should analyze and carefully examine the " free school principle," as well in its probable operation and effects upon the cause of education, as in its theory, and determine whether it owes most to intrinsic merit, or to the favorable regards of those who are interested in building up and centralizing a great state system of education.—*Binghamton Democrat, January 2, 1851*

The free school question excites considerable interest, and the members from the several districts are not satisfied to have the cities control them in all things. Many of them admit that the free school system works well in cities, but they contend that it is not adapted to the country.—*Syracuse Daily Star, January 7, 1851*

The School Law

Among the most important questions that will come before the Legislature during the ensuing session, will be the revision of the existing free school law. We say, the revision, because it is not to be expected that the law will be abolished or that the people desire to retain it in the present shape. Upon this subject, and the matter of assessments, the *New York Courier & Enquirer* has some very just remarks, which we annex—

But the most important subjects that will come before the Legislature, will undoubtedly be the free school Law. This was enacted in 1848 and submitted to the action of the people. It was approved by an immense majority, nearly a hundred thousand of the voters of the State. Great embarrassment was felt in putting it into practice, but this was obviated so far as possible, by instructions from the able and intelligent Secretary of State, Hon. Christopher Morgan, who was thoroughly devoted to the principles of the law, and who spared no pains to secure it successful and satisfactory operation. A year's trial, however, showed very great defects in the law. The peculiar system of assessment which it provided was found to throw most grievous burthens upon those not able to bear them; and in various ways the new law became distasteful to the people in very many districts of the State. Petitions were poured into the Legislature at its last session, some for the repeal, and others for the amendment of the law. Partly to escape the responsibility of acting upon so important a matter which was but partially understood, and partly to escape amendments which were felt to be unwise and unjust, the majority in the Legislature chose to refer the whole subject again to the people; and a bill was accordingly passed, calling upon the people to vote *for or against,* the free school *principle,*— for the present law is, of course open to such amendment as may be found expedient.

The result of the vote is somewhat singular. There is a majority of 25,139 *against* the repeal of the free school law. But the city of New York alone gave a majority of over 30,000, and all the large cities in the State also gave a very decided majorities on the same side. Now the law itself expressly *excepts the cities* from its operation. In all the incorporated cities of the State, free schools had already been established, and were in successful operation when the law was passed. The law, therefore, was, by its terms, confined to the country districts; and the vote of these districts had been very distinctly pronounced *against* it. But the cities step in and decide *for the whole State* that the law shall not be repealed,— that free schools shall be continued throughout the State. The question has thus been acted on as a state question, as one involving the interests of all sections,— of all the children in the State, without reference to their locality. The vote of the people seems to have decided, clearly and explicitly enough, *that all the property in the State shall be taxed to give free education to every child in the State.*

The first thing, therefore, to be expected, is the renewal of a proposition made at the last session to pay all the expenses of the free schools of the whole State *out of the general fund.* The entire annual expense of the system was estimated at $800,000; and it was proposed to collect this sum annually by a tax upon property, and to distribute it among the free schools of the State in proportion to the number of children taught, and the length of time in which the schools should be kept open. The effect of this will be to *increase* taxation for school purposes in all the large cities of the State, and especially in the city of New York. The proportion of the tax which will fall upon this city will be greater than the proportion of money they will receive. New York City will contribute about *one-third* of the whole State tax for free schools, while it will receive in return but about *one-fifth* of the amount collected. But when the New York delegation shall remonstrate against this as unjust — they will be told that New York has decided that the State shall have free schools, and she must, therefore, contribute her proportion of the expense required to carry their decision into effect. And the reply is one, the force of which they will find it exceedingly difficult to evade.

Our own belief is that the city of New York will not recede from the high ground she has taken in behalf of free schools, even at the risk of being saddled with what she may deem an unfair portion of the expense of sustaining them. Under such a law, New York City will be required to raise by tax, money enough to sustain her own free schools, and then to contribute nearly $200,000 annually, to sustain free schools in the country districts besides. And yet we believe she would prefer the passage of such a law, to the abandonment of the free school system for the Empire State. There is one boon, however, which the city has a right to ask in return, and one which we trust will not be refused: — we mean a law for *equalizing assessments* of real and personal property throughout the State. It is a fact universally known that property in this city is assessed at nearly its own value — while in the country districts, the assessments will not average more than *one-third* of the value of the property. The Comptroller, Hon. Washington Hunt, called the attention of the Legislature at its last session to the importance of remedying this inequality, the effect of which is to make the city contribute nearly double its due proportion of the state tax. We trust that the coming session will witness a renewed effort on the subject. If the Legislature will make assessments upon property *equal* throughout the State, we venture to predict that this city will uncomplainingly pay whatever may be her due proportion of the money required to support free schools in every district of the great State, to which it is her pride to belong.--*Syracuse Daily Standard, January 6, 1851*

MEETING OF CITIZENS OF MONROE COUNTY TO REGISTER OPPOSITION TO FREE SCHOOL LAW

Free School Convention

A meeting of those opposed to the present free school law is to be held in Minerva Hall today, commencing at 11 o'clock. The call for this meeting, which is published elsewhere, emanates from the country, where the greatest opposition to the law exists. This city, in common with every other in the State voted by a large majority in favor of it. It had no interest to do otherwise; as it has for some years supported a system of free schools, at some expense. Our country friends, however, are differently situated, and are indisposed to pay for the establishment and support of schools by money drawn indiscriminately from the body of taxpayers, without regard to the benefit to be received. The dislike of the law is not confined to any class of taxpayers but among those expressing their hostility are some of the wealthiest and most intelligent of the rural population. Their arguments were put forth with much plausibility and cogency; but, as it turned out, ineffectually. What they now propose to do, or wish to have done, will be set forth at the meeting. It is not unlikely that they will adopt to greater or less extent the views advanced by the school committee in the Assembly.— *Rochester Daily Democrat, February 14, 1851*

The Free School Convention

The representatives of the opponents of the new free school law, who met at Minerva Hall yesterday, were not numerous, but their action was summary and decided. Wm. Shepard, of Irondequoit, occupied the chair, and was assisted by several vice-chairmen. A committee, of which Calvin Huson, Esq., was chairman, reported in the afternoon a series of resolutions, expressing the most unqualified condemnation of the school law, and a preference for the old system before all others. The plan of amendment introduced into the Assembly by the majority of the school committee met with no better favor than the law which exists. The resolutions were agreed to with great unanimity and applause. The gentlemen composing this convention appeared to have fully settled in their own minds that the law is not to be tolerated in any shape, and they exhibited considerable restlessness when anything was said, or attempted to be said in its favor. We regret, for the sake of the objectors, that some degree of discourtesy was not shown toward one very much respected scholar of this city, who rose to speak in answer to Mr. McGonegal. We left the meeting before the conclusion of its proceedings, and while Gen. Brooks, of Livingston Co., was speaking. A full report will be given hereafter.— *Rochester Daily Democrat, February 15, 1851*

School Law Repeal Convention

A mass convention of the citizens of Monroe county, in favor of the repeal of the present school law, was held pursuant to a call for that purpose, at Minerva Hall in the city of Rochester, on the 14th day of February instant. The convention was largely attended, and when considered with regard to the character, standing and influence of the persons by whom it was composed, it has rarely been equalled by any convention ever held in this county.

His Hon. Judge Shepherd, was chosen president; John Colt, David McVean, John Shoecraft, Ebenezer Cook and John Brown, vice-presidents, and J. W. Stebbins, secretary.

On motion of C. Huson, jr., Esq., a committee of five was appointed by the president to prepare and present resolutions. The president appointed the following gentlemen as such committee:

C. Huson, jr., John McGonegal, David McVean, Wm. C. Bloss and A. W. Fisher.

On motion the president and secretary were added to the committee.

Mr Huson, in behalf of the committee, reported the following resolutions, which, after a full and interesting discussion, engaged in by a large number of the convention, were passed by acclamation.

Resolved, That the act passed March 26, 1849, entitled "An act establishing free schools throughout the State," deserves, and hereby receives, the unqualified disapprobation of this convention, and that the same ought to be repealed.

Resolved, That a general diffusion of knowledge is a chief corner-stone of our republican institutions — and that reason, revelation and experience dictate, that the education of youth is a parental duty, which, in a well-regulated community, is fully and generously discharged by parents, and which the State can not wholly assume without serious injury to the cause of education itself — that leaving the care of educating their offspring to parents, tends to promote studiousness and gratitude on the part of the child, and faithfulness and industry on the part of parent, thereby securing the highest mental and moral culture of the people, together with the greatest incitement to energy and perseverance in all the industrial pursuits.

Resolved, That the people of this State, under their long established system of education, have attained an elevation which challenges the admiration of the world; that although some of our sister states may show a smaller comparative number of persons who do not enjoy the advantages of a common education, yet, when we consider the large influx into this State of a hetrogeneous population from foreign countries, it is confidently believed that the State of New York is unparalleled in its educational advancement by any other community on the face of the globe.

Resolved, That no system of education, whatever may be its intrinsic merits, ought to be adopted in a republican state, which does not secure the general approbation of the people; that our former school laws did secure such approbation in an eminent degree; and that the present law has created dissatisfaction, wrangling and litigation, in nearly every school district in the State.

Resolved, That while we are in favor of the repeal of the present law, and of a return to the former law in relation to schools, yet we do not desire to close the door of our common school against any child in the State; and should it be shown that the former law contributed to that result, we should be in favor of such amendments to it, in regard to the distribution of the public money, and to exemption from payment of rate bills, as may effectually open the doors of our common schools to all the children in the State without respect to their pecuniary circumstances or condition.

Resolved, That the legislative power of this State is vested in a Senate and Assembly; that the submission of any legislative act to the people, except acts relating to finance, as specified in art. VII of the constitution, to be by them determined whether the same shall or shall not, become a law, is an unconstitutional exercise of authority. That the practice, if adopted and persevered in, if submitting legislative acts of doubtful propriety to a popular vote, and thereby yielding them to unthinking clamor or partisan importunity, to the fickleness or tyranny of ephemeral majorities, will lead to such a train of abuses and usurpation, as will speedily overthrow the constitution itself; and therefore,

Resolved, That so much of the action of the Legislature of 1849 as resulted in the submission of the new school law to a popular vote, and *particularly* so much of the action of the Legislature of '50 as resulted in the *resubmission* of that law to a popular vote, deserves, and hereby receives the deepest and most decided reprehensions of this convention.

Resolved, That the proceedings of this convention be published in the daily and weekly papers of this city, and that the secretary forward a copy of the same to each of the representatives of this county in the Legislature of the State.

Whereupon the convention adjourned.

WM. SHEPHERD, *Pres't.*
J. W. STEBBINS, *Sec'y.*

— *Rochester Daily Democrat, February 17, 1851*

STATE CONVENTION OF FRIENDS OF FREE SCHOOLS
(Town Superintendents)

State Convention

A state convention of the friends of free schools, is called to meet in this city on Wednesday, Feb. 26th. The object of the convention is, as we understand, to devise some means by which the present school law may be adapted to the sentiments of the people, and the advantages of free education be secured, without the inequalities of the new law. Amendments calculated to effect this will, it is said, be introduced on that occasion, and the delegated wisdom of the superintendents of schools throughout the state will be brought to bear in their consideration.— *Herald;* from *Utica Daily Gazette, February 15, 1851*

State Convention of Town Superintendents of Common Schools

The convention of town superintendents of schools met at the common council room in this city, yesterday A. M., pursuant to call, and was organized, on motion of Prof. Heffron, of Utica, by the appointment of Mr H. Putnam, of Onondaga, as chairman, and on motion of O. B. Pierce, of Oneida, L. Ingalls, of Jefferson, was chosen secretary.

The call having been read, on motion, a committee of six was appointed to prepare business for the consideration of the convention. Chair appointed as such committe, Messrs O. B. Pierce, of Oneida; Salisbury and Crandall, of Onondaga; Heffron and Perkins, of Oneida; and Ingalls, of Jefferson. Adjourned to 2 P. M.

Afternoon Session — 2 P. M.— Convention met pursuant to adjournment.

Mr Pierce, of Oneida, the chairman of committee on resolutions, reported the following:

1st. *Resolved,* That we indorse the principle, that the property of the State should educate the children of the State.

2d. *Resolved,* That there should be no going back in educational reform, and that any defects in the assessment laws of which the people justly complain should be remedied, and not be made the occasion of abandoning the free school principle.

3d. *Resolved,* That we approve the raising by state tax of $800,000, for the payment of teachers' wages, but that in the absence of a law equalizing the assessments as between the several counties, one-half of this sum should be assessed on a property basis and the other half on a basis of population.

4th. *Resolved,* That the balance of money necessary to pay the teachers' wages in any district, after applying its proportion of the public funds, shall be raised in the same manner as its contingent expenses.

5th. *Resolved,* That we approve the distributing of the public funds from the State, one-fourth equally among the several school districts, and the other three-fourths, as now, according to the number of children from 5 to 20 years of age, residing in the several districts.

6th. *Resolved,* That we believe provision by law should be made for having a school by a qualified teacher, at least eight months of the year, in each school district of the State.

On motion of W. L. Crandall, of Onondaga, the resolutions were considered separately, and passed unanimously, after discussion.

The president of the convention being compelled to leave, Mr George Spencer, of Utica, was appointed vice president, and took the chair.

On motion of Mr Heffron, of Utica, a committee was appointed to present in an appropriate way, the results of this convention to the literature committees of the Legislature. The committee were nominated, as follows: Mr Brinsmade, of New York; Mr Heffron, of Utica; Mr Ingalls, of Jefferson county.

On motion, the county papers, and such other papers as might see fit, were requested to publish the proceedings of the convention.

The convention then adjourned sine die.— *Utica Daily Gazette, February 27, 1851*

LEGISLATIVE ACTION

The transactions in the Legislature of 1851 and the passage of the free school law are here presented, as transcribed from the Senate and Assembly documents of that year.

In his annual message of 1851, Governor Hunt gives considerable attention to the establishment of free schools as follows:

It appears from the latest returns to the Superintendent of Common Schools that there are in the State 11,397 school districts; that the whole number of children taught therein, in the year 1849, was 749,500 of all ages; and that the whole amount paid for teachers' wages during that year was $1,322,696.24, of which $767,389.20 was contributed from the state treasury, and raised by county and town taxation.

The operations of the act of 1849, establishing free schools, have not produced all the beneficial effects, nor imparted the general satisfaction anticipated by the friends of the measure. It has been the policy of our State, from an early period, to promote the cause of popular education by liberal and enlightened legislation. A munificent fund created by a series of measures, all aiming at the same great result, has been dedicated by the Constitution to the support of common schools, and the annual dividend from this source will gradually increase. The duty of the State to provide such means and facilities as will extend to all its children the blessings of education, and especially to confer upon the poor and unfortunate a participation in the benefits of our common schools, is a principle which has been fully recognized and long acted upon by the Legislature and the people.

The vote of 1849, in favor of the free school law, and the more recent vote by a reduced majority against its repeal, ought doubtless to be regarded as a reaffirmation of this important principle, but not of the provisions of the bill, leaving it incumbent upon the Legislature, in the exercise of a sound discretion, to make such enactments as will accomplish the general design, without injustice to any of our citizens. An essential change was made by the law under consideration, in imposing the entire burthen of the schools upon property, in the form of a tax, without reference to the direct benefits derived by the taxpayer. The provisions of the act for carrying this plan into effect, have produced oppressive inequalities and loud complaints.

In some districts the discontent and strife attendant upon these evils, have disturbed the harmony of society. An earnest effort should be made to reconcile differences of opinion, to remedy the grievances arising from the imperfect operation of the law, and to equalize the weight of taxation by such principles of justice and equity as will ensure popular sanction. The success of our schools must depend, in a great degree, upon the united counsels and friendly co-operation of the people in each small community composing a district, and nothing can be more injurious to the system of common school education than feuds and contentions among those who are responsible for its healthful action and preservation.

It can not be doubted that all property, estates, whether large or small, will derive important advantages from the universal education of the people. A well considered system which shall insure to the children of all, the blessings of moral and intellectual culture, will plant foundations, broad and

WASHINGTON HUNT
Governor of New York, 1851–53

deep, for public and private virtue; and its effects will be seen in the diminution of vice and crime, the more general practice of industry, sobriety and integrity, conservative and enlightened legislation and universal obedience to the laws. In such a community the rights of property are stable, and the contributions imposed upon it for the support of government are essentially lightened. But I entertain a firm conviction that the present law requires a thorough revision, and that an entire change in the mode of assessment is indispensable.

In Assembly, February 6, 1851
No. 41
Report
Of the majority of the committee on colleges, academies and common schools, on the petitions for the amendment and repeal of the free school law.

Mr T. H. Benedict, from the majority of the committee on colleges, academies and common schools, to which was referred the petitions for the repeal and amendment of the free school law,

REPORTS:

That deeply impressed with the importance of the subject committed to their charge, they have given to it as full and impartial a consideration as circumstances would permit. They have been actuated in their deliberations solely by a desire to present some plan by which the educational system of the State might be established upon a basis sound and enduring; — knowing that a system that will not meet the views of a majority of the people of the State, is liable to be altered and amended at each successive session of the Legislature; and this vascillating policy cannot but prove extremely prejudicial to the cause of education. In view of this, your committee have endeavored to act in a spirit of justice to the 800,000 children of the State who are pleading with the natural eloquence of youth, for their undoubted right to taste some of the fruits of learning; and in justice also, to the great body of tax-payers who are affected, or seemingly so, by conceding this right.

The large number of petitions that have been referred to your committee, coming from different sections of the State, prove conclusively that there is existing among the people a deep feeling of discontent with the provisions of the present law. Many of your petitioners demand its unconditional repeal. Yet many of them, your committee are happy to observe, while expressing a dissatisfaction with the law, simply ask that such modifications may be made therein as will make it more acceptable to the taxable portion of the community, and, in consequence, more efficient in its operation.

It will not be deemed inappropriate in this connection to give a succinct sketch of the origin and progress of the common school system in this State; and, as incidental thereto, its first establishment upon this continent.

It was wisely forseen by that small band of men, who brought to this country, in 1620, the principles of civil and religious liberty, that to maintain and perpetuate those principles inviolate, it was indispensable that their children, who were to succeed them in the conduct of the government, should be trained to a knowledge of its duties and requirements, and thus be qualified to receive and sustain the inestimable privileges for which they had periled their lives and fortunes.

Experience had taught them that the foundations of despotism are built upon the ignorance and degradation of the masses; that to ensure freedom of action there must be freedom of thought; and, that liberty might not degenerate into licentiousness, it was necessary that the minds of the people should be early trained to the love of virtue and good order. With these truths impressed upon their minds, they felt it incumbent upon them to take some decisive action.

It would seem as if these heroic men had a prophetic vision of the greatness that would follow their feeble undertaking, for with a moral grandeur unsurpassed in any age, they set about the work of education, while their colony was yet in its infancy and their homes unprotected from the cruelty of the savages.

As early as 1635, in the city of Boston, a "schoolmaster was appointed for the teaching of the children amongst them," and a portion of the public lands given him for his support in 1642. The general court of the colony, by a public act, enjoined upon the municipal authorities the duty of seeing that every child within the jurisdiction should be educated; and the select men of every town were required "to have a vigilant eye over their neighbors, and see that they should endeavor to teach their children so much learning as might enable them perfectly to read the English language, and obtain a knowledge of the laws, upon penalty of 20 shillings for such neglect."

But they did not pause here. One thing yet was needed. The State claimed obedience from all its citizens, and, in return, guaranteed to them equal rights and privileges. It was therefore enjoined by law in 1647, that education should be free to all; and in consequence, the support of the schools was made compulsory.

Here may be found the germs of the common school system of this country. And thus early was established the principle that the property of the State should be taxed for the education of its citizens. It is idle to speculate upon the causes that induced these pioneers of republicanism to acquiesce so cheerfully in the correctness and soundness of the doctrine. It is sufficient for our purpose, to know that the justice and policy of the measure were never seriously questioned. It must be admitted that it bore heavily then as it does even now upon certain classes of the people. But no murmur or discontent was raised against it. It is remarked by an intelligent observer, that "in most of the towns of New England, one-fifth of the inhabitants pay at least one-half of the tax, and probably do not send more than one-sixth of the scholars." The school tax is, therefore, to a considerable extent, a tax upon the rich to educate the children of the poor; and this tax is repaid in the greater security afforded to life and property by the increased growth of intelligence and virtue throughout the community.

The same principle of taxation for the benefit of education has been recognised and followed by the general government, for upon the adoption of the federal compact, the most ample provision was made for the elementary instruction of all classes of the people. As new states began to be formed out of the public domain, one square mile in every township, or one thirty-sixth part of all the lands, has been reserved and devoted to the support of common schools.

In our own State, as early as 1795, an act was passed by which the sum of $50,000 was appropriated annually, for 5 years, among the several towns of the State — and the towns were required to raise an equal amount for the support of common schools. In 1805, a permanent fund for the same purpose was established, by the passage of an act appropriating 500,000 acres of land, "to raise a fund for the encouragement of common schools." The Surveyor General was authorized to sell the land, and the principal derived from such sale, with the interest accruing thereon, was to be loaned, until the whole interest should amount to $50,000 annually — which interest was to be distributed among the common schools as the Legislature should direct. This fund has, by various legislative enactments, been increased, until now the capital of our common school fund is $2,290,000 — which fund is being annually increased by the addition of $25,000 from the interest of the U. S. deposite fund. By an act of the Legislature in 1811, a commission was appointed to "report a system for the organization, regulation, and establishment" of common schools. This commission presented an elaborate report to the Legislature of 1812. Accordingly, a law was passed, which was, substantially, the basis of our very useful and efficient system of common schools until the year 1849. Under this system, the proceeds of the common school fund of the State were apportioned among the different towns of the State, according to the population therein; and the supervisors of each county were directed annually to levy by tax upon each town a sum corresponding with the amount received from the State. These sums made the public moneys of the town, and were to be distributed among the several school districts of the town, in proportion to the number of children therein, between the ages of 5 and 16 years, as should appear from the last report of the trustees of the district. It was required that the schools should be kept open during four months of the year, and for so much longer time as the trustees should direct. Whatever sums were required for the payment of the teacher's wages, after deducting the public money of the district, were to be raised by a rate bill, from those sending children to the school, in proportion to the number of days such children had been in attendance.

Such were, substantially, the main features of our common school system up to the year 1849. To say it had accomplished much good to the cause of education, and had realized the hopes of its originators and supporters, would be awarding it but a faint meed of approbation. It had surpassed the most sanguine expectations of its friends. Under its influence, as appears from reports furnished to the Superintendent of Common Schools for the year 1849, there had been organized 11,397 school districts, and the number of children that received instruction during the year was 794,500, being in excess of 59,312 over the number between the ages of 5 and 16 years, and 16,191 over the whole number taught during the preceding year, while the schools had been kept open during an average period of eight months. Well might the philanthropist point with admiration to a system productive of such results, and the skeptic in the science of free government banish his doubts, in view of such universal diffusion of knowledge.

Notwithstanding these grand results, the system was not perfect. A fatal defect was inherent therein, which if foreseen had not been deemed of sufficient importance to excite attention. A large and gradually increasing number of children in the State, were without any kind of education whatever; and though the school house was open and teachers ready to impart instruction, they entered not to receive it. The cause was apparent; they were the children of poverty; and their parents, with the inborn pride of freedom, could not brook the favor of an exemption from the rate bill, though such exemption could be had. It would naturally be supposed that this cause could have but a limited operation in deterring children from the school, but facts prove otherwise. From reports made to the State Superintendent in 1846, the startling discovery was made that over 46,000 children were deprived of the advantages of education, either through the remissness of the trustees of school districts, in exempting them from the rate bill, or from the pride of the parents in refusing to claim such exemption.

It is immaterial to enquire if such pride was justifiable. It is sufficient to know that the evil existed, and it behooved the friends of education and the friends of free government to devise some speedy remedy. It was deemed necessary where suffrage was universal, that education should be free. A system of free schools had already been established in many of the cities and large towns of the State, where the evil had become widespread, and the time seemed auspicious for the extension of the system over the whole State. Petitions to that effect were presented to the Legislature of 1849, and in accordance therewith an act was passed March 26th, 1849, establishing " free schools throughout the State." As this act would effect a radical change in the school system of the State, it was deemed proper by the Legislature to submit it to the people for their consideration. The act was sanctioned at the ensuing election by a majority of over 158,000 votes, but three counties in the State, Chenango, Tompkins and Otsego, having cast a majority against it. To say that the deed was rashly done, that the people acted without due reflection, is a libel on the intelligence and virtue of the people, is a libel on the great principle of free government. More than seven months had elapsed since the passage of the act, and its main feature — the free school principle — had been discussed in every quarter of the State; at county and town assemblages, in village gatherings, and at road-side inns. It had been the theme of conversation in the houses of the rich and in the homes of the poor. The learned had commended it in their ardent desire for the diffusion of knowledge, and the unlearned looked to its adoption for their children's release from the bondage of ignorance.

The conviction is irresistably forced upon the minds of your committee that the principle of the " free school " bill was the main feature considered, and that it was sanctioned by the people upon mature deliberation. The practical operation of the act was a matter that could be tested only by time. A brief period sufficed to show that the act was defective in its details. In less than four months after its adoption, the Legislature was flooded by petitions for the repeal or amendment of the law. Action, early action was needed, for discord and confusion had crept into the school districts throughout the State, and animosities were being engendered among all classes of the people, and a serious injury was inflicted upon the cause of education. Yet its friends, though disheartened, did not despair. The experiment of free education had been tried, and its partial failure was attributable to causes easily obviated. But the remedy was not applied. The people urged action upon their representatives. yet action was delayed, until, at the close of the session of 1850, it was resolved to submit the question again to the people, to decide either "for or against the repeal of the act." The wisdom and policy of this resolution it is not the province of your committee to question. They may be pardoned, however, for expressing the opinion that it afforded the opponents of the free school system an opportunity to destroy the principle through the agency of the obnoxious details that accompanied it, while the advocates of the principle were obliged to oppose the act to remove those obnoxious details, or throw their influence in its favor, and trust to the wisdom and justice of a succeeding Legislature to adopt such amendments as would render it perfect. The latter alternative was adopted, and already they are applying to this House for the remedy. At the annual election of 1850, the free school act was a second time sustained, by a popular majority of over 25,000 votes, although at this election a majority of the counties of the State — 42 in number — voted for repeal in majorities varying from 50 to 2500. Notwithstanding this apparently great opposition, it is the deliberate conviction entertained by the majority of your committee, that the large vote cast in those counties against the act, did not proceed from an opposition to the free school principle but was caused by the obnoxious and defective details of the act. This conviction is founded upon the representations made to your committee by members of this House from various sections of the State, and who, coming directly as the representatives from the people, are, it is to be presumed, informed as to their views.

It has been urged, with much pertinacity, by some of your petitioners, that the city of New York had a preponderating influence upon the question; that her majority of more than 37,000 votes in favor of the act had fastened the system upon the State; and that as she had an educational system of her own, separate and distinct from the State at large, she was not equitably entitled to vote upon the question. The plausibility of this objection is conceded; but, in the opinion of a majority of your committee, its ground is wholly untenable. If it can be shown that the city of New York is separate in interest and policy, and is in no way dependent on or advantageous to the other sections of the State, then might some weight be attached to the objection. But such is not the case. New York is the heart of the State, receiving and giving back wealth to every portion thereof. Her greatness as the commercial emporium of the Union is reflected upon every part of the State. But for her agency the abundant harvests of the farmer might rot in his fields,— but for the industry and thrift of the farmer, the city might fall from its greatness. The interests of both are homogenous. Whatever conduces to the prosperity and glory of the one, appertains in a proportionate degree to the other. If it is admitted, (and who in this State will deny the assertion?) that a republican form of government is the best adapted to the happiness of the people, and most conducive to their prosperity, the question then recurs as to the best method to continue that government. It will be conceded by every one, that the perpetuity of free institutions is based upon the intelligence and virtue of the people; and the chief agency for diffusing these is the common school. The educated child, it is fair to assume, will become a useful citizen,— it is equally fair to assert, as a general rule, that the uneducated child will prove the reverse. Facts warrant the assertion.

From the report of the inspectors of the state prisons for the year 1850, it appears that of 664 males in the Sing Sing prison 349 were under 20 years of age at the time of their conviction; 487 had never been taught a trade; 60 could not read, and 149 could read only, and that indifferently. Of 114 convicts at Clinton, 10 could not read, and 29 could read only. At the female prisons, of the 71 remaining in December last, 25 could neither read nor write; 17 could read only, and the balance had received a very limited instruction in the elementary branches. At the Auburn prison 109 convicts were, previous to admission, unacquainted with the alphabet, or could read but little, and 64 had no knowledge of arithmetic. The inspectors close with the remark, " that the frequent examinations into the causes of crime among the convicts almost invariably leads to the same result, and force upon the mind the startling truth, that a neglected education in youth is the source of all or nearly all the crime among us." These statistics are presented in corroboration of the general statement of your committee that crime and ignorance are generally found in unison. It can be no matter of surprise, therefore, that the citizens of New York, from a perusal of the daily records of their criminal courts, and their daily observation of the vice and misery that must ever cling to and flourish in great cities, should manifest a deep interest in the cause of education, and a desire for its universal diffusion. Philanthropy, at least, would prompt that they should be heard. Again: Prudential considerations demanded that New York should have a voice in the matter. She is a part of the State; subject to the same laws, and should be entitled to equal privileges with other portions of the State. With an aggregate valuation of real and personal estate amounting to $286,000,000 or more than one-third of the entire valuation of the State, and with this property liable to be affected by the legislation of a body elected by the universal suffrages of the citizens of the State, it would have been manifestly unjust that her vote should have been excluded. Your committee have been induced to present their views upon this subject from respect to the large number of your petitioners who have asked for the repeal of the Free School act, on the ground that such act would have been repealed by the popular vote had the city of New York been excluded from any action thereupon. Including this vote, therefore, the expression of the popular will of the State is emphatic in favor of the principle of free education; for no one, it is presumed, will hazard the opinion that the vote of New York was cast in favor of the act of 1849. Her citizens were unacquainted with the practical operation of that act, and the inference is natural that it was the principle only that was ratified at the ballot box.

Upon this view of the subject your committee entertain the opinion that it was the principle of the free school act only that was sanctioned and confirmed at the last election by the people of this State. In obedience to the popular will, therefore, they would recommend the retention of the free school principle. But as it is admitted by all parties interested in the subject, that the details of the act are seriously defective, it is proposed to make such modifications therein as will ensure greater efficiency to the system, and cause it to be more generally approved.

As the physician would enquire into the nature of the malady before prescribing for its cure, it is proper that your committee point out, what they deem the defects of the law under consideration, before proposing any modifications therein. A prominent objection to the act of 1849, is the mode in which the school moneys are required to be raised. By the 2d section of that act, it is made the duty "of the several Boards of Supervisors at their annual meeting, to cause to be levied and collected from their respective counties, a sum equal to the amount of State school moneys apportioned to such counties; and to apportion the same among the towns and cities in the same manner as the moneys received from the State are apportioned. They shall also cause to be levied and collected from each of the towns in their respective counties, a sum equal to the amount of State school moneys apportioned to said towns respectively." The income of the School Fund of the State is distributed among the different towns in proportion to their population. The county and town taxes levied by the supervisors, are, in consequence a tax upon the basis of population; and its operation is, therefore, unjust, unequal and oppressive. A large and populous county may, under this system of taxation, be compelled to raise more money than an adjoining county with a less population, though with a larger assessed valuation of real and personal property. It is obvious, therefore, that this inequality is peculiarly burdensome to the agricultural interests of the State, for in such districts the population is usually larger in proportion to the valuation of its property, than in the cities or large towns or villages. This inequality will appear by a glance at the following statement. In 1849 the taxable property and the school moneys (apportioned on the basis of population) in the following counties, were in this proportion:

	Taxable property	School money
New York	$256,197,143	$40,621.53
Albany	16,839,570	8,455.44
Allegany	3,797,486	3,459.07
Cattaraugus	3,824,598	3,394.28

The counties of New York and Albany are devoted to trade and commerce, while Allegany and Cattaraugus are purely agricultural counties. The same inequality will appear from a comparison of different rates of taxation in different towns. An illustration is afforded by some of your petitioners, in the case of the following towns in the county of Genesee, in 1849:

	Taxable property	School money
Batavia	$1,235,110	$479.72
Stafford	451,732	234.03
Bethany	323,928	221.43

Numerous instances of the same kind might be cited, to show the injustice of this mode of taxation, as applied to counties and towns. In the cities and larger towns are accumulated a vast amount of bank and insurance stocks, and other descriptions of personal property, which, under this system of taxing the population, is made to avoid their proportionate contribution for school purposes, while the poorer agricultural districts are borne down by the weight of taxation. This feature in the act of 1849 may be accounted one of the main causes of the heavy vote thrown for the repeal of the act throughout the central and western portions of the State. But the most serious objection to this act, in the estimation of your committee, is the plan of district taxation. By the 3d section of the act, it is made "the duty of the trustees within a specified time of the annual district meeting in each year, to prepare an estimate of the amount of money required for teachers' wages, (exclusive of the public moneys of the district, and the moneys raised by and under the 2d section of the act) and other expenditures for the year, and submit such statement to the legally qualified voters of the district, for their approval or rejection"; and in a following section it is provided that, "in case the voters of the district refuse to raise the estimate presented to them, it is enjoined upon the trustees to levy such tax as may be needed to keep the school open for the space of four months; and proceed to collect it in the same manner as other district taxes are collected." These two features of the act have wrought incalculable injury to the cause of education, by provoking animosities and bitter feuds among the inhabitants of the different districts; making the school houses of the State, where peace and harmony should blend, at each annual meeting a scene of strife and dissention. It would appear almost incredible that the inhabitants of any district in this State could be led by the simple act of being called upon to vote a certain amount for the education of the children of the district, to the exhibition of such feeling, but the fact, though lamentable, is nevertheless beyond dispute. Avarice hath its victims, and they are found as often in the quiet seclusion of the country, as in the busy marts of commerce.

It is obvious that any plan which submits the amount of tax to be raised for school purposes to the action of the voters of the district, is liable to serious objection. The childless, and those whose children have already received their education, deem it a hardship to be obliged to pay for the instruction of the children of their neighbors, and consequently vote against any appropriation. The rich, who are assessed upon the valuation of their estate, are oftimes unwilling to contribute to the support of a common school, inasmuch as they prefer the exclusiveness of a select institution for their own children, and feeling no interest whatever in the matter, with a short-sighted wisdom, they are often inclined to vote in the same way. This naturally produces a corresponding feeling of suspicion and hatred among the poorer classes of the districts, and opens wide a gap of social distinction that it is the true policy of the State to keep forever closed. Meantime the grossest injustice is inflicted upon the children of the State. In one district they are allowed by the magnanimity and public spirit of the voters to receive the priceless boon of education perhaps for eight months in the year, while in an adjoining district, it may be of the same town, and separated only by an imaginary line, they are permitted to enjoy only four months instruction in the public schools.

Thus are the children of the State — its future citizens, and, it may be, its law-givers, recognized by the spirit of our institutions, as born free and equal — thus early in life, without any agency of their own, made to feel the galling inequality of their social position, and waste the bright hours of their youth in ignorance.

Your committee cannot condemn in too strong terms, the injustice and impolicy of these features of the act. By reason of it the schools have languished during the past year, and it is the opinion, seriously entertained, that in a majority of the districts the schools have not been open over four months during the past year.

Having pointed out what they deem the imperfections of the act of 1849, it is incumbent upon your committee, in submitting a bill for the consideration of the House, to explain its provisions and the reasons that have induced their action. It is proposed that the common schools of the State shall be supported chiefly by a tax upon the property of the State. It is required, therefore, by the second section of the bill herewith presented, that the sum of $800,000 shall be raised by a tax on the real and personal property of the State.

This system of taxation is acquiesced in by all classes of the community when applied to the purposes of sustaining a military or naval establishment for the purpose of public defence, or for the establishment or maintenance of an efficient system for the prevention and punishment of crime or outrage, inflicted upon the persons or property of the citizens of the State, and it is conceived that the same system may be applied with far more justice towards the support of an institution designed for the diffusion of virtue and intelligence, and in consequence, for the suppression of crime and immorality. In this connection, your committee may well be pardoned for introducing an extract from the remarks of Daniel Webster, in a convention to revise the constitution of Massachusetts in 1821. "For the purposes of public instruction" said that eminent statesman, "we hold every man subject to taxation in proportion to his property; and we look not to the question whether he himself have or have not children to be benefited by the education for which he pays. We regard it as a wise and liberal system of police, by which property and life and the peace of society are secured. We seek to promote, in some measure, the extension of the penal code, by inspiring a salutary and conservative principle of virtue and of knowledge in an early age. By general instruction, we seek as far as possible to purify the whole moral atmosphere; to keep good sentiments uppermost, and to turn the strong current of feeling and opinion, as well as the censures of the law, against immorality and crime. And knowing that our government rests directly on the public will, that we may preserve it, we endeavor to give a safe and proper direction to the public will. It is every poor man's undoubted birthright — it is his solace in life — and it may well be his consolation in death, that his country stands pledged by the faith which it has plighted to all its citizens, to protect his children from ignorance, barbarism and vice."

By this system of taxation, it is to be expected, that as all classes of the people will contribute in proportion to their substance, that a universal interest will be felt in the cause of education throughout the State. And that in consequence, the character of our common schools will be elevated, and the children of wealth will be induced to enter and enjoy their advantages, and thus be brought to mingle in the early years of their life, when the kindly feelings of the heart are most active, upon terms of equality with the equally deserving, though more unfortunate children of want — and thus may be partially obliterated the distinctions of fortune, by investing wealth with the spirit of kindness and humility, and inspiring poverty with a feeling of honor and manly independence.

It is expected by your committee, that much opposition will be manifested against this provision of the bill. It will be objected by those who desire a return to the old system of the rate bill, that a parent should not be compelled to contribute towards the support of a school, without he desired its instruction for his child; and that the childless and those who have already educated their children should be exempted from the burden of supporting a school — or, in other words, that citizens of the State, who share in its prosperity and glory, and who derive an advantage from the universal diffusion of knowledge, by the safeguards it rears against vice and immorality, will desire to participate in the benefit without sharing the cost. These objections may be answered in the appropriate language of a friend* to humanity:

"But sometimes, the rich farmer, the opulent manufacturer, or the capitalist, when sorely pressed with his natural and moral obligation to contribute a portion of his means for the education of the young, replies, either in form or in spirit,— 'My lands, my machinery, my gold and my silver, are mine; may I not do what I will with my own?' There is one supposable case and only one where this argument would have plausibility. If it were made by an isolated, solitary being — a being having no relations to the community around him,— having no ancestors to whom he had been indebted for ninety-nine parts in every hundred of all he possesses, and expecting to have no posterity after him,— it might not be easy to answer it. If there were but one family in this Western hemisphere, and only one in the Eastern hemisphere, and these two families bore no civil and social relations to each other, and were to be the first and last of the whole race, it might be difficult, except on very high and almost transcendent grounds, for either one of them to show good cause why the other should contribute to help educate children not his own. But is this the relation which any man amongst sustains to his fellow? The society of which we necessarily constitute a part, must be preserved; and in order to preserve it, we must not look merely to what one individual or one family needs, but to what the whole community needs; not merely to what one generation needs, but to the wants of a succession of generations."

By the third section of the bill, the State Superintendent is directed to ascertain the portion of said tax to be assessed and collected in each of the counties of the State, by dividing the sum among the several counties according to the valuation of the real and personal estate therein, as shall appear by the assessment of the year preceding the one in which such sum is to be raised. Your committee are fully aware that serious objections will be raised against this provision of the bill, by reason of the great inequality existing in the present mode of assessment, and that in consequence thereof, several of the counties in the State will be obliged to contribute an undue amount towards the support of education; but it is respectfully suggested by your committee that they have performed the duty enjoined upon them by reporting (what is deemed in their opinion) the best plan for the support of the common schools of the State. It will devolve upon the select committee appointed by the House, with especial reference to the consideration of the subject of an equalization of assessments, to devise some remedy; and it is confidently expected that some plan will be adopted, by which general satisfaction will be afforded to the people of the State.

The 4th section of the bill provides for the apportionment and division of ¼th the amount raised by tax, and ¼th of all other moneys appropriated to

---
* Hon. Horace Mann.

the support of common schools, equally among the several school districts of the State, and an apportionment of 33 cents for each child, but not to exceed in the aggregate the sum of $24, is directed to be paid each separate neighborhood in the State. (It is proper to remark that this term is used to designate those parts of school districts, some 6 or 8 in number, adjacent to the borders of the States of Pennsylvania and Massachusetts). The provisions of this section were made with particular reference to the sparsely populated districts of the State, which, without such equal distribution, would be unable to sustain a good and efficient public school. Your committee could not reconcile it with a sense of justice to the larger districts, forming a majority in the State, to recommend the equal distribution of any greater sum.

By the 5th section of the bill, the remaining one-fourth of the amount raised by a state tax, together with three-fourths of all other moneys appropriated by the State for the support of common schools, is apportioned according to the number of children between the ages of 4 and 21 years of age, residing in said district. It is also enjoined that the schools shall be kept open during 8 months of the year, by a duly qualified teacher.

It is expected by your committee that the amount to be raised by the State tax, to wit: $800,000, in addition to the appropriation from the income of the common school fund, which, by the income of the fund, may be increased to $300,000, thus making the total sum of $1,100,000 for the payment of teacher's wages, will be sufficient to support the common schools for a period of eight months. But in case there should be a deficiency; or if it were deemed advisable by the trustees to continue the schools for a longer period, then it is required by the 6th section of the bill that " the balance to be raised in any school district for the payment of teacher's wages, beyond the amount provided by the previous section of the bill, shall be raised by a poll tax to be levied by the trustees upon each resident of the district entitled to vote at the school district meetings, of such an amount as will make up such balance." The qualifications requisite for a voter, as prescribed by law, are the following:

1 The voter must be a male.
2 Of full age, that is, twenty-one years old or more.
3 He must be an actual resident of the district.
4 He must be entitled by law to hold land in this State; and must own or hire real property in the district subject to taxation for school purposes, or
5 He must be authorized to vote at town meetings of the town in which the district, or part of the district is situated, or must own personal property liable to be taxed for school purposes in the district, exceeding fifty dollars in value, exclusive of what is exempt from execution.

During the year 1849, as appears by the last annual report of the Superintendent of Common Schools, there was expended for teachers' wages the sum of $1,322,696.24. Of this amount $767,389.20 was public money, $508,724.56 raised on rate bills from those sending to school, $31,934.27 raised by district taxation, to supply deficiency in the collection of such rate bills, and $14,748.21 raised in like manner, to defray the rate bills of indigent persons; the number of children placed in the list of indigent exempts having been 18,686. The sum of $22,226.26, included in the above amount of public money and appropriated for the payment of teachers' wages, was raised from local funds belonging to several of the counties and towns of the State.

Taking, therefore, these statistics as a basis, we can calculate with some degree of certainty the amount of poll tax to be paid by each person upon whom the trustees are authorized to levy it. To the $800,000 proposed to be raised by a State tax, there may be added the sum of $300,000, to be appropriated from the income of the income of the Common School Fund and of the U. S. Deposit Fund, and also the sum of $22,226, from the local funds belonging to different counties and towns, making a total sum of $1,122,226. There will then be required to make up the deficiency for the payment of teachers' wages, $200,470. There are nearly 12,000 school districts in this State, and it is fair to assume that the number of residents in each district entitled to vote at school meetings, will average twenty-five voters, thus making an aggregate of 300,000 persons upon whom to levy a poll tax. The average amount to be assessed upon each person, therefore, would not exceed the sum of 67 cents.

It is naturally to be expected, that under the free school system there would be an increase of scholars; though such increase would not necessarily imply a larger expenditure for the payment of teachers' wages, yet a liberal allowance may be made therefore, and the result will not vary materially. For, by the gradual increase of the appropriation from the income of the common school fund, by reason of the annual increase of its capital, and increase of the poll tax to average 75 cents per capita, would be amply sufficient to make up any deficiency.

It is deemed advisable, to ensure an economical administration of the schools, that a portion of the funds for their support should be raised from the districts, and your committee, upon mature deliberation, would suggest the plan of a poll tax as best adapted to accomplish this result, and least liable to objection. It cannot be said to be a tax upon the basis of population, inasmuch as it is not proposed to tax, indiscriminately, all the inhabitants of a district, but only those qualified to vote at school meetings. It may be said, therefore, with more propriety, to be a tax upon capital and labor combined.

The main support of our free institutions rests upon the virtue and intelligence of the great laboring class. It is desirable, therefore, that labor should be elevated by a spirit of honest independence. For this reason among others, the schools are made free, that the children of labor may, in the public schools of the State, claim a perfect equality with the more favored children of fortune. It is conceived, therefore, to be a wise and politic measure to give to labor the opportunity to contribute its share towards the support of an institution designed expressly for its moral and social elevation. There are many who are able and willing to contribute the price of a day's labor for the support of a school, who would be unable to raise the amount required to be paid upon a rate bill. A noble, manly pride belongs of right to labor, and when that pride is appealed to in aid of the 50,000 children of want in the State, who will not crave the boon of an exemption from the rate bill, it will not hear the appeal in vain. Again, the repeated demands of labor have made the common schools of the State, in reality, free. Yet it is denied the privilege of paying its due proportion of the means required to keep them free. It is not, therefore, morally free; and is but "as a guest eating a feast at the expense of its host, and does not feel at liberty to question the prudence or liberality of the giver, or to suggest improvement."

With this brief exposition of its leading features, the bill is respectfully submitted for the consideration of the House.

THEO. H. BENEDICT[1] (Westchester county)
CHARLES H. SWORDS[2] (New York county)
WM. H. FELLER (Dutchess county)

Albany, February 6th 1851

AN ACT TO ESTABLISH FREE SCHOOLS THROUGHOUT THE STATE

The People of the State of New-York, represented in Senate and Assembly do enact as follows:

Section 1 Common schools in the several school districts in this State shall be free to all persons residing in the district over five and under twenty-one years of age. Persons not resident of a district may be admitted into the schools kept therein, with the approbation in writing of the trustees thereof, or a majority of them.

2 There shall hereafter be raised by tax in each and every year, upon the real and personal estate within this State, the sum of eight hundred thousand dollars, which shall be levied, assessed and collected in the mode prescribed by chapter thirteen, part first of the Revised Statutes, relating to assessment and collection of taxes, and when collected, shall be paid over to the respective county treasures, subject to the order of the State Superintendent of Common Schools.

3 The State Superintendent of Common Schools shall ascertain the portion of said sum of eight hundred thousand dollars to be assessed and collected in each of the several counties of this State, by dividing the said sum among the several counties, according to the valuation of real and personal estate therein, as it shall appear by the assessment of the year next preceding the one in which said sum is to be raised, and shall certify to the clerk of each county, before the 10th day of July in each year, the amount to be raised by tax in such county; and it shall be the duty of the several county clerks of this State, to deliver to the boards of supervisors, of their respective counties, a copy of such certificate on the first day of their annual session, and the board of supervisors of each county shall assess such amount upon the real and personal estate of such county, and in the manner provided by law for the assessment and collection of taxes.

---

[1] Theodore H. Benedict was born in New York City March 31, 1821. He was a graduate of Yale College and lived most of the time on his estate at Tarrytown, being possessed of a considerable fortune. In 1850 he was elected to the Assembly on the Whig ticket in a district in Westchester county which had always given large Democratic majorities. Although the youngest member of the Assembly of 1851, he took a prominent part in the session. He was chairman of the committee on colleges, academies and common schools and made a report which received much commendation. He was prominently identified with the activities of his party but declined further public office as he was obliged to travel much of the time on account of ill health. During the Civil War he devoted his time and means to the raising and equipping of volunteers for the Union Army.

[2] Charles R. Swords descended from a family which settled in Saragtoga county in 1756. He was the son of James Swords who was a publisher in New York City and later the president of the Washington Insurance Company. Charles R. Swords was a merchant and after retiring from business devoted himself to literature and music.

4 The State Superintendent of Common Schools shall, on or before the first day of January in every year, apportion and divide, or cause to be apportioned and divided, one-fourth of the sum so raised by general tax, and one-fourth of all other moneys appropriated to the support of common schools among the several school districts, parts of districts, and separate neighborhoods in this State, from which reports shall have been received in accordance with law, in the following manner, viz: to each separate neighborhood there shall be apportioned and paid a sum of money equal to thirty-three cents for each child in such neighborhood, between the ages of four and twenty-one; but the sum so to be apportioned and paid to any such neighborhood, shall in no case exceed the sum of twenty-four dollars, and the remainder of such one-fourth shall be apportioned and divided equally among the several districts; and the State Superintendent of Common Schools shall by proper rgeulations and instructions to be prescribed by him, provide for the payment of such moneys to the trustees of such separate neighborhoods and school districts.

5 It shall be the duty of the State Superintendent of Common Schools, on or before the first day of January in every year, to apportion and divide the remaining three-fourths of the said amount of eight hundred thousand dollars, together with the remaining three-fourths of all other moneys appropriated by the State for the support of common schools, among the several counties, cities and towns of the State, in the mode now prescribed by law for the division and apportionment of the income of the common school fund; and the share of the several towns and wards so apportioned and divided, shall be paid over, on and after the first Tuesday of February, in each year, to the several town superintendents of common schools, and ward or city officers, entitled by law to receive the same, and shall be apportioned by them among the several school districts and parts of districts in their several towns and wards, according to the number of children between the ages of four and twenty-one years residing in said districts and parts of districts, as the same shall have appeared from the last annual report of the trustees.; but no moneys shall be apportioned and paid to any district or part of a district, unless it shall appear from the last annual report of the trustees that a school has been kept for at least eight months during the year, ending with the date of such report, by a duly qualified teacher, unless by special permission of the State Superintendent of Common Schools.

6 Any balance required to be raised in any school district for the payment of teachers' wages beyond the amount apportioned to such district by the previous provisions of this act, and other public moneys belonging to the district and applicable to the payment of teachers' wages, shall be raised in the following manner: It shall be the duty of the trustees of each school district within thirty days after the time of holding the annual meeting of such district in each year to levy a poll tax of such amount upon each resident of the district entitled to vote at school district meetings as will make up such balance, and to make out and deliver to the collector of the district their warrant therefor, which shall be executed by the said collector in the same mode in all respects as is provided by law in the case of other school district assessments, and the amount when collected shall be paid over to the trustees, or one of them, and be expended for the payment of teachers' wages.

7 The State Superintendent of Common Schools shall have exclusive jurisdiction on appeal, in such manner and under such regulations as shall be prescribed by him, over all controversies arising under the several laws relating to common schools, and his decision shall be final and conclusive.

8 Nothing in this act shall be so construed as to repeal or alter the provisions of any special act relating to schools in any of the incorporated cities or villages of this State, except so far as they are inconsistent with the provisions contained in the first, second, third and fourth sections of this act.

9 All provisions of law now in force requiring the several boards of supervisors to raise by tax, any sum of money for the support of common schools in this State, and all other laws and parts of laws, inconsistent or incompatible with the provisions of this act, are hereby repealed.

10 The State Superintendent of Common Schools shall cause to be prepared, published and distributed among the several school districts, and school officers of the State, a copy of the several acts now in force relating to common schools, with such instructions, digest and expositions as he may deem expedient; and the expense incurred by him therefor shall be audited by the Comptroller, and paid by the Treasurer.

11 All the moneys received or appropriated by the provisions of this act, shall be applied to the payment of teachers' wages exclusively.

12 This act shall take effect on the first day of July next: but nothing herein contained shall be so construed as to affect provisions already made in the several school districts, for the support of schools therein, under existing laws, for the current year.

STATE OF NEW YORK
No. 42
In Assembly, February 6, 1851
No. 42

Report

Of the minority of the committee on colleges, academies and common schools in the several bills and petitions referred to that committee relating to common schools.

The minority of the committee on colleges, academies and common schools to which were referred several bills and petitions relating to common schools,

REPORT:

That immediately after the organization of said committee, the several bills and petitions relating to common schools were taken up for consideration, and after two or three meetings had been held it was understood that the committee so far agreed in opinion upon the subject that a report could be made upon which there would be concurrence as to principles and substance; details only remaining subject of doubt and difficulty; and the chairman of the committee Mr T. H. Benedict, expressing a wish to prepare a report, an adjournment was agreed to for the purpose of giving necessary time, and the committee was afterwards, on the 4th instant, assembled to hear read the report prepared by the chairman, when, for the first time, a new method was proposed providing for the support in part, of common schools to which the minority could not assent.

It will be seen by reference to the bills submitted by the majority, and the minority, that the committee have unanimously agreed to recommend the levy of a general tax upon the real and personal property liable to taxation in the State at large, to the amount of $800,000, that the committee are also unanimous as to the mode of dividing and applying this sum, together with all other public moneys from whatever source to be derived, and that the only point of disagreement arose from the mode in which the balance required to support common schools should be raised.

This balance the majority proposes to raise by capitation or "poll tax upon persons having the right to vote at school district meetings" without reference to the pecuniary ability of the voter, the minority proposing to raise the balance by rate bill upon those sending to school, excepting from such rate bill all persons not having pecuniary ability to pay.

The majority by the first section of their reported bill, propose to declare all common schools free.

The minority bill contains no section which would authorize the application of the high-sounding title "free common schools," but it is believed by the minority that the bill which they have reported is better adapted to the wants of the people of the State than the system now in operation; and infinitely better adapted to the condition and prosperity of the common schools of this State than the poll tax system proposed by the majority.

It is believed that numerous weighty reasons could be adducted in proof of this opinion drawn from the experience of the past, and the practical working of a system of common schools which has been in operation in this State for a period extending over half a century. But the minority refrain at present from entering upon the reasons which decide their preference to a rate bill over a poll tax system, preferring in the first place to bring forward some reasons and suggestions in favor of adopting the bill reported by the minority as a substitute for the law now in force commonly called the "free school law."

And the undersigned will not at this point consult the theories of political philosophers or socialists to aid them in deciding the point in question, but will look rather to the condition of the State than theory and will assume as truth that which to by far the largest portion of the community interested appears to have been demonstrated during the existence of the present law.

It is assumed then that the present law is condemned throughout the State in every town where its practical effects are felt. In the cities where common schools have been supported by general tax upon the city at large the operation of a partial and unequal system of taxation are not felt.

And in considering the value of public opinion upon the existing law the vote cast in cities should for this reason be omitted; it will not be pretended that the vote cast in the rural districts against the repeal of the free school law should be counted in favor of the law as it stands. That vote should be understood as an expression of the opinion of so many votes in favor of the principles of "free schools," and as such the most respectful consideration should be given to it.

The principle, or sentiment, which prompted this vote, is nearly allied to the general maxim which has governed the Legislature of the State for more than a half a century.

To establish public schools, which all should be free to enter upon equal terms, and to endow these schools by appropriations from the treasury of the State, the common property of the people.

In this way education has been cheapened, and made accessible to all the children of the State living in districts sufficiently populous to organize a common school district; and from the year 1795, when $250,000 was appropriated for the support of common school for five years, $50,000 in each year,) to the present time, this policy has been pursued with a constancy of purpose which has known no change, and with an enlightened liberality worthy of all praise, until our system of common schools had, in 1848, acquired a position for usefulness almost without parallel in the world.

It is not necessary to attempt the defence of every item of policy which, during fifty-three years, contributed to this result; but it may be said, "without fear of dispute," that every measure adopted was the offspring of pure and honorable motives; and it is due to the venerated names associated with the past legislation of this State, to acknowledge; that to our wise and patriotic predecessors we are indebted for a system of common schools possessing many essential elements of great value and requiring only amendments and development to adapt it to the wants of the present age.

This age is esteemed by many as a radical, reformatory age, possessing more wisdom and virtue than any preceding it; and some persons fully possessed of this opinion, without pausing to inquire into its origin or truthfulness, and believing, doubtless, that upon themselves a large part of the business of reformation has been cast by providence, accident, or by virtue of their superior genius, have set themselves at work to hew down every institution of the State that they might enjoy the exclusive glory of rearing new institutions which should reflect their wisdom to posterity in such sublime effulgence as entirely to eclipse all who had gone before them.

Such lights have blessed our political firmament, and during the last few years many such have enacted their "fantastic tricks" for a season, and disappeared, not unlike those strange bodies which occasionally visit our solar system from the unexplored regions of the universe, to alarm the timid and instruct the wise for a season, and disappear again upon their pathless journey through "nameless regions void," and though in their passage the existing order has been disturbed, and the public mind convulsed, the names of Jay, Tompkins and Clinton, Young, Spencer and Savage, are still known and remembered with pride and veneration.

It is too common an error to invent theories and bring to their support hypotheses, and thence derive conclusions which have not a grain of experience to sustain them; such theories, put to the test of practical development, usually fail, to the astonishment of their inventors and perhaps the discomfiture of society.

Such has been the character of legislation respecting common schools; instead of improving the really excellent system which we had in 1848, by increasing gradually from year to year the amount of public moneys applicable to their support, until the point should be reached which would make our system available to every one upon terms entirely just and equitable, the idea of "free schools" was seized upon as a "popular element," and without waiting to enquire what the character of a school must be, or in what manner endowed or supported, to entitle it justly to that appellation, a law was adopted requiring every school district in the State to keep open a common school which should be " free to every child between the ages of 4 and 21 years, by levying a tax upon the property of the district to pay teachers' wages." A trifle more wisdom and logic of the "same sort" would have dictated a law that every man in the State should keep open a common school in his own house to educate his own children, levy a tax upon his own property to pay the teacher; the same logic could without difficulty demonstrate that this would be a " free school."

If each separate school district in the State constituted an independent community, having no relationship, political connection or commercial exchange with any other part of the State, such a free school system might with more propriety be adopted.

The proposition to endow public schools from the public treasury to cheapen education so that all might enjoy the advantages of learning, was the offspring of noble sentiment. To dignify it as one of the noblest sentiments of humanity, it must embrace the people of an entire State or empire, voluntarily agreeing to enact laws subjecting the entire property of the commonwealth to taxation for the support of schools, open to all the children of the State. Such a sentiment must rest upon the belief that mutual relations exist between the people of every commonwealth, rendering it obligatory upon all to give to every child in the State such a degree of learning as would be essential to success in the ordinary business of life, and to direct the mind in pursuit of virtue and happiness.

It is not intended to pause in this place to enumerate the various relations out of which such obligations grow, or to review the principle which claims for every child the fostering care of the State.

This principle, long ago adopted, is now universally admitted, and the only inquiry now remaining for us, how shall it be most successfully accomplished?

Shall we discard the principle and dishonor the State by an attempt to localize our duties, relations and sympathies, to those in sight of our own dwellings? Or shall the citizens of Albany and Rensselaer enjoying a rich commerce with every county in the State, recognize the children of Chautauqua and Steuben, Cattaraugus and St Lawrence, as within the range of their sympathies, within the pale of civilization, so far as to be entitled to receive from the treasury of the State substantial aid to assist in maintaining schools for their education? Will the people of the city of Albany, or any other wealthy cities or counties in the State encircle themselves with artificial geographical lines, and say to the rest of the State, " we will educate our own children within these lines, and you may take care of your own, we have more wealth than you, and cannot afford to be recognised as your relations."

If such a distinction is to be recognised, allow first the wealthy cities to say to the country, we cannot permit you to tax us to educate your children. We recognize no obligation which allows such a practice, we know of no relationship with you which admits of the adoption of such a rule.

The country villages, in imitation of such an example, claim the right of exemption from taxation to support schools in the rural districts, and the wealthy farmer in such districts, upon the same principle, claims to be exempt from taxes to educate the children of his less opulent or poorer neighbor.

Let these claims of selfishness be acknowledged, and we may justly inquire, who in our wide State holds such relations to the poor as to be willing to contribute to their education; and the children of the poor might justly exclaim, " We have appealed to the cities where wealth is located, and have been denied; we have proffered our petition to the wealthy villages of the State, and a deaf ear has been turned to us; we have implored our own neighbors, living within our sight, to help us, and in imitation of the example of others, our prayer has been spurned by them."

The undersigned, believing that the present school system of the State could not be sustained, have reported a bill, which, it is believed, will remove existing difficulties.

The bill presented by them, not proposing to make our common schools absolutely free to every one without any pecuniary charge, involves necessarily the question whether the Legislature shall regard the vote of the State upon the existing laws, as entitled to the respect due a superior authority.

The undersigned believe that the people of this State, by the emphatic majority, 158,000 votes cast in favor of free schools, in 1849, were governed by a desire to see our common schools improved, and their advantages secured to the largest possible number.

The aim was not so much to establish a theory as to attain a substantial, valuable reality; the statute to which they gave the sanction of their votes proved to be a theory only, which promised the substance and gave but a shadow, the discontent which followed brought to your Legislature last year numerous petitions for modification or repeal; and gathering the spirit of these petitions from the evils of which they complained, the members of the Assembly of 1850 passed with great unanimity a bill the same substantially as the one now presented by the undersigned, but at a period so late in the session that it failed to receive the consideration of the Senate; and on the last day of the session a bill was sent from the Senate to the House, providing for a resubmission of the law of 1849 to the people. It is unnecessary here to discuss the policy of such submission, and the fact is mentioned in this place only with the view of adding, that such was the force of public opinion against the existing law, that the Legislature of 1850 did not deem it proper to adjourn without passing some law upon the subject.

The people again voted upon the law of 1849, and the vote is here set down for the purpose of a canvass of its merits.

The following statement of the vote in the several counties of the State, for and against the repeal of the free school law, is derived from the official returns to the Secretary of State's office:

	For repeal of the new school law	Against repeal of the new school law	Majority for repeal	Majority against repeal
Albany	3,310	8,582	....	5,272
Allegany	3,787	2,161	1,626	....
Broome	3,021	1,846	175	....
Cattaraugus	3,175	2,196	979	....
Cayuga	3,639	3,409	230	....
Chautauqua	4,724	3,094	1,630	....
Chemung	2,315	2,135	180	....
Chenango	4,828	2,358	2,470	....
Clinton	1,963	1,893	70	....
Columbia	2,566	4,394	....	1,823
Cortland	3,150	1,153	1,997	....
Delaware	4,068	4,040	2,028	....
Dutchess	2,841	6,764	....	3,923
Erie	4,672	6,415	....	1,743
Essex	2,138	1,559	597	....
Fraaklin	1,664	1,221	443	....
Fulton	2,310	1,537	973	....
Genesee	2,830	1,698	1,132	....
Greene	3,217	1,847	1,379	....
Herkimer	3,588	3,038	50	....
Jefferson	6,064	3,959	2,106	....
Kings	1,060	11,136	....	10,076
Lewis	1,709	455	964	....
Livingston	3,599	2,548	1,051	....
Madison	3,896	3,254	642	....
Monroe	5,099	5,031	68	....
Montgomery	2,253	3,205	....	1,042
New York	987	38,816	....	37,827
Niagara	3,461	2,169	1,292	....
Oneida	7,414	6,517	897	....
Onondaga	4,657	6,583	....	1,926
Ontario	3,712	2,970	742	....
Orange	4,183	3,274	909	....
Orleans	2,835	1,523	1,312	....
Oswego	4,241	3,770	471	....
Otsego	3,816	4,096	1,720	....
Putnam	845	959	....	114
Queens	1,542	2,050	....	508
Rensselaer	3,370	7,176	....	3,806
Richmond	351	1,212	....	861
Rockland	826	948	....	112
St Lawrence	4,628	3,559	1,069	....
Saratoga	4,211	3,077	1,134	....
Schenectady	1,365	1,417	....	52
Schoharie	4,150	1,611	2,548	....
Seneca	1,810	2,113	....	303
Steuben	5,377	4,016	1,361	....
Suffolk	2,252	1,884	368	....
Sullivan	1,748	1,475	273	....
Tioga	2,784	1,130	1,654	....
Tompkins	4,441	1,924	2,517	....
Ulster	3,826	4,063	....	237
Warren	1,806	1,102	704	....
Washington	3,726	2,718	1,008	....
Wayne	4,742	2,605	2,136	....
Westchester	2,164	4,436	....	2,272
Wyoming	3,155	1,610	1,545	....
Yates	2,186	1,525	661	....
Total	184,308	209,346	46,874	71,912

Majority against repeal, 25,038

The above table shows that 41 counties gave an aggregate majority of 46,874 against the law, whilst the remaining 17 counties gave aggregate majorities amounting to 71,912 in favor of the law. Properly to estimate the value of this vote, those cities having special school laws for their government, which would not in any degree be affected by the vote should be excepted, and if we take from the vote the votes given in the following counties in each of which large cities are located, namely:

	Majorities
City and county of New York	37,827
Albany	5,272
Dutchess	3,923
Erie	1,743
Kings	10,076
Rensselaer	3,806
and you will have	62,647

to reduce the 71,912 aggregate majority for the law and leave only 8265 aggregate majorities in the remaining twelve of the 17 counties; and if you deduct this aggregate from the aggregate majorities in the 41 counties, the account stands thus:

For the repeal in 41 counties	46,874
Again repeal in 12 counties	8,265
	38,609

making 38,609 majority in the State in favor of repeal; but it is urged that the vote is not a fair test of public opinion, because given upon a law which was obnoxious to many objections for its defects; and that many voted against the law who were in favor of free schools; this is doubtless true to some extent; but it should be remembered that nearly all the public prints in the State, and a State convention of the friends of free schools urged upon every voter "friendly to free schools," the importance of voting against repeal and assured them that if the law was sustained amendments would be made to perfect the system; this fact, properly estimated, it is believed will warrant the conclusion that a majority of the people desired a repeal of the law of 1849.

Whether this large vote is to be understood as a condemnation of the free school principle or merely some of the most objectionable features of the law, may be a question of doubt, and the minority believe that it is not safe to assume, that it is not to be regarded as a condemnation of the principle merely because there was a majority of 158,000 in favor of the law when first submitted to the people. The vote on that occasion was far from being full, proving that a great many voters abstained from exercising their rights in this respect, either from indifference, or because they were willing to let the experiment be tried. Since then the subject has been more fully discussed in all its bearings, and the fact that a very great change has been manifested upon a full vote, coupled with the additional fact that numerous petitions are before us, praying for the unconditional repeal of the law, would seem to indicate that the principle itself had now been fairly recognized, or that a radical change had taken place in this respect. We know that many enlightened men are opposed to making schools entirely free upon the ground that that which costs nothing is apt to be cheaply estimated; and that the attendance of a larger number of pupils would be more likely to be secured by requiring some amount to be paid for tuition. It does not follow that all the children in the State between the ages of four and twenty-one would attend, were schools free, as seems to be somewhat too hastily assumed. In some instances parents do not sufficiently appreciate the benefits of even a common school education, and take no pains to secure them for their children. In others, and especially in remote farming districts, where the inhabitants are mostly in moderate circumstances, the children are detained from school at an early age to secure their services upon the farm. The fact that the Prussian government has resorted to coercive measures to compel the attendance of the children, proves that the adoption of the free school principle would not necessarily effect the object so confidently anticipated. Compulsion in this country, on this subject, is entirely out of the question. Our citizens cannot be compelled to receive these benefits for their children without adopting a despotic principle entirely at war with our free institutions.

The next point to be considered is whether we shall return to the law as it stood prior to the submission of this law to the people, or adopt a new method for the support of common schools.

In favor of the former system it is urged that it has gradually grown into existence; that the people are entirely familiar with its operations; that it produces as little contention and disturbance in the numerous school districts in the State as can be reasonably expected; and that it has been largely instrumental in diffusing the great benefits of education in the primary branches.

Many citizens of intelligence and unquestioned purity of motive, sincerely believe that upon the safe principle of "letting well enough alone," it is better to repeal the free school law unconditionally, and leave the law as it existed before. But it must be observed that the committee have not yet acted on any other proposition than that which relates to providing means for the support of common schools. A change in this respect does not essentially interfere with the machinery of the system as it has heretofore existed. A brief statement of the provisions of the law on this point will exhibit the extent of the change proposed.

The laws now in force provide

1st. That the State Superintendent should apportion the school monies to be annually distributed among the several counties of the State, and the share of each county among its respective towns and cities, according to the ratio of their population, as compared with the population of the whole State, according to the last preceding census.

2d. That the supervisors of each county should add to the sums of money to be raised on each of the towns of the county, for defraying the necessary expenses thereof, a sum equal to the school monies apportioned to such town, to be levied and collected as other monies directed to be raised in the town.

3d. That the balance required for the expenses of the school should be raised by a tax on the taxable inhabitants of the district.

An amount equal to the amount of the public money distributed was thus directed to be raised by a tax based upon population as distinguished from that of property.

The bill proposed by us abolishes all laws providing for the raising of money by vote at town meetings; and indeed every other statute authorizing the levying in districts taxes for the payment of teachers' wages. The only tax contemplated by the proposed act being a general tax upon all the property of the State amounting to $800,000; and the minority believe that the system which was in operation in 1848, with all the details of which the people were familiar, should be disturbed as little as possible, as violent changes in laws long established and well understood should never be made without weighty reasons; and notwithstanding the opinion of the majority, that the people have by their votes demanded a radical change, if it shall be assumed that a majority of the voters of the State have furnished the authority for innovation, the undersigned still repeat it can with equal truth be asserted that a very large majority prefer the old system; and as no system of common schools can long be sustained which arrays against it a large minority, it would seem that the friends of free schools would find their object best promoted by uniting with the friends of the old system in such amendments as would secure substantially the object at which they aim, and secure the concurrence and support of the great body of the community upon a plan embracing very nearly every feature desired by the most ardent friends of free schools.

It is believed that the bill proposed by the minority will if carried into effect secure general confidence and support, and greatly increase the usefulness of our common school system.

A little attention to the details of the proposed amendments will perhaps serve to illustrate its effects. The following extract from the report of the State Superintendent of common schools presents the condition of our common schools at the close of the year 1849:

"From the returns of the several town superintendents, made to the county clerks of the respective counties, and bearing date on the first day of July last, it appears that the whole number of school districts in the State, duly organized at that date, was 11,397, being an increase of 206 during the preceding year. Of this number, 8394 are composed of territory wholly situated in the town where the schoolhouse of the district stands, and the remainder are joint districts, formed from two or more adjoining towns.

"Reports, in accordance with law, have been received by the several town superintendents from the trustees of 11,173 of these districts, leaving 124 districts from which no returns were made. These reports bear date on the 1st day of January, 1850, and refer to the condition of the several schools during the year 1849. The average period during which the schools were taught, during that year, by duly qualified teachers, in accordance with law, was eight months. The whole number of children, between the ages of five and sixteen years, residing in the several districts of the State, on the 31st day of December, 1849, was 735,188; and the number of children taught during the preceding year was 794,500, being an excess of 59,312 over the number between the ages of five and sixteen, and 16,191 over the whole number taught in 1848. Of the number thus taught, 9079 had been under instruction during the entire year; 18,455 for ten months and less than twelve; 59,315 for eight months and less than ten; 106,100 for six months and less than eight; 167,732 for four months and less than six; 198,022 for two months and less than four; and 200,128 for a period less than two months. The period of attendance of the remaining 35,669 is not included in the reports of the trustees, which have been found very defective in this respect, from the difficulty of ascertaining the requisite data upon which to base these returns.

Estimates and Accounts of Expenditures of School Moneys

"During the year embraced in the report of the trustees, the whole amount of money paid for teachers' wages in the several districts from which reports were received was $1,322,696.24, of which $767,389.20 was public money, $508,724.56 raised on rate bills from those sending to school, $31,834.27 raised by district tax to supply deficiencies in the collection of such rate bills, and $14,748.21 raised in like manner to defray the rate bills of indigent persons, exempted by the trustees in the mode prescribed by law. The number of children thus placed on the list of indigent exempts during the year 1849, was 18,686.

"The balance of revenue now in the treasury, applicable to common school purposes, in addition to the revenue accruing from the United States deposit fund, is $137,524.07. The amount of revenue annually contributed to this object from the avails of the deposit fund is $165,000, which, added to the amount above stated accruing from the common school fund, gives an aggregate of $302,524.07 as the present revenue of the combined funds. As under the existing provisions of law, not only the capital but the revenue of this fund is constantly and steadily increasing, no good reason is perceived why the apportionment for the ensuing year, based upon the ratio of the population of the State, as ascertained by the census just completed, may not be increased from $285,000 to $300,000."

This amount, added to the sum of $800,000 proposed to be raised by the provisions of the bill reported by the undersigned, will supply the sum of one million one hundred thousand dollars, applicable to the payment of teachers' wages in 1852.

It is estimated that the number of children between the ages of 5 and 16, in the year 1852, will have reached 800,000; that one-half of this number will be in attendance at our schools a period averaging five months, and the other half a period averaging three months; so that the actual average of all the children attending school during that year would be four months.

It is estimated that $1,450,000 will be paid during the year 1852 for teachers' wages, leaving $350,000 to be raised by rate bills upon those sending to school, excepting those not having pecuniary ability to pay; and it will be seen that the rate bill, as an average, would be quite inconsiderable, and in no instance very large.

To participate in the distribution of public moneys, a school must be kept seven months during the year; and it is not doubted that every district in the State, where any attention is paid to education, would be able to sustain a good school during seven months, while in much the larger number of districts schools would be maintained from 8 to 10 months.

The third section of the bill provides for a division of one-fourth of all the public monies among the school districts of the State equally; the opinion is entertained by some that one-third of one-half of the public monies should be thus divided, the undersigned regard one-fourth as more equitable, for the following reasons: First — this will be found a sufficient discrimination in favor of small or sparsely populated districts to enable them to sustain schools from seven to eight months without imposing a high rate-bill. Secondly — to divide more in this manner would so materially abate the amount apportioned to the large districts that to sustain schools without oppressive rate-bills it would be necessary to place too many pupils under the charge of a single teacher, which all experience has proved to be unfavorable to the advancement of the pupil. Thirdly — it is believed by the committee that an examination into the comparative educational advancement of the children of populous districts and those having quite small numbers, even where schools have been kept open in the latter from a fourth to a third less period, that the children of the same age in the small districts will generally be found more advanced than those in the populous districts, owing entirely to the fact that their teachers, having fewer pupils, have been able to give to them more time and attention, and this the committee believe was the case previous to '49, when no discrimination was made in favor of small districts.

This first part of this section provides for paying separate neighborhoods 33 cents for each pupil, to an amount not exceeding $24. The term "separate neighborhoods" is applied only to small communities on the borders of the State, which maintain schools by uniting with similar communities in adjoining states, and though these separate neighborhoods are few and inconsiderable when compared with the rest of the State, they are equitably entitled to participate in the public monies, and the committee has endeavored by an approximate estimate to give these neighborhoods their fair proportion of this fund.

The assumed average of 33 cents to each pupil, or $24 to each separate neighborhood, has no application to the districts or parts of districts within the State.

The minority bill provides that a school shall be kept in each district seven months to entitle it to public monies; this change it is believed will furnish substantial relief to some weak districts; those of more ability will not be restricted by this section, and probably but few districts in the State will reduce the terms of their schools in consequence of this provision. If it should be found to operate unfavorably, it can easily be corrected.

The bill of the minority also provides that the first apportionment under this act may be made to any district in the State which was entitled to an apportionment in 1849.

Under the operation of the "free school" law, a very large number of districts in the State which were in prosperous condition previous to 1849 have become prostrated, and in many instances nearly disorganized, and without some provision favorable to their recovery and reorganization, the most unfortunate embarrassment would continue for some time to come. This provision of the bill is proposed to remove existing obstacles to a participation in the public school funds in such cases, and it is believed will produce the desired results.

The fourth section of the bill provides for the apportionment and division of the remaining three fourths among the districts of the State upon the basis of population, requiring that a school shall be kept for a period of seven months to entitle to a participation.

The fifth section provides that any balance required for the payment of teacher's wages beyond the amount apportioned from public moneys shall be raised by rate bill upon those sending to school, excepting all persons not having pecuniary ability, and paying the amount of such exemption from the public moneys.

To this section, the majority of the committee did not assent, and the bill introduced by the majority proposes to raise this balance by a "poll tax of equal amount, upon all persons having the right to vote at district meetings."

The minority do not question the motives of the majority in prefering the "poll tax" to a rate bill, but they cannot bring themselves to believe that any good reason can be assigned for adopting a system of taxation unknown to our laws in the present age, except the levy of one day's "service upon the highway" upon every male inhabitant of the State over the age of 21 years.

The exception referred to is not a tax payable in money, but a demand of labor-service, and the argument in favor of demanding this service, though doubtful in character is not good when it is proposed to substitute a capitation tax in money.

The framers of this highway poll tax law doubtless supposed that every poor man had it in his power to render labor to the State as an equivalent for his enjoyment of the privilege of the highway; they did not act upon the presumption that he had money or could pay a tax in money: to the honor of our State there is no money tax upon man imposed by any general law, taxes are levied upon property.

The highway poll service and the militia service alone rest upon the head, **the former is of doubtful utility and is not now uniformly enforced,** indeed it is believed that this highway poll service is seldom received from persons having no taxable property.

It is not denied that the country has a right to demand of every "able bodied" man such military service as the public safety shall require, but the claim to levy a money tax that exempts neither indigence nor age, which enters the humble home of the poor man and levies its demand upon his last bed, is denied — denied in the name of civilization and humanity! Such a statute would disgrace barbarian countries. For what purpose is it demanded? To sustain common schools! to make common schools nominally free!

The effect of such a statute would be to demand and extort from the hard earnings of every poor householder in the State a tax equal in amount to the tax levied upon the householder who possesses his thousands or millions of hoarded treasure.

The majority claim that the sum would be small, that it would average but about 67 cents; but they have omitted to state that in some cases it might amount to several dollars.

To illustrate the unequal effect of such a statute, let us suppose a case of a class of which there would be numerous examples: Take a farming community where a district should be composed of eight wealthy farmers, with an average of three children each, and five poor laborers living in cottages belonging to the farmers, and barely earning a subsistence for themselves and families, in the employment of their landlords; in such a case you will have 39 children to educate. Let a school be kept in such a district 8 months, at a cost of $16 per month, the aggregate would be $128; deduct from this $68, the amount of public moneys which such a district would receive, and there remains $65 to be supplied by "poll tax" upon persons entitled to vote at district meetings. The number of persons liable to this tax in such a district is 13, and the poll tax amounts to $5 upon each voter. Your five poor men, without an acre of their own, without any property belonging to them subject to ordinary taxation, are called upon to pay five dollars each. There is no clause to exempt the indigent — no provision in favor of the poor — and the only cow must be sacrificed, or the last bed sold, to answer the demand of this merciless, inexorable law, even though the poor laborer should have no children to be benefited by the school. His landlord, with one or two hundred acres of land, pays five dollars also, his poll tax, and by some mystery of logic not understood by us, this school is called free.

The annexed bill is submitted by the minority as a substitute for the bill reported by the majority.

SILAS M. BURROUGHS[1] (Orleans county)
BENJ. G. FERRIS[2] (Tompkins county)

AN ACT
To provide for the support of the common schools

The People of the State of New York, represented in Senate and Assembly, do enact as follows:

Section 1 There shall hereafter be raised by tax in each and every year, upon the real and personal estate within this State, the sum of eight hundred thousand dollars, which shall be levied, assessed and collected in the mode prescribed by chapter thirteen, part first of the Revised Statutes, relating to the assessment and collection of taxes, and when collected, shall be paid over to the respective county treasurers, subject to the order of the State Superintendent of Common Schools.

2 The State Superintendent of Common Schools shall ascertain the portion of said sum of eight hundred thousand dollars to be assessed and collected in each of the several counties of this State, by dividing the said sum among the several counties, according to the valuation of real and personal estate therein, as it shall appear by the assessment of the next year preceding the one in which said sum is to be raised, and shall certify to the clerk of each county, before the tenth day of July in each year, the amount to be raised by tax in such county; and it shall be the duty of the several county clerks of this State, to deliver to the board of supervisors of their respective counties, a copy of such certificate on the first day of their annual session, and the board of supervisors of each county shall assess such amount upon the real and personal estate of such county, in the manner provided by law for the assessment and collection of taxes.

[1] Silas Burroughs began his business career as a merchant but later became a very able lawyer in Medina, Orleans county. He was a colonel in the state militia, served in the Assembly of New York State and was twice elected to Congress.
[2] Benjamin G. Ferris was a college graduate and a leading lawyer of Tompkins county. He was district attorney of Tompkins county in 1840-45 and a member of the Assembly in 1851. In 1853 he was appointed secretary of Utah Territory but, after holding the position a short time, he returned to Ithaca, where he died in 1893.

3 The State Superintendent of Common Schools shall, on or before the first day of January in every year, apportion and divide or cause to be apportioned and divided, one-fourth of the sum so raised by general tax, and one-fourth of all other monies appropriated to the support of common schools, among the several school districts, parts of districts, and separate neighborhoods in this State, from which reports shall have been received in accordance with law, in the following manner, viz: To each separate neighborhood there shall be apportioned and paid a sum of money equal to thirty-three cents for each child in such neighborhood, between the ages of four and twenty-one; but the sum so to be apportioned and paid to any such neighborhood, shall in no case exceed the sum of twenty-four dollars, and the remainder of such one-fourth shall be apportioned and divided equally among the several districts; and the State Superintendent of common schools shall, by proper regulations and instructions to be prescribed by him, provide for the payments of such moneys to the trustees of such neighborhoods and school districts.

4 It shall be the duty of the State Superintendent of Common Schools, on or before the first day of January in every year, to apportion and divide the remaining three-fourths of the said amount of eight hundred thousand dollars, together with the remaining three fourths of all other moneys appropriated by the State for the support of common schools, among the several counties, cities, and towns of the State, in the mode now prescribed by law for the division and apportionment of the income of the common school fund; and the share of the several towns and wards so apportioned and divided, shall be paid over, on and after the first Tuesday of February, in each year, to the several town superintendents of common schools, and ward or city officers, entitled by law to receive the same, and shall be apportioned by them among the several school districts and parts of districts in their several towns and wards, according to the number of children between the ages of four and twenty-one years, residing in said districts and parts of districts, as the same shall have appeared from the last annual report of the trustees, but no money shall be apportioned and paid to any district or part of a district, unless it shall appear from the last annual report of the trustees that a school has been kept therein for at least seven months during the year, ending with the date of such report, by a duly qualified teacher, unless by special permission of the State Superintendent of Common Schools; excepting also that the first apportionment of money under this act may be made to all school districts, which were entitled to an apportionment of public money in the year 1849.

5 Any balance required to be raised in any school district for the payment of teachers' wages, beyond the amount apportioned to such district by the previous provisions of this act, and other public moneys belonging to the district applicable to the payment of teachers' wages, shall be raised by rate bill to be made out by the trustees against those sending to school in proportion to the number of days and of children sent, to be ascertained by the teachers' list, and in making out such rate bill it shall be the duty of the trustees to exempt either wholly or in part, as they may deem expedient, such indigent inhabitants as may, in their judgment, be entitled to such exemption, and such amount shall be paid out of the public monies received in such district applicable to the payment of teachers' wages.

6 The State Superintendent of Common Schools shall have exclusive jurisdiction on appeal, in such manner and under such regulations as shall be prescribed by him over all controversies arising under the several laws relating to common schools, and his decision shall be final and conclusive.

7 Nothing in this act shall be so construed as to repeal or alter the provisions of any special act relating to schools in any of the incorporated cities or villages of this State, except so far as they are inconsistent with the provisions contained in the first, second, third and fourth sections of this act.

8 Chapter one hundred and forty of the Session Laws of 1849, entitled "An act establishing free schools throughout the State," and chapter 404 of the Session Laws of 1849, entitled an act to amend an act entitled "An act establishing free schools throughout the State," sections sixteen, seventeen and eighteen of the Revised Statutes relating to common schools, requiring the several boards of supervisors to raise by tax on each of the towns of their respective counties, a sum equal to the school monies apportioned to such towns, and providing for its collection and payment, and all other provisions of law incompatible with the provisions of this act, are hereby repealed.

9 The State Superintendent of Common Schools shall cause to be prepared, published and distributed among the several school districts, and school officers of the State, a copy of the several acts now in force relating to common schools, with such instructions, digest and expositions as he may deem expedient; and the expense incurred by him therefor shall be audited by the Comptroller and paid by the Treasurer.

10 All the monies received or appropriated by the provisions of this act shall be applied to the payment of teachers' wages exclusively.

11 This act shall take effect on the first day of July next, but nothing herein contained shall be construed as to affect provisions already made in the several school districts, for the support of schools therein under existing laws for the current year.

Chapter 151

AN ACT to establish free schools throughout the State.

Passed April 12, 1851, "three-fifths being present."

The People of the State of New York, represented in Senate and Assembly, do enact as follows:

1 Common schools in the several school districts in this State shall be free to all persons residing in the district over five and under twenty-one years of age, as hereinafter provided. Persons not resident of a district may be admitted into the schools kept therein with the approbation, in writing, of the trustees thereof, or a majority of them.

2 There shall hereafter be raised by tax, in each and every year, upon the real and personal estate within this state, the sum of eight hundred thousand dollars, which shall be levied, assessed and collected in the mode prescribed by chapter thirteen, part first of the Revised Statutes, relating to the assessment and collection of taxes, and when collected shall be paid over to the respective county treasurers, subject to the order of the State Superintendent of Common Schools.

3 The State Superintendent of Common Schools shall ascertain the portion of said sum of eight hundred thousand dollars to be assessed and collected

in each of the several counties of this State, by dividing the said sum among the several counties, according to the valuation of real and personal estate therein, as it shall appear by the assessment of the year next preceding the one in which said sum is to be raised, and shall certify to the clerk of each county, before the tenth day of July in each year, the amount to be raised by tax in such county; and it shall be the duty of the several clerks of this State to deliver to the board of supervisors of their respective counties, a copy of such certificate on the first day of their annual session, and the board of supervisors of each county shall assess such amount upon the real and personal estate of such county, in the manner provided by law for the assessment and collection of taxes.

4 The State Superintendent of Common Schools shall on or before the first day of January in every year, apportion and divide, or cause to be apportioned and divided one-third of the sum so raised by general tax, and one-third of all other monies appropriated to the support of common schools, among the several school districts, parts of districts and separate neighborhoods in this State, from which reports shall have been received in accordance with law, in the following manner, viz: to each separate neighborhood belonging to a school district in some adjoining state there shall be apportioned and paid a sum of money equal to thirty-three cents for each child in such neighborhood (between the ages of four and twenty-one:) but the sum so to be apportioned and paid to any such neighborhood, shall in no case exceed the sum of twenty-four dollars, and the remainder of such one-third shall be apportioned and divided equally among the several districts and the State Superintendent of Common Schools shall, by proper regulations and instructions to be prescribed by him, provide for the payment of such monies to the trustees of such separate neighborhoods and school districts.

5 It shall be the duty of the State Superintendent of Common Schools, on or before the first day of January in every year, to apportion and divide the remaining two-thirds of the said amount of eight hundred thousand dollars, together with the remaining two-thirds of all other moneys appropriated by the State for the support of common schools among the several counties, cities and towns of the State, in the mode now prescribed by law for the division and apportionment of the income of the common school fund; and the share of the several towns and wards so apportioned and divided, shall be paid over, on and after the first Tuesday of February in each year, to the several town superintendents of common schools and wards or city officers entitled by law to receive the same, and shall be apportioned by them among the several school districts and parts of districts in their several towns and wards according to the number of children between the ages of four and twenty-one years, residing in said districts and parts of districts, as the same shall have appeared from the last annual report of the trustees; but no moneys shall be apportioned and paid to any district or part of a district, unless it shall appear from the last annual report of the trustees that a school has been kept therein for at least six months during the year ending with the date of such report by a duly qualified teacher, unless by special permission of the State Superintendent of Common Schools; excepting also, that the first apportionment of money under this act shall be made to all

school districts which were entitled to an apportionment of public money in the year eighteen hundred and forty-nine.

6 Any balance required to be raised in any school district for the payment of teachers' wages, beyond the amount apportioned to such district by the previous provisions of this act, and other public moneys belonging to the district applicable to the payment of teachers' wages, shall be raised by rate bill, to be made out by the trustees against those sending to school, in proportion to the number of days and of children sent to be ascertained by the teachers' list, and in making out such rate bill it shall be the duty of the trustees to exempt, either wholly or in part, as they may deem expedient, such indigent inhabitants as may, in their judgment be entitled to such exemption, and the amount of such exemption shall be added to the first tax list thereafter to be made out by the trustees for district purposes or shall be separately levied by them, as they shall deem most expedient.

7 The same property which is exempt by section twenty-two, of article two, title five, chapter six, part three of the Revised Statutes from levy and sale under execution, shall be exempt from levy and sale under any warrant to collect any rate bill for wages of teachers of common schools.

8 Nothing in this act shall be so constructed as to repeal or alter the provisions of any special act relating to schools in any of the incorporated cities or villages of this State, except so far as they are inconsistent with the provisions contained in the first, second, third and fourth sections of this act.

9 Chapter one hundred and forty of the Session Laws of 1849, entitled "An act establishing free schools throughout the State," and chapter four hundred and four of the Session Laws of 1849, entitled " an act to amend an act entitled 'An act establishing free schools throughout the State,'" and sections sixteen, seventeen and eighteen of the Revised Statutes relating to common schools, requiring the several boards of supervisors to raise by tax, on each of the towns of their respective counties, a sum equal to the school moneys apportioned to such towns, and providing for its collection and payment, and all other provisions of law incompatible with the provisions of this act, are hereby repealed.

10 The State Superintendent of Common Schools shall cause to be prepared, published and distributed among the several school districts and school officers of the State a copy of the several acts now in force relating to common schools, with such instructions, digest and expositions as he may deem expedient; and the expense incurred by him therefor shall be audited by the Comptroller and paid by the Treasurer.

11 All the moneys received or appropriated by the provisions of this act shall be applied to the payment of teachers' wages exclusively.

12 It shall be the duty of the trustees of the several school districts in this State to make out and transmit to the town superintendent of the town in which their respective school houses shall be located, on or before the first day of September next, a correct statement of the whole number of children residing in their district on the first day of August preceding the date of such report, between the ages of four and twenty-one; and such town superintendent shall embody such statement in a tabular form and transmit the same to the county clerk, in sufficient season to enable the latter to incorporate the information thus obtained in the annual report required by

him to be made to the State Superintendent of Common Schools for the present year.

13 It shall also be the duty of the trustees of the several school districts, in their annual reports thereafter to be made, to specify the number of children between the aforesaid ages, residing in their respective districts on the last day of December in each year, instead of the number of such children between the ages of five and sixteen.

14 This act shall take effect on the first day of May next; but nothing herein contained shall be so construed as to affect provisions already made in the several school districts for the support of schools therein under existing laws for the current year.

Chapter 425

AN ACT to amend the act entitled "An act to establish free schools throughout the State"

Passed July 9, 1851

The People of the State of New York, represented in Senate and Assembly, do enact as follows:

1 The act entitled an act to establish free schools throughout the State, passed April 12th, 1851, shall not be so constructed as to prevent or prohibit the distribution and application of library money in the manner heretofore prescribed by law.

2 Nothing in this act contained shall be so construed as to require the board of supervisors of each county to raise a sum of money for library purposes equal to the sum which it will receive from the State.

3 This act shall take effect immediately.

Superintendent Morgan in his last report makes the following comment on the new school law. This report was not printed until after his term expired, in 1852.

The returns contained in the annexed table show the condition of the common schools for the year ending on the 31st day of December, 1850, covering nearly the entire period during which the free school act of 1849 remained in operation; a period characterized beyond any other in the history of our common school system, for the agitation and excitement of the public mind consequent upon this measure; a period of transition between a system, nearly unanimously adopted by the people, but which in its practical operation had proved in many respects eminently disastrous, and a system more in accordance with the popular will; a period, consequently, peculiarly calculated to test not only the strength of the public sentiment in favor of our elementary institutions for popular education, but the stability and value of those institutions themselves. The unequal pressure of local taxation for the support of the schools, arising from an injudicious provision in the act referred to — a provision, the operation of which, in this respect, was almost entirely unforeseen — had originated a strong feeling of hostility against a system which a few months previously had received the deliberate sanction and approval of an immense majority of the people of the State. This hostility was manifested not only by a very general demand for the entire and unconditional repeal of the act itself, but by a virtual refusal, on the part of the inhabitants of a large proportion of the school districts, to carry its provisions into effect, beyond the point absolutely required as a condition for the receipt of their distributive share of the public money. The schools which had for a period of more than thirty years, uniformly been kept open for an average term of eight months during each year, were reduced in many instances to four, and the provision for their support limited to the avails of the public funds. So strong and general was the current of opposition to the obnoxious details of the law, that the most powerful efforts were required on the part of the friends of education generally, to prevent an entire abandonment of the great principle involved in its enactment, and which, wholly irrespective of the particular mode of its execution, had received the clear assent and full approbation of the people.

Pending a conflict so embittered and extensive, embracing within its range nearly every district and neighborhood of the State, and affecting so many and such powerful interests, it could scarcely have been expected that the prosperity and welfare of the schools should not have been seriously and generally affected. A careful inspection of the returns herewith submitted will, however, show that while in some few respects the statistical tables compare unfavorably with those of preceding years, their general results demonstrate a steady, reliable and gratifying improvement. And now that a crisis so perilous to the interests and the advancement of our noble system of primary education, has been safely passed, and the irritating causes of complaint which induced it, effectually removed, we may not unreasonably look forward to an uninterrupted progression and expansion of this most important department of our free institutions.

The proposed substitution of a permanent annual state tax of one mill upon every dollar of the real and personal property of the State, in lieu of the existing tax of eight hundred thousand dollars for the support of common schools, commends itself to the judgment of the undersigned as a measure fraught with incalculable blessings to the cause of universal education. If adopted, and permanently engrafted upon our existing system of common schools, its effect will be to carry out in the most simple, efficacious and perfect manner, the will of the people, repeatedly and distinctly expressed, that the property of the State shall provide for the elementary education of all its future citizens, and that all our common schools shall be entirely free to every child. This prinicple having been fully recognized and established, after mature consideration and discussion, it is unnecessary now to re-open the grounds upon which it was adopted, or to enter again upon the arguments which have so effectually demonstrated its soundness. The Legislature, at its last session, solemnly and definitively incorporated it as the basis of their enactment of a law, making a liberal appropriation from the aggregate property and funds of the State, for the maintenance and support of common schools. This appropriation, however, liberal and enlightened as it was, and worthy of the vast resources and immense wealth of the State, proves inadequate to the full accomplishment of the noble object in view — the education of all the children of the State, during the whole period ordinarily devoted in each year to common school instruction. An inconsiderable fraction of a mill upon each dollar of the increased valuation of real and personal estate is all that is requisite, in addition to the provisions already made, to secure the inestimable benefit of free schools, in all coming time, to every child of the State. It would be utterly unworthy of the enlightened forecast of the great majority of our fellow-citizens, to suppose that they are not prepared to make this slight additional sacrifice for the permanent accomplishment of an object of such great importance. The present State tax of $800,000 amounting as it did under the valuation in force at the period of its adoption to considerably more than a mill upon each dollar, is insufficient, with the aid of the annual revenue of the common school fund, to provide for the support of the schools of the State for an average period exceeding six months during each year. A permanent mill tax upon the existing valuation capable of adjusting itself from time to time to the fluctuating valuation of the property of the State, and to the increasing wants of the schools, will, in conjunction with the public funds already applicable to that object, provide liberally for the support of every school in the State during the entire year.

In opposition to these views it may probably be urged that the action of the Legislature at its last session providing for an annual state tax of $800,000, in addition to the annual revenue of the school fund, for the support of common schools, and directing that any deficiency in this respect should be supplied by rate bill, should, under the circumstances, be regarded as a final *compromise* between the views of the friends and opponents of an entirely free school system; that it is inexpedient and injudicious again to throw open to legislative and popular discussion, a subject upon which so considerable a diversity of feeling and of opinion is known to exist; that the very general acquiescence of the people in the present disposition of the matter is indicative of their satisfaction with the existing law; and that it is unwise at this early period to disturb these arrangements so recently and with such great unanimity adopted, especially in the absence of any experience of their practical workings, and of any general demand for their alteration or modification.

These objections are, unquestionably entitled to great weight, in the consideration of this subject; and unless they can be fairly overcome, the necessity or expediency of the proposed change must be regarded as doubtful.

Under the peculiar circumstances attending its passage, the act of the last session, was unquestionably the best that could be obtained by the friends of free schools. The only alternative presented was a return to the system in force in 1847, and a virtual abandonment of the principle for which the friends of universal education had so long struggled, and which had so repeatedly and signally triumphed. It will be recollected that although a popular majority of more than twenty thousand votes had been secured against the repeal of the act of 1849, forty-seven of the fifty-nine counties of the State had cast their votes nominally in favor of such repeal. The representatives from those counties, constituting a large majority of both branches of the Legislature, while fully aware that the popular expression of their respective constituencies adverse to the continuance of the law in question, was not to be regarded as in opposition to the *principle* of free schools, felt themselves bound by that expression to pursue a *middle course* between the entire rejection of that principle, and its unlimited adoption. Confident in the ultimate settlement of the question, on a basis in accordance with the dictates of public sentiment, and relying on the intrinsic justice and soundness of the principle involved, the friends of free schools consented to the adoption of the compromise proposed, without the slightest understanding on their part, or as it is believed on the part of those who favored and brought forward the amendment, that it was to be a permanent disposition of the subject. It was, on the other hand, regarded certainly by the former as a temporary arrangement merely.

If it be conceded that the public sentiment has unequivocally declared itself in favor of the adoption of the free school principle — and on this point there can not, in the judgment of the undersigned, be the slightest room to doubt — then any action of the Legislature, in contravention of or falling short of that principle, can not justly be regarded as final or conclusive. However desirable it may be, under ordinary circumstances, to avoid a reagitation of questions once fairly settled by legislative action, and especially where those questions affect an interest of such extent and importance as that under consideration, the will of the people, fairly and clearly expressed, is entitled to be carried into full effect; and, if for any reason their representatives have failed to embody that will in their legislation, there can be no such binding efficacy in a *compromise* measure at variance in any essential respect with the declared verdict of the popular voice, as to preclude subsequent action at the earliest practicable period, in conformity with such verdict. The act of the last session was clearly in contravention of the popular will, repeatedly and distinctly expressed, so far as the provision for meeting any portion of the expense of instruction in our common schools, by rate-bills, was concerned; and although after a long, animated and finally successful struggle at the ballot boxes for the complete recognition of the free school system, the people were disposed, in view of the manifold difficulties attendant upon the full embodiment of that principle by the Legislature, to rest satisfied with the important step finally taken, as the utmost that could, at that period, be accomplished, it is manifest that their compulsory acquiescence in this respect can not preclude them from insisting, at any subsequent period, upon a complete and practical legislative recognition of the right of every child in the State to free admission to the common schools, during the period in which they may be open for instruction, untrammelled by any pecuniary restriction, however slight.

There is another consideration connected with this subject, which cannot fail to address itself with great force to the statesmen and legislators of our State. Either the free school system is in accordance with the popular will, or it is not. Either the principles upon which it is based are in conformity with the dictates of a sound and enlightened public policy, or they are at irreconcilable variance with it. In either case there then should be no medium course between the full recognition and adoption of the system, and its practical incorporation as a portion of our institutions, and its rejection altogether, and a return to the system as it previously existed. It is utterly incompatible with all sound principles of legislation to declare in one breath that " common schools throughout the State shall be free to every child between the ages of five and twenty-one years," and in another to provide for the compulsory imposition of a rate bill for the expenses of such tuition, beyond a period embracing a portion only of the ordinary term of instruction. It is eminently unworthy of the representatives of the **Empire State**, thus to " hold the word of promise to the ear, and break it to the hope." Nearly two hundred and fifty thousand of the citizens and legal voters of the State, constituting a majority of one hundred and fifty thousand of all the votes cast, declared in 1849 their desire that the common schools of the state should be entirely free: and notwithstanding the obvious and universally conceded defects of the law enacted with the view of carrying their wishes into effect, they refused by a majority of more than twenty thousand to sanction its repeal, lest they should even seem to endanger the great principle they had so successfully vindicated and asserted. Having thus repeatedly and deliberately placed themselves upon the record, in this respect, they confided in their representatives to remove all the objectionable features of the law, without affecting the vital principle at stake. Had it been their desire to restore, either wholly or in part the old rate-bill system, it is reasonable to suppose they would have proceeded directly to the accomplishment of their object by a decisive vote in favor of the repeal of the act of 1849. Their vote against such repeal, in the face of unanswerable objection to the details of that act, is beyond all question conclusive of their intention, at all hazards, to preserve unimpaired the free school principle; and the strong vote of the direct representatives of the people, in favor of the first section of the act of the last session, declaratory of this principle, affords indubitable testimony of the strength of the public sentiment in this respect.

Let us look for a moment at the practical results of the existing law. It purports on its face to be "An act to establish free schools throughout the State," and the first section explicitly declares that "common schools in the several school districts in this State shall be free to all persons residing in the districts over five and under twenty-one years of age," as thereinafter provided. The annual revenue of the common school fund amounts to three hundred thousand dollars; and this sum (exclusive of $55,000 set apart for library purposes) together with the avails of an annual state tax of $800,000 is appropriated to the payment of teachers' wages. The average length of time during which the several schools are kept open during each year is eight months, or two terms of four months each. The aggregate amount paid for teachers' wages throughout the State falls a little short of $1,500,000, and is constantly increasing as teachers of a higher grade of qualification are brought into the schools. For the first term of four months, the schools may, therefore, be entirely free; in other words, free for one-third of the year. At the close of the second term, there will be a balance of nearly $400,000 to be collected by rate bill — an amount falling very little short of the sum heretofore contributed for this purpose under the act of 1847. This enormous balance will undoubtedly, in the great majority of instances, instead of being collected at the close of the second term, be diffused over the entire year — a portion only of the public money being appropriated to each term. Thus every child who enters the school, instead of finding it free, will at the end of each term, be charged with a rate bill; and unless exempted on the ground of indigence by the trustees, his parents or guardians will be compelled to pay the amount so assessed with fees for collection. Is it not absolute mockery to term such a system free?

The proposition to authorize a permanent mill tax on the property of the State, will, it is conceived, if adopted, effectually carry out the wishes of the people and their declared will. The amount is too trifling to be burdensome to any individual; while the object to be effected is one of the utmost magnitude and importance. Is there an individual in the State who would not cheerfully pay an annual assessment of one mill upon every dollar of his valuation, or one dollar upon every thousand, if thereby he could secure the blessings of education not only for his own children, but for every child of suitable age in the State, for the entire term during which the schools are kept open in each year, in all coming time? Is it not far better that the entire expenses of tuition should be met in this manner by one simple, definite, self-adjusting process, adapting itself to the varying standard of property and valuation, and to the increasing wants of the schools, than that the trustees of each of the eleven thousand districts should be periodically burdened with the trouble and parents with the expense of a vexatious and harassing rate bill? I cannot hesitate, therefore, cordially and earnestly to recommend the adoption of this measure as in my judgment best calculated to render our common schools in reality and permanently what they now are nominally, free; believing it to be due not only to the highest interests of education, but to a proper respect to the clearly expressed will of a majority of our fellow citizens, that the noble enterprise, the foundations of which have been so strongly laid in an enlightened public sentiment, should, without unnecessary delay, be prosecuted to a completion. . . .

Our schools are not yet entirely free. Deeply as this is to be regretted, after the noble, unyielding, and repeated efforts of the devoted friends of universal education — after the distinct and clear expression of the popular will, in this respect — and after the unassailable grounds of principle and expediency so successfully vindicated by the advocates of reform — there are ample and abundant sources of consolation in a review of the contest which has been waged for the adoption of this great measure. So far as public opinion is concerned, the question may, undoubtedly be regarded as definitely settled. Reforms of this nature when based upon sound reason and enlightened policy which underlie the principle of universal education, in a country such as ours, never go backwards. The indisputable right of every citizen of the American republic to such an education as shall enable him worthily and properly to discharge the varied and responsible duties incumbent upon him, as such, cannot long remain practically unrecognized in our republican institutions. It has already incorporated itself in the system of public instruction of several of our sister States; it has found its way into the municipal regulations of all our cities and many of the most important towns of our own State; and above and beyond all, it has entwined itself into the deepest convictions and soundest regards of the great mass of the people. Its full assertion may be deferred, but cannot ultimately be repressed.

Mr. S. L. Holmes, City Superintendent of Brooklyn, in his report under date of February 4, 1851, says, under the heading

Free Schools

The system of free common schools, thus established and conducted in the city, is now in general operation throughout the State. With us, it has existed since 1843; and the opinion formed of it, after a seven years' trial, was recently expressed by our citizens in their approving majority of nearly

8000 votes. In our cities, perhaps, this liberal system of public instruction is more fully appreciated than elsewhere. In them, too, it may be found of more urgent necessity and of more general application. Hence, the cities have called for its adoption almost unanimously, and in doing so, have given evidence of intelligence, generosity and patriotism, which do them honor. Overrun by the ignorant and destitute of all nations, the inhabitants of our cities seem nobly to have resolved, not only to welcome the crowds of homeless wanderers who seek an asylum among us, but to elevate them by mental and moral culture, and bless them by enabling them and their offspring to understand and prize the privileges they are permitted so freely to enjoy.

And this is done, with no view but to secure the public good; and with no intention of interfering, in the slightest degree, with the personal interest, the private views, or the religious preferences and scruples of any one. The social and civil welfare of all, and of all alike, forms the one great object of our free public school system wherever adopted. Happily, this institution of Free Schools is finding its way into most of the States of our Union; and in its progress is universally producing the belief that an institution so appropriate in its character, so magnanimous in its aim, so just in its operation, and so unlimited in the benefits it confers, cannot, if generally introduced and properly guarded, fail to prove, under Providence, the blessing and glory of our land.

Extract from report of Joseph McKeen, city superintendent of common schools New York City, to the board of education, January 28, 1852:

The *public school society's schools*[1] which were among the pioneer schools of the free common school system of this State, are still continued. The men who founded that society were men who loved their species and country. Their schools have done much for a numerous class of persons, who are now among us to speak their eulogium. But it is not in consonance with the voice of an intelligent community, that a voluntary or corporate body should assume, or perform the functions of the citizens at large except in cases of extreme dereliction on the part of the public. However beneficient their purposes, and however wise from experience the members of a society may become, there are many equally good and honest men who will doubt the policy of committing so great a matter, as the education of the majority of the children of the whole community to an incorporated society, over whose doings they have no direct control. It has been fortunate for the people of this city, that men of pure intention have continued to control the

---

[1] It is not intended to affirm that these were the first free schools in the State, nor the first which have been aided by the Colonial or State Legislature, but that they were the first unconnected with any church that were *common free schools.* There is a good school in the city under the patronage of the Collegiate Dutch churches, which has been in successful operation for near 150 years. Other churches have supported and still support free schools; some of them have at times received individual aid, and some have had grants from the public. It is not pretended that free schools are a new invention. The colony of Massachusetts, at an early day, had free schools. And before Massachusetts, the Scotch parliament, as early as 1494, had a school system, which was nearly *free.* And I find also in the writings of Bernard, the Fenelon of the 12th century, that the Vaudois had something like free schools, for this venerable man says — whether by way of exultation or reproof, the reader will judge: " *That the rustics and laymen of these valleys are taught to argue and confute their betters, upon subjects that they had no business to meddle with;* FOR THEY HAVE SCHOOLS EVERY WHERE, *in which the meanest of the people are allowed to attend."*

councils of this great society, until other municipal and State provisions are made for the education of a large portion of the children of this community.

Extract from report of Joseph McKeen, superintendent of common schools, New York City, to the State Superintendent, December 31, 1853:

That the course of education should receive countenance and support, people generally agree. Few or no complaints are made against the payment of so much tax as is necessary for the support of common schools. Thousands of respectable citizens, who, a few years ago, looked upon our public schools as a sort of commendable charity for the children of families of small means, now speak of them with pride or complacency, and send to them both their sons and their daughters, in the full confidence that in these schools they receive better elementary instruction than they could obtain elsewhere. . . .

At no period since the school system of the State was devised, has the city of New York presented so many gratifying evidences of progress, as at the present time. Formerly there may have been more signal sacrifices on the part of individuals in means and in services, to elevate the lowly. There may have been, and there probably *was,* more of personal effort to establish and sustain school organizations which were, from their constitution, partial or sectional, than can be shown or are needed at the present time. Public **sentiment has** been created in favor of free schools. The public purse has been opened for their support. Various society and corporate schools have been merged and consolidated into one organization. The schools are improved, better known, and more appreciated; the odor of charity is taken off, and the people at large recognise in them, under the smile of a benign Providence, a system of instruction yet to be matured and amplified, which we trust shall be for our children and their descendants for many generations.

Press Comment on Law of 1851

The following are newspaper editorials and comments in regard to the School Law, 1851:

We are informed that the Comptroller and Secretary of State have decided to withhold from this county our usual quota of school money, for the reason that the board of supervisors refused to levy a tax of like amount upon the county.

Truly we are in a pretty fix. The Supreme Court has decided the free school tax to be unconstitutional, and consequently the tax illegal. On the the other hand the Comptroller and Secretary say, impose the tax and raise the money, for until you do, you get no part of the school fund. Verily, we are between Syclla and Charybdis.— *Green County Whig, from Utica Daily Gazette, February 12, 1851*

The School Bills

We make, for the infomation of our readers, the following synopsis of the bills which have been reported to the Assembly by the committee on colleges, academies and common schools. We believe there are other propositions of different shades and complexions, before the Legislature, which have not yet been given to the public.

The bill reported by the majority of the committee, provides:

That the common schools of the State, shall be free to all persons residing in the several districts, over 5 and under 21 years of age.

That $800,000 shall be raised each year, by general tax upon the real and personal property within the State, the tax to be apportioned among the counties according to the valuation of the real and personal estate therein.

One-fourth of said $800,000, and one-fourth of all other moneys appropriated by the State for the support of schools, to be apportioned among the several districts, parts of districts and separate neighborhoods, from which report shall have been received, as follows: to each separate neighborhood, a sum equal to 33 cents for each child between the ages of 4 and 21 years, but not to exceed $24 in all, to each neighborhood; and the remainder of said one-fourth to be divided equally among the several districts.

The remaining three-fourths of the $800,000 and of all other moneys appropriated for the support of schools, to be apportioned to the several counties, cities and towns in the mode now prescribed by law, for the division of the income of the school fund; the share of each town to be paid to the town superintendents, and by them divided among the several districts according to the number of children between the ages of 4 and 21 years — but no money to be paid to any district which shall not have had a school taught by a duly qualified teacher at least 8 months during the year, unless by special permission of the State Superintendent.

Any balance necessary to be raised in any district for the payment of teachers' wages, to be raised by the trustees, by a poll tax upon each resident of the district entitled to vote at school district meetings.

All moneys appropriated by the act, to be applied to the payment of teachers' wages only.

This bill has the sanction of the following members of the committee: Messrs Benedict of Westchester, Swords of New York, and Feller of Dutchess.

The bill reported by the minority of the committee (Messrs Burroughs of Orleans and Ferris of Tompkins) omits the declaration that the schools "shall be free," but differs from the majority bill in substance, only, in providing that any balance necessary to be raised by the districts for the payment of teachers' wages, shall be raised by rate bill, against those sending to the school, in proportion to the number of days and children sent, and that the trustees may exempt any indigent inhabitant from payment, in whole or in part, in their discretion. It requires a school to be kept but 7 instead of 8 months, to entitle the district to share in the distribution, and provides that the first apportionment under the act may be made to all districts which were entitled to an apportionment of public money in the year 1849.— *Binghamton Democrat, February 20, 1851*

The Free School Law

Messrs Editors — It seems to be a settled fact, determined by the vote of the State, at two successive annual elections, by legislative action, by the necessity and propriety of the thing itself, and by the moral sense of the community, that we are to have free schools throughout the State, and must maintain them a certain portion of the year, free for all children of all classes of suitable age to attend them. This is all well, and as it should be; and for one, I am willing to be taxed my just proportion of the expense of supporting them, allowing the burdens and benefits of these schools are equally and justly distributed among all the districts of the State.

But there in one feature in the old school law, and the same is retained in the present law, and in substance embraced in the reports, both of the majority and the minority of the committee appointed to report on that subject to the present Legislature, which meets my decided disapprobation; and I think, on reexamination, it must meet the decided disapprobation of the majority of the people of the State. I allude to the unequal manner of distributing the aggregate of all the school funds possessed, and to be raised in the State, among the several districts within its limits. Both under the old law, and the present, and the one proposed by both branches of the committee (and, I am sorry to say, indorsed by the late state convention of town superintendents of common schools, held in this city) the operation is exceedingly unequal, unjust and onerous to the smallest districts. In these, the taxes and burdens on individuals of sustaining schools under the old law, have always been more than double, often quadruple, those imposed on the members of large districts. For while the large districts received public money enough to pay the entire amount of their teachers' wages through the year, the smallest districts were compelled to raise by rate bills or other means, from one-half to two-thirds or three-fourths of the teachers' wages among themselves, besides their incidental and other expenses. And this heavy burden has been borne by a small number (there being but few in the districts) whereas had the deficit occurred in the large districts, the burden would have been much less per individual than it was in the small. And what rendered this law still more oppressive was, that the inhabitants of these small districts were taxed equally with all others to raise the county and town school funds, which went into the common receptacle, and these were so unequally distributed, these districts not getting back what they had actually paid, and the large districts (drawing in proportion to the number of their children) getting more than they had paid of these county and town taxes. So it is under the present law.

The basis of distribution among the several districts by the new law proposed by both branches of the committee of the Assembly, and approved by the Utica convention of superintendents, is this: One-fourth of all the school funds from all sources, to be equally divided among all the districts of the State; and the other three-fourths to be divided according to the number of children between the ages of four and twenty-one, residing in the several districts. This, on a first or superficial view, may appear very fair and equal. But on a strict and careful consideration of all the circumstances of the case, and the expense of supporting a single school (whether large or small) for eight months of the year, I think it must appear exceedingly unequal and defective.

The difference in the expense between keeping up a large school and a small one, is very trifling — far less than most people imagine. In the first place, the small district must have a schoolhouse, as well as the large one; and, in proportion to their numbers, it will cost them quite as much, or more, than it will cost the large district to build theirs. In the next place, the small district must have a qualified teacher, teacher's board, and fuel for warming their house; and these will all cost nearly, if not quite, as much as the same will cost the larger district. Few or no rural districts in the State employ more than one teacher. Even in districts where there are 150 children between the ages of four and twenty-one, not more than from 70 to 90 generally attend school at once, and they employ but one teacher.

Now, here are two districts lying side by side in the same town: the one, situated in a small village, numbers 150 children between four and twenty-one years of age; and the other, spread over a larger space, but thinly peopled, has but 25 children of the age to draw public school money. Suppose now, the average sum of public money for distribution, is $100 per district; one-fourth of which is to be equally divided among them all, and the other three-fourths to be distributed according to the number of children of the above ages. Of course $200 would be the portion of these two districts. One-fourth of this sum ($50) divided equally, would give each district $25. Then the other three-fourths ($150) would have to be divided into seven equal parts, of which the small district would receive one, and the large district six parts, i.e. $21.43 lacking a few mills and $128.57, which added to the $25 each, before divided, would give a total to the small district of $46.43, and to the large district $153.51. Now both districts are required to support schools eight months in the year. Dividing these respective sums by 8, would give the small district $5.80 per month, and the large district $19.18 per month. Now, I ask, can the small district support a school eight months by a qualified teacher short of nearly double the amount above given it? And how is this additional sum to be raised in this small and poor district, already taxed its full proportion to raise the $800,000 State tax imposed by the law?

As before remarked, the difference in expense between supporting a large school and a small one, is but trifling, (as schoolhouse, fuel, teacher and board must alike be had for each,) and if a deficit of public money exist, the large is better able to supply it than the small. I sincerely hope, therefore, that this great inequality and injustice to small districts, will be corrected by the Legislature before the law passes. And I would respectfully submit to the Legislature and the public, whether it would not be less oppressive, more equal, more just, to divide two thirds of all the school moneys equally among the districts, and the other third according to the ratio of children in the districts. This would give the large district, in the case above supposed, and on that basis, $123.82 or $15.48 per month for eight months, and the small district $76.19, or $9.52 per month for eight months, which I think would be really more favorable to the large than to the small district, but altogether nearer to justice than the old law, or the new one proposed.

PHILO JUSTITIA
— Utica Daily Gazette, March 10, 1851

The school bill which passed to an engrossment in the Assembly, on Friday night, lays a state tax of $800,000 to be added to other public school funds and distributed among the school districts, one-third equally and the balance according to the number of scholars. The deficiency for the support of the schools is then to be raised by rate bills, as under the old common school system, property not liable under execution, being exempted from levy on a school warrant. The bill amounts to an increased appropriation of $800,000 for the support of common schools, to be raised by a state tax, and return to the old system, with some improvements. It is said that a large proportion of those who voted against the bill did so on the ground that a state tax would operate unequally upon the cities and larger counties, unless the assessment laws were modified. Several voted in the negative because the rate-bill system was retained, and a few others for minor and different reasons:

The Albany Argus remarks:

"The bill if accompanied by another equalizing assessments and taxation throughout the state, will probably find favor — without such an accompaniment, it can scarcely be expected that it will not create discontent. Such a bill is now in progress in the house, and now that the school bill is disposed of, will no doubt be perfected and passed." — *Binghamton Iris, April 4, 1851*

The New School Bill a Law

The school bill which has been pending in the Legislature since the commencement of the session, has passed through the Senate by the strong vote of 22 to 4. It now only waits the signature of the Governor to become law. It provides 1st. A state tax of $800,000. 2d. The equal distribution of one-third of this sum, together with the $300,000 from the school fund, among the school districts, and the residue per capita. 3d. The rate bill to make up deficiencies: and 4th. That all property exempt from execution shall be exempt from school warrants.

There are no other material changes in the details of the old law; and it is very generally believed that the measure will be reasonably acceptable to the People. It is a compromise measure, well calculated to allay the excitement which has existed during the last two years, and to restore that harmony in the districts so indispensable to the success of the schools, and the advancement of the cause of education.— *Rochester Daily Democrat, April 14, 1851*

Chapter 11

EDUCATIONAL DEVELOPMENTS AFTER THE ENACTMENT OF THE LAW OF 1851

This long period of statewide agitation for free schools had apparently brought about the consciousness of a need of further educational reform. As the State began to take upon itself more and more its educational responsibilities it became apparent that a State Department of Public Instruction would be necessary to fulfil this greater obligation. Such a department was created in 1853. The report of the committee on literature in regard to the matter of creating the office of Superintendent of Common Schools and separating it from that of the Secretary of State was as follows:

In Senate, February 1, 1854
No. 39

Report

Of the committee on literature, on the separation of the office of Superintendent of Common Schools from that of Secretary of State.

Mr Robertson,[1] from the committee on literature, to which was referred so much of the annual message of His Excellency the Governor as relates to the separation of the office of Superintendent of Common Schools from that of Secretary of State.

REPORTS:

That the office of Superintendent of Common Schools was originally a separate and distinct department of the state government, created when the first school law was passed in 1813, and remained such for a period of six or seven years; when, in consequence, as is believed, of some political reason, growing out of the appointment of the successor to the Hon. Gideon Hawley, it was merged in the office of Secretary of State. The duties then imposed upon that officer were comparatively light, either in his capacity as Secretary or Superintendent of Common Schools. Since that period, however, both have been immensely augmented; and, independently of his duties as a Commissioner of the Canal Fund and a member of the Canal Board, as a trustee of the capitol and of the State Library, and as a member of the

---

[1] William H. Robertson was born in Bedford, Westchester county, N. Y., October 10, 1823. After pursuing his preliminary studies at Union Academy, he read law and, in 1847, was admitted to the bar. Mr Robertson was early chosen for public positions. He served for several terms as town superintendent of the Bedford common schools, four years as supervisor of his town and twelve years as county judge of Westchester county. During the Civil War, Judge Robertson rendered effective service as chairman of the military committee and commissioner of the draft in his section of the State.

Mr Robertson was a Whig but in 1855 associated himself with the Republican party and served for twelve years as a member of the state committee of that organization. In 1849–50, he represented Westchester county in the Assembly and supported the free school bill of that year. He served in the State Senate in 1854–55. He was elected to the Fortieth Congress and in 1872–73 was again returned to the State Senate, where he served from 1872 to 1881 and again from 1889 to 1891, much of the time being president pro tempore. Senator Robertson was a delegate to many Republican national conventions and his action in the convention of 1880 in refusing to be bound by the "unit rule," thus making possible the nomination of General Garfield for President, made him a prominent figure of the time. He died December 6, 1898.

Regents of the University; duties, the performance of which absorb a very large share of his time; the constant aid of an efficient deputy and five clerks is necessary to enable him to discharge the duties appertaining to him as Secretary of State. He is also charged with the arrangement and supervision of the criminal statistics of the State, embracing returns from all the various criminal courts, with the returns of the overseers and superintendents of the poor in the several counties, with the disposition of the unsold lands belonging to the State and the records appertaining thereto, with the distribution of public documents, laws, &c., &c., and with a great variety of miscellaneous duties under the provisions of various acts; all which is deemed amply sufficient to occupy the time and exhaust the energies of the most faithful and competent public officer.

In consequence of this state of things, it has been found necessary, for years past, to devolve nearly the entire charge of the school department upon a deputy. There are nearly twelve thousand school districts in the State confided to his supervision, and a constant and burdensome daily correspondence with the officers and inhabitants of these districts, and with the several town superintendents, is necessary to be carried on, in reference to complicated and difficult questions of law, and protracted and angry controversies, growing out of their official acts and proceedings.

The amount of public money annually to be apportioned among the several counties, cities, and towns of the State, exceeds one million of dollars; and this, together with the annual apportionment, in the same manner of the State tax, of $800,000, required by the act of 1851, is sufficient of itself to occupy the time of a single officer for at least an entire month. In addition to all of these exhausting and responsible labors, the Secretary of State, in his official capacity as Superintendent of Common Schools, is charged with the preparation of forms, instruction, blanks, &c., for the use of the several school districts, with the annual visitation and inspection of several literary and charitable institutions in the city of New York, and with the general oversight and supervision of the State Normal School. It is also very desirable, in every point of view, that this general supervision should be extended so as to embrace the several academies and other incorporated literary institutions, and to cover, if possible, the entire educational interests of the State.

Both the late Secretary of State and his predecessor in office, have strongly recommended the organization of a distinct department, and the views of the present incumbent are understood to be decidedly in its favor. The commissioner appointed by the late Governor Hunt, in pursuance of a resolution of the Assembly in 1851, to codify the several statutes in relation to common schools, reported in favor of the adoption of this measure. The present Executive had added his sanction to this recommendation; and the State Association of Teachers, assembled at Rochester, in August last, and the convention of academical and classical teachers, recently in session in this city, unanimously adopted resolutions in favor of the separation of the two offices. The friends of popular education throughout the State, through the press and otherwise, have taken deep interest in this question, and with almost entire unanimity, have expressed their desire that the entire educational interests of the State should be represented by a distinct and efficient organization. Public sentiment is unequivocally and strongly in its favor;

and it is believed the time has fully arrived when this important and needed reform may advantageously be effected.

The election of State Superintendent by joint ballot of the Senate and Assembly, is deemed preferable to any other mode which has been suggested. The Regents of the University, representing the academical and collegiate branches of public instruction, are chosen in this manner; and the precedent thus established, is believed to be wise and judicious. The public interest demands an immediate and effective organisation of this department, independently of all political bias, and free from the agitation and excitement inevitably consequent upon a popular canvass at the polls. Political considerations, above all others, should be removed as far as possible from the choice of an officer entrusted with the supervisory charge of our noble system of public instruction; and the immediate representatives of the people can have no interests in the discharge of this responsible duty, not fully in accordance with the great mass of their constituents of all parties.

The term of office proposed for the State Superintendent, is of sufficient duration to enable him to become perfectly familiar with his duties, and sufficiently brief to render him amendable to public sentiment, in their discharge.

In conclusion, the separation of these two offices, and the organization of a distinct and independent department, charged with the general supervision of the educational interests of the State, are believed to be measures imperatively demanded by the best interests of the State — right and proper in themselves — in accordance with public sentiment, and conformably to the repeated and urgent recommendation of the several public functionaries, whose positions have enabled them to be the most competent judges of the necessity and expediency of the measure. On the other hand, the combination of the two is an anomaly which finds no precedent or countenance in our government. There is no more necessary or proper connection between these two officers, than between any other two independent departments of government; nor is there any stronger reason why the department of public instruction should be attached to the office of the Secretary of State, than to that of the Attorney General, Comptroller, Treasurer or State Engineer. Its duties have, it is true, been ably and satisfactorily discharged under the existing organisation, as beyond all doubt they would have been, under the same circumstances, by either of the state officers referred to. But it has been found impossible, and must continue to be utterly impracticable, to discharge them in person, or to give to them that attention and consideration which their importance demands. A division of labor in this respect would seem therefore not only to be wise in itself, but just to the officer whose time and energies are thus unreasonably taxed, and who is held responsible for acts the performance of which, to the full extent required at his hands is physically impossible.

Your committee accordingly, guided by these considerations, ask leave to introduce the accompanying bill.

In the report of the first Superintendent of Public Instruction V. M. Rice, under date of December 31, 1854, in speaking of union free schools, he says:

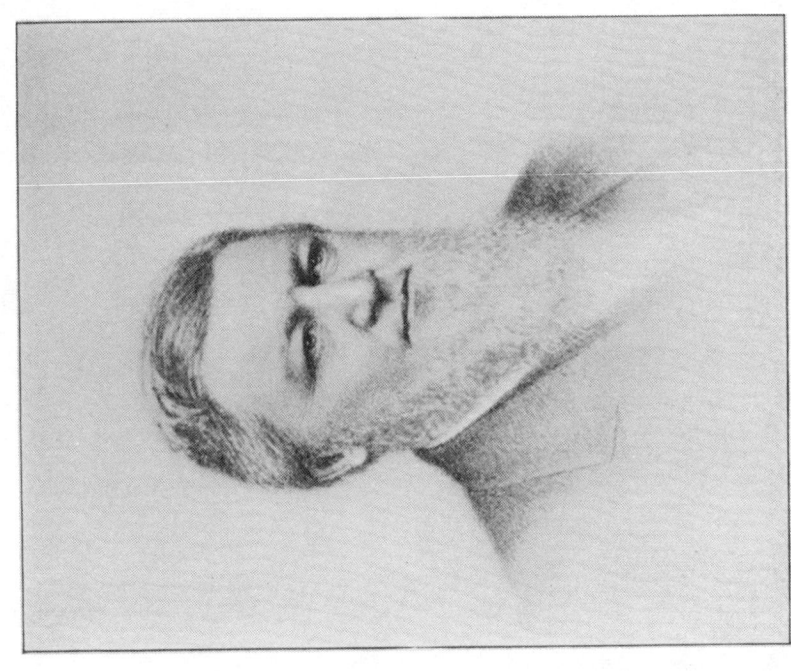

VICTOR M. RICE
First Superintendent of Public Instruction, 1854-57, 1862-68

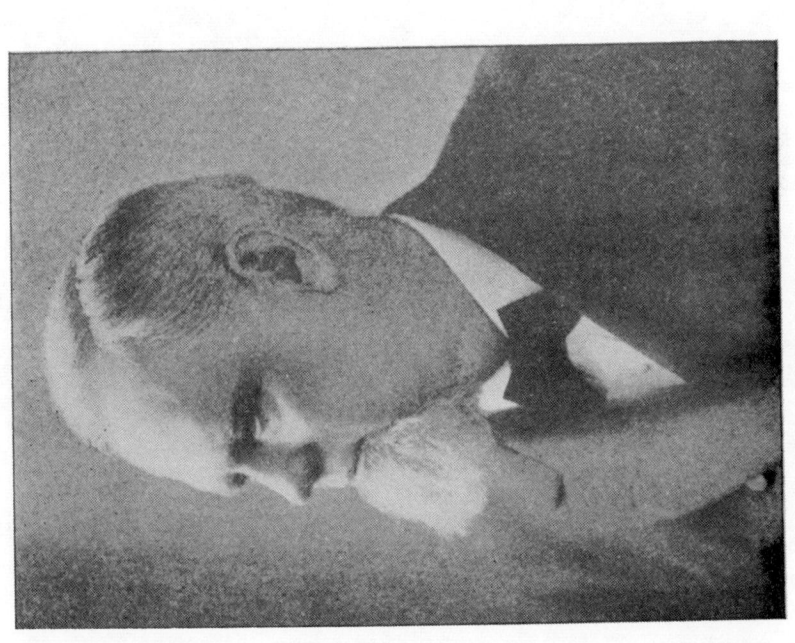

HON. WILLIAM H. ROBERTSON

The act to provide for the establishment of union free schools, passed June 18, 1853, is exerting a very beneficial influence. It is only necessary that its provisions be more fully understood to secure their general adoption by the districts throughout the State, as being decidedly preferable to the system of collection by rate bill. It is the opinion of the undersigned that universal free schools will result from the application of this law; for as rapidly as public opinion becomes enlightened, so as to appreciate and approve the principle, it will be adopted, and when thus adopted, it will have — what all laws and regulations in a free government should have — the free and cordial support of those for whose government or direction it was designed. The law, after receiving some verbal emendation, should be published with proper forms and instructions for general distribution.

A year later he writes upon the same subject as follows:

Twenty-five districts have been organized under chapter 433 of the Laws of 1853, for the establishment of union free schools. It is known to the Department that measures for the organization of several others have been abandoned, in consequence of the great obscurity of the statute in several vital points. Its main purpose appears to have been to enable the inhabitants of any school district, either singly or in conjunction with other districts, to provide for free instruction in the primary departments, and to defray the expense by tax instead of depending upon a rate bill for any portion. This purpose, however, is nowhere declared in express terms, and though it is clearly inferable in regard to such schools, when established in cities and incorporated villages, and is deducible, though with less certainty, from the provisions regulating the organization of rural districts, it is yet a matter of doubt whether such tax may be levied by the board of education without any popular vote (except that by which the inhabitants adopt an organization under the act) or requires a vote of a majority of the inhabitants, or finally must be sanctioned by the vote of two-thirds. There is no mode provided by which the inhabitants may abandon the system if found inconvenient or impracticable, but they are compelled to stumble along through doubts and difficulties which the statute does quite as much to create as to remove.

It is believed that the policy of conferring upon the inhabitants of school districts the power to devote their own resources to the support of entirely free schools — of encouraging the consolidation of contiguous districts, and thereby promoting the economy and efficiency of the schools — of permitting the union of an academical with the primary departments, and thereby facilitating the classification of pupils and preventing those who are able to pay for their education in the more advanced studies from being withdrawn from the public schools to private establishments — is a policy so eminently wise and beneficial, that the Legislature will not permit it to fail for want of the few amendments necessary to render the interpretation of the statute clear, and its administration easy and confident.

Extract from second annual report of V. M. Rice, Superintendent of Public Instruction, December 31, 1855:

The cities have been especially favored by legislation. Their schools are as free to every child as the air he breathes. It is their mission to give a practical education alike to the rich and the poor; and they are fulfilling it in a manner creditable to their particular localities and to the State. Thousands of parents have been induced to remove from the rural districts for the purpose of educating their children in these schools. With one or two exceptions, they are under a complete and a thorough supervision, which points out the most approved modes of school architecture, secures competent teachers, and incorporates into their plans of instruction every improvement of the day. How long the children of the cities shall enjoy privileges so much superior to those in other parts of the State remains for the Legislature to determine. I have visited with their superintendents some of the principal schools of New York and Brooklyn, and have seen great multitudes of children and youth congregated therein, fitting themselves for independence and extensive usefulness; some of whom, were it not for the liberal provision for schools, would be educated in the streets. Tax-payers have long since learned that they can not afford to encourage the education there acquired. Buffalo, Oswego, Rochester, Syracuse, Auburn, Utica, and other cities, are attracting the wealth and intelligence of less favored portions of the State in consequence of their excellent schools. I have received condensed reports of the character and operation of the school systems in several of the cities, which are appended to this report, and to which attention is invited.

Mr Emerson W. Keyes, Deputy Superintendent of Public Instruction, in his report dated January 8, 1862, discusses the question of taxation for schools under the heading

City Schools

The cities of our State comprise as it were, a system within themselves, or rather each is a system by itself, having a local organization through which its educational affairs are administered. The schools are made free by means of local taxation, the amount received from the State ranging from nineteen to eighty-five per cent only, of the sum raised by themselves for the support of their schools; while their proportion of the three-quarter mill state tax for school purposes, which forms a part of the general school fund distributed, exceeds the amount received back from the State out of that distribution, by many thousands of dollars.

This liberality on the part of the cities of the State whereby they maintain ample education facilities of a high order, for all the children within their limits, " without money and without price," is among the most encouraging and hopeful, as it is praiseworthy features of our system.

Superintendent H. H. Van Dyck, the successor of Superintendent Rice, makes the following comments in his annual reports of 1858 and 1860:

Under laws so diversified in their provisions as those which control the system of public education in this State, it is by no means surprising that defects in their practical operation should from time to time become manifest. Whilst it is comparatively an easy matter to point out these defici-

EMERSON W. KEYES
Third Superintendent of Public Instruction, 1861-62

HENRY H. VAN DYCK
Second Superintendent of Public Instruction, 1857–61

encies, the task of suggesting a remedy which shall prove both just and practicable, is far more difficult of performance. It is one of the fortunate characteristics of our population that they can so readily accommodate themselves to almost any state of circumstances — smoothing off the asperities of a system in one respect, and correcting its sinuosities in another, if they can only be assured of stability in the provisions of law to which they are called to conform. But a system which is perpetually changing, which vascillates from year to year, now adopting one mode of administration and then another; which provides at one time for all its necessities by a general tax on property, and at another throws it back on rate bills and local assessments, which fills a volume with laws, the crudities and inconsistencies of which, in many instances, no judicial officer can unravel, can not, while in this transition state, accomplish the important objects designed to be attained in a system of general education. I am not disposed, therefore, to regard with favor any alterations in the laws, beyond those simple amendments rendered obviously necessary by public convenience, and which will, without doubt, give greater efficiency to principles already well established. In this spirit, not less than in obedience to the pecuniary exigencies of the State and individuals, I refrain from urging any increase in the rate of taxation over that now provided, with a view of rendering the schools entirely free to those who attend them, a consummation deemed by many as highly desirable. To my mind it seems quite as important that means should be devised to render the money now contributed more diffusive in its benefits, and wider in its scope of application. If the State steps in, and by virtue of its sovereignty appropriates the property of the citizen to the education of all who choose to avail themselves of the benefit of the schools, the tax-payer has a right to demand that the sum thus contributed by him shall be made to confer the greatest amount of good of which its expenditure is capable. If the schools were full, and the means of instruction, as compared with those seeking to avail themselves thereof, deficient, a necessity would exist for extended accommodations and greater expenditure. But so far from this being the case, outside of the cities and villages, the almost universal concession is that the schools are too small — the number in attendance being so limited as to render their support, beyond the time for which the State contribution would pay, burthensome. The statistics presented with this report, when duly analyzed, will show that the average number of pupils to each teacher during the time in which the schools were taught, will not execeed twenty five. If, as is believed, double that number would not have been an excessive draft upon the capabilities of the teacher, it follows that the expenditure made was amply sufficient in amount to have educated all the children in the State, had they been in attendance on the schools. It further appears that the contribution of more money than is now expended, is not the only thing necessary to universal education. Indeed, the great obstacle to be contended against in reaching this desideratum is, not so much the want of facilities for imparting instruction, as the want of disposition on the part of a considerable portion of our population to avail themselves of those already furnished. The remedy for this evil of nonattendance, is not so apparent. The liberty of the citizen in controlling the time and occupation of his children, is not to be impinged for slight causes, or without great caution. Compulsory legislation in this respect, could scarcely be enforced. But it is a question worthy of the consideration of the Legislature, whether the same end might not to a considerable extent be attained by the application of a discrimination in the distribution of the State funds, founded on the proportional number in actual attendance? Such a provision would give to each tax-payer a direct pecuniary interest in securing the largest possible attendance on the schools, both as a means of securing a larger share of the State bounty, and as a defence against local taxation. If this, or some other mode should be found operative in diminishing this great evil, it would, in the estimation of the undersigned, form the most palpable improvement of which the system is at present susceptible. . . .

In accordance with the requirement of the statute, I have endeavored to present to the Legislature, as succinctly as the nature of the subjects would admit, the statistics gathered by this Department, " with such recommendations and suggestions are are deemed suitable." Though the common schools of the State are as yet far from exhibiting that perfection in character and extent of usefulness which is desirable, it is cause for congratulation that their progressive improvement is becoming each year more manifest. If the undersigned abstains from a lengthened disquisition upon the importance of general education, it is not attributable to an undervaluation of the benefits which knowledge in its most extended form is calculated to confer; but from a conviction that the representatives of the people must, from the distinguished post they occupy, be presupposed to hold in due estimation the advantages to be derived from a practical diffusion of education amongst the people. It is deemed enough, therefore, in conclusion, to offer the assurance of hearty co-operation in any measure which the Legislature may devise, to give greater scope, efficiency and perfection to the system of common school education, at once the highest glory and surest defence of the State.

Excerpts from report of H. H. Van Dyck, Superintendent of Public Instruction, January 31, 1860:

Popular education being in a great measure the offspring of the present century, has not yielded its full fruits — but here, as elsewhere, " as we sow, so also shall we reap." The greatest amount of practicable *education* should be our aim — and in this term is included much more than instruction in those primary branches which constituted the meagre fare imparted by the schools of other days, and still emulated in various localities. These form the tools by which education is achieved; and hold to it merely the relation which the chisel bears to the sculptor, or the brush to the painter. The material wealth of our citizens has increased beyond the conception of the most sanguine calculator in former days; and no limit to acquisition is yet discernable in the future. But there is reason to apprehend that general education in not advancing in the same ratio; in part from mistaken notions of economy, and partly from a self-satisfying view of the progress already attained. Surely whilst monarchial governments are seriously occupied in advancing the educational interests of their subjects, the citizens of a country whose institutions rest upon popular intelligence, can ill afford to neglect any practicable improvement in that which involves the perpetuity of the government under which they live. The problem is still to be solved, whether the American of the succeeding generation shall hold the same pre-eminence in general intelligence which he has hitherto enjoyed; or whether he shall be excelled in this respect by the natives of other climes, whom inclination or ill fortune may throw upon our shores. If we would maintain our national supremacy — if we would melt the mixed races with which our country is thronged into one homogeneous population, we must extend to all the benefits of thorough common school education — we must indoctrinate our youth with the advantages of superior knowledge, and endow them with all the educational facilties requisite to a life of honor, usefulness and virtue. You will, I doubt not, join in the aspiration that our educational system may eventuate in placing upon the stage of action a generation of intelligent citizens, who shall render our free institutions a blessing at home, as well as a beacon of hope to denizens of less favored lands.

Extract from seventh annual report of H. H. Van Dyck, Superintendent of Public Instruction, January 31, 1861:

The law under which union free school districts are formed needs revision. Its provisions are in many respects ambiguous, in some contradictory, in others odiously unequal. It purports to allow the inhabitants of any district, by a vote of two-thirds present, at a meeting called for the purpose, to decide whether an union free school shall be established therein; and after having decided by this preponderating vote to establish such free school, it requires, in every district whose limits do not correspond with those of any city or incorporated village, a vote of *two-thirds* at every annual meeting to raise the sum required for teachers' wages, and the other necessary expenses incidental to the school. In any incorporated village or city, however, the corporate authorities are imperatively required to raise " such sum or sums as the board of education established therein shall declare necessary," without any vote of the inhabitants thereon; and the authorities are especially prohibited from refusing " any supplies for the annual support of the teachers of said union free schools, and the necessary contingent expenses of the said schools." I am at a loss for any sound reason why this disparity should exist where the object to be accomplished is in each case precisely the same. There are other incongruities to the act, not amongst the least of which is that which admits of the imposition of a rate bill upon the pupils. A *free* school supported by rate bills, is such an anomaly as could be found sanctioned nowhere else save in the " Code of Public Instruction " in the State of New York.

Victor M. Rice was reappointed as Superintendent of Public Instruction in 1862 and served to see the " odious rate bill no longer preventing children from going to school." The following are extracts from his reports to the Legislature in 1864, 1865, 1866 and 1867:

Extracts from report of January 1, 1864:

In whatever light presented, the fact of this excessive prevalence of non-attendance and of irregular attendance at school, should command the serious attention of the Legislature; and any provision of law which, without infringing upon the free action of parents, as the natural and legal guardians of their children, will induce greater regularity of attendance while the schools are in session, must meet with general approval. The undersigned stated, in a report transmitted to the Legislature in 1857, that " in the rural districts greater regularity of attendance might be secured by distrubuting to the districts a part of the public money upon the basis of attendance; that a distribution upon such a basis would make it the pecuniary interest of every tax-payer in the district to encourage a regular and general attendance, and that parents would be less willing to permit their children to absent themselves from school for trifling causes." Subsequent reports from this department have substantially repeated the same suggestion; and it is hoped that your honorable body will provide by law for the apportionment, by the Commissioners, of a part of the public moneys (apportioned to the counties on the basis of population), to the several school districts in their respective counties, according to the actual average daily attendance, which shall be determined from a record to be kept by the teacher, and verified by him under oath.

This mode of apportionment has been adopted in sister States with happy results, and no reason is apparent why it would not operate equally well in this.

By the Law of 1851, which happily settled the controversy in this State as to the taxation of property for the support of schools, the tax for the purpose was made a fixed sum of eight hundred thousand dollars. While the number of children and the aggregate cost of their education was increasing, the state tax had remained the same. The increased cost was presented to the rural districts in the form of higher rate bills, and heavier local or district taxation. It will be understood that every fifth year a census of the population of this State is taken, and that the Superintendent of Public Instruction makes an apportionment of two-thirds of all moneys appropriated for the support of schools to the counties in which there is no city; and when a county is composed of city and country, to each separately, according to population, as reported in " the next preceding state or United States census." From 1850 to 1855 the aggregate population of the State had increased rapidly, but the increase was confined chiefly to the large cities, while the population of a large majority of the country towns had either remained stationary or had decreased. The effect of this, with a stationary tax, was to decrease correspondingly the apportionment made to the counties composed of these towns, and increase largely that made on the basis of the growing population of the cities. Concurring in the opinion that a state tax of eight hundred thousand dollars was proper to aid the rural districts, by so much as it diminished district taxation and decreased the sums collected by rate bills, the Legislature of 1856 deemed it proper to increase the aggregate of that tax to supply a growing want. It was better to establish a rate by which the tax would keep pace with the wealth and the increase of children and youth to be educated; hence the law of 1856, fixing the State tax for the support of schools at three-fourths of a mill upon every dollar of the property valuation. Every man assessed for one hundred dollars pays annually of this tax *seven and a half cents*; for one thousand dollars, *seventy-five cents* — certainly not an oppressive tax, to the payment of which any man of patriotic feelings and generous sympathies will object, in view of the fact that it is to be expended to educate his own children, and other children with whom his own must be associated politically if not socially, and to secure to them all alike the blessings of an enlightened and civilized community.

The argument for a state tax is grounded upon the fraternal relation and obligations established by the Creator among men and promulgated in that epitome of all wise conduct, the "Golden Rule:" "Whatsoever ye would that others should do unto you, do ye even so unto them." To feed the hungry, to clothe the naked, and to alleviate human suffering generally, is an acknowledged duty; and whoever possesses the power, and neglects or refuses to do it, disobeys the divine injunction, and thus does violence to his own enlightened conscience. And if any man apprehends that his brother will be in distress tomorrow or next year, or years hence, and has the power to make provision against such distress, by aiding him in becoming more enlightened and better, or in any other way, and neglects or refuses to do so, he just as clearly sets at naught that abiding rule, and the generous promptings of his better nature, as if he were to deny to a thirsty person a cup of water, or a morsel of bread to the hungry. In the one case, it is true, the suffering is present, and in the other, prospective; but both are within the compass of his understanding, and it is therefore equally his duty to alleviate the one, and provide against the occurrence of the other. Surely the rule of action which is binding upon one man in the case stated, is equally applicable to ten, an hundred or a thousand men, and to the whole people as an organized State. Every intelligent man knows that ignorance is the mother of disobedience, whence follow the frailties and miseries of mankind; that proper culture begets understanding, whence follow the greatest development of the natural powers and the highest enjoyment. It is, therefore, the duty of every man, and no less the duty of the whole people, to use every available means to save the rising generation from ignorance and its attendant calamities, by making ample provision for their highest development and consequent extensive usefulness.

A Christian state can not innocently disregard its obligations to protect the weak, to instruct the young, and to help the poor and dependent; nor can it innocently neglect to provide for its own safety, by providing for the safety and happiness of those composing it. The Legislature which provides for the definition, detection and punishment of crimes, has done but half its duty: it is bound also to make provision against the commission of crime; and for this object, experience proves that the school and the school master are more effective agencies than the detective police and the terrors of the law. Whilst it is not pretended that the best culture acquired in the schools is the sole means for the prevention of crime, yet it is abundantly proved by criminal statistics that the majority of those who suffer the penalty of violated law are ignorant, have not had the advantage of systematized instruction, have never been subjected to the smoothing and softening influence of obedience and discipline, and have never had their time or conduct regulated by wise authority; but on the contrary, have grown up unlettered and in the unrestrained indulgence of their appetites and baser passions. It is also as clearly proved that crime, vice, and disloyalty are most prevalent in those countries, and those parts of a country, where there is the least general education; whilst in those communities which have more nearly complied with their obligations to make provision for the instruction of the young in useful knowledge, there has always been, as there doubtless will ever be, the greatest regard for law and order, the most rational liberty, and, as a sequence, the greatest individual and national prosperity and happiness. No State, which had provided common schools and higher institutions of learning for the education of her people, could have made war upon our government, or attempted to tear down the good old flag, the emblem of liberty and union. No: intelligence foresees the danger, and shuns it; while ignorance leads her followers blindfold into the very abyss of ruin.

The general state tax produces a result which is sometimes overlooked. It compels those to perform their duty who would not, except upon legal compulsion. If the education of children were left entirely to the voluntary action of individuals, would not a great many, who now pay their just proportion for the support of schools, refuse or neglect to pay anything at all? Would not the whole burden then, if borne at all, fall upon the generous, the patriotic, the men of noble hearts? Surely such would be the result, if the principle were abandoned that "the property of the State should educate the children of the State." But experience has taught that the liberal and willing contributors to even so great a good are not equal to the task which would be thus imposed upon them, and that tens of thousands would soon lack an opportunity of acquiring even the first rudiments of an education essential to the safe exercise of the right of franchise.

This state tax, thanks to an enlightened public sentiment, lays hold of the property of the selfish and unwilling supporters of the public welfare, in whatever small corner they may have hoarded it: it extracts therefrom their equal share in the expense of educating all the children of the State.

The law imposing this tax has also the distinguishing merit of recognizing and inculcating a common brotherhood; that it is the bounden duty of the people of any part of the State to have the same solicitude for the welfare of those in every other part thereof, however remote, as they have for themselves; and its instructions are given with the majesty of an irresistible authority. It teaches the unity of the State, and a mutual dependence and obligation, in proportion to ability, to provide for the common weal; that the richer localities, where capital has concentrated on account of natural or artificial advantages, shall contribute of their abundance to the poorer, to those counties less favored by location and special legislation for school and other purposes. No county, not even New York, which pays a large sum annually to such counties as Otsego, Delaware, Schoharie, Franklin, Clinton and St Lawrence, has a right to complain. For the rule that would set off New York by itself, and free it from this tax, would also free every ward in that city from the city tax for the same purpose, and an individual in any ward could claim with equal propriety exemption from taxation for the support of schools therein; and following the same blind guide, he might claim exemption from every other tax imposed on account of the necessities and duties of an organized community. He could say to his neighbors and to the inhabitants of his ward, city and State, "I will take care of myself, and you may take care of yourselves;" and this rule having obtained, all organized action, regulated by law, would be at an end. I repeat, no part of the State has a right to complain of this tax. It is levied because it is the duty of the State to provide for the education of her children; and duty and right being correlative terms, her children have a right to demand that the doors of the schoolhouses shall be opened for their reception, and that competent teachers be employed to instruct them. The fact of their inability to enforce the observance of their rights in this respect, in the halls of legislation, has not heretofore failed, and, it is confidently believed, will never fail to bring to their aid the conscientious, patriotic and intelligent representatives of the people.

The amount appropriated by the State for the support of schools for last year, including the proceeds of this tax and the revenue derived from the common school and U. S. deposit funds, was less than *one dollar and forty-three cents* per pupil in attendance *upon the schools* — a sum hardly within the bounds of liberality — and yet sufficiently large to aid materially the rural districts of the State. How general is the conviction that the common schools, in which more than ninety per cent. of our people obtain all their instruction, must be supported under the most depressing circumstances, is evinced by the liberal support extended to them during the past year, by the people themselves in their district school meetings, and through their local authorities. It will be observed that, during that time, there were raised by local taxation and by rate bill, in the rural districts, $866,-922.33; and in the cities, $2,068,057.74, for their support. In no other way could the will of the people in regard to the schools have been more forcibly or fully manifested; and it is believed that the abandonment of a policy in furtherance of their will thus expressed — a policy to which they have been so long accustomed, and which has for its object the prosperity and independence of their children — could not meet with their approval, but would lead to a renewal of the controversy which was happily settled in 1851, in which settlement all parties have since acquiesced. I repeat the conclusion of what I said upon this subject in my last report, that the conception of the possibility, not probability, of an attempt to reduce the aggregate appropriation for the support of schools, by discontinuing that portion derived from the three-fourth mill tax, thus inflicting a lasting and irremediable injury upon the generation under tutelage, will account for my calling your attention to this subject.

In his report of January 11, 1864, Superintendent Rice speaks of free city schools as follows:

City Schools

The cities in this State have been especially favored by legislation. Their schools are as free to every child of proper age, as the air he breathes or the water he drinks. In them, the boy born in poverty and obscurity has an opportunity of competing on equal terms with the lad born and pampered in the palace and trained to indulgence. In the mind of the former, equality of privilege inspires hope, cheerfulness and courageous effort; whilst the latter, often for the first time, learns that wealth and affluence, in a democratic country, do not give legs to the laggard, by which he can hope to compete successfully in the race of life.

Thousands of parents have been induced to remove from the rural districts for the purpose of educating their sons and daughters in these excellent schools; and although the people annually tax themselves generously for their support and improvement, the fact is not to be denied that their real property is thereby largely enhanced in value. Were it not for this wise action on the part of the people of our cities, a numberless host that may now be daily seen wending their way to the schools, would be educated exclusively in the streets; and tax payers have long since learned that they cannot afford to encourage, by neglect of duty on their part, the instruction there acquired. With perhaps one exception, the schools in each of our large cities are under a complete and thorough supervision, which secures competent teachers, and incorporates into their plans of instruction every improvement of the day.

Extracts from report of January 1, 1865:

This subject [irregular attendance] was more fully discussed in my report to the Legislature of last year. That Legislature, in view of its importance, provided, by law, that, after the apportionment of the present school year, a part of the school moneys should be apportioned to the districts upon the basis of average daily attendance, thus making it the pecuniary interest of every tax-payer, to induce regular attendance of his own and his neighbors' children. I am gratified in being able to report that that simple provision of law, which went into practical operation on the first day of October last, has largely increased the number of pupils and the regularity of their attendance. . . .

The influence of the provision directing a portion of the public money to be apportioned to the districts outside of the cities, on the basis of average daily attendance, is, as yet, so far prospective as not to be susceptible of representation in the form of statistics; but as the attendance for the year commencing on the 1st of October last, is to be made a basis in the apportionment of next year, it is gratifying to learn, from all the sources of information at command, that a greatly increased interest is manifested in securing the largest possible attendance, and that the object aimed at by the Legislature is likely to be accomplished. To carry into full effect the provision just referred to, I prepared suitable registers for recording the attendance of pupils in the districts, for the current school year, and caused them to be distributed. The want of a school register, in the schools, had often been presented to the Legislature, in the reports from this Department, but no authority to supply it was granted. The opinion is still entertained that provision should be made for supplying each district with a register substantially bound and properly ruled, and of sufficient size to include the registration of the attendance at school, for several years.

The union free school law, as amended and embodied in that act, also meets with general favor. Many districts which were prevented from organizing on the free system, on account of the ambiguities and restrictions of the original law, are now availing themselves of the more clear and liberal provisions of the new act; and I may add the confident hope that within a few years all the districts will have dispensed with that relic of a by-gone age — the rate bill. . . .

It is impossible to read these reports (made by school commissioners) without being impressed with the conviction that the rate-bill is a serious impediment in the way of attendance upon the schools; that whatever other means must be employed to secure the education of all the youth of the State, the free school, at least, is absolutely essential to the accomplishment of that all-important end.

Extract from report of February 1, 1866:

Finally, the proposition that "the property of the State should educate the children of the State," should be carried out, by making the schools at once and forever FREE. From the inception of our school system, the support of schools by taxation of property has been sanctioned by successive legislative enactments. Since that early period, by authority of statute law, the property of school districts has been taxed for the purchase of sites, for erecting and furnishing schoolhouses, and for the payment of exemptions from and deficiencies in rate bills. The constitution of 1822 dedicated to the common school fund all the proceeds of the lands belonging to the State, and the income therefrom to the support of the schools. The constitution of 1846 confirms that dedication by declaring that the capital of that fund shall be preserved inviolate, and its revenues applied to the support of common schools; and the provision is included, that $25,000 from the revenue of the United States deposit fund shall be annually added to the common school fund. The Legislature of 1851, after the people had declared by an overwhelming vote in favor of taxation for the entire support of the schools, or, in other words, that the property of the State should educate the children of the State, authorized a state tax of $800,000 for this purpose; and the Legislature of 1856 increased that amount by making the tax three-fourths of a mill. Numerous special acts, based on the same just and wise policy, have been passed from time to time, by means of which the schools of our cities and of many of our villages are supported wholly by taxation upon property. Under authority of law, the people of other villages and thickly populated districts, have organized union free schools; thus by voluntary action sanctioning this policy, and acknowledging its justice.

If the hundreds of thousands intellectually starved by the operation of the *odious* rate bill should rise up in contrast with those generously nourished by the free system, the revolution in favor of the latter would become an "irrepressible conflict," which would result in the total overthrow of that slavish love of gain, which denies the common brotherhood of man, and ignores the divine command, "Love thy neighbor as thyself." I can conceive no higher legislative obligation than that of making provisions by which the portals to the school shall be thrown more widely open and attendance thus encouraged.

I may be allowed, in this connection, to manifest a special anxiety for the children of those soldiers and sailors who have died or been disabled while serving in the army or navy of the United States, by recommending that provision be made by which the public schools shall be required, and all other institutions of learning that participate in the distribution of any of the public moneys be induced, to give them instruction free of tuition. It is believed that this boon should be generously and freely extended and made an *inheritance,* a *right,* recognized and secured by the majesty of law. A manifestation of an *earnest gratitude* for the services and sacrifices of their fathers would be worthy of a grateful people. How so touchingly manifest that gratitude, as by such a provision for their children! If in other times the life of this nation shall be again imperiled, where so hopefully look for the loyal and brave, as to these foster-children whose incentive shall be, not only to imitate the manly and patriotic deeds of their fathers, but to shield the Protectress, who, in their early years, folded them in her arms with a loving kindness second only to that of Him who gave to us the victory!

Extract from annual report of February 1, 1867:

The number of districts in which the trustees did, to any extent, exempt indigent persons from payment of rate bills, is 2327, while in 7764 districts no exemption whatever was made. Thus it appears, that in over 80 districts in every 100, upon the confession of the trustees themselves, the law authorizing these officers to exempt the poor from this burden has proved of no effect. Section 39 of title 7 of the general school law of the State commences thus: "The common schools in the several school districts of this State shall be free to all persons over five and under 21 years of age, residing in the district." But, in fact, they are free only in the same sense that good dinners at our best hotels are free dinners. They are free to all those who will pay a good price for them. . . .

The greatest defect in our school system is, as I have urged in previous reports, the continuance of the rate bill system. Our common schools can never reach their highest degree of usefulness until they shall have been made entirely free. Although our common schools have made rapid progress in efficiency and usefulness during the past decade, I venture to prophesy that, if the Legislature shall comply with the public demand, and throw open the doors of the public school houses, so that all the children of the State may receive the benefits of education "without money and without price," their progress in the coming decade will be even greater than it has been in the past.

To meet this public demand, to confer upon the children of the State the blessings of free education, a bill has already been introduced into your honorable body entitled "An act to amend an act entitled an act to revise and consolidate the acts relating to public instruction," which meets with my fullest approbation. Every amendment to the school law, proposed by that bill, ought, in my judgment, to become a part of the law. The main features of the bill are the provisions to raise, by State tax, a sum about equal to that raised in the districts by rate bills, and to abolish the rate bill system; to facilitate the erection and repair of schoolhouses, whose character I have hereinbefore reported, by giving to the school commissioners and supervisors additional discretionary power in regard to them.

Number of Free Schools given in Superintendent's Reports, 1867

YEAR	CITIES	RURAL	TOTAL
1858	494	44	538
1859	457	205	662
1860	620	207	827
1861	695	216	911
1862	286	286	572
1863	372	437	809
1864	385	386	771
1865	285	378	663
1866	474	260	734
1867	462	299	761
1868	436	335	771

Henry S. Randall, Superintendent of Common Schools, in his report of January 4, 1853, says:

Our school system, so far as the means of its pecuniary support are concerned, represents but a series of adjustments between conflicting interests, and does not carry out strictly the theory on which the claims of any of these interests are sought to be established. The principle that education is a concern of government, that the government may of right, and is bound in duty to support it, and that the property of the country may be justly taxed for that support, has been distinctly recognized by the people of this State from its earliest organization. In 1789, but twelve years after the adoption of the constitution, the Legislature set apart public lands for school purposes. In 1795, the board of supervisors were required to raise by *a tax upon each town,* for the support of schools, half the amount of money received for the same purpose, under an Act passed that year. Laws involving the same principles, have been passed from time to time, from that day to this.

But while the right and the expediency of taxing property for the support of schools, has always been concurred in by the bulk of our population, the expediency of throwing the burthen of maintaining education exclusively on property, without any reference to the direct participation of the taxpayer in the benefits of the school, has never been declared by law until 1849. The "Free school act" of that year was intended to accomplish this object. Though the majority of the people twice expressed their approbation of free schools, by a vote on that distinct proposition, the law met with an opposition which neutralized the benefits which its friends anticipated from it. The strifes which it gave rise to, in the language of the Executive, in 1851, "disturbed the harmony of society." Districts were rent with contention; litigation in school matters rapidly increased; the inhabitants in many instances refused to carry out the provisions of the law, and in others, directly resisted it as unconstitutional and oppressive.

In 1851, the Legislature, with great unanimity, passed the law now in force. It is essentially a compromise between the views of the advocates and opponents of the law of 1849 — between the theories of an exclusively property basis of taxation for the support of schools, and that mixed one, previously obtaining, in which property, as such, bore a portion (but a smaller portion) of the burthen, and the persons directly benefitted, the remainder. While the present State tax of eight hundred thousand dollars is a greater concession from property than any made previously to 1849, it does not, as the title of the bill would seem to assume, render the schools entirely free, in the sense of being exempt from the payment of tuition fees. Rate bills to pay some portion of the teachers' wages have yet to be collected in many, if not most, of the districts of the State. But to the indigent, the schools are now, as they were under the laws anterior to 1849, absolutely free.

In the school code reported to the Legislature, during its last session, by the Commissioner, Mr S. S. Randall, and in the last annual report of the late Superintendent, it is proposed to substitute a mill tax for the present one. This is virtually, and indeed avowedly, a proposition to restore free schools.

A per centum tax, beyond all question, is more defensible in theory than one of fixed amount, when designed to meet a want which is varied by the same causes which vary the avails of the tax, viz: the increase or diminution of population and wealth. A fixed tax does not adapt itself to either of these contingencies; and among a rapidly increasing population, like our own, if it is exactly adequate to its purpose one year, it must necessarily fall short of it the next.

And that a mill tax cannot be fairly considered an onerous burthen on property, for the great object of maintaining popular education — for that protection which property itself derives from the dissemination of intelligence through all classes of society — has been very distinctly admitted by the opponents of free schools themselves, by their assenting to the eight hundred thousand dollar tax. When imposed, it amounted to more than a tenth of one per cent on the assessed value of the property of the State.

Should another leading feature of the present law — the equal division of one-third of the school moneys by districts — be permitted to remain in force, it is not probable that the class of districts which most strenuously opposed the free school law — the sparsely inhabited ones of the country — would object to the substitution of a mill tax for the present one; nor, on the other hand, that the wealthy city and village districts, which gave its popular majorities to that law, would press the change. Neither of these classes of districts would now desire it, except on conditions which would render it obnoxious to the other. This remark is thrown out to show that in settling this point, we are not permitted to view it as a separate and independent proposition to be decided on its abstract merits.

It constitutes, in fact, the principal in a series of measures, adopted as an adjustment between rival interests and opposing views. Experience may, and probably does, demand the modification of some of these measures. It certainly makes such demand, if it can be shown that they affect any portion of the community oppressively or injuriously. But whether it is expedient to so soon reopen the *whole* question — to reawaken the desolating controversies which preceded the enactment of the present law — and this too, not to correct any positive evil, but only to attain what a portion of the community regard as a greater good — it is for the wisdom of the Legislature to decide.

Not doubting that the wants of an advancing population will ultimately call for an increase of the state tax, and that when so increased, it would be better on all acounts to make it a per-centum, and therefore a self adjusting one, the undersigned feels constrained to express the opinion that the time has not arrived for such action. Nor is he disposed at present to recommend any action which will affect the interior polity of the schools, or the duties of trustees. The evils arising from too frequent changes in the latter particulars, have not been sufficiently appreciated.

The school system of New York is too vast, involves interests too important, to be rashly established or rashly changed. It requires permanency to adapt it to the circumstances of society, and to give facility and vigor to its operations. Where no serious practical evil is felt, it can scarcely be doubted that a reasonable degree of such permanency is preferable to incessant changes, even though, independently considered, those changes might promise some degree of improvement.

In the rapid transition from system to system, in the constant change of details, made without the benefit of sufficient experience, which has marked the school legislation of the last four years, the natural result has followed. Grave errors have been committed. To retrieve them, new ones have been plunged into. The local officers have been embarrassed to understand their duties, varied by each year's legislation. They have consequently performed them with diminished spirit and greatly diminished accuracy. Want of zeal or want of accuracy in the principal, soon extends to the subaltern, or paralizes his efforts. Even the teachers — a finer or more spirited professional body than whom is not to be found in our State — have lost something of that high enthusiasm which a few years since exhibited its kindling traces throughout our schools, or, as is more likely, their efforts unsupported from without, have fallen on a soil made sterile by indifference, or choked by angry contention. Melancholy as is the confession, and decided as are the exceptions to it, our schools, in the opinion of the undersigned, have deteriorated during the rapid changes of the last four years.

Whether we have reached a point in these mutations where it is best to pause, and let existing regulations where not obviously and seriously wrong, stand, until a further developed experience and a more settled public sentiment shall call for well-considered changes, is the grave question now to be settled. On it, the views of the undersigned are already expressed. . . .

Nothing can be more obviously true than the proposition that every dollar devoted by the State to educational purposes, should be so expended as to render its benefits, to the greatest practicable extent, equally open to all. The common schools alone, at this time, present this condition. In them, tuition is cheap to all, and absolutely free to the indigent. The academies and colleges, with the exception of certain beneficiary scholarships, and with some other exceptions which will be presently noticed, require tuition and other fees, and an expenditure for books, which shut their doors on a large class of our population. The public moneys which they receive does not, then, equally inure to the benefit of all, but to that of those who need it least, the wealthy, and in point of fortune, the middle classes.

There are two ways of removing this inequality. The one is to deprive academies and colleges of all share in the public moneys. What would be the effect of this? Wealth would still sustain these institutions, but necessarily in diminished numbers, as the cost of tuition in them, increased to counterbalance the withdrawal of the public aid, would exclude not only poverty, but that moderate competency which, united with effort and energy, now not unfrequently attains their benefits. Higher education would thus become the luxury, and the additional *power* of the wealthy. If the sons of the poor and of those in middling circumstances, were not excluded from the learned professions, and from all occupations demanding a higher grade of learning, they at least would start both in the attainment and the practice of those professions, on no equal footing with the educated sons of the rich; and they would require double talent and double industry to ensure equal success. Is this idea to be for a moment tolerated in a government which has enough for the reasonable wants of all? Are the public prepared to surrender, for the benefit of a small portion of our population, the treasure which they have been pouring for half a century into the coffers of our academies and colleges? Shall the monopoly, and hence the double power of learning, be made an appendage of the aristocracy of wealth?

It has been said that the increased amount of public money which might be distributed among the common schools, on depriving the academies and colleges of any participation in it, would put the former on such a footing that all the higher branches of education could be successfully taught in them. The proceeds of the literature fund and of the United States deposit fund, applicable to the support of academies, is about forty thousand dollars per annum. Add to this an equal amount, for annual aid to colleges — though, for a considerable term of years, they have received nothing like that amount. This eighty thousand dollars divided among the common schools of the State, would give to each, between six and seven dollars — a sum scarcely sufficient to purchase the text books which *one* scholar would annually require in pursuing the higher branches of literature and science! How far would it go towards purchasing the scientific apparatus necessary in teaching those higher branches of science? — how far towards collecting those libraries, without a knowledge of whose stores, scientific attainments lose half their value? How far would it go, added to present salaries, towards paying the wages of a class of teachers competent to instruct in academic and collegiate branches? These questions are asked to place in a strong light the futility of an idea, which has found advocates among those who have not sufficiently investigated the facts in the case, and who have probably formed exaggerated impressions of the aid which the State extends to its higher institutions of learning.

Union schools, with such additional aid, might, it is true, form a substitute for academies — but to what good? Few localities out of cities and villages will admit of them, until population and wealth have greatly advanced; and their benefits, it is believed, would not be as evenly disseminated as those of the academies now are. And why throw away what has already been lavished on academies — the acquisitions of years — merely to build up a *new* class of schools, to attain the same object? In their present sphere, the Union schools are productive of incalculable benefits; as substitutes for academies generally, they are uncalled for, and promise no improvement.

There is a method, in the judgment of the undersigned, by which the State can render the benefits of the funds which it appropriates to higher education equally accessible to all — throw open those benefits to the poor without curtailing any now enjoyed by another class — and in doing this, neither diminish the number, nor impinge the interests of the existing higher institutions of learning. That method would be to distribute among those institutions, as much money as now — and more, if necessary — but to require them to repay every dollar thus received, IN GRATUITOUSLY EDUCATING SUCH PUPILS AS THE STATE SHALL DESIGNATE.

By a proper method of designating the pupils, the inequalities of the present system would be done away, and results attained as accordant with enlightened philanthropy, as with the theory and spirit of our political institutions.

The following is an outline of the proposed plan. Let the common school districts of the State be arranged into as many academy districts, as there are now, or may hereafter be, of academies. Let each academy then be required to receive annually from the common schools in its district, and gratuitously educate a pupil for every $——— received from the State; a college to receive pupils from the free departments of a certain number of academies, on the same footing. The selection of the pupils should evidently be made on the basis of educational qualification and general merit. There are several methods of accomplishing this, which it is not necessary at this point to discuss. That the object is practically and readily attainable, is established by the experience of the free academy in the city of New York, and some other kindred institutions.

The free academy in the city of New York presents, in fact, a practical exemplification, in a single locality, of the plan above proposed for the whole State. It receives its pupils from the common schools on the basis above suggested, and *it educates them gratuitously*. The undersigned has, during the past season, visited this institution, personally, examined its records, investigated its plans of action in detail, and witnessed its operations. To say that it is eminently successful in accomplishing the objects of its foundation, is but faint praise of the men whose philanthropy originated, and whose energy secured that foundation — of the able and efficient corps of teachers who manage its concerns. Within its halls, the mark of caste and the distinctions of wealth, elsewhere so pervading — pervading the mansions of the living and even the mausoleums of the dead — are for once ignored. The sons of the rich and the poor — neither of them degraded beneficiaries, but the honored cadets of a parental government — meet on ground where neither has advantage. Sitting on the same benches, pursuing the same higher branches of science, drinking from the same rich foundations of classic literature, cultivating the same elegant tastes and personal accomplishments, the undersigned saw, with emotions he will not attempt to describe, the representatives of almost the extremes, and of every intermediate point, in social and pecuniary condition — the sons of the merchant whose vessels visit every ocean, and of the employees of his store-house and wharves — of fathers whose names are historic in professions, in literature, in arts and in arms, and of the obscure and toiling masses whose sinews support this social superstructure above them.

The following letter from Wheeler Trusdell of Fairmont, Onondaga county, is appended to Superintendent Randall's report of 1853:

Fairmount, Onondaga County, N. Y.
December 22, 1852

Hon. H. S. Randall
  State Superintendent of Common Schools:
  Having for several years been a trustee of "joint school district number one," of this place, I have been requested, by some of its inhabitants, to make a statement to you of the effects of the law of 1851 upon our school.

  The territory embraced in this district, originally constituted three school districts, each full the average size. For the purpose of establishing a department for the benefit of advanced scholars wishing to study the higher branches, these three districts were consolidated. We have now, as before, three schoolhouses, the centre house accommodating the high school and a primary department, the other two houses being used for primary purposes only.

  This was done nine years ago, when we were under the old school system. Since has followed the "free school law," which, with us, met with almost universal favor; the inhabitants cheerfully taxing themselves to pay the wages of four teachers for nine months in a year.

  Under the present law our county taxes for school purposes are largely enhanced, while we draw from the school moneys only thirty dollars more than we did the year previous. While we pay towards the state tax for school purposes $275, we receive in return thirty dollars. This is owing in part to the unjust division of one-third of the school moneys equally among all the districts. If this law is not entirely repealed, it should be so amended as to afford relief to districts employing several teachers, and especially to those sustaining schools in several schoolhouses at the same time.

  If no other basis is very soon adopted for the division of the school moneys, union districts that have been organized for the noble purpose of offering superior advantages to all, will be divided into their original number. Already the question is being discussed with us, and should the next Legislature fail to afford relief, a majority will feel themselves driven to the process of dividing.

  Is not the present method of dividing the school moneys a bid for small districts? The ruinous effects upon our common schools, by the division of districts and the consequent abandonment of our high schools, will be sorely felt by all who feel a deep interest in their prosperity, if not by the public at large.

  Our own high school, which has been nobly sustained to the credit and great benefit of our enterprizing inhabitants, has its origin in the union and consolidation of three former districts. To this school a large number of young men and women are already indebted for an education far superior to any obtained in any ordinary district. Had not this school have existed, a majority of these scholars would never have obtained a knowledge of the higher branches, in which many are now preeminently versed.

  Will our Legislature aid the friends of education to increase the number of *such* schools, while by so doing the number of small districts will be proportionally diminished? or will they destroy them by keeping in operation a law which offers great inducements to the multiplication of small and consequently feeble districts?

The evil of which we particularly complain may be partially remedied by either dividing one-third of the school moneys among the districts according to the number of teachers who may be employed at the same time for six months or more in a year, or according to the number of schoolhouses in which schools are kept by qualified teachers for a like term.

Very respectfully yours
WHEELER TRUSDELL

The following letter from Superintendent McKeen of New York City is appended to Superintendent Randall's report for 1853:

To the Hon. H. S. Randall
  Superintendent of Common Schools:

Allow me to make a few remarks and suggestions on the subject of the more recently enacted laws of the State regulating the manner of raising and dispensing moneys for the support of common schools in the State. The act of the Legislature to establish free schools throughout the State, passed April 12, 1851, is inequitable to large portions of the population of the State, and in many respects decidedly objectionable. The avails of the common school fund being inadequate for the entire sustentation of free schools throughout the State, and there being objections to, and clamor against the rate bill, which, for years, had been a main support in many places, it was discreetly considered that eight hundred thousand dollars should be raised by tax for the common benefit of all the children of the State from four to twenty-one years of age, in order, as it would seem, that all might enjoy alike the privileges of a beneficial legislation. At first no friend of such a law had the least conception that any discrimination or inequalities contravening the spirit of our government could be introduced. In the confidence that all the people of the State should share alike in the benefits and the burdens, according to their means and wants, the bill was urged upon the Legislature. It is believed that the unjust discriminations which go to benefit one portion of the State at the expense of another, were introduced into the bill for the purpose of making it odious and defeating it; rather than with the expectation that they would be accepted by the friends of free schools. There can be no question that a principle that can be carried through the legislature burdened with so many objectionable additions, must be deeply rooted in the minds of the people of this State. The bill, with all its defects, was finally accepted, in the hope that subsequent legislation and amendments would make it tolerable. It would seem that no sane man who had examined all its defects would have consented to it with the expectation of its remaining unaltered.

By this *act* $300,000 from the avails of the school fund, and $800,000 from the newly imposed tax making $1,100,000 is provided, which sum is to be annually distributed for the payment of instruction in common schools. This is certainly a liberal provision on the part of the State. The amount is large, and presents the State in an attitude of dignity that is very gratifying. The evil complained of is not that it is unreasonably large, but chiefly that the manner of distribution of the first third of this sum is wrong and unjust. It may safely be affirmed that the way provided by the act appropriating and distributing $366,666 of this money is neither equal nor in conformity with the principles and usages of the State government. It is contrary to the fundamental principles of a republican government. It does not proceed upon the basis of population in the districts, for it gives to a small district of twenty-five scholars who are taught for six months in the year by one teacher just as much of this one third of $1,100,000, as is given in New York or Kings county, to a large district of 2500 children who are taught for 11 or 12 months in the year by perhaps 30 teachers! This is a discrimination with a vengeance, the like of which has never before found a place in our Statute books. New York and Kings counties combined have, by the last census, 654,425 inhabitants. These two counties return 241 districts, and receive $66,433.31 from the first third of $1,100,000, while the counties of St Lawrence, Jefferson, Lewis, Herkimer, Delaware, Allegany, Broome, Cattaraugus, Chenango, Genesee, Madison, Otsego, Cortland, Essex, Greene, Hamilton and Warren, all combined, have but 646,807 inhabitants (less by 7615, than New York and Kings) which have 4161 school districts, and receive $126,213 from this same one-third. These last enumerated counties have fewer poor, their schools are certainly not better, and the average time of teaching is considerably less. What equitable claim can they have to receive in the division of $366,666, twenty times as much as New York and Brooklyn, in which places are to be educated most of the foreign poor. The injustice is plain, but what remedy is proposed that will conciliate and satisfy all parties and sections of the State, and encourage and keep up the district organization in the sparsely populated parts of the State? Every village that has as many as one hundred and fifty children at school, finds a great advantage by having a union classified school, with at least three teachers. In such school the teaching is better adapted and is more effectual, but the present law is a premium for small schools, and a bar to proper classification and improvement in teaching, where such advance is in every other respect entirely practicable and desirable.

This good school of 150, is but one district, and if it is cut up into four districts it will draw four times as much money from the first third of $1,100,000, and the little schools for the want of proper classification will not be half so effective as the large one. The defects of the present law have been sufficiently urged; now what change or remedy is proposed? simply this — *that the present district discrimination be changed; and that distribution be made according to the number of qualified teachers employed for at least six or eight months in the year.* In the large and graded schools twice as many are now taught by one teacher as can be properly taught in the lowest grade of district schools, and a discrimination of *two* to one instead of *twenty* to one is as much as ought to be asked in favor of the small rural districts.

I have the honor to submit the foregoing remarks with all due respect.

Your humble servant
JOSEPH MCKEEN
City Sup't of Common Schools, for the city and county of New York

To *Hon. Henry S. Randall*
Sup't Common Schools

As indicative of the sentiment in relation to free education, we include the following letter from President Hale to Superintendent Randall in relation to free tuition in Hobart College:

Hobart Free College
Geneva, Dec. 2, 1853

DEAR SIR: It gives me great pleasure to reply to your inquiries. This college " was made free " by the act of the corporation of Trinity Church, New York, of Nov. 14, 1851, granting to it an annuity of three thousand dollars, on condition of its taking its present name, and of its giving *free tuition and room rent,* so far as it might have rooms for the purpose, *to all, without restriction,* who, by acquirements and character, are properly qualified for admission. The grant was accepted by the trustees on the 9th of December following, and the college at the beginning of the next term, Jan. 15, 1852, as a *free college.*

These remarks may perhaps sufficiently answer your next question, " How far is it practically free to all? " But to prevent mistake, I will add that no condition whatever is required of candidates for admission, but the proper age, the prescribed amount of preparation, and correct moral character. No distinction is made in favor of any locality, or any creed. Besides members of the Protestant Episcopal church, there are students in college from as many as five different religious denominations, all deriving precisely the same advantages from the above mentioned grant of Trinity church.

" What expenses yet fall on the student? " No college charge, but a small one of three dollars a term or nine a year, to cover the expense of the janitor's services, the cost of ordinary repairs and some other necessary contingencies. The other expenses of the student are merely personal, as for board, &c., and are regulated by himself according to his means and his habits of economy.

" How the system works? " Having been in operation less than two years, its full effects have not had time to develop themselves. From our brief experience, however, I am satisfied that as it has worked well so far, so it will continue to do.

It is favorable to discipline. The students are not the patrons and supporters of the college, and there is therefore no inducement to retain the idle and vicious, whose presence hinders the proper work of a college, and tends to corrupt others. It is favorable also, as is obvious from this view, to the establishment of a high standard of scholarship and of character.

It will prove attractive to young men of moderate means; for it offers them free education, not as a special charity, but on an equal footing with others.

Our numbers are increasing with a moderate rapidity, just as we desire; for our wish is to establish a sound system of discipline and instruction, and wholesome precedents, and leave the rest to time. We have therefore taken no pains by advertising, or agencies, or other means to secure a rapid increase. During the years ending July, 1851 and 1852, the *admissions* were respectively 16 and 22. During that, ending July, 1853, 27 and so far in the current year, 26, with a prospect of more.

We are limited in the extent of our accommodations for students, having but 43 rooms for their use, and our present resources being no more than sufficient for the moderate support of the Faculty, we can not apply any part of them to the erection of additional buildings. We hope, as we offer free tuition and free room-rent, as far as we have rooms for the use of students, that public or private liberality will provide for the enlargement of our means.

I am, dear Sir,
Very respectfully,
Your friend and serv't,
BENJ. HALE, *President*

To the Hon. Henry S. Randall
Secretary of State, of the State of New York

UNPAID SCHOOL MONEYS

The difficulty in collecting the taxes for school purposes is well illustrated in the following report of the Superintendent of Common Schools to the Assembly on June 3, 1853:

In Assembly, June 3, 1853
No. 127

Communication From the Superintendent of Common Schools Relative to Certain Unpaid School Moneys

Secretary's Office
Department of Common Schools
Albany, June 3, 1853

To the Legislature:

Since the communication made by me to the Legislature on the 14th day of April, 1853, in regard to the portion of the eight hundred thousand dollar school tax, due from the counties of New York and Rensselaer, I have had an interview with the public authorities of the former, at which arrangements were made to have final action taken at an early day in regard to the payment of the sum due from the city and county of New York. That action was consummated on the 1st inst. and on the 2d inst. I was notified by the Comptroller that the money was placed subject to my draft, consequently the legislation asked in my former communication has become unnecessary.

As soon as the above is drawn there will only remain uncollected of the avails of the eight hundred thousand dollars school tax for the current year, to be applied to the payment of deficiencies in other counties besides Rensselaer, the sum of four thousand one hundred dollars and sixty-eight cents, which is still due from the county of Rensselaer. I am informed that a meeting of the supervisors of that county was held on the 10th of May last, and no provision was made for the payment of this money.

I have before called the attention of the Legislature to the serious evils which have resulted, and which are continuing to result to a large portion of the schools of the State from the non-payment of the school tax. To mitigate them as far as possible, I recently made a distribution of all the school money, (over and above that before in the hands of the treasurers of the counties,) collected up to the 12th day of May last, directing the treasurers to make a pro rata distribution of it among the towns. This put those officers to the trouble of making a second distribution, and the town superintendents of making a second collection, where but one is contemplated by law. Should I retain the money just obtained from New York, long in my hands, it would result in continued injury to the schools. Should I apportion it, and direct the treasurers to distribute it, before obtaining the Rensselaer county deficiency, the treasurers would be called upon to make a third, and should the Rensselaer deficiency be paid, a fourth distribution of school moneys during the year, thus putting them, the town superintendents, and this Department to much additional expense and trouble which is wholly out of the contemplation of the law. So far as this Department is concerned, these burthens would be willingly met, but it would be unjust to impose them on the other officers named above, except under the pressure of a necessity which does not exist.

No certainty exists that the Rensselaer county deficiency will be paid during the year. Though the sum is not large its nonpayment will compel collections of trifling sums by rate bills, in perhaps half the second districts of the State. This would be unjust, because the laws have made other provision for the payment of these moneys. It would lead to a vast amount of unnecessary trouble and expense, an amount perhaps really exceeding the value of the sum to be collected. Under these circumstances, I respectfully, but most urgently solicit the immediate attention of the Legislature to the subject. I recommend that the Comptroller be immediately authorized and directed to loan to the Superintendent of Common Schools from any moneys in the Treasury not otherwise appropriated, a sum equalling the amount due from Rensselaer county, to be paid out by the Superintendent in the same manner and in lieu of the sum due from said county; and that to pay the above loan, a like amount and interest thereon at the rate of six per cent per annum be withheld from the first school moneys hereafter apportioned to said county for common school purposes unless the same shall be sooner paid by the treasurer of said county.

HENRY S. RANDALL
Superintendent of Common Schools

The question whether State funds appropriated for use in common schools might be appropriated to private school systems was raised in 1853. The report of the committee on college, academies and common schools to the Assembly, April 2, 1853 in regard to this matter is of noted interest:

In Assembly, Apr. 2, 1853
No. 97

Report

Of the committee on colleges, academies and common schools, on petition of certain Roman Catholics of New York, Utica, Syracuse, &c., relative to instruction of their children.

Mr Patterson, from the committee on colleges, academies and common schools, to which was referred the petitions of certain Roman Catholic citizens of the cities of New York, Utica, Syracuse, Oswego, and of the villages of Auburn, Rome, &c., praying for the passage of a law, authorizing the establishment of schools where their children "may be instructed in religion; without which, they deem education more pernicious than useful;" and for granting such schools, "a portion of the school fund and taxes, proportioned to the numbers of children attending said schools," respectfully,

REPORTS:

That from the earnestness of the appeal that has been made to them, from this large and respectable class of our fellow citizens on this subject, they have given it, not only a respectful, but an anxious attention, with a sincere desire to recommend such measures to the Legislature, as should be most conducive to the harmony, usefulness and prosperity of the common schools of the State. The history of our common school system has been examined with careful attention, in the hope that we might deduce from this history the secret of its present prosperity, and the principles that will guide it, in its future triumphant career, towards an ultimate state of perfection.

Your committee find, that the smoke of the revolutionary battle fields was scarcely dissipated, before active measures were taken by the Legislature, at the instance of Gov. George Clinton, to "revive, strengthen and encourage our then feeble common schools." In 1789, the Surveyor General was directed to set apart, for gospel and school purposes, two lots in each township in the then unsurveyed portions of the State. Three or four years later, the Regents of the University called the attention of the Legislature "to the numerous advantages that would accrue to the citizens at large, from the institution of schools in various parts of the State, for the purpose of instructing children in the lower branches of education;" they also recommended that liberal provision be made to sustain the schools, by appropriations of the public lands, as the value of these lands would be enhanced by an increase of population. "The State will thus never want the means of promoting useful science, and will thereby secure the national happiness and fix the liberty of the people on the most permanent basis: that of knowledge and virtue."

In 1795, the Legislature on the recommendation of Gov. George Clinton, appropriated $50,000 annually for five years, for the support of the common schools of the State.

In 1800, Governor Jay, in his message to the Legislature, says: "Among other objects that will present themselves to you, there is one that I earnestly recommend to your notice and patronage: I mean our institutions for the education of youth. The importance of common schools is best estimated by the good effects of them when they most abound, and are the best regulated."

In 1802, Governor George Clinton again impresses upon the Legislature the importance of perseverance in the effort to elevate the character of our common schools, and to diffuse their blessings over the whole surface, and into all the ramifications of society. In his message to the Legislature, he says: "Education, by correcting the morals and improving the manners, tends to prevent those evils in society which are beyond the sphere of legislation."

Equally impressive are the words of Governor Lewis, (1804). "In a government resting on public opinion, and deriving its chief support from the affections of the people, religion and morality can not be too sedulously inculcated. To those, science is a handmaid; ignorance, the worst of enemies. Literary information should then be placed within the reach of every description of citizen, and poverty should not be permitted to obstruct the path to the fame of knowledge. Common schools, under the guidance of respectable teachers, should be established in every village, and the indigent be educated at the public expense. Learning would thus flourish, and vice be more effectually restrained, than by volumes of penal statutes." During this year, the net proceeds of 500,000 acres of public lands were reserved for school purposes.

This was the foundation of the present fund, which future Legislatures increased, until it has swollen to its present magnitude. In 1811, under the administration of Governor Tompkins, the school commissioners observe: "Perhaps there never will be presented to the Legislature a subject of more importance than the establishment of common schools.

"Education, as the means of improving the moral and intellectual faculties, is, under all circumstances, a subject of the most imposing consideration.

"To rescue man from that state of degradation to which he is doomed unless redeemed by education; to unfold his physical, intellectual and moral powers; and to fit him for those high destinies which his Creator has prepared for him, cannot fail to excite the most ardent sensibility of the philosopher and philanthropist. In proportion as every country has been enlightened by education, so has been its prosperity. When the heads and hearts of men are generally cultivated and improved, virtue and wisdom must reign, and vice and ignorance must cease to prevail.

"Virtue and wisdom are the parents of private and public felicity; vice and ignorance of private and public misery.

"As the people must receive the advantages of education, the enquiry naturally arises, how this end is to be attained? The establishment of common schools, which being spread throughout the State, and aided by its bounty, will bring improvement within the reach and power of the humblest citizen. This appears to be the best plan that can be devised to disseminate religion, morality and learning throughout a whole country. All other methods heretofore adopted are partial in their operation, and circumscribed in their effects."

In 1822, Gov. DeWitt Clinton called the attention of the Legislature to the subject of state instruction, in the following terms: "The first duty of a State is to render its citizens virtuous by intellectual instruction and moral discipline; by enlightening their minds, purifying their hearts, and teaching them their rights and obligations. Those solid and enduring honors which arise from the cultivation of science and the acquisition and diffusion of knowledge, will outlive the renown of the statesman and the glory of the warrior." Again, in 1827, he says: "I consider the system of our common schools as the palladium of our freedom; for no reasonable apprehension can be entertained of its subversion as long as the great body of the people are enlightened by education."

The committee have been induced to submit the above remarks from the different Governors and superintendents, the fathers and founders of our splendid system of common schools, for the purpose of exhibiting a few of the great principles that lay at the foundation of this stupendous superstructure.

The first is, that it is not only the right but the duty of the State to furnish and superintend the operation of a system of education for the children of the State.

Your committee believe that this point is not seriously controverted in this State, in the middle of the 19th century.

The second great principle (drawn from the history of our common school system, the consideration of which is involved in the petitions before us) is the eminently catholic nature of this system. Its entire exemption from every thing like a partizan or secretarian character, from its inception down to the present day, in every stage of its progress, amid the storm and the tempests that have attended the mutations of political parties; amid the rancor of theological controversy, and the heat of religious excitements, our common school system has moved quietly and majestically along, from the smallest beginning to its present magnificent proportions, under the guidance of those pure and patriotic statesmen (whose sentiments and opinions we have so liberally quoted), without participating in or ministering to the peculiarities of any party or any sect, its blessings falling upon the children and the youth of the whole state, like the dew of heaven, upon the high and low, the rich and poor, the catholic and protestant, upon every shade of religious and political opinion alike, without prejudice and without partiality.

In tracing down the history of the rise, progress and present state of our system of common schools, your committee has been impressed by the fact, that among the means that have been so successful in placing this system upon its present elevation, the government has never listened for a moment to the suggestion of fractionizing this system in favor of or against any political party, or any religious sect, or denomination. While the fathers, of our system of common schools have labored zealously and successfully, to place within the reach of the children of the State an education that shall qualify them for the discharge of their duties as citizens of the republic, and for the intelligent management of the ordinary avocation of life; while they have sought to blend with this education, a system of pure morality, indispenable to the future usefulness and respectability of the rising generation, they seem sedulously to have avoided all affinity with systems of faith or sects, whether religious or political. In their wisdom, they seem to have left the religious education, the sectarian discipline, the instruction in religious creeds and religious practises, where they rightfully belong — to the genial influences of the domestic fireside; the family altar, to the church; to pastoral instruction, the Sabbath school and the Bible class; or to such other means, outside of the school house, as the judgment or taste of parents or guardians should dictate.

Had the founder of this system, at any stage of its progress, parceled out the bounty of the State for the support of common schools, in favor of those based upon the peculiarities of any party or any sect; or upon any of the arbitrary or conventional distinctions that prevail in civilized society, your committee believe that its strength would have been frittered away, and lost amid the jealousies and contentions it would have engendered; that it would have added a new if not a fearful element to the bitterness of religious controversy, a controversy which this circumstance alone would have directed with crushing force against the utility and stability of our present great system of primary instruction. And your committee, instead of being able to report at this time nearly 12,000 school houses in the State in successful operation, in which nearly 1,000,000 of children have received the benefits of a common education during the past year, and supported at an expense (for teachers' wages alone) of more than $1\frac{1}{2}$ million dollars, it would have been called upon to report upon the wreck of a system efficient only in flooding the country with the bitter waters of partisan strife, and of religious and sectarian controversy.

The genius of our institutions is pre-eminently that of universal religious toleration, and it should never be overlooked for a moment, in our legislation upon the management of the common schools of the State; hence, by granting the prayers of these petitioners, we recognize the principle that each one of the organized sects or religious denominations of this State, may establish their schools, and be entitled to share of the common school fund for their support. Granting this privilege to one sect would open for applications for every sect and denomination in the State; and in view of their number, the conflicting and contradictory nature of their tenets, we should regard as suicidal the attempt to embrace them in the system of our common schools, or sustain them by its funds.

Grant the prayer of these petitioners, and a floodgate of ruin is opened upon our common school system which future legislation would hardly be able to restrain; for under our system of religious toleration, no resting place would be found until our magnificent school fund was subdivided among every denomination in the State, from the ancient and venerable establishment of the Roman Catholic Church, down to the conventicles of the spiritual mediums of these latter times.

The effects of fractionizing our School Fund among religious denominations, seems, to your committee, to be easily calculated. Hence, your committee should regard the first step of the government in that direction with the utmost anxiety and alarm, as a fatal blow struck at the prosperity and utility of a system of primary education, which has already become the pride of the State and the wonder of the age. Your committee, therefore, unanimously present the following resolution, and recommend its passage:

Resolved, That the prayers of the petitioners should not be granted.

>ASHBEL PATTERSON (Cortland county)
>WM. W. FORSYTH (Albany county)
>NICH. C. BLAUVELT (Rockland county)
>WM. TAYLOR (New York county)
>DANIEL STEWART (Delaware county)
>*Committee*

In passing it is of interest to note that the Court of Appeals in June 1853 (Barto v. Himrod, 8 N. Y. 483) declared the law of 1849 to be unconstitutional and void. The opponents of free schools pursued every possible avenue of attack upon the law and even instituted proceedings in the courts in four different counties to test its constitutionality. This decision was based upon the form and procedure in the enactment of the law and not upon the power of the Legislature or the authority of the people to provide free schools. The law was so drawn that its validity depended upon a majority of the votes being cast for its adoption and not upon the action of the Legislature. The court held that the Constitution conferred on the Legislature the power to enact laws and that the Legislature could not divest itself of this responsibility and delegate that power on the people.

This decision of the court, however, had no vital bearing upon the establishment of free schools.

Barto v. Himrod and Another
Constitutional Law — Reserved Point

If a legislative act be made to depend for its validity, upon the result of a popular election, it is unconstitutional; the legislature cannot delegate to the people, the power conferred upon them by the constitution.[1]

Thorne v. Cramer, 15 Barb. 112, and Bradley v. Baxter, Ibid. 122, affirmed; Johnson v. Rich, 9 Ibid. 680, overruled.

Distinguished in The People v. Fire Assn., 92 N. Y. 316; and in Matter of 34th St. R. R. Co., 102 N. Y. 352.

Where the jury pass upon the question of damages, subject to the opinion of the court, upon the law of the case, the facts admitted by the pleadings are before the court, on appeal from the decision upon the reserved point.

APPEAL from the general term of the Supreme Court, in the sixth district, where a judgment entered in favor of the plaintiff, upon a point reserved on the trial, had been affirmed.

This was an action of trespass for the wrongful taking of a wagon belonging to the plaintiff, by virtue of a warrant issued by the defendants, as trustees of a school district in Tompkins county, for the collection of a district school tax assessed under the provisions of the act of 26th March, 1849. The complaint merely alleged the unlawful taking of the wagon, in June 1850.

The defendants, in their answer alleged, that they were the trustees of the school district No. 1, in Ulysses and Covert, in Tompkins county; that on the 3d May 1850, a tax was ordered by a special district school meeting, amounting to $380.10, which they, in pursuance of their duty as trustees, assessed upon the property and inhabitants of the said district, and issued their warrant for the collection thereof; that the plaintiff was assessed $25.23, and that, upon his refusal to pay the same to the collector, the latter levied upon the plaintiff's wagon.

The plaintiff, in his reply, insisted, that the tax was unauthorized, among other reasons, because $250 thereof was assessed under the provisions of

---
[1] Cited in Phoenix Ins. Co. v. Walsh, 29 Kan. 675.

the act of 29th March 1850, entitled "an act establishing free schools throughout the State," and that such act was not constitutionally enacted; and even if it ever did become a law, it became so in a manner unknown to the constitution, and contrary to its provisions, by virtue of a vote at large of the electors of the state, in November 1849, when no legislative body recognised by the constitution was in session.

The act in question, under which this tax was assessed, provided, in the tenth section, that "the electors shall determine by ballot, at the annual election to be held in November next, *whether this act shall, or shall not, become a law.*" The 11th and 12th sections prescribed the manner in which the question should be voted on by the people, at the election. And the 13th and 14th sections provided as follows:

Sec. 13. "The inspectors of election, in the several election districts, shall furnish a separate ballot-box, in which shall be placed all the ballots given for or against the new school law. The inspectors shall canvass the ballots and make return thereof in the same manner as votes given for the office of governor and lieutenant-governor are by law canvassed and returned.

Sec. 14. "In case a majority of all the votes in the State shall be cast against the new school law, this act shall be null and void; and in case a majority of all the votes in the state shall be cast for the new school law, *then this act shall become a law,* and shall take effect, &c."

On the trial of the cause, before SHANKLAND, J., the only question raised was, as to the legality of the tax. The learned judge submitted to the jury the question of fact as to the value of the property taken, and reserved the law of the case for the consideration of the court.

The jury assessed the value of the property at $50, and the court subsequently decided the reserved point in favor of the plaintiff, and entered judgment in his favor for the damages assessed; which having been affirmed at general term, the defendants took this appeal.

The cause was submitted on printed briefs, and the court, at first, doubted whether they could go behind the verdict, and consider the facts admitted by the pleadings. They, however, reconsidered this question, and unanimously agreed that the facts admitted were before them for consideration; whereupon, they ordered a reargument upon the main question in the cause, to wit, the legality of the tax.

Dana, for the appellants.

Beardsley, for the respondents.

RUGGLES, C. J. (after stating the provisions of the statute)—It will be observed, that although the act directs the inspectors of election in each town to canvass the ballots for and against the law, and to make return thereof, in the same manner as votes for governor, and lieutenant-governor are canvassed and returned, it makes no such provision for the county or state canvass; and it gives no direction to the county clerks, or to the county or state canvassers, in relation to their duty. It provides, that, if a majority of all the votes in the State shall be against the law, it shall be void, and, if in its favor, it shall be valid; but it fails entirely in pointing out the mode in which the general result of the popular vote is to be ascertained and determined. The general election law contains no provision applicable to this case. The state canvassers could not have been made answerable, civilly or criminally, for neglecting or refusing to canvass the votes and certify the result, because they were not required to do so by the statute itself, nor by the general election law; whatever they may have done in regard to it, was voluntary and unofficial.

Courts are, in general, bound to take judicial notice of public statutes; they have the means of knowing, from the statute books, and, therefore, are presumed to know what laws are in force. But that rule is inapplicable to a case like the present; it cannot be ascertained from the statute book, whether the act of 1849 was adopted or rejected by the popular vote. The certificate of the state canvassers would not be legal evidence on that question, because it is not made so by the act, and because they had no authority to determine or certify the result of the vote; the act of 1849 does not prescribe the evidence by which it is to be known whether the act took effect or not. It was imperfect in its provisions; and there seems to be no mode of ascertaining by legal evidence, the result of the vote upon it, except by the production and examination of the returns of the town inspectors of elections; these officers only were empowered to make the certificates.

In the present case, the result of the popular vote was neither admitted in the pleadings, nor established by evidence; and there was a total defect in the proof that the act had been adopted by the vote of the people. We should, therefore, be compelled to affirm the judgment of the Supreme Court, for the want of this proof, whether the law is valid or not.

But upon the argument in this court, the case was rested mainly on the objection to the validity of the statute, on the ground that it was never enacted, in form or spirit, according to the constitution, and, therefore, never took effect, although it may have had the vote of the people in its favor. This objection to the validity of the act has been several times under consideration in the supreme court. In one of the districts it was held to be constitutionl and valid: in three others, it was adjudged to be void. The immediate practical importance of the question has been much diminished by the enactment, in the usual form, of "an act to establish free schools throughout the State," passed April 25th, 1851. (Laws 1851, p. 292.) To this statute, the objections made to the act of 1849 do not apply. The question is, however, still highly important in regard to future legislation, and as such it has been carefully considered; and we are of opinion, that the act in question is invalid, because the provisions contained in it in relation to free schools were never constitutionally enacted.

The legislative power in this State is vested by the constitution in the Senate and Assembly (art. iii., sec. 1). The power of passing general statutes exists exclusively in the legislative bodies; in one instance only, it is limited or qualified: "No law for the contracting of a debt shall take effect, until it shall, at a general election, have been submitted to the people, and have received a majority of all the votes cast for and against it at such election" (art. vii., sec. 12). In this special and single case, the people, by the constitution, reserved legislative power to themselves; the Legislature pass the bill, in the usual form of enactment, but the statute has no force or authority, until it is sanctioned by a vote of the people; in substance and reality, the Legislature propose the law; the people pass or reject it by a general vote; this is legislation by the people.

The exercise of this power by the people in other cases is not, expressly and in terms, prohibited by the constitution; but it is forbidden by necessary and unavoidable implication. The Senate and Assembly are the only bodies of men clothed with the power of general legislation; they possess the entire power, with the exception of above stated; the people reserved no part of it to themselves, excepting in regard to laws creating public debt; and can, therefore, exercise it, in no other case.

The act of 1849 does not, on its face, purport to be a law as it came from the hands of the Legislature, for any other purpose than to submit to the people the question whether its provisions in relation to free schools "should or should not become a law" (sec. 10); and by sec. 14, the act was to become law only in case it should have a majority of the votes of the people in its favor. Without contradicting the express terms of the 10th and 14th sections, it cannot be said, that the propositions contained in it, in relation to free schools, were enacted as law by the Legislature; they were not law, or to become law, until they had received a majority of the votes of the people, at the general election, in their favor, nor unless they received such majority. It results, therefore, unavoidably, from the terms of the act itself, that it was the popular vote which made the law; the Legislature prepared the plan or project and submitted it to the people to be passed or rejected.

The Legislature had no power to make such submission, nor had the people the power to bind each other by acting upon it. They voluntarily surrendered that power, when they adopted the constitution. The government of this State is democratic; but it is a representative democracy, and in passing general laws, the people act only through their representatives in the Legislature.

In *Johnson* v. *Rich,* 9 Barb. 680, it was held by the Supreme Court in the 7th district, that the act in question was a valid law, on the ground, that it was a conditional statute, made to take effect upon the happening of a future contingent event, to wit, the vote of a majority of the people in its favor. It is not denied, that a valid statute may be passed, to take effect upon the happening of some future event, certain or uncertain; but such a statute, when it comes from the hands of the Legislature, must be law *in praesenti* to take effect *in futuro.* If the observations already made are correct, the act of 1849 was not such a statute. But if, by the terms of the act, it had been declared to be law from the time of its passage, to take effect in case it should receive a majority of votes in its favor, it would nevertheless have been invalid, because the result of the popular vote upon the expediency of the law is not such a future event, as the statute can be made to take effect upon, according to the meaning and intent of the constitution.

The event or change of circumstances on which a law may be made to take effect, must be such as, in the judgment of the Legislature, affects the question of the expediency of the law — an event on which the expediency of the law, in the judgment of the law-makers, depends. On this question of expediency, the Legislature must exercise its own judgment, definitively and finally. When a law is made, to take effect upon the happening of such an event, the Legislature, in effect, declared the law inexpedient, if the event should not happen; but expedient, if it should happen. They appeal to no other man or men to judge for them in relation to its present or future expediency; they exercise that power themselves, and thus perform the duty which the constitution imposes upon them.

But in the present case, no such event or change of circumstances affecting the expediency of the law was expected to happen. The wisdom or expediency of the free school act, abstractly considered, did not depend on the vote of the people; if it was unwise or inexpedient before that vote was taken, it was equally so afterwards.

The event on which the act was made to take effect was nothing else than the vote of the people on the identical question which the constitution makes it the duty of the Legislature itself to decide. The Legislature has no power to make a statute dependent on such a contingency, because it would be confiding to others that legislative discretion which they are bound to exercise themselves, and which they can not delegate or commit to any other man or men to be exercised. They have no more authority to refer such a question to the whole people than to an individual. The people are sovereign, but their sovereignty must be exercised in the mode which they have pointed out in the constitution. All legislative power is derived from the people; but when the people adopted the constitution, they surrendered the power of making laws to the Legislature, and imposed it upon that body as a duty; they did not reserve to themselves the power of ratifying or adopting laws proposed by the Legislature, except in the single case of contracting public debt. They probably foresaw the evil consequences likely to arise from such a reservation; these are well and forcibly expressed by Mr Justice Johnson, in his opinion in the case of *Johnson* v. *Rich*, 9 Barb. 686. " I regard it," said he, " as an unwise and unsound policy, calculated to lead to loose and improvident legislation, and to take away from the legislator all just sense of his high and enduring responsibility to his constituents and to posterity, by shifting that responsibility upon others. Experience has also shown, that laws passed in this manner are seldom permanent, but are changed the moment the instrument under which they are ratified has abated or reversed its current; of all evils which afflict a state, that of unstable and capricious legislation is among the greatest."

For further illustration, let us suppose that the 10th and subsequent sections of the act of 1849 had directed the attorney-general, or the archbishop of the Catholic church, or the common council of the city of New York to certify, on the next general election day, whether, in his or their opinion, that act ought to become a law; and had further provided, that the act should or should not take effect, according to such certificate; it cannot be pretended, that the statute would have become operative, upon the making of the certificate in its favor. The constitution does not authorize the power of legislation to be so delegated.[1] If the Legislature can not delegate to an individual the authority to determine, by the mere exercise of his judgment, whether a statute ought to take effect or become a law, it follows, as a necessary consequence, that they can not delegate it to the whole people; the constitution has no more authorized it in the latter case than in the former. The people have limited the exercise of their own power to the modes

---

[1] See People's Railroad *v.* Memphis Railroad, 10 Wall. 50; Chase *v.* Miller, 41 Penn. St. 422; Chief Justice Read truly says, in Locke's Appeal, 72 Pa. St. 504, that if the Legislature can delegate the law-making power to a majority of the voters, they can also confer it upon the minority.

pointed out in the constitution; and although they hold the ultimate sovereignty of the State, they are subject, like other sovereigns, to established fundamental law. The people may change or abrogate that law, but they are bound by it, until changed or abrogated. The judgment of the Supreme Court ought to be affirmed.

WILLARD, J.— The objection to the law is, that it was not enacted in the manner prescribed by the constitution, but was submitted by the Legislature to the electors, to determine by ballot, at the annual election in November 1849, whether the act should, or should not, become a law.

By the 11th section of the 7th article of the constitution, the Legislature is prohibited from creating any debts, except such as are specified in the 10th and 11th sections of the same article, unless in the manner therein mentioned; and no such law shall take effect, until it shall, at a general election, have been submitted to the people, and have received a majority of all the votes cast for and against it, at such election. The section also provides, that on the final passage of such bill, in either house of the legislature, the question shall be taken by ayes and noes, to be duly entered on the journals thereof, and shall be — " Shall this bill pass, and ought the same to receive the sanction of the people?" A subsequent clause in the same section provides, that no such law shall be submitted to be voted on, within three months after its final passage, nor at any general election, when any other law, or any bill, or any amendment of the constitution, shall be submitted to be voted for or against. This is the only case in which a law is *required* to be submitted to the people; and there is no other part of the constitution that recognises, even by implication, the right of the Legislature thus to delegate their trust. It is worthy also of remark, that in this case, the Legislature are required to assume all the responsibility which attaches upon the passage of a law; for they are required to respond in the affirmative, not only to the question whether the bill shall pass their respective houses, but also whether it ought to receive the sanction of the people. The members of the Legislature, therefore, can not, in making a submission to the people, under this section, elude the responsibility which properly belongs to their station.

I pass by, as inapplicable to this discussion, the 13th article of the constitution, which provides for the submission to the people, by the Legislature, of proposed amendments to that instrument. And I do not mean to lay much stress upon the implication arising from the express provision to submit a law creating a debt to the people, and the silence of the constitution in relation to submitting to the people other matters of legislation. The maxim *expressio univus est exclusio alterius,* is more applicable to deeds and contracts than to a constitution, and requires great caution in its application, in all cases.

The present question must be decided with reference to our existing constitution. By that instrument, the legislative power of the State is vested in a Senate and Assembly (const., art. iii., sec. 1). The enacting clause of all bills is required to be, " The people of the State of New York, *represented in Senate and Assembly,* do enact as follows." It is not the people *at the polls,* who enact a law, but the people represented in Senate and Assembly. Every bill, before it becomes a law, must receive the assent of a majority of all the members elected to each branch of the Legislature, and the question upon its final passage must be taken immediately upon its last reading, and the yeas and nays entered on the journal (id., sec. 14, 15). The assent of two-thirds of the members elected to each house is requisite to every bill appropriating the public moneys or property for local or private purposes (art. i, sec. 9). On the final passage in either house, of every act which imposes, continues or revives a tax, or creates a debt or charge, or makes, continues or revives any appropriation of public or trust money or property, or releases, discharges or commutes any claim or demand of the State, the question shall be taken by yeas and nays, which shall be duly entered on the journal, and three-fifths of all members elected to either house, shall, in all such cases be necessary to constitute a quorum therein (id., art. vii, sec. 14). These various provisions are designed to insure the full attendance of both houses, when a bill is passed, and to cause the members to feel their individual responsibility. It is worthy of note, that the act under consideration falls within the 14th section of article vii, just quoted, and required a quorum of three-fifths of all the members elected to both branches of the Legislature to be present at the time of the final vote on its passage.

All the foregoing provisions contemplate that a law receives its vitality from the Legislature. The representatives of the people are the law-makers, and they are responsible to their constituents for their conduct in that capacity. By following the directions of the constitution, each member has an opportunity of proposing amendments; the general policy of the law, as well as the fitness of its details, is open to discussion. The popular feeling is expressed through their representatives; and the latter are enlightened and influenced more or less by the discussions of the public press.

A complicated system can only be perfected by a body composed of a limited number, with power to make amendments and to enjoy the benefit of free discussion and consultation. This can never be accomplished with reference to such a system, when submitted to a vote of the people; they must take the system proposed or nothing; they can adopt no amendments, however obvious may be their necessity. With respect to the single case, where the constitution *requires* a submission of the law to the people, the inconvenience is less felt, because only a single proposition is submitted, with respect to which no other answer can be given than yes or no.

The law under consideration is in conflict with the constitution in various respects. Instead of becoming a law by the action of the organs appointed by the constitution for that purpose, it claims to become a law by the vote of the electors; and it claims that the popular vote may make it void and restore the former law. All the safeguards which the constitution has provided are broken down, and the members of the Legislature are allowed to evade the responsibility which belongs to their office.

It is not denied, that a law may be passed to take effect on the happening of a future event; there are numerous examples of this species of legislation, which are not obnoxious to any objection. The general appropriation bill each year affords numerous specimens: thus, an appropriation of $4000 is usually made for the apprehension of fugitives from justice; the money is not payable, until a fugitive has been apprehended, and the requisite evidence of the arrest, together with the amount of expenses, furnished to the proper officer. There is also a standing appropriation for the apprehension of criminals, which does not become payable, until the criminal has been arrested, and the proof thereof has been produced. But in all these cases, the law does not derive its power from the arrest of the fugitive or the apprehension of the criminal, but from the Legislature. Those cases are widely different from this; here, the law was not in force until the people had cast a majority of votes for it in a given way: in the other case, the law is in force, whether there be a fugitive or a criminal or not. The future event gives no additional efficacy to the law, but furnishes the occasion for the exercise of its power.

The fundamental error of the court in *Johnson* v. *Rich* (9 Barb. 680) consists in confounding laws which become operative at a future day, with laws which do not become operative until approved by a popular vote. In the first case, the law is complete, when it has passed through the forms prescribed by the constitution, though its influence may not be felt until a subject matter has arisen upon which it can act. A law punishing murder with death, is inoperative, until a murder has been committed; it is not, however, the murder which imparts efficacy to the law; the latter was complete when first enacted; and the murder merely affords the opportunity for awakening its energies; had no murder ever been committed, it would still be a law, threatening vengeance on the crime whenever it should be perpetrated.

It was far otherwise with the free school law; had a majority of the electors failed to vote for it, no one pretends that it would have been a law. The voting by the electors does not furnish the occasion for the exercise of the power of the law, but was designed to give vitality to what was before lifeless. In short, the law was a mere proposition submitted to the people, to be adopted or rejected as they pleased. If this mode of legislation is permitted and becomes general, it will soon bring to a close the whole system of representative government which has been so justly our pride. The Legislature will become an irresponsible cabal, too timid to assume the responsibility of law-givers, and with just wisdom enough to devise subtle schemes of imposture to mislead the people. All the checks against improvident legislation will be swept away, and the character of the constitution will be radically changed.

Without enlarging upon this subject, or reviewing the decisions in other states, adverse to this mode of legislation, I think, it is in conflict with our constitution.

Judgment affirmed.

LEGISLATION FROM 1853 TO 1868

The following is some interesting legislation during the period 1853–68 in regard to free schools and the establishment of "tuition and rates."

Act of April 11, 1853; Chapter 155

Establishes a board of education in the village of Fort Covington and gives the board of education the power to regulate and to establish the terms of tuition fees for such resident and nonresident pupils as are enrolled in the institution.

Act of June 4, 1853; Chapter 305

In making possible the consolidation of the several school districts lying within the village of Polasky gives the board of education power to regulate and establish the terms of tuition fees and the rates of charges for instruction for all pupils entering the school.

Act of June 18, 1853; Chapter 417

Reference to an act providing free schools for the town of Bushwick as passed October 16, 1847.

Act of June 18, 1853; Chapter 433

An act providing for the establishment of union free schools.

" Whenever fifteen persons entitled to vote at any meeting of the inhabitants of any school district in the State shall sign or call for any such meeting to be held for the purpose of determining by a vote of such district whether an union free school shall be established therein in conformity with the provision of this act."

Act of July 18, 1853; Chapter 533

Provides for the establishment of free schools within the village of Jamaica in the county of Queens.

Act of April 15, 1854; Chapter 314

This act provides the village of Sing Sing shall be formed a permanent school district.

" The village of Sing Sing shall form a permanent school district; and the electors residing within the bounds of said village, at their annual charter election or at any time thereafter, upon the usual notice being given, may determine by a majority of votes, by ballot, upon the expediency of establishing free schools in said village. The trustees of the village shall conduct the election, and the ballots having written or printed on them the words " For free schools," or "Against free schools," shall be duly canvassed, and the result declared by them in the usual manner."

The Act of April 7, 1856; Chapter 129

In relation to the school district known as the Lyon Union School of the town of Lyon, Wayne county, provides that a board of education shall have power and it shall be their duties to fix the rate of tuition in the said school subject to the limitations and restrictions hereinafter contained and to designate some person or persons to whom the same may be paid and to exempt from payment of the whole or part of the tuition fee such persons as they may deem entitled to such exemption.

Act of April 7, 1857; Chapter 305

Provides for the town of Mentz in the county of Cayuga a free school district to be known as the Port Byron free school district, but in the act among the duties of the board of education is to establish and regulate the tuition fee for those scholars residing in the said district and attending the academy in that district.

Act of April 7, 1857; Chapter 296

In relation to the consolidated school district no. 1 in the town of Palmyra, Wayne county, provides that the tuition fee in the several departments or grades in the said school shall not for the pupils whose parents or guardians reside within the territory of said district exceed per term or quarter for each pupil as follows: that is to say, in the first grade such tuition shall not exceed $1.00; the second grade, $1.25; in the third grade, $2; in the fourth grade, $2.50.

Act of April 16, 1868; Chapter 222

Empowers the board of education of the union school in the school district no. 10 in the town of Warsaw to establish rates of tuition in the academical department of said union school and to collect.

Act of April 2, 1855; Chapter 140

Provides free schools for district no. 13 in the town of Taghanic in the county of Columbia.

Act of April 10, 1857; Chapter 333

Provides for free schools in the town of Lansingburgh in the county of Rensselaer.

Act of April 14, 1858; Chapter 192

Provides that the Clyde High School in the town of Clyde shall be free to all children between the ages of four and twenty-one years residing in that district.

Act of April 4, 1859; Chapter 113

An act in relation to the common schools in the village of Elmira, provides that all schools organized under this act shall be free to all pupils between the ages of four and twenty-one years who are actually resident of the said union school district.

Act of April 14, 1859; Chapter 303

Provides that the public schools in district no. 4 in the town of Orangetown in the county of Rockland shall be free to all children residing in that district.

Act of April 9, 1860; Chapter 211

Provides that the school in district no. 1 in the town of Salina, county of Onondaga, shall be free to all persons between the ages of four and twenty-one years residing in that district.

Act of February 27, 1865; Chapter 54

An act which states that the trustees of the school district no. 8 of the town of Phelps in Ontario county shall not hereafter collect or receive any fees or compensation for instruction in the schools under the charge of such trustees of said district of pupils whose parents or guardians reside within the territory embraced in said district.

Act of March 31, 1847; Chapter 51

In relation to the common schools of the village of Lockport, places among the duties of the board of education to fix the rate of tuition fee in said union schools and to exempt those who are unable to pay.

In March 18, 1850, chapter 77, another act relating to the common schools of the village of Lockport, was passed in which it was stated that the acts of March 31, 1847 were not altered or effected by the free school act of March 26, 1849 and authorized the board of education to increase the rate of tuition fees of the union schools under their charge. It also provides that the board shall not raise by tax any money for the teachers in the union school and likewise adds that after the first day of April, 1850, that so long as the common schools of this State shall be free, the said board of education shall cause each of the secondary schools under its charge to be taught by a competent male teacher and said secondary schools shall be free, but for the time prior to said first day of April next, said board may collect tuition fees for instruction therein.

Act of March 19, 1861; Chapter 60

States that the district no. 16 in the town of Ithaca in the county of Tompkins shall form a permanent school district and the said district shall be free to all children residing therein between the ages of four and twenty-one years and no rate bill shall hereafter be imposed.

Act of April 13, 1861; Chapter 212

States that the school district no. 18 in the town of Fishkill, in Dutchess county, shall be free to all children between the ages of five and twenty-one years residing in the district.

Act of April 19, 1861; Chapter 322

In the act relating to the schools of the village of Binghamton it provides that the school organized under this act shall be free to all pupils between the ages of four and twenty-one years.

Act of April 10, 1863; Chapter 116

Establishes a free school in district no. 1 in the town of Hempstead.

Act of May 2, 1864; Chapter 555, Title 9

An act to revise and consolidate the general acts relating to public instruction.

UNION FREE SCHOOLS

"Whenever fifteen persons entitled to vote at any meeting of the inhabitants of any school district in the State shall sign and call for a meeting to be held for the purpose of determining whether a union free school shall be established therein in conformity with the provisions of this title, it shall be the duty of the trustees of such district within ten days after such call shall have been presented to them to give public notice that a meeting of the inhabitants of such district entitled to vote thereat will be held for such purpose as aforesaid at the school house or other more suitable place.

"The establishment of the union free schools shall be determined by a two-thirds vote of those present and entitled to vote."

Act of April 29, 1863; Chapter 252

Provides free schools for the Gowanda union schools in Gowanda, this State.

Act of May 5, 1863; Chapter 459

Consolidates the school districts no. 1 and 9 of the town of Hancock in the county of Delaware and provides that the schools organized under this act shall be free to all pupils who are actually residents of the said district.

Act of April 15, 1864; Chapter 194

Provides for a free school in the town of Hoosick.

Act of April 23, 1864; Chapter 327

Provides that the several proceedings taken to organize the union free school of the town of Alika formed by consolidating districts nos. 1, 2, 3, 6, 10 and 16 in said town are hereby confirmed and legalized and the tax levied by the board of trustees of said union free school to purchase a site for the schoolhouse is declared valid.

Act of April 23, 1864; Chapter 309

Provides that the schools within the corporated limits of Owego village shall be free to all pupils between the age of five and twenty-one residing in its district and no rate bill shall hereafter be imposed therein.

Act of February 28, 1865; Chapter 63

Provides that the common school in school district no. 4 in the town of Fishkill, Dutchess county, shall be free to all children between the ages of five and twenty-one years residing in said district and rate bills therein are hereby abolished.

Act of March 7, 1865; Chapter 88.

Provides that every district or common school located in the village of Newburgh including the Newburgh High School and every school which may hereafter be located in said village under this act shall be free to all children between the ages of five and twenty-one residing in said village.

Act of April 11, 1865; Chapter 386

Confirms the proceedings under which a union free school was formed by the consolidation of school districts no. 8 of the town of Vernon, Oneida county, no. 22 of the town of Lenox, Madison county and the portion of the public square of Oneida-Castleton together with the academy building thereon to the board of education of said union free school for their sole use.

Act of April 17, 1865; Chapter 458

Provides that all that town of Schroeppel not included in the village of Phoenix and all that shall hereafter be added thereto and all the territory now included in what is known as school district no. 12 shall hereafter form but one school district to be known as the Phoenix free school district.

Act of May 1, 1865; Chapter 631

Establishes a union free school in district no. 2 in the town of Poughkeepsie.

Act of February 19, 1866; Chapter 57

Provides that the common schools in the village of Elmira shall be free to all pupils between the age of five and twenty-one.

Act of March 15, 1866; Chapter 151

Provides that the school district no. 16 with the town of Pittstown in the county of Rensselaer shall hereafter be a free school district.

Act of March 22, 1866; Chapter 193

Provides that the towns of Little Falls and Monheim, Herkimer county, is hereby constituted a free school district.

Act of April 7, 1866; Chapter 444

Creates a board of public instruction for the city of Albany and provides that the tuition of the pupils in the several schools under the charge of the board shall be free to all persons who are resident of the said city and entitled to attend same.

Act of May 8, 1867; Chapter 810

Provides for the consolidation of school districts nos. 1, 2 and 5 of the town of Plattsburg into one single school district free only to those members residing in the district.

MESSAGES FROM THE GOVERNORS.

The following extracts from the messages of the several Governors, during the period 1855–68, on education are of particular interest.

On June 2, 1855, Governor Clark presented the following discussion of the public school question:

Among the subjects which will require your attention there is none of more importance than the system of public education of the State. The magnitude of this interest has always been felt and appreciated by the people, and the State has shown from the earliest period of its existence, an earnest desire to provide the means for the adequate instruction of all the children within its limits. For a long time the system pursued was based on the assumption that education was mainly a matter of personal interest, and that the duty of providing it devolved exclusively upon parents; the instruction of the children of those whose poverty would not permit them to incur the expense of it themselves being made to depend upon the public charity. The inefficiency of this policy, its failure to accomplish the object aimed at, and especially its direct tendency to create distinctions hostile to the spirit and character of our institutions, led to its abandonment; and, a system, based upon the principle that the State is even more deeply and permanelty interested in the education of its children than their parents, and that the expense of providing it should be borne by the aggregate of the property within its limits, was adopted in its stead. Under the existing law, therefore, the State assumes the charge of public education,— committing its direction to local officers and paying the cost of it out of its own treasury. The system is comparatively new, and some practical defects are as yet exhibited in its workings; but they are such as spring chiefly from the failure to give full and complete development to its fundamental principles, and may easily be remedied by judicious legislation. The system itself is believed to be thoroughly rooted in the confidence and favor of the people.

The whole amount of money apportioned by the Superintendent of Public Instruction is $1,055,000, of which $800,000 was raised by a general tax, and $255,000 from the income of the common school and U. S. deposit funds. The whole amount expended for public schools is $2,666,609.36, of which $1,929,884.49 was applied to the payment of teachers, and $47,657.06 for the district libraries. The whole number of district schools reported for the year is 11,798; and the whole number of children in the State of the age required to draw public money 1,186,709. There have been 877,201 in attendance upon the district schools; in academies under the supervision of the Regents of the University, 37,406; 34,279 in unincorporated private schools, and 4,568 in colored schools. The average number of months during which the schools have been kept in the several districts is eight. The number of volumes in the district libraries is 1,571,270.

These results exhibit a gratifying increase in the number attending the district schools over the previous year. But it will still be seen that of the whole number of children of suitable age in the State there are 309,508, or nearly one-fourth of the whole number, who do not attend the district schools, and 233,255, or about twenty per cent, of the whole number, who do not attend any school. In view of the provision which has been made for the express purpose of securing the education of all, this proportion is much too large; and indicates some defect in the system pursued, because it does not completely attain the object at which it aims. That it does not, may be partly due to the mode of distributing the public funds. By the existing law, two-thirds of the public funds are distributed among the various districts of the State, in proportion to the whole number of children of a specified age within their limits, whether they attend the schools or not. If the apportionment of the public money were made to depend upon the number of attending school and upon the regularity of their attendance, it would become the interest of the citizens generally to promote the regular attendance of all the children within their limits. An amendment of the law which should give it this direction would, I believe, tend to secure, more fully, the desired result. The law is defective, also, in that it fails to carry out fully and completely the principle on which it is based. Education in the district schools is not yet entirely free. If the cost of the schools in any district exceeds the amount of money received from the State, the deficiency is made up by a rate bill, assessed upon those who send their children to school; and those who are unable to pay this assessment are received at the public expense, and thus become the recipients of public charity. The worst element of the old system is thus preserved, and the fundamental principle of the new law fails of its application in its most essential point. Education is still regarded as a matter of charity and not of right; and so long as this continues to be the case, in any degree or to any extent, it will detract from the full measure of usefulness which the system is designed to secure. This evil in the system can be remedied, only by making the schools entirely free.

The attention of the Legislature should also be directed to measures for improving the character of the schools, for increasing their efficiency, and for elevating and extending the instruction which they impart. In a State where every citizen should take an active interest in the administration of public affairs, and may be called upon to perform the highest duties of public life, it is important that popular education be carried to the highest point which the means of the State will allow. It has been objected to the system of free schools, that people do not prize that which costs them nothing, and that relieving individuals from the expense of educating their children will diminish their interest in the subject and lead them to relax the vigilance which is essential to the highest excellence in the public schools. There is undoubtedly some force in the suggestion, though experience shows that it is much less than is sometimes supposed. But whether it be more or less, it is entitled to consideration, and provision should be made for obviating the objection in any system of education which the State may adopt.

The connection of our common schools with the higher institutions of learning, with academies and colleges, making them all, in fact, parts of one great system, could not fail to contribute essentially to their elevation, and bring the means of a thorough and complete education within the reach of all. In the city of New York, where the free school system of the State has been, perhaps, more completely developed than in any other section, the benefits of substantially such a union are very conspicuous. A free academy has been added to the system, in which a large and competent corps of professors and tutors has been provided, a plan of study extending over five years and embracing all the branches of study pursued in the best colleges of the country has been adopted, scientific apparatus, libraries, and all the aids requisite for study have been furnished, and the general discipline and course of instruction have been made in all respects of the highest and most efficient character. Pupils who shall have attended any of the district schools for eighteen months, maintained throughout a good standing and character, and passed a satisfactory examination in certain specified studies, are admitted to the academy and entitled to the full enjoyment of its advantages, free of all expense. The academy has been in operation only three or four years, and the average number of its students is over four hundred. The attendance shows that its benefits are fully appreciated. But besides the thorough and most useful instruction conferred upon so large a number of the children and youth of the community, its most marked advantages are seen in the influence which it exerts upon the common schools, stimulating their teachers, trustees, inspectors and pupils alike to a generous rivalry, increasing their vigilance and their industry, and rendering them zealous and emulous in sending the best pupils to the academy, whose facilities for education are the prize for which all may alike contend. While I am aware that large cities afford facilities for such a system, which cannot be fully enjoyed in the rural districts, I think that something may be done throughout the State in this direction. A voluntary beginning, indeed, has already been made in some sections, by the establishment of union schools; and their success shows that the system is not wholly impracticable. I think that the time has come when higher purposes and broader views may be entertained in rgard to our system of State education; and that our academies may be brought into a more direct and immediate connection with the general plan, and thrown more widely and more freely open to the advantages they are intended to confer. The character of their instruction should be elevated, and its range extended; and they should be more completely furnished with apparatus and the means of imparting knowledge in those sciences which are of the most service in practical life. By making free admission to the thorough and complete education they would then afford, the reward of excellence in our district schools, a stimulus would be furnished which could not fail to be felt beneficially upon their discipline and character. It would be highly desirable to bring the colleges of the State into harmonious connection with such a plan, so that they might become more directly recognized as members of our general system of State education and as essential to its completeness and perfection.

In the following year, 1856, Governor Clark again calls attention to the policy of free schools as follows:

I would also suggest the expediency of making the schools of the State entirely free. Twice when this question has been submitted to the people, their verdict has been rendered by a large majority in favor of it.

There is evidently a growing repugnance to the rate bill system, and it is now time that the subject of its final abolition was fully discussed. The imposition of an additional tax for the maintenance of public schools for a given time, not less than eight months, to be assessed upon the several towns in conformity with the recommendation of their respective boards of education, would supply all the means requisite for schools during each year. If, instead of school districts as now organized, it should be left discretionary with the educational officers of each town to establish schools whenever necessary in different localities in the town, it would be far easier to disburse the school moneys equitably than under the present arrangement, where districts are formed of different sizes, and with no general regulation as to population or available resources. This policy has been adopted in several States with decided advantage. The interminable controversies between school districts, the adjudication of which occupies so large a proportion of the attention of the State Superintendent, and which seem every year to become more numerous, more bitter, and more mischievous, would be obviated. A more equitable division of the school moneys, greater economy in their application, and the convenience of the public, would be effected.

The amount of school moneys apportioned by the Superintendent of Publice Instruction for the current year is $1,110,000, of which $800,000 are derived from a general tax, $165,000 from the income of the United States deposit fund, and $145,000 from the income of the common school fund.

The amount reported as having been expended for the payment of teachers wages for the year 1854 was $2,301,411.25; for libraries, $55,216.31; for school house sites, school houses and fuel, $863,990.53; total, $3,220,618.08. The amount of money raised by tax in those districts where free schools are maintained, and the amounts raised by rate bill, are not separately stated, but it is certain that the former considerably preponderate. . . .

Defects in our public school policy, and the legislation necessary to remedy them, will demand your earnest attention. A modification, that shall secure greater economy of the public treasury and an extension of the system to all the children of the State, seems to me obviously necessary. Particular attention should be directed to the academies now deriving a revenue from the literature fund. I would suggest that a board of commissioners be appointed to visit them, examine their management, ascertain to what extent they have complied with the regulations prescribed by the Board of Regents, and report the results of the investigation to the Legislature at its next session.

I cannot regard our school system as complete until it shall extend free academical instruction to every child residing in the State desirous of its benefits.

Governor Morgan, in 1861, reported:

Our educational system is justly the pride of the commonwealth. Granting to all a thorough course of common school education, New York fully recognizes the duty of the State to educate her children. Depending for their stability and perpetuity, as due our institutions, and the safety of life and property, upon the intelligence and moral worth of the people, it becomes a matter of the first importance to retain, unimpaired, so far as may be, the plan which thus far has been productive of such inestimable benefits. The provisions of our laws as they affect the school system are generally approved, and should not be lightly disturbed. It is bad to commit errors in financial and political policy, but infinitely worse to do so in matters pertaining to the education and future happiness of our children. Although heavily taxed, our people show no disposition to avoid assessments for the support of schools; and it may be remarked as an evidence of their liberality, that more than thirteen hundred thousand dollars are paid out of the public treasury annually for this purpose. The Superintendent of Public Instruction, who, in the discharge of his duty has visited nearly every portion of the State, will submit to you in his annual report many interesting facts and conclusions respecting the workings of the system; and that in the improved style of school houses, the qualifications of teachers, and the general improvement in other respects, we have proof that these educational advantages are appreciated by the people.

The academies of the State, under the supervision of the Regents of the University, are in a condition of advancing prosperity. Their reports for the last year show an increase in the number of pupils over those of the preceding year, and an advance in the course of instructions. They furnish an education well adapted to the practical purposes of life, and provide, especially for the rural districts, a large portion of the teachers of the common schools.

In his message in 1866, Governor Fenton reported:

Intelligent and philanthropic citizens evince a deep interest in the promotion of regular and general attendance at our schools. The law directing the apportionment of part of the school money on the basis of average daily attendance, seems to be operating favorably, by inducing a more general attendance; but the great object of public concern is the education of all the children, and the question may well be raised, whether some additional incentive is not required to secure this result. For valuable views bearing upon this point, I refer you to the report of the Superintendent. He also recommends that free tuition in our common schools shall be furnished to the destitute children of those who have died in the military or naval service of the United State. It is presumed that such a special recognition of

MYRON H. CLARK
Governor of New York, 1855-57

REUBEN E. FENTON
Governor of New York, 1865–68

the patriotic services and sacrifices of the heroes who have died, could not fail to meet the approval of an intelligent and grateful people. More than ninety per cent of all the children and youth who receive scholastic instruction, go only to the common schools. In view of this fact, and of the intimate dependence of good government upon the education of the people, these institutions are of paramount public importance, and provision for their liberal support and prosperity cannot be safely neglected.

In his annual message, January 2, 1867, Governor Fenton, in relation to education in New York State, said:

At an early day, general attention was directed to the subject of education, which was deemed essential to the security, progress and power of the people. Provision was made for the incorporation and endowment of colleges and academies. It soon became evident, however, that institutions of learning thus organized could not meet the demand of a people whose government was founded upon the theory of the general education of the masses. A more comprehensive system was needed, embracing in its operation the entire State, and making available to every family, instruction in the primary branches of education. It does not appear that the views of Governor Clinton upon this subject, communicated to the Legislature as early as 1795, resulted in the adoption of a general common school system until 1814. Since that period the progress of the system has been marked, gaining steadily in character, and extending yearly its beneficent influence. More than ninety per cent of all the children and youth who receive scholastic instruction in our various institutions of learning attend only the common schools.

The following brief summary is gathered from the records of the Department of Public Instruction, and from the report of the efficient Superintendent:

For support of common schools

Public school moneys, including ¾ mill tax	$1,406,080 43
Voluntary taxation in the school districts	4,550,111 86
Rate bill	708,003 03
Other sources	714,684 90

Expended during the year

Teachers' wages	$4,586,211 09
Libraries	27,560 06
School apparatus	186,508 90
Building and repairs of schoolhouses	969,618 12
Miscellaneous	858,246 12
Balance reported on hand	750,735 93
Total number of children and youth between the ages of five and twenty-one years	1,354,967
Number of children between the ages of six and seventeen years	931,404
Number of children of school age who have attended the public schools during some portion of the year	919,033

Teachers employed in public schools for twenty-eight weeks, or more, during the year	15,664
Whole number of male teachers	5,031
Whole number of female teachers	21,450
Total number of school districts	11,732
Total number of school houses	11,552
Aggregate number of weeks' school	369,571
Number of volumes in district libraries	1,183,017
Aggregate number of pupils attending the Normal schools at some time during the year	451
Number of teachers instructed in teachers' institute	8,553
Number of teachers in teachers' classes in academies	1,469
Amount of money to be apportioned for the support of common schools, for the current fiscal year	$1,468,422 22

The report shows that the number of children and youth in daily attendance at the public schools is 30.02 per cent of the entire number between five and twenty-one years of age, or 43.67 per cent of the entire number of children between six and seventeen years of age.

Although this average attendance upon the public schools is the largest ever reported, it is, nevertheless, believed that, by judicious legislation it may be essentially increased. If, to the number who have attended school during some portion of the year, we add those instructed for a longer or shorter time in the private schools, including colleges and academies, still the proportion neglecting these opportunities for education cannot fail to excite serious attention. With the conviction that universal education is a necessity of the State, I recommend that all impediments in the way of its free acquisition be removed, whether in the form of rate bills, poor and incommodious schoolhouses, or the want of teachers specially trained to their vocation.

In his annual message, January 7, 1868, Governor Fenton said:

There are probably few among us who, even amid the pressure of the active affairs of life, fail to recognize the importance and magnitude of our system of popular education. Our people have acted upon the theory that the extension to every class and condition of society, of the means of early education, and facilities for the acquisition of knowledge in after life, contributes to the prevention of crime, the preservation of social order, and the security and stability of the government, and the thrift and prosperity of all who are engaged in the various departments of industry. Our legislation has been based on this liberal and enlightened policy, and the practical result is that our schools are open to the children, even of the poor and the homeless. We have been steadily extending facilities for instruction in the higher departments. The State has generously and wisely given aid, from time to time, to institutions struggling to rise under the disadvantage of a feeble endowment or a limited patronage. The revenue of a permanent fund, wisely established for the development of the sciences, has been liberally dispensed, and there is reason to believe that our system of education, as a whole, is meeting the just expectations of the people.

The following summary is gathered from the records of the department of Public Instruction, and from the interesting report of the Superintendent:

For the support of common schools

Public moneys, including three-quarters mill tax	$1,403,163 84
Voluntary loan taxation in the school districts	5,591,871 06
Rate bills	743,306 72
Other sources	1,134,890 74

Expenses during the year

Teachers' wages	$4,881,447 53
Libraries	24,414 86
School apparatus	211,637 82
Building and repairs of schoolhouses	1,712,523 36
Miscellaneous and incidental	850,884 73
Balance reported on hand	1,192,324 06
Total number of children and youth between the ages of five and twenty-one years	1,372,853
Number of children between the ages of six and seventeen years	943,699
Number of children of school age who have attended the public schools during some portion of the year	947,162
Teachers employed in public schools for twenty-eight weeks or more	15,606
Number of male teachers	5,263
" female teachers	21,218
" school districts	11,724
" school houses	11,580
Aggregate number of weeks	357,137
Volumes in district libraries	1,113,147
Number of pupil teachers attending the three Normal schools	689
Teachers instructed in teachers' institutes	9,682
Teachers in teachers' classes in academies	1,373
Amount of money to be apportioned for the support of common schools for the current fiscal year	$2,400,134 65

The report further shows that the number of children and youth in daily attendance at the public schools is 30.62 per cent of the entire number between five and twenty-one years of age, or 44.54 per cent of the whole number of children between six and seventeen.

In my last annual message, I expressed the opinion that the propositions for the location of normal and training schools in the villages of Fredonia, Brockport, Cortland, and Potsdam, would be carried into full effect at the earliest practicable period. That opinion has been confirmed. The erection of the buildings has been vigorously prosecuted, and when they are finished and furnished, with the grounds upon which they are located, the value cannot be less than four hundred thousand dollars. The schools at Fredonia and Cortland will be open for the reception of pupils during the ensuing summer or early autumn. The main part of the building at Brockport is completed and occupied for a normal school, which is in successful operation. The Oswego and Albany normal schools are reported to be in a prosperous condition, each numbering as many pupil teachers as can well be provided with instruction.

The establishment of two additional normal schools has been authorized by law, one at Buffalo and one at Geneseo. The liberality and public spirit of the people of these places will not fail to consummate an enterprise of so much local and general importance. I am informed by the Superintendent of Public Instruction, that the law of last winter, which abolished rate bills and charges, though it has been in operation only since the first of October last, is producing a very large increase of the aggregate number of pupils at the schools, and greater regularity in their attendance. It is believed that the additional tax imposed by that law, will equal the amount of money which has heretofore been raised by rate bills. It has the effect, as will be seen, to decrease local or school district taxation, by so much as it increased the general State tax. It simply transfers the burden from the few to the many; from those with limited means, but possibly with large families, to the aggregate property of the commonwealth. An examination of the assessed valuation of taxable property in the several school districts of the State, will show that even for the support of inferior schools the percentage of taxation in certain districts often largely exceeds that in neighboring districts in which there are superior schools, and the same or a greater number of children of school age. Conceding that the education of the people is a matter of common concern, to which each one should contribute according to his pecuniary ability, the justice of reducing this local district taxation by the general state tax for the support of schools, is apparent. Even should the support of free schools require an increase of this tax, I should still concur in the opinion "that in promoting the great interest of moral and intellectual cultivation, there can be no prodigality in the application of the public treasury."

In all our cities, and in most of our large villages, the education of youth is provided for by special acts, giving enlarged powers to the local authorities, or creating boards with exclusive control of the schools. They are generally well managed, and it is believed that our schools in the city, as well as in the country, have advanced the character of our population above that of any other people. If it is true, however, as asserted, that poverty, crime and ignorance, still largely prevail in our most populous cities, the result, in part at least, of neglect to educate all the young, should we not extend and improve our schools and bring every child within their influence? In some of our cities, and especially in New York and Brooklyn, the school accommodations are insufficient, and thousands of children are unable to gain admission. The provision for higher classes and more advanced pupils, is not deficient, but the rooms for primary scholars are overcrowded. It is probable that the city authorities have power to correct this defect, but if otherwise, I feel confident that the Legislature will apply the appropriate remedy.

Chapter 12
ABOLISHING THE RATE BILL

One begins to see signs in the annual report of the school commissioners, from 1864 on, that the rate bill was doomed. Although there were considerable differences in opinion, the majority seemed to think that the rate bill was objectionable, but it is probable that in reporting upon this matter the various commissioners reflected the sentiments of their localities quite as much as they expressed their own judgment.

Commissioner W. D. Renwick of Allegany county said:

These have a bad effect both on attendance and the quality of the schools. Whole families of children are sometimes taken out of school to save a rate bill. Trustees in some instances endeavor by employing cheap teachers to make the public money cover the expenses of the school for six months, and secure as the reward of their economy sickly and inefficient schools.

Commissioner A. McIntosh, jr. of Cayuga county, in speaking of the rate bills, said:

These have the effect of reducing the attendance in many districts. This is shown by the fact that many children are withdrawn from school as soon as it is ascertained that the public money is expended and also from the fact that in many cases school is continued just long enough to comply with the statutes.

Commissioner B. Bisbee of Chenango county said:

As far as my observation has extended rate bills have had a tendency to decrease the attendance and this is most noticeable in those rural districts where the children can least afford to lose a part of the little time they give to securing an education.

Commissioner G. W. Lewis of Franklin county said:

There are evils, I think, arising from the present system of rate bills that prove a detriment to the interest of many of the schools. In many cases it causes irregularity of attendance. The inhabitants of many of the districts calculate to support a school only as far as the public money will defray the expenses. Trustees are often instructed that in hiring teachers they must keep within the limits of the public money. Only thirty-two districts have subjected themselves to a rate bill during the past year.

Commissioner L. F. Burr of Fulton county said:

Rate bills are much dreaded in many districts by those who patronize our schools, especially in country districts where schools are sometimes feeble. Trustees often calculate so closely that they hire cheap teachers, third grade, to save raising any money by rate bill.

Commissioner George C. Mott of Greene county said:

Rate bills do in some districts make a material difference in the attendance. There would be far better attendance if the schools and text books were perfectly free to all.

Commissioner George A. Ranney of Jefferson county said:

Rate bills have been collected in all but seventeen districts amounting in the aggregate to $3866.96. I am of the opinion, formed by observation and inquiry that rate bills do not materially affect the attendance in school districts, but in villages they are often an excuse for patronizing private schools.

Commissioner Elbridge R. Adams of Lewis county said:

Often parents in appreciating the benefits of education consider it better to take their little ones from the hand of the teacher than to be subjected to the expense of helping carry on the school by rate bill. Is it not reasonable to suppose that the free school system would obviate this difficulty as it has done in other states of our union.

Commissioner Joseph A. Tozier of Monroe county said:

I am of the opinion that a better attendance would be had were a free school system adopted. Several instances have come under my observation here in which injury was done to schools through fear of a large rate bill.

Commissioner G. W. Sutphen of Ontario county said:

The amount raised by rate bills during the year was $4394, being an average of $38 per district. The system of paying a balance of teachers' wages by means of rate bills I believe to be unfavorable to attendance.

Commissioner John J. Barr of Orange county said:

I do not think rate bills have any effect on the attendance. In many districts rate bills and tax lists are unknown. The trustees keep up their school for six months in order to draw the public money, and the public money generally pays the teacher, or, in other words, they bargain with the teacher to teach the school for six months for the public money.

Commissioner Lemuel P. Storms of Oswego county said:

The amount raised in the district by rate bills during the past year is $4023.79, being nearly one-half as much as the public money apportioned to the district. There are fourteen school districts that raise nothing by rate bills.

Commissioner W. Townsend 2d of Putnam county said:

From information derived from conversation with school trustees and patrons, I am inclined to believe that the rate bill system is more acceptable to the people than the free school system, and that the attendance is not less than it would be under any other arrangement not yet proposed.

Commissioner Charles W. Brown of Queens county said:

Wherever the free school system has been adopted a sufficient length of time, there may be found good school houses with modern improvements upon pleasant sites and with large and ample playgrounds. Upon the other hand, there is not a good building nor a playground, except the street, in a single district which has the rate bill system. I did not intend to say any more in regard to rate bills, but they seem to be the cause of all our drawbacks.

Commissioner William D. Wood of Queens county said:

The rate bill seems to be unfavorable to attendance. It has a tendency to keep a lower grade of teachers in some of the schools. Trustees in many instances engage teachers of limited qualifications because their services can be obtained for a compensation which the public money will nearly cancel.

Commissioner Barney Whitney of St Lawrence county said:

In those localities where there are the most enlightened and liberal public sentiments rate bills affect the interest of the schools but little, but in the majority of districts in which schools are *kept,* rarely *taught,* they offer a premium for cheap teachers, and greatly diminished attendance.

Commissioner N. T. Van Atta of Schenectady county said:

Rate bills with the great majority of people are not considered burdensome but are paid cheerfully. I believe that they exert a salutary influence, stimulating the people to secure the services of able teachers, since they expect to pay for them. Rate bills are the true index of a school, and the interest taken by the inhabitants therein. Wherever large rate bills have been collected I have found our best teachers engaged.

Commissioner Bartholomew Becker of Schoharie county said:

The people are in favor of the present rate bill system and pleased with the present school system.

Commission I. Runyan of Seneca county said:

The present system of rate bills in accordance with my judgment and observation is not prejudicial to a general attendance in our schools in rural districts, but in our large villages the cause of popular education would be best promoted by free schools.

Commissioner E. H. Brown of Steuben county said:

I think the public sentiment generally is in favor of the rate bills, yet in many small schools they tend to lessen the already small attendance.

Commissioner Albert T. Parhill of Steuben county said:

There is very little complaint in reference to rate bills, and but few scholars have been kept out of school on that account. In a few instances districts have not exceeded in expenditure the money apportioned.

In the report of the Superintendent of Public Instruction for 1867, we find the rate bill discussed by the commissioners of the following districts.

Broome County — First District

Upon this point my views have changed very much since writing my last report; for, in my humble opinion, there is no greater curse to our school system than these rate bills. Let trustees have the means at their disposal (without collecting a heavy rate bill from the patrons of the school), and the order of things will be changed. Instead of cheap, ordinary teachers, the call will be for good, well qualified ones. And whoever is instrumental in bringing this about, whether Superintendent or legislator, shall have monuments erected by grateful hearts, while the State reaps its rich rewards and humanity enjoys its blessings.

Fulton County — Sole District

Rate bills are a perfect dread in some of our weak districts. We have a few schools of this sort, in which the schools are most generally failures, as the trustees most generally employ third-rate teachers because they are cheap. As a consequence, no person " likes the school," while one person after another withdraws his children from school after the " public money " is used up, so that in many cases that have come under my obsevation, only two, three or four pupils remain, and those either out of sympathy for the teacher, or through the generosity of some well disposed persons, who support their schools at a great cost, in order that their districts may participate in the distribution of school moneys for the next succeeding year. What can a school commissioner do in such a case?

Greene County — Second District

Rate bills continue to damage our schools. Taxes are paid to the town collector without grumbling; yet it is difficult to get a collector for each district to collect rate bills and school district taxes. If each town was formed into one consolidated district, with a board of education to take charge of all the schools within the town, I am fully convinced we should have better attendance and better schools. Rate bills should be done away with.

Jefferson County — First District

In my first report to the Department I took occasion to say that I did not think the rate bill system materially affected the interests of our public schools. A longer experience with and a more extended inquiry into the working of the system compel a change of opinion. I now fully believe that our schools can never attain the highest standard of excellence until every child in the State is entitled to an education " without money and without price." The shortest possible term of school and the cheapest teachers are the natural outgrowth of the present system.

We want no more legislative patching of the old law, but a new one, making the schools free, and recognizing the great principle that on the enlightenment of the masses depend the stability of free institutions and a popular form of government.

Jefferson County — Third District

And if the rate bill were abolished and our State tax increased to the amount necessary to make all our schools free, we should take a long step in the right direction.

Montgomery County — Sole District

The rate bill, in many districts, injures very much the efficiency of the school. For fear of a high rate bill many parents do not send their children to school, or send them but a part of the time. Trustees employ second-rate teachers at low wages, to make a cheap school; perhaps keep them just long enough to use up the appropriation from the State; and thus, year after year, this programme is gone through with, to save a few paltry dollars, at the expense of the education of the children. Never will our schools be what they should be until this odious rate bill is abolished. I take pleasure in reporting that two districts, during the past year, have voted free schools; and I think there are others that will soon follow in the wake, unless the Legislature, the present session, give us a general free school law, which I hope and pray they may.

Niagara County — First District

In several of the 54 districts subject to rate bills, the fear of high tuition has caused a number of parents to keep their children out of school portions of the year. Such a course by patrons is prejudicial to the best interests of the school, and is a positive injury to the unfortunate children of such parents. The sentiment in favor of free schools is gaining ground among the people, and there is reason to believe that the time is not far distant when, justly appreciating the correctness of the principle involved, they will demand free schools for the education of the people.

Oneida County — First District

Rate Bills, in some instances, tend to diminish the attendance at school; nevertheless, they meet the approbation of the public as well as any system of taxation.

Oneida County — Third District

The amount of money raised and paid on rate bills, as shown by the reports of trustees, is $4816.97, against $87.87 exemptions, showing a willingness on the part of patrons of the schools to pay debts incurred for the education of their children, truly commendable, and furnishing a strong argument in favor of the rate bill system; as it is confidently believed that no country merchant, however prudent and cautious, can be found, whose account books will show so small a percentage of slow pay; and this, too, while schools are open to all, without distinction, and all are invited to become district debtors.

Orleans County

I hail with great pleasure an increasing disposition, on the part of men of property, heavy tax payers, to give their adhesion to the support of schools by taxation. I have taken special pains everywhere to discuss the subject of free schools; and I believe that if the question could be submitted to the voters of the county today it would result in an affirmative vote.

Schenectady County

I have changed my mind in reference to rate bills. Let there be none. In a majority of cases they greatly diminish the attendance.

It will be of interest to know what the commissioners of the State had to say in regard to the Free School law after it had been in operation a few months. I submit extracts as follows:

Cattaraugus County — First District

The present term is the beginning of a new era in the history of our school system. I know we will show a greater average attendance next fall under the new law. I have not seen a man who does not approve of the new law, abolishing rate bills. The schools open well; I think the teachers are fully alive to the importance of the work, and, in conclusion, on this branch of the subject, I think I can truly say, that the schools in my district generally, are doing well.

Broome County — First District

The free school law meets with much less opposition than I feared it would. I have heard but very little complaint, while on the other hand I have often heard it commended as just and right. The grumbling has not come from the heaviest taxpayers, but from those who pay but little tax or none at all.

Cayuga County — Second District

The new school law was greeted with general satisfaction and has a growing interest in the hearts of the people.

Jefferson County — First District

The amendment to the laws, making the schools of the State free, receives the approval of a very great majority of the tax payers of this district. The "rate bills" under the old law were, in many cases, so excessive as to greatly diminish the attendance, and, in numerous instances, greatly exceeded the tuition charged at the academies for instruction in the same branches. The schools have opened under the new law, with an attendance very much greater than that of the corresponding term of the past school year. The increase, as far as I have received reports, varying from ten to twenty per cent. There are fewer private schools than heretofore — one of the direct results of the new law; and, in my judgment, the wants of the people of this section require no material change in the law at present. I am, however, of the opinion that, in districts where there are no academies, there might with great profit, be established one or more "central" schools to be supported by public funds, in about the same manner as ordinary district schools, where pupils, when sufficiently advanced, could enjoy the advantages of an ordinary academic course without charge for tuition.

Orange County — First District

I have no doubt that a large majority of the people in this district approve of the law making the schools free. The beneficial effects of this law have already been such as to dispel whatever fears may have been entertained respecting its successful operation. The information regarding it that reaches me, from nearly every part of the District, is more satisfactory than its most ardent friends could reasonably have anticipated. The teachers' reports received since the law took effect indicate a very large increase in the attendance. In four districts, additional teachers have been employed; and in several other districts the necessity of employing additional teachers is becoming apparent to trustees.

Otsego County — Second District

I think the free school law may be hailed as the second Declaration of Independence; and without flattery, allow me to say that when the monuments erected to the memory of the achievers of our first declaration shall dim and crumble by age, the monument you have erected to your hard-earned fame in securing the passage of this law will rise higher and grow brighter as long as intelligence and virtue bear sway, and unborn generations will rise up and call you blessed.

Steuben County — First District

The attendance so far, this term, in this commissioner district, is at least sixty per cent above the attendance during the same period last year. The increase is universally attributed to the influence of the free school system. This system is popular with all teachers and school officers in this section; and, if it can have a fair trial, it will receive the almost unanimous approval of the people of the State.

Mr Victor M. Rice, Superintendent of Public Instruction, in his special report on "The Present State of Education in the United States and Other Countries and on Compulsory Education," of February 15, 1867, discusses the abolishment of rate bills as follows:

Lastly, the schools should be made free for obvious reasons. Indigent parents, having too much pride to ask to be exempted from paying their rates, keep their children away rather than be put down upon the list of indigents. The parsimonious keep their children at home rather than pay the amount required to defray teachers' wages after the public money has been applied.

The law, it is true, allows trustees to exempt poor parents from the rate bill, but the record shows that this has been generally neglected. The whole amount collected by rates, during the last school year, was $709,025.36, and the sum of all the exemptions was only $48,873.56. The two sums added together show the aggregate sum on the rate bills, viz.: $757,898.92. It appears, therefore, that the liberality of the trustees extended to the pitiful exemption of only 6½ per cent of the sum charged in the rate bills.

The number of children in the rural districts, between 5 and 21 years of age, is reported at 844,259, and the whole attendance at school at 592,511, while the average daily attendance was 263,401. The aggregate attendance is, therefore, 70 per cent of the entire number, and the average attendance only 31 per cent.

If we make allowance for sickness, for distance from the schoolhouse, for impassable roads and bad weather, for employment in various kinds of labor, on the farm, in the shop or manufactory, or in household duties, for vagrancy and truancy, the number of absentees will be still a formidable sum, to be accounted for by some reason operating generally and powerfully. In the state of Virginia, the school system was established for the indigent only, and the pride and self respect of the really poor revolted against such a discrimination. The schools were comparatively worthless, were unattended, and the system failed. The same causes operate in this State to diminish attendance, and admonish us to abolish the rate bill.

The schools can be made free in the rural districts without materially adding to the burden of taxation, and without doing injustice, by an increase of the state tax to one mill and one-fourth of a mill upon every dollar of the assessed valuation of property.

The amount raised by rate bill during the last school year was $709,025.36. The proposed increase of the state tax would add to the sum now raised $765,614.82. A ratable proportion of this tax would be apportioned to the cities, thus lessening their local taxation. The proportion which would go to the rural districts would be nearly equal to the amount now raised by rate bill. The local taxation in those districts for teachers' wages, to maintain a school for 28 weeks, over and above the amount of public moneys which will be received, will be merely nominal.

The proposed mode of raising the money is strictly in accordance with the principle which may now be deemed a settled policy of this and other states, and of the civilized world, that "the property of the State shall educate the children of the State."

The practice of raising any part of the money for the schools by local taxation, can be supported only upon the assumption that, if cities and districts are compelled thus to raise a part of the money, they will be more economical in its expenditure. But as the State requires a school to be kept 28 weeks each year in every district, it is just and equitable to raise a general tax sufficient to defray the expense for that term.

If the inhabitants desire to build schoolhouses that will add to their reputation as public-spirited and enlightened citizens, and to the comfort and instruction of their children, the power is given, and its exercise is left to their discretion. If they wish to have their schools in session for ten months instead of twenty-eight weeks, they have the authority to tax themselves to pay for the additional time. If they wish to have teachers of a higher order of mind and superior acquirements, and able to awaken in their children noble and generous aspirations, and the public money be not sufficient to command their services, the privilege of taxing themselves for any necessary additional sum surely ought not to be withheld.

The education of the people is a matter of common concern, and a state tax for the support of schools is the most equitable and just, since it distributes the burden of taxation in proportion to the ability of tax-payers. The rate bill is a violation of equity and justice, for it imposes upon the indigent and the poor a tax, under a plausible name, not upon their property, for they have none, but upon their affection and solicitude for their children.

The rate bill, it is true, falls partly upon tax-payers and partly upon non-tax-payers, and so far as it falls upon tax-payers is substantially a tax. A change of the law will merely shift the burden from a rate bill to a tax list, and the district tax for deficiencies will not probably equal the annual tax for a fair and generous exemption.

A statement of the amount raised by voluntary or local taxation for the support of schools, and that raised by the State for the same purpose, during the last school year, will show their relative proportion. The amount raised by local taxation, including board of teachers, was $4,855,013.43. The state tax was $1,148,422.22. The local taxation exceeds the state tax more than four to one. At least half the proposed addition to the state tax will be saved in local taxation. If one half the proposed addition to the state tax be added to the present tax, and the same amount be deducted from the local taxation, the latter would still be equal to three times the former.

Thus, by transferring to the general state tax the burden of local taxation and rates now borne by the school districts, as has been shown, the schools of the State of New York will be made *free* — not nominally free, but absolutely free.

The following are extracts from an address delivered before the New York State Teachers Association by Andrew S. Draper, July 8, 1890:

The early legislation seems to have been framed on the belief that the income of the state school fund, and the tax equal to one-half its share, which each district was required to raise, would support the schools, but this was found to be inadequate, and then it was provided that the schools should be maintained a specified time each year, and that any deficiency in funds should be collected from the patrons of the schools in proportion to the attendance of their children. This gave rise to the "rate bill." It was only a tax levied upon parents in proportion to the number of days which their children attended the school. The amounts raised in this way were not inconsiderable. In 1830 it was $374,000; in 1840, $475,000; in 1867, the last year of the system, it was $709,000. The average sum annually collected by rate bill in the forty years from 1828 to 1868, was $410,685.66.

The greatest contest concerning schools which the State has known was over the abolition of the rate bill and the consequent establishment of absolutely free schools. Every man here, past 50 years of age, who is accustomed to be interested in affairs, will feel the blood coursing more rapidly through his veins at the remembrance of the fight for schools, free to all and maintained at public expense. I fear none of the ladies are old enough to recall it.

The system became odious. It discriminated against the poor. Although it permitted trustees to excuse such from paying fees, no self-respecting man could suffer himself to be publicly adjudged to be poor, by a school trustee. It afforded a good excuse, or plausible pretext for non-attendance. It was attended with many misunderstandings and disputes, and promoted demoralization in many ways. Sentiment was deeply agitated, and found expression in every direction. In 1849, the Legislature submitted the question to a vote of the people, and the returns showed 249,872 in favor of making "the property of the State educate the children of the State," and 91,951 against it. The opponents were not content. In 1850, they procured legislation resubmitting the question, and the returns showed 209,616 against the rate bill, and 184,303 for the old system. Still the opponents were not content. In 1850, a kind of compromise was effected, and the controversy was attempted to be settled by restoring the rate bill and levying a State tax for $800,000, to be distributed with the school money. This tax increased to larger amounts has been annually raised since, and is technically known as the " free school fund."

But, as a general thing, the cities would not tolerate the rate bill. At their solicitation the Legislature, from time to time, passed special acts creating a board of education with general powers and duties, and in this manner set up an organized school system in each city. These special laws ordinarily authorized taxation adequate to the entire support of the schools, and thus the rate bill became obsolete in most of the cities at a comparatively early day.

In the meantime, the "union free school district system" became legally permissible, and met with considerable favor. It authorized districts to combine and establish a graded school, and meet the expenses by a general tax, thus obviating the necessity for the rate bill, in communities adopting it. In 1867, under the impetuous and able leadership of Victor M. Rice, the rate-bill system was finally abolished, and the principle that the schools should be absolutely free to all and supported at public and general expense, was fully and triumphantly established.

Smith M. Weed has been interested in public education all his life. He served as a member of the board of education in Plattsburg for over fifty-four years. When he entered the Assembly in 1857, he took up this question of the rate-bill system with Superintendent Rice and assisted him in the preparation of the bill, introduced the measure in the Assembly and succeeded in obtaining its passage.

In a letter of October 29, 1918, Mr Weed writes as follows:

Education and the schools have been of great interest to me from a very early day, and I became a member of the Plattsburg board at an early day, and continued in the high school board of education of Plattsburg for a little over fifty years, taking the place of the Hon. William Swetland who had been a member for fifty-four years. In the early days the common schools were very poor, but I take it that at that time they were so practically all over the country districts of the United States.

When in the Legislature about fifty years ago, I helped Mr Rice, the State Superintendent, draft the bill abolishing the rate bill, and introduced the bill and advocated its passage successfully. So that from that time all common schools of the State were and still are free. In 1811 a law was passed creating the Plattsburg Academy. This institution for a great many years was a very creditable school, and in it a large number of men were educated who became important personages in Plattsburg and other places. In time, however, it ceased to be an important educational institution, and later was by an act of the Legislature created a part of the Plattsburg High School.

After a little over fifty years of service, and after the completion of the new high school building in Plattsburg, and getting to be an "old man," I resigned from the board, thinking that I had done my full duty. During my

HON. SMITH WEED

service I had helped to build five intermediate and primary school buildings, which I think compare favorably with such buildings in any city of the size of Plattsburg in the State, and also the new high school building.

For many years the school board employed from three to six sisters of the Grey Nunnery as teachers. They made admirable teachers, and drew to the school a large number of pupils whose parents were French Catholics. This primary school was under the full control of the board of education as to their studies, and in every other respect, and continued for twenty-five or thirty years, to the great advantage of the young men and women of that religious belief.

From the Journal of the Assembly of the State of New York of the nineteenth session:

On Wednesday, January 30, 1867: " Mr Weed gave notice that he would at an early date ask leave to introduce a bill to make the common schools of the State of New York free to all and to provide for the government and maintenance of said schools."

On Monday, March 18, 1867: " Mr Speaker announced the special order being Assembly bill entitled "An act to amend an act entitled an act to revise and consolidate the General Acts relating to public instruction passed May 2, 1864." The house reserved this into a committee of the whole on special bill and after some time spent therein Mr Travis, from said committee, reported in the favor of the passage of said bill with an amendment and the title amended so as to read: "An act to amend an act entitled an act to revise and consolidate the General Acts relating to public instruction passed May 2, 1864 and to abolish rate bills authorized by special acts," which report was agreed to and said bill ordered engrossed and to a third reading.

On Friday, March 22, 1867: By unanimous consent the bill entitled "An act to amend an act entitled an act to revise and consolidate the General Acts relating to public instruction passed May 2, 1864 and to abolish rate bills authorized by special acts " was read a third time. Mr Speaker put the question whether the house would agree to the final passage of said bill and it was determined in the affirmative, a majority of the members elected to the Assembly voting in favor thereof and three-fifths of said members being present, the ayes 82 and the noes, 0. Then it was ordered that the clerk deliver said bill to the Senate and request their concurrence therein.

The following are extracts from the Journal of the Senate of the State of New York, nineteenth session, 1867:

An act to amend an act entitled "An act to revise and consolidate the general acts relating to public instruction," passed May 2, 1864, and to abolish rate bills authorized by special acts, which was read the first time, and by unanimous consent was also read the second time ,and referred to the committee on literature.   March 23, 1867, p. 484

Mr Andrews, from the committee on literature, to which was referred the Assembly bill entitled "An act to amend an act entitled 'An act to revise and consolidate the general acts relating to public instruction,' passed May 2, 1864," reported in favor of the passage of the same, and said bill was committed to the committee of the whole.   March 28, 1867, p. 550

Assembly, "An act to amend an act entitled 'An act to revise and consolidate the general acts relating to public instruction,' passed May 2, 1864."
April 4, 1867, p. 674

Mr Platt presented a petition of citizens of Warren county, for the passage of a law to amend the act relating to public instruction; which was referred to the committee of the whole.
April 8, 1867, p. 724

"An act to amend an act entitled 'An act to revise and consolidate the general acts relating to public instruction,' passed May 2, 1864."
April 9, 1867, p. 750

The Assembly bill entitled "An act to amend an act entitled 'An act to revise and consolidate the general acts relating to public instruction,' passed May 2, 1864, and to abolish rate bills authorized by special act," was read a third time.
April 11, 1867, p. 777

"An act to amend an act entitled 'An act to revise and consolidate the general acts relating to public instruction,' passed May 2, 1864, and to abolish rate bills authorized by special act."
April 16, 1867, p. 878

"An act to amend an act entitled 'An act to revise and consolidate the general acts relating to public institutions,' passed May 2, 1864, and to abolish rate bills authorized by special acts."
April 20, 1867, p. 1157

Chapter 406

AN ACT to amend an act entitled "An act to revise and consolidate the general acts relating to public instruction," passed May 2, 1864, and to abolish rate bills authorized by special act.

Passed April 16, 1867; three-fifths being present.

The People of the State of New York, represented in Senate and Assembly, do enact as follows:

Section 1 Chapter 555 of the Laws of 1864 is hereby amended as follows: Section 3 of title 2 is hereby amended so as to read as follows:

§ 3 The school commissioner for each school commissioner district shall be elected by the electors thereof, by separate ballot, at the general election, in the year one thousand eight hundred and sixty-six, and triennially thereafter, and the ballots shall be indorsed " school commissioner." The laws regulating the election of and canvassing the votes for county officers shall apply to such elections. And it shall further be the duty of county clerks, and they are hereby required, as soon as they shall have official notice of the election or appointment of a school commissioner, for any district in their county, to forward to the Superintendent of Public Instruction a duplicate certificate of such election or appointment, attested by their signature and the seal of the county.

§ 2 Subdivisions 3 and 4 of section 13 of title 2 are hereby amended so as to read as follows:

3 Upon such examination, to direct the trustees to make any alteration or repair on the schoolhouse or out-buildings which shall, in his opinion, be necessary to the health or comfort of the pupils, but the expense of making such alterations or repairs shall, in no case, exceed the sum of two hundred dollars, unless an additional sum shall be voted by the district. He may

also direct the trustees to abate any nuisance in or upon the premises, provided same can be done at an expense not exceeding twenty-five dollars.

4 In concurrence with the supervisor of the town in which a schoolhouse is situated, by an order under their hands, reciting the reason or reasons, to condemn such schoolhouse, if they deem it wholly unfit for use and not worth repairing, and to deliver the order to the trustees, or one of them, and transmit a copy to the Superintendent of Public Instruction. **Such order, if no** time for its taking effect be stated in it, shall take effect immediately. They shall also state what sum, not exceeding eight hundred dollars, will in their opinion, be necessary to erect a schoolhouse capable of accommodating the children of the district. Immediately upon the receipt of said order, the trustee or trustees of such district shall call a special meeting of the inhabitants of said district, for the purpose of considering the question of building a schoolhouse therein. Such meeting shall have power to determine the size of said schoolhouse, the material to be used in its erection, and to vote a tax to build the same; but such meeting shall have no power to reduce the **estimate made by the commissioner and supervisor** aforesaid by more than twenty-five per cent of such estimate. And where no tax for building such house shall have been voted by such district within thirty days from the time of holding the first meeting to consider the question, then it shall be the duty of the trustee or trustees of such district to contract for the building of a schoolhouse capable of accommodating the children of the district, and to levy a tax to pay for the same, which tax shall not exceed the sum estimated as necessary by the commissioner and supervisor as aforesaid, and which shall not be less than such estimated sum by more than twenty-five per cent thereof. But such estimated sum may be increased by a vote of the inhabitants at any school meeting subsequently called and held according to law.

§ 3 Section 1 of title 3 is hereby amended so as to read as follows:

§ 1 There shall be raised by tax, in the present and succeeding year, upon the real and personal estate of each county within the state, one mill and one-fourth of a mill upon each and every dollar of the equalized valuation of such estate, for the support of common schools in the State; and the proceeds of such tax shall be apportioned and distributed as herein provided.

§ 4 Section 4 of title three is hereby amended.

§ 4 The Comptroller may withhold the payment of any moneys, to which any county may be entitled, from the appropriation of the incomes of the school fund and the United States deposit fund for the support of common schools, until satisfactory evidence shall be furnished to him that all moneys required by law to be raised by taxation upon such county, for the support of schools throughout the State, have been collected and paid, or accounted for to the State Treasurer; and whenever, after the first day of March in any year, in consequence of the failure of any county to pay such moneys on or before that day, there shall be a deficiency of moneys in the treasury applicable to the payment of school moneys, to which any other county may be entitled, the Treasurer and Superintendent of Public Instruction are hereby authorized to make a temporary loan of the amount so deficient, and, such loan and the interest thereon at the rate of twelve per cent per annum, **until payment shall be made to the treasury, shall be a charge upon the** county in default, and shall be added to the amount of State tax, and levied upon such county by the board of supervisors thereof at the next ensuing assessment, and shall be paid into the treasury in the same manner as other taxes.

§ 5 Section 2 of title 6 is hereby amended so as to read as follows:

§ 2 With the written consent of the trustees of all the districts to be affected thereby, he may, by order, alter any school district within his jurisdiction, and fix, by said order, a day when the alteration shall take effect.

§ 6 Section 3 of title 6 is hereby amended so as to read as follows:

§ 3 If the trustees of any such district refuse to consent, he may make and file with the town clerk his order making the alteration, but reciting the refusal, and directing that the order shall not take effect, as to the dissenting district or districts, until a day therein to be named, and not less than three months after the notice in the next section mentioned.

§ 7 Section 12 of title 7 is hereby amended so as to read as follows:

§ 12 Every male person of full age residing in any neighborhood or school district, and entitled to hold lands in this State, who owns or hires real property in such neighborhood or school district liable to taxation for school purposes, and every resident of such neighborhood or district authorized to vote at town meetings of the town in which he resides, who has permanently residing with him a child or children of school age, some one or more of whom shall have attended the district school for a period of at least eight weeks within one year preceding, or who owns any personal property liable to be taxed for school purposes in any such district, exceeding fifty dollars in value, exclusive of such as is exempt from execution, and no other shall be entitled to vote at any school meeting held in such neighborhood or district.

§ 8 Section 16 of title 7 is hereby amended by adding thereto the following subdivision:

§ 16 To vote a tax to pay whatever deficiency there may be in teachers' wages after the public money apportioned to the district shall have been applied thereto; but if the inhabitants shall neglect or refuse to vote a tax for this purpose, or if they shall vote a tax which shall prove insufficient to cover such deficiency, then the trustees are authorized, and it is hereby made their duty, to raise by district tax, any reasonable sum that may be necessary to pay the balance of teachers' wages remaining unpaid, the same as if such tax had been authorized by a vote of the inhabitants.

§ 9 Section 18 of title 7, is hereby amended so as to read as follows:

§ 18 No tax voted by a district meeting for building, hiring or purchasing a schoolhouse, exceeding the sum of one thousand dollars, shall be levied by the trustees, unless the commissioner, in whose district the schoolhouse of said district is situated, shall certify in writing, his approval of such larger sum.

§ 10 Section 19 of title 7 is hereby amended so as to read as follows:

§ 19 Whenever the majority of all the inhabitants of any school district entitled to vote, to be ascertained by taking and recording the ayes and noes of such inhabitants attending at any annual, special or adjourned school district meeting, legally called or held, shall determine that the sum proposed and provided for in the next preceding section shall be raised by installments, it shall be the duty of the trustees of such district, and they are hereby authorized, to cause the same to be raised, levied and collected in equal installments, in the same manner and with the like authority that other school district taxes are raised, levied and collected, and to make their tax list and warrant for the collection of such installments, with interest thereon as they become payable, according to the vote of the said inhabitants; but the payment or collection of the last installment shall not be extended beyond five years from the time such vote was taken, and no vote to levy any such tax shall be reconsidered except at an adjourned, general or special meeting, to be held within thirty days thereafter, and the same majority shall be required for reconsideration that was had to impose such tax.

§ 11 Section 28 of title 7 is hereby amended so as to read as follows:

§ 28 It shall be the duty of the district clerk, and of the neighborhood clerk, or of any person who shall act as clerk at any district or neighborhood meeting, when any officer shall be elected, forthwith to give the person elected notice thereof in writing; and such person shall be deemed to have accepted the office, unless within five days after the service of such notice, he shall file his written refusal of it with the clerk. The presence of any such person at the meeting which elects him to office, shall be deemed a sufficient notice to him of his election.

§ 12 Section 42 of title 7 is hereby amended so as to read as follows:

§ 42 No part of the school moneys apportioned to a district can be applied or permitted to be applied to the payment of the wages of an unqualified teacher; nor can his wages, or any part of them, be collected by a district tax.

§ 13 Section 49 of title 7 is hereby amended as follows:

Subdivision 5 is hereby amended so as to read as follows:

5 To purchase or lease a site for the district schoolhouse or schoolhouses, as designated by a meeting of the district, and to build, hire or purchase such schoolhouse as may be so designated, and to keep in repair and furnish such schoolhouse with necessary fuel and appendages, and to pay the expense thereof by tax, but such expense shall not exceed fifty dollars in any one year, unless authorized by the district or by law.

Subdivisions 10 and 11 are hereby amended so as to read as follows:

10 To pay toward the wages of such teachers as are qualified, the public moneys apportioned to the district and legally applicable thereto, by giving them orders on the supervisor therefor, and to collect as herein provided, the residue of such wages by district tax.

11 To divide such public moneys apportioned to the district, whenever authorized by a vote of their district, into two or more portions for each year; to assign and apply one of such portions to each term during which a school shall be kept in such district, for the payment of teachers' wages during such term; and to collect the residue of such wages not paid by the proportion of public money allotted for that purpose, by district tax as herein provided.

Subdivisions 12, 13, 14, 15, 16 and 17 are hereby stricken out and repealed, and subdivisions 18 and 19 are numbered 12 and 13 respectively, and another subdivision is hereby added, as follows:

14 After having paid toward the wages of such teachers as are qualified,

the public moneys of the district legally applicable thereto, by giving them orders on the supervisor therefor, to collect the residue of such wages by a district tax, or, if the same shall have been already collected, to give such teacher an order on the district collector for the balance of his or her wages still remaining unpaid.

§ 14 Section 50 of title 7 is hereby amended so as to read as follows:

§ 50 The trustees may expend, in necessary and proper repairs of each schoolhouse under their charge, a sum not exceeding twenty dollars in any one year. They may also expend a sum not exceeding fifty dollars in the erection of necessary out buildings, where the district is wholly unprovided with such buildings. They may also make any repairs, and abate any nuisances, pursuant to the direction of the school commissioner as hereinbefore provided; and provide fuel, pails, brooms, and other implements necessary to keep the schoolhouse or houses clean, and make them reasonably comfortable for use, and not provided for by a vote of the district; and may also provide for building fires and cleaning the schoolroom, by arrangement with the teacher or otherwise. They shall provide the bound blank books for the entering of their accounts, and the keeping of the school lists, the records of the district, and the proceedings of district and trustee meetings. Whenever it shall be necessary, for the due accommodation of the children of the district, they may hire, temporarily, any room or rooms for the keeping of schools therein. Any expenditure made or liability incurred, in pursuance of this section, shall be a charge upon the district.

§ 15 Section 53 of title 7 is hereby amended so as to read as follows:

§ 53 They shall procure two bound blank books for the district, and when necessary, others in their place. In one of them, at or before each annual district meeting, they shall enter at large, and sign a statement of all movable property belonging to the district, and their accounts of all moneys received or drawn for or paid by them, and they shall deliver this book to their successors. In the other, the teachers shall enter the names of the pupils attending school, their ages, the names of the persons who send them, and the number of days each pupils attends; and also the facts and the dates of each inspection of the school by the school commissioner or other official visitor, and any other facts and in such form as the Superintendent of Public Instruction shall require; and each teacher, shall by his oath or affirmation, verify his entries in such book, and the entries shall constitute the school lists from which the average daily attendance shall be determined; and such oath or affirmation may be taken by the district clerk, but without charge. Until the teacher shall have so made and verified such entries, the trustees shall not draw on the supervisor for any portion of his wages.

§ 16 Section 60 of title 7 is hereby amended so as to read as follows:

§ 60 The trustees of each school district shall, between the first and second Tuesdays of October in each year make and direct to the school commissioner a report in writing, dated on the first day of October of the year in which it is made, and shall sign and certify it, and deliver it to the clerk of the town in which the schoolhouse of the district is situated; and every such report shall certify:

1 The whole time any school has been kept in their district during the year ending on the day previous to the date of such report, and distinguishing

what portion of the time such school has been kept by qualified teachers, and the whole number of days, including holidays, in which the school was taught by qualified teachers.

2 The amount of their drafts upon the supervisor, for the payment of teachers' wages during such year, and the amount of their drafts upon him for the purchase of books and school apparatus during such year, and the manner in which such moneys have been expended.

3 The number of children taught in the district school or schools during such year by qualified teachers, and the sum of the days' attendance of all such children upon the school.

4 The number of children residing in the district on the last day of September previous to the making of such report, between the ages of five and twenty-one, and the names of the parents or other persons with whom such children respectively reside, and the number of children residing with each.

5 The amount of money paid for teachers' wages, in addition to the public money paid therefor, the amount of taxes levied in said district for purchasing schoolhouse sites, for building, hiring, purchasing, repairing and insuring schoolhouses, for fuel, for district libraries, or for any other purpose allowed by law, and such other information in relation to the schools and the district as the superintendent of public instruction may, from time to time, require.

§ 17 Section 66 of title 7, as amended by section 12 of chapter 647 of the Laws of 1865, is hereby amended so as to read as follows:

§ 66 In making out a tax list, the trustees of school districts shall apportion the same on all taxable inhabitants of the district, and upon corporations and persons holding property therein, according to the valuation of the taxable property which shall be owned or possessed by them at the time of making out such list within such district, or partly within such district, and partly in an adjoining district, and upon all unoccupied real estate lying within the boundaries of such district, the owners of which shall be non-residents, and which shall be liable to taxation for town or county purposes; and upon the amount of rents reserved in any leases in fee, or for one or more lives, or for a term of years exceeding twenty-one years, and chargeable upon lands within such district, which rents shall be assessed to the person or persons entitled to receive the same as personal estate, which it is hereby declared to be, for the purposes of taxation for school purposes, at a principal sum, the interest of which, at the legal rate per annum, shall produce a sum equal to such annual rents; and in case such rents are payable in any other thing except money, the value of such annual rents in money shall be ascertained by the trustee or trustees, and the same shall be assessed in manner aforesaid. But when it shall be ascertained that the proportion of any tax upon any lot, tract or parcel not occupied by any inhabitant, or upon rents reserved, would not amount to fifty cents, the trustees, in their discretion, may omit such lot, tract or parcel, or reserved rents, from the tax list. Banks or banking associations, organized under the laws of Congress or of this State, shall be taxed by assessing the individual stockholders for the amount of stock owned or possessed by them; but such assessment shall be made only in the district where the bank is located. And it is hereby made the duty of the president or cashier of any such banking association, or of the person temporarily performing the duties of either of them to furnish the trustee or trustees, or board of education of the school-district in which the bank of such association is located, whenever the same shall be called for, for the purpose of making out a tax list for the collection of a district tax, a list of all persons and bodies corporate, owning or holding stock in said bank, which list shall also show the amount of stock owned or held by each such person or body corporate. A refusal to comply with the requirements of this section by the officers of any such banking association herein named, shall be punished by a fine of not less than fifty nor more than two hundred dollars for each and every refusal, to be sued for by the supervisor of the town in which the bank of such association is located, in his name of office; which penalty, when collected, shall be for the benefit of the school district in which such bank is located; individual bankers shall be assessed in accordance with the provisions of section 2 of chapter 761 of the Laws of 1866.

§ 18 Section 81 of title 7 is hereby amended so as to read as follows:

§ 81 The warrant for the collection of a district tax shall be under the hands of the trustees, or a majority of them, with or without their seals; and it shall have the like force and effect as a warrant issued by a board of supervisors to a collector of taxes in the town; and the collector to whom it may be delivered for collection shall be thereby authorized and required to collect from every person in such tax list named, the sum set opposite to his name or the amount due from any person or persons specified therein, in the same manner that collectors are authorized to collect town and county charges.

§ 19 Section 82 of title 7 is hereby amended so as to read as follows:

§ 82 A warrant for the collection of a tax voted by the district shall not be delivered to the collector until the thirty-first day after the tax was voted. A warrant for the collection of any tax not so voted may be delivered to the collector whenever the same is completed.

§ 20 Section 85 of title 7 is hereby amended so as to read as follows:

§ 85 Any collector to whom any tax list and warrant may be delivered for collection, may execute the same in any other district or town in the same county, or in any other county where the district is a joint district and composed of territory from adjoining counties, in the same manner and with the like authority as in the district in which the trustees issuing the said warrant may reside, and for the benefit of which said tax is intended to be collected; and the bail or sureties of any collector, given for the faithful performance of his official duties, are hereby declared and made liable for any moneys received or collected on any such tax list and warrant.

§ 21 Section 86 of title 7 is hereby amended so as to read as follows:

§ 86 If the sum or sums of money, payable by any person named in such tax list, shall not be paid by him or collected by such warrant within the time therein limited, it shall and may be lawful for the trustees to renew such warrant in respect to such delinquent person; or, in case such person shall not reside within their district at the time of making out a tax list, or shall not reside therein at the expiration of such warrant, and no goods or chattels can be found therein whereon to levy the tax, the trustees may sue for and recover the same in their name of office.

§ 22 Section 87 of title 7 is hereby amended so as to read as follows:

§ 87 Whenever the trustees of any school district shall discover any error in a tax list made out by them, they may, with the approbation and consent of the Superintendent of Public Instruction, after refunding any amount that may have been improperly collected on such tax list, if the same shall be required by him, amend and correct such tax list, as directed by the superintendent, in conformity to law; and whenever more than one renewal of a warrant for the collection of any tax list may become necessary in any district, the trustees may make such further renewal, with the written approbation of the supervisor of any town in which a schoolhouse of said district shall be located, to be indorsed upon such warrant.

§ 23 Section 5 of title 11 is hereby amended so as to read as follows:

§ 5 The trustees of every school district are hereby directed to give to the teacher or teachers employed by them the whole of the time spent by such teacher or teachers in attending at any regular session or sessions of an institute in a county embracing the school district, or a part thereof, without deducting anything from his or their wages for the time so spent; and whenever the trustees' report shows that a district school has been supported for the full time required by law, including the time spent by the teacher or teachers in their employ in attendance upon such institute, and that the trustees have given the teacher or teachers the time of such absence, and have not deducted anything from his or their wages on account thereof, the Superintendent of Public Instruction may include the district in his apportionment of the State school moneys, and direct that it be included by the school commissioner or commissioners in their apportionment of school moneys, provided always that such school district be in all other respects entitled to be included in such apportionment.

§ 24 Section 3 of title 13 is hereby amended so as to read as follows:

§ 3 Any person who shall willfully disturb, interrupt or disquiet any district school or school meeting in session, or any persons assembled, with the permission of the trustees of the district, in any district schoolhouse, for the purpose of giving or receiving instruction in any branch of education or learning, or in the science or practice of music, shall forfeit twenty-five dollars for the benefit of the school district.

§ 25 This act shall take effect on the first day of October, eighteen hundred and sixty-seven. The state tax of one and one-fourth mills upon the dollar shall be imposed for the fiscal year commencing the first day of October, eighteen hundred and sixty-seven, and shall be assessed, raised, levied and collected in the manner prescribed by law.

§ 26 Hereafter all moneys now authorized by any special acts to be collected by rate bill for the payment of teachers' wages, shall be collected by tax, and not by rate bill.

§ 27 Nothing in this act contained shall be construed to authorize the common council of any city to increase the local city tax for the support of the schools therein, beyond the amounts they are now authorized by law to raise for local school purposes, and such local tax shall be reduced in such city, by an amount equal to the amount it shall receive by the additional tax authorized by this act, for the support of schools, in the State generally.

The rate bill was abolished and Superintendent Rice in his special report of 1867 speaks as follows:

The law of the present year, abolishing rate bills, and establishing free schools, has done away with that feature in the system which has been most prolific of dispute and controversy; which has imposed the heaviest and most perplexing duties upon trustees; which has been burdensome and odious to the poor; which has imposed an unequal and unjust tax upon the families more blessed in their children than in their basket and store; and which has been the great cause of irregular attendance and absenteeism.

The average sum yearly collected by rate bill for the forty years (1828-1866) included in the table is $410,685.66.

For the fourteen years prior to 1828, it is probable that the amount collected by rate bill was $250,000 a year; and we may reasonably suppose that the sum for the year ending September 30, 1867, will be $700,000. The aggregate will be, therefore, increased to $20,627,426.66 for fifty-four years, and the yearly average will be $381,989.38.

It will be observed that the sum raised by rate bill has uniformly exceeded and generally quadrupled the amount distributed from the income of the common school fund. It has as regularly exceeded the whole public money apportioned from the school fund and the United States deposit fund, and added to the county and town taxes until the imposition of the state tax in 1851. The years to be excepted from these statements are 1850-1-2, the years of the free school controversy. The rate bill has been the special tax upon the patrons of the common schools. It may justly be styled a tax upon knowledge. The present law has merely transferred this burden from the fathers of families to the taxable property of the whole State.

If the rate bill shall be abolished, the common schools will hereafter be supported from the following sources:

1 The income of the common school fund.
2 The amount that the Legislature may annually set apart from the income of the United States deposit fund.
3 The general state tax.
4 District, village and city taxation.
5 The income of local funds.

(1) The revenue of the common school fund is about $170,000 a year, The distribution from it is, at present $155,000 yearly.

(2) The appropriation from the income of the United States deposit fund is $165,000 annually; but it depends upon the Legislature, which may at any time divert the income to some other object.

(3) The main dependence of the schools, so far as relates to the payment of teachers' wages, must be upon the state tax, which, being fixed at one and a quarter mills upon each dollar, of valuation, will probably yield about two millions of dollars a year. The income of the two funds is about one-eighth of the sum annually needed to pay teachers.

(4) District, village and city taxation is voluntary, and the amount raised annually varies with the exigencies of the year. The purchase of sites, the building of schoolhouses, and the furnishing of them with seats, desks, chairs, stoves, fuel and apparatus are all done by local taxation. No money

has ever been appropriated for these objects from the income of the State funds, or the avails of the state tax.

(5) The income of local funds, chiefly gospel and school lands, was last year $19,182.60. It does not vary much from year to year.

Four months after the abolishing of the rate bill the Superintendent of Public Instruction was able to make the following comments (Report of February 10, 1868):

The union free school act which was passed in 1853 and amended in 1864 has contributed materially to the establishment and maintenance of a superior class of graded schools, and has diminished the number of applications for special laws to meet the increasing demand for such schools in districts thickly populated. In many cases there was a consolidation of two or more school districts for the purpose. Under the operation of this law enlarged powers are exercised, and sufficient property is associated to permit the incurring of heavier expenditure for school houses and the employment of a proper number of competent teachers. Owing to the fact that in such districts the schools were free, the aggregate and regular attendance of pupils was largely increased. There being in many of them a gradation of department from primary to academical, the labor of the teachers was more effectively divided. It may be said in respect to their higher departments that in range and quality of instruction they have compared favorably with the best academies. They are generally provided with all necessary scientific apparatus, and are all under the immediate charge and supervision of boards of education, to whose zeal, fidelity and intelligence as school officers I have pleasure in bearing testimony.

Special reports from these boards and from the officers of other districts in which free schools have been established by special laws, comparing the condition of the schools at the time they became free, with their condition at the time of making these reports, show the following results:

Average increase of the time of maintaining schools per year. 9.4 per cent
Aggregate increase of the number of teachers employed twenty-eight weeks or longer per year.................... 88 do
Aggregate increase of the amount paid for teachers' wages per year .... 141 do
Average increase of compensation to each teacher per year.. 28 do
Aggregate increase of the number of children of school age. 32 do
Aggregate increase of the daily attendance of pupils at school. 74 do
Aggregate increase of value of school houses and sites...... 178 do

Prior to their organization as union free school districts there was a great destitution in the matter of comfortable school houses; and even in cases where the schools were large, it was not found easy to pay for a sufficient number of qualified teachers. Little attention could be paid o the individual wants of the pupils; the schools were not graded; and the rate bills, by which they were principally supported, served to keep from them, to a great degree, the children of the poor and parsimonious. But, immediately after their organization upon the new plan, the children crowded the schools, and the inhabitants made ampler provision for schoolhouses and for teachers, competent in number and ability to instruct all the pupils that came.

The law passed at the last session of the Legislature, commonly known as the " free school act," is meeting the most sanguine hopes of its advocates. It took effect on the first day of October, 1867; and already the local school officers report an average daily attendance of pupils at the school twenty to thirty-five per cent greater than it was during the same period of the year previous. In many districts, and particularly where there is a large proportion of foreign-born population, it has been found necessary to increase the accommodation, from this cause. They also report that the provision of the act by which a general State tax is substituted for the " odious rate bill " is almost unanimously approved.

PRESS COMMENTS

The following are various press comments in regard to the abolishing of the rate bill:

The Glens Falls Messenger under dae of May 10, 1867 says under the heading " The Free School Law ":

The Legislature, at the late session passed an act denominated the free school law. We have not yet seen a copy of the law, but the Albany Evening Journal contains the following remarks concerning it:

" The act abolishing rate bills, and making the common schools in the rural districts free, does not take effect until the first of October next, the beginning of the fiscal and school year. In the meantime the wages of teachers employed in all districts except " union free school districts," and districts in which rate-bills have been abolished by special acts, will be paid as heretofore, by the application of the school moneys in the hands of the supervisors, and by collections made by rate-bills. The public schools of our cities have for many years been free; and every year the Legislature has, for twenty years past, erected free schools in one or more of our large villages. The " union free schools " number about two hundred. The rate bill had been banished from almost every populous district; and it was time to relieve the rural districts from their oppression, and give their children the same opportunities enjoyed by those living in cities and villages. With free soil, free schools, a free press, and free men, the future is full of hope and promise."

A New School System

Mr Weed, of Clinton, has introduced into the Assembly a very important bill, which in effect substitutes a general system of " free schools " for the present one. It extends to the whole State. The bill provides that with the year commencing Oct. 1st, 1867, the schools of the State shall be free to all; and that for their support there shall annually be levied and collected by the State a tax of one and one-fourth mills to the dollar. The amount thus obtained shall be distributed among the various schools, in proportion to the attendance of the pupils. The teachers are to be employed by trustees, as at present, and if the amount of money received from the State be insufficient to pay their salaries, the deficiency shall be made a local district tax. The bill gives school trustees enlarged powers as to repairs, school buildings, &c. No tax exceeding $1000 can be voted by the district for building, hiring or repairing schoolhouses, unless the school commissioners having jurisdiction over that district approve, in writing, of all larger sums. This bill was drafted by Hon. V. M. Rice, State Superintendent of Public Instruction, and has been drawn with care. Its model is from the German. No bill has been introduced this session whose provisions so thoroughly permeate every hamlet and city of the State, as well as every country school district as this.— *Kingston Argus (editorial), February 13, 1867*

Compulsory Education

The opinion expressed by the Rev. Mr Beecher on Sunday last, that education should be compulsory, agrees precisely with the views hitherto urged by the Sun. One of the essential requisites for good citizenship is a fair elementary education, such as is within the scope of every intellect, in all grades of society. The acquisition of this knowledge need not interfere materially with other duties, yet it is very common to find children totally neglected in this respect, either through the indifference or the avarice of parents. The early years, when the mind is plastic, and most capable of receiving the ground work of education, are in many cases allowed to pass in other occupations; or as is too often the case, in idleness and mischief. What is lost before the age of fifteen is seldom regained in later years. The necessities of life begin to make themselves felt, and between the cares of mind and physical toil, it is not easy to find time for systematic education. It would be well, therefore, if parents and guardians were compelled by law to send their children between certain ages, to the public or other schools. A law to this effect would be no hardship to those who are disposed to do their duty, but it would oblige delinquents to give their children the advantages which the State provides for all. The system has long prevailed in Prussia and the German states, and the consequence is, that education there is more universal than in any other country. Ignorance is especially inexcusable in this country, where every male citizen has a share and interest in the government under which he lives. Without some education, men and women are wholly unfit to do their part in the civilized society of this republic, and since children of tender age have themselves no discretion or choice in the matter, it is eminently proper that their natural and legal protectors should be obliged by law to afford them every facility for obtaining a substantial and practical English education. The stability and credit of our nation depends in no small degree on the efficiency of our system of popular education, and every state should take measures to render compulsory such a share of education as is indispensable to intelligent citizens. This subject will be an appropriate one for discussion in the forthcoming constitutional convention in this State.— *New York Sun (editorial), April 16, 1867*

A New School Plan

Mr Weed, of Clinton, has introduced a bill to establish the free school system throughout the entire State. It takes effect on the first of October next. It requires an annual state tax of one and one-fourth mills per dollar, from which fund, thus collected, the schools are to be supported. The distribution of money is to be made in proportion to the averge attendance of pupils, and if the amount be not sufficient to pay the teachers employed, the amount of deficiency is to be a local district tax. No teacher can receive pay from the State or district without having a written certificate from the school commissioner as to his fitness to teach. The bill also gives enlarged powers to the school commissioners. Repairs on school buildings to a cost not exceeding $200, can be made on order of a commissioner. No tax exceeding $1000 for building, hiring or purchasing a schoolhouse, can be collected unless the school commissioner approve such larger sum. This bill, it is understood, was drafted by Victor M. Rice, State Superintendent.—*Kingston Democratic Journal (editorial) February 20, 1867*

Our Common Schools

Do the people of New York know that nearly three-fifths of the children of the State between the ages of six and seventeen are every day in the year absent from the schoolroom, and knowing this fact, will they realize its fearful significance and at once set about applying the remedy which they alone can apply? The statistics of the last report of the Superintendent of Public Instruction show that there are in the State 1,398,759 children between the ages of five and twenty-one, and 961,518 between the ages of six and seventeen. Of the former class, an average number of 395,617 were in attendance upon school every day in the year and obviously a less number of the latter class. Taking 395,617 from 961,518 we have 565,901 — less than the average number out of school every day in the year, between the ages of six and seventeen. To put this fact in the startling words of the Superintendent's report, "This amounts to an annual loss by children of this age only, of 565,901 school years of instruction. Thus more than half a million years' instruction have been lost in a single year!"

It may seem astonishing to the hopeful and yet thoughtful friend of free institutions, that in the State of New York, right in the midst of conditions the most favorable to popular progress and development, apathy should be growing up in regard to the matter of education — so often spoken of as the bulwark of those institutions, their only assurance of permanent safety, and satisfactory advancement. Such is the fact, astonishing as it certainly is; for figures do not lie. We do not propose, at present, to inquire into the causes of this apathy, but to examine briefly the excuse which is about the best offered by parents for the nonattendance of their children at school. That excuse is the same as that offered for the existence of 202 log schoolhouses in the State of New York; for the existence of hundreds of such school buildings as "good farmers would not stable their cattle in during the inclement season of winter;" for the employment of wretchedly incompetent teachers, viz: the expense. Yet that expense is comparatively insignificant, but a tithe of what so many men tax themselves for tobacco and like harmful indulgencies. It is estimated by a commissioner, that "while upon an average, a man may send his children to school by the payment of the labor of one day and a half in each year, still the rate bill is first consideration." "In my opinion," says another commissioner, "rate bills affect the attendance at the schools more than all other causes combined." Says another: "I have known cases where the dread of a large rate bill has broken up the best schools in the district." Another adds: "As soon as it is ascertained that the public money is expended, the children are withdrawn from school." Still another: "Rate bills operate badly in some districts, by causing 'cheap teachers' to be hired, whose inexperience and inefficiency will be spread out, 'warranted and defended' over the required twenty-eight weeks for the public money, be the same more or less."

The facts are humiliating and disgraceful, besides being fearfully ominous. But they are too well attested to be denied. In a great number — not by any means all — the school districts of the State, there exists remarkable apathy in regard to education, and whatever its real cause, an insignificant rate bill is frequently brought forward as the primary and efficient one. What is the remedy? Obviously the rate bill should be abolished. Let the alleged excuse be swept away. Let the schools everywhere be made absolutely free. A relatively equal tax must be assessed for the support of common schools. The principle that "the property of the State should educate the children of the State," should be carried out. The principle is absolutely just. It is more; it is, when carried into operation, self-remunerative. Says the report of the Dutchess county commissioner: "Our city (Poughkeepsie) raises nearly three times as much money for the support of paupers as it does for the support of schools. Were the amount provided for schools doubled, I believe we might soon diminish in the same proportion the amount required for paupers." In our own city of Utica, about $40,000 are annually paid for the support of the poor, but only half that sum for the support of schools.

A bill, amendatory of the present school law is now before the Legislature, having already passed the lower House, which is intended to meet by its provision, the necessities of the situation. Its main features are the abolition of the entire system of rate bills and the increase of the state tax for the support of schools from three-fourths to one and one-fourth of a mill per dollar. This proposed tax will yield a revenue of $2,074,315.77. The state appropriation of $155,000 from the common school fund, and $165,000 from the United States deposit fund, makes the aggregate $2,394,315.77. This, it is thought, will be sufficient to support the schools of the State, except in the large cities, for twenty-eight weeks in the year. This bill will no doubt become a law. The educational interests of the State — second in importance to no other interests — demand its adoption and the practical application of its provisions to the schools of the State.

But this will not be sufficient. It is not enough that the State generously assist in the payment of teachers' wages. Twenty-eight weeks of school each year are a much fewer number than is demanded for the satisfactory mental progress of the children. Two million three hundred and ninety thousand dollars is an aggregate sum much too small to procure the services of competent teachers for all the common schools of this great State. No amount of legislation, of appropriation of money, or of any merely external appliances, can make up for the lack of interest on the part of the people. Money can be distributed, teachers may be employed, commissioners may do their whole duty, and yet there is wanting the one thing needful if the active and earnest encouragement and support of the people themselves, are withheld. At least let us have everywhere as much interest as will induce parents to send their children to the schools that are provided. For the daily detention of hundreds of thousands from the schoolroom, there can be, in a vast majority of cases, no reasonable excuse. It is as much the duty of a parent to provide for his children, at least such an amount of instruction as qualifies them to

perform the ordinary requirements of intelligent citizenship, as it is to feed and clothe their bodies. The amendatory bill, if it becomes a law, will no doubt do considerable toward remedying the evil of nonattendance; but it cannot do all that ought to be done. And what if measures already devised and under contemplation fail to secure the desired results? What if the apathy remains, and our common schools continue year by year to lapse towards inefficiency? Will not the time come, when the State will be called upon, by its obligations to generations of the immediate and distant future, the nonperformance of which it can not evade, to make attendance upon such instruction as is necessary for the safety of our institutions, in a greater or less degree compulsory?
— *Utica Morning Herald and Daily Gazette, April 5, 1867*

Free Schools

A bill establishing free schools throughout the State, has passed the Assembly, without opposition, and it is to be presumed that it will soon pass the Senate, and become a law. It increases the three-fourths mill tax now imposed for the support of schools, to one and one-fourth mills on the dollar, which will net $2,075,315.77. In addition to this the State appropriates $155,000 from the common school fund, and $165,000 from the United States deposit fund each year, making $2,304,315.77 in all. For this twenty-eight weeks of school are to be held in every school district, and whatever further is required, the school districts, villages and cities must make up by local taxation. The passage of this bill completes an effort persisted in by educational men ever since 1848.

Of this tax New York City will pay about $800,000, a handsome portion of which will be absorbed by other counties, as only New York, Kings and Albany counties draw back from the state treasury, a less amount than they pay. In 1865, New York paid for schools into the state treasury $445,088.27; the aggregate for the State being $1,148,422.22.

The entire valuation of the State is $1,659,552,615; of New York, $736,088,908; Kings, $143,817,295, so that of the state tax these two counties pay more than half.— *Schenectady Republican (editorial), April 13, 1867*

The School Bill

The bill to make the schools of the State absolutely free, has been signed by the Governor. This law increases the annual state tax from three-quarters of a mill to one and a quarter mills on the dollar, and will permit schools to be taught throughout the year. This is an excellent measure, and is one of the redeeming acts of the present legislative session.
— *Utica Morning Herald and Daily Gazette, April 10, 1867*

Our Common Schools

The Legislature passed, and the Governor has just signed, a most important bill in relation to the common schools of the State. It is denominated the free school law, and it accomplishes just what its title expresses. Our schools have heretofore been called free, but they have not been literally free, and experience has shown that the comparatively trifling expense attached to attendance has kept large numbers of children away. What are the facts?

The reports show that of 1,398,759 children in the State, between the ages of five and twenty-one, an average number of only 395,617 were in attendance upon school every day in the year. Or taking the number of those between the ages of six and seventeen, 961,518, it appears that there is at least an average number of 565,901 out of school every day in the year. This is certainly a startling statement. In the language of the Superintendent of Public Instruction: "This amounts to an annual loss, by children of this age only, of 565,901 school years' instruction. Thus more than half a million years' instruction have been lost in a single year."

After all that has been said about the value of education, and about common schools as the bulwark of freedom, these figures seem almost unaccountable. The conditions have been favorable to educational progress. There has been no lack of the enlightenment which enforces the importance of constant instruction for the young. There has been no want of such facilities and advantages as, although far from perfect, should have drawn out a full attendance. Yet the fact remains that far less than one-half of the children between the ages of six and seventeen have daily attended the schools. Upon what principle is it to be accounted for? Strange as it may seem the insignificant rate bill has been the controlling cause. Look at the testimony.

One commissioner says that "while upon an average a man may send his children to school by the payment of the labor of one day and a half in each year, still the rate bill is the first consideration."

"In my opinion," says another, "rate bills effect the attendance at the schools more than all other causes combined."

"I have known cases," says a third, "where the dread of a large rate bill has broken up the best schools in the district." This is the uniform testimony. — The paltry rate bill keeps the children at home. Undoubtedly there are other causes, but that is the main one. It is not a satisfactory thing to confess, but it must nevertheless be accepted and acted upon. This the new law does. It abolishes the whole system of rate bills. It makes the schools absolutely free. It opens them to all without price. The state tax for the support of schools is increased from three-fourths to one and one-fourth of a mill, and it is calculated that this will yield a revenue of $2,074,315.77. To it must be added $155,000 from the common school fund and $165,000 from the United States deposit fund, making an aggregate of nearly $2,400,000.

It is estimated that this sum will support the schools of the State, except in the larger cities, during twenty-eight weeks of the year. It marks an era in our educational history and will greatly promote the educational interests of the State. That it will bring all the children into the schools cannot be expected. In every community there are those who fail to appreciate and accept the advantages which are placed directly before them, and the figures show that there has been marked indifference and apathy among the people. But the bill removes what experience has shown to be a common excuse, and its effect cannot fail to be an increase in the attendance upon our schools.

The new law does not take effect until the close of the school year — October 1st. Until that time the schools are to be supported as heretofore.

— *Kingston Democratic Journal* (editorial), *May 15, 1867*

The law, taking effect October 1, 1867, had increased state taxation for the schools, and made them free in fact, as well as in name, throughout the State, as they had been, for years, in the cities. The rate bill was abolished. This was a glorious consummation. The blot upon the 'scutcheon was effaced. The principle that the property of the State should educate the children of the State was vindicated. The doors of the common school were opened wide; all could enter upon equal terms; there would be no further exemptions as the stigma of the indigent and no further burdens to make up deficiencies for the well-to-do to bear. The schools were democratized. The free school was, above all else, a basal principal of a commonwealth, long apprehended, by statesmanship and expressed by the municipalities, yet long waiting for full legal recognition. As such, the statute of 1867 is to be commemorated in educational annals, and, credit is to be accorded to those who are instrumental in securing it, and conspicuously to Victor M. Rice, who, as the head of the common school system, was its consistent champion and tireless promoter.— *The Public School, by Charles E. Fitch*

Chapter 13
THE IMPORTANT EDUCATIONAL LAWS OF 1917

In 1869 it could already be said that the cause of public instruction during the last fiscal year had brought results unequaled in all the past. We are now enabled to study the influence of this measure not only from the limited experience of one year but through the period of half a century. The State had committed itself " to the liberal and progressive policy of providing for all its children within its limits, the opportunity to acquire at least a sound elementary education sufficient for the duties of good citizenship and personal usefulness." That that progressive liberal spirit that authorized these possibilities " has not failed to watch its workings with unabated interest," is manifested in the continued efforts for better and better schools.

The following legislation of 1917 is a fitting tribute to that liberal spirit and a worthy contribution to the fiftieth anniversary of the free school movement.

COMMUNICATION FROM THE PRESIDENT OF THE UNIVERSITY[1]

July 19, 1917

To the Honorable The Board of Regents:

Legislation in 1917

The legislative program of 1917 approved by the Board of Regents was adopted almost in its entirety by the Legislature of 1917 and approved by the Governor. The legislature enacted will practically result in the reorganization of the administration of the school system of the entire State. More legislation of far-reaching importance in its influence on public education was enacted by the Legislature of 1917 than has been enacted by the Legislatures of any decade.

While credit can not here be apportioned to all who have had part in its enactment, the Legislature and the Governor are deserving of a special vote of appreciation from this body, and with them Doctor Finegan, who has for years had charge of legislation for the Department. His persistency, patience, courage and complete acquaintance with the problems are in a good measure responsible for the gratifying results.

The following important educational legislation was obtained:

1 The enactment of the township law, which substitutes the town for the school district as the unit of administration in rural schools. This measure was before the Legislature thirty years ago, and was introduced again, with the approval of the Board of Regents, in the Legislatures of 1915, 1916 and 1917.

---

[1] From the Regents Journal.

2 The city school law, which repeals about 250 special laws relating to the school systems of the cities and substitutes therefor one measure. This, like the township law, has been before three Legislatures, with the approval of the Board of Regents. It has become known as a home rule measure, because the provisions of the law are such as to confer large powers upon local school authorities in the administration of city school system.

3 School elections are held in about one-half of the cities of the State but there has been no general law regulating and controlling such elections. The Legislature of 1917 enacted a school election law applicable to the cities in which the people elect members of boards of education.

4 A law increasing the salary of the 207 district superintendents of schools, who are charged with the supervision of the rural schools of the State, from $1200 to $1500 a year, was also enacted and approved by the Governor.

5 Two or more adjoining union free school districts are authorized to unite and maintain one central high school for the benefit of all the high school children living within the territory of such districts, under a measure which was enacted this year. While this measure is purely optional, it offers the opportunity to several districts in the populous centers of the State to unite and maintain one strong, effective high school where two or more are now maintained. There are sections of the State where the operation of this law will result not only in affording more efficient high schools but in economy in the administration of such schools.

6 While not approved by the Board of Regents, the bill before the Legislature reorganizing the retirement act for the city of New York had the support of the Department officials. This is an important law as it affects about 25,000 teachers, or nearly one-half of the teaching force of the State. The laws rests upon a sound actuarial basis and has the approval of the State Department of Insurance. It will undoubtedly furnish a model for other large cities in the country as well as for other states.

7 The secondary agricultural schools of the State are placed under the direct supervision and control of the Education Department. Hereafter, this Department will exercise the same control and management over these schools which it now exercises over state normal schools. This bill was not initiated or approved by the Board of Regents or officers of the Education Department but was enacted after a conference between leading members of the Legislature and members of the Education Department.

8 Each town board of education as well as the board of education of each union free school district or city is authorized to employ a director of agriculture to supervise practical and scientific instruction in agriculture. Under the terms of this law the State will pay an annual quota of $600 to each town, school district or city which employs such director. In connection with the township law this measure will be an important one in the development of agricultural education.

9 The Board of Regents was designated by the Legislature as the State authority to cooperate with the authorities of the national government in the proper enforcement and administration of the national vocational education law, known as the Smith-Hughes law.

10 Another important measure approved by the Board of Regents and enacted into law is one which requires each city and union free school

district to take an enumeration of all children who are three years or more retarded in mental development. The Board of Regents will be required under the terms of this law, to prescribe regulations for the segregation of such children and for providing special instruction adapted to their mental attainments.

11 Another equally important law, and a companion to the one relating to the children of retarded mental development, is the one enacted requiring each union free school district or city to take an enumeration of the children who are physically defective, such as deaf, blind or crippled. The enactment of these two laws affords the Department the opportunity to make an important contribution in providing for the proper education of these two types of unfortunate children and in the elimination of many evils which now exist.

12 The amendments to the compulsory attendance law make that law more effective and easily enforced. Provision was also made for a permanent census board in each city of the State. These boards must be organized under regulations prescribed by the Board of Regents and will furnish information in each city as to the number of children within compulsory attendance age, and their residence. This will be of material assistance in the proper enforcement of the compulsory attendance law.

13 The increase in appropriations for the work of the Education Department this year over the appropriations last year is in excess of $400,000. The greater part of this increase is for the automatic increase in apportionments to the public schools, yet through these appropriations provision is made for two additional inspectors in the Attendance Division, for an assistant medical inspector and a registered nurse in the bureau of medical inspection, and for two additional specialists in the Examinations and Inspections Division. Provision is also made for an officer to organize and develop the work of education for adult illiterates.

14 An additional state normal school was authorized for Westchester county. This school is not to be established until proper provision has been made for improvements to the other normal schools of the State and until the Board of Regents certifies the necessity for this additional school.

15 The Commissioner of Education was given discretionary power to meet situations such as those which arose last year by reason of the prevalence of infantile paralysis and which prevented many schools from being in session the required period of 180 days. In such cases the Commissioner of Education is given discretion to apportion to the districts the full amount of public money to which they are entitled.

16 Laws were also enacted strengthening the statutes which regulate the practice of dentistry, optometry, veterinary medicine and architecture.

17 The general education law was also amended by conferring on the Board of Regents discretionary power relative to the licensing of persons to practise the various professions. The object of this amendment is to enable the Board of Regents to relieve individuals from hardships which would otherwise result because of their failure to meet technical requirements of the statutes.

The Laws Enacted

The more important of these laws are given in full as follows:

Chapter 328

AN ACT to amend the Education Law, by creating town boards of education and providing for the support and maintenance of schools in towns.

Became a law May 2, 1917, with the approval of the Governor. Passed, three-fifths being present.

The People of the State of New York, represented in Senate and Assembly, do enact as follows:

Section 1 Chapter 21 of the Laws of 1909, entitled "An act relating to education, constituting chapter 16 of the Consolidated Laws," as amended by chapter 140 of the Laws of 1910, is hereby amended by inserting therein a new article, to be known as article 11-a, and to read as follows:

ARTICLE XI-A.
TOWN BOARD OF EDUCATION

Section 330 School districts continued
331 Town board of education
332 Qualification of members of board of education
333 Appointment of officers by board
334 Bond of treasurer
335 Vacancies in school offices
336 Board to constitute a body corporate
337 Meetings of board
338 Duties of clerk
339 Duties of treasurer
340 Powers of board of education
341 Schools to be free to children of town
342 Transfer of pupils
343 Schoolhouse sites
344 Erection, repair and improvement of school buildings
345 Annual school budget
346 Levy and collection of taxes
347 Borrowing money in anticipation of collection of taxes
348 Submission of certain questions to a vote of the town
349 Issue and sale of school bonds
350 State funds to be used for schools of town
351 Certain union free school districts not subject to provision of article
352 School district officers abolished; terms continued to collect funds, pay claims, et cetera.
353 Outstanding bonds; existing school property
354 Election of board of education
355 Time and place of annual meeting
356 Notice of annual school meeting
357 Special school meetings in towns
358 Qualifications of voters at school meetings
359 Preparation of list of qualified electors
360 Nominations and ballots
361 Inspectors of election

362 Conduct of school meetings; challenges
363 Canvass of votes; declaration of result
364 Successful candidates to be notified of election
365 Appeals to the Commissioner of Education

§ 330 **School districts continued.** Each school district in the State is hereby continued as such district exists at the time this act goes into effect or until modified as provided in this chapter. No order consolidating two or more school districts shall be effective until such order is approved by a majority vote of the town board of education of the town or towns in which such districts are located, and thereafter approved by a majority vote of the qualified electors of each district present and voting at a meeting of the districts consolidated by said order.

§ 331 **Town board of education.** 1 A town board of education in each town of the State, having jurisdiction over all the schools in the town as hereinafter provided, except in union free school districts having a population of fifteen hundred or more or employing fifteen teachers or more at the time this act takes effect, and the school districts in the several towns of a county which adjoins a city having a population of one million or more and in which there are only two district superintendents, is hereby established to begin on the first day of August, 1917. Such board shall consist of three members in each town in which the number of school districts under its jurisdiction is five or less and shall consist of five members in all other towns. The term of office of each member shall be three years except that, of the members first elected hereunder, in a town having three members on such board, one shall hold office until August 1, 1918, one until August, 1, 1919, and one until August 1, 1920, and in a town having five members, two shall hold office until August 1, 1918, two until August 1, 1919, and one until August 1, 1920. The terms of office of such members shall begin on the first day of August following their election.

2 Where there are two or more union free school districts each having a population of less than fifteen hundred, each maintaining an academic department which has been admitted to The University of the State of New York and the principal schoolhouse in each is situated wholly in the same town, the district superintendent shall issue an order dividing the town into as many units as there are such union free school districts situated in the town and designating the several school districts of the town to be associated with such union free school districts to form such units. The said units shall be known as town school units and shall be numbered by the district superintendent at the time of such division. Each union free school district and the districts so associated with it in forming such unit shall have a separate board of education to be elected in the same manner as boards of education in towns are elected. Such board shall have and exercise the jurisdiction and powers, and perform the duties in respect to the schools in the districts forming said unit, conferred or imposed upon a town board of education as to the schools of the several districts in a town. Wherever in this article reference is made to the town board of education, to the school officers of the town, to the school meeting of the town, or to the school electors of the town it shall be construed as referring also to the boards of education, school officers, school meeting or school electors of such units as the case may be.

3 Whenever twenty-five duly qualified voters from each of such separate units in a town having two or more boards of education shall present a petition to the district superintendent to have all of the schools situated within the limits of the town united under one town board of education as provided by subdivision 1 of this section, the district superintendent shall direct each separate board of education to submit to the voters of their unit at the next annual school meeting the question "Shall all the schools in the town of .... be placed under the jurisdiction of one town board of education?" If a majority of the voters in each separate unit, voting at such election, shall vote in favor thereof, the terms of office of each of the members of the boards of education in such town shall terminate one year from the first day of August next following such annual meeting, and there shall be elected at the next annual meeting a new town board of education as provided by section three hundred and fifty-four of this act, which board shall take charge of all the schools of the town on the first day of August following such election.

4 In a town in which there is, wholly or in part, a union free school district having a population of fifteen hundred or more or employing fifteen teachers or more, the principal schoolhouse of which is situate in such town, such district may by resolution, duly submitted and adopted as provided by law at a district meeting, determine to become subject to the provisions of this article. The board of education shall, upon the petition signed by not less than fifteen per centum of the qualified electors of such district, give notice of the submission of such resolution to an annual or special meeting, in the manner provided by law. If such resolution be adopted at such meeting, the board of education of the town in which the schoolhouse of such district is situate, shall, upon petition signed by fifteen per centum of the qualified electors of such town, residing outside of such union free school district, submit a resolution to an annual or special meeting of such town as provided in this article, for the purpose of determining whether such union free school district shall become subject to the provisions of this article. If such resolution be adopted by such town, the schools of such union free school district shall become subject to the jurisdiction of the board of education of such town and the provisions of this article shall apply to such district and the schools thereof, notwithstanding the exception contained in subdivision 1 of this section, and thereupon the terms of office of the officers of such union free school district shall terminate.

§ 332 **Qualifications of members of board of education.** A member of a board of education must be a qualified elector at the school meetings of the town for which he is chosen. A district superintendent of schools, or a supervisor shall not be eligible to the office of member of a board of education. Not more than one member of a family shall be a member of the same board of education in a town. A person who is removed from his office as a member of a board of education shall be ineligible to appointment or election to any school office in the town for a period of five years from the date of such removal.

§ 333 **Appointment of officers by board.** The board of education of each town shall elect one of its members chairman who shall serve until the next annual meeting of the board, and shall also appoint a clerk of the board and a town school treasurer to serve during the pleasure of such board. Any person who is qualified to vote at a school meeting in the town may be appointed as clerk or treasurer. A member of the board or a teacher employed in a public school of the town shall not hold the office of clerk or treasurer. The board shall determine the duties and fix the compensation of such clerk and treasurer.

§ 334 **Bond of treasurer.** The treasurer within ten days after the receipt of notice in writing of his appointment, duly served upon him, and before entering upon the duties of his office, shall execute and deliver to the board of education a bond, in a sum to be prescribed by the board and with sureties to be approved by it, conditioned for the faithful discharge of the duties of his office.

§ 335 **Vacancies in school offices.** 1 A school office becomes vacant by death, resignation, refusal to serve, incapacity, removal from the town or from office.

2 A member of a board of education who publicly declares that he will not accept or serve in the office of member of the board of education, or refuses or neglects to attend three successive meetings of the board of which he is duly notified, without rendering a good and valid reason therefor to the board of education, vacates his office by refusal to serve.

3 A member of a board of education vacates his office by the acceptance of either the office of district superintendent of schools or of supervisor.

4 A treasurer vacates his office by failure to execute a bond to the board of education as herein required.

5 A vacancy in the office of member of a board of education may be filled by the board. A person appointed to fill such vacancy shall hold office until the next annual school meeting of the town, when such vacancy shall be filled by election for the balance of the unexpired term.

6 When a vacancy has existed in the office of a member of a board of education for thirty days, the district superintendent of schools shall appoint a person qualified to vote at school meetings in the town to fill such vacancy and the person so appointed shall hold office until the next annual school meeting of the town, when the vacancy shall be filled for the balance of the unexpired term.

§ 336 **Board to constitute a body corporate.** The board of education of each town shall be a corporation. All property which is now vested in, or shall be hereafter transferred to, the board of education of a town for the use of schools therein shall be held by such board as a corporation.

§ 337 **Meetings of board.** The annual meeting of a board of education of a town shall be held on the first Tuesday in August of each year. A regular meeting of the board shall be held at least once in each quarter. The board may adopt by-laws prescribing the time and place where regular meetings shall be held, and regulate the conduct of such meetings. Such board shall also prescribe a method of calling special meetings. The meetings of the board shall be open to the public but the board may hold executive sessions at which business may be transacted which should not, in its judgment, be transacted in an open session, at which sessions only member of the board or persons invited shall be present.

§ 338 **Duties of clerks.** The clerk of the board of education of each town shall have the powers and perform the duties of the clerk of a school district as provided in this chapter. In addition to such powers and duties, such clerk shall

1 Act as clerk at all meetings of the board and record the proceedings of such meetings, and the orders and resolutions adopted thereat, in proper books.

2 Draw and sign warrants upon the treasurer for all moneys to be disbursed by the town for school purposes and present them to the chairman to be countersigned by that officer. Each warrant shall specify the object for which it is drawn, the fund from which it is payable and the name of the individual or corporation to whom the amount thereof is payable.

3 When directed by the board of education, prepare all reports required by law and forward the same to the proper officers.

4 Perform such other duties as are or shall be required by law or by the board of education.

§ 339 **Duties of treasurer.** The treasurer shall have the powers and perform the duties of a district treasurer as provided in this chapter, and in addition thereto shall

1 Be the custodian of all school moneys of the town and be responsible for the safekeeping and accurate account thereof.

2 Pay all orders or warrants lawfully drawn upon him out of the moneys in his hands belonging to the funds upon which such orders or warrants are drawn.

3 Keep accurate accounts of all moneys received and disbursed by him, the sources from which they are received and the persons to whom, and the objects for which, they are disbursed.

4 Prepare and submit as required by law annual reports of receipts and disbursements, and render at such times as may be required by law or directed by the board of education, a report or statement relative to the school funds of the town.

§ 340 **Powers of board of education.** The board of education of each town shall, in respect to the public schools and school officers of the town.

1 Exercise the powers and perform the duties conferred or imposed by law upon boards of education or trustees of school districts, so far as they may be applicable to the schools or other educational affairs of the town and not inconsistent with the provisions of this article. Any power, duty, liability or obligation which is conferred or imposed by this chapter, or any other statute, upon the board of education of a union free school district or the trustees of a school district, shall be exercised or performed by the board of education of a town, and such board shall be subject to such liability or obligation, in respect to the schools in the town, in the same manner and to the same extent as in the case of boards of education in union free school districts or trustees of school districts.

2 Determine the number of teachers to be employed in the several schools of the town and to contract with principals and teachers for the maintenance and operation of such schools pursuant to the provisions of this chapter; employ or appoint medical inspectors, nurses, attendance officers, janitors and other employees required for the proper and efficient management of the schools and other educational affairs under their direction and control.

3 Provide transportation when necessary for children attending school, under regulations to be prescribed by it.

4 Have the care, custody, control and safekeeping of all school property or other property of the town used for educational, social or recreational work and not specifically placed by law under the control of some other body or officer, and prescribe rules and regulations for the preservation of such property.

5 Purchase and furnish such apparatus, maps, globes, books, reproductions of standard works of art, furniture and other equipment and supplies as may be necessary for the proper and efficient management of the schools.

6 Establish and maintain elementary schools, high schools, vocational, industrial, agricultural and homemaking schools or classes, night schools, or such other schools and classes as shall be deemed necessary to meet the needs and demands of the town.

7 Establish and maintain school libraries which may be open to the public as provided by law.

8 Prescribe courses of study which shall be followed in the schools or classes established and maintained in the town.

9 Contract with boards of education of other towns, and of union free school districts and cities for the instruction of pupils of the town, and when any such contract is made the public money or state tuition apportioned for such instruction shall be paid to such town.

§ 341 **Schools to be free to children of town.** Each school maintained in a town under the supervision and control of a town board of education, and each department of such school and each course of study maintained therein, shall be free to the children of school age residing in such town.

§ 342 **Transfer of pupils.** Where pupils of school age residing in a town may be more conveniently instructed in the school or schools of an adjoining town, or of a union free school district or city, the board of education of such town may provide for the transfer of such pupils to the school or schools in such adjoining town or an adjoining union free school district or city in or out of the town. The board of education making such transfer shall send notice thereof to the board of education of the town, union free school district or city to which it is proposed to transfer such pupils, and provisions shall thereupon be made by the board of education of the town, union free school district or city wherein such pupils are to be instructed, for the accommodation of such pupils, upon the approval of the commissioner of education. The commissioner of education shall not approve the transfer of such pupils, when such action shall require the town, union free school district or city receiving such pupils to provide additional teachers or other school accommodations, without the consent of the board of education of such town, district or city. Whenever pupils have been transferred as herein provided, the board of education of the town, union free school district or city to which the transfer is made shall submit, through its chairman and clerk, to the board of education of the town where the pupils reside, a verified statement of the cost of the instruction of such pupils. The cost of the instruction of such pupils shall be a charge against the town wherein such pupils reside, and the board of education thereof shall direct the payment of the cost of such instruction out of the school funds of the town, in the same manner as other charges upon such funds are paid.

The amount charged for such instruction may be determined by agreement between the board of education of the town wherein the pupils reside and the board of education of the town, union free school district or city in which such pupils are to be instructed, or if such boards are unable to make such agreement the matter may be referred to the commissioner of education for determination; and in making such determination the per capita cost of the instruction of the pupils of the town, village or city to which such pupils have been transferred may be used as a basis.

§ 343 **Schoolhouse sites.** The board of education of a town, whenever in its judgment it is necessary for the interest of the schools of the town, may designate a new site for the schoolhouse, or enlarge the site of an existing schoolhouse. Whenever a new site is designated, or an existing site is enlarged, the board shall pass a resolution stating the necessity therefor, describing by metes and bounds the land to be acquired for either of such purposes, and estimating the amount of funds necessary therefor. Such resolution must be adopted by the votes of at least a majority of the members of the board of education. When such resolution is adopted the land described therein may be acquired by the board of education in the manner provided by law for the acquisition of real property for school purposes.

§ 344 **Erection, repair and improvement of school buildings.** The board of education of a town shall provide for the repair of school buildings in the town, or other buildings under its control and management, and shall expend therefor an amount not exceeding the amount included in the annual school tax budget. The board may also remodel, enlarge or improve such school buildings or other buildings under its control and management, and may construct new buildings, whenever required, for the proper accommodation of the school children of the town. The board of education shall not expend in any one year for the remodeling, improvement or enlargement of existing school buildings or for the construction of new buildings an aggregate amount in excess of one-half of one per centum of the assessed valuation of the town and in no case an amount in the aggregate in excess of five thousand dollars without a vote of the school meeting of the town, except as hereinafter provided.

§ 345 1 **Annual school budget.** On or before the first day of July in each year the board of education shall prepare in triplicate an itemized tax budget containing the amounts required to be raised by tax for school purposes in the town for the ensuing school year. Such tax budget shall contain a statement of the probable amount to be received by the town in the next apportionment of school funds from the state and the estimated amount to be received from all other sources, and shall specify the several amounts to be raised for the following purposes:

a The salaries and compensation of principals, teachers, medical inspectors, nurses, attendance officers, janitors and other employees appointed or employed by said board of education.

b All necessary incidental and contingent expenses of the schools of the town, including transportation, the purchase of fuel and light, supplies, textbooks, school apparatus, furniture and other articles and services necessary for the proper maintenance, operation and support of the schools of the town.

c The ordinary repairs of school buildings and other buildings under its control and management.

d The remodeling, improvement or enlargement of existing buildings, and the construction of new buildings and the furnishing and equipment thereof.

e The amount required to be raised for the payment of the interest and principal of bonds and other indebtedness lawfully incurred or to be incurred for school purposes and which are a charge against the town.

f The amount which may be required for the payment of any other claim against the town arising from the support and maintenance of the schools of the town.

g The amount voted at the annual or a special school meeting in the town on a proposition or question lawfully submitted at such meeting.

h The amount determined upon as the proportionate share of the cost of maintaining a school in a district partly in two or more towns, required to be paid by said board.

2 The clerk shall cause such budget to be published at length once in each week for the four weeks next preceding the first day of August, in two newspapers if there shall be two, or in one newspaper if there shall be but one, published in such town. A written or printed copy of such budget shall be posted in at least five of the most public places in the town at least twenty days before the first day of August.

3 Such tax budget shall be signed in duplicate by a majority of the members of the board of education. On or before the first day of September such duplicate tax budgets shall be filed as follows: one in the office of the clerk of the board of education and one in the office of the clerk of the town.

4 The board of education of a town may, in the manner herein provided, prepare a supplemental budget to raise money for any lawful purpose,

a When authorized by a vote of an annual or special school meeting in the town,

b When the amounts stated in the annual tax budget for the purposes specified are insufficient therefor and such amounts may be raised by tax without a vote of a school meeting in the town.

Such supplemental budget shall not authorize the levy of a tax for the purposes therein specified, or be effectual for any purpose unless there shall be endorsed thereon the certificate of the district superintendent of the supervisory district in which such town is situated, to the effect that the purposes for which the amount therein specified is to be raised are lawful. Such supplemental tax budget shall be prepared in the same manner and filed with the same officers as the annual tax budget.

5 The Commissioner of Education may prescribe the form of such budget. He may adopt regulations not inconsistent with law, providing for the examination, review, correction and the modification of such budgets and the instruction and assistance of school authorities in the performance of duties in respect thereto.

6 District superintendents shall, during the month of August in each year, examine the tax budgets on file in the office of each clerk of the board of education of each town in his supervisory district, and shall advise with

and aid boards of education in the preparation and correction of such budgets, and perform such other duties in respect thereto as may be prescribed by the Commissioner of Education.

§ 346 **Levy and collection of taxes.** 1 The board of education of the town shall, within ten days after the first day of September in each year, cause the amounts specified in such tax budget and supplemental tax budgets, if any, to be levied and assessed against the taxable property within that portion of the town which is subject to the provisions of this article. The board of education shall immediately upon the completion of its tax list annex thereto a warrant for the collection thereof, which shall direct the collector of the town to collect the tax so levied and assessed and to pay over the amount thereof to the town school treasurer. The town collector of taxes shall have the same power and jurisdiction in respect to the collection of such taxes as he has in respect to the collection of other taxes levied upon taxable property in the town, and the provisions of law relative to the collection of such taxes, except as otherwise provided in this chapter, shall apply to the collection of such school taxes.

2 The town collector shall before receiving the warrant for the collection of such taxes execute a bond to the board of education of the town, with one or more sureties to be approved by the board, and in the amount to be prescribed by such board, conditioned for the due and faithful collection of the taxes under such warrant and the return thereof to the proper officer.

3 The provisions of article 15 of this chapter relating to the assessment and collection of taxes shall apply to the assessment of school taxes in a town by the board of education thereof, and to the collection of the taxes assessed and levied as herein provided, except so far as the provisions thereof may be in conflict with the provisions of this article.

4 If a district is situated partly in two or more towns, the taxable property in that portion of such district lying in a town other than that in which the principal schoolhouse is situated, shall be assessed for school purposes at the same rate as the taxable property of the town in which such principal schoolhouse is located. The valuation of the real property in the portions of such district lying in two or more towns, as appearing upon the several assessment rolls of such towns, may be equalized by the supervisors of such towns upon the request of the boards of education of such towns, or of three or more persons liable to pay taxes upon real property in either of such towns, and the provisions of section 414 of this chapter shall apply to such equalization. The taxable property in the portions of such district located in a town or towns other than the town in which the principal schoolhouse of such district is located, shall not be assessed for such purposes in such towns.

§ 347 **Borrowing money in anticipation of collection of taxes.** The board of education of a town may borrow money in anticipation of the levy and collection of a tax, for any of the purposes specified in a budget or supplemental budget filed with the clerk of the board of education and the other officers with whom the same is required to be filed as herein provided. Certificates of indebtedness may be issued by such board of education which shall be signed by the president of the board and countersigned by the treasurer thereof. Such certificate shall not be issued for more than one year from the date thereof, and shall bear interest at a rate not exceeding six per centum per annum. The money borrowed shall be placed in the custody of the treasurer and shall be paid out by him on the order of the board of education in the same manner as money collected by taxes levied against the taxable property of the town.

§ 348 **Submission of certain questions to a vote of the town.** 1 Whenever the board of education of a town shall deem it necessary to expend an amount exceeding the sum of five thousand dollars for the repair, remodeling, improvement or enlargement of existing school buildings or the construction of a new school building it shall submit a proposition therefor to a vote of the qualified school electors of the town at either an annual school meeting of the town or a special school meeting called for such purpose.

2 If a school building in the town shall have been condemned by the district superintendent as unfit for use and not worth repairing and the amount required to be raised by tax therefor shall exceed the sum of five thousand dollars the board of education shall submit a proposition for the construction of such new building to the qualified school electors of the town as above provided. If the amount to be raised for the erection of a new building in place of a building which has been condemned is less than five thousand dollars the amount thereof shall be included in the annual school tax budget of the town. Except as herein provided the board of education of a town shall be subject to the same powers and duties in relation to the erection of a new schoolhouse, when the schoolhouse in a district in such town has been condemned, which are imposed upon trustees of school districts under the provisions of the Education Law.

3 The board of education of a town may in its discretion submit a proposition to the qualified electors of the town at an annual or special school meeting of the town for the voting of a tax in an amount not less than one thousand dollars for the erection of a new building, the repair, remodeling, improvement or enlargement of an existing building, the purchase of a new site or of an addition to an existing site.

4 When the electors at a school meeting in a town adopt a proposition for any of the purposes specified in this section they may direct the levy of a tax to meet the expense incurred thereby either in one levy or by instalments.

5 The provisions of section 467 of this chapter relative to the notice of the meeting and the levy of a tax by instalments in a union free school district shall apply, except when inconsistent with this act, to the submission of the propositions herein authorized and the levy and collection of taxes for the purposes specified.

§ 349 **Issue and sale of school bonds.** Whenever a tax shall have been voted to be collected in instalments for any of the purposes specified in the preceding section the board of education of the town may borrow so much of the sum voted as may be necessary at a rate not exceeding six per centum per annum. The board may issue bonds or other evidences of indebtedness for such purposes which shall not be sold below par. The interest and principal of such bonds or other evidences of indebtedness shall be a charge upon the town, and shall be paid when due. Such bonds or other evidences of indebtedness shall be sold by the board of education in the manner provided by section 480 of this chapter.

§ 350 **State funds to be used for schools of towns.** Funds hereafter apportioned by the State under the provisions of this chapter to school districts under the supervision and control of a town board of education shall be apportioned on the basis provided in this chapter, but the funds so apportioned to the several school districts of a town shall be paid by the county treasurer to the town school treasurer. Funds apportioned for teachers' salaries shall be paid on the order of the board of education of the town for the payment of the salaries of teachers employed in such town and funds apportioned for school libraries, apparatus, maps or works of art, shall be paid respectively in like manner for school libraries, apparatus, maps or works of art, in such town

§ 351 **Certain union free school districts not subject to provisions of article.** This article shall not apply to a union free school district having a population of fifteen hundred or more or employing fifteen teachers or more at the time this act takes effect unless a resolution shall have been adopted by such district making such article applicable to such district as provided in section 331 of this article and the provisions of such article shall not apply to the school districts in the several towns of a county which adjoins a city having a population of one million or more and in which there are only two district superintendents. Unless such resolution shall have been adopted, a school tax in a town in which the whole or any portion of such a district is situate shall be levied only against the taxable property in the town outside of the boundaries of such union free school district and the inhabitants of such district shall not be permitted to vote for candidates for members of the town board of education or upon any proposition or question submitted at an annual or regular meeting in the town. School districts which, under the provisions of this section, are exempt from the provisions of this act shall continue to be subject to and regulated by the provisions of law which now regulate and control the affairs of such districts.

§ 352 **School district officers abolished; terms continued to collect funds, pay claims, et cetera.** 1 All trustees, members of boards of education and other school officers of school districts subject to this article, in office when this act takes effect shall continue in office to and including the thirty-first day of July, 1917, when the offices of trustees, members of boards of education, district clerks, collectors, treasurers and other school district officers of such districts shall be and are hereby abolished and the terms of such officers shall cease except as herein provided.

2 The trustees, boards of education and other officers, of each district, enumerated in subdivision 1 of this section are hereby continued in office with all the powers and duties conferred on such officers by the education law or other statutes, including the power to levy, assess and collect taxes for the purpose of closing up the business and financial affairs of such district and of satisfying its obligations, except bonded indebtedness, adjusting its claims, collecting funds due it and paying its just debts. After liquidating all outstanding obligations except bonded indebtedness, and settling or adjusting all claims against such district, and closing up all its financial affairs as a district, such officers shall apportion any funds remaining in the treasury, except moneys received from the State, among the taxpayers of the district in the manner now provided by law. Such apportionment shall be based upon the relation of the assessed valuation of such taxpayers to the

aggregate assessed valuation of the district. The portion of such funds which consists of moneys received from the State shall be paid into the town school treasury.

§ 353 **Outstanding bonds; existing school property.** 1 The bonded indebtedness of the school districts in a town which are subject to the provisions of this article, including a union free school district having a population of fifteen hundred or employing fifteen teachers or more, which has adopted a resolution pursuant to the provisions of section 331 of this article, existing and outstanding at the time of the taking effect of this article shall be a charge against the property which is subject to tax for the maintenance of the schools in such town or union free school district.

2 Within one year from the taking effect of this article the value of the school property in the several districts which are made subject to the provisions hereof shall be appraised and determined by a commission consisting of the supervisor of the town, the chairman of the town board of education and the district superintendent of schools.

3 The value of the school property in each district as so appraised shall, after deducting the outstanding bonded indebtedness of such district, be credited to such district and charged against the town. The total amount charged to the town as a result of such appraisal shall be raised by tax upon the taxable property of the town in the same manner as other school expenses are raised. Such tax shall be levied and collected in five equal, annual instalments and the amount required shall be included by the board of education in the annual tax budget of the town.

4 The commission hereinbefore created shall, upon appraising such property and determining the credit to be allowed to each district, apportion the amount so credited to such district among the owners or possessors of taxable property in the district in the ratio of their several assessments on the last corrected assessment roll of the town. The said commission shall report to the board of education of the town the apportionment so made and the board shall cause to be issued to each of such owners or possessors, a certificate of credit stating the amount so apportioned. Such certificates of credit shall be transferable by the persons to whom they are issued, and shall be payable only out of moneys raised by tax as herein provided for the payment of the charge against the town on account of the school property acquired by such town. They shall be issued in such denominations and shall be due at such times as to provide for their payment out of the moneys raised by tax for the payment of such charge.

5 The Commissioner of Education shall prescribe rules governing the commission in the appraisal of school property as herein provided and regulating the distribution and apportionment of the credits and charges herein referred to and the form and denomination of such certificate. An appeal will lie from such appraisal or from any act of such commission or board of education in respect to the apportionment of credits, the distribution of charges and the levy and collection of a tax on account of such school property to the Commissioner of Education in the same manner and under the same conditions as in the case of other appeals to the Commissioner of Education. A like appeal will lie from the apportionment of the bonded indebtedness of any town.

§ 354 **Election of board of education.** 1 The first board of education of each town thereof shall be elected by the trustees and members of the boards of education of the several school districts in such town, subject to the provisions of this article. The said trustees and members of boards of education shall meet for such purpose on the second Tuesday in June, 1917, in one of the schoolhouses in the town to be designated by the district superintendent of schools. The said trustees and members of boards of education shall organize by the election of a chairman and clerk. They shall thereupon proceed to elect members of the board of education of the town to hold office for the term specified in section 331 of this article. The persons elected as members of such board shall be residents of the town and qualified electors at school meetings therein. Not more than three of the members of such board of education shall reside in the same school district, except in towns in which there are less than three school districts. The chairman and clerk of the meeting shall canvass the votes cast for the candidates for the offices to be filled and the candidate receiving a majority of the votes cast shall be elected. The chairman and clerk of the meeting shall thereupon notify the district superintendent in writing of the persons declared elected as members of said board, and the district superintendent shall give notice of such election to the persons so elected. As the terms of office of such members expire their successors shall be elected at the annual school meeting.

2 The district superintendent of schools shall call a meeting of the board of education of each town in his supervisory district, elected as above provided, on the first day of August in 1917, at the principal schoolhouse of the town, for the purpose of organization and the transaction of any other business which may properly come before such board. Upon the election of a clerk of such board, the chairman and clerk of the meeting held for the purpose of electing members of the board of education shall file the minutes of the meeting with such clerk.

§ 355 **Time and place of annual meeting.** 1 The annual school meeting in each town shall be held on the first Tuesday in May in each year, at which members of the board of education shall be elected and such business as may legally come before such meeting shall be transacted. Such meeting shall be held at the schoolhouse in the town which is the most conveniently accessible to a majority of the qualified electors of such town. The board of education shall designate the schoolhouse at which such meeting shall be held.

2 The board of education may divide the town into school election districts, whenever it deems it necessary for the convenience of the qualified electors, because of the territorial extent of the town or the number of such electors. If a town is divided into school election districts, the board shall designate the schoolhouse in each district where the annual meeting shall be held.

3 The polls for the election of members of the board of education at such meeting shall be open from nine o'clock in the morning to four o'clock in the afternoon.

§ 356 **Notice of annual school meeting.** The clerk of each board of education shall give notice of the time when and the places where the annual school meeting in the town is to be held, by publishing such notice once in each week for the four weeks next preceding such meeting, in two newspapers, if there shall be two, or in one newspaper, if there shall be but one, published or circulated in such town. If no newspaper shall be published or circulated therein, such notice shall be posted on the door of each schoolhouse in the town and in at least ten other public places in said town, at least twenty days before the time of such meeting.

§ 357 **Special school meetings in towns.** The board of education of each town shall have power to call a special meeting of the qualified electors of the town, whenever it deems necessary and proper, and whenever required by law, in the manner prescribed for the giving of a notice of the annual meeting. Such special meetings shall be held at the schoolhouse or schoolhouses at which the annual school meeting of the town is required to be held.

§ 358 **Qualifications of voters at school meetings.** 1 To be eligible to vote at annual or special town school meetings, a person must possess the qualifications prescribed in section 203 of this chapter, except as provided in the following subdivision:

2 In a school district located in two or more towns, those persons possessing the qualifications required under subdivision one of this section shall be entitled to vote at annual or special town school meetings in the town in which the principal schoolhouse of the district in which they reside is located, irrespective of the town in which they reside. A person entitled to vote under this subdivision, at an annual or special town school meeting in a town other than the town in which he resides shall not be entitled to vote at such meetings in the town in which he resides.

§ 359 **Preparation of list of qualified electors.** 1 The clerk of the board of education in each town shall, on or before the first day of April in each year, prepare a list of the persons qualified to vote at annual or special school meetings held in the town. If the town is divided into school election districts, a separate list shall be prepared, as herein provided, containing the names of the qualified electors, residing in each district. The names on such list shall be arranged alphabetically, according to the surnames of such electors, and shall contain a statement as to the place of residence of each elector.

2 Such list shall be placed on file in the office of the clerk of the board of education or at some other place, to be designated by the board, where it may be examined by any person interested therein, from four to eight o'clock in the evening of each Friday and Saturday of the four weeks immediately preceding the annual school meeting. The clerk of the board of education or some person to be designated by the board, shall attend at such office or place, at such time, and permit public inspection of such list. A person, whose name is not upon such list, who is or will be a qualified voter at the annual meeting, may submit to the clerk of the board, evidence, showing such fact, and the clerk shall correct such list, by inserting his name therein. If the name and residence of a qualified elector are incorrectly stated upon such list, the clerk, upon satisfactory evidence being presented to him, may correct such errors.

3 A qualified voter at the annual school meeting of the town may, upon the examination of such list, file with the clerk of the board, a written challenge of the qualifications as an elector of any person, whose name appears upon such list. The board of education of the town shall meet on the Monday

preceding the annual school meeting and may, upon satisfactory evidence being presented to it, correct the errors in such list of qualified electors and add thereto the names of persons, ascertained by it to be qualified electors at such annual meeting. The board shall also indicate upon the list of qualified electors, the persons whose qualifications as electors have been challenged.

4 If the annual school meeting is held in election districts, a separate list for each district, revised and corrected as above provided, shall be delivered by the clerk of the board of education to the inspectors appointed, as hereinafter provided, to conduct such school meeting in each of such districts.

§ 360 **Nominations and ballots.** 1 Candidates for members of the board of education in a town shall be nominated by petition. Such petition shall be directed to the clerk of the board of education of the town and shall be signed by at least twenty-five qualified electors thereof. It shall state the names and residences of the candidates and whether such candidates are nominated for full terms or for the unexpired portion of such terms. Each petition shall be filed with the clerk of the board of education on or before the fifteenth day preceding the day of the annual school meeting.

2 The board of education shall cause to be printed official ballots, containing the names of all candidates nominated as above provided. Such ballots shall separately state whether the persons named thereon are candidates for full terms or for portions of terms. The names of the candidates shall be arranged alphabetically according to their surnames, in columns under titles or designations, showing whether they are to be elected for full terms or portions of terms. Blank spaces shall be provided so that persons may vote for candidates who have not been nominated for the offices to be filled at such election. Such ballots shall have printed thereon instructions as to the marking of the ballots and the number of candidates for the several offices for which an elector is permitted to vote.

3 Whenever a question is required to be submitted at an annual or special school meeting, the ballots therefor shall conform as nearly as may be to the ballots required to be used, under the election law, for the submission of questions or propositions, at a general election.

4 The number of ballots to be used at an annual or special school meeting shall at least equal the number of qualified electors in the town, as appears from the list of qualified electors thereof. The clerk of the board shall cause to be delivered to the inspectors in each of such election districts, on the day of the meeting, a sufficient supply of such ballots for the use of the qualified electors thereof. Such ballots shall be printed at the expense of the town and the cost thereof shall be paid out of school funds, in the same manner as other school expenses. An election of a member of a board of education shall not be declared invalid or illegal because of the use of ballots which do not conform to the requirements of this section or to the provisions of the election law, provided the intent of the elector may be ascertained from the use of such irregular or defective ballot and such use was not fraudulent and did not substantially affect the result of the election.

§ 361 **Inspectors of election.** The board of education shall designate three inspectors of election for each election district into which such town has been divided. The clerk of the board of education shall give written notice of appointment to the persons so appointed. If a person, appointed as inspector of election, refuses to accept such appointment, the board of education may appoint a qualified elector of the district to fill such vacancy. Such boards of inspectors shall before opening the polls in the election district for which they are appointed, organize by electing one of their number as chairman and one as poll clerk. Each inspector shall receive for his services a compensation of three dollars, to be paid out of the school funds of the town and in the same manner as other expenses are paid.

§ 362 **Conduct of school meetings; challenges.** 1 All elections, held as provided herein, shall be conducted, so far as may be, in accordance with the provisions of the election law relative to general elections, except as otherwise provided herein. Suitable ballot boxes shall be provided by the board of education, to be used at such school meetings. Such ballot boxes shall conform as nearly as may be to the provisions of the election law relative to ballot boxes at general elections. All persons, whose names appear upon the list of qualified electors, as residing in the town or election districts, shall be permitted to vote and shall be given ballots for such purpose. Persons whose names do not appear upon such list may be permitted to vote, upon satisfactory evidence being presented showing that they are qualified electors of town or district and upon making the declaration hereinafter prescribed. The ballots when presented to the inspectors shall be folded so as to conceal the names of candidates for whom or the proposition or question for which the elector has voted. All electors entitled to vote, who are in the places where the election is held at or before the time of closing the polls, shall be allowed to vote. The poll clerk shall keep a poll list, containing the names of the qualified electors who vote at such election for the candidates or propositions or questions voted for thereat.

2 Any qualified elector may challenge the right of a person to vote, at the time when he requests a ballot. All persons, named upon the list of electors as having been challenged prior to the day of the meeting, shall also be challenged before ballots are given to them. The chairman of the board of inspectors shall require the person so challenged, or a person whose name does not appear upon the list of qualified electors, and who requests the privilege of voting, to make the following declaration: "I do declare and affirm that I have been for the thirty days last past an actual resident of this town and that I am qualified to vote at this meeting."

If such person makes such declaration, he shall be permitted to vote at the meeting but if he shall refuse to make such declaration he shall not be permitted to vote for candidates or upon any question or proposition at such meeting.

3 A person who wilfully makes a false declaration as to his right to vote at such meeting, is guilty of a misdemeanor. A person who is not qualified to vote at such meeting but who shall vote thereat, shall be subjected to a penalty of fifty dollars which may be recovered in a suit brought therefor by the board of education for the benefit of the schools of the town.

§ 363 **Canvass of votes; declaration of result.** 1 Immediately upon the close of the polls, the board of inspectors shall count the ballots found in the ballot boxes, without unfolding them, except so far as is necessary to ascertain that each ballot is single. They shall compare the number of ballots found in the ballot boxes with the number of persons recorded on the poll list as having voted for the candidates or the questions or propositions submitted at such meeting. If the number of ballots found in the ballot boxes shall exceed the number of names so recorded on such list, such ballots shall be replaced, without being unfolded, in the boxes from which they were taken and shall be thoroughly mingled in such boxes and one of the members of the board of inspectors designated by such board shall publicly draw out as many ballots as shall be equal to the number of excess ballots. The ballots so drawn out shall be inclosed, without unfolding, in an envelop which shall be sealed and indorsed with a statement of the number of such excess ballots withdrawn from the box and shall be signed by the inspector who withdrew such ballots. Such envelop shall be delivered to the clerk of the board of education and shall be preserved by him for a period of at least one year.

2 The ballots shall be counted or canvassed by the inspectors in the manner provided for the canvassing of ballots at a general election, except as otherwise provided herein. The votes cast for each question or proposition shall be tallied and counted by the inspectors and a statement shall be made, containing the number of votes cast for and against each question or proposition submitted at such meeting. Such statement shall also give the number of ballots which are declared void and describe the defects therein and shall also specify the number of wholly blank ballots cast. Such statement shall be signed by the inspectors. A ballot shall not be declared void unless the defects are such as to clearly indicate that the ballot was marked for identification or that the intent of the elector in voting such ballot can not be ascertained therefrom. The ballots which are declared void and not counted shall be inclosed in an envelop, which shall be sealed and indorsed as containing void ballots and shall be signed by the inspectors. Such envelop shall be filed with the clerk of the board of education and preserved by him for a period of at least one year. After the ballots are counted and the statements have been made as required herein, such ballots shall be replaced in the ballot boxes. Each box shall be securely locked and sealed and deposited with the clerk of the board of education. The unused ballots shall be placed in a sealed package and be returned to the clerk of the board of education, at the time when such ballot boxes are delivered to him.

3 The inspectors shall deliver the statement of the votes cast at such meeting, in each election district, to the clerk of the board of education on the day following such meeting. The board of education shall meet at the usual place of meeting, at eight o'clock in the evening of the day following such election and shall forthwith examine and tabulate the statement of the results of the election in the several election districts of such town. The board of education shall canvass the returns as contained in the statements of the inspectors and shall determine the number of votes cast for and against each candidate at such election and for and against each question or proposition voted upon in the several election districts of the town. The board shall thereupon declare the result of the canvass of the votes in each election district.

4 The candidates receiving a plurality of the votes cast respectively for the several offices shall be declared elected. The clerk of the board of education shall record the result of the election as announced by the board of education, in the minutes of the meeting.

§ 364 **Successful candidates to be notified of election.** The clerk of the board of education shall, within twenty-four hours after the result of the election has been declared, serve a written notice either personally or by mail upon each person declared to be elected as a member of the board of education. A person upon whom such notice has been served shall be deemed to have accepted the office unless within five days after the service of such notice he shall file his written refusal with the clerk.

§ 365 **Appeals to the Commissioner of Education.** An appeal may be taken to the Commissioner of Education from such election or from any of the acts or proceedings of a school meeting or the board of education, in the same manner and with the same effect as in the case of an appeal to him from the acts or proceedings of a school meeting or election or of a board of education, under the provisions of this chapter. The Commissioner of Education may, in his discretion, order a new election in any town.

§ 2 **Repeal of inconsistent provisions: effect of repeal.** All acts or parts of acts, general or special, inconsistent with the provisions of this act are hereby repealed. The repeal of the acts hereinafter specified or of such inconsistent acts of parts of such acts shall not affect any right existing or accrued or any liability incurred prior to the passage of this act. This act shall not affect a pending action or proceeding brought by or against a trustee, trustees or a board of education of a school district but the same may be prosecuted or defended in the same manner and for the same purpose by the board of education of the town of which such district forms a part, as though this act had not been passed. All contracts entered into by a trustee, trustees or the board of education of a school district prior to the taking effect of this act, under and pursuant to the provisions of the education law, shall be carried into effect according to the terms thereof by the board of education of the town of which such school district forms a part, in the same manner and for the same purpose as though this act had not been passed. Any right, existing or accrued, or any liability incurred by a trustee, trustees or board of education of a school district, prior to the passage of this act, may be asserted and enforced by or against the board of education of the town of which such school district forms a part, in the same manner and to the same extent as though this act had not been passed.

§ 3 **Sections renumbered.** Sections 340 and 341 of the Education Law are hereby renumbered sections 364 and 365; sections 360, 361, 362, 363, 364 and 365 of such law are hereby renumbered respectively sections 370, 371, 372, 373, 374 and 375.

§ 4 **Time of taking effect.** This act shall take effect immediately.

Chapter 786

AN ACT to amend the Education Law, by providing for a board of education in the several cities of the State.

Became a law June 8, 1917, with the approval of the Governor. Passed, three-fifths being present.

The People of the State of New York, represented in Senate and Assembly, do enact as follows:

Section 1 Chapter 21 of the Laws of 1909, entitled "An act relating to education, constituting chapter 16 of the Consolidated Laws," as amended by chapter 140 of the Laws of 1910, is hereby further amended by inserting therein a new article, to be known as article 33-a, and to read as follows:

ARTICLE 33-A
Board of Education in the Several Cities of the State

Section 865 Board of education
866 Board of education; eligibility; how chosen; term of office; vacancies
867 Meetings of board of education
868 Powers and duties of board of education
869 Superintendent of schools
870 Powers and duties of superintendent of schools
871 Board of examiners
872 Appointment of associate, district or other superintendents, teachers, experts and other employees; their salaries, et cetera
873 Local school board districts
874 Bonds of employees
875 Building, sites, et cetera
876 Purchase and sale of real property
877 Education budget
878 Tax election
879 Bond issue
880 Funds; custody and disbursement of
881 Continuation in office of boards, bureaus, teachers, principals and other employees

§ 865 **Board of education.** 1 A board of education is hereby established in each city of the State. The educational affairs in each city shall be under the general management and control of a board of education to consist of not less than three and not more than nine members, to be chosen as hereinafter provided, and to be known as members of the board of education. The number of members on the board of education of each city shall be as follows:

a A city having nine members or less on its board of education shall continue to have such number of members on said board as such board contains at the time this law goes into effect.

b A city having a population of one million or more shall have a board of education to consist of seven members.

c In all other cities of the State the number of members of the board of education shall be nine.

2 A board of education in office at the time this law goes into effect except as hereinafter provided shall continue in office and possess the powers and duties of a board of education under this article until its successor shall be chosen as provided herein.

3 The provisions of this act shall apply to and govern the operation and administration of the public school system and other educational affairs in a city which is created after this act goes into effect. The authorities in charge of the operation and administration of the schools and other educational affairs of the school districts included within such city at the time the act creating such city goes into effect shall continue in charge thereof

until the first Tuesday in May thereafter. On such first Tuesday in May a board of education consisting of five members shall be elected at the annual school election in accordance with the provisions of this chapter. One member of such board shall be elected for one year, one member for two years, one member for three years, one member for four years, and one member for five years from the said first Tuesday of May. As their terms expire their successors shall be chosen for a full term of five years.

§ 866 **Board of education; eligibility; how chosen; term of office; vacancies.** 1 No person shall be eligible to the office of member of a board of education who is not a citizen of the United States and who has not been a resident of the city for which he is chosen for a period of at least three years immediately preceding the date of his election or appointment.

2 In a city having a population of one million or more and divided into boroughs, there shall be a board of education consisting of seven members. Two members of such board shall be residents of the borough having the largest population. two shall be residents of the borough having the second largest population, and one shall be a resident of each of the other boroughs in such city. The mayor shall appoint such members on the first Wednesday in January, 1918, and in appointing them shall designate the terms of office of such members so that the term of one member shall expire on the first Tuesday in May, 1919; one on the first Tuesday in May, 1920; one on the first Tuesday in May, 1921; one on the first Tuesday in May, 1922; one on the first Tuesday in May, 1923; one on the first Tuesday in May, 1924; and one on the first Tuesday in May, 1925. Their successors shall be chosen for full terms of seven years. Thereafter, as vacancies occur on such board they shall be filled from the several boroughs so that each borough shall always be represented on such board as required under this subdivision. A vacancy occurring otherwise than by expiration of term shall be filled for the unexpired term.

3 In each city in which the law provides, prior to the time this article goes into effect, that the members of the board of education shall be chosen by vote of the people at an election separate from the general or municipal election, the members of the board of education of that city shall hereafter be elected by the voters at large at the annual school election.

4 In each city in which the law provides, prior to the time this article goes into effect, that the members of the board of education shall be chosen by vote of the people at a general or municipal election, the members of such board of education shall continue to be so chosen by the voters at large at either a general or municipal election, or at both, and for the terms prescribed by such law.

5 In each other city of the State members of the board of education shall be appointed from the city at large by the mayor except as otherwise provided herein, but in a city having a population of four hundred thousand or more and less than one million, such appointments shall be subject to confirmation by the council. The members of the board of education in a city having a population of four hundred thousand or more and less than one million shall be appointed by the mayor on January 15, 1918, subject to confirmation by the council, for terms of one, two, three, four and five years from the first Tuesday in May, 1917, and their successors shall be appointed as provided herein for five years.

6 If the number of members on a board of education in a city in which the members of such board are chosen at an annual school, general or municipal election exceeds nine, no person shall be elected to membership thereon as vacancies occur until the number of members on such board shall be less than nine.

7 If the number of members on a board of education in a city in which the members of such board are appointed by the mayor exceeds nine, the term of office of each member of such board shall cease and terminate when this act takes effect, except as otherwise provided herein, and the mayor in each of such cities shall thereupon appoint a board of education to consist of nine members. Such members shall be appointed for the following terms: two members to serve until the first Tuesday in May, 1918; two to serve until the first Tuesday in May, 1919; two until the first Tuesday in May, 1920; two until the first Tuesday in May, 1921, and one until the first Tuesday in May, 1922. As their terms expire, their successors shall be chosen for a full term of five years.

8 The persons either elected or appointed to membership for a full term on a board of education, and their successors in office, shall be elected or appointed for terms of five years each, except at otherwise provided in this act.

9 In a city having less than five members on its board of education the term of office of such members shall be for the period of time specified in the law in effect prior to the time this act goes into effect. As the terms of office of such members expire their successors shall be chosen for like terms.

10 When a vacancy occurs in a board of education by expiration of term prior to the first Tuesday in May, 1922, such vacancy shall be filled at the time it occurs, and the person chosen shall take office immediately and hold the same for a term of five years, except as otherwise provided herein, from the first Tuesday in May following the date on which such vacancy occurs and thereafter his successor shall be chosen for a full term of five years.

11 If a vacancy occurs other than by expiration of term of office in the office of a member of a board of education in a city in which such members are elected at a school, or general, or municipal election, such vacancy shall be filled by appointment by the mayor until the next annual school election is held, and such vacancy shall then be filled at such election for the unexpired portion of such term.

12 If such vacancy occurs in such office in a city in which the members of the board of education are appointed by the mayor, such vacancy shall be filled by appointment by the mayor of such city for the unexpired portion of such term, but in a city having a population of four hundred thousand or more and less than one million, such appointment shall be subject to confirmation by the council.

§ 867 **Meetings of board of education.** 1 The annual meeting of a board of education shall be held on the second Tuesday in May, at which meeting the board shall select a president for the ensuing year.

2 Each of such boards shall also fix a time for holding regular board meetings which shall be at least as often as once each month and shall also prescribe a method for calling special meetings of such board.

§ 868 **Powers and duties of board of education.** Subject to the provisions of this chapter, the board of education in a city shall have the power and it shall be its duty

1 To perform any duty imposed upon boards of education or trustees of common schools under this chapter or other statutes, or the regulations of The University of the State of New York or the Commissioner of Education so far as they may be applicable to the school or other educational affairs of a city, and not inconsistent with the provisions of this article.

2 To create, abolish, maintain and consolidate such positions, divisions, boards or bureaus as, in its judgment, may be necessary for the proper and efficient administration of its work; to appoint a superintendent of schools, such associate, district and other superintendents, examiners, directors, supervisors, principals, teachers, lecturers, special instructors, medical inspectors, nurses, auditors, attendance officers, secretaries, clerks, janitors and other employees and other persons or experts in educational, social or recreational work or in the business management or direction of its affairs as said board shall determine necessary for the efficient management of the schools and other educational, social, recreational and business activities; and to determine their duties except as otherwise provided herein.

3 To have the care, custody, control and safekeeping of all school property or other property of the city used for educational, social or recreational work and not specifically placed by law under the control of some other body or officer, and to prescribe rules and regulations for the preservation of such property.

4 To purchase and furnish such apparatus, maps, globes, books, furniture and other equipment and supplies as may be necessary for the proper and efficient management of the schools and other educational, social and recreational activities and interests under its management and control. To provide textbooks or other supplies to all the children attending the schools of such cities in which free textbooks or other supplies are lawfully provided prior to the time this act goes into effect.

5 To establish and maintain such free elementary schools, high schools, training schools, vocational and industrial schools, kindergartens, technical schools, night schools, part-time or continuation schools, vacation schools, schools for adults, open air schools, schools for the mentally and physically defective children or such other schools or classes as such board shall deem necessary to meet the need and demands of the city.

6 To establish and maintain libraries which may be open to the public, to organize and maintain public lecture courses, and to establish and equip playgrounds, recreation centers, social centers, and reading rooms from such funds as the education law or other statutes authorize and the state appropriates for such purposes, and from such other funds as may be provided therefor from local taxation or other sources.

7 To authorize the general courses of study which shall be given in the schools and to approve the content of such courses before they become operative.

8 To authorize and determine the textbooks to be used in the schools under its jurisdiction, but in a city having a board of superintendents, the books thus authorized and determined shall be from lists recommended by such board.

9 To prescribe such regulations and by-laws as may be necessary to make effectual the provisions of this chapter and for the conduct of the proceedings of said board and the transaction of its business affairs, for the general

management, operation, control, maintenance and discipline of the schools and of all other educational, social or recreational activities and other interests under its charge or direction.

10 To perform such other duties and possess such other powers as may be required to administer the affairs placed under its control and management, to execute all powers vested in it, and to promote the best interests of the schools and other activities committed to its care.

§ 869 **Superintendent of schools, associate superintendents, board of superintendents.** The superintendent or an associate superintendent of schools of a city in office when this article goes into effect shall hold his position for the term for which he was chosen and until his successor is chosen. A superintendent or associate superintendent appointed after this article goes into effect shall hold his position in a city of the first class for a period of six years from the date of his appointment subject to removal for cause and in all other cities subject to the pleasure of the board of education. In a city having a population of one million or more there shall be eight associate superintendents, and the superintendent of schools and such associate superintendents shall constitute a board of superintendents. The superintendent of schools shall be the chairman of such board. A superintendent or an associate superintendent may vacate his position by filing a written resignation with the board of education. No person shall be eligible to the position of superintendent of schools or associate, district or other superintendent of schools or a member of the board of examiners unless he is

1 A graduate of a college or university approved by The University of the State of New York, and has had at least five years' successful experience in the teaching or in the supervision of public schools since graduation; or

2 A holder of a superintendent's certificate issued by the Commissioner of Education under regulations prescribed by the Regents of The University of the State of New York, and has had at least ten years' successful experience in teaching, or in public school administration, or equivalent educational experience approved by the Commissioner of Education.

§ 870 **Powers and duties of superintendent of schools.** The superintendent of schools of a city shall possess, subject to the by-laws of the board of education, the following powers and be charged with the following duties:

1 To enforce all provisions of law and all rules and regulations relating to the management of the schools and other educational, social and recreational activities under the direction of the board of education, to be the chief executive officer of such board and the educational system, and to have a seat in the board of education and the right to speak on all matters before the board, but not to vote.

2 To prepare the content of each course of study authorized by the board of education, but in a city having a board of superintendents the content of each of such courses shall be prepared and recommended by the board of superintendents, submitted to the board of education for its approval and, when thus approved, the superintendent or board of superintendents, as the case may be, shall cause such courses of study to be used in the grades, classes and schools for which they are authorized.

3 To recommend suitable lists of textbooks to be used in the schools, but in a city having a board of superintendents such board of superintendents shall recommend to the board of education such lists.

4 To have supervision and direction of associate, district and other superintendents, directors, supervisors, principals, teachers, lecturers, medical inspectors, nurses, auditors, attendance officers, janitors and other persons employed in the management of the schools or the other educational activities of the city authorized by this chapter and under the direction and management of the board of education; to transfer teachers from one school to another, or from one grade of the course of study to another grade in such course, and to report immediately such transfers to said board for its consideration and action, but in a city having a board of superintendents such transfers shall be made upon the recommendation of such board; to report to said board of education violations of regulations and cases of insubordination, and to suspend an associate, district or other superintendent, director, supervisor, expert, principal, teacher or other employee until the next regular meeting of the board, when all facts relating to the case shall be submitted to the board for its consideration and action.

5 To have supervision and direction over the enforcement and observance of the courses of study, the examination and promotion of pupils, and over all other matters pertaining to playgrounds, medical inspection, recreation and social center work, libraries, lectures and all the other educational activities and interests under the management, direction and control of the board of education, but in a city having a board of superintendents rules and regulations for the promotion and graduation of pupils shall be made by such board.

6 To issue such licenses to teachers, principals, directors and other members of the teaching and supervising staff as may be required under the regulations of the board of education in cities in which such board requires its teachers to hold qualifications in addition to or in advance of the minimum qualifications required under this chapter. In a city having a board of examiners, such licenses shall be issued on the recommendation of such board.

§ 871 **Board of examiners.** In a city having a population of one million or more there shall be a board of examiners to consist of four members. No person while in the supervising or teaching service in the city shall serve on such board. It shall be the duty of the board to hold examinations whenever necessary, to examine all applicants who are required to be licensed or to have their names placed upon eligible lists for appointment in the schools in such city, except examiners, and to prepare all necessary eligible lists. Eligible lists shall not be merged and one eligible list shall be exhausted before nominations are made from a list of subsequent date. No eligible lists, except a principals' eligible list shall remain in force for a longer period than three years. The board of examiners may employ temporary assistants at a compensation fixed by the board of education. It shall perform such other duties as the board of education may require.

§ 872 **Appointment of district or other superintendents, teachers and other employees; their salaries, et cetera.** 1 District superintendents, directors, supervisors, principals, teachers and all other members of the teaching and supervising staff, except associate superintendents and examiners, authorized by section 868 of this article, shall be appointed by the board of education, upon the recommendation of the superintendent of schools, but in a city having a board of superintendents on the recommendation of such board, for a probationary period of not less than one year and not to exceed three years; such period to be fixed by the board of education in its discretion. The service of a person appointed to any of such positions may be discontinued at any time during such probationary period, on the recommendation of the superintendent of schools, and in a city having a board of superintendents on the recommendation of such board, by a majority vote of the board of education.

2 Associate superintendents, examiners and all other employees authorized by section 868 of this article, except as otherwise provided in subdivision 1 of this section, shall be appointed by the board of education.

3 At the expiration of the probationary term of a person appointed for such term, the superintendent of schools, and, in a city having a board of superintendents, such board shall make a written report to the board of education recommending for permanent appointment those persons who have been found competent, efficient and satisfactory. Such persons and all others employed in the teaching, examining or supervising service of the schools of a city, who have served the full probationary period, or have rendered satisfactorily an equivalent period of service prior to the time this act goes into effect shall hold their respective positions during good behavior and efficient and competent service, and shall not be removable except for cause after a hearing by the affirmative vote of a majority of the board. In a city in which teachers have not permanent tenure under the laws in force prior to the time this act goes into effect, such teachers shall be entitled to receive permanent appointments after serving the probationary period fixed by the board of education as herein provided.

4 No principal, supervisor, director, or teacher shall be appointed to the teaching force of a city who does not possess qualifications required under this chapter and under the regulations prescribed by the Commissioner of Education for the persons employed in such positions in the schools of the cities of the State, but a board of education may prescribe additional or higher qualifications for the persons employed in any of such positions.

5 In a city having a population of four hundred thousand or more, recommendations for appointment to the teaching and supervising service, except for the position of superintendent of schools, associate superintendent or district superintendent, or director of a special branch, principal of or teacher in a training school, or principal of a high school, shall be from the first three persons on appropriate eligible lists prepared by the board of examiners. Eligible lists in force at the time this act takes effect and the relative standing of persons whose names are on said lists shall not be affected by the passage of this act. The board of education, on the recommendation of the superintendent of schools, and in a city having a board of superintendents on the recommendation of such board, shall designate, subject to the other provisions of this chapter, the kind and grades of licenses which shall be required for service as principal, branch principal, director, supervisor or teacher of a special branch, head of department, assistant or any other position of the teaching staff together with the academic and professional qualifications required for each kind or grade of

license. No person required to have a license under the provisions of this chapter in order to be employed in a position who does not have such license shall have any claim for salary.

6 The salaries of all members of the supervising and teaching force and of all employees and for all positions authorized under section 868 of this act shall continue to be on the same basis as such salaries and positions are when this article goes into effect, and such salaries shall continue to be regulated and increased in the same manner, by the same provisions of law and under the same conditions as such salaries are regulated and increased under the laws governing such salaries at the time this article goes into effect. Rules and regulations shall be adopted governing excusing of absences and for the granting of leaves of absence either with or without pay.

§ 873 **Local school board districts.** 1 The local school board districts in a city having a population of one million or more are hereby continued as they exist at the time this article goes into effect subject, however, to the provisions contained herein. The board of education of such city may modify the boundaries of such districts, consolidate two or more of such districts, and establish new districts.

2 There shall be in each of such districts a local school board of five members appointed by the president of the borough in which such district is located. The board of education shall designate as a member of a local school board one member of the board of education and the city superintendent of schools shall assign one district superintendent to advise with such board.

3 The members of such local school boards in office prior to the time this article goes into effect shall serve for the term for which they were appointed. The full term of office of a member of such board shall be five years. A vacancy on such board shall be filled by the borough president for the unexpired term.

4 Subject to the provisions of this chapter a local school board shall within its district have the power and it shall be its duty to visit the schools at least once every quarter; to make recommendations to the board of education with respect to matters affecting the interests of the schools; subject to the by-laws of the board of education, to transfer teachers from school to school, to excuse absences of teachers, to hear charges against principals or teachers and make recommendations thereon to the board of education, and to perform such other duties as may be required under said by-laws; to provide by-laws regulating the exercise of the powers and duties vested in it, provided such by-laws are not in conflict with the by-laws of the board of education; to elect a secretary and determine his duties. The secretary is hereby authorized to administer oaths and take affidavits in all matters pertaining to the schools in his district, in which a local school board has power to act, and for that purpose shall possess all the powers of a commissioner of deeds, but shall not be entitled to any fees or emoluments thereof. The board of education shall provide for the expenses of a local school board and for its places of meeting.

§ 874 **Bonds of employees.** The board of estimate and apportionment of a city or in a city having no board of estimate and apportionment the body or officer performing the duties performed by a board of estimate and apportionment which may now legally require bonds of such employees may continue to require bonds of such employees in such amount as such board of estimate and apportionment or other body or officer shall determine. In all other cities bonds may be required of such employees by the board of education. The premiums on such bonds shall be paid by the city.

§ 875 **Buildings, sites, et cetera.** 1 A board of education is authorized and it shall have power to purchase, repair, remodel, improve or enlarge school buildings or other buildings or sites, and to construct new buildings, subject to such limitations and restrictions and exceptions as are herein provided.

2 Whenever in the judgment of a board of education it is necessary to select a new site, or to enlarge a present site, or to designate a playground or recreation center, or to acquire title to or lease real property for other educational purposes authorized by this chapter, such board may take options on property desirable for such purposes but before taking title thereto shall pass a resolution stating the necessity therefor, describing by metes and bounds the grounds or territory desired for each of these purposes, and estimating the amount of funds necessary therefor. An item for such amount if funds are not available for the purchase or lease of such property may be included in the next annual budget if not included in a special budget as herein provided.

3 Whenever in the judgment of a board of education the needs of the city require a new building for school purposes or for recreation or other educational purposes authorized by this chapter, or when in its judgment a building should be remodelled or enlarged, such board shall pass a resolution specifying in detail the necessity therefor and estimating the amount of funds necessary for such purpose. An item for such amount if funds are not available for the construction of such building may be included in the next annual budget if not included in a special budget as herein provided.

4 No site shall be designated except upon a majority vote of a board of education and no building shall be constructed, remodelled or enlarged until the plans and specifications therefor are approved by the board of education.

5 After a site has been selected and plans and specifications for a building thereon have been approved as provided herein, a board of education in a city having a population of more than four hundred thousand but less than one million may, in its discretion, by regulation deliver such plans and specifications to the council which may thereupon, in its discretion, award a contract for the erection of such building in the same manner and in accordance with the provisions of law regulating the awarding of contracts for the construction of municipal buildings of such city.

6 In a city of the second class in which the common council, the board of estimate and apportionment and the board of contract and supply and the commissioner of public works or other city officials, or any one or more thereof, has the authority under the law in force prior to the time this act takes effect to erect, remodel, improve, or enlarge school buildings or to purchase supplies or real property for any school purpose, such officers, board or boards shall continue to possess such powers and duties and to perform such functions.

7 When the real property of a city under the control and management of the board of education is no longer needed for educational purposes in the

city, such board shall notify the common council of such fact and in a city having no common council, the council or the commissioners of the sinking funds, as the case may be, may then sell or dispose of such property in the manner in which other real property owned by the city may be sold or disposed of and the proceeds thereof shall be credited to the funds under the control and administration of the board of education in such city, except that in cities where the proceeds of such sales are required by statute, in effect prior to the time this article goes into effect, to be paid to the credit of the sinking fund established and maintained therein, the proceeds of such sales shall continue to be paid to the credit of the sinking fund of such city or cities as required by statute, and except that in a city having a council or a board of estimate and apportionment, such council or board may, by resolution, authorize the use of the proceeds of such sale for other municipal purposes.

8 No contract for the purchase of supplies, furniture, equipment, or for the construction or the alteration or remodelling of any building shall be entered into by a board of education involving an expenditure or liability of more than one thousand dollars unless said board shall have duly advertised for estimates for the same and the contract in each case shall be awarded to the lowest responsible bidder furnishing the security as required by such board.

§ 876 **Purchase and sale of real property.** The board of education may purchase real property for any of the purposes authorized by law and shall take title thereof in the name of the city, and when the owner of such property refuses to sell the same or such board is unable to agree with the owner of such property on the purchase price thereof, it shall have the power and authority to institute such proceedings and take any action necessary to acquire title to such property under and pursuant to the provisions of the condemnation law, city charter, or of any special statute authorizing proceedings to acquire title by right to eminent domain, except that in a city in which the common council, board of contract and supply or other city officers or body are authorized and empowered by law to acquire title to real property for school purposes under the laws in force at the time this act goes into effect, said council, board, officers or body shall continue to possess such powers and shall exercise the same, including the power to condemn real property for said purposes, under the provisions of law relating thereto notwithstanding any of the provisions contained in this act.

§ 877 **Annual estimate.** 1 The board of education in each city having a population of less than one million shall prepare annually an itemized estimate for the current or ensuing fiscal year of such sum of money as it may deem necessary for the purposes stated in this section, after crediting thereto the amount anticipated in the next apportionment of school funds from the state and the estimated amount to be received from all other sources. Such itemized estimate in such cities shall be filed at such times and in such manner as city departments or officers are required to submit estimates for such departments or officers. The board of education in each other city shall prepare annually an itemized estimate for the ensuing fiscal year and file the same on or before the first day of September. Such estimate shall be for the following purposes:

a The salary of the superintendent of schools, associate, district or other superintendents, examiners, directors, supervisors, principals, teachers, lecturers, special instructors, auditors, medical inspectors, nurses, attendance officers, clerks and janitors and the salary, fees or compensation of all other employees appointed or employed by said board of education.

b The other necessary incidental and contingent expenses including ordinary repairs to buildings and the purchase of fuel and light, supplies, textbooks, school apparatus, books, furniture and fixtures and other articles and service necessary for the proper maintenance, operation and support of the schools, libraries and other educational, social or recreational affairs and interests under its management and direction. The provisions of this section in regard to the purchase of light shall not apply to a city having a population of one million or more.

c The remodelling or enlarging of buildings under its control and management, the construction of new buildings for uses authorized by this chapter and the furnishing and equipment thereof, the purchase of real property for new sites, additions to present sites, playgrounds or recreation centers and other educational or social purposes, and to meet any other indebtedness or liability incurred under the provisions of this chapter or other statutes, or any other expenses which the board of education is authorized to incur.

2 In a city which had, according to the state census of 1915, a population of less than fifty thousand such estimate shall be filed with the clerk of the common council and the common council shall include, except as otherwise provided herein, in the next annual tax and assesment roll of the city the amount specified in such estimate and the same shall be collected in the same manner at other city taxes are collected and shall be placed to the credit of the board of education as herein provided. In each city in which the law provides, prior to the time this article goes into effect, that such assessment shall be included in a school tax and assessment roll, separate and distinct from the annual tax and assessment roll, and at a different time, such assessment shall continue to be included in a school tax and assessment roll, to be prepared and levied at the same time each year as the law provides in respect to said cities prior to the time this article goes into effect. In case more than twenty-five thousand dollars is required to be raised by tax for the purposes specified in paragraph *c* of subdivision 1 of this section, the common council, or the board of education, or either, may provide for the submission to the voters of the city, at a tax election, the proposition for the expenditure of such sum or may levy a tax to be payable in installments, for such purposes, and may issue and sell municipal bonds as hereinafter provided. In cities in which the board of education is either appointed, or is elected at a general or municipal election, the submission of such question shall be to the voters of such city at either a general or municipal election.

3 In a city of the third class in which the common council, under statutes in effect prior to the time when this act takes effect, has the power to determine the amount of funds which shall be included in the estimate for the support and maintenance of public schools, and in any such city in which the mayor under such statutes has the power to consider and determine the amount included in such estimate for the support and maintenance of public schools, such common council and mayor shall have the same power and shall perform the same duties as are required under the statutes in effect

prior to the taking effect of this act, and the provisions of such statutes shall continue in full force and effect notwithstanding the provisions of this act. Nothing in this act shall be construed as conferring upon the common council of a city of the third class the power to determine the amount which shall be used for school purposes, which was not specifically conferred upon the common council of such city under the statutes in effect prior to the taking effect of this act. Where the mayor, under a statute in effect prior to the taking effect of this act, reduces, or eliminates items in the estimate for the support and maintenance of the public schools in the city, he must return such estimate to the board of education, stating his reasons for making such reductions or eliminations, within ten days after the filing of such estimate, and thereupon the board of education may take action on such estimate and may by a three-fourths vote of the members of the board restore the items so reduced or eliminated, and the estimate shall thereupon become effective and the amounts specified therein shall be levied and collected in the same manner as other city taxes are collected.

4 In a city of the second class in which the board of estimate and apportionment has authority, under the statutes in effect prior to the time this act goes into effect, to determine the amount of funds which shall be included for the support and maintenance of public schools in the estimate to be submitted to the common council, and in a city of the first class having a population of less than four hundred thousand, according to the federal census of 1910, such estimate shall be filed with the mayor. The mayor shall place such estimate before the board of estimate and apportionment at the same time and in the same manner as estimates from city departments or officers are placed before said board of estimate and apportionment, and such estimate shall thereafter be subject to the same consideration, action and procedure as all other estimates from city departments or officers. The said board of estimate and apportionment may increase, diminish or reject any item contained in said estimate, except for fixed charges for which the city is liable. When such estimate is adopted the board of estimate and apportionment shall file it with the common council.

5 The board of education in each other city of the second class shall file such estimate with the mayor. The common council of each city included within the provisions of this subdivision shall include the amount of such estimate in the tax and assessment roll of the city and the same shall be collected and placed to the credit of the board of education as herein provided, except that a tax for the purposes specified in paragraph *c* of subdivision one of this section shall be levied payable in installments and bonds therefor shall be issued and sold as hereinafter provided.

6 In a city which had, according to the federal census of 1910, a population of four hundred thousand or more but less than one million such estimate shall be filed with the officer authorized to receive other department estimates and the same acted on by such officer and by the council of such city in the same manner and with the same effect as other department estimates. The council is also authorized, in its discretion, to include in such budget a sum for any of the purposes enumerated in paragraph *c* of subdivision one of this section, and any further amount for such purposes as may be authorized by a tax election held in such city pursuant to the provisions of this chapter. After the adoption of such budget the council shall cause

the amount thereof to be included in the tax and assessment roll of the city and the same shall be collected in the same manner and at the same time as other taxes of the city are collected, and placed to the credit of the board of education.

7 In a city which had, according to the federal census of 1910, a population of one million or more such estimate shall be filed with the board of estimate and apportionment. If the total amount requested in such estimate shall be equivalent to or less than four· and nine-tenths mills on every dollar of assessed valuation of the real and personal property in such city liable to taxation, the board of estimate and apportionment shall appropriate such amount. If the total amount contained in such estimate shall exceed the said sum of four and nine-tenths mills on every dollar of assessed valuation of the real and personal property in such city liable to taxation, such estimate shall, as to such excess, be subject to such consideration and such action by the board of estimate and apportionment, the board of aldermen, and the mayor as that taken upon departmental estimates submitted to the board of estimate and apportionment. The board of estimate and apportionment is authorized to make additional appropriations for educational purposes authorized by this chapter. The general school fund shall consist of all moneys raised for the payment of the salaries of all persons employed in the supervising and teaching staff, including the superintendent of schools and all associate, district and other superintendents, members of the board of examiners, attendance officers, supervisor of lectures, lecturers and director and assistant director of the division of reference and research. The special school fund shall contain and embrace all moneys raised for educational purposes not comprised in the general school fund. The general school fund shall be raised in bulk and for the city at large. The board of education shall administer all moneys appropriated or available for educational purposes in the city, subject to the provisions of law relating to the audit and payment of salaries and other claims by the department of finance.

8 A board of education may, to meet emergencies which may arise, submit a special estimate in which items for extraordinary expenses may be submitted to meet such emergencies. Such estimate shall contain a complete statement of the purposes for which the items are requested and the necessity therefor. The same method of procedure shall be followed in submitting such estimate and such estimate shall be subject to the same consideration and action as is required in the submission, consideration and action upon the regular annual estimate submitted by a board of education. The common council in such a city shall have power to make the appropriations requested by a board of education in such special estimate. The common council of a city of the third class, the common council, the board of estimate and apportionment of a city of the second class and, in a city having a population of four hundred thousand or more and less than one million, according to the federal census of 1910, the council may temporarily borrow the amount appropriated on city certificates of indebtedness or by the issuance of revenue bonds, or other municipal bonds, which certificates of indebtedness or bonds shall be payable at such time and in such manner as shall be provided by general laws or the charter of such city for other certificates of indebtedness or revenue bonds.

9 In cities in which the boundaries of the school district or districts are

not coterminus with the city boundaries and in which the board of education, under the provisions of law existing at the time of the passage of this act, is authorized to levy taxes for school purposes, the board of education is hereby authorized and empowered to prepare, fix and determine the education budget for all the purposes set forth in this section, and said board of education shall levy and collect the necessary tax or taxes for all the purposes specified in said budget in accordance withe provisions of the education law. In the event the boundaries of said city or cities are hereafter made coterminous with the school district boundaries this provision shall no longer apply.

10 A board of education shall not incur a liability or an expense chargeable against the funds under its control or the city for any purpose in excess of the amount appropriated or available therefor or otherwise authorized by law.

11 In a city in which, under the statutes in effect prior to the time of the taking effect of this act, it is provided that the estimate of expenditures for the support and maintenance of the public schools of the city shall not be less than a specified per capita sum, based on the number of pupils enrolled in the public schools of the city, the amount authorized or required to be included in the estimate of school expenditures as provided in this act shall not be less than the per capita sum specified in such statute.

§ 878 **Tax election.** 1 In a city having a population of less than seventy-five thousand, according to the federal census of 1910, the board of education may call a tax election, by giving notice thereof as notice is required under the education law of an annual school election and submit to those qualified to vote at such election a proposition to expend a sum of money in excess of twenty-five thousand dollars for any of the purposes enumerated in paragraph *c* of subdivision 1 of section 877 of this chapter. The provisions of law relating to and governing annual school elections, including inspectors, notices, qualifications of voters, challenges, hours for keeping polls open, penalties, canvass of votes, filing returns, supplying ballots, and all other matters relating to an annual election shall apply to and govern, so far as may be practicable, a tax election except in a city in which the election of members of the board of education is held at the general or municipal election. In such cities the law applying to and governing such general or municipal elections shall apply to and govern such tax election.

2 In such a city in which the members of the board of education are elected at the general or municipal election, a tax election for like purposes may be held by direction of the board of education. The provisions of law regulating such general or municipal elections in such cities shall apply to and govern the method of calling and holding tax elections in said cities.

§ 879 **Bond issue.** 1 When the common council or the voters of a city authorize an appropriation to be raised by a tax in installments for any of the purposes enumerated in paragraph *c* of subdivision 1 of section 877 of this chapter, city bonds shall be issued in the same manner and under the same provisions as other bonds are or may be issued by such city. The principal and interest of such bonds shall be paid out of moneys raised by tax therefor in the same manner as other school moneys are raised, when such bonds and the interest thereon shall become due and payable. In a city having a population of four hundred thousand or more but less than one million, according to the federal census of 1910, such bonds shall be issued by the council.

2 In a city of the second class and in a city of the first class having a population of less than four hundred thousand, according to the federal census of 1910, the common council and the board of estimate and apportionment shall have power to determine upon the necessity of issuing bonds for any of the purposes enumerated in paragraph *c* of subdivision 1 of section 877 of this chapter, and when bonds shall be thus authorized such bonds shall be issued by the municipal authorities.

3 In a city having a population of four hundred thousand or more but less than one million, the council of such city may, by a vote of four-fifths of its members, authorize from time to time the issuance of bonds of said city to defray the expense of the construction, improvement and equipment of school buildings or the purchase or acquisition of school sites, which expense shall not have been included in the budget, in such amounts and payable at such times and places and having such rates of interest, not exceeding six per centum per annum, as said council may determine, interest to be paid semiannually, said bonds, however, to be due in not more than fifty years from their date and to be sold for not less than their par value and accrued interest. Such bonds may be made payable in equal proportions during a number of successive years not exceeding a period of fifty years from their issuance, as the council shall determine. Such bonds shall be issued and sold by the authorities of the city in the same manner that bonds for other municipal purposes are issued and sold and the proceeds of the sale of such bonds shall be paid into the treasury of the city and placed to the credit of the board of education. As such bonds become due the municipal authorities of the city shall include in the tax levy, and assess upon the property of the city, the amount necessary to pay such bonds and interest thereon.

4 In a city having a population of one million or more, the board of estimate and apportionment may in its discretion annually cause to be raised such sums of money as may be required for the purposes enumerated in subdivision *c* of section 877 of this act, in the manner provided by law for the raising of money for such purposes.

§ 880 **Funds; custody and disbursement of.** 1 Public moneys apportioned to a city by the state and all funds raised or collected by the authorities of a city for school purposes or to be used by the board of education for any purpose authorized in this chapter, or any other funds belonging to a city and received from any source whatsoever for similar purposes, shall be paid into the treasury of such city and shall be credited to the board of education.

2 Such funds shall be disbursed only by authority of the board of education and upon written orders drawn on the city treasurer or other fiscal officer of the city. Such orders shall be signed by the superintendent of schools and the secretary of the board of education or such other officers as the board may authorize. Such orders shall be numbered consecutively and shall specify the purpose for which they are drawn and the person or corporation to whom they are payable.

3 It shall be unlawful for a city treasurer or other officer having the custody of city funds to permit the use of such funds for any purpose other

than that for which they are lawfully authorized and such funds shall not be paid out except on audit of the board of education and the countersignature of the comptroller, and in a city having no comptroller by an officer designated by the officer or body having the general control of the financial affairs of such city. The board of education of such city shall make, in addition to such classification of its funds and accounts as it desires for its own use and information, such further classification of the funds under its management and control and of the disbursements thereof as the comptroller of the city, or the officer or body having the general control of the financial affairs of such city, shall require, and such board shall furnish such data in relation to such funds and their disbursements as the comptroller or such other financial officer or body of the city shall require.

§ 881 **Continuation in office of boards, bureaus, teachers, principals and other employees, et cetera.** 1 Except as otherwise provided herein the boards, bureaus, teachers, principals, supervisors, superintendents, heads of departments, assistants to principals, examiners, supervisor of lectures, directors and all other officers and employees of the school system or of boards of education of the several cities of the State, lawfully appointed or assigned before this act takes effect, shall continue to hold their respective positions for the term for which they were appointed or until removed as provided in subdivision 3 of section 872 of this article.

2 If a board of education abolishes an office or position and creates another office or position for the performance of duties similar to those performed in the office or position abolished, the person filling such office or position at the time of its abolishment shall be appointed to the office or position thus created without reduction in salary or increment, provided the record of such person has been one of faithful, competent service in the office or position he has filled.

3 If an office or position is abolished or if it is consolidated with another position without creating a new position, the person filling such position at the time of its abolishment or consolidation shall be placed upon a preferred eligible list of candidates for appointment to a vacancy that may thereafter occur in an office or position similar to the one which such person filled without reduction in salary or increment, provided the record of such person has been one of faithful, competent service in the office or position he has filled. The names of such persons shall be placed upon such preferred list in the order in which their services have been thus discontinued.

§ 2 **City school district.** Each city in which the school district boundaries are coterminus with the city boundaries is hereby declared to be a city school district. In a city in which the city boundaries and the school district boundaries are not coterminus the school district boundaries shall remain as they existed prior to the time this act takes effect and until such time as such school district boundaries may be changed as provided by law. In each city where the school district boundaries are not coterminus with the city boundaries the school district which contains the whole or the greater portion of the inhabitants of the city shall be the city school district of said city and shall be subject to the provisions of this act.

§ 3 **Repeal of inconsistent provisions; effect of repeal.** All acts or parts of acts, general or special, inconsistent with the provisions of this act are hereby repealed. The repeal of the act specified in the schedule hereto annexed, or of such inconsistent acts or parts of such acts, shall not affect any right existing or accrued or any liability incurred prior to the passage of this act, and all acts or parts of acts, general or special, not specifically repealed by this act and not inconsistent with the provisions of this act shall remain in full force and effect.

§ 4 **Pending actions or proceedings; existing rules.** The repeal of a law or any part of it specified in the annexed schedule and any provision of this act shall not affect pending actions or proceedings brought by or against the board of education of a city, or by or against a city, in respect to the public schools thereof, under or in pursuance of any of the provisions of the laws hereby repealed, but the same may be prosecuted or defended in the same manner and for the same purpose by the board of education of the city under the provisions of this chapter as though such laws had not been repealed. The rules and regulations adopted by a board of education in pursuance of any law hereby repealed shall continue in full force and effect notwithstanding such repeal, until the same are modified, amended or repealed by the board of education as provided in this chapter. Nothing in this act shall affect titles to school property, but such property may be held either in the name of the city school district or of the board of education, as provided in this act or in any other act relating to titles to such property.

§ 5 **Time of taking effect.** This act shall take effect immediately.

§ 6 **Laws repealed.** Of the laws enumerated in the schedule hereto annexed, that portion specified in the last column is hereby repealed.

SCHEDULE OF LAWS REPEALED

Laws of	Chapter	Section	Laws of	Chapter	Section
1829	234	All	1868	729	All
1842	137	All	1869	43	All
1844	131	All	1869	122	All
1844	175	All	1869	363	All
1846	7	All	1870	118	All
1847	51	All	1871	186	All
1849	184	105, 106	1873	234	All
1850	66	All	1873	386	All
1850	77	All	1873	623	All
1852	156	All	1873	666	All
1852	258	All	1875	169	All
1853	252	All	1875	577	All
1854	348	All	1877	243	All
1856	164	5	1877	441	All
1857	382	All	1879	318	All
1857	572	All	1880	17	2
1858	34	1–9, 11–21	1880	524	All
1858	95	All	1881	70	All
1858	269	All	1881	180	All
1859	105	All	1881	294	All
1859	298	All	1882	168	All
1862	18	124	1883	163	All
1863	377	All	1884	61	All
1864	98	All	1885	26	174–183
1865	88	All	1885	313	All
1866	9	All	1886	120	58, 268
1866	58	All	1887	279	All
1866	378	All	1887	368	16
1866	579	All	1888	103	All
1867	115	All	1888	381	All
1867	353	All	1889	15	All
1867	573	All	1889	18	All
1867	787	All	1889	220	All
1867	822	All	1889	387	All
1868	82	All	1890	15	All
1868	249	All	1890	215	All
1868	312	All	1891	105	324–343, 343-a, 344–348
1868	630	All			

FREE SCHOOLS

Laws of	Chapter	Section
1892	22	All
1892	182	229, 229-a–229-s
1892	626	5
1892	671	Title 6, §§ 1–125
1893	10	All
1893	216	All
1893	345	7
1893	381	All
1893	454	All
1893	524	All
1893	531	20–24
1894	10	All
1894	33	All
1894	454	All
1895	123	All
1895	189	All
1895	370	All
1895	394	156–177
1895	526	All
1895	565	5, 42
1895	751	144–150, 150-a–150-c, 151–155
1895	831	All
1895	950	23–27
1895	998	All
1895	1032	All
1896	146	All
1896	161	All
1896	416	All
1896	425	161–169
1896	710	All
1896	747	161–181
1897	372	All
1897	378	1056, 1059–1064, 1067, 1068, all of 1069, except subdivision 8, 1070–1090, 1093
1897	402	All
1897	479	All
1897	752	All
1897	700	84, 85, 86, subds. 1–12; 87–97, 99
1898	48	All
1898	182	240–252
1898	232	6
1898	298	All
1898	430	All
1898	431	All
1898	498	All
1899	40	All
1899	275	74, 185–197
1899	304	1–20
1899	586	All
1899	627	All
1900	152	All
1900	160	150–166
1900	562	All
1900	563	All
1900	573	All
1900	659	8, part amending §§ 161–163, 166, 167
1901	56	2, 3
1901	110	All
1901	127	All
1901	196	18, 19
1901	204	16–19
1901	285	All
1901	298	All
1901	466	1056, 1059–1064, 1067, 1068, all of 1069 except subdivision 8, 1070–1090, 1093
1901	473	All
1901	718	All
1902	63	150–167
1902	223	All
1902	269	98–113
1902	284	All
1902	494	1
1902	560	All
1902	572	160–174
1903	43	All
1903	46	All
1903	71	All
1903	187	All
1903	249	2
1903	295	5
1903	399	6, 8
1903	416	All
1903	449	3, parts amending §§ 99–101
1903	555	All
1903	562	All
1904	189	All
1904	242	All
1904	300	340–353
1904	319	6, parts amending §§ 106–109, 113
1904	542	199–208
1904	650	All
1905	109	All
1905	357	Title 22, §§ 1–13
1905	364	All
1905	468	20
1905	486	All
1905	593	220–241
1906	68	All
1906	335	17
1906	495	All
1907	118	All
1907	130	All
1907	165	All
1907	203	Title 12, § 4
1907	537	All
1907	543	All
1907	595	All
1907	653	6
1907	751	384–405
1907	752	Title 18, §§ 1–3
1907	755	90, 381–404
1908	29	167, 168, 168-a, 169, 170
1908	51	All
1908	336	All
1908	406	All
1908	452	Article 9, §§ 1–17, 20
1908	454	150–166
1908	481	All
1908	503	170–199
1909	85	All
1909	365	2, 3
1909	550	24, 25
1909	574	150–153
1909	591	All
1910	49	All
1910	101	All
1910	391	All
1910	464	All
1910	466	All
1910	491	1, part amending §§ 152, 153
1910	559	351–365
1910	632	93–99
1911	77	All
1911	184	165–184, and so much of section 17 as relates to the salary of the city superintendent of schools
1911	187	7, 8
1911	242	116–129
1911	340	2
1911	386	All

Laws of	Chapter	Section	Laws of	Chapter	Section
1911	422	All	1914	226	All
1911	522	All	1914	228	All
1911	617	32–34	1914	281	20
1911	645	19, 20	1914	286	All
1911	648	44, subd. 7; 240–256	1914	289	All
			1914	354	200
1911	699	36–38	1914	476	1
1912	438	All	1915	13	11
1912	455	All	1915	69	279–289
1913	13	All	1915	113	All
1913	45	All	1915	229	120
1913	314	All	1915	356	257–268
1913	481	250–257	1915	359	3
1913	507	127–142	1915	611	49–51
1913	539	102	1916	229	23
1913	659	1, part amending § 383, subd. 7	1916	271	All
			1916	431	All
1913	688	All	1916	464	15, 16
1913	749	All	1916	488	All
1914	4	1	1916	530	92, 281–294
1914	217	290–293	1916	575	80–84

Chapter 791

AN ACT to amend the Education Law, relative to school elections in certain cities

Became a law June 8, 1917, with the approval of the Governor. Passed, three-fifths being present.

The People of the State of New York, represented in Senate and Assembly, do enact as follows:

Section 1. Chapter 21 of the Laws of 1909, entitled "An act relating to education, constituting chapter 16 of the Consolidated Laws," as amended by chapter 140 of the Laws of 1910, is hereby amended by inserting therein a new article, to be known as article 7-a, and to read as follows:

ARTICLE 7-A
School Elections in Certain Cities

Section 208 Application of article
　　　　 209 Annual school election
　　　　 210 Qualifications of electors
　　　　 211 Division of city or district into districts; elections held in schoolhouses
　　　　 212 Notices of election
　　　　 213 Preparation of poll lists; correction
　　　　 214 Inspectors of election; organization
　　　　 215 Nomination and ballot
　　　　 216 Conduct of election; challenges
　　　　 217 Canvass of votes and return to board of education; declaration of result
　　　　 218 Use of voting machines

§ 208 **Application of article.** This article shall apply to each city in the State, in which members of the board of education are elected by the qualified electors of such city at an election other than a general or municipal election.

§ 209 **Annual school election.** 1 An annual election shall be held on the first Tuesday of May in each city to which this article applies.

2 The polls of such election shall be open from twelve o'clock noon until eight o'clock in the evening.

§ 210 **Qualifications of voters.** A person shall be entitled to vote at a school election in such city who is:

1 A citizen of the United States.
2 Twenty-one years of age.
3 A resident within the election district for a period of thirty days next preceding the election at which he offers to vote; and who in addition thereto possesses one of the following four qualifications.

a Owns or hires real property in such district or is in the possession of such property under a contract of purchase, assessed upon the last preceding assessment roll of the city, or

b Is the parent of a child of school age, provided such child shall have attended the public schools in the city in which the election is held for a period of at least eight weeks during the year preceding such election, or

c Not being the parent, has permanently residing with him a child of school age who shall have attended such public schools for a period of at least eight weeks during the year preceding such election, or

d Owns personal property, assessed on the last preceding assessment-roll of the city, exceeding fifty dollars in value, exclusive of such as is exempt from execution.

No person shall be deemed to be ineligible to vote at any such election, by reason of sex, who has the other qualifications required by this section.

§ 211 **Division of city into districts; elections held in schoolhouses.** The board of education of each such city shall adopt a resolution on or before the first day of April, preceding the first annual school election held hereunder, dividing the city into school election districts. The city shall be so divided, that if circumstances will permit, there shall be a schoolhouse in each district and each district shall contain not more than one thousand qualified voters. The districts thus formed shall continue in existence until modified by resolution of the board of education. Such resolution shall accurately describe the boundaries of such districts by streets, alleys and highways, when practicable, and shall, so far as may be, include one or more of the regular election districts of such city. School elections shall be held in such districts so far as may be possible in the public schoolhouses therein. If there is no public schoolhouse in a district the board of education shall by resolution designate the place where the election in such district shall be held.

§ 212 **Notices of election.** The board of education shall cause a notice of the annual school election to be published at least once in each week for the four weeks preceding such election, in at least two newspapers published in such city. Such notice shall state the day of the election and the hours during which the polls are to be open, shall accurately describe the boundaries of the school election districts into which the city is divided, and shall specify the schoolhouses or other places therein where such election will be held. Such notice shall also state that poll lists prepared by the clerk of the board of education as required by this article containing the names of the qualified electors of each school election district are on file and may be examined at the office of such clerk or of the superintendent of schools of such city.

§ 213 **Preparation of poll lists; correction.** 1 The secretary or clerk of the board of education in each such city shall on or before the first day of April in each year prepare a poll list for each school election district which shall contain the names of all persons residing in such district who shall be qualified to vote for candidates for the offices of members of the board of education at the ensuing election. The names on such list shall be arranged alphabetically by the surnames, and the place of residence by street and number of each person named on such list, if any, and if not, some description accurately locating such place of residence shall be given on such list.

2 Such list shall be placed on file in the office of the secretary or clerk of the board of education or some other suitable and accessible place to be designated by the board of education where it may be examined by persons interested therein during the office hours of such secretary or clerk for thirty days preceding the annual school election and from four to eight o'clock in the evening of each Friday and Saturday of the four weeks immediately preceding the election. The secretary or clerk of the board of education or some person to be designated by such board shall attend at such office at such times, and shall permit such lists to be examined by the public.

3 Any person whose name is not upon such list, who is or will be a qualified voter of the city at such election, may file a written statement with the secretary or clerk of the board of education giving his name, place of residence, occupation and the school election district in which he resides, and specifying the qualifications which entitle him to vote at such election. The name of such voter shall thereupon be placed on such poll list. If such person appears before the secretary or clerk of the board of education and furnishes the information above required, such secretary or clerk shall place his name upon the poll list.

4 If a qualified voter is a resident of a school election district and his name appears on a poll list as a resident of another district, a written statement may be filed by such voter with the secretary or clerk of the board of education showing his correct residence and the name of such voter shall thereupon be stricken from such poll list and placed upon the proper poll list.

5 The board of education shall furnish blanks for such statements, which shall be used by the voters in presenting the facts above prescribed. No change or alteration of such list shall be made by any person before the correction and revision thereof as hereinafter provided.

6 Such statements and challenges shall be received and preserved by the secretary or clerk of the board or other person designated by the board, and on the Monday preceding the annual election such secretary or clerk shall correct and revise each of such duplicate lists by striking therefrom and inserting in their proper places the names of persons who have filed the statements above referred to and shall indicate on such lists the persons whose qualifications as voters have been challenged.

7 Such corrected and revised lists shall be filed in the office of the secretary or clerk of the board of education. Such board shall cause a copy of the list of each election district to be delivered on the day of the election, before the opening of the polls therein, to the inspectors of such districts, at the place where the election in such district is to be held.

8 A qualified voter may, upon the examination of such list, file a written challenge of the qualifications as a voter of any person whose name appears on such list. Such challenge shall be written and shall be on blanks to be furnished by the board of education.

§ 214 **Inspectors of election; organization.** The board of education shall appoint not less than ten days prior to each school election three qualified voters residing in each school election district to act as inspectors of elections in such district at the annual election. The secretary or clerk of the board of education shall given[1] written notice of appointment to the persons so appointed. If a person appointed an inspector of election refuses to accept such appointment or fails to serve, the board may appoint a qualified voter of the school election district to fill the vacancy. Not more than two additional inspectors of elections for each district may be appointed for one more of such school election districts, when, in the opinion of the board, special circumstances exist requiring the services of such additional inspectors. Such inspectors shall, before opening the polls in the election district for which they are appointed, organize by electing one of their number as chairman, and one as poll clerk. Each inspector shall receive for his services a compensation of three dollars, to be paid out of the school funds in the same manner as other claims against the city or district.

§ 215 **Nomination and ballot.** 1 Candidates for members of the board of education in a city to which this article applies shall be nominated by petition directed to the board of education and signed by at least thirty persons qualified to vote at school elections in such city. Such petition shall contain the name and residences of the candidates for the vacancies in the board of education to be filled at the annual election and shall state whether such candidates are nominated for full terms or for the unexpired portions of such terms. Such petitions shall be filed with the secretary or clerk of the board of education, on or before the tenth day preceding the day of the annual election.

2 The board of education shall cause to be printed official ballots containing the names of all candidates as above provided. The ballots shall separately state whether the persons named thereon are candidates for full terms or for unexpired terms. The names of the candidates shall be arranged alphabetically according to their surnames in columns under titles or designations showing whether they are to be elected for full terms or unexpired terms. Blank spaces shall be provided so that voters may vote for candidates who have not been nominated for the offices to be filled at such election. The form of such ballots shall conform substantially to the form of ballots used at general elections as prescribed in the election law. Such ballots shall be printed at the expense of the city and the cost thereof shall be paid out of funds appropriated for school purposes and available therefor.

3 There shall be delivered to the inspectors in each school election district on the day of the annual election a supply of such ballots which shall at least equal the number of qualified voters in such district as appears from the poll list thereof.

4 Such ballots shall have printed thereon instructions as to the marking of the ballots and the number of candidates for the several offices for which a voter is permitted to vote.

[1] So in original.

5 If official ballots are not furnished as above provided, an election of members of a board of education in such city shall not be declared invalid or illegal because of the use of ballots which do not conform to the requirements of this section or of the provisions of the election law, provided the intent of the voter may be ascertained from the use of such irregular or defective ballots and such use was not fraudulent and did not substantially affect the result of the election.

§ 216 **Conduct of election; challenges.** 1 Such election shall be conducted, so far as may be, in accordance with the provisions of the election law, relative to general elections, except as otherwise provided herein. Ballot boxes shall be provided by the board of education for each school election district, one to contain the ballots voted and the other for the rejected or defective ballots.

2 All persons whose names appear upon the poll list as residing in such election district shall be permitted to vote and shall be given ballots for such purpose.

3 Booths shall be provided and voters shall be required to enter such booths for the purpose of marking their ballots. The ballots when presented to the inspector shall be folded so as to conceal the names of the candidates for whom the voter has voted.

4 All voters entitled to vote who are in the place where the election is held at or before the time of closing the polls shall be allowed to vote. The inspector shall keep a poll list, containing the name and address of each qualified elector who votes at such election for the candidates or propositions or questions voted for thereat.

5 Any qualified voter of a district may challenge the right of a person to vote at the time when he requests a ballot. All persons named upon the poll list as having been challenged prior to the day of the election shall also be challenged before they are given ballots to vote. The chairman of the board of inspectors shall administer to each person so challenged the following oath: "I do solemnly swear (or affirm) that I am a citizen of the United States; that I am of the age of twenty-one years or more; that I have been for the thirty days last past an actual resident of this city; and that in addition thereto I possess one of the four qualifications prescribed by section two hundred and ten of the education law, to wit: — (Here state facts upon which qualifications are claimed), and am therefore qualified to vote at this election." The chairman of the board of inspectors shall before administering such oath inform the person so challenged of the four qualifications prescribed by such section. If the person challenged so swears or affirms, he shall be permitted to vote at such election; but if he shall refuse to so swear or affirm, he shall not be given a ballot or be permitted to vote.

6 A person who wilfully swears or affirms falsely as to his right to vote at such election after his right to vote has been challenged is guilty of perjury and may be punished in the manner provided by law for the punishment of such crime. A person who is not qualified to vote at such election who shall vote thereat, although not challenged, shall be guilty of a misdemeanor, punishable by a fine of not less than twenty-five dollars, or by imprisonment for not less than thirty days, or by both such fine and imprisonment.

§ 217 **Canvass of votes and return to board of education; declaration**

of result. 1 Immediately upon the close of the polls the inspectors of each school election district shall count the ballots found in the ballot box without unfolding them, except so far as is necessary to ascertain that each ballot is single. They shall compare the number of ballots found in the ballot box with the number of persons recorded on the poll list as having voted at the election. If the number of ballots found in the ballot box shall exceed the number of names, such ballots shall be replaced without being unfolded in the box from which they were taken and shall be thoroughly mingled in such box and one of the inspectors designated by the board shall then publicly draw out as many ballots as shall be equal to the number of excess ballots. The ballots so drawn out shall be enclosed without unfolding in an envelop which shall be sealed and endorsed with a statement of the number of such excess ballots withdrawn from the box and shall be signed by the inspector who withdrew such ballots. Such envelop with the excess ballots therein shall be placed in the box for the defective or spoiled ballots.

2 The ballots shall be counted or canvassed by the inspectors in the manner provided for the canvassing of ballots at a general election except as otherwise provided herein. The votes cast for each candidate shall be tallied and counted by the inspectors and a statement shall be made containing the names of each candidate receiving votes in such district and the number of votes cast for each candidate. Such statement shall also give the number and describe the ballots which are declared void and shall also specify the number of wholly blank ballots cast. Such statement shall be signed by the inspectors. The ballots which were declared void and not counted shall be enclosed in an envelop which shall be sealed and endorsed as containing void ballots and signed by the inspectors. Such envelop shall be placed in the ballot box containing the defective and spoiled ballots.

3 After the ballots are counted and the statements have been made as required herein the ballots shall be replaced in the ballot box. Each box shall be securely locked and sealed and deposited by an inspector designated for the purpose with the secretary or clerk of the board of education. The unused ballots shall be placed in a sealed package and returned by the inspector designated for such purpose to the said secretary or clerk at the same time that such ballot boxes are delivered to him. The statement of the canvass of the votes shall be delivered to the secretary or clerk of the board of education on the day following the annual election.

4 The board of education shall meet at the usual place of meeting at eight o'clock in the evening of the day following such election and shall forthwith examine and tabulate the statements of the result of the election in the several school election districts. The said board shall canvass the returns as contained in such statements and shall determine the number of votes cast for each candidate in the several school election districts. The board shall thereupon declare the result of the canvass. The candidates receiving a plurality of the votes cast respectively for the several offices shall be declared elected. The secretary or clerk of the board of education shall record the result of the election as announced by the board of education.

5 The secretary or clerk of the board of education shall within twenty-four hours after the result of the election has been declared serve a written notice either personally or by mail upon each person declared to be elected as a member of the board of education.

§ 218 **Use of voting machines.** In a city in which voting machines are used at general or municipal elections, it shall be lawful for the board of education of such city to authorize the use of such voting machines at a school election. When such voting machines are used the law relating to the use of such machines at a general or municipal election shall apply to and govern the use of such machines in a school election.

§ 2 This act shall take effect immediately.

Chapter 303

AN ACT to amend the Greater New York charter and to repeal sections 1092–a, 1092–b and 1092–c, thereof, in relation to teachers' retirement fund.

Became a law May 1, 1917, with the approval of the Governor. Passed, three-fifths being present.

Accepted by the city

The People of the State of New York, represented in Senate and Assembly, do enact as follows:

Section 1 Section 1092 of the Greater New York charter, as reenacted by chapter 466 of the Laws of 1901, and amended by chapter 530 of the Laws of 1902, chapter 177 of the Laws of 1903, chapter 661 of the Laws of 1905, chapter 167 of the Laws of 1907 and chapter 476 of the Laws of 1914, is hereby amended to read as follows:

§ 1092 The following words and phrases as used in this act, unless a different meaning is plainly required by the context, shall have the following meanings:

(1) "Retirement system" shall mean the arrangement for the payment of retirement allowances, under the provisions of this act.

(2) "Retirement association" shall mean the teachers' retirement association provided for in subdivision B of this act.

(3) "Retirement board" shall mean the teachers' retirement board provided for in subdivision C of this act.

(4) "Medical board" shall mean the board of physicians provided for in subdivision T of this act.

(5) "Board of education" shall mean the board of education of the city of New York.

(6) "Public school" shall mean any class, school, high school, normal school, training school, vocational school, truant school, parental school, and all schools or classes conducted under the order and superintendence of the board of education, and the schools or classes maintained by the department of public charities or by the department of correction in pursuance of the rules established or to be established by the board of education, or by the commissioner of public charities or by the commissioner of correction for schools or classes maintained by such commissioners, respectively.

(7) "Teacher" shall mean the city superintendent of schools, the associate city superintendents, the district superintendents, the director and the assistant director of the divisions of reference and research, the director and the assistant directors of the bureau of compulsory education, school census and child welfare, the members of the board of examiners, the directors and the assistant directors of special branches, the supervisor and the assistant

supervisors of lectures, all principals, vice-principals, assistants-to-principals, heads of departments, and all regular and special teachers of the public day schools of the city of New York, and all employees of the board of education appointed to regular positions in the service of the public schools at annual salaries and whose appointments were made or shall hereafter be made from eligible lists prepared as the result of examinations held by the board of examiners of the department of education.

(8) "Present-teacher" shall mean any teacher employed in the public schools at a teacher on the first day of August, 1917, or on leave of absence on said date.

(9) "New-entrant" shall mean any teacher appointed to serve in the public schools after the first day of August, 1917.

(10) "Contributor" shall mean any member of the retirement association.

(11) "Transferred-contributor" shall mean a contributor as defined in subdivision I of this act.

(12) "Beneficiary" shall mean any person in receipt of a pension, an annuity, a retirement allowance, or other benefit as provided in this act.

(13) "City-service" shall mean any service as an employee of the city of New York or of any department, bureau, board or corporation created under the provisions of the Greater New York charter, or as an employee of any of the municipalities, counties or parts thereof which are included within the boundaries of the city of New York or which have been incorporated into said city.

(14) "Prior-service" shall mean all city-service and all teaching or supervisory service in schools or colleges not maintained by the city of New York computed to and including the sixteenth day of September, 1917, in the case of a present-teacher and in the case of a new-entrant to the date of his appointment as a teacher, subject to the limitations and restrictions imposed by subdivision H of this act.

(15) "Total-service" shall mean all prior-service together with all subsequent service as a teacher or contributor as provided in this act.

(16) "Service retirement" shall mean retirement as defined in subdivision K of this act.

(17) "Disability retirement" shall mean retirement as defined in subdivision L of this act.

(18) "Average salary" shall mean the average annual salary earnable by a contributor for the ten years immediately preceding retirement except that in case a contributor shall retire prior to the first days of January, 1922, average salary shall mean the average annual salary earnable by the contributor since the first day of January, 1912.

(19) "Minimum contribution" shall mean (a) the amount realized by deducting from the salary of a contributor three per centum of his earnable salary; or (b) such per centum thereof, if less than three per centum, as shall be computed to be sufficient, with regular interest, when paid until age sixty-five, to provide for him on retirement at that age with an annuity which, when added to his pension provided for in this act, will provide a retirement allowance of fifty per centum of his average salary.

(20) "Minimum accumulation" shall mean the amount created by the accumulation of the minimum contributions, together with the regular interest thereon.

(21) "Accumulated deductions" shall mean the total of the amounts deducted from the salary of a contributor and standing to the credit of his individual account in the annuity savings fund, together with the regular interest thereon.

(22) "Regular interest" shall mean interest at four per centum per annum, compounded annually.

(23) "Pension" shall mean payments for life derived from appropriations made by the city of New York and from any other sources of revenue of the pension reserve funds as provided in this act.

(24) "Annuity" shall mean payments for life derived from contributions made by a contributor as provided in this act.

(25) "Retirement allowance" shall mean the pension, plus the annuity.

(26) "Pension reserve" shall mean the present value computed on the basis of such mortality tables as shall be adopted by the retirement board, with regular interest, of the future payments to be made on account of any pension granted under the provisions of this act.

(27) "Annuity reserve" shall mean the present value computed on the basis of such mortality tables as shall be adopted by the retirement board, with regular interest, of the future payments to be made on account of any annuity or benefit granted and based on the accumulated deductions of the contributor.

(28) "Expense fund" shall mean the fund provided for in paragraph numbered 1 in subdivision F of this act.

(29) "Contingent reserve fund" shall mean the fund provided for in paragraph numbered 2 in subdivision F of this act.

(30) "Pension reserve fund number one" shall mean the fund provided for in paragraph numbered 3 in subdivision F of this act.

(31) "Pension reserve fund number two" shall mean the fund provided for in paragraph numbered 4 in subdivision F of this act.

(32) "Annuity savings fund" shall mean the fund provided for in paragraph numbered 5 in subdivision F of this act.

(33) "Annuity reserve fund" shall mean the fund provided for in paragraph numbered 6 in subdivision F of this act.

(34) "Fiscal year" shall mean the year commencing with January first and ending with December thirty-first next following.

A The retirement system shall be established on the first day of August, 1917.

B A teachers' retirement association is hereby organized among the teachers of the public schools; its membership shall consist of the following:

1 All teachers who have been granted or shall hereafter be granted permanent licenses pursuant to section 1089.

2 All teachers, without a permanent license, who shall file a statement in writing with the retirement board consenting to membership in the retirement association and to the deductions for annuity purposes prescribed in this act.

3 All transferred-contributors.

C 1 A retirement board of seven members is hereby constituted which shall consist of the following:

(a) The president of the board of education.

(b) The comptroller of the city of New York.

(c) Two members appointed by the mayor of the city of New York, one of whom shall be a member of the board of education; they shall serve until their successors are appointed. Should the board-of-education member of the retirement board cease to be a member of the board of education, he shall thereupon cease to be a member of the retirement board.

(d) Three members of the retirement association elected from the contributors as follows: On the first Thursday of May, 1917, and in each year thereafter, the contributors in each public school shall meet in their respective schools at three o'clock in the afternoon, or if the administrative conditions in any school are such that the meeting ought to be held at some other hour, then at such hour in said school as shall be designated by the city superintendent of schools after consultation with the principal of said school; the prinicipal of the school, and in his absence the acting principal, shall call the meeting to order, and the contributors present at the meeting shall proceed to elect from their number by ballot a chairman and a secretary, and shall then elect from their number by ballot one delegate for each ten contributors and major fraction thereof in said school; each school shall have at least one delegate. At the close of the meeting the secretary thereof shall transmit to the district superintendent in charge of the school the names of the delegates so elected. On the second Thursday of May, 1917, and in each year thereafter, said delegates shall meet at three o'clock in the afternoon in one of the schools in the district designated by the district superintendent; said designation shall be made and mailed by the district superintendent to each delegate at least three days before the second Thursday of May. For the purpose of attending the meeting each delegate shall leave his school not later than two-thirty o'clock in the afternoon on said second Thursday of May. No delegate shall suffer loss of pay by reason of attendance at said meeting. Said delegates shall be called to order by the principal of the school, and in his absence by the acting principal of the school, in which the meeting is held. Two-thirds of the delegates elected in a district shall constitute a quorum for that district. The delegates present at the meeting shall proceed to elect from their number by ballot a chairman and a secretary, and shall then elect from their number by ballot a representative and an alternate for said representative. Immediately after the meeting, the secretary thereof shall transmit to the secretary of the board of education the name of the representative and the name of the alternate so elected. The representatives shall meet at three o'clock in the afternoon of the third Thursday of May in each year at the hall of the board of education; for the purpose of attending said meeting, the representatives shall leave their respective schools at two o'clock in the afternoon on said third Thursday of May. No representative shall suffer loss of pay by reason of attendance at said meeting. Said meeting shall be called to order by the city superintendent of schools, or, in his absence, by the acting city superintendent of schools; two-thirds of the said representatives shall constitute a quorum; said representatives shall elect from their number by ballot a chairman and a secretary, and shall then elect by ballot a contributor to serve as a member of the retirement board for three years. At the first meeting of the representatives after this act takes effect, said representatives shall elect by ballot three contributors to serve as members of the retirement board; the three so elected shall determine by lot their terms of office as, one, two, and three years, respectively. Should a vacancy occur among the members of the retirement board elected by the representatives, said representatives shall meet within ten days thereafter at a special meeting at the call of the president of the board of education, and they shall proceed to elect by ballot a contributor to serve on said retirement board for the unexpired term. The proceedings at this special meeting shall be in all respects the same as the proceedings at the regular meeting held on the third Thursday of May. Should a vacancy occur among the representatives, or should any representative be unable to attend any meeting, his place shall be taken at said meeting by his alternate.

(e) For the purpose of voting for delegates on the first Thursday of May, 1917, all teachers shall be considered to be contributors.

(f) For the purpose of voting for delegates, teachers and contributors, not appointed as regular teachers to any public school, shall be considered to be teachers regularly appointed to teach in such schools as the board of education by its by-laws shall prescribe.

2 The members of the retirement board shall serve as such without compensation but shall be reimbursed from the expense fund for any necessary expenditures and no contributor shall suffer loss of salary or wages through serving on the retirement board.

3 The retirement board shall elect from its membership a chairman, and shall appoint a secretary, an actuary, and such medical, clerical and other employees as may be necessary.

4 The compensation of all employees of the retirement board shall be fixed by said retirement board subject to the approval of the board of estimate and apportionment.

5 Subject to the limitations of this act and of law, the retirement board shall from time to time establish rules and regulations for the administration of the funds created by this act and for the transaction of its business.

6 The retirement board shall keep in convenient form such data as shall be necessary for actuarial valuation of the various funds created by this act.

7 In the years 1919 and 1922, and in every fifth year thereafter, the actuary of the retirement board shall make an actuarial investigation into the mortality and service experience of the contributors and beneficiaries as defined in this act, and shall make a valuation of the various funds created by this act, and on the basis of such investigation and valuation the retirement board shall

(a) Adopt for the retirement system one or more mortality tables and such other tables as shall be deemed necessary;

(b) Certify the rates of deduction from salary necessary to pay the annuities authorized under the provisions of this act; and

(c) Certify the rates of contribution, expressed as a percentage of salary of new entrants at various ages, which shall be made by the city of New York to the contingent reserve fund.

8 Immediately after the passage of this act the actuary of the retirement board shall make such investigation of the mortality, service, and salary experience of the teachers as the retirement board shall authorize. On the basis of such investigation and upon the recommendation of the actuary the retirement board shall adopt such tables and certify such rates as are **required in subsections** *a, b,* **and** *c* **of paragraph 7 immediately preceding.**

On the basis of such tables the actuary of the retirement board shall as soon as practicable after the first day of August, 1917, make a valuation of the various funds created by this act.

9 The retirement board shall publish annually a report certified to by each member showing the condition of the various funds created by this act, and setting forth such other facts, recommendations, and data, as may be of use in the advancement of knowledge concerning teachers' pensions and annuities; and said retirement board shall submit said report to the mayor of the city of New York and shall file at least fifty copies thereof with the board of education for the use of said board and of its members; and at least one copy in each school for the use of the teachers thereof. It shall also file one copy in the office of the city superintendent of schools, and of each associate city superintendent of schools, and of each district superintendent of schools.

10 Each member of the retirement board shall take an oath of office that he will, so far as it devolves upon him, diligently and honestly administer the affairs of said retirement board and that he will not knowingly violate or wilfully permit to be violated any of the provisions of law applicable to this act. Such oath shall be subscribed by the member making it, and certified by the officer before whom it is taken, and shall be immediately filed in the office of the clerk of the county of New York.

11 The concurrence of the comptroller or of one member appointed by the mayor, of a member elected by the retirement association, and of at least two other members shall be necessary for a decision of the retirement board.

12 The retirement board shall keep a record of all its proceedings open to public inspection.

13 The retirement board shall perform such other functions as are required for the execution of the provisions of this act.

D For the purposes of this act, the retirement board shall possess the powers and privileges of a corporation, and as such may sue and be sued. The corporation counsel of the city of New York shall be the legal adviser of said retirement board.

E The funds created by this act shall be managed as follows:

1 The members of the retirement board shall be the trustees of the several funds created by this act, and shall have exclusive control and management of said funds, and shall have full power to invest the same, subject, however, to all the terms, conditions, limitations, and restrictions imposed by this act upon the making of investments and subject also to the terms, conditions, limitations, and restrictions imposed by law upon savings banks in the making and disposing of investments by savings banks; and, subject to like terms, conditions, limitations, and restrictions, said trustees shall have full power to hold, purchase, sell, assign, transfer, or dispose of any of the securities and investments in which any of the funds created by this act shall have been invested as well as of the proceeds of said investments, and of any moneys belonging to said funds. The retirement board shall annually allow regular interest on each of the funds as provided for in this act with the exception of the expense fund and pension reserve fund number two. The amount so allowed shall be due and payable to said funds and shall be annually credited thereto by the retirement board.

2 The comptroller of the city of New York shall be the custodian of the several funds created by this act.

3 Payments from the funds created by this act shall be made by the comptroller of the city of New York upon warrant signed by the chairman and countersigned by the secretary of the retirement board; and no warrant shall be drawn except by order of the retirement board duly entered in the record of its proceedings.

4 For the purpose of meeting disbursements for pensions, annuities and other payments in excess of the receipts, there may be kept an available fund, not exceeding ten per centum of the total amount in the several funds created by this act, on deposit in any bank in this State, organized under the laws thereof or under the laws of the United States, or with any trust company incorporated by any law of this State, provided said bank or trust company shall furnish adequate security for said funds and provided that the sum so deposited in any one bank or trust company shall not exceed twenty-five per centum of the paid-up capital and surplus of said bank or trust company.

5 Except as herein provided no member and no employee of the retirement board shall have any interest, direct or indirect, in the gains or profits of any investment made by the retirement board, nor as such, directly or indirectly, receive any pay or emolument for his services. And no member or employee of said retirement board, directly or indirectly, for himself or as an agent or partner of others, shall borrow any of its funds or deposits, or in any manner use the same except to make such current and necessary payments as are authorized by the retirement board; nor shall any member or employee of said retirement board become an endorser or surety or become in any manner an obligor, for moneys loaned by or borrowed of said retirement board.

F The funds hereby created are the expense fund, the contingent reserve fund, pension reserve fund number one, pension reserve fund number two, the annuity savings fund and the annuity reserve fund.

1 The expense fund shall consist of such amounts as shall be appropriated by the board of estimate and apportionment, on estimates submitted by the retirement board, to defray the expenses of the administration of this act, exclusive of the payment of pensions, of annuities, or retirement allowances, and of the other benefits provided for in this act.

2 Beginning in the month of August, 1917, the city of New York shall pay each month into a fund to be known as the contingent reserve fund, on account of each new-entrant who is a contributor, such amount as shall be certified by the retirement board as necessary to provide during the prospective active service of such new-entrant for the death benefit and for the pension reserve required at the time of retirement to pay the disability or service pension allowable by the city under the provisions of this act. The amount so certified by the retirement board shall be computed to bear a constant ratio to the salary of such new-entrant during his entire period of prospective active service and shall be based on such mortality and other tables as shall be adopted by the retirement board, and on regular interest. Beginning in the year 1918 the city of New York shall further pay each year into the said contingent reserve fund one million dollars on account of present-teachers, which payment shall continue until the present

value of such amounts so paid into the contingent reserve fund, together with the amounts restored to the contingent reserve fund from pension reserve fund number one on account of present-teachers restored to active service, shall equal the present value of all amounts which have been transferred from the contingent reserve fund to pension reserve fund number one on account of present-teachers plus the present value of all amounts thereafter to be transferred from the contingent reserve fund to said pension reserve fund number one on account of present-teachers; said amounts shall be computed on the basis of such mortality and other tables as shall be adopted by the retirement board, and on regular interest.

3 Upon the retirement of a new-entrant, an amount equal to his pension reserve shall be transferred from the contingent reserve fund into a fund to be known as pension reserve fund number one; his pension shall be paid from said pension reserve fund number one. Should said new-entrant be subsequently restored to active service his pension reserve shall thereupon be transferred from pension reserve fund number one to the contingent reserve fund. Upon the retirement of a present-teacher, an amount equal to the amount of his accumulated deductions not exceeding the amount of his pension reserve shall be transferred from the contingent reserve fund into pension reserve fund number one; a pension which shall be the actuarial equivalent of the amount so transferred shall be paid to said retired present-teacher from pension reserve fund number one. Should said present-teacher be subsequently restored to active service the pension reserve on such pension shall thereupon be transferred from pension reserve fund number one to the contingent reserve fund.

4 Pension reserve fund number two shall consist of the following:

(*a*) The balance remaining in the permanent fund of the retirement fund of the board of education of the city of New York on the thirty-first day of July, 1917.

(*b*) The balance remaining in the permanent fund of the retirement fund of the board of education of the city of New York on the thirty-first day of July, 1917.

(*c*) Five per centum of all excise moneys or license fees belonging to the city of New York, and derived or received by any commissioner of excise or public officer from the granting of licenses or permission during the year 1917 to sell strong or spirituous liquors, ale, wine, or beer in the city of New York under the provisions of any law of this State authorizing the granting of such license or permission.

(*d*) The donations, legacies, and gifts which may be made to the retirement system.

(*e*) The sums now due and which hereafter may become due to the retirement fund of the board of education of the city of New York.

(*f*) The amounts contributed by the city of New York to pay the pensions of the teachers retired on or before the thirty-first day of July, 1917, and to pay that part of the pensions and the other benefits of present-teachers who shall be retired or who shall become eligible for retirement after the thirty-first day of July, 1917, which are not payable from any other fund created by this act. Pensions and other benefits, or such part thereof allowable to present-teachers and to present pensioners, provision for the payment of which out of any other fund created by this act is not specifically made, shall be paid out of pension reserve fund number two.

5 The annuity savings fund shall consist of the accumulated deductions from the salaries of contributors made, under such rules and regulations as the retirement board shall prescribe, as follows:

(a) From the salary of each present-teacher who is a contributor there shall be deducted such per centum of his earnable salary as he shall elect, provided, however, that such contributor shall be limited in his choice to one of the following rates:

(1) Three per centum of his earnable salary.

(2) Such per centum of his earnable salary as shall be computed to be sufficient, with regular interest, when paid until age sixty-five, to provide for him on retirement at that age an annuity which, when added to his pension, provided for in this act, will provide a retirement allowance of fifty per centum of his average salary.

(3) A per centum of his earnable salary greater than three per centum thereof.

Should any present-teacher, on becoming a contributor, fail to make such an election, he shall be deemed to have elected a deduction from his salary at the rate of three per centum of his earnable salary.

(b) From the salary of each new-entrant who is a contributor, there shall be deducted such per centum of his earnable salary as shall be computed to be sufficient, with regular interest, to procure for him on service retirement an annuity equal to twenty-five per centum of his average salary; the rate per centum of said deduction from salary shall be based on such mortality and other tables as the retirement board shall adopt, together with regular interest, and shall be computed to remain constant during his prospective teaching service prior to eligibility for service retirement; but no beneficiary restored to duty shall be required to contribute a per centum of his earnable salary greater than the per centum thereof which he was required to contribute prior to his retirement.

(c) And the head of each department shall deduct on each and every payroll of a contributor for each and every payroll period subsequent to July thirty-first, 1917, such per centum of the total amount of salary earnable by the contributor in such payroll period as shall be certified to said head of department by the retirement board as proper in accordance with the provisions of this act. In determining the amount earnable by a contributor in a payroll period the retirement board shall consider the rate of salary payable to such contributor on the first day of each regular payroll period as continuing throughout such payroll period and it may omit salary deductions for any period less than a full payroll period in cases where the teacher was not a contributor on the first day of the regular payroll period; and to facilitate the making of the deductions it may modify the deductions required of any contributor by such amount as shall not exceed one-tenth of one per centum of the salary upon the basis of which the deduction is to be made; the deductions provided herein shall be made notwithstanding that the minimum salaries provided for by section 1091 shall be reduced thereby; and said head of each department shall certify to the comptroller on each and every payroll the amounts to be deducted; and each of said amounts so deducted shall be paid into said annuity saving fund, and shall be credited together with regular interest to an individual account of the contributor from whose salary the deduction was made.

6 Upon the retirement of a contributor, his accumulated deductions shall be transferred from the annuity savings fund to a fund to be known as the annuity reserve fund; his annuity shall be paid out of said annuity reserve fund. Should such a beneficiary be restored to active service his annuity reserve shall thereupon be transferred from the annuity reserve fund to the annuity savings fund.

7 No contributor shall be required to continue to contribute to the annuity savings fund after he shall have become eligible for service retirement; all contributions made thereafter to said fund shall be voluntary.

G Regular interest charges payable, the creation and maintenance of reserves in the contingent reserve fund and the maintenance of annuity reserves and pension reserves as provided for in this act and the payment of all pensions, annuities, retirement allowances, refunds, death benefits, and any other benefits granted under the provisions of this act are hereby made obligations of the city of New York. All income, interest, and dividends derived from deposits and investments authorized by this act shall be used for the payment of the said obligations of the city of New York. Upon the basis of each actuarial determination and appraisal provided for in this act, the retirement board shall prepare and submit to the board of estimate and apportionment on or before the fifteenth day of September in each year an itemized estimate of the amounts necessary to be appropriated by the city to the various funds to complete the payment of the said obligations of said city accruing during the ensuing fiscal year. The board of estimate and apportionment and the board of aldermen shall make an appropriation which shall be sufficient to provide for such obligations of the city of New York and the amounts so appropriated shall be included in the tax levy and shall be paid by the comptroller into the various funds created by this act.

H In computing the length of service of a contributor for retirement purposes under the provisions of this act, full credit up to the nearest number of years and months shall be given each contributor by the retirement board (a) for all city-service; and (b) in the case of present-teachers for all teaching or supervisory service in schools and colleges not maintained by the city of New York; and (c) in the case of new-entrants for all teaching or supervisory service not exceeding fifteen years, in schools and colleges not maintained by the city of New York. Under such rules and regulations as the retirement board shall adopt, each teacher shall file with the retirement board a detailed statement of all such service rendered by him. As soon as practicable thereafter, the retirement board shall verify such statement as to prior-service and shall issue to each teacher a certificate certifying to the aggregate length of his prior-service. Such certificate shall be final and conclusive as to his prior-service unless thereafter modified by (a) the retirement board upon application by the teacher; or (b) by the board of education upon application by the teacher or by the retirement board, provided such application for modification be made to said board of education within one year after the issuance of a certificate or a modified certificate by the retirement board. A certificate for prior-service issued to a present-teacher shall certify the total length of prior-service allowance for said present-teacher through the sixteenth day of September, 1917. The time during which a contributor was absent on leave of absence without pay shall not be counted in computing the prior-service or the total-service of a contributor, unless allowed both by the head of the department in which the said contributor was employed at the time said leave of absence was granted and by the retirement board; the time during which a contributor was absent on leave of absence on full pay or part pay from city-service shall be counted in computing the prior-service and the total-service of said contributor. For the purpose of computing prior-service the retirement board shall fix and determine by appropriate rules and regulations how much service rendered on the basis of the hour, day or session, or any other than a per annum basis, shall be the equivalent of a year of service. No allowance shall be made for such service as a substitute teacher, night school teacher, vocational school teacher, or for any service rendered in a position to which the contributor was not regularly appointed and served on a per annum salary unless such service was city-service. But all service allowed by the board of examiners of the board of education pursuant to section 1091 shall be allowed by the retirement board.

I Any contributor who resigns his position to accept and who, within sixty days thereafter, does accept another position in the city-service shall continue to be a contributor while in said city-service and shall be known as a transferred-contributor provided he executes and files with the retirement board a statement in writing that he elects to leave with the annuity savings fund his accumulated deductions and to continue to contribute to said fund at a rate of salary deduction not less than the rate of deduction theretofore required from his salary, and further provided that he shall waive and renounce any present or prospective benefit from any other retirement system or association supported wholly or in part by the city of New York.

J Withdrawals from the retirement association shall be by resignation, by transfer, or by dismissal.

1 Should a contributor resign from the position by virtue of which he is a contributor under the provisions of this act, or should he, upon transferring from such a position to another position in the city-service, fail to become a transferred-contributor as provided in subdivision I of this act, his membership in the said retirement association shall cease and he shall be paid forthwith the full amount of the accumulated deductions standing to the credit of his individual account in the annuity savings fund.

2 Should a contributor be dismissed from the position by virtue of which he is a contributor under the provisions of this act, his membership in the retirement association shall cease and there shall be paid him forthwith:

(a) Out of the annuity savings fund the full amount of the accumulated deductions standing to the credit of his individual account; and

(b) In addition thereto, out of the pension reserve fund number two, an amount equal to the contributions made by him to the teachers' retirement fund of the board of education of the city of New York as it existed prior to the first day of August, 1917.

K Retirement for service shall be as follows:

1 Any contributor may retire for service upon written application to the retirement board setting forth at what time subsequent to the execution of

said application he desires to be retired. Said application shall retire said contributor at the time so specified, provided,

(a) He has reached or passed the age of sixty-five years; or

(b) If a present-teacher, he has a total-service of thirty-five years or more; or

(c) If a new-entrant, he has a total-service of thirty-five years or more, at least twenty of which shall have been city-service.

2 Each and every contributor who has attained or shall attain the age of seventy years shall be retired by the retirement board for service forthwith or at the end of the school term in which said age of seventy years is attained.

L Retirement for disability shall be made and discontinued as follows:

1 Upon the application of the head of the department in which a contributor is employed, or upon the application of said contributor or of one acting in his behalf, the retirement board shall retire said contributor for disability, provided the medical board after a medical examination of said contributor made at the place of residence of said contributor or at a place mutually agreed upon shall certify to the retirement board that said contributor is physically or mentally incapacitated for the performance of duty and that said contributor ought to be retired and provided further that said contributor has had ten or more years of city-service.

2 Once each year, the retirement board may require any disability pensioner while still under the age of sixty-five years to undergo medical examination by physician or physicians designated by the medical board, said examination to be made at the place of residence of said beneficiary or other place mutually agreed upon. Should the medical board, as the result of such examination, report and certify to the retirement board that such disability beneficiary is no longer physically or mentally incapacitated for the performance of duty, the head of the department in which said beneficiary was employed at the time of his retirement shall, upon notification by the retirement board of such report of the medical board, reappoint said beneficiary to such a position as was held by, and at such a rate of salary as was paid to, said beneficiary at the time of his retirement; but after the expiration of ten years subsequent to the retirement of such beneficiary, his restoration to duty, notwithstanding the recommendation of the medical board, shall be optional with said head of the department.

3 Should any disability beneficiary while under the age of sixty-five years refuse to submit to at least one medical examination in any year by a physician or physicians designated by the medical board, his pension shall be discontinued until the withdrawal of such refusal and should such refusal continue for one year, all his rights in and to the pension constituted by this act shall be forfeited.

4 Upon application of any beneficiary under the age of sixty-five years drawing a pension or a retirement allowance under the provisions of this act, approved by the retirement board, said beneficiary may be restored to active service by the head of the department in which said beneficiary was employed at the time of his retirement. Upon the restoration of a beneficiary to active service his retirement allowance shall cease.

M A contributor, on retirement, shall receive a retirement allowance which shall consist of:

1 A pension calculated as follows:

(a) For disability retirement twenty per centum of his average salary.

(b) For service retirement, or for disability retirement after he becomes eligible for service retirement, twenty-five per centum of his average salary.

(c) If the contributor retiring is a present-teacher, he shall receive, in addition to the pension prescribed in subdivisions (a) or (b) a pension computed at the rate of one-thirty-fifth of twenty-five per centum of his average salary for each year of prior-service as certified to said present-teacher in the certificate issued to him by the retirement board under the provisions of subdivision H of this act, but in no event shall the total pension exceed fifty per centum of his average salary.

2 An annuity, in addition to the pension, which shall be the actuarial equivalent of his accumulated deductions at the time of his retirement, provided that in no case shall such annuity be less for each one hundred dollars of accumulated deductions of a present-teacher at the time of retirement than is shown in the following schedule:

Age at retirement	Annuity in case of men teachers	Annuity in case of women teachers
48	$7.20	$6.52
49	7.34	6.64
50	7.49	6.77
51	7.65	6.90
52	7.82	7.04
53	8.00	7.19
54	8.19	7.35
55	8.39	7.52
56	8.61	7.70
57	8.84	7.89
58	9.09	8.10
59	9.35	8.31
60	9.63	8.54
61	9.93	8.79
62	10.25	9.05
63	10.60	9.33
64	10.96	9.63
65	11.36	9.95
66	11.78	10.30
67	12.24	10.67
68	12.72	11.06
69	13.25	11.48
70	13.81	11.94

N Upon the death of a contributor before retirement there shall be paid to his estate or to such person as he shall have nominated by written designation duly executed and filed with the retirement board (a) his accumulated deductions; and in addition thereto (b) an amount equal to the salary earnable by him during the six months immediately preceding his death, provided that at the time of his death he had attained the age of sixty-five years or had a total-service of thirty-five years and was eligible for service retirement; said amount to be paid out of the contingent reserve fund in the case of a new-entrant, and out of pension reserve fund number two in the case of a present-teacher.

O At the time of his retirement any contributor may elect to receive his benefits in a retirement allowance payable throughout life or he may on retirement elect to receive the actuarial equivalent at that time of his annuity, his pension, or his retirement allowance in a lesser annuity, or a lesser pension, or a lesser retirement allowance, payable throughout life, with the provision that:

Option I. If he die before he has received in payments the present value of his annuity, his pension, or his retirement allowance, as it was at the time of his retirement, the balance shall be paid to his legal representatives or to such person, having an insurable interest in his life, as he shall nominate by written designation duly acknowledged and filed with the retirement board at the time of his retirement.

Option II. Upon his death, his annuity, his pension, or his retirement allowance, shall be continued throughout the life of and paid to such person, having an insurable interest in his life, as he shall nominate by written designation duly acknowledged and filed with the retirement board at the time of his retirement.

Option III. Upon his death, one-half of his annuity, his pension, or his retirement allowance, shall be continued throughout the life of and paid to such person, having an insurable interest in his life, as he shall nominate by written designation duly acknowledged and filed with the retirement board at the time of his retirement.

Option IV. Some other benefit or benefits shall be paid either to the contributor or to such other person or persons as he shall nominate, provided such other benefit or benefits together with such lesser annuity, or lesser pension, or lesser retirement allowance shall be certified by the actuary of the retirement board to be of equivalent actuarial value and shall be approved by the retirement board.

P The pensions of all persons who are now receiving a pension paid out of the teachers' retirement fund of the board of education of the city of New York shall not be increased or decreased, and all such pensions now due shall be paid forthwith and those hereafter becoming due shall be paid as they become due out of pension reserve fund number two.

Q A pension, an annuity or a retirement allowance, granted under the provisions of this act, shall be paid in equal monthly instalments, and shall not be decreased, increased, revoked or repealed except as otherwise provided in subdivision L of this act.

R Subject to such terms and conditions and to such rules and regulations as the retirement board may adopt, any contributor from time to time may:

(*a*) Increase or decrease his rate of contribution to the annuity savings fund, but in no event shall the contribution of a present-teacher be less than the minimum contribution, nor shall the contribution of a new-entrant be at a rate less than the per centum rate provided for said new-entrant in subdivision F-5-*b* of this act;

(*b*) If a present-teacher, withdraw from his individual account in the annuity savings fund the amount in excess of his minimum accumulation;

(*c*) Withdraw, after having become eligible for service retirement, such part of his accumulated deductions as shall be in excess of the amount necessary to procure for him an annuity which, if added to his prospective pension, will yield a retirement allowance of fifty per centum of his average salary;

(*d*) Borrow from the retirement board, if a present-teacher and if the application is made prior to July first, nineteen hundred and twenty, on a policy of life insurance, a sum of money not exceeding the loan value of said policy as set forth in the body thereof, and at a rate of interest not exceeding five per centum per annum, provided that:

1 The applicant has a policy of life insurance in which he is designated as the assured and said policy is issued by a life insurance company permitted to transact business in the State of New York, and said policy is free from any liens or claims and is in full force and effect at the time of the making of the loan.

2 The applicant on securing the loan shall deposit said life insurance policy with the retirement board accompanied with an assignment of said policy to the retirement board; said assignment shall be executed by the applicant and by all adult beneficiaries named in said policy. Should any of the beneficiaries named in said policy be infants, said retirement board shall not grant the loan until after it has made a careful investigation into the merits thereof and an order has been made and entered by the supreme court directing such loan after due notice to such insurance company. If, thereafter, the retirement board shall grant the loan, its action shall be binding on said infant beneficiaries with the same force and effect as if they were adult beneficiaries and had executed the assignment required herein.

3 After said policy has been assigned to and deposited with the retirement board for the purposes herein stated, said policy shall not be assigned, transferred, or disposed of, or changed in any of its terms without the written consent of the retirement board.

4 The retirement board shall notify the life insurance company carrying said policy of the assignment thereof and said assignment shall be binding on said company.

(*e*) If a present-teacher, retire upon written application to the retirement board after he has completed thirty years of service upon a retirement allowance consisting of

(1) An annuity which shall be the actuarial equivalent of his accumulated deductions; and, in addition thereto,

(2) Such pension as shall be certified by the actuary of the retirement board to have an actuarial value equivalent to the reserve which would be in the contingent reserve fund had the city contributed on account of such present-teacher from the date of his entrance into service, in such manner as is provided for the city's contributions on behalf of new-entrants in subdivision F, paragraph two, of this act, the amount determined by the actuary of the retirement board to be necessary to provide for the death benefit and for the pension reserve required at the time of retirement to pay the pension allowable by the city as provided in this act. In determining the amount of the reserve the actuary of the retirement board shall base his calculations on the tables then in use as the basis for determining the rates of contribution required of the city on account of new-entrants.

S Teachers hereafter appointed in the schools or classes maintained in the institutions controlled by the department of public charities or by the department of correction, shall be appointed by the commissioner of the appropriate department upon the nomination of the city superintendent of schools and shall be licensed by the board of examiners of the department of education. The department of education through such representatives as it may designate shall maintain an effective visitation and inspection of all such schools and classes.

T There shall be a medical board of three physicians constituted as follows:

(*a*) One physician appointed to serve to August 1, 1922, who shall be appointed by the members of the retirement board who are contributors.

(*b*) One physician appointed to serve to August 1, 1921, who shall be appointed by the members of the retirement board who are not contributors.

(*c*) One physician appointed to serve to August 1, 1920, who shall be appointed by the retirement board. Said physician shall be an expert in women's diseases and in diseases of the nervous system.

Their successors shall be appointed to serve for a term of three years; vacancies shall be filled for the unexpired term. All appointments for a full term or for an unexpired term shall be made in the manner provided in this section for the original appointment.

U The retirement system created by this act shall be subject to the supervision of the department of insurance in accordance with the provisions of sections 39 and 45 of the insurance law, so far as the same are applicable thereto and are not inconsistent with the provisions of this act.

V If, after August 1, 1917, any present-teacher shall recover a judgment for arrears of salary covering in whole or in part any period prior to said date, the comptroller of the city of New York before paying said judgment shall deduct therefrom the per centum of salary theretofore contributed by said teacher to the retirement fund of the board of education, as it existed prior to said date, and said deduction shall be paid into pension reserve fund number two.

W The right of a person to a pension, an annuity, or a retirement allowance, to the return of contributions, the pension, annuity, or retirement allowance itself, any optional benefit, any other right accrued or accruing to any person under the provisions of this act, and the moneys in the various funds created under this act, are hereby exempt from any state or municipal tax, and exempt from levy and sale, garnishment, attachment, or any other process whatsoever, and shall be unassignable except as in this act specifically otherwise provided.

§ 2 Section 1092-a, as amended by chapter 107 of the Laws of 1905, section 1092-b, as amended by chapter 505 of the Laws of 1909, and section 1092-c, as amended by chapter 613 of the Laws of 1916, are hereby repealed.

§ 3 This act shall take effect on August 1, 1917, except as to subdivisions B, C, D, E, paragraph 5; subdivision F, paragraph one, and the provision of subdivision F, paragraph 5, part (a), which provides for the election of a rate of salary deduction by any person entitled to make such election and the further provision of the same part which provides that if any person entitled to make such election fails so to do he shall be deemed to have elected a deduction from his salary at the rate of three per centum of his earnable salary; subdivisions H, T, and U, and as to provisions of such subdivisions, paragraphs and parts of paragraphs this act shall take effect immediately.

Chapter 560

AN ACT to amend the Education Law, relative to the employment of directors of agriculture, mechanic arts and homemaking in cities, towns and school districts.

Became a law May 18, 1917, with the approval of the Governor. Passed, three-fifths being present.

The People of the State of New York, represented in Senate and Assembly, do enact as follows:

Section 1. Sections 601 and 604 of chapter 21 of the Laws of 1909, entitled "An act relating to education, constituting chapter 16 of the Consolidated Laws," as amended by chapter 140 of the Laws of 1910 and chapter 747 of the Laws of 1913, are hereby amended to read as follows:

§ 601 **Establishment of such schools; directors of agriculture, mechanic arts and homemaking.** The board of education of any union free school district shall also establish, acquire and maintain such schools for like purposes whenever such schools shall be authorized by a district meeting. The trustees or board of trustees of a common school district may establish a school or a course in agriculture, mechanic arts and homemaking, when authorized by a district meeting. The board of education of a city, town or union free school district, not maintaining a school of agriculture, mechanic arts and homemaking, may employ a director of agriculture. The boards of education or trustees of two or more districts or towns may by joint contract **employ** such a director and determine in such contract as to the portion of the compensation which is to be paid by each district. The qualifications of a person employed as such director shall be prescribed by the Commissioner of Education, as provided by law in respect to teachers employed in public schools of the State.

§ 604 **State aid for general industrial schools, trade schools, and schools of agriculture, mechanic arts and homemaking.** 1 The Commissioner of Education in the annual apportionment of the state school moneys shall apportion therefrom to each city and union free school district for each general industrial school, trade school, parttime or continuation school or evening vocational school, maintained therein for thirty-six weeks during the school year and employing one teacher whose work is devoted exclusively to such school, and having an enrolment of at least fifteen pupils and maintaining an organization and a course of study, and conducted in a manner approved by him, a sum equal to two-thirds of the salary paid to such teacher, but not exceeding one thousand dollars.

2 He shall also apportion in like manner to each city, union free school district or common school district for each school of agriculture, mechanic arts and homemaking, maintained therein for thirty-six weeks during the school year, and employing one teacher whose work is devoted exclusively to such school, and having an enrolment of at least fifteen pupils and maintaining an organization and course of study and conducted in a manner approved by him, a sum equal to two-thirds of the salary paid to such

teacher. Such teacher may be employed for the entire year, and during the time that the said school is not open shall be engaged in performing such educational services as may be required by the board of education or trustees, under regulations adopted by the commissioner of education. Where a contract is made with a teacher for the entire year and such teacher is employed for such period, as herein provided, the commissioner of education shall make an additional apportionment to such city or district of the sum of two hundred dollars. But the total apportioned in each year on account of such teacher shall not exceed one thousand dollars.

3 The Commissioner of Education shall also make an additional apportionment to each city and union free school district for each additional teacher employed exclusively in the schools mentioned in the preceding subdivisions of this section for thirty-six weeks during the school year, a sum equal to one-third of the salary paid to each such additional teacher, but not exceeding one thousand dollars for each teacher.

4 The Commissioner of Education shall also apportion in like manner to each city, town and school district employing, or joining in the employment of, a director of agriculture, as authorized by section six hundred and one of this chapter, and establishing, maintaining and conducting an organization and course of instruction in such subject, approved by the Commissioner of Education, a sum equal to one-half of the salary paid to such director by such city, town or district, or by two or more of such towns or districts, not exceeding in each year the sum of six hundred dollars for each director employed. Where the apportionment is made on account of a director employed by two or more towns or districts, it shall be apportioned to such towns or districts in accordance with the proportionate amount paid by each of such towns or districts under the contract made with such director.

5 The Commissioner of Education, in his discretion, may apportion to a district or city maintaining such schools or employing such teachers for a shorter time than thirty-six weeks, or for a less time than a regular school day, an amount pro rata to the time such schools are maintained or such teachers are employed. This section shall not be construed to entitle manual training high schools or other secondary schools maintaining manual training departments, to an apportionment of funds herein provided for.

Any person employed as teacher as provided herein may serve as principal of the school in which the said industrial or trade school or course, or school or course of agriculture, mechanic arts and homemaking, is maintained.

§ 2 This act shall take effect immediately.

Chapter 553

AN ACT to amend the Education Law by providing for the education of children with retarded mental development.

Became a law May 18, 1917, with the approval of the Governor. Passed, three-fifths being present.

The People of the State of New York, represented in Senate and Assembly, do enact as follows:

Section 1 Chapter 21 of the Laws of 1909, entitled "An act relating to education, constituting chapter 16 of the Consolidated Laws," as amended by chapter 140 of the Laws of 1910, is hereby further amended by inserting therein a new article to be known as article 20-b, and to read as follows:

ARTICLE 20-B

CHILDREN WITH RETARDED MENTAL DEVELOPMENT

§ 578 **Children with retarded mental development.** 1 The board of education of each city and of each union free school district, and the board of trustees of each school district shall, within one year from the time this act becomes effective, ascertain, under regulations prescribed by the Commissioner of Education and approved by the Regents of the University, the number of children in attendance upon the public schools under its supervision who are three years or more retarded in mental development.

2 The board of education of each city and of each union free school district in which there are ten or more children three years or more retarded in mental development shall establish such special classes of not more than fifteen as may be necessary to provide instruction adapted to the mental attainments of such children.

3 The board of education of each city and of each union free school district, and the board of trustees of each school district which contains less than ten such children may contract with the board of education of another city or school district for the education of such children in special classes organized in the schools of the city or district with which such contract is made.

§ 2 This act shall take effect immediately.

Chapter 559

AN ACT to amend the Education Law by providing for the education of physically defective children.

Became a law May 18, 1917, with the approval of the Governor. Passed, three-fifths being present.

The People of the State of New York, represented in Senate and Assembly, do enact as follows:

Section 1 Chapter 21 of the Laws of 1909, entitled "An act relating to education, constituting chapter 16 of the Consolidated Laws," as amended by chapter 140 of the Laws of 1910, is hereby further amended by inserting therein a new article to be known as article 39-a, and to read as follows:

ARTICLE 39-A

PHYSICALLY DEFECTIVE CHILDREN

§ 1020 **Physically defective children.** 1 The board of education of each city and of each union free school district, and the board of trustees of each school district shall, within one year from the time this act becomes effective, ascertain, under regulations prescribed by the Commissioner of Education and approved by the Regents of the University, the number of children in such city or district under the age of eighteen years who are deaf, blind, so crippled or otherwise so physically defective as to be unable to attend upon instruction in regular classes maintained in public schools.

2 The board of education of each city and of each union free school district in which there are ten or more children who are deaf, blind, crippled or otherwise physically defective shall establish such special classes as may be

necessary to provide instruction adapted to the mental attainments and physical conditions of such children.

3 The board of education of each city and of each union free school district, and the board of trustees of each school district, which contains less than ten children who are deaf, blind, crippled or otherwise physically defective, is hereby authorized and empowered to contract with the board of education of another city or school district for the education of such children in special classes organized in the schools of the city or district with which such contract is made.

§ 2 This act shall take effect immediately.

Chapter 14
THE EVENING SCHOOLS OF COLONIAL NEW YORK CITY.
(after 1664)

ROBERT FRANCIS SEYBOLT PH. D.

University of Wisconsin

The principle of free schools is broad in its scope. It not only intends that educational opportunities should be afforded to the young in day schools but also that the many who, because of economic conditions, must leave school as soon as law permits, should likewise be afforded the opportunity of free schooling. It was appreciated a long time ago that many of these could not be reached in any other form of school except through evening schools. The history of the free school movement in this State would hardly be complete without a history of the evening schools inaugurated in the city of New York.

The evening schools of New York City have a history well worth recording. Established in the seventeenth century, and continuing uninterruptedly to the present day, they have played a prominent part in the solution of the problem of providing education for all classes. The essential characteristics of evening school practice at the present time find their origins in the colonial period.

There were several types of evening schools in colonial New York City. The available records indicate that the earliest, those of the late seventeenth and early eighteenth centuries, offered instruction only in the rudiments — reading, writing and cyphering. It is probable that these were attended exclusively by apprentices. In some few instances, adults may have received such evening instruction, but on this matter the records are silent.

One of the earliest references to the practice of sending apprentices to school, in New York City, occurs in a Harlem indenture dated November 25, 1690, in which the master promised that his apprentice " shall have the privilege of going to the evening school."[1] According to a New York City indenture of October 1, 1698, the apprentice was to be given " his winter's schooling."[2] From

---

[1] Harlem Records, II, 529. (Manuscript folio volume, owned by Title Guarantee and Trust Company of New York City.)

[2] City of N. Yorke Indentures, begun February 19, 1694 and ends Jan. ye 29th 1707, 47. (Manuscript folio volume, preserved at the city hall of New York City.) See also Harlem Records, II, 543; Citty of N. Yorke

indentures of a later date we learn that the evening school was kept in the winter. An indenture of November 18, 1701 contains the provision: "in the Evenings to go to School each Winter to the End he may be taught to write and read."³ In some instances the master promised to give his apprentice " One Quarter of a year's Schooling,"⁴ in others " Every winter three Months Evening Schooling."⁵ An indenture dated January 20, 1720 combines the two preceding provisions into "a Quarter or three Months Schooling in every Winter."⁶ And the particular three months, or quarter, during which the evening school was held is indicated in an indenture of February 24, 1719, in which the master agreed to " put him to school three Months in Every Year during the said apprenticeship Immediately after Christmas in Every Year to the Evening School to learn to Read and Write."⁷ Frequently the indentures refer to these three months as " the usual times in the Winter Evenings," or the " Customary " period.⁸ That the evening school was held only at this time is indicated by these references, and by an indenture of June 9, 1726, in which the apprentice is " to go to School during the time that is customary here to keep Night School."⁹

The records also reveal the fact that there was more than one evening school in New York City. An indenture of October 17, 1705 contains the master's covenant " to lett him [the apprentice] have in Every Winter three Months Learning *att any Evening School within this City,* and to pay for the same."¹⁰ Another master, in

---

Indentures, 90, 81, 155; Liber 29, 19, 7, 31, 60, 67, 73, 117, 230, for indentures of 1698–1724. (Manuscript folio volume, labeled " Liber 29," containing " Indentures Oct. 2, 1718 to Aug. 7, 1727. Library of N. Y. Hist. Soc.)

³ Citty of N. Yorke Indentures, 81.

⁴ Ibid, 60. Indenture of Jan. 20, 1700.

See also indentures of 1718–1726 in Liber 29, 1, 39, 14, 54, 110, 123, 129, 152, 156, 181, 196, 199, 220, 227, 241, 244, 261, 264, 266, 268, 270, 275, 284, 286, 303, 312, 314, 324, 325, 327, 354, 358.

⁵ Citty of N. Yorke Indentures, 62, 107, 128, 143, 158.

See also indentures of 1701–1726 in Liber 29, 3, 13, 44, 45, 55, 59, 70, 86, 90, 102, 112, 119, 151, 158, 168, 172, 216, 232, 239, 242, 320, 349.

⁶ Liber 29, 94.

⁷ Ibid, 55. See also Ibid, 123, indenture of July 30, 1705: " to allow him Evening Schooling Every Winter from Christmas as is Customary"; 139, indenture of Jan. 18, 1722: " Schooling in Winter Evenings from Christmas " ; 289, indenture of June 1, 1725: " Every Quarter after Christmas"; 346, indenture of May 1, 1726; " Eavening scholling from Christemis Eavery year of the said term."

⁸ Ibid, 34, 36, 102, 212, 216, 225. Indentures of 1717–1724.

⁹ Ibid, 318.

¹⁰ Citty of N. Yorke Indentures, 128.

1720, agreed to send his apprentice "One Quarter of a Year in Each Year of the said Term to a good Evening School."[11] A 1690 indenture mentioned above reveals the existence of an evening school in Harlem, which was within the jurisdiction of New York City.

It may be fairly assumed that many New York apprentices went to evening schools. As a rule apprentices could not be spared during the day; they were more or less constantly employed by their masters. Thrifty schoolmasters keen to take advantage of this situation opened evening schools. The writer found one hundred eight indentures which contained provisions for sending apprentices to evening schools. Of this number, not one indicates that girls attended these schools. It is safe to say that they did not. Some few girl-apprentices did attend day schools, however. An indenture of June 11, 1724 contains the following provision for a girl: "Schooling to Learn to read."[12] A certain number of apprentices, boys and girls, attending schools conducted by the Society for the Propagation of the Gospel in Foreign Parts, and it is probable that the education of many poor-apprentices was taken care of by this society.

The province of New York made no provision for establishing free evening schools. These schools were privately conducted, and tuition fees were charged. It was customary for the master to pay all charges for the instruction of his apprentices. Sometimes this was specifically mentioned in the indenture: the master "shall at his own Charge put his said Apprentice to School."[13] In one instance the apprentice was "to go to the winter Evening School at the Charge of his father"; in another, it was agreed that the apprentice should go to "Night School three Months in every Year dureing the said term his father to pay one halfe of Said Schooling and his Master the other halfe;"[15] and in a third, he was "to go to

---

[11] Liber 29, 80.

[12] Ibid, 218.

[13] Ibid, 36. Indenture of Aug. 1, 1717.

Ibid, 128. Indenture of Oct. 17, 1705: master "to pay for the same"; 14. Indenture of Dec. 4, 1717; 5. Indenture of Sept. 1, 1718: "at the Charge of the said Master"; 15. Indenture of Oct. 15, 1718; 90. Indenture of May 1, 1719; 32. Indenture of Aug. 1, 1719; "Masters Cost and Charge"; 158. Indenture of Feb. 7, 1722; 236. Indenture of Feb. 26, 1723: "at my one Cost and Charge"; 327. Indenture of Nov. 26, 1725.

[14] Ibid, 31.

[15] Ibid, 13. See also Citty of N. Yorke Indentures, 90. Indenture of Oct. 20, 1701: "the father shall provide and pay for two winters Nights scooling and his said Master Shall allow him two halfe Winters Schooling."

School during the time that is customary here to keep Night School his friends paying for the same."[16] But these were exceptions; the master in most cases assumed all expenses of maintaining and educating his apprentices.

The curriculum of the evening schools conformed to the educational needs of the New York apprentice. According to the records, they offered instruction in reading, writing and cyphering. The evidence of the indentures indicates that these subjects were taught singly, or in any combination desired. An indenture of October 14, 1700 provides for sending the apprentice to the " winter school *to learn to read* as long as the school time shall last."[17] In other instances the apprentice was permitted " in the evenings to go to School Each Winter to the End that he may be taught *to write and Read*,"[18] or to " Learn *Writing and Cyphering* at the usuall Winter Seasons."[19] The most popular provision, however, was: " One Quarter of a Year in Each Year of said Term to a good Evening School in Order to be well instructed in *reading, writing Accounting* and the like."[20]

[16] Liber 29, 318. Indenture of June 29, 1726.
[17] Harlem Records, II, 543.
[18] Citty of N. Yorke Indentures, 81. Indenture of Nov. 18, 1701. See the following indentures in Liber 29:
59 (Feb. 9, 1719) : " three Months to School to Learn to Write and Read."
55 (Feb. 24, 1719) : " School . . . Every Year . . . to learn to Read and Write."
69 (Dec. 9, 1719) : " school at Suitable Times . . . to learn to Read and Write."
83 (Apr. 26, 1720) : " Schooling to Read and Write."
119 (Nov. 18, 1720) : " Every Winter . . . Evening School . . . to Read and Write."
117 (Feb. 1, 1721) : " Evening Schooling . . . to Read and write English."
212 (July 10, 1722) : " to Read and write English . . . in Winter Evenings."
[19] Liber 29, 36. Indenture of Aug. 1, 1717. See the following in Liber 29:
36 (Aug. 1, 1717) : " School to Learn Writing and Cyphering."
78 (Apr. 16, 1718) : " Evening School . . . to learn to write and cypher."
34 (Aug. 6, 1719) : " write and cypher at the usual times in the winter."
102 (May 1, 1720) : " School . . . Evenings to Learn Writing and Cyphering."
193 (Sept. 1, 1723) : " Night School . . . writeing and Arithmetick."
[20] Liber 29, 80. Indenture of Aug. 1, 1720. See the following in Liber 29:
82 (Nov. 8, 1720) : " Evening School . . . Reading and Writing and Arithmetick."
190 (Nov. 6, 1722) : " Schooling to Read write and Arithmetick."
241 (Jan. 31, 1723) : " Evening School to Read write and Cypher."
197 (Aug. 1, 1723) : " School . . . on Winter Evenings . . . to Read write and Cypher."

The purpose of this education for apprentices may be well expressed in the words of an indenture of December 7, 1724, which made provision for teaching the boy to "Read write and Cypher so far as will be Sufficient to Manage his Trade."[21]

It is interesting to note the content of the course in "cyphering," or arithmetic, pursued by the apprentice. A Westchester indenture of July 1, 1716 makes provision for teaching the apprentice to "Read Write & Cast Accompts to so far as the Rule of three."[22] Sometimes this description was added to in the following manner: "Cypher as far as the rule of three direct inclusive."[23] The most complete statement of the composition of this subject occurs in a New York City indenture of May 20, 1720, in which the master agreed to provide instruction in "writing and cyphering So far as Addition Subtraction and Multiplication."[24] In some instances the apprentice was to be taught "to Cypher so as to keep his Own accounts,"[25] or "so far as he be able to keep his Booke.[26]

Obviously the evidence of the indentures of apprenticeship is somewhat incomplete. They indicate in a matter-of-course manner,

266 (Dec. 25, 1723): "Every Winter one Quarter . . . to Read writ and Cypher."

314 (Jan. 4, 1724): "Every Winter . . . Eveven Skool . . . to Read write en syfer."

225 (July 26, 1724): "School . . . in the Winter . . . to Reade write and Cypher."

278 (Oct. 5, 1724): "Winters to School . . . to Read write and Cypher."

229 (Oct. 26. 1724): "Winter Season . . . to School . . . to Reade write Cypher."

280 (June 1, 1725): "Reading writing and Cyphering at the Cost . . . of Master."

289 (June 1, 1725): "to read and write . . . every Quarter . . . and Syfer two Quarters."

[21] Liber 29, 282.

[22] Westchester Records, 1707–1720, 254½. (Manuscript folio volume in New York Hall of Records.)

[23] Flushing Town Records, 1790–1833, 104. Indenture of Oct. 31, 1816. See Ibid, 16. Indenture of Jan. 4, 1817: "to cypher as far as the rule of three direct." (Manuscript folio volume in N. Y. Hall of Records.)

[24] Liber 29, 97.

[25] Ibid, 276. Indenture of Feb. 1, 1722.

[26] Westchester Records, 1711–1730. July 23, 1725. (Manuscript folio volume in New York Hall of Records. Pages not numbered.)

Huntington Town Records, II, 518. Indenture of Sept. 7, 1772: "to read write & Arethmatick so as to keep a good Book."

(The material embraced by notes 1–26 is taken from R. F. Seybolt, Apprenticeship and Apprenticeship Education in Colonial New England and New York, N. Y., 1917.)

that elementary evening schools were common during the period considered, and that the customary curriculum comprised reading, writing and arithmetic. Additional light is thrown upon these schools by the newspapers; in fact, for this purpose, they constitute our best sources. After the establishment of the first New York newspaper, in 1725, advertisements of evening schools are numerous, and by piecing them together we can build up a more complete account of the actual schools.

In the New York Gazette of December 18, 1749, we find the following advertisement:

> Reading Writing and Arithmetick, taught by Thomas Evans, at the House of Mr. Bingham, Shoemaker, near the New-Dock, where he will give due Attendance for Night School, commencing the first Day of January next.[27]

From the New York Mercury of August 31, 1761, we learn that "Samuel Bruce . . . Opens his Night School in Wall Street, the 21st of September next, where he continues teaching Reading, Writing, and Arithmetic in the best Manner,"[28] and from the New York Gazette and Weekly Mercury, September 29, 1777, that Thomas Wiley, "Late Usher to Mr. Joseph Hildreth, Master of the Charity School," who taught "Reading, Writing, and Arithmetic," "has now opened his Night School."[29]

These advertisements not only contain information concerning the names of the schoolmasters, and the places where the schools were kept, but they reveal the fact that the earlier custom of conducting evening schools only during the winter, i. e., the "three Months . . . Immediately after Christmas," no longer obtained.[30] Two of the schools mentioned above opened in September, but the length of the term was not indicated in either case. It seems probable that by the middle of the eighteenth century, the demand for evening instruction of this character could not be satisfied by schools kept only during the winter season. Schoolmasters, here and there in the city, were advertising longer periods of tuition. There was no uniformity in this matter; some taught the time-honored "quarter," and others six months, or even all year round. Hugh Hughes, in 1767, advertised that his school would

---

[27] Repeated in New York Gazette, Dec. 25, 1749; Jan. 1, Jan. 8, 1750.
[28] Repeated in New York Mercury, Sept. 7, Sept. 28, 1761.
[29] In 1779 Thomas Wiley opened his evening school, "opposite Trinity Church," on Sept. 20 (N. Y. Gazette and Weekly Mercury, Sept. 13, 1779); and in 1782, on Nov. 19 (Ibid, No. 4. 1782).
[30] See notes 1-9.

"commence the first of April next and continue to the first of October following."[31] A particularly pertinent advertisement, in this connection, is one inserted by Robert Leeth in the New York Evening Post, May 27, 1751:

> I find it has been a Custom here immemorial, for School Masters to keep Evening Schools Winter only; But as it may suit many young People's Conveniencies to write and cast Accompts at other Seasons of the Year, I do hereby give Notice that I intend to keep an Evening School from six o'Clock till Eight, the Year round.[32]

Additional material for our description of these schools is to be found in the following advertisement:

> New York, March 20, 1767.
>
> The Subscriber proposes to open a Morning and Evening School, for the Instruction of Youth in Writing, and Arithmetic, to commence the first of April next, and to continue to the first of October following. Attendance will be given from six to eight in the Morning, and from five to seven in the Evening precisely. It is imagined that this Plan may suit some of both Sexes, who attend other Places of Education at different Periods, for other Purposes . . . .
>
> HUGH HUGHES.[33]

Here the hours of "Attendance" are indicated — "from five to seven." But it must not be inferred that there was any agreement, on this matter, among the masters; in fact, considerable variation obtained. The most popular hours, however, were from six to eight.

Furthermore, this advertisement would seem to indicate that girls, as well as boys, attended evening schools. But a positive statement to this effect would not receive support from the sources. It is very probable that the girls attended the morning school, in this case. Many masters, during the eighteenth century, advertised morning schools, or morning hours, for girls exclusively.

Information concerning the rates of tuition in the elementary evening schools is not abundant. The writer was unable to find more than one advertisement containing the tuition fees of evening schools of this type. Robert Leeth, in 1752, taught "Writing at 9s. per Quarter; Vulgar and Decimal Arithmetick at 12s.," in his day school, and "Writing at 8s. per Quarter, and vulgar and decimal Arithmetick

---

[31] New York Gazette and Weekly Mercury, April 16, 1767. This advertisement was written by Hughes on March 20, 1767.

[32] Repeated in New York Evening Post, June 3, 1751. (Stone Street.)

[33] New York Gazette or Weekly Post Boy, April 16, April 23, April 30, May 7, May 14, May 21, June 4, 1767.

at 10s." in his evening school.[34] If we are justified in making any conclusion from this one document, we may say that the evening rates were lower than those of the day school.

More complete information on this matter is available for the practice of day schools, and it may be profitable to make a brief examination of their rates. In an elementary day school of 1735 the master taught "Reading, Writing, and Arithmetick at very reasonable Terms, which is per Quarter for Readers 5s, for Writers 8s., for Cypherers 1s."[35] Two years later, in 1737, one Joshua Ring advertised that he would "teach carefully (After the Easter Holidays) Reading, Writing, and Arithmetic at 12s. per Quarter; Reading and Writing at 10s."[36] Evidently Robert Leeth, in 1752, considered "writing at 8s. per Quarter" as fair a price as it was in 1735. The rate for arithmetic seems to have risen, but it is probable that with Leeth arithmetic was a more advanced subject than cyphering. In 1766, John Young "continues to teach as usual, Reading at 9s., Writing at 11s., and Arithmetic at 13s. per Quarter,"[37] and in 1776 Amos Bull taught "English Grammar, Reading, Writing, and Arithmetic . . . at 25s. per Quarter for each Scholar."[38] If Leeth's advertisement represents a common practice, namely, of charging lower rates in the evening schools, it may be fairly assumed that the prevailing elementary evening school rates were slightly lower than those just examined. At any rate, the day school advertisements indicate approximately the current prices for the elementary subjects.

Another type of evening school offered instruction in practical subjects of secondary grade, in addition to the rudiments. In these schools certain hours were set apart for those who were learning to read, write and cypher. In some, only the higher subjects were taught. The higher classes were patronised not only by older apprentices who had received an elementary education, but also by young men and adults of independent economic status. Like the

[34] New York Gazette Revived in the Weekly Post Boy, Sept. 18, Sept. 25, Oct. 2, Oct. 9, Oct. 16, Oct. 23, Oct. 30, 1752.
[35] New York Gazette, July 14-21, July 21-28, July 28-Aug. 4, Aug. 4-11, 1735. (Smith Street.)
[36] New York Weekly Journal, April 4, 1737. ("lower End of Stone Street")
[37] New York Mercury, May 19, May 26, 1766. (French Church Street)
[38] New York Gazette and Weekly Mercury, May 13, May 20, 1776. (King Street)

evening schools of elementary grade, they were designed for "those who cannot spare time in the day time."

As in the case of evening schools offering instruction only in the three R's, there was no agreement among the masters that all the evening schools in the city should begin their terms at the same time. Thomas Metcalfe, in 1747, conducted his evening school "all the Summer,"[39] and in 1759, James and Samuel Giles also decided to keep theirs "during the Summer Season."[40] In most instances, however, these schools were advertised to begin in the months of September,[41] October,[42] and December,[43] and an appreciable number still observed the "Custom here immemorial" of running "during the Winter Season."[44]

In none of the advertisements of evening schools of this class is the length of the term definitely stated, but we may safely infer from evidence of several kinds that the schools were run on a quarterly plan. Some were kept "during the Winter Season," and others during the "Summer Season." It is very probable that the expressions "during the Summer Season," and "during the Winter Season," refer to the three months of summer, or winter. Further-

[39] New York Evening Post, Aug. 3, 1747. (Wall Street)

[40] Parker's New York Gazette or Weekly Post Boy, April 30, May 14, May 21, May 28, 1759. (Maiden Lane)
See also advertisements of John Nathan Hutchins (Courtlandt Street) in New York Mercury, April 25, May 2, 1763; and Thomas Carroll (Broad Street), in Ibid, May 6, May 13, May 20, 1765.

[41] New York Gazette or Weekly Post Boy, Aug. 14, Aug. 28, Sept. 4, 1758 (Edward Willett, and George Adams, French Church Street); Ibid, Sept. 8, Sept. 15, Sept. 22, Oct. 6, Oct. 13, Oct. 20, Oct. 27, 1755 (James Wragg, Ferry Street); Ibid, Sept. 15, Sept. 19, Sept. 29, Oct. 6, Oct. 13, 1755 (John Searson, "opposite to the Post-Office"); New York Mercury, Sept. 7, Sept. 14, Sept. 21, Dec. 7, Dec. 14, 1761 (James and Samuel Giles); Ibid, Sept. 7, 1761 (John Young); New York Gazette and Weekly Mercury, Sept. 30, 1782 (J. Mennye, 56 Beekman Street).

[42] Royal Gazette, Oct. 6, 1781 (Mr. Davis, 63 Maiden Lane); Ibid, Oct. 18, Oct. 22, 1783 (J. Mennye, "32 Gold Street, Corner of Beekman Street"); Rivington's New York Gazetteer, or Connecticut, New Jersey, Hudson's River, and Quebec Weekly Advertiser, Oct. 6, 1774 (Gollen and Mountain, "Crown Street, near the North River"); New York Gazette or Weekly Post Boy, Oct. 8, Nov. 26, 1753 (John Lewis).

[43] New York Gazette or Weekly Post Boy, Oct. 24, 1757 (Edward Willett, "next Door to Mr. Richards, in the Broadway"); New York Mercury, Nov. 10, 1766 (Thomas Carroll); Ibid, Nov. 23, 1761 (Thomas Johnson); New York Packet and American Advertiser, Fishkill, Nov. 20, 1783 (Edward Riggs, Little Queen Street).

more, in the advertisements that mention the rates of tuition, the various subjects were taught at so much " per Quarter."

Similarly, when we attempt to ascertain the evenings of the week on which these schools were kept, we find that pertinent advertisements are not numerous. In some instances, instruction was given every evening, and in others, certain evenings were " excepted." From an advertisement of 1772, we learn that James Gilliland taught "every Evening."[45] We may infer that Mr. Evans, who advertised, in 1781, that he would teach " in the evenings," kept school every evening.[46] Some masters stated definitely that their schools would be open on certain evenings only; James and Samuel Giles, in 1759, taught " in the evenings of all School Days, Wednesday and Saturday Evenings excepted;"[47] and John Nathan Hutchins, in 1763, omitted " Saturday evenings."[48]

The hours of instruction were not uniform throughout the city. Thomas Metcalfe, in 1747, " proposes to teach an Evening School, beginning at five to be continued till Sunset."[49] In most cases the hours were definitely stated, as: " from 5 to 7 in the Evenings,"[50]

---

[44] New York Gazette Revived in the Weekly Post Boy, Sept. 17, Sept. 24, 1750 (Gabriel Wayne, " near the Watch-House in the Broad Street," " during the Winter Season "); Royal Gazette, Oct. 17, Oct. 20, Oct. 31, Nov. 21, 1781 (Mr. Evans, 18 Great Dock Street, " during the winter ").
See also New York Gazette or Weekly Post Boy, Dec. 12, 1768 (James Lamb, Rotten Row); Ibid, Jan. 12, Feb. 16, 1764 (William Cockburn, Hanover Square); New York Gazette and Weekly Mercury, Dec. 14, Dec. 28, 1772 (James Gilliland, " near the old City Hall "); Ibid, Jan. 14, Oct. 14, Oct. 21, 1782 (Mr. Davis); Ibid, Jan. 1, Jan. 8, Jan. 15, Jan. 22, Jan. 29, 1770 (George Robinson, Golden Hill); Ibid, Jan. 19, Jan. 26, 1778 (John Davis, " Maiden Lane between Nassau and William Streets "); New York Gazette Revived in the Weekly Post Boy, Jan. 21, Jan. 28, 1751 (Benjamin Leigh and Garrat Noel, " lower End of Broad Street, near the Long-Bridge "); New York Gazette, Jan. 18, 1762 (Thomas Johnson, " almost opposite to Leonard Lispenard's "); Rivington's New York Gazetteer, or Connecticut, New Jersey, Hudson's River, and Quebec Weekly Advertiser, Jan. 12, Jan. 19, 1775 (James Gilliland, Broad Street).

[45] New York Gazette and Weekly Mercury, Dec. 14, Dec. 28, 1772.

[46] Royal Gazette, Oct. 17, Oct. 20, Oct. 31, Nov. 21, 1781.

[47] Parker's New York Gazette or Weekly Post Boy, April 30, May 14, May 21, May 28, 1759.

[48] New York Mercury, April 25, May 2, 1763.

[49] New York Evening Post, Aug. 3, 1747.

[50] Parker's New York Gazette or Weekly Post Boy, April 30, May 14, May 21, May 28, 1759 (James and Samuel Giles); New York Mercury, April 25, May 2, 1762 (John Nathan Hutchins).

"from 6 to 7 o'Clock,"[51] "from 6 to 8,"[52] and "from Six to Nine."[53] The most popular hours seem to have been from six to eight.

Our chief interest is in the curriculum of these secondary evening schools. We shall find, upon examining the evidence of the advertisements, that these schools met the demand of a large class for practical instruction beyond the rudiments. In schools of this type, open during the day, as well as in the evening, the bookkeepers, merchants, surveyors and navigators of the period received their technical training.

The typical curriculum of these secondary evening schools comprised, in addition to the elementary subjects, bookkeeping, and the "practical Branches of the Mathematicks." Thomas Metcalfe's advertisement, of 1747, contains the simple statement that he would teach "Reading, Writing, Arithmetick, Mathematicks, &c."[54] For an interpretation of "Mathematicks &c." we must examine a more detailed advertisement, such as the following, of 1755:

NOTICE is hereby GIVEN that
JOHN SEARSON

Who teaches School at the House of Mrs. Coon, opposite to the Post-Office, proposes (God Willing) to open an Evening School, on Thursday the 25th of this Instant September; where may be learn'd Writing, Arithmetick Vulgar and Decimal, Merchants Accounts, Mensuration, Geometry, Trigonometry, Surveying, Dialling, and Navigation, in a short, plain, and methodical Manner, and at very reasonable Rates. Said Searson having a large and commodious Room, together with his own diligent Attendance,

---

[51] Royal Gazette, Oct. 17, Oct. 20, Oct. 31, Nov. 21, 1781 (Mr. Evans).

[52] New York Gazette and Weekly Mercury, Jan. 1, Jan. 8, Jan. 15, Jan. 22, Jan. 29, 1770 (George Robinson); Ibid, Dec. 14, Dec. 28, 1772 (James Gilliland); Ibid, Jan. 19, Jan. 26, 1778 (John Davis); Rivington's New York Gazetteer, or Conn., N. J., H. R., and Quebec Weekly Advertiser, Oct. 6, 1774 (Gollen and Mountain).

[53] New York Mercury, May 6, May 13, May 20, Sept. 30, Oct. 7, 1765 (Thomas Carroll).

[54] New York Evening Post, Aug. 3, 1747.

New York Gazette Revived in the Weekly Post Boy, Sept. 17, Sept. 24, 1750. Gabriel Wayne taught "Reading, Writing, Arithmetick, Navigation."

Ibid, Nov. 13, 1752. Nicholas Barrington ("near St. George's Chapel in Beekman's Street"): "Reading, Writing, and Arithmetick, both Vulgar and decimal, as also Navigation and Merchants Accounts."

New York Gazette or Weekly Post Boy, Oct. 8, Oct. 15, Nov. 26, Dec. 3, 1753. John Lewis: "Reading, writing, Arithmetic, Navigation, Surveying &c."

FREE SCHOOLS 641

the Scholars will have it in their Power to make good Progress in a short Time.[55]

As early as 1723, John Walton taught, among other subjects, "Reading, writing, Arethmatick, whole Numbers and Fractions, Vulgar and Decimal, The Mariners Art, Plain and Mercators Way; Also Geometry, Surveying."[56] Further enlightenment is supplied by the course of study advertised by James and Samuel Giles, in 1759, which included the subjects just mentioned, and, in addition, "Interest and Annuities," "Extraction of Roots of all Powers," "Mensuration of Superficies and Solids," "Book-Keeping in the true Italian Manner of Double Entry," "Guaging," "Algebra," "Conic Sections," and "&c.&c."[57] The curriculum of Benjamin Leigh and Garrat Noel, in 1751, contained "Geography and the Use of Globes,"[58] and that of James Wragg, in 1755, "Astronomy."[59] "Gunnery" is added by Edward Willett and George Adams, in 1758,[60] and "Fortification," by William Cockburn, in 1764.[61]

An excellent summary of this comprehensive curriculum is given in Thomas Carroll's advertisement, of 1765. It follows:

Taught by Thomas Carroll, At his Mathematical School, in Broad-street, in the City of New York.
Writing, Vulgar and Decimal Arithmetic; the Extraction of the Roots; Simple and Compound Interest; how to purchase or sell Annuities, Leases for Lives, or in Reversion, Freehold Estates, &c. at Simple and Compound Interest; The Italian Method of Book-Keeping; Euclid's Elements of Geometry; Algebra and Conic Section; Mensuration of Superficies and Solids. Surveying in Theory, and all its different Modes in Practice, with two universal Methods to determine the Areas of right lined Figures, and some useful Observations on the whole; Also Guaging, Dialling, Plain and Spheric Trigonometry, Navigation; the Construction and Use of the Charts, and Instruments necessary for keeping a Sea-Journal (with a Method to keep

---

[55] New York Gazette or Weekly Post Boy, Sept. 15, Sept. 19, Sept. 29, Oct. 6, Oct. 13, 1755.
Ibid, April 7, April 21, May 5, 1755. James Wragg: "Writing, Arithmetick, Merchants Accounts, Navigation, Surveying, Mensuration, Guaging, Dialing, and Astronomy."
[56] American Weekly Mercury Philadelphia, Oct. 17-24, Oct. 24-31, Oct. 31-Nov. 7, 1723.
[57] Parker's New York Gazette or Weekly Post Boy, April 30, May 14, May 21, May 28, 1759.
[58] New York Gazette Revived in the Weekly Post Boy, Jan. 21, Jan. 28, 1751. The curriculum of this school included "a new invented Short-Hand."
[59] New York Gazette or Weekly Post Boy, July 14, July 28, Aug. 4, Aug. 11, Aug. 18, Sept. 1, 1755.
[60] New York Gazette or Weekly Post Boy, Aug. 14, Aug. 28, Sept. 4, 1758.
[61] Ibid, Jan. 12, Feb. 16, 1764.

41

the same, were the Navigator deprived of his Instruments and Books &c. by any Accident) the Projection of the Sphere, according to the Orthographic and Stereographic Principles; Fortification, Gunnery, and Astronomy; Sir Isaac Newton's Laws of Motion; the mechanical Powers, viz. The Balance, Lever, Wedge, Screw, and Axes in Peritrochio explained, Being not only an Introduction necessary to the more abstruse Parts of Natural and Experimental Philosophy, but also to every Gentleman in Business.

He will lecture to his Scholars, every Saturday, on the different Branches then taught in his School, the Advantage of which may in a little Time, make them rather Masters (of what they are then learning) than Scholars. He invites Gentlemen to visit his School, and be Judges of the Progress his Pupils will make, and the Benefit they must receive from him.

He will attend a Morning School in Summer from 6 to nine for young Ladies only, from Nine to Twelve and from Two P.M. to Five for all others who choose to attend; and a Night School from Six to Nine for young Gentlemen; or he will divide the time in any other Way, if thought more agreeable. Young Gentlemen and Ladies may be instructed in the more easy and entertaining Parts of Geography with the true Method of drawing the Plan of any Country &c. without which they cannot properly (be said to) understand that useful Branch of Knowledge; during this Course, Care will be taken to explain the true Copernican or Solar System, the Laws of Attraction, Gravitation, Cohesion &c. in an easy and familiar Manner, and if he is encouraged to purchase proper Apparatus, he will exhibit a regular Course of experimental Philosophy. He will not accept any but decent Scholars, nor crowd his School with more than he can teach at a Time. On this plan, if the Gentlemen of this City are convinced of the vast Utility it must be to the Youth here, and are of the Opinion that he may be a useful Member amongst them, and encourage him as such, he will do all in his Power to merit their Approbation, and give general Satisfaction; but if otherwise, he will accept of any Employment in the Writing Way, settling Merchant's Accounts, drawing Plans, &c. or of a decent Place in the Country till the Return of the Vessels from Ireland, to which he has warm Invitations. He must observe that he was not under the Necessity of coming here to teach, he had Views of living more happy, but some unforeseen and unexpected Events have happened since his Arrival here, which is the Reason of his Applying thus to the Publick.

N.B. Mrs. Carroll proposes teaching young Ladies plain Work, Samples, French Quilting, Knotting for Bed Quilts, or Toilets, Dresden, flowering on Cat Gut, Shading (with Silk, or Worsted) on Cambrick, Lawn, and Holland.[62]

---

[62] New York Mercury, May 6, May 13, May 20, Sept. 30, Oct. 7, 1765. See also detailed advertisements of J. N. Hutchins, in New York Mercury, April 25, May 2, 1763; and J. Mennye, in Royal Gazette, Oct. 18, Oct. 22, 1783. J. Mennye's advertisement contains the following: "And in order that no Part may be wanting, the Method of making Logarithms to any Number of Places will be taught in as extensive a Manner as they have hitherto been in any University in Europe; And whoever may be curious in these Arts, will be taught the Construction of his Mathematical Instruments, by which Means he can always prove any Instrument already made."

It is not known whether this school was actually established in 1765, but from an advertisement of November 10, 1766, we learn that "Thomas Carroll has opened a night school."[63]

It may not be inappropriate, at this point, to set out an interesting advertisement written by Mr Davis, in 1781. The item follows:

EDUCATION
Evening School, by Mr. Davis
in Maiden Lane, No. 63.

Where is taught Reading, a grace of the schools,
Writing, Arithmetic by easy rules,
Book-keeping, Geometry, too very plain,
And Navigation to steer o'er the main:
Surveying and Mensuration as well,
With rare Algebra to make you excell.
All those — and more he has got in his plan,
To rouse the genius, and furnish the man.

The Pupils may depend on an easy, elegant, perspicuous explication of things, being most conducive to rouse the genius, and invigorate the thought, or to inspire the mind, with a true and lively sense of what is taught, which cannot fail to enrich it with fruitful ideas; and as they shoot will not only be cherished, but made to flourish.[64]

In most advertisements of the colonial period, and in all colonies, merchant's accounts, or bookkeeping, was taught " after the Italian Method of double Entry." An interesting exception to, and criticism of, this method is to be found in an advertisement of 1770:

This is to inform the Public, That George Robinson, Late of Old England, purposes opening an EVENING SCHOOL, at his house on Golden Hill, New York, January the 8th for book-keeping as used in London, either in the wholesale or retail way: Has practised it upwards of twenty years, having served an apprenticeship in the mercantile way, and ever after constantly used to it. Presumes it necessary almost every Person intended

---

[63] New York Mercury, Nov. 10, 1766.
[64] Royal Gazette, Oct. 6, 1781.
Appended to Mr. Davis' notice of 1782, in New York Gazette and Weekly Mercury, Jan. 7, Jan. 14, Oct. 14, Oct. 21, 1782, is the following:

"These lively fields pure pleasures do impart,
  The fruit of science, and each useful art,
 Which forms the mind, and clears the cloudy sense,
  By truth's powerful pleasing eloquence.
Ye hopeful youths, be sensible of this.
  O! mark the fleeting time and profer'd bliss,
The only time when learning makes it way
  Thro' dark ignorance, brightening into day;
Bright'ning into day, you'll in knowledge shine
  Full orb'd with wisdom to the human mind
Ye hopeful Youths, come learn what he has told
  Exalt your Minds and be what ye behold;
While Genius soaring, great Heights explore,
  And grace your Talents with true Beauties o'er,
Till ornamented with the Flowers of Truth,
  Ye shine bright Patterns for unlearned Youth."

for business should learn a course of book-keeping; but begs leave to say, not in the customary way: Witness the complaints among merchants and tradesmen, that the boys when they first come to business, are almost as ignorant in the management of their books as if they had never learnt any method. There is boys who have not had time to learn, or perhaps a capacity to understand a compleat course of the Italian, which is commonly promiscuously alone taught to all; there are also many intended for such business as that the Italian method is thrown away upon them. Hours from 6 to 8."[65]

Mr Davis, in 1782, taught " Book-keeping in an exemplary manner, so that the Book-keeper can adapt his ideas to any circumstance in trade and business."[66]

The practical purpose of trigonometry is seen in its relation to navigation and surveying. In the courses of study examined, it was usually allied with these two subjects. Several interesting records indicate this relationship. In advertisements of 1753 and 1754, John Lewis informs us that " What is called a new Method of Navigation, is an excellent method of Trigonometry here particularly applied to Navigation; But is of great Use in all kinds of Measuring and in solving many Arithmetical Questions."[67] William Cockburn, in 1764, taught " Trigonometry, with its Application to the taking of Heights and Distances . . . Spherical Trigonometry, with its Application to Great Circle Sailing and Astronomy."[68]

In some instances the " Theory of Surveying " was taught, in others, " both theoretical and practical." Obviously, the " Theory of Surveying " could easily be taught within doors. How the subject was taught in a practical manner is indicated by but one advertisement. John Nathan Hutchins, in 1763, announced, in an advertisement of his day school, that " Young Gentlemen inclined to learn Surveying, will be instructed in the Practick as well as the Theorical Part, he being provided with Chain and Compass, and has obtained Liberty of exercising his Scholars on a convenient Tract of Land not far distant."[69]

More detailed information is available for the course in navigation. By putting together the significant portions of many evening school advertisements, we are able to get a fairly adequate notion of

---

[65] New York Gazette and Weekly Mercury, Jan. 1, Jan. 8, Jan. 15, Jan. 22, Jan. 29, 1770.
[66] Ibid, Jan. 7, Jan. 14, Oct. 14, Oct. 21, 1782.
[67] New York Gazette or Weekly Post Boy, Dec. 24, 1753; Ibid, Jan. 7, Jan. 14, Jan. 21, 1754.
[68] Ibid, Jan. 12, Feb. 16, 1764.
[69] New York Mercury, April 25, May 2, 1763.

the scope of this subject. John Walton, in 1723, taught "The Mariners Art, Plain and Mercators Way."[70] From an advertisement of 1763, we learn that John Nathan Hutchins taught "Navigation by all the various Ways ever yet taught, whether Tabular, Logarithmetical, or Instrumental, also without the Help of Books or Scales. Gentlemen Mariners &c., may be taught the making and Use of all Sorts of Charts, Plain or Globular."[71] Further evidence of the practical character of the subject is supplied by an advertisement of 1764, in which the master proposed to teach "Navigation after an easy Method, by which a Man may be able to work a Day's Work in a few Weeks; also a new Method of observing the Latitude at any Time of Day, so very much wanted in thick Weather at Noon."[72] Some masters were able to give their students the benefit of actual experience; James Lamb, in 1768, announced that "he has had 16 years Experience at Sea," and "flatters himself he can render Navigation (in some Measure) familiar to the young Navigator the first Voyage."[73] Mr Davis, in 1782, advertised that he would teach "Practical Navigation by the most expeditious and approved methods, whereby the Navigator can never be at a loss upon any occasion, to find the ship's place, by dead reckoning and celestial observation, and to this purpose also are taught the doctrine of the Orthographic and Stereographic Projections of the Sphere, Spheric Trigonometry, with its application to Astronomy, by which he will be led to the summit of his wishes, it being supposed, a thorough knowledge of the New Method of finding the Latitude by two altitudes of the Sun, and of finding the Longitude by the Moon's distance from the Sun, &c."[74]

---

[70] American Weekly Mercury, Philadelphia, Oct. 17–24, Oct. 24–31, Oct. 31–Nov. 7, 1723.

[71] New York Mercury, April 25, May 2, 1763.

Royal Gazette, Oct. 18, Oct. 22, 1783. "The method of making a chart fitted to any Voyage, or to any extent of Land and Water." (J. Mennye)

[72] New York Gazette or Weekly Post Boy, Jan. 12, Feb. 16, 1764 (William Cockburn).

[73] Ibid, Dec. 12, 1768.

[74] New York Gazette and Weekly Mercury, Jan. 7, Jan. 14, Oct. 14, Oct. 21, 1782.

An advertisement of 1781 mentions this new method of "finding the latitude by two Altitudes of the Sun, and the longitude by the distance of the Moon from the Sun," and informs us that it was described in "John Hamilton Moore's Navigation." (Royal Gazette, Oct. 17, Oct. 20, Oct. 31, Nov. 21, 1781)

See also J. Mennye's advertisement in the Royal Gazette, Oct. 18, Oct. 22, 1783. "Navigation, together with the new Method of finding the Latitude

The evening school advertisements examined do not contain information concerning the fees for instruction in the practical subjects. Nothing more definite appears than the expressions " reasonable,"[75] " all at reasonable Rates,"[76] and " upon very reasonable Terms."[77] We must again rely upon the evidence of the advertisements of day schools. Robert Leeth, in 1752, taught " Book Keeping after the true Italian Method," for £4, " The Art of Navigation " for £3, and " Mensuration of Superficies and Solids, Surveying, &c &c. at a Price in Proportion to the other Branches of the Mathematicks."[78] If £4 was the prevailing rate for double-entry bookkeeping, it remained constant during the next fourteen years, at least; John Young, in 1766, advertised " Common Accounts for 40s., Merchants ditto after the Italian method for £4."[79] The incompleteness of the records makes it impossible to quote the fees for other secondary subjects.

In New York City there were many evening schools other than those belonging strictly to the types just considered. An interesting type was the evening academy,[80] a good illustration of which is given in the following advertisement:

> There is a school in New York, in the Broad Street, near the Exchange, where Mr. John Walton, late of Yale Colledge, Teacheth Reading, Writing, Arethmatick, whole Numbers and Fractions, Vulgar and Decimal, The Mariners Art, Plain and Mercators Way; Also Geometry, Surveying, the Latin Tongue, the Greek and Hebrew Grammers, Ethicks, Rhetorick, Logick, Natural Philosophy and Metaphysicks, all or any of them for a Reasonable Price. The School from the first of October till the first of March will be tended in the Evening. If any Gentlemen in the Country are disposed to send their Sons to the said School, if they apply themselves to the Master he will immediately procure suitable Entertainment for them, very Cheap. Also if any Young Gentlemen of the City will please to come in the Evening

will be taught in a short Time to those who are already acquainted with Figures."

Messrs. Gollen and Mountain, in 1774, taught " the use of Davis's and Hadley's quadrants." (Rivington's N. Y. Gazetteer, or Conn., N. J., H. R., and Quebec Advertiser, Oct. 6, 1774)

[75] New York Gazette or Weekly Post Boy, Sept. 8, Sept. 15, Sept. 22, Oct. 6, Oct. 13, Oct. 20, Oct. 27, 1755. (James Wragg)

[76] New York Mercury, April 25, May 2, 1763. (J. N. Hutchins)

[77] New York Packet and American Weekly Advertiser, Fishkill, Nov. 20, 1783. (Riggs)

[78] New York Gazette Revived in the Weekly Post Boy, Sept. 8, Sept. 15, Oct. 2, Oct. 9, Oct. 16, Oct. 23, Oct. 30, 1752.

[79] New York Mercury, May 19, May 26, 1766

[80] The term is here used in the traditionally accepted sense.

and make some Tryal of the Liberal Arts, they may have oppertunity of Learning the same Things which are commonly Taught in Colledges.[81]

This is the earliest available record of an academy in New York City, and the fact that it had evening, as well as day, classes, makes it doubly interesting.

Evening schools offering instruction in the ancient and modern languages were by no means uncommon. In Thomas Metcalfe's advertisement, of 1747, we find the statement that "At the Same Place in a separate Apartment will be taught Greek, Latin, Rhetoric, Prosody by a Person lately arrived from London, thoroughly acquainted with Classical Authors."[82] In addition to teaching the rudiments, Garrat Noel, in 1751,[83] gave instruction in Spanish, Thomas Ross, in 1754, French, Low-Dutch, and Latin,[84] and Timothy Wetmore, in 1777, Latin and Greek.[85] In schools emphasizing the practical subjects, Gabriel Wayne, in 1750, taught Latin,[86] and Benjamin Leigh and Garrat Noel, in 1751, Latin, Greek French, and Portuguese.[87] John L. Mayor, in 1753, offered courses only in French, Latin and Greek,[88] and Anthony Fiva, in 1774, in English, French, Spanish, and Italian.[89] Fiva taught these subjects with the view of fitting "his pupils in a short time to carry on an epistolary correspondence, so useful particularly to young persons in business."

Other subjects that appear in the curriculums of the period are English, geography and history. English was usually taught "grammatically;" in fact, grammar as a foundation for all higher work in "English reading and speaking" received a great deal of attention at this time. A long advertisement of Hugh Hughes's plan,

---

[81] American Weekly Mercury, Philadelphia, Oct. 17-24, Oct. 24-31, Oct. 31-Nov. 7, 1723.

[82] New York Evening Post, Aug. 3, 1747.

[83] New York Gazette Revived in the Weekly Post Boy, Sept. 2, Sept. 9, Sept. 16, Sept. 23, 1751. (Beaver Street)

[84] New York Mercury, Oct. 7, 1754 ("opposite the Merchant's Coffee House").

[85] New York Gazette and Weekly Mercury, Jan. 27, 1777 ("two Doors below Peck's Slip").

[86] New York Gazette Revived in the Weekly Post Boy, Aug. 13, Aug. 27, 1750.

[87] Ibid, Jan. 21, Jan. 28, 1751.

[88] New York Gazette or Weekly Post Boy, Nov. 26, Dec. 3, 1753 ("near the Long Bridge").

[89] Rivington's New York Gazetteer, or Conn., N. J., H. R., and Quebec Weekly Advertiser, May 19, May 26, 1774.

in 1772, throws considerable light upon the methods of teaching the subject.

To the PUBLIC

THE SUBSCRIBER proposes, if encouraged, to teach the English Language grammatically. And, for the Satisfaction of those who may be disposed to encourage such a necessary Mode of Education as that of instructing Youth in the grammatical Knowledge of their native Tongue, confessedly is, he gives the following sketch of a Plan which he has adopted. When the Pupil can read fluently and write a legible Hand, he will be taught the English Accidence, or the Properties of the Parts of Speech, as divided and explained in the latest and most eminent English Grammarians; that is DOCTOR LOWTH, and DOCTOR PRIESTLY, and others. After which he will be taught how to parse disjunctively, then modally, and instructed in the Rules of English Syntax; and, when he is sufficiently skilled in them to account for the Construction of the Sentences in general, he will receive Lessons of false Spelling and irregular Concord &c. taken from some classic Author, but rendered ungrammatical for the Purpose of trying his Judgment. When he has reduced these as near their Originals, as his Knowledge of Grammar will permit, he will be shown all such irregularities as may have escaped his Notice, either in the orthographical or syntactical Part. These Lessons will also be selected from different Authors on various Subjects; and frequently from the Works of those who are the most celebrated for the Elegance of their Epistolary Writings; as this Kind of Composition is acknowledged to be as difficult as any, and of greater utility. The erroneous Part in every Lesson will likewise be modified. At one Time, it will consist of false Spelling alone. At another of only false Concord. The next perhaps, will consist of both. The 4th may not be composed of either of them, but may contain some Inaccuracies or Vulgarisms &c. The 5th may retain all the foregoing Improprieties, and the last, none of them, of which the Pupil needs not to be apprised, for Reasons that are too evident to require a Recital. To the preceding Exercises will succeed others on the Nature and Use of Transposition — The Ellipses of all Parts of Speech, as used by the best Writers, together with the Use of synonymous Terms — A general Knowledge of all which joined to Practice, will enable Youth to avoid the many orthographical Errors, Barbarisms, inelegant Repetitions, and manifest Solecisms, which they are otherwise liable to run into, and in Time, render them Masters of an easy elegant Style by which Means they will become capable of conveying their Sentiments with Clearness and Precision, in a concise and agreeable manner; as well with Reputation to themselves, as Delight to their Friends — Lastly tho' the pointing of a Discourse requires riper Judgment, and a more intimate Acquaintance with the syntactical Order of Words and Sentences than the Generality of Youth can be possessed of, to which may be added the unsettled State that Punctuation itself is really in; so that very few precise Rules can be given, without numerous Exceptions, which would rather embarrass than assist the Learner: Yet, some general Directions may be given, in such a Manner as greatly to facilitate so desirable an Acquisition; and they will be attended to on the Part of the Tutor, in Proportion to the Susception of the Pupil.

But he doth not mean to insinuate that the most tractable of mere Youth can be perfected in all the Varieties of the Language in a few Quarters, as Perfection is not to be acquired by Instruction alone, any more than it is by Practice without Instruction. On the Contrary he knows that it is a Work which requires considerable Time and close Application, on the Part of the Pupil as well as great Care and Much Labour, on the Part of the Teacher; and that all hasty Performances in Grammar, have a greater Tendency to raise a slender Superstructure, than lay a permanent Foundation. Much more might be said on the Advantage resulting from this Mode of Education, were they not so very plain, that they scarcely require mentioning, and that this is only a Sketch. However, it may not be amiss to observe, that the Pupils by continually searching of their Dictionaries, in Quest of Primitives and their Derivatives, as well as the constituent Parts of compound Terms; besides learning the Dependence that native Language has on itself; will also treasure up in their Memories a vast Stock of Words from the purest Writers And, what is of infinitely more Value, their just Definitions, as every One of this Class will have Johnson's Dictionary in Octavo. Therefore, if it be true, that 'He who knows most Words, will have most Ideas,' and that on the 'Right Apprehension of Words depends the Rectitude of our Sentiments,' May it not be presumed, that such a Plan, in its full Extent, bids fair for improving the Minds of Youth in Necessary Knowledge, and consequently, is likely to produce intelligent Men and useful Citizens? The Consideration of which, is, with all due Deference most humble submitted to the respectable Public; by its greatly obliged and very humble Servant,

H. Hughes.

P.S. He intends, as soon as Opportunity will permit, to publish a Series of Ratios; calculated for converting, by Multiplication alone, any Sum of New York Currency or the Currency of any other Colony, into Sterling; but may be equally useful for finding the Value of a lower Currency in a higher; when the difference between them increases, or decreases, as it does between Sterling and Currency.

N.B. His Night School will be opened on Monday Evening the 6th of Jan. 1772.[90]

Messrs Gollen and Mountain, in 1774, taught "the method of reading and writing the English language with propriety, so as to avoid a vitiated pronunciation and a false orthography, qualifications too often neglected in the education of youth."[91] John Davis, in 1778, exercised "the greatest care, not only that they shall learn to read grammatically, but be taught properly and syntactically; whence they can discover the beauty and elegance of their mother tongue; that they may be able to construe what they read, thro' every part of speech. By this means, the scholar is fully taught to understand

---

[90] New York Gazette and Weekly Mercury, Dec. 30, 1771; Ibid, Jan. 6, Jan. 13, Jan. 20, Jan. 27, 1772.

[91] Rivington's New York Gazetteer, or Conn., N. J., H. R., and Quebec Weekly Advertiser, Oct. 6, 1778.

the science of what he reads; &, is enable to express himself with propriety."[92]

Another popular type of evening school, for " Young Gentlemen and Misses and Adults of both Sexes," was the " French Night School." The records indicate, that by the middle of the century, French was considered a " very fashionable and necessary language." A notice of 1757 informs us that " Young Gentlemen and Ladies may be taught the FRENCH language in a Manner the most modern and expeditious, by one lately arrived from London, who has made his Tour through France."[93] John Girault, in 1773, instructed " his pupils in all the variations of this polite tongue, after the rules of the most approved grammars, founded on the decisions of the Academy at Paris."[94]

[92] New York Gazette and Weekly Mercury, Jan. 19, Jan. 26, 1778.
See also the Royal Gazette, Oct. 18, Oct. 22, 1783. " J. Mennye, At No. 32 Gold-Street, Corner of Beekman-Street, proposes to open an Evening School, the 21st Instant; in which, and in the Day-School, the following Branches of Education will be taught: The English Language agreeable to the Rules laid down by the most approved Grammarians, and that the Memory may be as little burthened as possible, the Rules are compressed in as few Words as the Nature of the Subject will permit; and, in order that no Inconveniency may arise from this Conciseness, a greater Variety and Number of Examples are given to the Scholars, by way of Exercises than are to be met with in any English Grammar yet published; Besides, that no Illustration of the Rules which can possible be wanting, many Passages will be produced from our most celebrated Authors, to prove, that they themselves, have in many Instances, proved themselves to have been ignorant or inadvertant to several of the Rules which are now universally received as Canons; whence this Inference may fairly be drawn, that English Grammar has hitherto been too much neglected."

[93] New York Gazette or Weekly Post Boy, Oct. 17, Oct. 24, Nov. 21, Nov. 28, Dec. 19, 1757.
Ibid, Jan. 30, Feb. 6, Feb. 20, March 6, 1758 (John Philipse: "every Evening, from the Hour of Five till Eight").
New York Gazette and Weekly Mercury, Jan. 10, 1780. " THE FRENCH LANGUAGE Taught in the most perfect and easy Manner, by THOMAS EGAN Whose residence for many years in some of the first compting-houses in France, enables him to assure those Ladies and Gentlemen, who please to receive his instructions, that they will not be disappointed in his abilities." (30 King Street)

[94] Rivington's New York Gazetteer, or Conn., N. J., H. R., and Quebec Weekly Advertiser, Sept. 16, Sept. 23, Oct. 7, Oct. 14, 1773.
New York Gazette and Weekly Mercury, Sept. 9, Sept. 16, Sept. 23, 1771; Ibid, Sept. 7, Sept. 14, Sept. 21, Oct. 12, Oct. 19, 1772 (John Girault, " upper End of Stone Street").
Rivington's New York Gazetteer, or Conn., N. J., H. R., and Quebec Weekly Advertiser, Oct. 26, Nov. 9, Nov. 16, 1775. Francis Vandale, " next door to Mr. Rivington." taught " French and other languages."

The advertisements do not give definite information concerning the rates of instruction in the languages. Francis Vandale, in 1775, in his "day and evening school," taught "French and other languages . . . at very reasonable rates, " i. e., £2 " a piece (½ entrance) a quarter."[95] More detailed, but equally indefinite, information is available for the tuition fees of day schools. Robert Leeth, in 1751, taught " Latin, Greek, and the most useful Branches of the Mathematicks at a Pistole per Quarter, exclusive of a Pistole Entrance as has always been the Custom at Grammar Schools in this City."[96] William Clajon, in 1766, announced that " My terms are as follows, viz. For the French, Latin and Greek Languages, besides English Grammar, &c. . . 36s. entrance and 20s. per Quarter. . . I will teach . . . for 24s per Month, and 24s entrance, those of riper Years who incline to learn the French Language."[97] In the same year, Edward Riggs taught " the Latin and Greek languages . . . rhetoric, geography, &c. . . without entrance," for "five pounds a year."[98] Josiah Stoddard, in 1770, gave instruction in the " Latin and Greek Languages . . . for the small sum of four or five and twenty pounds per ann,"[99] and John Copp, in 1774, announced that for " the Latin and Greek languages, and arithmetic. . . Reading, and Writing, and the principles of English grammar. . . The price of tuition will not exceed fifteen dollars yearly; no entrance fee expected."[100]

The evening school of colonial New York was a unique institution. Whatever its type, it provided " at convenient Hours," for those " who cannot attend in the Day Time." In some cases it was patronised by pupils who attended " other Places of Education at different Periods, for other purposes." From these standpoints alone it rendered a distinct service to the period in widening the scope of educational opportunity.

The most popular evening school was the one that gave instruc-

---

[95] Rivington's New York Gazetteer, or Conn., N. J., H. R., and Quebec Weekly Advertiser, Oct. 26, Nov. 9, Nov. 16, 1775.
[96] New York Gazette Revived in the Weekly Post Boy, Sept. 18, Sept. 25, Oct. 2, Oct. 9, Oct. 16, Oct. 23, Oct. 30, 1752.
[97] New York Mercury, May 19, May 26, 1766. ("Consistory Room of the French Church")
[98] Ibid, May 26, 1766. (Kingston)
[99] New York Gazette and Weekly Mercury, Oct. 22, Oct. 29, Nov. 5, Nov. 26, 1770. (Kingston)
[100] Rivington's New York Gazetteer, or Conn., N. J., H. R., and Quebec Weekly Advertiser, July 7, July 14, July 21, 1774. (Flatbush)

tion in the "practical branches." New York was a city of many trade and commercial activities, operating on land and sea; and the advertisements indicate that higher technical instruction was needed to prepare young men for these pursuits. Trade-training was provided by the apprenticeship system, but that institution could not adequately equip apprentices "for business either as mechanic, merchant, seaman, engineer, etc."[101] Very few men, outside the teaching profession were capable of giving thorough courses in arithmetic, algebra, geometry, trigonometry, astronomy, geography, navigation, surveying, bookkeeping etc.; and fewer could spare the time. Furthermore, merchants, engineers and ship-owners were demanding that the young men entering their employ, have this technical preparation. Undoubtedly, these schools exercised an appreciable influence in the direction of raising the "entrance requirements" of many pursuits. They were the commercial schools, or business colleges, of the colonial period. Their contribution constitutes a valuable chapter in the history of trade, as well as in the history of education, in colonial New York City.

---

[101] New York Mercury, May 6, May 13, May 20, Sept. 30, Oct. 7, 1765.

Chapter 15
NEW YORK COLONIAL SCHOOLMASTERS
(From the first English Occupation to the Evacuation)
1664–1783
ROBERT FRANCIS SEYBOLT, Ph.D.

University of Wisconsin

Although this list of schoolmen has no direct bearing upon the history of the free school movement, yet we must appreciate the part they played. History is probably the best proof as to the part schools have played in its making. We can probably, without injustice, attribute a great deal to these schoolmen as being among those who from the beginning were conscious of the responsibility the State had in the education of its youth, and this probably laid in the minds of the young the principles that came to pass in the generations to come.

	Name	Date	Place
1	Evert Pietersen	(1664–1669)	New York City
2	Johannes la Montagne	(1664–1670)	New Harlem
3	John Schutte	(1665)	Albany
4	Willem la Montagne	(1666)	Wildwyck, Ulster co.
5	Jan Tiebout	(1666–1670, 1681–82, 1685–98)	Flatbush and New Harlem
6	Abram de La Noy	(1668–1702)	New York City
7	Philip Alcock	(1669)	Jamaica
8	.... Houlding	(1669)	Hempstead
9	Richard Charlton	(1670)	Hempstead
10	Richard Gildersleeve	(1670)	Hempstead
11	Jacob Joosten	(1670–1676)	Flatbush
12	Hendrick Jansen Van der Vin	(1670–1685)	New Harlem
13	Michael Hainelle	(1674–1675)	Flatbush
14	Ebenezer Kirtland	(1674–1676)	New York City

[1] The Records of New Amsterdam (B. Fernow, editor. 7 v. N. Y., 1897), V. 137; VI, 168.
[2] W. H. Kilpatrick, The Dutch Schools of New Netherland and Colonial New York (U. S. Bureau of Education. Bulletin 1912, No. 12), 133, 160.
[3] The Annals of Albany (J. Munsell, editor. 10 v. Albany, 1850–59), III, 327.
[4] Olde Ulster (B. M. Brink, editor. 10 v. Kingston, N. Y., 1905–1914), X, 69.
[5] Kilpatrick, 167, 172, 174.
[6] Abstracts of Wills, 1665–1686 (17 v. N. Y. Hist. Soc. Coll. 1892–1908), I, 342.
[7] Records of the Town of East Hampton, N. Y. (4 v. Sag Harbor, 1887–89), I, 322.
[8] D. J. Pratt, Annals of Public Education in the State of New York, 1626–1746 (Albany, 1872), 58.
[9] Pratt, 58.
[10] Pratt, 122.
[11] Kilpatrick, 167, 170.
[12] Kilpatrick, 160, 164.
[13] Pratt, 63.
[14] Minutes of the Common Council of the City of New York, 1675–1776 (8 v. New York, 1905), I, 22–23.

	Name	Date	Place
15	John Laughton	(1675)	Jamaica
16	Mathew Hillyer	(1676)	New York City
17	Asher Long	(1676)	New York City
18	Luykas Gerritse (Wyngaard)	(1676)	Albany
19	Arien Appel	(1676)	Albany
20	Jan Becker	(1676)	Albany
21	Gerret Swartt	(1676)	Albany
22	Jan Gerritz Van Marken	(1676-1680)	Flatbush
23	Richard Jones	(1677)	Jamaica
24	Rem Remse	(1677)	Flatbush
25	Thomas Webb	(1678)	Oyster Bay
26	Derick Storm	(1680-1681)	Flatbush
27	John Bowne	(1680-1693)	Flushing
28	Dirck Wessels	(1681)	Marbletown, Ulster co.
29	Peter Benson	(1682-1683)	East Hampton
30	Johannes Van Ekelen	(1682-1700)	Flatbush
31	Goody Davis	(1685)	Jamaica
32	Rachel Spencer	(1685)	Hempstead
33	Henry Harrison	(1685)	New York City
34	Charles Gage	(1686-1687)	New York City
35	Jores Van Spyk	(1687-1688)	Flatbush
36	Guilliam Bertholf	(1690-1691)	New Harlem
37	Johannes Schenk	(1691-1711)	Flatbush and New York City
38	Joost de Baare	(1692)	New Utrecht
39	Daniel Martineau	(1692-1700)	Flatbush
40	David Vilant	(1693-1697)	New York City
41	John Mowbray	(1694)	Southampton

[15] East Hampton Records, I, 380.
[16] Min. Com. Coun. City of N. Y., I, 24.
[17] Mayor's Court Minutes, Nov. 1675–Nov. 1677. Item dated April 11, 1676. (Manuscript folio. Pages not numbered.)
[18] Pratt, 62.
[19] Pratt, 62.
[20] Pratt, 62.
[21] Pratt, 62.
[22] Kilpatrick, 170, 172.
[23] Records of the Town of Jamaica, N. Y., 1656–1751 (Brooklyn, 1914, 3 v.), I, 69.
[24] Pratt, 64.
[25] Oyster Bay Town Records (v. 1, N. Y., 1916), I, 235.
[26] Pratt, 63.
[27] Pratt, 68.
[28] Olde Ulster, II, 60; X, 69.
[29] East Hampton Records, II, 107, 131.
[30] Kilpatrick, 174, 176, 177; Pratt, 63.
[31] Pratt, 69.
[32] Pratt, 69.
[33] Pratt, 71.
[34] Pratt, 71.
[35] Kilpatrick, 189.
[36] Kilpatrick, 165.
[37] Kilpatrick, 176, 177; Pratt, 63; Roll of Freemen of New York City, 1675–1866 (in N. Y. Hist. Soc. Coll. 1885, p. 39–443), 71.
[38] Calendar of New York Historical Manuscripts (E. B. O'Callaghan, editor. P. 2, Albany, 1866), 226.
[39] Kilpatrick, 189.
[40] Min. Com. Coun. City of N. Y., II, 21.
[41] Pratt, 75.

FREE SCHOOLS 655

	Name	Date	Place
42	William Huddlestone	(1695, 1702–1725)	New York City
43	Isaac Selover	(1695–1708)	Flatlands
44	Alexander Paxton	(1698)	New York City
45	Adrian Vermeule	(1699)	New Harlem
46	William de Meyer	(1700)	Albany
47	Cornelis Bogardus	(1700)	Albany
48	Jan Langestraat	(1700–1706)	Flatbush
49	Peter Bontecou	(1702)	New York City
50	Robert Parkinson	(1702)	New York City
51	John Sellwood	(1702)	New York City
52	Paulus Van Vleck	(1702)	Kinderhook
53	Dan Thwaites	(1703)	New York City
54	Evert Ridder	(1703)	Albany
55	Andrew Foucautt	(1703)	New York City
56	Stephen Gasheris	(1704)	Kingston
57	Joseph Cleator	(1704–1731)	Rye and New York City
58	George Muirson	(1704)	New York City
59	Prudent de la Fayole	(1705)	New York City
60	Andrew Clarke	(1705)	New York City
61	Henry Lindley	(1705)	Jamaica
62	Elias Bon Repos	(1705)	New Rochelle
63	Elizabeth Hand	(1706)	East Hampton
64	Alexander Baird	(1706, 1708)	Hempstead
65	Edward Fitzgerald	(1706)	Westchester
66	James Jeffray	(1706)	New York City
67	Thomas Barclay	(1707–1722)	Albany
68	John Stevens	(1708)	New York City

[42] Abstracts of Wills, VII, 55; W. W. Kemp, The Support of Schools in Colonial New York by the Society for the Propagation of the Gospel in Foreign Parts (New York, 1913), 80, 92; Pratt, 112.
[43] Pratt, 69, 117.
[44] Roll of Freemen of N. Y. City, 62.
[45] Kilpatrick, 165.
[46] Annals of Albany, IV, 100.
[47] Annals of Albany, IV, 106.
[48] Kilpatrick, 189.
[49] Roll of Freemen of N. Y. City, 83.
[50] Roll of Freemen of N. Y. City, 76.
[51] Roll of Freemen of N. Y. City, 82.
[52] E. B. O'Callaghan, The Documentary History of the State of New York (4 v. Albany, 1849–51), III, 894.
[53] Roll of Freemen of N. Y. City, 85.
[54] Annals of Albany, IV, 177; Ecclesiastical Records of the State of New York (6 v. Albany, 1901–1905), III, 1522; Pratt, 90.
[55] Pratt, 90.
[56] Pratt, 91.
[57] Pratt, 07, 114; Kemp, 77, 122, 126; A List of Emigrant Ministers to America, 1690–1811 (G. Fothergill. London, 1904), 20.
[58] Ecclesiastical Records, III, 1552; Pratt, 87.
[59] Pratt, 92.
[60] Min. Com. Coun. City of N. Y., III, 69; Kemp, 72; A List of Emigrant Ministers to America, 20.
[61] Pratt, 91.
[62] Pratt, 92.
[63] East Hampton Records, III, 154.
[64] Pratt, 92.
[65] Pratt, 93.
[66] Pratt, 92.
[67] Kemp, 197.
[68] Kemp, 77.

	Name	Date	Place
69	Thomas Meeken .... (1708–1709)		Jamaica and Flushing
70	John Bashford .... (1708)		New York City
71	Cornelius Lodge .... (1708)		New York City
72	John Humphreys .... (1708)		New York City
73	Thomas Huddlestone...... (1708; 1714; 1725–31)		Southold, Rye and New York City
74	Daniel Clarke .... (1710)		Westchester
75	Adam Brown.............. (1710–11 to 1712–13)		Staten Island
76	Jan Gancell .... (1711–1719)		Flatbush
77	Allane Jarrat .... (1712)		New York City
78	Francis Williamson .... (1712–1713)		Staten Island
79	John Dupuy .... (1712–1713)		Staten Island
80	Benjamin Drewitt .... (1712–1713)		Staten Island
81	Thomas Potts .... (1712–1713)		Staten Island
82	Charles Glover .... (1713–1715)		Westchester
83	Robert Macbeth .... (1713)		Huntington
84	Benjamin Miller .... (1713–1715)		Staten Island
85	Thomas Gildersleeve........ (1713–14 to 1739–40)		Hempstead
86	Charles Taylor .... (1714–1742)		Staten Island
87	John Conrad Codwise................... (1715)		New York City
88	James Battersby .... (1715)		Flushing
89	Robert Jenney .... (1716–1722)		New York City
90	David Jamison .... (1716)		New York City
91	Jacobus Goelet .... (1717)		New York City
92	William Forster .... (1717–1744)		Westchester
93	Samuel Jones .... (1718–1719)		Yonkers
94	Pieter Van der Lyn..................... (1719)		New York City
95	.... Jones .... (1719–1720)		Westchester
96	Adriaen Hegeman .... (1719–1741)		Flatbush

[69] Kemp, 77; Pratt, 94.
[70] Kemp, 77.
[71] Kemp, 77.
[72] Kemp, 78.
[73] Kemp, 77, 92; Pratt, 112, 116.
[74] Pratt, 114.
[75] Pratt, 113.
[76] Pratt, 63.
[77] Pratt, 93.
[78] Pratt, 113; Kemp, 165.
[79] Pratt, 113; Kemp, 165.
[80] Pratt, 113.
[81] Kemp, 165.
[82] Pratt, 114; Kemp, 146.
[83] Huntington Town Records, 1653–1688 (3 v. Huntington and Babylon, 1887), II, 310.
[84] Pratt, 113; Kemp, 165.
[85] Pratt, 111; Kemp, 174.
[86] Kemp, 166: Pratt, 113.
[87] Mayor's Court Minutes, May 24, 1715, to April 29, 1718, 26.
[88] Pratt, 121; Cal. N. Y. Hist. MSS., 427.
[89] Kemp, 74.
[90] Pratt, 122.
[91] Mayor's Court Minutes, May 24, 1715, to April 29, 1718, 317.
[92] Pratt, 114; Ecclesiastical Records, III, 2140; Kemp, 147.
[93] Kemp, 160–1.
[94] Mayor's Court Minutes, May 1718 to June 1720, 232.
[95] Pratt, 113.
[96] Kilpatrick, 181, 182.

FREE SCHOOLS

	Name	Date	Place
97	Peter Parvisol	(1720)	New York City
98	Johannes Glandorf	(1721)	Albany
99	Georgius Sheriosby	(1721)	Westchester
100	George Browning	(1721)	New York City
101	George Brownell	(1722, 1731, 1733)	New York City
102	William Glover	(1722)	New York City
103	James Loquart	(1722)	Jamaica
104	Thomas Lynstead	(1723)	Oyster Bay
105	James Weeks	(1723)	New York City
106	John Carhart	(1723)	Rye
107	James Wetmore	(1723-24 to 1724-25)	New York City
108	Daniel Denton	(1724-25 to 1730-31)	Oyster Bay
109	Peter Finch	(1725)	New York City
110	Jonathan Sherer	(1725)	New York City
111	Thomas Colgan	(1725-26 to 1729-30)	New York City
112	Barend de Forest	(1725-1732)	New York City
113	Flint Dwight	(1728-1735; 1735-1745)	Rye and White Plains
114	Johannes Glundorff	(1728)	New York City
115	Edward Gatehouse	(1728, 1731, 1740)	New York City
116	Mitchell Somersett	(1729)	New York City
117	James Delpech	(1729)	East Chester
118	Edward Davies	(1729-1735)	Southampton
119	Edward Willett	(1729-30 to 1741-42)	Jamaica
120	.... Charlton	(1729-30 to 1743-44)	New York City
121	Samuel Purdy	(1729-30 to 1752-53)	Rye
122	Thomas Keble	(1730-1748)	Oyster Bay
123	James Lyde	(1730)	New York City
124	John Beasley	(1730-1734)	Albany

[97] Liber 29 (manuscript folio in library of N. Y. Hist. Soc.), 63.
[98] Annals of Albany, VIII, 262.
[99] Pratt, 118.
[100] Mayor's Court Minutes, May 1720 to August 1723, 179.
[101] Liber 29, 145; New York Gazette, June 14 to June 21, 1731; New York Weekly Journal, Feb. 18, Feb. 25, March 4, March 11, 1733.
[102] Roll of Freemen of N. Y. City, 102.
[103] Pratt, 118.
[104] Pratt, 118.
[105] Roll of Freemen of N. Y. City, 103.
[106] Pratt, 114.
[107] Pratt, 113.
[108] Pratt, 111; Kemp, 183.
[109] Roll of Freemen of N. Y. City, 106.
[110] Roll of Freemen of N. Y. City, 105.
[111] Pratt, 113.
[112] Kilpatrick, 150-151.
[113] Pratt, 114, 116; Kemp, 142, 143.
[114] Roll of Freemen of N. Y. City, 111.
[115] Roll of Freemen of N. Y. City, 111; New York Gazette, Oct. 4 to Oct. 11, 1731. New York Weekly Journal, March 24, March 31, April 7, 1740.
[116] Mayor's Court Minutes, Jan. 26, 1724 to June 1729 (Manuscript folio, in N. Y. Hall of Records).
[117] Kemp, 161.
[118] Pratt, 111; Kemp, 191.
[119] Pratt, 111; Kemp, 188.
[120] Pratt, 113.
[121] Pratt, 114; Kemp, 67, 130-131.
[122] Pratt, 111; Kemp, 185.
[123] New York Gazette, Aug. 31 to Sept. 7, 1730.
[124] Kemp, 200; Pratt, 111.

	Name	Date	Place
125	Thomas Noxon	(1730–31 to 1742–43)	New York City
126	William Rock	(1731)	Jamaica
127	Alexander Malcolm	(1732–1739)	New York City
128	William Thurston	(1732)	New York City
129	Gerrit Van Wagenen	(1732–1742)	New York City
130	Peter Stoughtenburgh	(1735)	New York City
131	Daniel Shatford	(1735)	New York City
132	John Cavelier	(1736)	New York City
133	Charles Henley	(1737)	New York City
134	Joshua Ring	(1737)	New York City
135	Walter Hetherington	(1739)	New York City
136	Thomas Temple	(1739–40 to 1752–53)	Hempstead
137	James Foddey	(1740)	New York City
138	Thomas Allen	(1740–41, 1752; 1763)	New York City and Cortlandt
139	John Campbell	(1741)	New York City
140	John Ury	(1741)	New York City
141	John Moore	(1741–1743)	Jamaica
142	Jores Remsen	(1741–1755)	Flatbush
143	Henry Peckwell	(1741–1769, 1771)	New York City
144	Elward Mariner	(1742)	New York City
145	Andrew Wright	(1742–1748)	Staten Island
146	Samuel Seabury	(1742–1764)	Hempstead
147	Abraham de Lanoy	(1743–1747)	New York City
148	Huybert Van Wagenen	(1743)	New York City
149	Samuel Dunlop	(1743–1744)	Cherry Valley
150	Basil Bartowe	(1743–44 to 1760–61)	Westchester
151	Thomas Hildreth	(1743–44 to 1775–76)	New York City

[125] Pratt, 112; Kemp, 97, 100.
[126] Pratt, 118.
[127] Kemp, 73; Pratt, 124–141; Min. Com. Coun. City of N. Y., IV, 174–5.
[128] New York Gazette, Aug. 28 to Sept. 4, 1732.
[129] Kilpatrick, 151–2.
[130] Roll of Freemen of N. Y. City, 127.
[131] Roll of Freemen of N. Y. City, 128.
[132] Roll of Freemen of N. Y. City, 130; Mayor's Court Minutes, Feb., 1735 to Aug., 1742, 48. (Manuscript folio, in N. Y. Hall of Records).
[133] Roll of Freemen of N. Y. City, 131; Mayor's Court Minutes, Feb., 1735 to Aug., 1742, 100.
[134] New York Weekly Journal, April 4, April 11, 1737.
[135] Pratt, 142; Cal. N. Y. Hist. MSS., 538.
[136] Pratt, 111; Kemp, 176–7.
[137] New York Weekly Journal, March 24, March 31, April 7, 1740.
[138] Roll of Freemen of N. Y. City, 142; Abstracts of Wills, VIII, 235; Mayor's Court Minutes, Feb., 1735 to Aug., 1742, 432; New York Gazette Revived in the Weekly Post-Boy, March 16, March 23, April 6, 1752.
[139] Cal. N. Y. Hist. MSS., 552; New York Weekly Journal, April 6, April 13, April 27, May 4, May 18, May 25, May 31, June 15, June 22, 1741.
[140] Cal. N. Y. Hist. MSS., 553, 565.
[141] Pratt, 111; Kemp, 190.
[142] Kilpatrick, 182.
[143] Abstracts of Wills, VI, 106, 307; VII, 56, 304; Roll of Freemen of N. Y. City, 209 New York Gazette and Weekly Mercury, April 15, April 22, May 6, 1771.
[144] Roll of Freemen of N. Y. City, 144; Mayor's Court Minutes, Feb. 1735 to Aug. 1742, 571.
[145] Pratt, 113; Kemp, 168.
[146] Kemp, 182.
[147] Ecclesiastical Records, IV, 2828–9; Kilpatrick, 153.
[148] Pratt, 144; Ecclesiastical Records, IV, 2938.
[149] Pratt, 143.
[150] Pratt, 114; Kemp, 153.
[151] Pratt, 112.

FREE SCHOOLS

	Name	Date	Place
152	Charles Johnston	(1744, 1748, 1752)	New York City
153	Abraham De Lancey	(1744)	New York City
154	John Carhart	(1744–1770)	Rye
155	Joseph Hildreth	(1744–1776)	New York City
156	William Sturgeon	(1745–1746)	Rye
157	George Gorden	(1745–1761)	Rye
158	Malcolm Campbell	(1746)	New York City
159	Christian Schultz	(1746, 1769)	Rhinebeck
160	George Bingham	(1747)	New York City
161	Joseph Blanchard	(1747)	New York City
162	Thomas Metcalfe	(1747)	New York City
163	Henry Moore	(1747)	New York City
164	Augustus Vaughan	(1747)	New York City
165	Archibald McEuen	(1747, 1750)	New York City
166	Charles Johnson	(1747)	New York City
167	Samuel Auchmuty	(1747–48 to 1763–64)	New York City
168	Cornelius Linch	(1748)	New York City
169	.... Seabury	(1749)	Oyster Bay
170	John Clarke	(1749–1750)	Brooklyn
171	Thomas Evans	(1749–1750)	New York City
172	Daniel Bratt	(1749–1754)	New York City
173	Nicholas Barrington	(1749–52; 1752, 55, 57)	Staten Island and New York City
174	Richard Smith	(1749–50, 1753–1757)	New York City
175	Mary Giles	(1749, 1761)	New York City

[152] New York Weekly Post-Boy, March 5, 1744; Records of the Town of New Rochelle, 1699–1828 (J. A. Forbes, editor. New Rochelle, 1916), 273; New York Gazette Revived in the Weekly Post-Boy, May 11, May 18, May 25, June 1, 1752.
[153] Roll of Freemen of N. Y. City, 151.
[154] Abstracts of Wills, VI, 176, 254, 425; Ibid, VII, 10, 247, 383.
[155] Roll of Freemen of N. Y. City, 165; Abstracts of Wills, VI, 24; Calendar of Wills, 1626–1836 (B. Fernow, editor. N. Y., 1896), 161; Kemp, 106.
[156] Pratt, 114.
[157] Abstracts of Wills, VI, 77, 128.
[158] Roll of Freemen of N. Y. City, 156.
[159] Abstracts of Wills, V, 420; Ibid, VII, 333; Calendar of Wills, 224.
[160] New York Evening Post, Aug. 3, 1747.
[161] New York Evening Post, Aug. 3, 1747.
[162] New York Evening Post, Aug. 3, 1747.
[163] New York Gazette Revived in the Weekly Post-Boy, June 1, June 8, 1747.
[164] New York Evening Post, Oct. 26, 1747.
[165] Roll of Freemen of N. Y. City, 159; The New York Gazette Revived in the Weekly Post-Boy, Aug. 6, Aug. 13, Aug. 27, 1750.
[166] Roll of Freemen of N. Y. City, 158.
[167] Pratt, 113.
[168] New York Gazette Revived in the Weekly Post-Boy, July 4, July 11, July 18, July 25, 1748.
[169] Kemp, 186.
[170] New York Gazette Revived in the Weekly Post-Boy, Dec. 4, Dec. 11, Dec. 18, 1749; Jan. 1, Jan. 8, 1750.
[171] New York Gazette Revived in the Weekly Post-Boy, Dec. 18, Dec. 25, 1749; Jan. 1, Jan. 8, 1750.
[172] Ecclesiastical Records, IV, 3025; Kilpatrick, 153.
[173] Pratt, 113; Kemp, 169; New York Gazette Revived in the Weekly Post-Boy, Nov. 13, 1752; New York Mercury, May 19, June 2, 1755; New York Gazette or Weekly Post-Boy, May 29, June 6, June 13, June 20, June 27, July 4, 1757.
[174] New York Gazette Revived in the Weekly Post-Boy, Dec. 25, 1749; Ibid, Jan. 1, Jan. 8, Jan. 15, Jan. 22, Jan. 29, 1750; Abstracts of Wills, V, 246; New York Gazette or Weekly Post-Boy, April 23, April 30, June 11, June 18, June 25, July 2, July 9, July 16, 1753; Ibid, Feb. 16, March 8, 1756.
[175] Abstracts of Wills, VI, 65.

	Name	Date	Place
176	James Giles.............	(1749, 1758–59, 1761–62)	New York City
177	William Wilson	(1750)	New York City
178	Gabriel Wayne	(1750)	New York City
179	Michael C. Knoll.......................	(1750)	New York City
180	Reinhold Jan Klockhoff..................	(1751)	New York City
181	Benjamin Leigh	(1751)	New York City
182	Jan Paulus Ostome......................	(1751)	New York City
183	Edward Smith	(1751)	New York City
184	Garrat Noel	(1751–1753)	New York City
185	Robert Leeth..................	(1751–1752, 1755)	New York City
186	John Nathan Hutchins.....	(1751–52, 1755, 1763, 1765, 1770, 1772)	New York City
187	Rebecca Furman	(1752)	New York City
188	John Baptiste Guerbois..................	(1752)	New York City
189	James Hutchins	(1752)	New York City
190	Thomas Price	(1753–1760)	Staten Island
191	John Lewis	(1753–1754)	New York City
192	John Lewis Mayor..................	(1753–1754)	New York City
193	William Elphinstone.......	(1753–1766, 1775–1776)	New York City

[176] Abstracts of Wills, VI, 65; New York Gazette or Weekly Post-Boy, March 27, April 3, April 17, May 1, 1758; Ibid, April 30, May 14, May 21, May 28, 1759; New York Mercury, Sept. 7, Sept. 14, Sept. 21, 1761; New York Gazette or Weekly Post-Boy, Sept. 2, Sept. 23, Sept. 30, 1762.
[177] New York Gazette Revived in the Weekly Post-Boy, June 18, June 25, July 2, 1750.
[178] New York Gazette Revived in the Weekly Post-Boy, July 30, Aug. 6, Aug. 13, Aug. 27, Sept. 17, Sept. 24, 1750.
[179] New York Gazette Revived in the Weekly Post-Boy, Aug. 6, Aug. 13, 1750.
[180] New York Gazette Revived in the Weekly Post-Boy, April 22, 1751.
[181] New York Gazette Revived in the Weekly Post-Boy, Jan. 14, Jan. 21, Jan. 28, 1751.
[182] New York Gazette Revived in the Weekly Post-Boy, Aug. 26, Sept. 2, Sept. 16, Sept. 23, 1751.
[183] New York Gazette Revived in the Weekly Post-Boy, April 29, 1751.
[184] Roll of Freemen of N. Y. City, 177; New York Gazette Revived in the Weekly Post-Boy, Jan. 21, Jan. 28, June 3, June 10, Sept. 2, Sept. 9, Sept. 16, Sept. 23, 1751.
[185] New York Evening Post, May 27, June 3, 1751; New York Gazette Revived in the Weekly Post-Boy, June 17, June 24, July 8, July 15, July 22, 1751; Ibid, Sept. 18, Sept. 25, Oct. 2, Oct. 9, 1752; N. Y. Gazette or Weekly Post-Boy, May 12, May 19, 1755.
[186] Roll of Freemen of N. Y. City, 177; Abstracts of Wills, VI, 147, 225, 266; Ibid, VII, 434; Ibid, VIII, 12; Ibid, IX, 299; New York Gazette Revived in the Weekly Post-Boy, May 13, May 27, June 3, 1751; Ibid, June 26, July 6, July 13, July 20, 1752; New York Mercury, May 12, May 19, 1755; Ibid, April 25, May 2, 1763; Ibid, Oct. 21, Oct. 28, 1765; New York Gazette and Weekly Mercury, Oct. 22, 1770; Ibid, Sept. 21, 1772.
[187] Abstracts of Wills, VI, 459.
[188] New York Gazette Revived in the Weekly Post-Boy, Nov. 6, Nov. 27, 1752.
[189] New York Gazette Revived in the Weekly Post-Boy, June 26, July 6, July 13, July 20, 1752.
[190] Pratt, 113; Kemp, 170.
[191] New York Gazette or Weekly Post-Boy, June 4, June 11, June 25, July 9, July 16, July 23, Oct. 15, Nov. 26, Dec. 3, Dec. 24, 1753; Ibid, Jan. 7, Jan. 14, Jan. 21, Jan. 28, Feb. 11, Feb. 25, 1754.
[192] New York Gazette or Weekly Post-Boy, Nov. 26, Dec. 3, 1753; Ibid, Sept. 30, Oct. 14, Nov. 4, Nov. 11, 1754.
[193] New York Gazette or Weekly Post-Boy, Oct. 15, Oct. 22, Oct. 29, Nov. 12, Nov. 19, Dec. 3, 1753; Ibid, Jan. 6, Jan. 13, Jan. 20, Jan. 27, 1755; Ibid, April 26, May 10, May 17, 1756; Ibid, May 22, May 29, June 5, June 12, June 26, July 3, 1758; Parker's New York Gazette or Weekly Post-Boy, Sept. 18, Oct. 9, 1760; New York Mercury, June 22, July 27, Aug. 3, Sept. 14, Sept. 21, Sept. 28, Dec. 7, Dec. 14, 1761; New York Mercury, Jan. 10, Jan. 17, Feb. 7, Sept. 19, Sept. 26, Oct. 3, 1763; New York Gazette or Weekly Post-Boy, May 17, May 31, 1764; New York Mercury, Feb. 4, Feb. 11, March 25, April 1, Sept. 23, Sept. 30, Oct. 14, Oct. 21, 1765; Ibid, April 14, May 19, Aug. 4, Aug. 11, 1766; Rivington's New York Gazetteer or The Connecticut, Hudson's River, New Jersey, and Quebec Weekly Advertiser, Aug. 31, 1775; New York Gazette and Weekly Mercury, Jan. 1, 1776.

	Name	Date	Place
194	Timothy Wetmore............	(1753–1767; 1777)	Rye and New York City
195	Adrianus Van der Swan................	(1754)	Albany
196	Jeremiah Owen	(1754)	New York City
197	Thomas Ross	(1754)	New York City
198	John Cooper	(1755)	Southampton
199	.... Graham	(1755)	Rumbout Precinct, Dutchess co.
200	John Searson......................	(1755, 1757)	New York City
201	James Wragg	(1755–1757)	New York City
202	Anthony Whelp	(1755–1767)	New York City
203	Peter Durand	(1756)	New York City
204	James Farrill	(1756)	New York City
205	Elizabeth Wragg	(1756)	New York City
206	John Thompson	(1756)	New Windsor
207	Luke Cummins	(1756)	Hempstead
208	Thomas Johnson..............	(1756, 1761–1762)	New York City
209	Gerard Smith	(1757)	New York City
210	Thomas Clark	(1757)	New York City
211	John Philipse	(1757–1758)	New York City
212	William Penn	(1757–1759)	New York City
213	Edward Willet................	(1757–1758, 1764)	New York City
214	John Davis	(1758)	Westchester co.
215	George Adams	(1758)	New York City
216	Nathaniel Havens	(1758)	New York City

[194] Pratt, 114; Kemp, 134; New York Gazette and Weekly Mercury, Jan. 27, 1777.
[195] Ecclesiastical Records, V, 3521.
[196] Abstracts of Wills, V, 112.
[197] New York Mercury, Oct. 7, 1754.
[198] Abstracts of Wills, V, 59.
[199] New York Mercury, May 19, June 2, 1755.
[200] New York Gazette or Weekly Post-Boy, April 28, May 5, May 12, May 19, June 2, Sept. 15, Sept. 19, Sept. 29, Oct. 6, Oct. 13, Oct. 27, 1755; Ibid, May 16, May 23, May 30, June 13, 1757.
[201] New York Mercury, Feb. 17, 1755; New York Gazette or Weekly Post-Boy, April 7, April 21, May 5, May 12, May 19, May 26, June 16, July 14, July 28, Aug. 4, Aug. 11, Aug. 18, Sept. 1, Sept. 8, Sept. 15, Sept. 22, Oct. 6, Oct. 13, Oct. 20, Oct. 27, 1755; Ibid, April 5, April 12, Sept. 19, Sept. 26, May 3, May 10, May 17, June 4, July 19, Sept. 13, Sept. 20, Oct. 25, Nov. 29, 1756; Ibid, April 4, April 11, April 18, April 25, 1757.
[202] Docs. Rel. Col. Hist. N. Y. (E. B. O'Callaghan and B. Fernow, eds. 15 v. Albany, 1853–1887), III, 312; Kilpatrick, 185–6; Pratt, 63.
[203] New York Gazette or Weekly Post-Boy, May 31, 1756.
[204] New York Mercury, July 12, July 26, Aug. 2, Aug. 9, Aug. 16, 1756.
[205] New York Gazette or Weekly Post-Boy, April 5, April 12, April 19, April 26, May 3, May 10, May 17, June 4, July 19, 1756.
[206] Calendar of Wills, 387.
[207] Abstracts of Wills, V, 376.
[208] New York Gazette or Weekly Post-Boy, May 10, May 17, June 7, June 21, 1756; New York Mercury, Nov. 23, 1761; New York Gazette, Jan. 18, 1762; The American Chronicle, May 17, May 24, 1762.
[209] Abstracts of Wills, VI, 340.
[210] New York Gazette or Weekly Post-Boy, May 2, May 9, May 30, June 13, 1757.
[211] New York Gazette or Weekly Post-Boy, Oct. 17, Oct. 24, Nov. 21, Nov. 28, Dec. 5, Dec. 19, 1757; Ibid, Jan. 30, Feb. 20, Mar. 6, 1758.
[212] Abstracts of Wills, V, 226.
[213] New York Gazette or Weekly Post-Boy, Oct. 24, 1757; Ibid, Aug. 14, Aug. 28, 1758; Ibid, March 29, April 5, 1764.
[214] Muster Rolls of the New York Provincial Troops (in N. Y. Hist. Soc. Coll. 1891), 66, 76.
[215] New York Gazette or Weekly Post-Boy, July 31, Aug. 14, Aug. 28, 1758.
[216] New York Gazette or Weekly Post-Boy, May 8, May 15, May 22, May 29; June 12, 1758.

	Name	Date	Place
217	William Wilson	(1758)	Queens co.
218	Alexander Graham	(1758)	Orange co.
219	Joseph Gibbs	(1758)	Southampton
220	Samuel Giles	(1758–59, 1761, 1763–64)	New York City
221	John Wingfield	(1758, 1777)	New York City
222	Samuel Moore	(1759, 1763)	Phillipsburgh, Westchester co.
223	William German	(1760)	Queens co.
224	John MacGie	(1760)	Suffolk co.
225	Daniel Moor	(1760)	Dutchess co.
226	John Wallas	(1760)	Westchester co.
227	John Watts	(1760–1761)	Staten Island
228	William Barker	(1761)	Dutchess co.
229	John Chandler	(1761)	Orange co.
230	Nathaniel McCaul	(1761)	New York City
231	John Kean	(1761)	Dutchess co.
232	William Rudge	(1761)	New York City
233	Robert Butcher	(1761)	Poughkeepsie
234	William Hanna	(1761)	Albany
235	Caleb Heustis	(1761)	North Castle, Westchester co.
236	Ephraim Avery	(1761–1763)	Rye
237	Samuel Bruce	(1761–1763, 1765)	New York City
238	William Clajon	(1761, 1764, 1766)	New York City
239	Petrus Van Steenburgh	(1761–1792)	Flatbush
240	John Young	(1761, 1766, 1768–1793)	New York City

[217] Muster Rolls of the N. Y. Provincial Troops, 108.
[218] Abstracts of Wills, V, 272.
[219] Abstracts of Wills, V, 308.
[220] New York Gazette or Weekly Post-Boy, March 27, April 3, April 17, May 1, 1758; Parker's New York Gazette or Weekly Post-Boy, April 30, May 14, May 21, May 28, 1759; New York Mercury, Sept. 7, Sept. 14, Sept. 21, Dec. 7, Dec. 14, Dec. 21, 1761; Ibid, April 11, Sept. 19, Sept. 26, Oct. 3, 1763; New York Gazette or Weekly Post-Boy, April 12, Sept. 20, Sept. 27, 1764.
[221] New York Gazette or Weekly Post-Boy, Oct. 23, Oct. 30, Nov. 13, Nov. 27, Dec. 4, 1758; New York Gazette and Weekly Mercury, Sept. 15, Sept. 22, Sept. 29, Oct. 13, 1777.
[222] Muster Rolls of the N. Y. Provincial Troops, 182, 336; Abstracts of Wills, VII, 9.
[223] Muster Rolls of the N. Y. Provincial Troops, 242.
[224] Muster Rolls of the N. Y. Provincial Troops, 236.
[225] Muster Rolls of the N. Y. Provincial Troops, 254.
[226] Muster Rolls of the N. Y. Provincial Troops, 316.
[227] Pratt, 113; Kemp, 171.
[228] Muster Rolls of the N. Y. Provincial Troops, 414.
[229] Muster Rolls of the N. Y. Provincial Troops, 404.
[230] New York Mercury, Sept. 21, 1761.
[231] Muster Rolls of the N. Y. Provincial Troops, 382.
[232] New York Mercury, Sept. 28, 1761.
[233] Abstracts of Wills, VI, 123.
[234] New York Mercury, Nov. 23, 1761.
[235] Abstracts of Wills, VI, 319.
[236] R. Bolton. History of the Protestant Episcopal Church in the County of Westchester (N. Y., 1855), 314. (Taken from Abstracts of the Venerable Propagation Society).
[237] Abstracts of Wills, VI, 409; New York Mercury, Aug. 31, Sept. 7, Sept. 28, 1761; Ibid, April 4, 1763; Ibid, May 13, 1765.
[238] New York Mercury, Jan. 26, Nov. 2, 1761; New York Gazette or Weekly Post-Boy, Oct. 25, Nov. 1, Nov. 15, Nov. 22, 1764; Ibid, Jan. 2, Jan. 9, May 15, May 22, 1766.
[239] Abstracts of Wills, VII, 335, 350, 398; Ibid, VIII, 269; Ibid, XIV, 195; Kilpatrick, 183, 185.
[240] Roll of Freemen of N. Y. City, 214; Abstracts of Wills, VII, 252; Ibid, XIV, 130, 173, 222, 247; Parker's New York Gazette or Weekly Post-Boy, April 9, 1761; New York Mercury, May 19, May 26, Sept. 7, 1766.

	Name	Date	Place
241	Frederic Rothenbuhler	(1762)	New York City
242	John Wallis	(1762)	Westchester
243	Cornelius Cregier	(1762)	New York City
244	Stephen Dwight	(1763)	New York City
245	William Jones	(1763)	New York City
246	Alexander Leslie	(1763)	New York City
247	Daniel Thane	(1763)	Staten Island
248	Dunlap Adems	(1763)	New York City
249	George Harrie	(1763)	Rye
250	William Cockburn	(1763–1764)	New York City
251	Tunis Egberts	(1763–1783)	Staten Island
252	John Roorback	(1764)	Albany
253	Richard Fletcher	(1764–1769)	New York City
254	Nathaniel Seabury	(1764–65 to 1767–68)	Westchester
255	William Adams	(1764, 1766; 1770)	Coldenham, Ulster co. and Harlem
256	George Rynhard	(1764–1784)	Catsbaan, Albany co.
257	Mary Bosworth	(1765)	New York City
258	Peter Wilson	(1765)	New York City
259	Richard Bunn	(1765)	Rye
260	James McCarrell	(1765)	Newtown
261	Jeremiah Connor	(1765)	Staten Island
262	Seth Moore	(1765)	New York City
263	.... Jackson	(1765)	New York City
264	Thomas Carroll	(1765–1766)	New York City
265	Edward Riggs	(1765–1766, 1783)	New York City
266	Leonard Cutting	(1766–1769)	Hempstead
267	Godfrey Hains	(1767)	Harrison's Purchase

[241] New York Gazette or Weekly Post-Boy, July 8, 1762.
[242] Muster Rolls of the N. Y. Provincial Troops, 422.
[243] Abstracts of Wills, VII. 165.
[244] New York Mercury, May 2, May 9, 1763.
[245] New York Mercury, April 25, May 2, Nov. 21, Nov. 28, 1763.
[246] New York Mercury, April 25, May 2, 1763.
[247] New York Mercury, Nov. 14, 1763.
[248] New York Mercury, Jan. 10, Jan. 17, Jan. 24, May 9, May 16, 1763.
[249] Abstracts of Wills, VI, 329.
[250] New York Mercury, Dec. 5, Dec. 12, 1763; New York Gazette or Weekly Post-Boy, Jan. 12, Feb. 16, 1764.
[251] Pratt, 113; Kemp, 171.
[252] Abstracts of Wills, VI, 405.
[253] Abstracts of Wills, VI, 437; Ibid, VII, 299; Ibid, VIII, 17.
[254] Pratt, 114; Kemp, 156.
[255] New York Gazette or Weekly Post-Boy, April 26, 1764; New York Mercury, April 14, Sept. 16, 1766; New York Gazette and Weekly Mercury, June 11, June 18, June 25, July 30, Aug. 6, 1770.
[256] Abstracts of Wills, VII, 375; Calendar of Wills, 195, 229, 275, 471.
[257] New York Mercury, May 20, 1765.
[258] New York Mercury, April 22, April 29, 1765.
[259] Westchester Wills, 210.
[260] New York Mercury, April 15, June 3, 1765.
[261] Abstracts of Wills, VII, 165.
[262] Abstracts of Wills, VII, 25.
[263] New York Mercury, April 22, April 29, 1765.
[264] New York Mercury, May 6, May 13, May 20, Sept. 30, Oct. 7, 1765; Ibid, May 12, May 19, June 2, Nov. 10, 1766.
[265] New York Mercury, April 22, April 29, 1765; Ibid, May 26, 1766; New York Packet and American Advertiser, Nov. 1783.
[266] Kemp, 182.
[267] Westchester Wills, 261.

	Name	Date	Place
268	George Murray	(1767)	New York City
269	William Hider	(1767)	Staten Island
270	Hugh Hughes	(1767, 1771–1772)	New York City
271	George Meader	(1768)	New York City
272	James Lamb	(1768, 1770)	New York City
273	Edward Wall	(1768–1775)	Johnstown
274	George Youngs	(1768–69 to 1775–1776)	Westchester
275	Cornelius Van Velzor	(1769)	Westchester co.
276	Lewis Donovan	(1769)	Woodbury Clove, Orange co.
277	John Rand	(1769–1770)	Rye
278	William Leahy	(1769–1770)	South Hempstead
279	George Robinson	(1770)	New York City
280	James Carpenter	(1770)	Goshen
281	Josiah Stoddard	(1770)	Kingston
282	Robert Pigot	(1770)	Orange co.
283	Joseph Coddington	(1770)	Shawangunk, Ulster co.
284	Stephen Van Voorhis	(1770)	New York City
285	John Avery	(1770)	Huntington
286	.... Hall	(1770–1771)	Canajoharie
287	John Girault	(1770–1773)	New York City
288	Jacob Tyler	(1770–1775)	New York City
289	Colin McLeland	(1770–71 to 1781–82)	Canajoharie
290	Mary Pack	(1771)	New York City
291	John Bay	(1771)	Albany
292	Michael Bechades	(1771)	New York City

[268] New York Gazette or Weekly Post-Boy, June 18, July 2, July 23, July 30, Aug. 6, Sept. 3, Sept. 10, Sept. 24, 1767.
[269] Abstracts of Wills, VII, 464.
[270] New York Gazette or Weekly Post-Boy, April 16, April 23, April 30, May 7, May 14, May 21, June 4, 1767; New York Gazette and Weekly Mercury, Dec. 30, 1771; Ibid, Jan. 6, Jan. 13, Jan. 20, Jan. 27, 1772.
[271] Abstracts of Wills, VII, 466.
[272] New York Gazette or Weekly Post-Boy, Dec. 12, 1768; New York Gazette or Weekly Mercury, May 14, May 21, 1770.
[273] Pratt, 112; Kemp, 204.
[274] Pratt, 114; Kemp, 157.
[275] Abstracts of Wills, VII, 467.
[276] Abstracts of Wills, VII, 359.
[277] Doc. Hist. N. Y., IV, 408–9; Pratt, 114; Kemp, 139.
[278] Pratt, 111; Kemp, 118.
[279] New York Gazette and Weekly Mercury, Jan. 1, Jan. 8, Jan. 15, Jan. 22, Jan. 29, 1770.
[280] Abstracts of Wills, VII, 403.
[281] New York Gazette and Weekly Mercury, Oct. 22, Oct. 29, Nov. 5, Nov. 26, 1770.
[282] Calendar of Wills, 359.
[283] Abstracts of Wills, VII, 405.
[284] Roll of Freemen of N. Y. City, 229.
[285] Abstracts of Wills, VII, 341.
[286] Pratt, 112.
[287] New York Gazette and Weekly Mercury, Jan. 29, Feb. 5, Feb. 12, Oct. 1, Oct. 8, 1770; Ibid, Sept. 9, Sept. 16, Sept. 23, Sept. 30, 1771; Ibid, Sept. 7, Sept. 14, Sept. 21, Oct. 12, Oct. 19, 1772; Rivington's New York Gazetteer or The Connecticut, Hudson's River, New Jersey, and Quebec Weekly Advertiser, Sept. 16, Sept. 23, Oct. 7, Oct. 14, 1773.
[288] Roll of Freemen of N. Y. City, 230; Abstracts of Wills, VIII, 374.
[289] Pratt, 112.
[290] New York Gazette and Weekly Mercury, April 22, April 29, May 6, 1771.
[291] Abstracts of Wills, VIII, 60; Early Wills of Westchester County, 1664–1784 (W. S. Pelletreau, editor. New York, 1898), 309.
[292] New York Gazette and Weekly Mercury, July 22, July 29, Aug. 19, 1771.

FREE SCHOOLS 665

	Name	Date	Place
293	Frederick John	(1771)	Jamaica
294	James Wetmore	(1771–72 to 1781–82)	Rye
295	William Andrews	(1771–1773)	Schenectady
296	J. Tanner	(1771, 1774)	New York City
297	M. Tanner	(1771, 1774	New York City
298	James Gilliland	(1771–1772, 1774–1775)	New York City
299	James O'Brien	(1771, 1780)	New York City
300	John Bryan	(1772)	Brooklyn
301	Francis H. De La Roche	(1772)	New York City
302	John Haumaid	(1772)	New York City
303	James Duffie	(1772)	Staten Island
304	Samuel McCorkle	(1772)	New York City
305	Terence Reilly	(1772)	Staten Island
306	Anthony Fiva	(1772–1774)	New York City
307	J. Peter Tetard	(1772–1773, 1775)	Kings Bridge
308	J. Hughes	(1773)	New York City
309	Robert Gilmore	(1773)	Westchester
310	.... Austin	(1773)	Albany
311	Alexander Miller	(1773)	Schenectady
312	John Leffert	(1773)	South Hempstead
313	John Doty	(1773–1777)	Schenectady
314	Frances Brien	(1774)	New York City
315	John Addison	(1774)	Kingston
316	Joseph Cozani	(1774)	New York City

[293] Abstracts of Wills, VII, 451, 457.
[294] Pratt, 114; Kemp, 139.
[295] Doc. Hist. N. Y., IV, 467, 470; Kemp, 202.
[296] New York Gazette and Weekly Mercury, Jan. 14, Jan. 21, Jan. 28, Feb. 4, Feb. 11, 1771; Rivington's New York Gazetteer or The Connecticut, Hudson's River, New Jersey, and Quebec Weekly Advertiser, Feb. 24, March 3, April 7, April 14, 1774.
[297] New York Gazette and Weekly Mercury, Jan. 14, Jan. 21, Jan. 28, Feb. 4, Feb. 11, 1771; Rivington's New York Gazetteer or The Connecticut, Hudson's River, New Jersey, and Quebec Weekly Advrtiser, Feb. 24, March 3, April 7, April 14, 1774.
[298] New York Gazette and Weekly Mercury, May 27, June 3, 1771; Ibid, Dec. 14, Dec. 28, 1772; Roll of Freemen of N. Y. City, 237; Rivington's New York Gazetteer or Connecticut, Hudson's River, New Jersey, and Quebec Weekly Advertiser, Jan. 12, Jan. 19, 1775.
[299] New York Gazette and Weekly Mercury, May 6, May 13, May 27, 1771; Ibid, June 5, 1780.
[300] Abstracts of Wills, VIII, 18.
[301] New York Gazette and Weekly Mercury, March 2, 1772.
[302] New York Gazette and Weekly Mercury, Sept. 21, 1772.
[303] Abstracts of Wills, VIII, 38.
[304] New York Gazette and Weekly Mercury, Dec. 21, Dec. 28, 1772.
[305] Abstracts of Wills, VIII, 38.
[306] Rivington's New York Gazetteer or Connecticut, Hudson's River, New Jersey and Quebec Weekly Advertiser, July 22, Aug. 12, Dec. 9, Dec. 16, 1773; Ibid, May 19, May 26, Dec. 22, 1774.
[307] New York Gazette and Weekly Mercury, Sept. 7, Sept. 14, Oct. 5, 1772; New York Journal or General Advertiser, Feb. 17, 1774; Rivington's New York Gazetteer or Connecticut, Hudson's River, New Jersey, and Quebec Weekly Advertiser, June 1, June 15, June 22, July 13, July 21, July 27, 1775.
[308] Rivington's New York Gazetteer or Connecticut, Hudson's River, New Jersey, and Quebec Weekly Advertiser, Oct. 21, Oct. 28, Nov. 11, 1773.
[309] Abstracts of Wills, VIII, 359.
[310] Rivington's New York Gazetteer or Connecticut, Hudson's River, New Jersey, and Quebec Weekly Advertiser, April 29, 1773.
[311] Rivington's New York Gazetteer, or Connecticut, Hudson's River, New Jersey, and Quebec Weekly Advertiser, Nov. 4, Nov. 11, Nov. 25, Dec. 2, 1773.
[312] Kemp, 180.
[313] Kemp, 203.
[314] New York Gazette and Weekly Mercury, March 14, 1774.
[315] Rivington's New York Gazetteer or Connecticut, Hudson's River, New Jersey, and Quebec Weekly Advertiser, May 5, May 12, Sept. 1, 1774; Olde Ulster, X, 75.
[316] Rivington's New Yoork Gazetteer or Connecticut, Hudson's River, New Jersey, and Quebec Weekly Advertiser, June 16, 1774.

	Name	Date	Place
317	John Ostrander	(1774)	Albany
318	Thomas Byerley	(1774)	New York City
319	Josiah Day	(1774)	New York City
320	Daniel Hamill	(1774)	Dutchess co.
321	George Shannon	(1774)	New York City
322	Catherine Lugrin	(1774)	New York City
323	Simeon Lugrin	(1774)	New York City
324	John Copp	(1774)	Flatbush
325	David Monell	(1774)	Hanover, Ulster co.
326	.... Gollen	(1774)	New York City
327	.... Mountain	(1774)	New York City
328	William Horton	(1774)	Phillipsburg, Westchester co.
329	Sarah Long	(1774–1775)	New York City
330	William Long	(1774–1775)	New York City
331	Mrs. Cozani	(1774–1775)	New York City
332	George Gott	(1774–1776)	Westchester
333	Samuel Seabury	(1775)	Westchester
334	Francis Vandale	(1775)	New York City
335	John Campbell	(1775)	Orange co.
336	Cornelly Ferran	(1775)	Goshen
337	Robert Frayer	(1775)	Orange co.
338	Thomas Hart	(1775)	Goshen
339	James Howard	(1775)	Goshen

[317] Abstracts of Wills, IX, 285.
[318] Rivington's New York Gazetteer or Connecticut, Hudson's River, New Jersey, and Quebec Weekly Advertiser, Feb. 17, April 14, June 22, June 30, July 7, 1774; New York Journal or General Advertiser, Feb. 17, Feb. 24, March 3, March 10, March 17, March 31, April 21, April 28, 1774.
[319] Rivington's New York Gazetteer or Connecticut, Hudson's River, New Jersey, and Quebec Weekly Advertiser, Feb. 17, April 14, June 22, June 30, July 7, 1774; New York Journal or General Advertiser, Feb. 17, Feb. 24, March 3, March 10, March 17, March 31, April 21, April 28, 1774.
[320] Abstracts of Wills, VIII, 349.
[321] Abstracts of Wills, VIII, 373.
[322] Rivington's New York Gazetteer or Connecticut, Hudson's River, New Jersey, and Quebec Weekly Advertiser, April 21, April 28, 1774.
[323] Rivington's New York Gazetteer or Connecticut, Hudson's River, New Jersey, and Quebec Weekly Advertiser, April 21, April 28, 1774.
[324] Rivington's New York Gazetteer or Connecticut, Hudson's River, New Jersey, and Quebec Weekly Advertiser, July 7, July 14, 1774.
[325] Abstracts of Wills, VIII, 265.
[326] Rivington's New York Gazetteer or Connecticut, Hudson's River, New Jersey, and Quebec Weekly Advertiser, Oct. 6, 1774.
[327] Rivington's New York Gazetteer or Connecticut, Hudson's River, New Jersey, and Quebec Weekly Advertiser, Oct. 6, 1774.
[328] Abstracts of Wills, VIII, 259.
[329] Rivington's New York Gazetteer or Connecticut, Hudson's River, New Jersey, and Quebec Weekly Advertiser, Jan. 27, Feb. 24, March 3, March 31, 1774; Ibid, Nov. 2, 1775; New York Journal or General Advertiser, Jan. 27, Feb. 3, 1774.
[330] Rivington's New York Gazetteer or Connecticut, Hudson's River, New Jersey, and Quebec Weekly Advertiser, Jan. 27, Feb. 24, March 3, March 31, 1774; Ibid, Nov. 2, 1775; New York Journal or General Advertiser, Jan. 27, Feb. 3, 1774.
[331] Rivington's New York Gazetteer or Connecticut, Hudson's River, New Jersey, and Quebec Weekly Advertiser, July 21, 1774; Ibid, April 20, April 27, July 21, 1775.
[332] Pratt, 114; Kemp, 159.
[333] Rivington's New York Gazetteer or Connecticut, Hudson's River, New Jersey, and Quebec Weekly Advertiser, March 16, March 23, 1775.
[334] Rivington's New York Gazetteer or Connecticut, Hudson's River, New Jersey, and Quebec Weekly Advertiser, Oct. 26, Nov. 9, Nov. 16, 1775.
[335] Calendar of Wills, 78.
[336] Docs. Rel. Col. Hist. N. Y., XV, 116.
[337] Docs. Rel. Col. Hist. N. Y., XV, 169.
[338] Docs. Rel. Col. Hist. N. Y., XV, 170.
[339] Docs. Rel. Col. Hist. N. Y., XV, 167.

	Name	Date	Place
340	Owen Madden	(1775)	Shawangunk
341	.... Rose	(1775)	Johnstown
342	James Leasley	(1776)	New York City
343	William Denn	(1776)	Goshen
344	Amos Bull	(1776, 1778-1782)	New York City
345	Gabriel Ellison	(1776-1790)	Flatbush
346	John McClenachan	(1777)	New York City
347	John McKillop	(1777)	New York City
348	Thomas Kyle	(1777)	Goshen
349	William Thompson	(1777-1778)	Goshen
350	.... Teniere	(1777-1778)	New York City
351	Jacob Taylor	(1777-1779)	New York City
352	.... Panton...................	(1777, 1779)	New York City
353	Thomas Wiley...........	(1777, 1779, 1782)	New York City
354	James Wetmore	(1777-1783)	Oyster Bay
355	William Hume	(1778)	Ulster co.
356	Thomas Kingston	(1778)	Staten Island
357	Peter Sparling	(1778)	New York City
358	John Davis..................	(1778, 1781-1782)	New York City
359	Thomas L. Moore.......................	(1779)	Newtown
360	Lionel Watts	(1779)	New York City
361	James Foley	(1779-1780)	Bushwick
362	Thomas Egan	(1780)	New York City
363	John Clints	(1780)	Albany
364	Robert Davis	(1780)	Norman's Kill
365	Edward Finn	(1780)	Ballstown
366	Philip Doyle	(1781)	Gray Court, Orange co.

[340] Docs. Rel. Col. Hist. N. Y., XV, 171.
[341] Kemp, 207.
[342] Abstracts of Wills, VIII, 331.
[343] Abstracts of Wills, IX, 183.
[344] New York Gazette and Weekly Mercury, May 13, May 20, 1776; Pratt, 113; Kemp, 116.
[345] Pratt, 63.
[346] New York Gazette and Weekly Mercury, Dec. 15, Dec. 22, 1777.
[347] New York Gazette and Weekly Mercury, Sept. 8, Sept. 15, Sept. 22, 1777.
[348] Abstracts of Wills, IX, 169.
[349] Abstracts of Wills, IX, 157; Calendar of Wills, 40.
[350] New York Gazette and Weekly Mercury, Sept. 1, Sept. 8, Sept. 15, Oct. 6, Oct. 13, Oct. 20, Dec. 8, 1777; Ibid, July 13, July 27, 1778.
[351] Abstracts of Wills, IX, 41, 82.
[352] New York Gazette and Weekly Mercury, Dec. 15, Dec. 29, 1777; Ibid, Jan. 18, 1779.
[353] New York Gazette and Weekly Mercury, Feb. 17, Feb. 24, March 3, March 10, March 24, 1777; Ibid, Sept. 13, Sept. 20, 1779; Ibid, Nov. 4, 1782.
[354] Kemp, 186.
[355] Calendar of Wills, 120.
[356] Abstracts of Wills, IX, 24.
[357] Abstracts of Wills, IX, 49.
[358] New York Gazette and Weekly Mercury, Jan. 19, Jan. 26, 1778; Ibid, Jan. 7, Jan. 14, Oct. 14, Oct. 21, 1782; Royal Gazette, Oct. 6, 1781.
[359] New York Gazette and Weekly Mercury, Aug. 2, Aug. 9, Aug. 16, Aug. 23, 1779.
[360] Abstracts of Wills, VIII, 353.
[361] New York Gazette and Weekly Mercury, June 14, June 21, Aug. 30, Oct. 4, 1779; Ibid, March 27, April 10, 1780.
[362] New York Gazette and Weekly Mercury, Jan. 10, Jan. 17, 1780.
[363] Calendar of Wills, 472.
[364] Minutes of the Commissioners for detecting and defeating Conspiracies in the State of New York (3 vols. Albany, 1909-10), II, 506.
[365] Min. Com. for detecting and defeating Conspiracies in the State of New York, II, 436.
[366] Abstracts of Wills, IX, 240.

	Name	Date	Place
367	William Kerr	(1781)	New York City
368	Mrs. Shackerly	(1781)	New York City
369	John Klint	(1781)	Rennselaerwyck
370	.... Evans	(1781)	New York City
371	Thomas Madden	(1781)	New York City
372	Christopher Witting	(1781)	Rennselaerwyck
373	Alexander Campbell	(1782)	Goshen
374	John H. Hentz	(1782)	New York City
375	George Huggan	(1782)	New Windsor, Ulster co.
376	Isaac Rysdyk	(1782)	Dutchess co.
377	Ebenezer Street	(1782)	New York City
378	Benoni Bradner	(1782)	Goshen
379	Edward Haswell	(1782–1783)	New York City
380	J. Mennye	(1782–1783)	New York City

[367] Royal Gazette, April 25, 1781.
[368] New York Gazette and Weekly Mercury, July 16, July 30, 1781.
[369] Min. Com. for detecting and defeating Conspiracies in the State of New York, II, 651.
[370] Royal Gazette, Oct. 17, Oct. 20, Oct. 31, Nov. 21, 1781.
[371] Abstracts of Wills, XIV, 219.
[372] Min. Com. for detecting and defeating Conspiracies in the State of New York, II, 716.
[373] Abstracts of Wills, IX, 293.
[374] New York Gazette and Weekly Mercury, May 27, 1782.
[375] Abstracts of Wills, IX, 295.
[376] New York Packet and American Advertiser, June 13, 1782.
[377] Kemp, 120.
[378] New York Packet and American Advertiser, Sept. 26, Oct. 3, Oct. 10, 1782.
[379] Kemp, 121.
[380] New York Gazette and Weekly Mercury, Sept. 20, 1782; Royal Gazette, Oct. 18, Oct. 22, 1783.

This list is not exhaustive. It would be impossible to name all the schoolmasters of the English colonial period. Even if all the names could be secured, the number would still seem to be inadequate for so long a period. In this connection, one must keep in mind the fact that instruction of various grades was also given by parents, older children, tutors and ministers.

No attempt has been made to classify the schoolmasters; in many cases this would be impossible. Many are mentioned, in the records, merely as schoolmasters. We know that most of them were English, and taught in English elementary and secondary schools. A relatively small number were Dutch, and most of these taught in Dutch schools. Ministers and catechists, as such, are not included in the list.

Kemp and Kilpatrick, as sources of information for the colonial period, are reliable. Only verifiable references have been taken from Pratt.

Probable duplications: numbers 107 and 294, or 107 and 354 (James Wetmore); 98 and 114 (Johannes Glandorff or Glundorff); 106 and 154 (John Carhart); 93 and 95 (Samuel Jones and . . . Jones); 177 and 217 (William Wilson); 146 and 333 (Samuel Seabury).

Chapter 15

BIBLIOGRAPHY OF FREE SCHOOLS

Selected list of references compiled by Martha L. Phelps, reference assistant in education, New York State Library.

Adams, Francis. The free school system of the United States. Lond. 1875

American Association for the Advancement of Education. Proceedings. 1851–58

American doctrine of public instruction. American Journal of Education, 15:5–16 (March 1865)
   Includes Address to people of New Jersey by the Rt. Rev. Bishop Doane (1838), American authorities and Massachusetts doctrine of free schools.

American Journal of Education: organ of the New York State Teachers Association. 1846

Barnard, Henry. History of common schools in Connecticut. American Journal of Education, 4:657–710 (March 1858); 5:114–54 (June 1858)

Barney, H. H. Report on the American system of graded schools. Cincinnati. 1851

Blackmar, F. W. History of state and federal aid to higher education in the United States. (U. S. Bureau of education. Circular of information, 1890, no. 1)

Boese, Thomas. Public education in the city of New York. 1869

Boone, R. G. Education in the United States; its history from the earliest settlement. 1903
——— History of education in Indiana. 1892

Bourne, E. G. The history of the surplus revenue of 1837. N.Y. 1885

Bowman, H. M. The administration of Iowa: a study in centralization (Columbia University studies in history, economics and public law. V. 18, no. 1) N.Y. 1903

Brown, E. E. The making of our middle schools. 1903
   Bibliography, p. 481–518.

Burns, J. J. Educational history of Ohio. 1905

Bush, G. G. The first common schools of New England. U.S. Com'r of education. Report 1896–97, v.1:1165–86
——— History of education in Florida (U.S. Bureau of education. Circular of information 1888, no. 7)
——— History of education in New Hampshire. (U. S. Bureau of education. Circular of information, 1898, no. 3)
——— History of education in Vermont. (U. S. Bureau of education. Circular of information 1900, no. 4)

Caldwell, H. W. Education in Nebraska. (U. S. Bureau of education. Circular of information 1902, no. 3)

Carleton, Frank. Economic influence upon educational advance in the United States, 1820–50. (Bulletin of the University of Wisconsin. Economics and political science series, v.4, no. 1, 1908)

Carroll, Charles. Public education in Rhode Island. 1918 (Rhode Island Education circular)

Carter, J. G. Essays upon popular education. 1826

────── Letters to Hon. William Prescott LL.D. on the Free schools of New England with remarks on the principles of instruction. 1824

Clark, W. G. History of education in Alabama, 1702–1889 (U. S. Bureau of education. Circular of information. 1889, no. 3)

Cews, E. W. Educational legislation and administration of the colonial government. 1899
(Columbia University. Contributions to philosophy, psychology and education v. 6, no. 1–4)

Colonial period in American education. Monroe's Cyclopedia of education 2:114–22

Columbian history of education in Kansas: compiled by Kansas educators. Topeka 1903

Common schools and public instruction. American Journal of Education, 24:225–329 (June 1873)
> Development from 1800 to 1870.

Connecticut. State Department of education. Report. 1868 Free schools in various states. p. 16–30

Constitutional provisions respecting education. American Journal of Education 17:81–124 (Sept. 1867)

Cook, J. W. Educational History of Illinois. Chicago, 1912

Cubberley, E. P. School funds and their apportionment. 1906 (Teachers college contributions to education, no. 2)

Dexter, E. G. History of education in the United States. 1904

District school journal of the state of New York, 1840–52.
> This periodical contains many references on the subject of free schools in general as well as discussions of the question in the State of New York. It was considered by the State Superintendent of Public Instruction as the official organ of communication with the officers of the several districts.

Dix, J. A. School system of New York. Connecticut Common School Journal, 1:75, 77

Doane, G. W. The state and education: an address delivered to the people of New Jersey in 1838. American Journal of Education, 15:5–11 (March 1865)
> Also in U. S. Commissioner of education. Report 1895–96, v.1:250–54

Draper, A. S. Origin and development of the New York common school system. 1890
> Address before New York State Teachers Association.

────── Public school pioneering in New York and Massachusetts. Educational Review, 3:313–36 (April 1892)

Draper, A. S. Public school pioneering in New York and Massachusetts: a reply to a reply. Educational Review, 4:241–52 (October 1892)
—— Public school pioneering: a final reply. Educational Review, 5:345–62 (April 1893)
—— —— Editorial. Educational Review, 5:406–7 (April 1893)

Dunshee, H. W. History of the school of the Reformed Protestant Dutch Church in the city of New York from 1633 to the present time. 1853

Earliest form of public schools in New England. American Journal of Education, 27:59–156 (January 1877)

Early school movements in Virginia. American Journal of Education, 27:33–57 (January 1877)

Education: A national interest. Historical development. American Journal of Education, 17:41–63 (September 1867)

Emerson, G. B. Education in Massachusetts. Early legislation and history. Boston 1869

Fay, E. W. History of education in Louisiana. (U. S. Bureau of education. Circular of information, 1898, no. 1)

Fees, (U. S.) Monroe's Cyclopedia of education, 2:587–89

Fellow, Henry. A study in school supervision and maintenance. Topeka 1896

Finegan, T. E. Struggle for free schools in New York. State Service (Albany, N. Y.), 2:3–14 (November 1918)
  Story of a fight which lasted half a century before victory crowned the efforts of the pioneer advocates.
—— The establishment and development of New York's school system. 1913
  Address before New York State Teachers Association, November 26, 1912, at Buffalo.

Fitch, C. E. A history of the common schools in New York. 1904
  Reprint from New York State Department of Public Instruction. Annual report, 1902–3, p. 1–144.

Free School Clarion. (Syracuse, N. Y.) Ten issues.
  July 1850 until after election.

Free School Clarion (Massilon, Ohio) October 1846–48

Free schools: American usage. Monroe's cyclopedia of education, 2:699

Germann, G. B. National legislation concerning education. New York 1899

Great Britain. Report of the commissioners appointed . . . to inquire into the education given in schools in England . . . and . . . in Scotland (and) on the common school system of the United States and Canada, by Rev. James Fraser. Sydney 1868.
—— Schools inquiry commission. Report . . . on the school system of the United States and of the provinces of Upper and Lower Canada. London 1866

Good, H. G. Benjamin Rush and his services to American education. 1918
  Bibliography, p. 259–75.

Greer, J. N. History of education in Minnesota. (U. S. Bureau of education. Circular of information. 1902. no. 2)

Hale, H. M. Grove, Aaron & Shattuck, J. C. Education in Colorado, 1861–85. Denver 1885

Hall, E. W. History of higher education in Maine. (U. S. Bureau of education. Circular of information. 1903, no. 3)
  Public schools, p. 17–28.

Henry, James. Address upon education and common schools. Albany 1843

Hinsdale, B. A. Documents illustrative of American educational history. U. S. Commissioner of education. Report 1892-3, v.1:1223–1414

——— Educational influence and results of the ordinance of 1787. National Education Association. Proceedings 1887, p. 135–40

——— History of popular education on the Western Reserve. 1898. (Ohio Archaeological and Historical Society. Publications, 6:35–58)

Hobson, E. G. Educational legislation and administration in the state of New York, 1777–1850. Menasha, Wis. 1918
  Published also as Supplementary educational monographs, University of Chicago, v. 3, no. 1, November 1918.

Hough, F. B. Historical and statistical record of the University of the State of New York during the century 1784–1884. Albany 1885

Hoyt, C. O. & Ford, R. C. John D. Pearce, founder of Michigan school system, and study of education in the Northwest. Ypsilanti 1905

Illinois. Prairie Farmer (1841–55)
  An agricultural paper which devoted much space to important educational discussions.

Indiana. Department of public instruction. Education in Indiana: an official monograph prepared for the Louisiana Purchase Exposition, St Louis 1904. Indianapolis 1904

Jackson, G. L. The development of school support in colonial Massachusetts. New York 1909

Jones, C. E. Education in Georgia. (U. S. Bureau of education. Circular of information, 1888, no. 4)

Kemp, W. W. Support of schools in colonial New York, by the Society for the Propagation of the Gospel in Foreign Parts. 1913. Teachers College, Columbia University. Contributions to education. no. 56

Kent, R. A. State aid to public schools in Minnesota. (University of Minnesota. Studies in social science, no. 11 April 1918)

Kiehle, D. L. Education in Minnesota. Minneapolis 1903

Kilpatrick, W. H. The Dutch schools of New Netherland and colonial New York. (U. S. Bureau of education bulletin, 1912, no. 12)

Knight, G. W. History and management of land grants for education in the northwest territories. Papers of the American Historical Association, v. 1, no. 3, 1885)

Lane, J. J. History of education in Texas. (U. S. Bureau of education. Circular of information, 1903, no. 2)

Lewis, A. F. History of higher education in Kentucky. (U. S. Bureau of education. Circular of information, 1899, no. 3)
Public school system, p. 328–43.

McCaskey, J. P. Samuel Breck who wrote the first common school law, Thaddeus Stevens, the "Old Commoner," Thomas Henry Burrowes, the organizer of the school system. Pennsylvania School Journal, 67:185–202 (November 1918)

McCrady, Edward. Education in South Carolina prior to and during the Revolution. (In South Carolina Historical Society. Collections, v.4, 1887)

Maddox, W. A. Free school idea in Virginia before the Civil War; a phase of political and social evolution. 1918. Teachers College, Columbia University. Contributions to education, no. 93

Martin, G. H. The evolution of the Massachusetts public school system. 1894

Martin, George. Public school pioneering: a reply. Educational Review, 4:34–46 (June 1892)
A reply to Doctor Draper. See Educational Review, 3:313–36 (April 1892).

——— Public school pioneering: final statement of the Massachusetts claim. Educational Review, 5:232–42 (March 1893)

Massachusetts doctrine of free schools. American Journal of Education, 27:63 (January 1877). Also in 15:15–16 (March 1865)

Mayes, Edward. History of education in Mississippi. (U. S. Bureau of education. Circular of information, 1899, no. 2)

Mayo, A. D. The American common school in New England from 1790–1840. U. S. Commissioner of education. Report 1894–95, v.1:1551–1651

——— The American common school in New York, New Jersey and Pennsylvania during the first half century of the republic. U. S. Commissioner of education. Report 1895–96, v.1:21966

——— The American common school in the southern states during the first half century of the republic, 1790–1840. U. S. Commissioner of education. Report 1895–96, v.1:267–338

——— Common school in the southern states beyond the Mississippi river from 1830–60. U. S. Commissioner of education. Report 1900–01, v.1:357–402

——— Development of the common schools in the western states from 1830–65. U. S. Commissioner of education Report 1898–99, v.1:357–450

——— Education in the northwest during the first half century of the republic, 1790–1840. U. S. Commissioner of education. Report 1894–95, v.1:1513–50

——— Horace Mann and the great revival of the American common school, 1830–50. U. S. Commissioner of education. Report 1896–97, v.1:715–67

——— Organization and development of the American common school in the Atlantic and central states of the south, 1830–60. U. S. Commissioner of education. Report 1899–1900, v.1:427–562

Mayo, A. D. The organization and reconstruction of state systems of common school education in the North Atlantic states from 1830 to 1865. U. S. Commissioner of education. Report 1897–98, v.1:355–486

——— Original establishment of state school funds. U. S. Commissioner of education. Report 1894–95, v.2:1505–11

——— Public schools during the colonial and revolutionary period in the United States. U. S. Commissioner of education. Report 1893–94, v.1: 639–738

Mead, A. R. The development of free schools in the United States as illustrated by Connecticut and Michigan. 1918. Teachers College, Columbia University. Contributions to education, no. 91.

Meriwether, Colyer. History of higher education in South Carolina, with a sketch of the free school system. (U. S. Bureau of education. Circular of information, 1888, no. 3)

Miller, E. A. History of educational legislation in Ohio from 1803 to 1850. 1918
  Thesis (Ph.D.) University of Chicago, 1915. Reprinted from Ohio Archaeological and Historical Quarterly, 27:1–2 (January and April 1918).

Moore, E. C. Fifty years of American education: a sketch of progress of education in the United States from 1867 to 1917. 1917

Moores, C. W. Caleb Mills and the Indiana school system. (Indiana Historical society publications v.3; n.6, 1905, p. 360–638)

Morley, John. The struggle for national education. London 1873. p. 105

Morrison, A. J. The beginnings of public education in Virginia, 1776–1860. 1917
  Issued by Virginia State board of education.

Mowry, W. A. The first American public school. U. S. Commissioner of education. Report 1902, v.1:541–50

Murray, David. History of education in New Jersey. (U. S. Bureau of education. Circular of information, 1899, no. 1)

National convention of the friends of education, Philadelphia. Proceedings, 1849, 1850

New Jersey. An address to the people of New Jersey on the subject of common schools. 1838

——— Addresses in reference to free high schools before the legislature, March 1, 1871 (Doc. 37)

——— Maclean, John. A common school system for New Jersey. January 23, 1828
  Address before the Literary and Philosophical Society of New Jersey.

——— New Jersey life board and literary standard, published twice a month. v.1, no. 1, issued September 24, 1853

——— Proceedings of public meeting of the friends of education at Trenton, November 11, 1828

——— Newark sentinel of freedom: twenty essays on education between August 26, 1828, and January 27, 1829
  Probably contributed by Professor John Maclean.

New Jersey. Hoagland, C. C. Address advocating free schools before educational convention held at Trenton, New Jersey, October 20, 1853
    "Address printed and widely circulated."

New York state convention of teachers and friends of education. Proceedings, October 1830
    First convention held in Utica. Recommended a more general assemblage at a future day and recommended a United States convention of teachers to be held in May 1831.

―――― Address, Utica, 1831
    Address of state convention held at Utica January 12–14, 1831, with an abstract of the proceedings of said convention.

New York state. Messages from the governors, edited by C. Z. Lincoln. II vol. 1683–1906. 1906
    See also entry Wyer & Groves Index to governors' messages, 1777–1901.

Noble, S. G. Forty years of the public schools in Mississippi with special reference to the education of the negro. 1918. Teachers College, Columbia University. Contributions to education, no. 94

Orth, S. P. The centralization of administration in Ohio. New York 1903
    (Columbia University, Faculty of political science. Studies in history, economics and public law, v. 16, no. 3).

Parker, L. F. Higher education in Iowa. (U. S. Bureau of education. Circular of information, 1893, no. 6. Public schools, p. 19–46)

Patterson, J. W. National aid to education. Education 5:413–24 (May 1881)

Pennsylvania society for the promotion of public economy. Report of the committee on public schools. Philadelphia 1817

Perry, W. F. The genesis of public education in Alabama. (Alabama historical transactions, 2:14–27)

Phillips, C. A. A history of education in Missouri; the essential facts concerning the history and organization of Missouri's schools. Jefferson City 1911

Plan for public schools in Pennsylvania; added thoughts on education in a republic

Powell, L. P. History of education in Delaware. (U. S. Bureau of education. Circular of information, 1893, no. 3)

Pratt, D. J. Annals of public education in the state of New York from 1626 to 1746. Albany 1872

Putnam, Daniel. Development of primary and secondary public education in Michigan. Ann Arbor 1904

Rammage, B. J. Social government and free schools in South Carolina. Johns Hopkins University studies, v. I, no. 12. 1883

Randall, S. S. Common school system of the state of New York. Troy 1851
―――― Digest of the common school system of the state of New York. Albany 1844
―――― History of the common school system of the state of New York from its origin in 1795 to the present time. N. Y. 1871

Rawles, W. A. Centralizing tendencies in the administration of Indiana. New York 1903
    (Columbia University. Faculty of political science. Studies in history, economics and public law, v. 17, no. 1.)

Riggs, J. H. National education. 1873
    Contains chapter on School education in the United States.

Schafer, Joseph. The origin of the system of land grants for education. (Bulletin of the University of Wisconsin. History series v. 1, no. 1, 1902)

Shinn, J. H. History of education in Arkansas. (U. S. Bureau of education. Circular of information, 1900, no. 1)

Smith, C. L. History of education in North Carolina. (U. S. Bureau of education. Circular of information, 1888, no. 2)

(The) state and education: the right and duty of the state to establish public schools. American Journal of Education, 11:323–29 (June 1862); 13:717–24 (December 1863); 14:401–8 (September 1864)
    Includes American opinions and practice, also the First school law of the colonies of Massachusetts, Connecticut, New Haven and Plymouth, and leading English authorities.

Stearns, J. W., ed. Columbian history of education in Wisconsin. Milwaukee 1893

Steiner, B. C. History of education in Connecticut. (U. S. Bureau of education. Circular of information, 1893, no. 2)

—— History of education in Maryland. (U. S. Bureau of education. Circular of information, 1894, no. 2)

Stevens, Thaddeus. A plea for public schools. U. S. Commissioner of education. Report 1898–99, v. 1:518–24.

—— Two memorable speeches on behalf of general education. Pennsylvania School Journal, 39:325–37 (February 1891). Speeches of 1835 and 1838

Stewart, R. M. Cooperative methods in the development of school support in the United States. 1914
    Ph.D. degree thesis, State University of Iowa.

Stockwell, T. B. History of public education in Rhode Island, 1638–1876. Providence 1876

Suzzallo, Henry. The rise of local school supervision in Massachusetts. New York 1906

Swett, John. History of the public school system of California. San Francisco 1876

Swift, F. H. A history of public permanent common school funds in the United States, 1795–1905. 1911

—— Early sources of school support and evolution of public permanent school funds. (In his History of public permanent school funds in the United States, 1795–1905, p. 23–38)

Teachers' Advocate, 1845–52
    Official organ of the New York State Teachers Association. Contains many references on the discussion of the free school question in the State of New York.

Thomas, T. P. The public school system of Tennessee. In Merriam, L. S. Higher education in Tennessee. U. S. Bureau of education. Circular of information, 1893, no. 5, p. 282–87

Tolman, W. H. Higher education in Rhode Island. (U. S. Bureau of education. Circular of information, 1894, no. 1) Public schools, p. 13–31

Updegraff, Harlan. The origin of the moving school in Massachusetts, 1908. Teachers College, Columbia University. Contributions to education no. 17)

Van Slyke, Nicholas. The right and duty of the state to educate its children. American institute on instruction. Proceedings, 1886, p. 191–201

(Mr) Wadsworth's efforts in behalf of common schools. American Journal of Education, 5:395–406 (September 1858) Also in v. 15:249–60 (June 1865)

Webster, Daniel. Tribute to the policy of New England concerning common schools. American Journal of Education, 1:591 (May 1856)
  Extract from Centennial address at Plymouth 1822.

Whitehill, A. R. History of education in West Virginia. (U. S. Bureau of education. Circular of information, 1902, no. 1)

Whitten, R. H. Public administration in Massachusetts. New York 1898 (Columbia University Faculty of political science. Studies in history, economics and public law, v. 8, no. 4)
  Includes Public schools, p. 19–36.

Wickersham, J. P. A history of education in Pennsylvania. 1886

Woodburn, J. A. Common school system of Indiana. In his Higher education in Indiana. U. S. Bureau of education. Circular of information, 1891, no. 1, p. 36–73

Wyer, M. G. & Groves, C. E. Index of New York governors' messages, 1777–1901. 1906 (New York State Library. Bulletin: Legislation no. 26)

INDEX

Academies, authorized, 7
Acts, early legislative references to free schools, 76–82; appropriations for the support of common schools for year *1849* and *1850*, text, 197
  1702, for the encouragement of a grammar free school in the city of New York, 22
  1732, to encourage a public school in the city of New York for teaching Latin, Greek and mathematics, 22
  1784, providing funds for the support of the schools, 25
  1795, 7; *1795*, and *1796*, text of 26–33
  1812, 34–51; text of, 43–51
  1842, applying to New York City, text, 73–76
  1849, see Free school act of *1849*
  1851, free school law of, 419–85
  1853–1868, 523–28
  1867, on rate bill, text, 548–55
  1917, important laws, 565–629
Agriculture, act to amend Education law, relative to employment of directors of, 626–27
Appropriations, act for the support of common schools for year *1849* and *1850*, text, 197

Bibliography of free schools, 670–78
Board of education in the several cities of the State, text of law, 586–604
Bowdish, John, sketch of, 119–20

Campaign before the November election in *1850*, 314–418
Clark, Governor, on public school question, 528–32

Clinton, Governor De Witt, extracts from messages on the "State and education," 52–53
Clinton, Governor George, recommended that provision be made for education of children of the State, 7; interest in public schools, 25
Coffin, Alexander J., sketch of, 181
Cole, Almeron Hyde, sketch of, 181–82
Colleges, colonial, in New York, 9–24
Colonial New York City, evening schools, 630–52
Colonial schoolmasters, New York, list, 653–69
Colonial schools in New York, 9–24
Columbia college, Kings college reorganized as, 24
Common school state convention, *1846*, 101–29
Common schools, foundation of our state system of, 8; act of *1795*, text of, 26–33; appointment of committee to report system for organization and establishment of, 34; report of committee appointed by Governor Tompkins, 37–43; act of *1812* for establishment of, text, 43–51; extracts from Governors' messages on the "State and education," 52–58. *See also* Free schools
Common schools, Superintendent of, communication from relative to certain unpaid school moneys, 510–11
Compulsory education, 559
Constitutional convention of *1846*, 83; committee on education, 118; journal, 121–29; editorial comment on the consideration of free schools by, 129–47; views of superintendents, 148–61

Cook, James M., sketch of, 180
Cooper, Edward, sketch of, 118
Court of Appeals, decisions on free school law, 515–23
Crandal, W. L., address before Onondaga county teachers institute, 314–34

Defective children, act to amend Education law by providing for education of, 628–29
Draper, Andrew S., on rate bills, 545–46
Dutch, schools under, 9–19

Editorial comments, on the consideration of free schools by constitutional convention of *1846*, 129–47; on free school act of *1849*, 199–230; on free school act of *1849*, fight for resubmission, 237–64; on campaign before November election in *1850*, 334–418; on free school act of *1851*, 433–41, 481–85; on abolition of rate bills, 558–64
Education, after the Revolution, 25–33; extracts from Governors' messages on, 52–58, 528–36
Education law, amendments of *1917*, 568–629
Educational developments after enactment of law of *1851*, 486–510
English, schools under, 19
Evening schools of colonial New York City, 630–52

Fenton, Governor, on public school question, 532–36
Fine, John, sketch of, 178–79
Finley, John H., communication to Regents on legislation in *1917*, 565–68
Fish, Governor, message of *1850* on establishment of free schools, 265
Free school act of *1849*, views of county superintendents, 162–67; views of state superintendents, 167–69; passage of the bill, 169–77; references to taken from Assembly

Free school act of 1849 (*continued*):
journal, 182–88; text, 188–90; references to taken from Senate journal, 190–95; amendments to, 196; vote by counties, 197–98; editorial comments, 199–230; memorial of the Onondaga county teachers institute, 203–6; fight for resubmission, 231–64; fight for resubmission, press comment, 237–64; act of resubmission, action of Legislature on, 265–79; act of resubmission *1850*, text, 280–81; act of resubmission, report of Attorney General in answer to a resolution of the Assembly, 282–83; petition of inhabitants of Pompey for repeal, 283–85; report of committee on petitions for amendment, 286–308; report of committee on literature on a bill to provide for the support of common schools, 308–12; resubmission law *1850*, text, 312–13; campaign before November election in *1850*, 314–418
Free school act of *1851*, 419–85; press comment, 433–41, 481–85; legislative action, 442–85; to provide for the support of the common schools, text, 469–71; to establish free schools throughout the State, text, 471–74; amending law of *1851*, text, 474; educational developments after enactment of, 486–510
Free schools, early schools, 7–8; education after the Revolution, 25–33; period *1826–46*, 52–82; early legislative references to, 76–82; constitutional convention *1846*, 83–101; support, discussion on, 83–101; legislation from *1853–1868*, 523–28; bibliography, 670–78. *See also* Acts

Geddes, George, sketch of, 181
Governors' messages, extracts from 52–58, 528–36
Grammar school, first founded west of Albany at Cherry Valley in *1743*, 23

INDEX 681

Hale, Benjamin, letter from, 509–10
Hamilton, Alexander, interest in public schools, 25
Harrington, Henry Francis, sketch of, 117
Hawley, William M., sketch of, 177–78
Henry, Mr, remarks and report on free school resolution, 112–16
Homemaking, act to amend Education law relative to employment of directors of, 626–27
Hunt, Governor, message on free schools, 442–43
Hunt, John H., sketch of, 121

Jay, John, interest in public schools, 25
Judicial decisions on free school law, 515–23

Kings college, established, 23

Latin schools, 21
Lawrence, John L., sketch of, 180–81
Laws, *see* Acts
Legislative references, early, to free schools, 76–82
L'Hommedieu, Ezra, interest in public schools, 25
Livingston, interest in public schools, 25
Long Island, schools of, 24

Mann, Horace, address, 102–11
Marcy, Governor William L., extracts from messages on the "State and education," 53–55
Marion, General, remarks, 85–89
Martin, Frederick Stanley, sketch of, 179
Massachusetts public school system, evolution of, 68–70
Mechanic arts, act to amend Education law relative to employment of directors of, 626–27
Morgan, Governor, on public school question, 532

Morgan, Superintendent, comments upon act for establishment of free schools, 231–37; comments on educational situation. 419–25; on the new school law, 474–79
Munro, David, sketch of, 118–19

New Rochelle, school buildings in, 24
New York City, colonial, evening schools, 630–52
New York City, Legislature in *1842* extended provision of general school law to apply to, 73
New York colonial schoolmasters. list, 653–69
Newspapers, editorial comments, on consideration of free schools by constitutional convention of *1846*, 129–47; on free school act of *1849*, 199–230; on the fight for resubmission of free school act of *1849*, 237–64; on free school law of *1849* campaign before November election in *1850*, 334–418; on free school act of *1851*, 433–41, 481–85; on abolishment of rate bills, 558–64
Nicoll, Henry, sketch of, 118

Potter, Professor, address, 89
Private schools, 7, 19; opposition to use of public funds for, 511–15
Public Instruction, State Department of, created. 486; extracts from reports, 488–510
Public schools, *see* Common schools; Free schools

Randall, Henry S., on free school act of *1851*, 425–33; report on school system, 501–5
Rate-bill system, 33–51; comments on, 537–48; act to abolish, text. 548–55; press comments on abolishment of, 558–64
Retarded mental development, act to amend Education law by providing for education of children with, 627–28

Regents, Board of, statement setting forth needs of a system of public schools, 25
Revenue, sources of, 35–36
Rhode Island, comments on history of free schools in, 70–72
Rice, Victor M., extracts from reports, 488–90, 493–501; on abolishment of rate bills, 543–45; comments on abolishment of rate bills, 556–58
Roman Catholics, report of committee on colleges, academies and common schools, on petition of certain, 511–15
Ryerson, Egerton, sketch of, 72–73

Scholarships, act of *1732* as germ of law of *1912* establishing, 23
School elections in certain cities, text of law, 604–10
School moneys, unpaid, 510–23
Schoolmasters, New York colonial, list, 653–69
Schools, *see* Common schools; Free schools
Seward, Governor William H., extracts from messages on the "State and education," 55–58
Seybolt, Robert Francis, Evening schools of colonial New York City, 630–52; New York colonial schoolmasters, list, 653–69

Society for the Propagation of the Gospel in Foreign Parts, 20
State aid for public schools, 7
Statistics, comparative table of in the cities, etc., of this State, 93
Stevens, Thaddeus, a plea for public schools, 59–66; sketch of, 67–68

Tamblin, John W., sketch of, 181
Taxes, *see* School moneys
Teachers retirement fund, New York city, text of law, 610–26
Thomson, Professor James Bates, remarks and report on free school resolution, 112–16; sketch of, 117
Tompkins, Governor, appointment of committee to report system for the organization and establishment of common schools, 34; report of committee appointed by, 36–43
Town board of education, text of law, 568–85

University of the State of New York, 7, 25

Valentine, Thomas Weston, sketch of, 116
Van Dyck, H. H., excerpts from reports, 490–93

Willard, Horace Kemper, sketch of, 121

Young, Andrew W., sketch of, 120

AMERICAN EDUCATION: ITS MEN, IDEAS, AND INSTITUTIONS
An Arno Press/New York Times Collection

Series I

Adams, Francis. **The Free School System of the United States.** 1875.

Alcott, William A. **Confessions of a School Master.** 1839.

American Unitarian Association. **From Servitude to Service.** 1905.

Bagley, William C. **Determinism in Education.** 1925.

Barnard, Henry, editor. **Memoirs of Teachers, Educators, and Promoters and Benefactors of Education, Literature, and Science.** 1861.

Bell, Sadie. **The Church, the State, and Education in Virginia.** 1930.

Belting, Paul Everett. **The Development of the Free Public High School in Illinois to 1860.** 1919.

Berkson, Isaac B. **Theories of Americanization: A Critical Study.** 1920.

Blauch, Lloyd E. **Federal Cooperation in Agricultural Extension Work, Vocational Education, and Vocational Rehabilitation.** 1935.

Bloomfield, Meyer. **Vocational Guidance of Youth.** 1911.

Brewer, Clifton Hartwell. **A History of Religious Education in the Episcopal Church to 1835.** 1924.

Brown, Elmer Ellsworth. **The Making of Our Middle Schools.** 1902.

Brumbaugh, M. G. **Life and Works of Christopher Dock.** 1908.

Burns, Reverend J. A. **The Catholic School System in the United States.** 1908.

Burns, Reverend J. A. **The Growth and Development of the Catholic School System in the United States.** 1912.

Burton, Warren. **The District School as It Was.** 1850.

Butler, Nicholas Murray, editor. **Education in the United States.** 1900.

Butler, Vera M. **Education as Revealed By New England Newspapers prior to 1850.** 1935.

Campbell, Thomas Monroe. **The Movable School Goes to the Negro Farmer.** 1936.

Carter, James G. **Essays upon Popular Education.** 1826.

Carter, James G. **Letters to the Hon. William Prescott, LL.D., on the Free Schools of New England.** 1824.

Channing, William Ellery. **Self-Culture.** 1842.

Coe, George A. **A Social Theory of Religious Education.** 1917.

Committee on Secondary School Studies. **Report of the Committee on Secondary School Studies, Appointed at the Meeting of the National Education Association.** 1893.

Counts, George S. **Dare the School Build a New Social Order?** 1932.

Counts, George S. **The Selective Character of American Secondary Education.** 1922.

Counts, George S. **The Social Composition of Boards of Education.** 1927.

Culver, Raymond B. **Horace Mann and Religion in the Massachusetts Public Schools.** 1929.
Curoe, Philip R. V. **Educational Attitudes and Policies of Organized Labor in the United States.** 1926.
Dabney, Charles William. **Universal Education in the South.** 1936.
Dearborn, Ned Harland. **The Oswego Movement in American Education.** 1925.
De Lima, Agnes. **Our Enemy the Child.** 1926.
Dewey, John. **The Educational Situation.** 1902.
Dexter, Franklin B., editor. **Documentary History of Yale University.** 1916.
Eliot, Charles William. **Educational Reform: Essays and Addresses.** 1898.
Ensign, Forest Chester. **Compulsory School Attendance and Child Labor.** 1921.
Fitzpatrick, Edward Augustus. **The Educational Views and Influence of De Witt Clinton.** 1911.
Fleming, Sanford. **Children & Puritanism.** 1933.
Flexner, Abraham. **The American College: A Criticism.** 1908.
Foerster, Norman. **The Future of the Liberal College.** 1938.
Gilman, Daniel Coit. **University Problems in the United States.** 1898.
Hall, Samuel R. **Lectures on School-Keeping.** 1829.
Hall, Stanley G. **Adolescence: Its Psychology and Its Relations to Physiology, Anthropology, Sociology, Sex, Crime, Religion, and Education.** 1905. 2 vols.
Hansen, Allen Oscar. **Early Educational Leadership in the Ohio Valley.** 1923.
Harris, William T. **Psychologic Foundations of Education.** 1899.
Harris, William T. **Report of the Committee of Fifteen on the Elementary School.** 1895.
Harveson, Mae Elizabeth. **Catharine Esther Beecher: Pioneer Educator.** 1932.
Jackson, George Leroy. **The Development of School Support in Colonial Massachusetts.** 1909.
Kandel, I. L., editor. **Twenty-five Years of American Education.** 1924.
Kemp, William Webb. **The Support of Schools in Colonial New York by the Society for the Propagation of the Gospel in Foreign Parts.** 1913.
Kilpatrick, William Heard. **The Dutch Schools of New Netherland and Colonial New York.** 1912.
Kilpatrick, William Heard. **The Educational Frontier.** 1933.
Knight, Edgar Wallace. **The Influence of Reconstruction on Education in the South.** 1913.
Le Duc, Thomas. **Piety and Intellect at Amherst College, 1865-1912.** 1946.
Maclean, John. **History of the College of New Jersey from Its Origin in 1746 to the Commencement of 1854.** 1877.
Maddox, William Arthur. **The Free School Idea in Virginia before the Civil War.** 1918.
Mann, Horace. **Lectures on Education.** 1855.
McCadden, Joseph J. **Education in Pennsylvania, 1801-1835, and Its Debt to Roberts Vaux.** 1855.
McCallum, James Dow. **Eleazar Wheelock.** 1939.
McCuskey, Dorothy. **Bronson Alcott, Teacher.** 1940.
Meiklejohn, Alexander. **The Liberal College.** 1920.
Miller, Edward Alanson. **The History of Educational Legislation in Ohio from 1803 to 1850.** 1918.

Miller, George Frederick. **The Academy System of the State of New York.** 1922.
Monroe, Will S. **History of the Pestalozzian Movement in the United States.** 1907.
Mosely Education Commission. **Reports of the Mosely Education Commission to the United States of America October-December, 1903.** 1904.
Mowry, William A. **Recollections of a New England Educator.** 1908.
Mulhern, James. **A History of Secondary Education in Pennsylvania.** 1933.
National Herbart Society. **National Herbart Society Yearbooks 1-5, 1895-1899.** 1895-1899.
Nearing, Scott. **The New Education: A Review of Progressive Educational Movements of the Day.** 1915.
Neef, Joseph. **Sketches of a Plan and Method of Education.** 1808.
Nock, Albert Jay. **The Theory of Education in the United States.** 1932.
Norton, A. O., editor. **The First State Normal School in America: The Journals of Cyrus Pierce and Mary Swift.** 1926.
Oviatt, Edwin. **The Beginnings of Yale, 1701-1726.** 1916.
Packard, Frederic Adolphus. **The Daily Public School in the United States.** 1866.
Page, David P. **Theory and Practice of Teaching.** 1848.
Parker, Francis W. **Talks on Pedagogics: An Outline of the Theory of Concentration.** 1894.
Peabody, Elizabeth Palmer. **Record of a School.** 1835.
Porter, Noah. **The American Colleges and the American Public.** 1870.
Reigart, John Franklin. **The Lancasterian System of Instruction in the Schools of New York City.** 1916.
Reilly, Daniel F. **The School Controversy (1891-1893).** 1943.
Rice, Dr. J. M. **The Public-School System of the United States.** 1893.
Rice, Dr. J. M. **Scientific Management in Education.** 1912.
Ross, Early D. **Democracy's College: The Land-Grant Movement in the Formative Stage.** 1942.
Rugg, Harold, et al. **Curriculum-Making: Past and Present.** 1926.
Rugg, Harold, et al. **The Foundations of Curriculum-Making.** 1926.
Rugg, Harold and Shumaker, Ann. **The Child-Centered School.** 1928.
Seybolt, Robert Francis. **Apprenticeship and Apprenticeship Education in Colonial New England and New York.** 1917.
Seybolt, Robert Francis. **The Private Schools of Colonial Boston.** 1935.
Seybolt, Robert Francis. **The Public Schools of Colonial Boston.** 1935.
Sheldon, Henry D. **Student Life and Customs.** 1901.
Sherrill, Lewis Joseph. **Presbyterian Parochial Schools, 1846-1870.** 1932.
Siljestrom, P. A. **Educational Institutions of the United States.** 1853.
Small, Walter Herbert. **Early New England Schools.** 1914.
Soltes, Mordecai. **The Yiddish Press: An Americanizing Agency.** 1925.
Stewart, George, Jr. **A History of Religious Education in Connecticut to the Middle of the Nineteenth Century.** 1924.
Storr, Richard J. **The Beginnings of Graduate Education in America.** 1953.

Stout, John Elbert. **The Development of High-School Curricula in the North Central States from 1860 to 1918.** 1921.
Suzzallo, Henry. **The Rise of Local School Supervision in Massachusetts.** 1906.
Swett, John. **Public Education in California.** 1911.
Tappan, Henry P. **University Education.** 1851.
Taylor, Howard Cromwell. **The Educational Significance of the Early Federal Land Ordinances.** 1921.
Taylor, J. Orville. **The District School.** 1834.
Tewksbury, Donald G. **The Founding of American Colleges and Universities before the Civil War.** 1932.
Thorndike, Edward L. **Educational Psychology.** 1913-1914.
True, Alfred Charles. **A History of Agricultural Education in the United States, 1785-1925.** 1929.
True, Alfred Charles. **A History of Agricultural Extension Work in the United States, 1785-1923.** 1928.
Updegraff, Harlan. **The Origin of the Moving School in Massachusetts.** 1908.
Wayland, Francis. **Thoughts on the Present Collegiate System in the United States.** 1842.
Weber, Samuel Edwin. **The Charity School Movement in Colonial Pennsylvania.** 1905.
Wells, Guy Fred. **Parish Education in Colonial Virginia.** 1923.
Wickersham, J. P. **The History of Education in Pennsylvania.** 1885.
Woodward, Calvin M. **The Manual Training School.** 1887.
Woody, Thomas. **Early Quaker Education in Pennsylvania.** 1920.
Woody, Thomas. **Quaker Education in the Colony and State of New Jersey.** 1923.
Wroth, Lawrence C. **An American Bookshelf, 1755.** 1934.

Series II

Adams, Evelyn C. **American Indian Education.** 1946.
Bailey, Joseph Cannon. **Seaman A. Knapp: Schoolmaster of American Agriculture.** 1945.
Beecher, Catharine and Harriet Beecher Stowe. **The American Woman's Home.** 1869.
Benezet, Louis T. **General Education in the Progressive College.** 1943.
Boas, Louise Schutz. **Woman's Education Begins.** 1935.
Bobbitt, Franklin. **The Curriculum.** 1918.
Bode, Boyd H. **Progressive Education at the Crossroads.** 1938.
Bourne, William Oland. **History of the Public School Society of the City of New York.** 1870.
Bronson, Walter C. **The History of Brown University, 1764-1914.** 1914.
Burstall, Sara A. **The Education of Girls in the United States.** 1894.
Butts, R. Freeman. **The College Charts Its Course.** 1939.
Caldwell, Otis W. and Stuart A. Courtis. **Then & Now in Education, 1845-1923.** 1923.
Calverton, V. F. & Samuel D. Schmalhausen, editors. **The New Generation: The Intimate Problems of Modern Parents and Children.** 1930.
Charters, W. W. **Curriculum Construction.** 1923.
Childs, John L. **Education and Morals.** 1950.

Childs, John L. **Education and the Philosophy of Experimentalism.** 1931.
Clapp, Elsie Ripley. **Community Schools in Action.** 1939.
Counts, George S. **The American Road to Culture: A Social Interpretation of Education in the United States.** 1930.
Counts, George S. **School and Society in Chicago.** 1928.
Finegan, Thomas E. **Free Schools.** 1921.
Fletcher, Robert Samuel. **A History of Oberlin College.** 1943.
Grattan, C. Hartley. **In Quest of Knowledge: A Historical Perspective on Adult Education.** 1955.
Hartman, Gertrude & Ann Shumaker, editors. **Creative Expression.** 1932.
Kandel, I. L. **The Cult of Uncertainty.** 1943.
Kandel, I. L. **Examinations and Their Substitutes in the United States.** 1936.
Kilpatrick, William Heard. **Education for a Changing Civilization.** 1926.
Kilpatrick, William Heard. **Foundations of Method.** 1925.
Kilpatrick, William Heard. **The Montessori System Examined.** 1914.
Lang, Ossian H., editor. **Educational Creeds of the Nineteenth Century.** 1898.
Learned, William S. **The Quality of the Educational Process in the United States and in Europe.** 1927.
Meiklejohn, Alexander. **The Experimental College.** 1932.
Middlekauff, Robert. **Ancients and Axioms: Secondary Education in Eighteenth-Century New England.** 1963.
Norwood, William Frederick. **Medical Education in the United States Before the Civil War.** 1944.
Parsons, Elsie W. Clews. **Educational Legislation and Administration of the Colonial Governments.** 1899.
Perry, Charles M. **Henry Philip Tappan: Philosopher and University President.** 1933.
Pierce, Bessie Louise. **Civic Attitudes in American School Textbooks.** 1930.
Rice, Edwin Wilbur. **The Sunday-School Movement (1780-1917) and the American Sunday-School Union (1817-1917).** 1917.
Robinson, James Harvey. **The Humanizing of Knowledge.** 1924.
Ryan, W. Carson. **Studies in Early Graduate Education.** 1939.
Seybolt, Robert Francis. **The Evening School in Colonial America.** 1925.
Seybolt, Robert Francis. **Source Studies in American Colonial Education.** 1925.
Todd, Lewis Paul. **Wartime Relations of the Federal Government and the Public Schools, 1917-1918.** 1945.
Vandewalker, Nina C. **The Kindergarten in American Education.** 1908.
Ward, Florence Elizabeth. **The Montessori Method and the American School.** 1913.
West, Andrew Fleming. **Short Papers on American Liberal Education.** 1907.
Wright, Marion M. Thompson. **The Education of Negroes in New Jersey.** 1941.

Supplement

The Social Frontier (Frontiers of Democracy). Vols. 1-10, 1934-1943.